DEDICATION

To the strong, loving women in my life: My wife Sarah, my daughters Patricia and Christy, my granddaughter Samy, my sister Elizabeth Ann, my Mother Helen, my mother-in-law Mary Hunt, and to my nieces Jennifer and Marley — I dedicate this book. No man has ever had more loving and caring women in their life. You are my angels and my inspiration.

I also dedicate this book to my Dad David, and Sarah's Dad, George, her brother, George Jr., my brother-in-law Joe, my nephew Jeff, my sons-in-law Al and Brian, my nieces' husbands Dave and Patrick, and to my stillborn twin sons, Joshua and Stephen (who The Lord took unto Himself), I look forward to being introduced to you and being with you and all my loved ones in Heaven.

Love to all,
David

D1716745

THE COSMOGONY OF THE ANCIENT OF DAYS:
MODERN SCIENCE AGREES WITH MOSES & NAHMANIDES
A COMMENTARY ON THE GENESIS CREATION ACCOUNT
INTRODUCTION & BOOK I: BOOK II: & BOOK III (three books in one)
COPYRIGHT © 2024 by Dr. David E. Marley, JR. M.D. ISBN 9798329973433
Printed in the United States of America by: Amazon Kindle Direct Publishing

ON 15 MAY 2022, DR. GERALD L. SCHROEDER GAVE ME HIS WRITTEN PERMISSION TO REFERENCE AND QUOTE THREE OF HIS BOOKS.

- GENESIS AND THE BIG BANG: The Discovery of the Harmony between Modern Science and the Bible. Dr. Gerald L. Schroeder, PhD. Bantam Books, New York, Toronto, London, Sydney, Auckland, © 1990.
- THE SCIENCE OF GOD: The Convergence of Scientific and Biblical Wisdom. Dr. Gerald L. Schroeder, PhD. Broadway Books, New York, N.Y. © 1997.
- THE HIDDEN FACE OF GOD: Science reveals the Ultimate Truth. Dr. Gerald L. Schroeder, PhD. Touchstone Books, Simon and Schuster, New York, N.Y. © 2001.

THE COSMOGONY OF THE ANCIENT OF DAYS:
MODERN SCIENCE AGREES WITH MOSES & NAHMANIDES

A COMMENTARY ON THE GENESIS CREATION ACCOUNT

INTRODUCTION

IN THE BEGINNING, DARKNESS WAS THE 1ST THING GOD CREATED.

BLACK WAS THE COLOR OF GOD'S CREATION ON "DAY ONE."

BLACK IS THE PRESENCE OF ALL COLOR.

AT THE END OF "DAY ONE" GOD SAID: *"LET THERE BE LIGHT!"*

WE ARE ALL CREATED IN DARKNESS.

ALL CHRISTIANS STEP OUT OF THEIR DARKNESS,

AND ENTER GOD'S LIGHT— WHEN THEY LEARN OF,

BELIEVE IN & FOLLOW JESUS CHRIST.

AT THEIR DEATH, ALL CHRISTIANS SING:

"Swing Low, Sweet Chariot; Coming for to Carry Me Home.

Swing Low, Sweet Chariot; Coming for to Carry Me Home.

I looked over Jordan and What did I See — Coming for to Carry Me Home?

A Band of Angels Coming after Me. Coming for to Carry Me Home!"

BY: Dr. David E. Marley, Jr. M.D. (O. David)

⚜

Prelude: Our Country (the USA) is Broken

There was a time when a chosen people turned their backs on their God and did what was evil in His sight. They abandoned the worship of their God and removed His name from their memory. They forgot who they were. They did not honor their history and did not teach it to their young. They worshipped the pagan gods of the heathen among them, and adopted their religious practices of free love, ritual prostitution, and human sacrifice. They burned their unwanted children (born of their licentious sexual behaviors), on their altars to pagan gods. All people did what was "Right in Their Sight." It was a "Me-First Culture." People cheated, stole, lied, took from the weak, persecuted widows and orphans, shed innocent blood, devised wicked plans, and did evil. False witnesses were everywhere. The borders of their land were porous and insecure. Foreigners regularly invaded and overran their land. The invaders roamed freely and like locusts, devoured their crops, took their livestock, and destroyed their economy. It was a time of "Mob Rule and Persecution." "Might was Right." There was no "Law and Order." The standard of living was so degraded that people abandoned their homes and hid in caves! I have just described what Gideon experienced during the Midianite Oppression of Israel circa 1200 BC (Judges 6-8).

When Solomon finished building his Temple to God, The Lord appeared to him at night and said: *14 "If My people who are called by My name will humble themselves and pray and seek My face, and turn from their wicked ways, then I will hear their prayers from heaven, and I will forgive their sins, and heal their land"* (II Chron. 7:14 KJV). Then God warned Solomon: *"If you turn away and forsake My statutes and My commandments and go and serve and worship other gods, then I will uproot you from My land, which I have given you, and this house which I have consecrated for My name I will cast out of My sight, and I will make it a proverb and a byword among all peoples"* (II Chron. 7:19-20 circa 950 BC).

Sadly, in his old age, Solomon turned from God. He served pagan gods and sacrificed children on pagan altars. God was true to his word. Solomon's kingdom was divided by Civil War. *"When the fullness of time had come,"* both the Northern and Southern Kingdoms of Israel were defeated by foreign powers, enslaved, and carried away to foreign lands. Solomon's Temple to God was destroyed, and for 2500 years, the nation itself—*"became a proverb and a byword among all people."*

For decades politicians, judges, prosecutors, bureaucrats, teachers, and the liberal left media sowed dissension in our society, and kicked God out of our government, institutions, and schools. Our youth were not taught the history of *how* our Freedom was won! They have been insidiously indoctrinated in Marxist, Communist, and Socialist ideologies, with the goal of converting us to a "new religion of Humanism." (See Chapter 21 The Agenda of Darwinists in Book II.) The politics of our nation has become so polarized and contentious that the true purpose of all policies and legislation is not trusted and is hard to discern. Most politicians profess belief in God, but some serve mammon! It seems many politicians spin the truth and lie. Some purposefully foment violent, destructive protests. Current open border policies are causing an invasion of our country! The autocratic immigration policies of the current Democrat Administration supports giving illegal aliens the right to vote! Why? To maintain their political rule and power! Since

2021, political policy decisions have been marching our country toward the abyss of economic destruction! Apparently, the ruling autocrats do not see their policies are tearing our nation apart and are destroying our economy and lives! With the cooperation of the liberal left media, the current administration seeks to control and regulate public opinion to do its bidding. Their leadership is currently driving us all pall mall into "Democratic Socialism" (an oxymoron if I ever heard one). History has shown socialism has caused untold millions to <u>suffer</u> and <u>die</u>! [1] Everywhere Socialism has been tried, it has failed! The goal of socialists the world over is to create a "One-World Order." Socialism turns countries into welfare-states that control everything from the cradle to the grave. From time immemorial, there has been a struggle between the rights of the working people versus the so-called "divine rights" of kings and "ruling elites." Socialism is a tyranny that says: *"You work and toil and earn bread and I'll eat it"* (quoting Abraham Lincoln out of context, 1858)! Adding "Democratic" to Socialism is a distinction without a difference!

So-called *"'Woke' Liberal Left Progressives"* are now saying the *"Bigoted Basket of Deplorable Conservatives"* must be — *"Deprogrammed!"*[2,3] *"Deplorables"* say the *"Liberal Left"* needs to be — *"Cognitively Recalibrated!"* Why? Because they are changing our lives, and <u>we do not like and did not vote for their arrogant ignorant autocratic changes</u>! Their *"Cognitive Dissonance"* has blinded them. Conservatives believe the *liberal left needs to be EDUCATED! Political Liberal leftists have been corrupted by their lust for political power and riches! Money and Power are their gods! What happened to: "Thou shalt have no other gods before Me," "Treat others as you would want to be treated," "Love others the way you love yourself," "Love others as Jesus loved,"* Civility, Loving Kindness, and *"Thou shalt not murder?"*

The people of the USA are divided. It seems half our nation have turned away from God, have forsaken God's statutes and commandments, and are now serving and worshiping other "gods." For more than half a century, people in our country have been shaking their fists at God! Since 1973, we have sacrificed more than 63 million innocent children on the pagan altar of *"Freedom of Choice!"* See INTRODUCTION—PART VI: MYTH vs. FACT: under "INFANT SACRIFICE TO FALSE GODS," — "WE HAVE DONE THE SAME THING: BEAM ME UP SCOTTY!" We have made the same mistakes ancient Israel did! If we don't humble ourselves, turn from our wicked ways, pray for forgiveness, and return to God; The Lord God Almighty will uproot us from our land, cast us out of His sight, and the USA will become a proverb and a byword among all peoples! Our "Land of Freedom" will no longer exist! We need a spiritual revival that leads our nation to repent our sins and return to God. Furthermore, we need to re-educate ourselves and our youth. We must understand — Jesus Christ is the answer to all problems!

Where should we begin? Let's start <u>our</u> re-education by going back to—*"In The Beginning!* O. David

---

[1] *"WHERE DO WE GO FROM HERE" Chapter 1: A Cultural Prophecy—Socialism: © 2021 by Dr. David P. Jeremiah.*
[2] https://nypost.com › 2016/09/12 › clintons-basket-of-d... Clinton's 'basket of deplorables' gaffe stuns both parties
[3] **Hillary Clinton calls for 'formal deprogramming' of Trump ' ...**

OPEN MY EYES, THAT I MAY SEE

[1]Open my eyes, that I may see.
Glimpses of truth Thou hast for me.
Place in my hands the wonderful key
That shall unclasp and set me free.

CHORUS

Silently now I wait for Thee,
Ready, my God, Thy Will to see.
Open my eyes, illumine me, Spirit divine!

[2]Open my ears, that I may hear,
Voices of truth Thou sendest clear.
And while the wave-notes fall on my ear,
Everything false will disappear.

CHOURS

Silently now I wait for Thee,
Ready, my God, Thy Will to see.
Open my ears, illumine me, Spirit divine!

[3]Open my mouth and let me bear.
Gladly the warm truth everywhere.
Open my heart and let me prepare,
Love with Thy children thus to share.

CHORUS

Silently now I wait for Thee,
Ready, my God, Thy Will to see.
Open my heart, illumine me, Spirit divine!

Words: Clara H. Scott, 1895
Music: Clara Scott, 1895
The United Methodist Hymnal
Copyright © 1989 The United Methodist Publishing House
Page 454

[15]"Some indeed preach Christ even from envy and strife, and some also from good will: [16]The former preach Christ from selfish ambition, not sincerely, supposing to add affliction to my chains: [17]but the latter out of love, knowing that I am appointed for the defense of the gospel." (The Apostle Paul, writing the church at Philippi, from prison: Philippians 1:15-17 The Jeremiah Study Bible NKJV — The New King James Version).

Dear God, I love You.
Thank You for loving me. (*O. David*)

Go Tell it on the Mountain! Jesus Christ is Lord!

ARE YOU PUZZLED BY THIS IMAGE?

ANSWER

1) *GET CLOSE TO THIS IMAGE.*
2) *Look at the 4 small irregular rectangles near the center of the image, and count to 20.*
3) *When you say "20," look at the wall and blink your eyes.*
4) *You will see a man. Who do you think He is?*
5) *Now, just for fun, REPEAT # (2) then close your eyes & KEEP THEM CLOSED.*
6) *WAIT FOR IT! After a moment, "your mind's eye" will "see" a circle of light. Then, for a fleeting moment (within the circle of light), you will see the face of JESUS.*

THIS IMAGE IS COURTESY OF:
"FREE OUIJA WEDGE OPTICAL ILLUSION JESUS IMAGE"
The more you study the Bible, the more you "see" Jesus!

KING DAVID'S PRAYER

[17] "O God, Thou hast taught me from my youth.
And I still declare Thy wondrous deeds.

[18] And even when I am old and gray,
O God, do not forsake me until I
declare Thy strength to this generation,
Thy power to all who are to come."

(Psalm 71:17-18 NASB. A Psalm of David)

Since I am in my 9th decade,
This prayer has special meaning to me. (*O. David*)

SEVEN THINGS GOD HATES

[16] "There are six things which the Lord hates,
Yes, seven which are an abomination to Him:
[17] [a]Haughty (conceited) eyes, a [b]Lying Tongue,
And Hands that [c]Shed Innocent Blood,
[18]A Heart that Devises [a]Wicked Plans,
And [b]Feet that Run Rapidly to Evil.
[19] [a]A False Witness Who Utters Lies,
And One Who [b]Spreads Strife
Among Brothers."

(Proverbs 6:16—19 NASB)

THE FEAR (I.E., THE REVERENCE FOR)[4] THE LORD REQUIRES:

"The Fear of the Lord:
Is to [1]Hate Evil,
[2]Hate Pride,
[3]Hate Arrogance,
[4]Hate the Perverted Mouth,
And [5]Hate the Evil Way."

(Proverbs 8:13 NASB)

----

[4] Fear of the Lord = Reverence for the Lord more than anyone else. (Ryrie Bible Study Note on Genesis 22:12) Synonyms for Reverence are Admiration, Amazement, Astonishment, *Awe*, Devotion, Respect, Veneration, Worship. Synonyms for Hate are Abhorrence, Animosity, Aversion, Disgust, Dislike, Distaste, Hatred, Loathing, Odium, Revulsion. Evil, Pride, Arrogance, the Perverted Mouth & the Evil Way: are "actions" Christians should "Hate." Hate the act/action. Do not hate the person.

FROM: HENRY WADSWORTH LONGFELLOW'S CHRISTUS POEM

SAMARITAN WOMAN
Oh, come see a man
Who hath told me all things that I ever did!
Say, is not this the Christ?

THE DISCIPLES
Lo, Master, here is food
That we have brought thee from the city.
We pray thee eat it.

CHRISTUS
I have food to eat ye know not of.

THE DISCIPLES (TO EACH OTHER).
Hath any man been here,
And brought Him aught to eat, while we were gone?

CHRISTUS
The food I speak of is to do the will
Of Him that sent me, and to finish his work.
Do ye not say, Lo! There are yet four months
And cometh harvest? I say to you,
Lift up your eyes, and look upon the fields
For they are white already unto harvest! [5]

---

[5] From Longfellow's *Christus Poem* (based on John 4:1-42). The Ryrie Study Bible Note on these scripture verses interprets — *"They are white already for harvest"* as: *"The mission fields — Christ says are ripe and waiting for harvesters."* The Jeremiah Study Bible (NKJV) says: *"It was winter; the just planted crops were green (not ready for harvest), but Jesus saw a crop that **was** ready for harvesters—**the Samaritans**."* Christ told His Apostles: *"Go therefore and make disciples of all the nations, baptizing them in the name of the Father and of the Son and of the Holy Spirit, teaching them to observe all that I commanded you. And lo, I am with you always, even to the end of the age (Matt. 28:19-20)."*

MY PRAYER FOR THIS BOOK

Our Father in heaven, please hear my cry.
For some strange reason, I know not why—
Christus called me this season.

W. C. Colley,[6] often would bellow.
"Come little David, come blow your horn.
Sheep in my meadow, Cows in my corn![7]

You must contend with Satan's scorn!"

Why me Dear Lord, an unknown sinner?
When others renown, better could sound.
For when they emote, people take note.

Oh, Holy Father, I think I know why.
Dear Christus, I now see this book is my cry!

I pray this work, was Heaven-sent.
For Father I see your fields are bent.[8]
They are white & full ripe unto harvest.

O.David

---

[6] W.C. Colley, a Deacon in the First Southern Baptist Church of Brundidge, who lived on South Main Street (U.S. Highway 231) in my hometown — had a garden next to his home. He often shouted this to me when I walked by his garden on my way to town. I played the cornet in the Baptist and Methodist Churches, accompanied by my mother on the piano, or my sister on the organ.

[7] It has been said this English children's rhyme means: *"The fences need mending."* Things are *"topsy-turvy."* **THE WORLD IS UPSIDE DOWN.** The sheep have come into the cow-meadow, and the cows have broken into *"my"* corn. The deeper meaning is: **THERE IS A NEED FOR A RELIGIOUS REVIVAL!** *Many English children's rhymes of this period are tied to the English Reformation.* Mr. Colley was a much beloved elder who loved Jesus.

[8] The fields are bent by the weight of their fruit—**I.E., THE NUMBERS OF PEOPLE WHO NEED JESUS!**

✠
THE ROLE OF THE PRE-INCARNATE JESUS CHRIST — *"IN THE BEGINNING."*

What does Jesus Christ have to do with The Beginning? Answer: Everything! As you shall see, Jesus Christ was with God in the Beginning. Jesus Christ is *"the Word of God"* spoken of by the apostle John in the first chapter of his gospel. *"In the beginning was the Word, and the Word was with God, and the Word was God (John 1:1)." "All things were made by Him* (in the Beginning), *and without Him was not anything made that was made (John 1:3)." "He was in the world, and the world was made by Him, and the world knew Him not (John 1:10 KJV)."* He is also *"the First Wisdom of God"* spoken of in Genesis 1:1 (in the Onkelos Aramaic Translation of the Hebrew Bible). Jesus Christ is the heart and the center of the Bible. He is *"the Alpha and the Omega — the beginning and the end."*

The Old Testament is the story of a Nation. The New Testament is the story of the most unique Man who ever lived — Jesus Christ of Nazareth. The Nation of Israel was founded by God to be a blessing to all the peoples of the earth. That nation was intended by God to give mankind a concrete, definite, tangible idea of how God wants all people to be and to live. But ancient Israel failed God! So, *"When the fullness of time had come,"* (cf. Appendix II in Book III), God sent His son, Jesus Christ to preach, and teach men how they should live. Jesus was sent to show us what God is like. God is like Jesus Christ. God also sent His Son to save man. In His first advent, when Jesus Christ came to earth, He was God incarnate — in human form. But He was also — man! The dual nature of Jesus Christ (*"Very God of very God"* — and at the same time, *"Son of Man and Son of God"*) [9, 10] is just one of the many mysteries of Jesus Christ (cf. Matt: 22:41-46).[11]

The appearance of Jesus Christ on earth — is the central event of all history! The Old Testament sets the stage for His appearance. The New Testament describes it. Everything about the Old points to the New. The New clarifies the Old. The New is in the Old — concealed. The Old is in the New — revealed. This means Jesus Christ is hidden in the Old Testament. But He is openly revealed to man in the New Testament.

Jesus Christ is the most important person who ever lived. He is also the most controversial. There is no middle ground with Jesus. Christians believe Jesus Christ is who He says He is. We believe how we respond to Him determines our eternal destiny. Our acceptance (or rejection) of Him determines for each of us either eternal glory, or eternal ruin —Heaven or Hell— One or the other. The Bible was written for man so that we might understand, believe in, know, love, live for, and follow Jesus Christ.

---

[9] **Nicene Creed I History & Text - Encyclopedia Britannica**

[10] **The Nicene Creed: Where it came from and why it still matters**

[11] See Psalm 110:1 (*The son of David i.e., The Messiah, is also the Lord of David*). Also see the Ryrie Study Bible note on Matt: 22:44.

All Christians know the story of Jesus Christ of Nazareth. The New Testament story of Jesus Christ is the most important good news mankind has ever received! It is also essential all Christians be thoroughly familiar with it because the New Testament explains — why belief in Jesus Christ is essential for our salvation. He is our only pathway to God! (John 14:6)

However, very few Christians have any understanding of the essential role the Pre-Incarnate Jesus Christ played in God's Creation. Many think the role Jesus played occurred only in New Testament times. Not so! Jesus Christ has been active in the affairs of the earth since *"The Beginning"* and He has been active in the affairs of "*Man*" ever since He "*Made*" and "*Created*" him (cf. with [I.] "Man first *Made* and later *Created*"— in CHAPTER 23: THE 6TH DAY — MAN "MADE IN HIS IMAGE" — in Book III). This book talks about what I now believe was the role of the Pre-Incarnate Jesus Christ in Creation — *"In the Beginning."*

O. David

INTRODUCTION CONTENTS

INDEX OF ILLUSTRATIONS, CHARTS, EXPLANATIONS & IMAGES

⚜

INTRODUCTION —PART I: SYNOPSIS:
THE COSMOGONY OF THE ANCIENT OF DAYS:
MODERN SCIENCE AGREES WITH MOSES & NAHMANIDES

"In the Beginning..."

These are the first words English-speaking people read in their Bibles. They are also the first words in the ancient Hebrew "Bible." Jewish tradition claims Moses wrote them. However, atheists and skeptics say the Genesis Creation Account is a myth. They claim it is a story for children, and allege it is a simple fairytale. Furthermore, they argue Moses did not write it! Sixty years ago, when I was a college sophomore, I was shocked when I discovered some Protestant Christian Seminarians teach a theory that asserts Moses did not write the Torah. Furthermore, some Seminarians and Christian Ministers believe the supernatural "stories" in the Bible are "myths." I believe these disparagements of the Bible's Creation Account and the Bible in general, are an attack on the "Judeo" part of our Judeo-Christian faith. So, I started reading. This series of books is my attempt to relate what I found.

NAHMANIDES

In the middle of the 13th century AD, an ancient Jewish sage, Nahmanides, wrote his concept of: "The Beginning." He based his hypotheses on his knowledge of the first Chapter of the Hebrew Book of Genesis — what Jews say is the first chapter of the first book of the Torah. Nahmanides believed Moses wrote the Torah. He also said his understanding of the deeper meaning of the ancient Hebrew text was: **"Divinely Inspired by God." Nahmanides' 13th century "Commentary on the Beginning" reads like a modern-day physics textbook on the Big Bang Theory. [12] Nahmanides believed: God dictated The Genesis Creation Account to Moses! He was convinced God told Moses how He created, made, and has continued to make and form all that exists "out of nothing"— i.e., *"Creation Ex Nihilo"* — something only God can do.**

CONFLICT

For centuries, a conflict of beliefs between science and the Bible has been the result of bad science and flawed religious interpretations of translations of the Hebrew Bible. However, a renaissance in science and religion has caused a convergence of agreement in the views of each discipline. Science has now proved — Creation happened the way Moses described it!

A RENAISSANCE IN JUDEO-CHRISTIAN RELIGION

Discoveries of ancient religious texts, such as the 1947 discovery of The Dead Sea Scrolls at Qumran (Israel) have caused Bible scholars to reexamine their doubts about the antiquity and accuracy of the Hebrew Bible. In 1854, Babylonian cuneiform tablets were discovered that verified the actual existence of Belshazzar (the last of the Babylonian kings who succeeded Nebuchadnezzar II). At a drunken feast on the very night a besieging army broke through the defenses of his capital city (Babylon), Belshazzar saw a hand — writing these words on his banquet room wall — "MENE, MENE, TEKEL, UPHARSIN." [13] Daniel interpreted the message for him: 'MENE' — "*God has numbered the days of your*

---

[12] Schroeder: *Genesis & the Big Bang* Chapter 3 p 64d-68
[13] PERES (the singular of UPHARSIN) The Ryrie Study Bible Notes on Daniel 5:25, 5:28, and 5:30.

reign, and they are ended. 'TEKEL' — *You have been weighed in God's balances and found wanting.* 'PERES' — *Your kingdom will be divided and given to the Medes and Persians*" (Daniel 5:25-28 and 5:30). 'PERES' is the singular of 'UPHARSIN.' That very night, General Gobyras captured Babylon and killed Belshazzar. Gobyras' Persian King, (Cyrus II), entered the city seventeen days later. Both Herodotus and Xenophon stated — on October the 11th or 12th of 539 BC, the Medes and Persians broke into the city of Babylon after they diverted the Euphrates River. They found the people drunk and celebrating — and their King drunk and reveling with his guests in a private inebriated banquet.

Before the discovery of the Babylonian cuneiform tablets that proved his existence, Belshazzar's "story" was thought to have been a biblical myth, because the only places his name had been found were in the Old Testament Book of Daniel [14] and in Xenophon's fictive history; *Cyropaedia: The Education of Cyrus* — an imaginative history of King Cyrus II of Persia. [15,16,17,18*]

When Belshazzar brought out the golden goblets Nebuchadnezzar II had stolen from Solomon's Jerusalem Temple of God (70 years earlier) — to serve wine to his guests for a toast to the false gods of Babylon — he profaned the sacred goblets and blasphemed the God of the Jews.

Two Hundred years before it happened, Isaiah warned the tribe of Judah of the coming Babylonian captivity. He also prophesied the Persians would defeat the Babylonians and free Judah. Isaiah mentions the Persian king's name ("*Cyrus*") in Isaiah 44:28 and 45:1, and says he is *"God's anointed, God's shepherd, who will perform God's desire!"* Cyrus is also mentioned several times in Isaiah 43, 46, and 48. So, the Bible tells us — 200 years before King Cyrus was born, God not only told Isaiah the Kingdom of Judah would be destroyed and enslaved by Nebuchadnezzar II, but God also told Isaiah the name of the Persian King who would free the Judeans from Babylonian captivity!

All happened as Isaiah said it would. Daniel validated Isaiah's prophecies when he told his story of his experiences of the Babylonian Captivity in his Book of Daniel. Seventy years after Nebuchadnezzar II conquered Judah, Cyrus defeated the Babylonians and decreed a small remnant of captive Judean Jews be returned to Judea to rebuild Jerusalem, and God's Temple (just as Isaiah and Jeremiah had foretold). [19]

NINEVEH DISCOVERED

Nineteenth century archeological discoveries of ancient Biblical cities such as the discovery of the ruins of the ancient Assyrian Empire Capital (Nineveh), in 1845 [20,21,22] — have quelled the claims of skeptics that some cities in the Bible were mythical because

---

[14] The Biblical Book of Daniel: Chapters 5-10

[15] Belshazzarl King of Babylonial Britannica.com https://www.britannica.com/biography/Belshazzar

[16] The Belshazzar of Daniel & The Belshazzar of History...Lester L Crabbe, The University of Hull, Hull, HU6 7RX, England *https://digitalcommons.andrews.edu/cgi/viewcontent.cgi?article=1868&context=auss*

[17] Halley's Bible Handbook: by Henry H. Halley, Zondervan Publishing House, Grand Rapids, Michigan, 24th Edition, © 1965, p. 212, and p. 344-345

[18] *Belshazzar's Feast and the Fall of Babylonl https://bible.org/seriespage/5-belshazzar-s-feast-and-fall-babylon

[19] Read about it in the Ryrie Study Bible (Isaiah 41:5, 41:25, 43:3, 44:28, 45:1-2, 45:20-21, & 46:2; Jeremiah 25, and Daniel Chapters 5-10) and pay special attention to the Ryrie Study Bible notes on these scriptures.

[20] Nineveh, Capital of Assyria: Isaiah 37:37, Jonah 1:2, and Nahum 1:1

[21] Discoveries At Nineveh - Assyrian International News Agency http://www.aina.org/books/dan.html

[22] Halley's Bible Handbook: by Henry H. Halley, Zondervan Publishing House, Grand Rapids, Michigan, 24th Edition, © 1965, p.369-371.

there was no evidence of their existence. The discoveries of the archeological ruins of several ancient Biblical cities are only a few examples of important archeological discoveries that have verified the accuracy of the Bible and have helped bring about a renaissance in religious thought.

A RENAISSANCE IN SCIENCE

In the last 85 years scientists have theorized the beginning started with a "Big Bang." I've just said Nahmanides' interpretation of the 1st two chapters of Genesis reads like a modern-day physics textbook on the Big Bang Theory. However, **it is not widely known *The Big Bang Theory* agrees with Nahmanides' 13th Century Hebrew Cosmogony!** Furthermore, a few scientists have now realized the massive amounts of fossil evidence discovered since the 1st Edition of Darwin's Book was published (~165 years ago), **absolutely disproves Darwin's theory!** Darwin claimed evolution occurred at the level of the "phyla." However, science has now verified the Bible's ten-fold repeated statement of — "*according to its kind*"— in the 1st Chapter of Genesis means: ***"Evolution would occur at the level of the 'species.'"*** [23] Moreover, the renaissance in religion and science that has caused a convergence of agreement in both disciplines, **has also proved the Mosaic Genesis Account of Creation is accurate.** We now know Nahmanides' explanation of the deeper meaning of the Hebrew words Moses wrote (that God dictated to him) in his Genesis Creation Account, **accurately explains *The Cosmogony of the Ancient of Days (i.e., God)!* This means the 1st two chapters of Genesis are not a myth! The Bible's Creation Account is History, Religion, and Science!** This book tells the story of why it is highly probable Creation and Evolution happened the way Moses said!

I published my first book: *"THE GENESIS CODE: Moses & Modern Science Agree"* with Xulon Press in 2016. But I was not pleased with my first effort. I felt the book should be improved. So, I did not promote my book, and I immediately started a re-write. I changed the title to:

THE COSMOGONY OF THE ANCIENT OF DAYS: MODERN SCIENCE AGREES WITH MOSES & NAHMANIDES

Eight years later I completed my second effort. During that re-write, the world has suffered through and is still suffering from a horrific Pandemic. Millions have suffered, and millions have died! But *"THE CHINA VIRUS"* is still with us! I now have a new understanding of what people experienced in the *"Spanish Flu" Pandemic of 1918-1919*. At that time, there were no antiviral medications, and there were no vaccines against the disease. There were also no antibiotics to treat the bacterial pneumonia that followed on the heels of the flu that caused most of the deaths! I dare say those of us who have survived have been forever changed. I have a new perspective of how temporary we are—and I say that as a Doctor of Medicine, a Physician, who had already spent four decades walking the halls of medicine serving and ministering to the injured, the sick, and trying to ease the pain and suffering of those who were dying. *That is the work God gave me to do.* I've seen the

---

[23] In the Interlinear Bible (a Hebrew to English translation), *"according to its kind,"* is repeated ten times in Genesis One. The King James Bible says, *"after its kind," 9 times. Both translations interpret the Hebrew word "miyn" this way.* The deeper meaning of "*miyn*" is: "*species*" (Explained in Book II).

majority of my patients recover their health, and their vitality. But I have also seen a lot of suffering, dying, and death. I've seen terminally ill patients prepare for their mortal end, and I have witnessed the difference faith in God makes for those who have time to prepare for *their "Eternity Future!"* True Christians see their death as a doorway to Heaven where they will be given new bodies — *"bodies that will never be sick again and will never die."*

"vs.23 And even we Christians, although we have the Holy Spirit within us as a foretaste of future glory, also groan to be released from pain and suffering. We, too, wait anxiously for that day when God will give us our full rights as his children, including the new bodies he has promised us—bodies that will never be sick again and will never die (Romans 8:23 The Living Bible)."

I honestly don't understand why I felt compelled to write this book. And I have no idea of how it may be received. I can only hope it might help some people appreciate this gift God gave us that we call — *"life."* I have always believed: If we study history, we can profit by avoiding the mistakes of the past. Otherwise, we are doomed to repeat them.

My new book is now a *series* of three books: (1) Introduction & Book I: *Day One—From Darkness to Light.* (2) Book II: *The 2nd Day through the 6th Day—"The Six Days of The Ancient of Days" were Different from Our Days—* And (3) Book III: *The 1st Sabbath was Adam's 1st Day—Our Time-Flow Started with Adam.*

NINE-PART INTRODUCTION

This nine-part Introduction is necessary because there has been a history of conflict between religion and science for centuries. As you read this series of books, you will understand what I now believe, and how I have resolved many conflicts in my own mind. I have studied and reconciled the findings of recent scientific discoveries with what two ancient Jewish sages (from the 12th and 13th centuries) have concluded about the *Torah Creation Account.* I believe the last 85 years of scientific discovery; and a parallel renaissance in religious studies, have brought about a convergence of agreement between science and religion. My life-long belief in Jesus Christ has been affirmed and strengthened by what I have learned.

O. David

✤

INTRODUCTION— PART II: "INHERIT THE WIND" — THE REASON I WROTE THIS BOOK

"O. David! What have you done?"

"Ah-ha! I think your Moses shall have been a fool!" (The King of Siam: Chapter 5 Book I)

"Some people think: I — 'Shall have been a fool'— for writing this book." (O. David)

"But the natural man receiveth not the things of the Spirit of God for they are foolishness unto him. Neither can he know them because they are spiritually discerned." (I Cor. 2:14 KJV)

"INHERIT THE WIND"

In 1960, when I was a 20-year-old Pre-Med College sophomore, I saw *"Inherit the Wind."* That movie planted the seeds of discontent that (56 years later), caused me to publish the 1st Edition of this book. I am currently working on this rewrite of the manuscript — 60 years later. *"Inherit the Wind"* mocked the Christians in a small rural Tennessee town. They were portrayed as a march of brainwashed lemmings who blindly followed and parroted a fictional dogmatic Christian Fundamentalist preacher. The pastor in the movie was an angry arrogant bigot. He preached hellfire, brimstone, and damnation. The preacher-man in the movie was full of judgment! There was no love in him! He damned his own daughter because her fiancée taught Darwin's Theory of Evolution! With furrowed brow and a primeval energy, he shouted out his version of the first chapter of the Book of Genesis. As he thundered out his description of each Biblical Day of Creation, his "lemmings" punctuated his every sentence with — "Amen!"

While the preacher preached in the central town square, a crowd of visitors who had come to witness the trial of John Scopes, flooded into the nearby town park, and gathered around a circus hawker. The hawker was part of a carnival that had come to town for that festive occasion. His chimpanzee was a caricature of a poor southern farmer. Wearing overalls and a battered straw hat, the chimp was smoking a cigarette. The hawker was telling people — Darwin was wrong about man evolving from monkeys. The sign behind his chimp read: *"Monkeys devolved from Man!"*

Every day, the townspeople burned effigies of John Scopes (called Bertram Cates in the film) as they paraded around the town singing: *"We'll hang Bert Cates to a sour apple tree. Our God is marching on."*

The movie treated Darwin's theory as if it were true science and a proven law. In truth, after 165 years of searching, Darwin's Theory of Evolution remains a theory — because science has not proved it. *"Inherit the Wind"* is a clever mockery of a real-life 1925 trial that took place in Dayton, Tennessee — a small country town near Chattanooga. When I left the movie, I was angry, because the movie venerates Darwinism, maligns the Judeo-Christian God, pillories Christians, and ridicules the Bible. I also think it mischaracterizes the people of Dayton, Tennessee.

The people of my small rural southeast Alabama hometown are not like the people in the movie. For the most part, they are honest, intelligent, forgiving, kind, hardworking people. In one way only, my hometown is sort-of-like a southern version of the Boston Cheers Bar. It's a place where: *"Everybody knows your name."* If I got into mischief, my mother would hear about it before I got home, because in Brundidge, news and gossip spread like wildfire! She often said:

"O. David! What have you done?"

You see, most all the telephones in my hometown were on "party lines." That means all the telephones on our street were on the same phone line. When the phone rang, we were supposed to count the number of rings before we answered. If the phone rang once, we all knew the phone call was for the Fleming sisters. If the phone rang seven times, the call was for us. Our phones were not private. We assumed a lot of people would always be quietly listening in. There was no such thing as anonymity in Brundidge. Therefore, we were careful about what we said. They were good people, but one thing was sure: some were gossips. The lesson of the party line was — God is listening too! I always told the truth — not because I was a *"goody-two-shoes,"* but because I knew my mother *always* knew. Most of the folks in my hometown are Christians, but they don't wear God on their sleeves. I don't remember anyone with a better-than-thou-attitude. Okay, since *"Pobody's Nerfect,"* maybe there were a few. But I didn't know them. As for me and my childhood friends, we all thought our hometown was our own private *"Finian's Rainbow Glocca Morra."* After the movie I wondered: What's this movie really saying? It was clear: Charles Darwin was the center of it all. Then I thought: What if the Bible is right — and Darwin is wrong?

THE BURGESS PASS FOSSILS

At the time, I did not know the fossils that proved Darwin wrong had already been found! Charles Doolittle Walcott discovered them in the Burgess Pass in NW Canada in the summer of 1909, two years after my dad was born. He returned every summer for the next 10 years to collect more fossils. But their significance would not be known until the first analysis of all 60,000 of his fossils had been completed.[24] That happened in the mid 1980s after Dad died in 1985. That was almost 80 years after Walcott discovered them. Chapter 14: *"The 5th Day and The Cambrian Explosion of Visible Life"* is devoted to that subject. And Chapters 15—21 tell the instructive tale of the delayed realization of the full impact of Walcott's fossils. Those eight chapters are in Book II. After I saw *"Inherit the Wind,"* I started studying Darwin's book: *"The Origin of Species."* I wanted to see what his book said. I soon discovered Darwin's 19th century style of writing, would not be considered scientific writing today. Although common in his day, his style of writing has long since fallen out of favor. His book is full of unproved assumptions, beliefs, conjectures, circular logic, excuses, justifications, opinions, philosophies, rationalizations, speculative schemes, and suppositions.

I also read a few books about other theories of our origins — none of which have been proved. Today, scientific proof is required before a theory can be accepted as "Law." Nevertheless, because his theory is the only theory of evolution that is popularly touted as *"science,"* Darwin's theory may be the exception to that rule. *Because Darwinists have for so long claimed his theory is a proven law, most people now believe Darwin was right. Nothing could be further from the truth.* My quest continued for the next four decades.

In 1960, I did not know why the scriptwriters fictionalized and falsely characterized the people and the town in *"Inherit the Wind."* Neither did I know their intentions. Their motives were not revealed until one of the playwrights stated them in an interview in 1966

---

[24] *Schroeder The Science of God* Chp. 2 p 37b,e & 39b,c,d,e and p 40a

— the year I graduated from Medical School. However, I was focused on becoming a physician, and did not read the report of that interview until after I retired from Medicine and concentrated on completing the research that led to this book. So, I wondered: Why did they invent a false narrative and rewrite history by fictionalizing the people, the town, and the trial? To understand, one must consider the times, and the scriptwriter's beliefs, motives, and objectives.

THE TIMES: CHRISTIAN FUNDAMENTALISM — & — "THAT OLD-TIME RELIGION"

The real-life 1925 trial was the result of a perfect storm of colliding religious, political, cultural, and so called "scientific" events. In the 1920s, religious Christian Fundamentalists believed in a literal interpretation of The King James Bible. They still do. The theme song of *"Inherit the Wind"* is: *'Give Me that Old-Time Religion.'* It is clear: Christian Fundamentalism, with its literal interpretation of the King James Bible, is one of the targets of the film. Christian Fundamentalism is: *'That Old-Time Religion'* that *"Inherit the Wind"* maligns. The lyrics say: *"It was good for my ole mother, ole father, and everybody."* Other verses say: *"It was good for the Hebrew children, Ole Jonah, the prophet Daniel, and Paul & Silas."* However, the King James Bible did not exist in biblical times. I guess Christian Fundamentalists never considered: The 1st Edition of the King James Bible was published in 1611 AD. Therefore, the King James Bible is only slightly more than 400 years old. But, the Hebrew children of ancient biblical times were descendants of Abraham and his first wife Sarah, who lived about 2,000 years BC. And, Ole Jonah (about 786 BC) — and Daniel (who was taken in captivity to Babylon in 605 BC) — all lived several hundreds of years before Christ — between 4000 to 2600 years ago. Judaism was their religion. Furthermore, Paul and Silas (also known as Silvanus) lived in the 1st century AD — about 1500 years before the 1st Edition of the King James Bible was published. Paul and Silas were Christians. They converted to Christ and took the Gospel to the Gentiles in the 1st century AD after Christ arose from the dead and ascended into Heaven. My point is this: American Christian Fundamentalism, which was so onerous to "Progressives" in the 1920s, was a relatively new phenomenon that started in the late 19th century in opposition to the growth of 19th century Theological Liberalism, which aimed to reconcile traditional Christian beliefs with new developments in the natural and social sciences — especially regarding Darwin's Theory of Evolution. There really was nothing that is "Old-Time" about it. So, while American Christian Fundamentalism was good enough for *"my ole mother and father,"* it couldn't have been — good enough for the Hebrew children, Ole Jonah, the prophet Daniel, or even Paul and Silas.

THE RELATIVITY OF TIME

Christian Fundamentalists believe the *"Six Days of Creation"* were literally six 24-hour days, which were exactly like our days. The *"exactly like our days"* belief has been scientifically refuted. Chapter 5 (Book I) explains *the time-conundrum* in the Genesis Creation Account. It has everything to do with *Einstein's Laws of the Relativity of Time.* In the 13th century AD, Nahmanides deduced the concept of the Relativity of Time in the "Six Days of Creation" through his knowledge of the deeper meaning of the Hebrew words Moses wrote in the 1st Chapter of Genesis. I'll talk about that in Book I.

With his understanding of the deeper meaning of the Genesis Creation Account and the *Tanakh* (i.e., the rest of the Hebrew Old Testament), Maimonides concluded

Jehovah-Elohim reset the earth's clock on the First Sabbath (i.e., *the 7th Day*), and got rid of all those billions of earth-year-equivalents those *"Six Days of Old"* represented. He believed: On the First Sabbath (which was Adam's first full day), God changed the time-flow on earth — to its present 24-hour day. I'll talk about that in detail in Chapter 25 (in Book III).

Some Christian Fundamentalists not only refuse to accept *the Relativity of Time in Creation*, but they also reject the scientific discoveries that prove the earth is very old and the universe is even older. They believe the earth is young, about 5700 years old. Their belief in a *"young earth"* is based upon calculations derived from the genealogy lists in the book of Genesis. They are *"Young Earth Creationists"* who have founded the *"Creation Research Society,"* and claim: *"Extensive Messianic prophecy corruptions, and Flood-related chronology errors disqualify the Septuagint (LXX) as a reliable source for Creationist research."* [25] Do they not know: *The Septuagint* is a time-honored Greek translation of the Hebrew Bible that dates to the 3rd Century BC? [26] It was the work of 70 (LXX) Jewish religious scholars who were commissioned by Ptolemy II. I'll talk more about that in Part V of this Introduction: *"The Bible, Religion & Science."*

One Christian Fundamentalist told me she ignores the fossil record because "God is love," and "fossils would mean too much death." Apparently, she has never considered her skeleton will someday be the fossil evidence, that will prove — she once walked on earth. Others, who deny the fossil evidence of life-forms earlier than 5700 years ago, give other reasons. I think Christian Fundamentalists are right about their belief in Jesus Christ. But when it comes to science, I believe some Christian Fundamentalists are blinded by their own *"Cognitive Dissonance."* [27] (See the definition below.)

THE TIMES: THE POLITICAL ACTIVISM OF CHRISTIAN FUNDAMENTALISTS

In the 1920s, John W. Butler, a Tennessee farmer, State Representative, and head of the World Christian Fundamentals Association, lobbied the Tennessee state legislature to pass an anti-evolution law. He opposed the teaching of any theory of evolution that contradicted a literal interpretation of the Bible. He succeeded when The Butler Act was passed in 1925. That was a year after President Woodrow Wilson died and my dad graduated from High School (in Elba, Alabama). That law prohibited the teaching of Darwin's Theory of Evolution in all Tennessee state-funded schools.

THE TIMES: THE POLITICAL ACTIVISM OF "PROGRESSIVE" SECULARISTS

In 1925, the American Civil Liberties Union strongly opposed the Butler Act and all similar religious laws passed in other states. The legislative actions of ultraconservative religious fundamentalists were the reasons for the opposition of the ACLU. The ACLU believed a trial that challenged the constitutionality of Tennessee's Butler Act would be an opportunity to defend intellectual freedom and oppose Religious Fundamentalism. So, the ACLU looked for a teacher in Tennessee who would be willing to teach Darwin's

---

[25] https://creationresearch.org/crsq-2019-septuagint/

[26] www.britannica.com>topic>Septuagint

[27] *Cognitive Dissonance:* "The mental conflict caused by beliefs that are contradicted by new information." Cognitive Dissonance causes people to reject, avoid, or reconcile new information if it contradicts their preconceived notions about how things are or were. People will resort to any means available to preserve their ideas about stability and order in their conceptions of the world. (www.britannica.com/science/cognitive-dissonance)

theory, and advertised it would hire a defense attorney, and pay all legal expenses if the teacher were prosecuted for violating Tennessee's new religious law.

THE TIMES: DAYTON, TENNESSEE

Aware of what was happening, a businessman in Dayton thought a trial in his impoverished town would stimulate its economy. After obtaining the consent of Dayton's community leaders, he persuaded John Thomas Scopes to be the first teacher to challenge the new law. So, Scopes began teaching Darwin's Theory, and in the summer of 1925 the town constable charged him with violating Tennessee's new Butler Act.

The trial was set, and the upcoming legal battle would feature two nationally prominent lawyers. William Jennings Bryan volunteered to prosecute John Thomas Scopes, and Clarence Seward Darrow volunteered to defend him. Both men provided their services pro bono. These two nationally prominent antagonists dominated the trial. Thousands of local people and scores of national press reporters flocked to Dayton. The Scopes Trial became the first trial in the USA to be broadcast live on national radio. People called it *"The Monkey Trial."*

"THE MONKEY TRIAL"

In the 1960 *"Inherit the Wind"* movie, two of my favorite actors played key roles. Fredrick March played Bryan, who was given the fictional name, Matthew Harrison Brady. Spenser Tracy played Darrow, who was called Henry Drummond. Dick York (Bertram Cates in the film) played Scopes. Dayton was called — Hillsboro. That movie was a masterful blend of fact and fiction. To the uninformed there was enough fact to render the storyline believable. Fiction clearly won the day.

THE INTENT (OR MOTIVE) OF THE SCRIPTWRITERS

"Inherit the Wind" was written to ridicule and vilify Christian Fundamentalism. So, the writers twisted the facts and misrepresented the people, the town, and the trial. The movie portrayed the people of Hillsboro as childlike mindless southerners who blindly followed their evil pastor. In truth, the people of Dayton were intelligent, courteous, friendly, welcoming people — like the people of my hometown.

Drummond played the part of an enlightened freethinker who was the epitome of intellectual prowess and the champion of those who wished to be allowed to think, speak, and be free of the chains of religious dogma. In truth, the real-life Clarence Darrow was an Agnostic. He admired Christ's teachings but doubted His divinity. Nevertheless, at a meeting of nonbelievers in Chicago, when other speakers went too far in ridiculing Jesus Christ, Darrow jumped in and defended Christ so eloquently that he won the heart of George Schilling, a socialist, and a prominent Chicago trade unionist. They became fast friends.

Darrow's real-life character was in keeping with the way he was portrayed in the film. He really was a rough and tumble litigator — emphasis on the "gator" part of that word. His opponents literally felt the ferocity of his passionate arguments. Known as *"the Attorney for the Damned,"* Darrow was comfortable in his courtroom defenses of murderers, assassins, anarchists, bombers, and what he considered the poor, disadvantaged, downtrodden, defenseless masses. In his mind, Corporate America, with its boundless wealth was the Great Satan. He was also equally comfortable in the wild and blighted habitat of corrupt Chicago city politics *("There is nothing new under the sun"*

... Ecclesiastes 1:9) — where he worked, thrived, and honed his courtroom oratory. His tactics bewildered prosecutors. His verbal parries and thrusts always turned the argument and placed the prosecutors of his clients on the defensive. Many have said William Jennings Bryan was *"the silver-tongued orator of his time."* I argue the real master of courtroom oratory was Clarence Seward Darrow — not Bryan. Although Darrow had supported Bryan in two of his three previous campaigns for President of the United States, it was no secret Darrow eventually became an antagonist of Bryan. He developed a scornful loathing for *Religious Fundamentalism* — which is what he later decided Bryan represented. [28,29]

In Drummond's cross-examination of Brady, the movie shows Brady declaring, *"The original sin was sex."* (I was taught the original sin was *disobedience* — Romans 5:19.) In truth, the subject of original sin was never mentioned in the actual trial. In the film and in the real trial, Darrow (i.e., Drummond) treated Darwin's Theory of Evolution as if it were true science. In the movie, Drummond also questioned the veracity and truth of the Bible. His "*scientific*" arguments assumed God could not change or control His natural laws of nature, therefore if God stopped the sun for a day (Joshua 10:12-14) the earth would have been destroyed. Ergo, that "*story*" in Joshua could not have happened! (cf. Chapter 28 Book III: The Garden of Eden, under part III: *Separation for Holiness and God's Covenant with Abraham*).

There are numerous scenes in the movie, which depict Brady as a glutton. One scene shows him ravenously eating in the courtroom, just before the judge called the court to order. The movie fabricated the court scene where Brady badgered Cates' fiancée, when he tried to get her to admit Cates was teaching a heretical theory to young impressionable students. The innocent pastor's daughter that Brady interrogated and bullied — *never existed!* There was no evil bigoted pastor in Dayton, and Scopes was not dating the pastor's daughter! Scopes (i.e., Cates in the film) was not engaged! Neither did he have a love interest at the time of the trial! He was fined, but never jailed!

Brady was also portrayed as a pompous, arrogant, religious fanatic who collapsed at the end of the trial while frantically shouting out his belief in the truth of the Bible (as the crowd walked away). In the movie, Brady never recovered from his collapse, and he died that night. Drummond was told he died from *"a busted belly!"* In truth, the real William Jennings Bryan was not a glutton. He was courteous to all, exhibited a calm demeanor during the trial, and offered to pay Scope's fine. Although Bryan did die after the trial, he did not exhibit any fanatical behavior during the trial or after the verdict — did not suffer a stroke in the courtroom — and did not collapse at the end of the trial. He died peacefully in his sleep — five days later.

THE SCRIPTWRITER'S MOTIVES AND OBJECTIVES—FINALLY REVEALED

Six years after the movie, in a 1966 interview, Jerome Lawrence Schwartz admitted his purpose in writing *"Inherit the Wind"* was "to criticize McCarthyism and defend intellectual freedom!" Schwartz explained: *"We used the teaching of evolution as a parable, a metaphor for any kind of mind control. It's not about science versus religion. It's about the*

---

[28] Clarence Darrow: Attorney for the Damned, by John A. Farrell Copyright 2011
[29] Who is Clarence Darrow? faculty.smu.edu/jclam/science_religion/trial_darrow.html: by Douglas O. Linder, Professor of Law, University of Missouri, 1997

right to think." [30] Schwartz said he chose the title, *"Inherit the Wind,"* to show religious fundamentalists had caused unnecessary trouble in their own house. The title comes from Proverbs 11:29 — *"He that troubleth his own house shall inherit the wind. And the fool shall be servant to the wise of heart."*

MCCARTHYISM? REALLY?

In the 1950s, and without any regard for proper evidence, Wisconsin's ultra-conservative Republican Senator, Joseph McCarthy, accused several prominent American citizens and U.S. Government officials of being Communists. He claimed they were guilty of subversion and treason against the Government of the United States. Some of the accused were not guilty and did not belong to the Communist Party. Nevertheless, they were blacklisted and lost their jobs!

"McCarthyism" was an egregious, reprehensible, unlawful assault on the civil liberties of politically targeted citizens of our country. But McCarthyism happened 25 years after the Scopes Trial. I suspect a lot of people who saw the film and the earlier play, never realized the playwrights thought there was a connection between the Scopes trial and McCarthyism. However, I get it. Some Fundamentalist Preachers are scary, and Religious Fundamentalists overstepped their bounds with their 1925 Butler Act. That law violated the Constitutional principle of *"Separation of Church and State."*

"SEPARATION OF CHURCH AND STATE"

This principle has been interpreted and re-interpreted several times in the history of our country. When our country was founded, people remembered the evils state-sponsored religions in Europe had inflicted upon their people for centuries. Large numbers of people who came to our shores were fleeing from the persecutions of state-sponsored religions. That is why I think the 1st Amendment in our Constitution says:

"Congress shall make no law respecting an establishment of religion."

The original intent of our 1st Amendment was to ensure people would be free to worship (or not worship) as they please. Congress may not dictate if, how, or what, we believe — or when we worship or how American churches are financed. Government must stay out of religion altogether! This is how I interpret the original intent of our First Amendment. I suppose my interpretation is more consistent with the so-called minimalist view of church-state separation because I think it is more consistent with our history, and more accurately represents the intent of its framers. Nevertheless, the subject remains highly controversial, and (*at the moment in time in 2021 — when I first wrote these words*), the pendulum of public opinion and the Supreme Court interpretation of the 1st Amendment had for some time, swung from the original conservative view of the framers — to the views of the present-day liberal left. [31] Furthermore, I think the ridicule Schwartz heaped on Christianity with *"Inherit the Wind"* was unconscionable, and I also think there is an even greater danger today. Secular Darwinists and *"Progressives"* (a misnomer, in my view) want to change our constitutional right to freedom *of* religion — into freedom *from* religion. They want to outlaw all religions and erase God from our history. The demonstrations of young socialist progressives are now being joined by violent anarchists

---

30 Tennessee Attempts to Inherit the Wind Again I HuffPost https://www.huffington post.com/alex-simon/tennessee-attempts-to-inh_b_7082644.html

31 The Separation of Church and State in the United States: Oxford Research: Article by Steven K. Green: Dec. 2014: ·
http://americanhistory.oxfordre.com/view/10.1093/acrefore/9780199329175.001.0001/acrefore-9780199329175-e-2

who say they are *"left-wing reformers."* I disagree with *"reformers,"* because their tactics are not peaceful. They have become confrontational mobs of lawless, murderous, vicious, violent, rioters, arsonists, liars, looters, thieves, and thugs. In just the last few years, everywhere they *"protest,"* they destroy the property, homes, and businesses, of innocent citizens, and devastate the economies of entire cities! The same applies to the unlawful actions of *the alt-right!* Both extremes practice coercion and should be called: *"Coercionists,"* because they are mobs of fanatical people whose goal is to influence government through violence and coercion. Current-day extreme leftists now openly suppress the free-speech rights of conservatives. (This will be discussed in Chapter 21 of Book II*: The Agenda of Darwinists.*)

Likewise, I think Schwartz's *"parable"* and *"metaphor"* characterizations of the film were a *façade.* Jesus Christ often spoke in parables and metaphors to enlighten His listeners. However, He explained His parables to His disciples. But Schwartz's metaphoric *"Inherit the Wind"* was a satirical false narrative, which was an outright assault on Judeo-Christianity. It was an unprincipled fable — a depraved, dishonest, amoral, folktale. It should be clear to all: Schwartz and his co-writer, Robert E. Lee (the irony in that name) acted on the premise — *"The ends justify the means."* Stated another way: It's Okay to misrepresent, mischaracterize, fabricate, cheat, lie, riot, burn, and steal — if you think your reason is just. No wonder they fictionalized the people, the trial, and the town in the movie. I wonder how many people realize *"Inherit the Wind"* was political and social propaganda?

The movie debut was a fanfare event, which was attended by the rich and famous — many of whom were members of the so-called *"Hollywood Elite."* They arrived in chauffeured limousines, wearing formal attire dripping with diamonds, and were filmed on the red carpet, as they waved like royalty to their admiring fans. Who said: *"There are no 'Royals' in America?"*

SCHWARTZ RIDICULED RELIGIOUS FUNDAMENTALISM

"Not about science versus religion" — is simply not true. Of course, it was all about science versus religion! But the *"science of Darwinism"* is not science! It is PSEUDO-SCIENCE! I'll discuss that in detail in Book II. Nevertheless, it is clear — Schwartz's purpose was to convince people:

   (1) The Bible's Creation Account is myth.
   (2) Darwin's Theory of Evolution is science.
   (3) People who believe in the creation *"story"* are mindless idiots.
   (4) And Religious Fundamentalism is a form of mind control.

Is Schwartz saying: belief in God is a mindless choice? Does he think people who believe in God are not intelligent and don't exercise their right to think? Does he suppose: If science can't prove God exists, we shouldn't believe in God? I say: *"Arrogant secular 'progressives' and atheists know no bounds!"* Dr. Schroeder (cf. Chapter 1 in Book I) has written: *"Judaism, Christianity, and Islam all draw their understanding of creation from the opening chapters of the Book of Genesis. Genesis claims that a single, eternal, omnipotent and incorporeal God created the universe."*[32]

---

[32] This is a direct quote from Dr. Schroeder's book: The Hidden Face of God: Chapter 1 p 10a

Jews, Christians, and Muslims recognize the existence of a Superior Being whose intellect and power are greater than man's. Although Jews call "God" *Jehovah*, Muslims say "God" is *Allah*, and Christians believe Jesus Christ is the *"The Messiah and the Son of Jehovah"* — all three religions say the generic name of the Supreme Being they worship is — *"God."* They all believe what the Bible proclaims: *"God" is the Creator of all that exists!* Furthermore, all three great *monotheistic religions deny the secular claim — their belief in "God" is a form of "mind control!"*

Nevertheless, when the 1925 Butler Act was passed, Religious Fundamentalists did cross the line. The state legislators of Tennessee made a law that violated the first three of the five rights guaranteed citizens in the 1st Amendment to the US Constitution:

(1) "Congress shall make no law respecting an establishment of religion—

(2) Or prohibiting the free exercise thereof (meaning the free exercise of religion) —

(3) Or abridging the freedom of speech, or of the press—

(4) Or the right of the people peacefully to assemble, and

(5) To petition the Government for a redress of grievances." (The underlining is mine.)

Hit the pause button right now! The 1st Amendment begins with a specific prohibition of Congress. Congress shall not make any law that establishes or sponsors any religion, and Congress shall not interfere in any way with the free exercise of any religion. Also notice, the word *"protest"* doesn't appear in the 1st Amendment of our Constitution. The 1st Amendment does not guarantee citizens the right to assemble to — intimidate, riot, fight, kill, loot, and deface, damage, burn, or destroy property! Furthermore, we do not have the right to suppress the freedom of speech of other people, or of the press. It simply says the freedom of speech and of the press shall not be abridged! Conservatives interpret that to mean: if people are unhappy with what is happening in society, they only have the right to assemble *peacefully* to demonstrate their disagreement, and petition (i.e., to peaceably assemble to speak and parade with their signs — to lobby, plea, and implore) the Government for a redress of their grievances!

By making it illegal to teach Darwin's theory in Tennessee's public schools, the Butler Act attempted to legislate the preeminence of a religious fundamental interpretation of the Genesis Creation Account. It clearly was an unconstitutional law that outlawed the free exchange of ideas. There is no doubt it was an egregious assault on the right to think.

On the other hand, I think *"Inherit the Wind"* falsely characterized Christian Fundamentalism, and I also think it tarred and feathered all of Christianity with the broad brush of its mischaracterizations.

DARWIN—THE CHAMPION OF ATHEISTS

Ever since his book was first published ~ 165 years ago, Darwin has been proclaimed the champion of atheists. That is why Richard Dawkins wrote in his book, "The Blind Watchmaker:" *"Darwin made it possible to be an intellectually fulfilled atheist."* [33]

Influential atheists in Darwin's time encouraged Darwin to publish his book because they wanted to use his theory to attack the Bible and defend atheism. When Darwin's book: *"The Origin of Species"* was published, atheists used it to support their claim: *"There is no God!"* Some who won't go that far claim: *"If God exists, He is irrelevant — because*

[33] D'Souza: What's So Great About Christianity Chapter 3 p. 26

Darwin has proved creation and evolution could have happened without God." They believe Darwin's claim of random chance origins and natural selection development has proved God irrelevant. After scientists proposed *"The Beginning started as a Big Bang,"* atheists said, *"'The Big Bang Theory' was acceptable to them because no God was required. All could have happened by Darwin's idea of random chance."* They claimed: *"No God (i.e., no Big Banger) was necessary!"*

In *"Inherit the Wind,"* Darwinism and atheism clearly won the day. Schwartz may be the most successful propagandist in American history. Today, it seems Darwinism has triumphed. Many Americans now think all religions are myths. Since 1960, *"Inherit the Wind"* has not only achieved all the ACLU had hoped the 1925 trial would accomplish, but I believe it was a turning point in American public opinion. Before *"Inherit the Wind,"* the literal interpretation of the Bible's Creation Account could be taught in American public schools. Now, more than half a century after *"Inherit the Wind,"* not only is it unlawful to teach the Biblical Creation Account, but it is also unlawful to pray to God and mention God's name in public schools and public events. There are some who want to ignore our history and remove the generic name — *"God"* — from our monuments, government buildings, Pledge of Allegiance, and money. Now Darwinism and Neo-Darwinism are the only explanations of our origins that can be taught in our country's public schools. This will be discussed in Chapter 21, in Book II.

DARWINISM IS PSEUDO-SCIENCE.

If you want to tout your science, you should be certain your science is correct. People think Darwinism is science. In truth, this book will explain why it is pseudo-science. The truth of this statement will become evident if you continue reading. Nevertheless, I think it was a good thing the Butler Act was declared unconstitutional, because (in 1925) the pendulum of public opinion had swung too far to the extreme conservative religious right. But I also think it has turned into a bad thing, because the pendulum is now stuck — too far to the so-called *"progressive"* secular left.

WE NEED A RELIGIOUS REVIVAL.

The Biblical Creation Account begins in chaos (Book I). On each day of creation, the Creator imposed a degree of order on the chaos of The Beginning. Remove the Creator, and everything will revert to chaos. I think that is what has happened to us. I believe all that is wrong with our society today is the result of the denial of our Creator, and a turning away from God. More, and more, we are beginning to look to government to solve all our problems. I think the only thing that can prevent the implosion of our government and society is a nation-wide revival that brings about humility, prayer, repentance, forgiveness, worship, and a return to God—and His loving kindness. We need to return to the beliefs of our founding fathers, and we must learn to follow *the commandment of Christ to love others as we love ourselves.* (cf. Chapter 23 — *"Image, Likeness, & Image of God"* in Book III.)

When I left that movie in 1960, I felt Christianity, and the Bible were under an attack. I did *not* know the 19th and 20th century discoveries of modern science would eventually *refute Darwin's theory and verify the truth of the Bible's Creation Account.* In 1960, no one had stepped back and looked at *"The Big Picture."* Now, when viewed as a whole, the scientific discoveries of the last 85 years actually confirm the accuracy of the sequences of creation presented in the Bible! [34] Moreover, in 1965 — five years after the 1st showing of *"Inherit the Wind"* — **Cosmic Microwave Background Radiation (CBR)** was discovered. The existence of CBR has proved the validity of Lemaitre's 1927 Big Bang Theory and has also verified Nahmanides' 13th Century Hebrew Cosmogony, which Nahmanides derived from his interpretation of the Hebrew Torah — specifically Genesis One! CBR is *"the smoking gun of the Big Bang!"* It is the irrefutable scientific proof of something the Bible first proclaimed 3300 years ago — There actually was a beginning! [35,36,37,38] The Hebrew Bible had been correct all along! Dr. Gerald L. Schroder says: "Arguments concerning cavemen, dinosaurs, and other controversies embraced by critics of the Bible's Creation Account, now pale in significance when compared to the bold opening statement of the Bible — there actually was a beginning!" [39]

Book I in this series discusses the scientific discoveries that prove the truth of these statements. Furthermore, the accumulating millions of fossil discoveries over the past 165 years since Darwin 1st published his book *("The Origin of Species"), have provided the undeniable evidence that absolutely refutes Darwinism and Neo-Darwinian theory!* [40] The case for the proof of this statement is presented in detail in Chapters 14-21 in Book II. These are the things science has discovered in the last 85 years. **These discoveries happened after Darwin died.** *They are things Darwin did not know!*

For years after I retired from practicing Diagnostic Radiology, Nuclear Medicine, and Radiation Therapy, I struggled with the idea I should write about what I have learned. I realized any attempt to do so would not only consume me but worried many Christians would misunderstand my intent. However, there is nothing in this book that contradicts the basic tenets of Christianity! Furthermore, I felt Darwinism is now so entrenched, and the mores of society have so drastically changed, that anything I might write would be like trying to empty an ocean with an eyedropper. So, I procrastinated. Nevertheless, I continued to feel strangely unsettled. Finally, I decided to start putting some thoughts on paper. I promised myself — If I should find any conflict between religion and science that cannot be attributed to bad science, or faulty religious interpretations of the Bible, I would quit writing and walk away. What criteria would I use in making those determinations? I would use the opinions of ancient Jewish sages, which are recorded in their written interpretations of the ancient Hebrew Scriptures. I would also use the opinions of current-day scientists and religious leaders who are considered principled enlightened authorities on the issues involved. These people will be identified when their written opinions are discussed and referenced in the narrative, which follows.

[34] Schroeder *The Science of God* Chapter 4 p 66c and Chp 2 p 39c-40a (the Genesis Sequence of Creation is 3300 years old!)
[35] Article: Georges Lemaitre-Father of the "Big Bang" IThe Catholic…http://www.vofoundation.org/blog/priests-science-georges-lemaitre-father-big-bang/)
[36] Article: 'A Day Without Yesterday': Georges Lemaitre & the Big Bang
https://www.catholiceducation.org/en/science/faith-and-science/a-day-without-yesterday-georges-lemaitre-a
[37] Article: Discovery of Cosmic Background Radiation: http://hyperphysics.phy-astr.gsu.edu/hbase/astro/penwil.html
[38] Article: Arno Penzias and Robert Wilson: Bell Labs, Holmdel, NJ http://hyperphysics.phy-astr.gsu.edu/hbase/penwil.html
[39] Schroeder The Science of God Chapter 2 p 22 (A direct quote.)
[40] Charles Darwin The Origin of Species Chp VI Difficulties of the Theory—Modes of Transition p 155

After three decades of research and study, and an additional twelve years of post-retirement writing, re-writing, and editing — I finally completed *"THE GENESIS CODE: Moses & Modern Science Agree."* My book, published by Xulon Press in April 2016, makes the case — a 20th century renaissance in science and religion has reconciled differences and has brought about a convergence of agreement between the two disciplines.

This book starts with a nine-part Introduction, which discusses the conflicts that have historically existed between religion and science. Then, the discussion of the Cosmogony of the ancient Jewish sages and how it relates to the Genesis Creation Account is discussed in the three books, which follow. My reasons for doing this are explained in this nine-part Introduction. I have not only added new material, but I have removed several redundancies, and I have made corrections to typographical errors that are in the 1st Edition.

PAUL — THE APOSTLE TO THE GENTILES — SAID:

"For the word of the cross is folly to those who are perishing, but to us who are being saved it is the power of God. For it is written: 'I will destroy the wisdom of the wise, and the cleverness of the clever I will thwart.' Where is the wise man? Where is the scribe? Where is the debater of this age? Has not God made foolish the wisdom of the world? For since, in the wisdom of God the world did not know God through wisdom, God was pleased, through the folly of what we preach — to save those who believe. For Jews demand signs and Greeks (i.e., Gentiles) [41] *seek wisdom. But we preach Christ crucified, a stumbling block to Jews and a folly to Gentiles. But to those who are called, both Hebrews and Greeks* (i.e., Jews and Gentiles), *Christ is the power of God and the wisdom of God. For the foolishness of God is wiser than men, and the weakness of God is stronger than men (I Cor. 1:18-25 RSV)."*

No work of this nature can ever be complete, nor can it be free of error! This book represents my opinions, beliefs, and faith in Jesus Christ — all of which were formed by my upbringing, and tested by my formal education, 80+ years of life-experiences, my four-decades of studying, practicing, and teaching Medicine, and the opinions of the people referenced in this book. This book will give you a different perspective of the Biblical *"Six Days of Creation."* It looks at the deeper meaning of the Mosaic Account. No doubt, this book will be anathema to all Darwinists, all Atheists, and to a lot of Liberal and Fundamental Christians. Hopefully, those believers who have similar views, proclaim the same faith, and may continue the quest — will correct the errors I have made in this manuscript. I share this now with those who care to read it because of what this work has done for me. I am now convinced the words of Moses (in the Genesis Account of Creation) are absolute truth and were Divinely Inspired by God. The Bible's Creation Account is not a fairy tale! The first two chapters of Genesis are not a myth! They are history, religion, and science. They are — God's words!   *Soli Deo Gloria!*

"O. David! What have you done?"

---

[41] Gentiles: Anyone who is not a Jew. Jews are descendants of Abraham and Sarah. This is a simplistic explanation. If you research "Jew," "Hebrew," "Eber," "Shem," "Noah," "Ur," "Chaldean," "Haran," et cetera. You will find yourself feeling somewhat like *the dog that chases his tail.*

❖
INTRODUCTION—PART III:
MACBETH—THE WAY OF THE WORLD VS. GOD'S WAY.

"Tomorrow, and tomorrow, and tomorrow
Creeps in this petty pace from day to day,
To the last syllable of recorded time.
And all our yesterdays have lighted fools,
The way to dusty death.

Out, out, brief candle.
Life is but a walking shadow, a poor player,
That struts and frets his hour upon the stage,
And then is heard no more.

It is a tale told by an idiot,
Full of sound and fury,
Signifying nothing."

Shakespeare's Macbeth: Upon hearing of his wife's death...From Act V: Scene V:

In this moment of crisis, Macbeth heard a horrific shriek echoing throughout his castle. Someone discovered his wife committed suicide! He thinks —death, our return to dust— seems insignificant. It is the last act of a very bad play. To him, life is meaningless, an idiot's tale, full of sound and fury, signifying nothing! These are the words of a wicked Godless person — a fool who lusted for the power and prestige of another's throne — an evil man who murdered a king to achieve the objects of his lust. He and his wife planned the murder and afterward, they inaugurated a reign of homicidal terror to bolster their power. Their guilty consciences eventually drove them both to the edge of madness. Just before he was told his wife committed suicide, he learned an avenging army was stealthily advancing upon his castle. *Birnam Wood was indeed coming to Dunsinane!* [42] Realizing he would soon be dead — he began to reflect upon his criminal deeds — the ultimate futility of his ghastly works and the meaninglessness of his own vicious life. Macbeth was a man, who followed the way of the world. Near his end, and in the face of imminent justice, he decided all his evil ambitions, his foul murders, his heinous deeds, and the very essence of his fetid life — had been futile. The Bible points to another way. The other way is in God's Play.

For a Life full of Meaning, and Filled with Purpose:
Agape's the Way, Belief's the Seed, and
Faith's the Kernel, that Lead Believers
to Life Eternal.

(My Rhyme —cf. "GOD'S PLAY @ the end of the next Chapter. *O. David*).

---

[42] In Shakespeare's play, Macbeth is told he will be defeated when *"Birnam Wood comes to Dunsinane."* When the attack comes, the enemy's army advances on his castle through *Birnam Wood*. Each soldier cut a large branch of a tree to disguise himself. When the army marches on Macbeth's castle, it looks like: *"Birnam Wood — is coming to Dunsinane."*

❧
INTRODUCTION—PART IV: BELIEF & FAITH
Jesus: "I am the way, the truth, and the life. No one comes to the Father, but through Me." (John 14:6)
"Know what to answer a skeptic." (Maimonides—an Ancient Jewish Sage)

This is a book about origins. It focuses on what the Bible first declared 3300 years ago, and what science now says about our origins. It is also a book about belief and faith in God, Jesus Christ, the Holy Spirit— and the Christian commitment to act in God's Play, by living our lives in God's Way.   O. David

"MADE FROM MONKEYS?"

It was a magnificent day. A glorious array of blooming fall perennials beautified the park. The pleasing smell of tea olive filled the coastal air. The crowd in Forsyth Park had begun to flow towards the bandstand behind the park's giant ornate water fountain. The first concert of Savannah's Annual Jazz Festival was about to begin. Bob James was the main attraction. The well-known jazz pianist had just returned to the States from a very successful concert tour in Japan. The Japanese love him. Mr. James is also popular in Georgia. A large crowd was gathering. I was looking forward to his performance and hoped to meet him after the concert. My wife and I had come with two friends who were close friends of Mr. James. As we settled into our portable chairs (near the bandstand) and watched as the crowd gathered, a young man sat on the ground in front of me. On the front and back of his black T-shirt were capitalized white bold letters that read:

"MADE FROM MONKEYS!"

I wondered: Does he believe the message he is wearing, or does he think he's just making a hip statement? Then I thought: What do I believe? Do I believe I was: *"Made from Monkeys?"*

WHAT IS BELIEF?

Belief is the acceptance of the truth of something. Belief comes after one realizes something is true, is real. Belief is often underpinned by an emotional or spiritual sense of certainty and conviction. How does one get to the acceptance of the truth of something? One must first gain knowledge and then become convinced the knowledge is true. In short, knowledge + assent = belief. Over time, as we experience the truth of our knowledge, our belief will become — a conviction of belief.

THE THREE GREAT QUESTIONS FOR ALL TIMES CONCERN OUR ORIGINS.

If you are like me, the first question is: Where did I come from? Next, I look around and ask: Where did we come from? Then I wonder: Where did everything come from? The scientist in me shortened that list to:
- How did I originate?
- How did life originate?
- How did the universe originate?

When I looked at that list, I realized the order of the questions should be — What was the origin of:
- The Universe—
- Of Life—
- Of Humans?

WHAT DO YOU BELIEVE?

How do you think you came to be? Have you given the subject of your origins any serious thought? Do you believe Charles Darwin, or do you believe God's word — the Bible?

A WONDERFUL ANCIENT BOOK—THE BIBLE:

I was raised in a Christian home. In our home the Bible played a major role. My father often read to us from the Bible after supper. I loved the sound of his voice and looked forward to hearing God's word. Early on, I developed a love for the Bible.

MY ORIGINS? I HAVE ALWAYS BELIEVED THE BIBLE.

[27]*"So, God created man in His own image. In the image of God created He him. Male and female created He them."* (Gen. 1:27 KJV)[7] *"And the LORD GOD formed man of the dust of the ground. And breathed into his nostrils the breath of life. And man became a living soul."* (Gen. 2:7 KJV)

DARWIN VERSUS THE BIBLE:

Ever since Charles Darwin, Christians have asked themselves: Which is true — the Bible, or Darwin? Some Christians have accommodated Darwin by thinking: Maybe God created monkeys before he created man, and maybe the way he created man was by evolving some monkeys into the first man. I have admiration and empathy for Mr. Darwin. He was a brilliant man. However, he seems to have been a tormented man. But we'll get to that later. Nevertheless, at some point, everyone needs to decide—

- What knowledge have I bought into?
- Do I assent to the truth of that knowledge?
- Do I have the conviction of the truth of that belief?

A VALUABLE LESSON FROM MY FATHER

I will never forget the day my father talked to one of my best friends about Jesus Christ. My parents had come for a visit during my freshman year at the University of Alabama in Tuscaloosa. My friend Henry had doubts about Jesus and wanted to talk with my dad. We were on the front porch. The year was 1958. Dad suggested we walk away from the crowd. Then, he turned to Henry and asked if he believed in God. The conversation, as I remember it, went something like this—

Dad: "Henry, do you believe there is a God?"

Henry: "Yes Sir."

Dad: "Do you believe the Old and New Testaments of the Bible are the Word of God?"

Henry: "Yes Sir."

Dad: "Do you believe the God of the Bible would ever lie?"

Henry: "No Sir."

Dad: "Who was Jesus Christ?"

Henry: "He was a good man who did a lot of good things, but I don't believe he was the Son of God."

"THIS IS MY BELOVED SON, IN WHOM I AM WELL PLEASED."

Dad took out the small New Testament he always carried in his inside coat pocket, and asked Henry if he would like to hear what God said about His son. When Henry said: "Yes," Dad read the account of the Baptism of Jesus by John the Baptist (in the 3rd Chapter of Matthew). Dad emphasized the words God spoke from the heavens in verse 17: *"This is My beloved Son, in whom I am well pleased"* (Matt. 3:17 NASB).

"THIS IS MY BELOVED SON, IN WHOM I AM WELL PLEASED. LISTEN TO HIM."

Next, Dad read one of the narratives of the Transfiguration of Jesus recorded in the gospels of Matthew (17:1-5), Mark (9:2-7), and Luke (9:28-35). All three scriptures say

Peter, James, and John witnessed this miraculous event. These accounts of Christ's Transfiguration are almost identical even though they were written several years apart, 50-60 years after the crucifixion and resurrection of Christ. Dad told Henry: Matthew was a disciple of Jesus who wrote his gospel to the Jews. Mark, a close friend, and disciple of Peter wrote his gospel to the Gentiles. Luke was probably the only Gentile author of any part of the New Testament. Luke wrote the Gospel of Luke and the Book of Acts. He was a beloved physician and a close friend and companion of the apostle Paul. [43] Each account says Jesus took Peter, James, and John to a high mountain where He was transfigured before them (cf. 2 Peter 1:16-21). They all agree—

- Christ's face shown like the sun.
- His garments became radiant and as white as light.
- Elijah and Moses appeared and were talking to Jesus.
- The three disciples became terrified.
- A bright cloud formed and overshadowed them, and then,
- A voice came out of the cloud saying:
- *"This is my beloved Son, in whom I am well pleased. Listen to Him." (Matt. 17:5)*
- *"This is my beloved Son, Listen to Him." (Mark 9:7)*
- *"This is my Son, my chosen One: Listen to Him." (Luke 9:35)*
- *"This is My beloved Son with whom I am well-pleased" (2 Peter 1:17 — all from the NASB).*

THE SIGNIFICANCE OF THE CLOUD

My father explained — the disciples understood the voice from the cloud was God's voice — because (in Old Testament times) God frequently cloaked Himself in a cloud to protect His people from His appearance (cf. Exodus 33:18-23). During the Exodus, God appeared to Moses and the Israelites as a "pillar of cloud by day" and "a pillar of fire by night." When the Egyptians were pursuing and thought they had trapped the Israelites against the seashore that night, God stood before the Egyptians as a pillar of cloud that obscured their vision, because all was in darkness on their side of the pillar of cloud. But, on the side facing the Israelites, He was a pillar of fire that lighted their way through the parting of the waters that night (Ex. 14:20 the KJV). God led his people in the Sinai during the Exodus in the form of a pillar of cloud by day. When He wanted them to travel at night, God's pillar of cloud turned into a pillar of fire by night — that lighted their way. When He wanted them to stop for the night, the pillar of cloud would stop moving; they would erect the tent tabernacle, and the pillar of cloud would move into the Holy of Holies. Then, God would settle on the Ark of the Covenant as a pillar of fire that did not consume! The people (who were encamped around the tent tabernacle) could see the light of God coming from within the Holy of Holies at night! Thus, God was a constant presence among His people during the Exodus, leading and protecting them as a pillar of cloud by day, and a pillar of fire by night. (Ex. 13:21-22; 14:19-20; 16:10; 19:9; 40:34-38 Num. 9:15-23).

"I AND THE FATHER ARE ONE."

Dad then read the first eleven verses of the 14th Chapter of John. This scripture is part of John's account of "the Last Supper" on the night Jesus was betrayed and arrested. At the

---

[43] Ryrie Study Bile Notes — Introductions to the Gospels Matthew, Mark, and Luke.

conclusion of the Last Supper, Christ told His disciples He would soon be leaving them. He would be going to His Father's house of many rooms in heaven. There, He would prepare a place for them so that where He was, they would be also. Then Jesus said: [4]*"And you know the way where I am going"* (John 14:4). Thomas said: [5]*"Lord, we do not know where you are going, how do we know the way?"* Jesus responded: [6]*"I am the way, and the truth, and the life. No one comes to the Father but through Me. [7]If you had known Me, you would have known My Father also. From now on you know Him and have seen Him"* (John 14:6-7). To this: [8]Philip said to Him *"Lord, show us the Father, and it is enough for us" (14:8).* Then (in verse 9-10), Jesus told Philip: [9]*"He who has seen Me has seen the Father.[10]Do you not believe I am in the Father and the Father is in Me? The words that I say to you I do not speak on My own initiative, but the Father abiding in Me does His works.*

After that, Dad read John 10:30, where Jesus said: [30]*"I and the Father are One."*

THE ASCENSION OF JESUS

Next, Dad read Luke's account of the Ascension of Christ in the 1st Chapter of Acts. He emphasized Acts 1:9 and explained, after Jesus arose from the dead, the last time the disciples saw Him was on the Mt. of Olives (Acts 1:1-12). There, they watched Him ascend into heaven. While they were looking, a cloud received Him out of their sight. Then, two angels told them Jesus would return in the same way. At that point, Dad told Henry the disciples understood: God the Father, cloaked in a cloud, had come to earth to embrace His beloved, and wounded Son — to carry Him back to paradise. Finally, Dad looked at Henry and asked:

"Henry, when God said: *'This is My Son in whom I am well pleased, Listen to Him,'* and when Jesus said: *'I and the Father are One,'* do you believe God and Jesus lied?"
Henry looked at Dad — paused for a long moment and then — with a big smile on his face, said: *"NO SIR!"*

Understanding Henry had just learned the central truth of the New Testament, and confessed his belief in Jesus Christ, my Father smiled and said: "At this very moment, Jesus has reserved a room in Heaven for you!"

"KNOW WHAT TO ANSWER A SKEPTIC."

With a few questions my father learned Henry was not an atheist. Neither was he an Agnostic, nor a Gnostic. When Dad discovered Henry believed in God, believed in the Bible, and did not question Jesus was a good man who helped people — he knew how to state the case to help Henry overcome his doubts about Jesus Christ. Later, when I told my father I had been amazed with the wisdom of the way he had chosen to help Henry, my father said to me: "Son, a highly respected ancient Jewish Sage and Physician, Maimonides, once said: *'Know what to answer a skeptic.'"*

"LOVE THY NEIGHBOR AS YOU LOVE YOURSELF" (MARK 12:28-31).

As I thought about what Dad did for Henry, I realized he did it out of love. By sharing his knowledge of God, which came from the Bible; my father used the Bible to help Henry free himself from the bondage of his doubt of the truth of Jesus. Henry finally understood Jesus Christ is the Son of God in whom God is well pleased. We must listen to Him. Living our lives in the service of others is the ultimate goal of a firm belief and faith in God and

Jesus. Serving the needs of others is what Jesus did. Serving others is what believers do.

THE DISCIPLES' KNOWLEDGE & ASSENT TO THE TRUTH OF CHRIST

The disciples' faith in a belief in Jesus came from their daily walk with Him. They saw Him raise people from the dead, witnessed His miracles of healing, and heard His many parables and sermons. Their faith was based on their own personal experience of Jesus. For three years, they walked, talked, ate, slept, and lived with Him. We know they had a conviction of faith in Christ and in God, because of what they did after Christ's crucifixion, resurrection, and ascension. They all went into the world and preached the Gospel. They obeyed Christ's commandment to: *"Go therefore and make disciples of all the nations; baptizing them in the name of the Father, and of The Son, and of the Holy Spirit." (Matt. 28:19 NASB)*.

They were all persecuted for preaching the Gospel. Because of their conviction of faith in a belief in Jesus and God, all but one of the disciples (John), died a martyr's death as Christ had foretold (Matt. 27:1-10; John 15:18-20, John 16:2, John 21:18-23; and John Foxe's: *Book of Martyrs*). John lived to write the Gospel of John, the three Epistles of John, and the Book of Revelation. He died a natural death. Judas Iscariot did not preach the Gospel after Christ's crucifixion. He was not persecuted or martyred. Full of remorse after he betrayed Jesus, he tried to return his 30 pieces of silver to the priests, but they refused, so he threw the pieces of silver into the temple, left, and committed suicide (Matt. 27:3-10).

HOW DO WE GET TO KNOW & ACCEPT THE TRUTH OF CHRIST?

Regular worship at Church services, Sunday school, Bible study groups, and fellowship with other believers strengthens and renews our faith. But our primary source for gaining our knowledge of God and Jesus Christ should be from reading and studying the Bible.

FAITH: THE BASIS OF A BELIEF IN AND DEVOTION TO GOD.

The Bible teaches us: *"Faith is the assurance of things hoped for and the conviction of things not seen"* (Hebrews 11:1). Faith gives reality and proof of things unseen, helping us to treat them as if they are already objects of sight, and not mere objects of hope. *"For we walk by faith, not by sight" (II Cor. 5:7)*. Walking by faith and not by sight is a daring walk because it asks us to look beyond logic and believe what we cannot prove. It requires us to ignore the wisdom of the world, and place confidence in the Wisdom of God (I Cor. 1:18-25). Faith enables us to believe the Wisdom of God revealed to us through God's Spirit. The Bible says: *"But as it is written, Eye hath not seen, nor ear heard, neither have entered into the heart of man, the things which God hath prepared for them that love him. But God hath revealed them unto us by his Spirit — for the Spirit searcheth all things, yea, the deep things of God" (I Cor. 2:9-10)*.

People of faith do not ignore the truth. They seek it. They do not scorn reason, but neither do they worship it, nor expect reason to reveal all that is to be known. The faithful recognize — God's wisdom and knowledge far exceed the wisdom and knowledge of man. They do not expect to understand all mysteries (Isa. 55:8-9). Yet, if something remains beyond their understanding, they must hold to the mystery of faith with a clear conscience (I Tim. 3:9) and accept that many of the truths of God are embraced not by logic, but by faith. There are certain concrete beliefs and truths faith brings.

- *"By faith we understand the worlds were prepared by the Word of God so that what is seen was <u>not</u> made out of things which were visible" (Heb. 11:3).* When I read this scripture I not only think about the universe, but I also think about atomic structure and the subatomic "world!"
- Through faith we believe: *"God so loved the world that He gave His only begotten Son, so that whosoever believeth in Him should not perish, but have eternal life" (John 3:16).*
- When Jesus Christ of Nazareth 1st came to earth (that is, in His 1st advent), *"...God did not send the Son into the world to judge the world, but that the world should be saved through Him" (John 3:17).*
- *"He who believes in Him is not judged. But he who does not believe has been judged already, because he has not believed in the name of the only begotten Son of God" (John 3:18).*
- By faith: Understanding is enlarged, blessings are claimed, divine responsibilities are assumed, miracles are fashioned, and dramatic victories are won (a synopsis of Hebrews 11:1-40).

It has been said: Belief comes from knowledge and an assent to the truth of that knowledge. From that process comes the conviction of the truth of that belief. When one trusts his conviction of the truth of his belief, then his belief turns into faith. In our journey into the process of belief in God: Faith adds Trust. In short, knowledge of God + assent to the truth of our knowledge of God = belief in God. Belief in God + Trust in God = Faith in a Belief in God. Over time, as our knowledge and experience of the truth of God grows, our faith in a belief in God grows, and becomes a conviction of our faith in a belief in God. This leads to a devotion to God. This process frees us from all doubt. A faith, which is free of doubt, is a living faith. And a living faith empowers us to live our lives in a way that pleases God. We possess a true faith in God when we finally reach the point where we always take God at His Word. What I just described as a stepwise process is, in our actual experience, a seamless process that naturally occurs without any conscious effort on our part. The whole process is the result of the work of the Holy Spirit within us. Do you know the truth of Jesus Christ? Do you know what to answer a skeptic?

WHEN I TALKED ABOUT MACBETH (IN PART III), I MENTIONED "GOD'S PLAY."

By "God's Play," I meant: "We must live according to God's Way." We must continually seek God's Will for us "to finish God's work" by preaching the Gospel of Jesus Christ to all others (cf. Longfellow's Christus Poem). God sent His Son Jesus Christ to show us how we should live. Jesus Christ is our example. Remember these words? *"The Bible points to another way. The other way is in God's Play.*

For a Life full of Meaning, and Filled with Purpose, Agape's the Way, Belief's the Seed, and Faith's the Kernel, That Lead Believers to Life Eternal."

THE GREATEST OF THESE IS THE AGAPE OF CHRIST.

Agape (i.e., sacrificial love) + the seed of belief in the Gospel of Jesus Christ + the "Kernel" of Christian Faith (i.e., the nucleus and center of our faith in Christ Jesus) — are the three elements necessary for a life full of meaning and filled with purpose. Christ's sacrifice on the Cross was "Agape Love." The Father's and Christ's Agape for us — was the reason Jesus died for us!

His sacrifice atoned for the sins of the world, (past present and future) *and washed believers as clean and pure as the driven snow so that they might be made acceptable to God!*

He died so that we may have eternal life! That is the *Kernel*, which is the *Nucleus*, and/or the *Active Ingredient* in the *"Seed of the Central Truth of Christian Faith!"* (See the Parable of the Sower in the Epilogue — in Book III.) Jesus Christ died for us so that we might be resurrected to eternal life in Heaven, where we will live *"in Eternity Future"* in the presence of the Holy Trinity, the Heavenly Host of God's Angels, and all our loved ones who are now God's saints who have preceded us in mortal death. We must emulate Christ's agape love for all mankind by the way we treat others. We absolutely must treat all others in the same way we would wish to be treated! Saint Francis of Assisi said: *"Preach the Gospel every day, and if necessary, use words."* [44] This emphasizes the age-old axiom — *words without actions are not signs of God's Spirit.* They are just *wind. Agape* is the type of love where one puts the needs of others first — ahead of our love for ourselves. *Agape* is more than *wind.* Agape is *actionable caring* for the needs, interests, and welfare of others.

"ETERNITY PAST, ETERNITY PRESENT, ETERNITY FUTURE"

On his last Sunday on this earth, my dad stood before his Sunday School class and said: "This morning we are going to talk about: *'Eternity Past, Eternity Present & Eternity Future.'* " He then suddenly dropped to the floor — dead! My father died from a sudden, massive, painless, heart attack! God took him when he was doing what he loved best — teaching God's Word. For years I wondered what he would have said in his lesson that day. But he always spoke extemporaneously and never took any notes. However, after doing the research for this book, I now think I know. *"Eternity Past, Eternity Present, and Eternity Future"* will be defined and discussed in Chapter 10: *The 3rd Rock from the Sun* — in Book II.

Summary points:
- Maimonides said: "Know how to answer a skeptic."
- When Jesus was baptized, God said: *"This is My beloved Son, in whom I am well pleased."*
- When Jesus was transfigured, God said: *"This is My beloved Son, in whom I am well pleased. Listen to Him!"*
- Jesus said: *"I am in the Father, and the Father in Me. He who has seen Me has seen the Father. I and the Father are One."*
- Jesus also said: *"I am the way, the truth, and the life. No one comes to the Father but through Me."*
- Knowledge + assent to the truth of that knowledge = Belief.
- Belief + experience over time = a Conviction of Belief.

---

[44] Memories of Family and Faith with Coach Dale Brown, Cover ...

- A Conviction of Belief + Trust = Faith.
- *"Faith is the assurance of things hoped for and the conviction of things not seen."*
- *"Faith gives reality & proof of beliefs not seen, helping us to trust without seeing, for we walk by faith — not by sight."*
- *"By faith we understand the worlds were prepared by the Word of God so that what is seen was <u>not</u> made out of things which were visible."*
- Faith in a belief in God requires knowledge of God and an assent to the truth of that knowledge.
- A conviction of faith in a belief in God leads to a devotion to God.
- Devotion to God frees us from all doubt.
- A faith that is free of doubt is a living faith.
- A living faith empowers us to express agape love for our fellow man and live our lives by serving others.
- This pleases God.

THE REST OF THE STORY

Yes, my father literally died teaching his Sunday school class that Sunday morning. But a nurse in his class gave him CPR and revived him. He was taken to the hospital in Troy, Alabama but they could not medically control a dangerous arrythmia the heart attack caused. The University of Alabama sent a jet plane to transfer him to Birmingham for an Electrophysiologic Study of his heart. If the EPS could identify the irritable focus in Dad's heart that was causing the dangerous arrythmia, they planned to proceed immediately to an electrical ablation of that focus via a catheter procedure (we were told). Dad told me he did not want surgery. I told him they were only going to do an electrical study of his heart by placing an electrode through a catheter they would place in his heart through the vessels that led to his heart. If they found the focus that was causing his dangerous arrhythmia, they would ablate that focus by passing an electrical charge through the electrode they had inserted.

Mom and I drove to Birmingham (about a 2 ½—3-hour drive in 1985). When we got there, we were surprised he was in surgery. They performed an open-heart coronary-artery bypass instead. For five days, Dad suffered. Then, Dad's coronary artery bypass grafts clotted, and my father died (again), but this time — he died in pain! On the day before my father died, he curled up into the fetal position, and I heard him say: *"Oh Mama! Oh Mama! Your little David Escar Marley boy is in so much trouble — so sick! So sick! Oh Mama! Oh Mama!"* On the day my father died he asked me: *"Son I can't feel my legs. They are so cold! Why?"* I could barely talk, but through my tears, I managed to say: *"Dad, I think you will soon be with Jesus."* Oh, how he suffered!

THE WAY DAD DIED DERAILED MY FAITH. I BECAME ANGRY. I BECAME ANGRY — AT GOD!

- See the discussion about Satan in the next chapter.
- See the 3rd Summary Point in Book II, Chapter 16: *Charles Darwin: The Man* — concerning *"angry at God."*

❖
INTRODUCTION—PART V: THE BIBLE, RELIGION, & SCIENCE

"Study astronomy and physics if you desire to comprehend the relation between the world
and God's management of the world.." Maimonides

"Conflicts between science and religion result from misinterpretations of the Bible. We must form a conception of the existence of the Creator according to our capacities; this is, we must have a knowledge of 'metaphysics' (*The Science of God*), which can only be acquired after the study of 'physics' (*The Science of Nature*), for the science of 'physics' is closely connected with 'metaphysics' and must precede it in the course of our studies. Therefore the Almighty commenced the Bible with the description of Creation — that is with 'physics' (i.e., *The Science of Nature*)."   Maimonides

The '' & () are mine — for reasons I will now explain.

Here, Maimonides is saying the Genesis Creation Account is — 'Physical Science,' which today some people "reason" is the same thing as — 'The Science of Nature' &/or 'Natural Science' &/or 'Natural Law.' Some people use 'Circular Logic' to conflate their concept of 'Natural Law' with 'The Science of Nature.' I caution, there are some people today who use "logic and reason" to justify the legalization of "abortion on demand" under the umbrella of the so-called "Natural Law of Reproductive Rights."   O.David

Maimonides also said: "Science is not only the surest path to knowing God, it is the only path, and for that reason, the Bible commences with a description of Creation (i.e., The 1st Two Chapters of Genesis are 'Physics').

I disagree with "Science is the surest path to knowing God." I believe the only path to knowing God is through Belief and Faith. Belief and Faith can take us to those places that science can never go. *O.David*

THE PACE OF THE CREATION ACCOUNT MOVES LIKE LIGHTNING!
The first two chapters of the Bible are a verifiable "blitzkrieg" [45] of the history of creation. The description of the "Six Days of the Ancient of Days" is so sparse — it seems as if God is an impressionist artist, who has painted a magnificent, broad-stroke canvass of color that astounds and awes us, but seemingly lacks detail. The words of our English translations are beautiful and are like reading poetry. But when we read the first two chapters of the Book of Genesis, we are left with more questions than answers.

- Was there really a beginning, or has the universe always existed?
- Is there truly a God, a Creator, or did things just randomly happen, as Darwin claimed?
- Did He (or She) actually make the heavens and the earth? If so — How?
- How did He make our sun?
- How did He make our earth?
- From where did I come?
- Did He make me from dirt, from dust?
- Where did dirt and dust come from?
- What does it mean when the Bible says: *"The earth was without form and void?"*

---

[45] Blitzkrieg: German for "lightning war"—a German innovation of a fast-paced form of offensive warfare used in WWII—used here in the vernacular to reflect the rapid tour de force pace of the description of Creation as told in the Genesis Creation Account.

- What was: *"The face of the deep?"*
- What is the Bible talking about when it says: *"The surface of the waters?"*
- What are those billions of lights in the black of the night sky?
- Do they have anything to do with me?

QUEST FOR TRUTH—BELIEF, FAITH, RELIGION, & SCIENCE

The black of space is punctuated with billions of brilliant points of light. Primitive man stared at the night sky much more than we do today. He was less distracted by his society, and more concerned with his survival. From time immemorial, man has sought answers to the most basic questions by observing the heavens.

THE BELIEFS OF ASTROLOGY AND THE SCIENCE OF ASTRONOMY ARE AS OLD AS MAN HIMSELF. At first, men sought to determine the meaning of the positioning of the stars — how those stars affected man! Thus, the first astrologers observed the skies seeking to discover their fate! The edifices of Stonehenge in England (*circa* 2500 BC), and the Goseck Circle near Berlin, Germany (*circa* 5500 BC) — approximately 3000 years older than Stonehenge — are examples of early Bronze Age and Neolithic Age solar observatories. However, modern scientists believe they had religious significance as well.

PRIMEVAL RELIGION

Early on, men began to think the heavens were the abode of the gods. When primitive men started drawing imaginary lines between the stars, they began to see patterns. Next, primeval men began to think these stellar patterns in the night sky, were significant imprints of the forces of nature. The forces that govern man's existence were poorly understood at first. In an effort to ingratiate themselves to these mystical forces of nature — aboriginal men often deified, worshipped, and made sacrifices to the imagined "god-like" signs in the heavens. Much later, men called them *constellations* — and gave them names. At Goseck, the orientation of the graves and the cut marks on the bones of the buried suggest ritual sacrifices were performed. So, Goseck is believed to have been both a stellar observatory and a temple. At Goseck, stellar observations led to beliefs that morphed into a primitive form of religion. Thus, in many places around our globe, *astrology* and *polytheism* were born.

PRIMEVAL SCIENCE

The mythical beliefs of *Astrology* eventually gave rise to the science of *Astronomy*, which came forth from man's efforts to read "the signs in the heavens." Primitive men believed their imagined heavenly signs helped them determine the changing seasons and the optimum times for planting and harvest. It must have been difficult for primeval men to determine the difference, but from the mythical beliefs of Astrology came the first baby-steps of the scientific observations of Astronomy.

This begs the question — is it religion *and* science, or religion *versus* science? Are science and religion at odds or do they agree? Are they one and the same or are they different? Some say they are different. They claim science answers the "*how*" of the question — *How did things come to be?* They say religion is best suited to address the "*why*" of things — *Why are things the way they are?* Is it really that simple? The answer lies in our understanding.

SIMPLE OBSERVATIONS OF THE SKIES OFTEN LED TO WRONG CONCLUSIONS.

If all we have to draw conclusions from what we observe is our *experience* — then our conclusions will be limited by *our inexperience.* When we look at the universe, we get the sense we are the center of everything we see. From our view of the cosmos, it seems earth is the only fixed point. We seem stable. Everything else seems to be moving and revolving around us. Right? Wrong! Earth isn't fixed. It is not the center of anything. The whole history of the science of cosmology [46] is one of a relentless retreat of the earth from center stage. For very good reasons, man cannot determine the center of the universe.[47] However, as you shall see in Chapter 2 of Book I, man has determined — our sun is the center of our solar system. Earth's life forms could not survive even a brief moment of up-close exposure to its heat. If earth were any closer or any farther from the sun, earth would be a very different place. Either way, earth would be rendered incapable of supporting life. Although our earth isn't the center of anything — it is unique. Earth's location is unique, preeminent, and momentous. The positioning of our earth in the grand scheme of things is extremely important. Our Creator put our earth in the only place within our solar system where life (as we know it), could survive and flourish. The unique location of our earth ensures our survival and nourishment, just as our Creator intended.

MODERN SCIENCE

Science is almost as old as man himself. Since his inception, man's struggle to come to grips with the laws of the universe and of nature, has slowly advanced out of the mythical and imaginary into what man now calls — Modern Science. In the last 85 years modern science has matured and made some significant advances in the quest to answer the question of our origins. These are some of the questions modern science has addressed.

- Is the universe eternal, or did it have a beginning?
- What is the structure of the universe?
- What are its laws?
- Do the laws that govern the universe have anything to do with us?
- Does the universe govern change?
- If so, how did we come to be?

Mankind has considered these questions since his beginning. He started his investigations by looking at the skies with his bare eyes! Next, he began to chart his observations. Then, he pondered his findings. Finally, man began to postulate causes and effects. Modern science is well equipped to answer the first five questions in the list. But it is doubtful if science can ever answer the last one. We now realize 'Natural Science' &/or 'Natural Law' (i.e., the 'Science of Man' &/or 'Physical Science') — has its limits. *There are some places the 'Science of Man' can never take us!*

THE SCIENTIFIC METHOD

As man's experience expanded, so did his understanding. Early conclusions were re-examined, tested, and refined. Old thoughts became the platforms upon which new platforms of thought were built. Many faulty platforms were constructed, but each re-examination by later generations of scientists provided corrections and new advances along the pathway to better understanding. Over time, experience built on previous

---

[46] Cosmology: The scientific study of the universe.

[47] Schroeder *The Science of God* Chp. 12 p. 190 We are circle people.

experience. What tested to be true became accepted law. We now call this process — *"the Scientific Method."* That is how science works — or is supposed to work. In Book II, we will discuss the theory Darwin proposed 165 years ago. His theory has been thoroughly investigated by modern science and has now been proved to be false (at every level) beyond every shadow of a doubt! However, this is not widely known. In our institutions of learning, students are still being taught Darwin's ideas as if they have been proved to be true laws of nature, and the way life evolved on our planet. As you shall see, nothing could be further from the truth!

MONOTHEISM—ABRAHAM

The Biblical Account of the monotheism of Abraham is a divinely inspired departure from the polytheism of primitive men. As mankind matured, the concept of the One, All-powerful, Almighty God evolved. In the Book of Genesis, we find the story of Abraham, the Father of the Jews, and the Arabs. Abraham grew up in the polytheistic society of Ur. But through faith, Abraham rejected the polytheism of his father when he discovered *the One True God — Jehovah.*

MONOTHEISM—JOB

In another ancient book of the Bible, the Book of Job (which some say is the oldest book in the Bible), we are told the story of another prominent ancient monotheist who also worshipped Jehovah. The times in which Job lived and the date the Book of Job was written are uncertain. Scholars have speculated several dates for the book that range from the middle of the second millennium BC (near the time of Abraham), to the second Century BC. In his exhaustive, scholarly 248-page Introduction to his book: *"Job 1-21, Interpretation & Commentary,"* C.L. Seow discusses the origins of this mystical book. He also talks about the numerous translations of the Book of Job into other languages from the more ancient Masoretic Hebrew text. He does this from every conceivable point of view. Seow seems to favor the Transjordan region near the Dead Sea as the most likely location for Job's *"Land of Uz."* [48]

The Bible tells us Job was a devout, wealthy, influential man who also worshipped the God of Abraham. Job was the priest of his family. Because Abraham and Job discovered the One True God and worshipped Him, Biblical history has considered them to be enlightened men. Both men had an intimate relationship with Jehovah. Even though Abraham may have preceded Job and moved from Ur of the Chaldeans to Canaan, whereas Job lived in another land — for those who believe *Uz* was a real place and Job was a real person — the case can be made that Job would have heard about Abraham. How do we know this? Job 1:1 tells us Job lived in *"the Land of Uz."* Genesis 22:20-21 informs us the first son of Abraham's brother (*Nahor*), was named *Uz.* So, Job lived in a land that may have been settled and named for a nephew of Abraham. [49] One of Job's

---

[48] *Job 1-21, Interpretation & Commentary:* William B. Eerdmans Publishing Company, Grand Rapids, MI/Cambridge, UK: Copyright © 2013 C. L. Seow. cf. pages 44, 46-47, 251

[49] There are apparently 3 people in the Bible who were named *"Uz."* The *Uz* of Genesis 10:21-23 & I Chron. 1:17 was a son of *Aram,* who (like Abraham) was in the lineage of *Shem* (who was one of Noah's three sons). Another *Uz* is mentioned in Gen. 36:28 & I Chron. 1:42 who was a son of *Dishan, a Horite (descended from the sons of Seir in the land of Edom). The Land of Uz could have been named for either of them. The Uz, Buz, & Elihu in the Book of Job were more closely related to Abraham through Abraham's brother—Nahor. T*he Land of Uz (in which Job lived), could have been named for this *Uz.* It is highly probable that *Bildad* was *a direct descendant of Abraham* (for the reasons just given).

critics, "*Elihu, the son of Barachel the Buzite*" — (cf. Job 32:2 with Gen. 22:20-21), *was a descendant of Buz*. Nahor's second son was named — *Buz*. So, Elihu may have been a descendant of another nephew of Abraham. *Bildad*, a *Shuhite* (i.e., a descendant of *Shuah*, who was the 6th son of Abraham and his 2nd wife *Keturah* — *Gen. 25:1-2*), was one of Job's friends. So, Bildad was a descendant of one of Abraham's sons, and therefore was a direct descendant of Abraham! So, it is highly probable Abraham preceded Job, and Job would have known about Abraham.

FOUR CELESTIAL SIGNS ARE MENTIONED IN THE BOOK OF JOB.

I have just said ancient men stared at the night sky much more than we do today, and noted signs in the heavens, which they deified and worshipped. We have all heard of the Pleiades, Orion, Arcturus (the Guardian of the Bear), and Mazzaroth. These constellations and heavenly signs are cited in the Book of Job. God answered Job "out of the whirlwind," and said to him:

> "*Who is this that darkens counsel by words without knowledge? Now gird up your loins like a man, and I will ask you, and you instruct Me. Where were you when I laid the foundations of the earth? Tell me, if you have understanding…Canst thou bind the sweet influences of Pleiades, or loose the bands of Orion? Canst thou bring forth Mazzaroth in his season, and guide the Arcturus with his sons? Knowest thou the ordinances of heaven? Canst thou set the dominion thereof in the earth?*" (Job 38:1-4 & 31-33 KJV)

In this scripture, God put His finger on one of man's most serious faults. History is full of examples of men who have — "**Darkened counsel by words without knowledge.**" God told Job his complaints betrayed his ignorance of God's Divine Omniscience! So, in a venerated book of the Hebrew Bible, the Book of Job: God mentioned the names of four celestial signs in the heavens known to man. *Arcturus* has been called "*Job's star*," because it is one of the few stars mentioned in the Bible. [50] The point I am trying to make by mentioning "Job's star" is this: Throughout man's oral and written history, humankind has searched for answers by gazing at the stars.

The fact that four constellations are mentioned by God in the ancient Book of Job is *prima facia evidence* that early men searched the heavens for answers to their most basic questions. When most of the ancients in the time of Job looked at the stars, they deified certain constellations and worshipped them. But, when Abraham, Job, and Job's friends gazed at the stars, they saw the God of the entire universe and worshipped Him. Jehovah was The One True God for them.

THE TORAH, PENTATEUCH, TANAKH, SEPTUAGINT, & THE KING JAMES BIBLE

You may have wondered how the Greek names for the star Arcturus, and the constellations, Pleiades, Orion, and the 12 signs of the zodiac (Mazzaroth), found their way into our English Bibles.

Alexander the Great started his conquest of the known world in 333 BC. Persia was the first empire to fall. After his death in 323 BC, his empire was divided between his generals. Ptolemy controlled the western provinces of Judea and Egypt. His capital

---

[50] Arcturus-Alpha Bootis I Constellation Guide: August 31, 2014

was Alexandria, Egypt—a city founded and named by Alexander the Great. All the Greek rulers in Ptolemy's lineage had 'Ptolemy' in their names. The Ptolemies dealt kindly with the Jews and permitted religious freedom. Tradition says Ptolemy Philadelphus (also known as Ptolemy II, 285-247 BC), requested the Torah (the Hebrew name for the first five Books of Moses in the Old Testament), be translated into Greek. Seventy Jews, who were skillful linguists, were sent from Jerusalem to Alexandria. The Pentateuch (the name for the Greek translation of the Torah) was translated first. Later, the rest of the Hebrew Old Testament books (i.e., the Tanakh) were added to the translation. The Greek translation of the Tanakh was called the Septuagint for the 70 translators (LXX) who did the work.

The first widely accepted English translation (i.e., the King James Bible of 1611 AD), was based on the 2,200-year-old Septuagint, and the Latin Vulgate of St. Jerome, which dates from the 4th century AD. Thus, the Greek names for these heavenly signs appear in our English Bibles.

These stellar signs were known the world over by peoples of many cultures who gave them different names. The Babylonians, Persians, Hindus, and Chinese knew about the Pleiades. The Maori (i.e., the Australian Aborigines), Maya, Aztecs, and the Sioux Indians of North America also knew of them. Each culture had its own name for this constellation. This is evidence for the claim—from time immemorial; man has sought the answers to the most basic questions by observing the heavens. [51] We have their Greek names in our English Bibles because the Septuagint was one of the sources upon which the King James Bible was based.

ARE RELIGION AND SCIENCE STILL AT ODDS?

Some would say religion is different from science. They claim religion is based only on belief. They think belief cannot be tested — cannot be proved. Unless they can see it, feel it, and touch it, they will not believe it. People of this opinion have no use for religion. They see all religion as a distraction from reality, a soporific that dulls the senses of the masses. In their view, science enlightens and frees us. Religion blinds us and keeps us in bondage to a false set of primitive beliefs.

⊙ [52]

Are you puzzled by this symbol? Its meaning will be revealed in Chapters 6 and 7 (in Book I).

If it were possible to put this belief to Job, he would strongly disagree. Job's experience with God was up close and personal. Job talked with God and God talked back. As we shall later discuss, the Hebrew concept of the degree of Divine Direction in a person's life depends on how close to the Creator one chooses to be. Our closeness to God is a matter of our choice, our own free-will choice. The truth is, those who believe in God and those who do not, have one very fundamental thing in common — belief. Those who believe in God try to follow Him. Those who do not believe in God reject Him. If you have rejected God don't kid yourself. You still believe in something. No man lives in a vacuum. If you

[51] Article: The Pleiades: the celestial herd of ancient timekeepers. By Amelia Sparavigna, Dipartimento di Fisica, Politecnico di Torins http://arxiv.org/ftp/arxiv/papers/0810/0810.1592.pdf
[52] ⊙ Are you puzzled by this symbol? Its meaning will be revealed in Chapters 6 and 7 (in Book I).

are not a disciple of God, you are a disciple of something else, even if that something else is nothing more than yourself. If this describes you, know this — you are living your life in the *"flesh"* (cf. Rom. 8:1-16) — you are living life *"backwards."* What is *"the FLESH?"* Spell it backwards and eliminate the *"H."* This is what you get — *S-E-L-F!* Do you get it now? The *"H"* stands for *"Him!"* *"Him"* is *Jesus Christ*. You are living your life without *Jesus!* In my 40 years of medical practice, I've seen many patients prepare for their death. Believers in Jesus Christ see death as a *"Doorway to Heaven,"* and look forward to their reunification with their loved ones in *Eternity Future*. Non-believers are fearful of the unknown. Some are terrified.

BELIEF IN GOD: A RICH HERITAGE OF EXPERIENCE

Those who believe in the One Almighty Creator God, look to the past for the foundation of their belief. They look to the oral and recorded history of their ancestors. They have two things in common:

- The belief there is only One God,
- And the small geographic location on the face of the earth from which their ancestors came.

They can trace their beliefs back to their patriarchs, and to the oral and recorded experiences of their patriarchs with their Creator. Theirs is a rich heritage of experience. The three religions that believe there is One True God originate from the cradle of civilization — that part of the earth we refer to today as the Middle East. There is strong evidence this is the part of the earth from which modern man originated. The three great monotheistic religions are Judaism, Christianity, and Islam. They all draw their understanding of "Creation" from the first two chapters of the first Book of the Hebrew Prophet Moses — the Book of Genesis![53]

A HISTORY OF MISUNDERSTANDING BASED ON BAD SCIENCE & FAULTY RELIGIOUS DOCTRINES.[54]

The origins of modern science are rooted in the works of many great thinkers who were also religious believers — men such as Copernicus, Galileo, Kepler, Bacon, and Newton. We know the scientific discoveries of these men often caused conflict with the religious doctrines of their day. The leaders of the early Christian Church often claimed the opinions of early scientists contradicted their interpretations of the Bible and were therefore heresy. In those days, Christian hierarchy felt science was God's enemy. It is a matter of historical record the Christian Church persecuted some scientists after they published their discoveries. Most of the conflict was the result of faulty science or misinterpretations of the Bible. In some cases, both. Early scientists often made mistakes. Furthermore, some religious doctrines were the inventions of men whose misinterpretations of the Bible led to false doctrines. False doctrines come from men — not God. Thus, conflict was born out of *Cognitive Dissonance* on both sides. Cognitive Dissonance will be discussed in Chapter 1 of Book I. However, regarding the question of our origins, in just the last few decades of the 20th century, a massive paradigm change has occurred in scientific opinion. If you continue reading this book you will discover — Modern science *now* agrees with the Hebrew Bible!

---

[53] Schroeder The Hidden Face of God Chapter 1, p. 10 a
[54] Schroeder The Science of God Chapter 2 p. 20

SOME CHRISTIANS FEEL THREATENED BY SCIENCE.

Sadly, some Christians still find the discoveries of modern science such a threat they vigorously oppose the truth of recent scientific discoveries. There are some Christians who claim the fossil evidence of a very old earth, and the mountains of accumulating scientific data, which prove an even older universe, are deceptions of God because God wishes to punish the arrogant men who believe in those discoveries. According to these Christians, God purposefully planted fossils in geologic strata for the explicit purpose of deceiving man. [55] These believers (who claim their interpretation of the Bible proves the earth is very young), have claimed the author of truth (God), has done something God would never do — practice deception to punish the arrogance of man. How could they think God would do such a thing? When you read Chapter 16 (in Book II), you will discover Charles Darwin met people in his day that had the same belief and gave the same explanation. With our prejudicial judgments of others, we the people of God have been hurting God and eachother ever since He made us.

GOD IS TRUTH!

The Bible makes the case: God is truth, the ultimate and perfect truth — the very essence of truth! In the Old Testament, God used the might of nations to punish the unfaithful. There are also many examples of other ways God was active in the affairs of men. The Bible teaches us God is in control. His original Dispensation of Innocence occurred in the Garden of Eden, where He created a Paradise on earth for man. There was no death or enmity. All of that changed after Man sinned against God. That ushered in mortal death and enmity between men, enmity between man and nature, and the separation of man from God.

SATAN

The message of the 3rd Chapter of Genesis is — *Satan is the father of all lies and deceptions!* Job 1:7 & 2:2 tell us Satan roams the earth and walks among us. Satan is the great deceiver and the first mass murderer because he deceived Eve and brought about the mortal death of all humanity! His conversation with God in the first Chapter of Job tells us Satan seeks to do harm to those who believe in God. He is *The Great Deceiver* whose mission is to bring such calamity and sorrow upon God's faithful that we (in our suffering and misery) will curse God to His face (Job 1:11 & 2:5)! Job 2:6 makes it clear Satan is the cause of all suffering on earth. I believe if my wife and I had been Eve and Adam, we would have fallen from grace just as Eve and Adam did. We have all sinned and fallen short of the glory of God (Romans 3:23). Satan is to blame for the enmity between men, between man and the earth, and between man and nature. When man sinned against God in Eden, man destroyed the Paradise God had created for him in the Garden, and God's initial *"heaven on earth"* was taken back to Heaven. So, when bad things happen to good people don't blame God! Blame Satan and blame human nature (cf. "The Lessons of the Garden of Eden" — Chapter 28, in Book III). Yet, God is still in control. Satan cannot do anything without God's permission. That is *man's conundrum.* Why does God allow Satan to roam the earth seeking to do us harm? There was a time in the Garden when God protected Adam and Eve from Satan's harm. They were not protected from his deceptions and temptations because God gave them *free will.* But so

---

[55] Stephen Parker: Bridges: Reconnecting Science and Faith. p. 40-45

long as they were obedient to God, Satan was powerless to physically harm them. Everything in the Garden was permitted except for one forbidden thing—*the fruit of the Tree of the Knowledge of Good and Evil.* They were warned — eating the fruit of that tree would bring them mortal death. I believe their disobedience is the root cause of all of the enmity in our world. We cannot know God's ultimate purpose in all of this while we await our mortal death. But on the last page of this chapter, I will share with you some thoughts about this mystery. It has everything to do with our inability to fully understand God's thoughts and God's ways.

THE DISPENSATION OF THE GRACE OF JESUS CHRIST

John 5:22 and 24, & John 3:16 and 18 clearly say: ~ 2,000 years ago, God gave all judgment to Jesus Christ. All who hear Christ Jesus and believe in Him shall have eternal life: *"For not even the Father judges anyone, but He has given all judgment to the Son...He who hears My word, and believes Him who sent Me, has eternal life, and does not come into judgment, but has passed out of death into life" John 5:22,24 NASB.*

"For God so loved the world, that He gave His only begotten Son, that whoever believes in Him should not perish, but have eternal life.... He who believes in Him is not judged; He who does not believe has been judged already, because he has not believed in the name of the only begotten Son of God" John 3:16,18 NASB.

CHRISTIANS BELIEVE THE BASIC TENETS OF THE NEW TESTAMENT ARE—

1. Sin separates us from God.
2. The Original Sin of Disobedience to God in the Garden of Eden was the root cause of all disease, suffering, enmity, and death in our world.
3. The sacrifice of Jesus Christ cancels all our sins.
4. Confession and repentance of our sins, and the profession of our belief in Jesus Christ, cleanses us of all unrighteousness.
5. This makes us acceptable to God, so that we can enter His presence, and experience His eternal rest and peace.
6. Jesus died for all people in all times to set us free from all of our sins. [56] Jesus is our Savior!

Summary points:

- The beliefs of astrology and the science of astronomy are as old as man himself.
- At first, men sought to determine the meaning of the positioning of the stars — how those stars affected man. Thus, the first astrologers observed the skies seeking to discover their fate.
- Early on, men began to think the heavens were the abode of the gods.
- When primitive men began to see patterns in the night sky, polytheism was born.
- The Biblical Account of the monotheism of Abraham is a *divinely inspired* departure from the polytheism of primitive men.
- As mankind matured, the concept of the One, All-powerful, Almighty God evolved.
- Abraham, Job, and Job's friends worshipped the same God — Jehovah.

---

[56] Hebrews 9:25-28 & Hebrews 10:10

- The genealogies of Job's friends suggest Abraham preceded Job, and Job probably knew about Abraham.
- The three great monotheistic religions are Judaism, Christianity, and Islam. They all draw their understanding of Creation from the first two chapters of the first Book of the Hebrew Prophet Moses — the Book of Genesis.
- *Torah* is the Hebrew name for the five books of Moses (Genesis, Exodus, Leviticus, Numbers and Deuteronomy). Torah means: "*Instruction.*"
- The Pentateuch is the Greek translation of the Torah.
- The Tanakh is the Hebrew name of the Hebrew Bible — i.e., the Old Testament.
- The Septuagint is the Greek translation of the Tanakh.
- The King James Bible of 1611 AD is an English translation of the Bible that is based on the 2200-year-old Septuagint and the Latin Vulgate of Saint Jerome, which dates to the 4th Century AD.
- The Greek names of stars and constellations in the Book of Job appear in the King James Bible because the 2200-year-old Septuagint (which is the Greek translation of the Hebrew Tanakh), was one of the translations on which the King James Bible was based.
- For centuries, religious beliefs and the opinions of scientists have often caused conflicts that were either the result of faulty religious interpretations of scripture, or the result of bad science.
- Some current-day Christians feel threatened by modern science.
- However, a recent renaissance in science and religion has produced a convergence of agreement between the two disciplines. Unfortunately, this is not yet widely known.
- God is truth — the ultimate and perfect truth — the very essence of truth!
- Satan is the father of all lies and deceptions! Satan murdered all life on earth!
- Satan is responsible for all the evil done on our planet! He is the author of all the misery and calamity on earth. He is the cause of the enmity that exists between men—the enmity between man and predatory animals—and all the enmity that exists between man and nature (i.e., misfortune, disease, and so-called "natural disasters").
- Eve and Adam's "original sin" — *Disobedience to God* — caused their separation from God and their eviction from the Garden. They yielded to Satan's temptation and brought on God's judgment of mortal death to all living creatures and vegetation on earth.
- The central message of the New Testament is — the sacrifice of Jesus Christ is the solution for the separation from God the original sin caused.
- Jesus is our Savior! He died once — for all people in all times! He died so that we might have Life Eternal—if we confess, repent, and call on His name.

THE SCIENCE OF MAN VS. THE SCIENCE OF GOD

The Science of Man is 'Physics.' The Science of God is 'Metaphysics.' Isaiah 55:8-9 says:

"My thoughts are not your thoughts. Neither are your ways My ways...For as the heavens are higher than the earth, so are My ways higher than your ways and My thoughts than your thoughts."

I Corinthians 13:12 says: *"For now we see in a mirror dimly, but then face to face. Now I know in part, but then I shall know fully just as I also have been fully known."*

Putting the two together, mortal man has demonstrated he can learn '*the Science of Nature*' &/or 'Natural Science' &/or 'Natural Law' (i.e., Life Science and The Physical Sciences). Where we are now (in that process) has taken us many hundreds of years, and yet we have only just begun. However, the Bible tells us man is not capable of understanding *"The Science of God."* God's thoughts and God's ways cannot be understood by mortal man. Mortal man sees dimly in a mirror and can only know in part. But when we get to heaven, we will enter into the consciousness of God. Then we will be capable of understanding "The Science of God" and we will fully know God— just as He has fully known us. Therefore, in this life, man cannot prove the existence of God through the science of nature or fully know Him. '*The science of nature*' &/or '*Physics*' *(as Maimonides called it),* is <u>not</u> capable of helping us *understand The Creator.* Our <u>only</u> pathway to God in this mortal life is <u>*Belief*</u>. Belief in God's Son (Jesus) will lead us to belief in our Creator. We call that process <u>*Faith*</u>. <u>Jesus Christ is our only pathway to God</u>. *But belief in Jesus must involve <u>our surrender of self-control, and our acknowledgment of His Lordship.</u>*

I have a dear friend (since childhood) who says: "**<u>If you prove to me God exists, I will believe in Him.</u>**" For years he has tried to find God through his intellect. His problem is his *"if"*— i.e., his *"doubt."* He will not surrender *his "if"* — i.e., his <u>*I*ndividual *F*reedom and his personal freedom of self-determination to God.* In his scheme, God must first:

- Come to him.
- Explain Himself.
- And prove to him — *He exists!*
- Only then *will* he believe in God!

He says he has fervently prayed to God many times to simply speak to him. But God has remained silent. He doesn't realize Jesus has been knocking on his door for years. But his door can only be opened from the inside. He has refused to open his door of belief. He has refused **to invite Jesus in!** My friend says if I can convince him Jesus died for him, then and only then will he accept Christ's gift of salvation. My friend does not understand his scheme for belief has — "the-cart-before-the-horse." That configuration cannot take him anywhere. Jesus will come to those who willingly invite Him in and receive Him. But therein lies his problem. **My friend will not invite, receive, or believe!** Every time I answer his questions with my reasons for believing, he always says: "I can't make myself believe that." He has turned God's gift of free will — against God. He has turned his back on Jesus and has been running from the faith of his grandparents for years. He must first invite Jesus to come into him, believe Jesus is Who He says He is, and believe Jesus died for him — before Jesus will come into him, and grant him absolution. Only then will Jesus say to him what He said to the thief on the cross who believed in Him—"*Truly, I say to you, today you shall be with Me in paradise (Luke 23:43)."*

We truly can't understand why bad things happen, or why natural disasters, wars, disease, enmity, and mortal death exist. Truly, on this side of *"the river Jordan"* we see dimly through a darkened glass. We cannot understand the thoughts and ways of God. But in Heaven, we will fully know Him as we have been fully known. In Heaven there will be no enmity, disease, suffering, or death. For the sufferings of the world (Genesis 3:8-24 — since man was expelled from the Garden) are not worthy to be compared with the glory that is to be revealed in heaven to us (Rom. 8:18). For Creation itself was subjected to futility and suffering after Adam sinned (Rom. 8:20). From the eviction of man from the Garden until the 2nd Coming of Christ, the whole of creation groans and suffers together with us (Rom. 8:22), and enmity has existed between men, and between man and nature. But we must hold firm in our belief that:

> *"God causes all things to work together for good to those*
> *who love God, to those who are called according to His*
> *Purpose" (Romans 8:28).*

In Heaven, God will make all things new, and God will wipe away every tear and sorrow (Rev. 21:4-5). God will give all believers new eternal bodies that can never get sick again and can never die (**Romans 8:23 — see The Living Bible**). And, for believers, God will correct every wrong ever done — when He makes all things new. All memory of suffering, and all sin and death will be forgotten — and all losses will be restored to God's faithful.

I BELIEVE THIS BECAUSE I TRUST GOD'S WORD!

AND I TRUST GOD!

❧
INTRODUCTION—PART VI MYTH VS. FACT

"Trust in the Lord with all your heart, and do not lean on your own understanding." Prov. 3:5 NASB

"Fear of God is the beginning of wisdom, and knowledge of the Holy One is understanding." Prov. 9:10

"Fear of the Lord is instruction for wisdom. Before honor comes humility." Prov. 15:38

"The steadfast of mind Thou wilt keep in perfect peace because he trusts in Thee.
Trust in the Lord forever, for in God the Lord, we have an everlasting Rock." Isaiah 26:3-4 NASB

God is Omnipotent, Omniscient, and Omnipresent. God will not tolerate sin. We fear God because we know we sin, and we fear His Judgment. But God is also All-Loving, All-Forgiving, Pure, Kind, Just, Righteous, and Merciful. When we realize God Loves us and will forgive us – if we humble ourselves and ask – We discover God is faithful to forgive all our sins. That is when our "Fear" of God turns into "Awe" – a reverential respect, love, and trust of God. (See Ryrie Study Bible note on II Timothy 1:7)   *O. David*

SECULARISTS[57] & SOME THEOLOGIANS THINK THE BIBLICAL CREATION ACCOUNT IS A MYTH. Years ago, I watched a man argue with Anne Graham Lotz on his TV show. Mrs. Lotz is the second daughter of Billy and Ruth Graham. I have always thought Mrs. Lotz is an effective Christian advocate. The host of the show was a self-described "apathetic atheist" meaning: He doesn't believe in God — claims there is no God — and is unworried about his unbelief. On the other hand, Mrs. Lotz was confident and gracefully defended her conviction of a well-grounded belief and faith in God. The host repeatedly questioned her faith. Nevertheless, she was composed, and her responses were kindhearted, dignified, and poised. When her segment was over, the host ridiculed her faith and attacked the Bible. I will not repeat what he actually said about God after she left the set. His contempt for her belief and faith cannot be fully expressed by mere words. But the gist of his comments was:

- The creation story is a myth, born from the oral tradition of a primitive Stone-Age people.
- The Bible is a Bronze-Age text — God only knows was written by who?
- The Bible is an irrelevant mythical history of an angry god and his barbaric warring tribe!

These angry indictments of the Bible and Christianity incited an enthusiastic cheering applause from his audience. It was as if those people were gloating over his pummeling of Mrs. Lotz. I remember thinking: *Public opinion is swayed by the clap-response on programs like this.* At times like that I sometimes think: "We the people" have strayed far from the religious principles of the founding fathers of our country, and their firm belief in *The One True God,* who they believed was the Creator and the Giver of our lives and liberty. Nevertheless, he was certainly right about one thing. God knows who wrote the book of Genesis and all the other books of the Bible.

Questions about the author of the Genesis Creation Account, the Torah, and the rest of the Bible have caused a lot of controversy. Many Western Christian Seminarians now teach Moses did not write the Torah! This idea originated with some academics who called themselves — The *School of Higher Biblical Criticism*, or SHBC. This "school"

---

[57] Secularism, Secularists: A system of political & social philosophy that rejects all forms of religious faith and worship.

claims there are differences in the literary styles and two different names for God in the first two chapters of the book of Genesis. So, let's take a little bit of time, ink, and paper, and talk about that now.

QUESTIONING THE IDENTITY OF THE AUTHORS OF THE TORAH & THE TANAKH

Some respected modern-day seminarians also believe the Bible's Creation "story" is a "myth," and the thrust of that "story" is religious — having nothing to do with science or reality. On the mythical part, a surprising number of Christian ministers, theologians, and priests; and many secularists, gnostics, agnostics, and atheists — agree. Anti-God people use the term "myth," in its usual sense. But some Christians qualify their use of the term by claiming — when they say "myth" — they do not necessarily mean the "stories" in the Bible are not true, but the "*mythical stories*" the Bible tells (while not factually accurate),[58] reveal more truth, and are more valuable, than facts alone can disclose." [59]

Does that explanation satisfy you? I think that line of "reasoning" is *Circular Logic*. "Circular Logic" is nothing more than just a lot of meaningless words that start at ground zero and take a long circular detour that eventually comes back to the starting point — "ground zero!" The people who use that line of "reasoning" are trying to redefine the meaning of — "*myth*." The notion people can decide what parts of the Bible are myth, and what parts actually happened seems risky to me. God gave us our gift of intellect, and every person has the right to question and wrestle with the mysteries of life and his own existence. People have the right and duty to decide what they believe. I believe the choice they make will determine their eternal future!

My problem with the SHBC is two-fold. The SHBC takes issue with the Hebrew tradition that Moses wrote the Torah, and it questions the Jewish belief that Moses was *Divinely Inspired* by God! Those beliefs are cornerstones of Judaism! So, I unabashedly ask 'academics' these questions:

- Does a change in literary style really mean a change in authors?
- Could it be Moses exercised an author's "poetic license," and changed his style of writing when he wrote the 2nd Chapter of Genesis?
- Aren't the hypotheses of the SHBC based on the SHBC's interpretations of their Greek translations of the Hebrew Torah?

THE TRUTH IS — **The SHBC concentrated on the Greek translation of the Torah (i.e., the *Pentateuch*) and absolutely ignored the *Hebrew Torah!***

THERE ARE MANY LITERARY STYLES IN THE BIBLE.

The Bible is full of allegory, history, hyperbole, imagery, metaphor, poetry, simile, and symbolism. Our Lord Jesus Christ told his disciples he often spoke in parables. But he also interpreted his parables for them. Nevertheless, most of us can tell when an ancient writer is using a different *genre*, especially when his writing uses the literary device of "*personification*" when proclaiming the magnificence, the majesty, and the mystery of God. Such statements as: *"The very heavens declare His righteousness"* (Ps. 97:6), and *"Let the mountains sing together for joy"* (Ps. 98:8)— are common in the Bible. We

---

[58] I think the things we cannot explain, we call *myth*. We forget: *"Nothing is impossible for God!"* (cf. Gen. 18:14 a, Job 42:2, Jeremiah 32:27, Matt. 19:26, Mark 10:27, Luke 1:37 & Luke 18:27).
[59] Parker, Stephen: *BRIDGES: Reconnecting Science and Faith*. p. 37-45, *A Breath of Fresh Air Blows Through the Bible*.

understand these inanimate features are not actually declaring and singing. But the author is saying — "The very existence of the heavens and the mountains proclaims the Creator's 'righteousness' and 'joy' in creation."

A SLIPPERY SLOPE

People are on a slippery slope when they decide certain parts of the Bible are myth. Pretty soon, nonbelievers can convince themselves and persuade others the Bible is irrelevant. The Bible will always be relevant. If you read the Bible, you will see history repeating itself. History teaches us the past is all too often the harbinger of the future because *people will always be people!* A friend of mine says: *"People are worse than anybody!"* Our ignorance of the past, and our arrogance in our present (i.e., *our ignorant arrogance*) — doom each generation to repeat the errors of the past. One cannot deny the truth of the words of King Solomon in Ecclesiastes 1:2, and 8-11:

2"Vanity of vanities! All is vanity...8All things are wearisome; Man is not able to tell it. The eye is not satisfied with seeing, nor is the ear filled with hearing. 9That which has been, is that which will be. And that which has been done, is that which will be done. So, there is nothing new under the sun. 10Is there anything of which one might say, 'See this, it is new?' Already it has existed for ages, which were before us. 11There is no remembrance of earlier things. And also, of the later things which will occur — there will be for them no remembrance among those who will come later still." (Eccl. 1:2 & 8-11 NASB)

Jewish Tradition attributes these words, and the authorship of the Book of Ecclesiastes to King Solomon. It can be argued Jewish Tradition is correct. While Ecclesiastes does not specifically say Solomon was its author — The Ryrie Study Bible's Introduction to the Book of Ecclesiastes says — "The author identifies himself as 'the son of David, king in Jerusalem (Eccl. 1:1).'" And also says — "References in the book to the author's unrivaled wisdom, unequaled wealth, opportunities for pleasure, and extensive building activities all point to Solomon, since no other descendant of David measured up to such specifications."

"POWER CORRUPTS, & ABSOLUTE POWER CORRUPTS ABSOLUTELY!" [60]

I'm going to exercise an author's poetic license here and take a short detour away from the discussion of the SHBC. When the sad tale you are about to read is finished, I will resume the discussion of the SHBC.

David and Bathsheba gave Solomon all possible advantages in life. Raised a son of privilege, Solomon became the wealthiest man in his time. He not only expanded the borders of his inherited kingdom to its zenith, but he also built an impressive navy, army, fortresses, and public-works buildings. Furthermore, he constructed new cities, and his magnificent Temple to God in Jerusalem was proclaimed one of the wonders of the world. But all his building projects were constructed with the forced labor of the descendants of the Canaanites who were not driven out of Israel during Joshua's conquest. Later, Solomon imposed forced labor on *all* his people. Because of his wisdom and his political alliances, great wealth flowed to Solomon from foreign nations, but he spent lavishly and

---

[60] **Search for: Sir John Dalberg-Acton writes to Bishop Creighton**
Sir John Dalberg-Acton made this remark in a letter to an Anglican bishop in which he claimed: "Power tends to corrupt, and absolute power corrupts absolutely." (Sir John believed — as a person's power increases, their moral sense diminishes.)

took on much debt. [61] Sadly, he also constructed pagan temples on all the high places in Israel to the foreign gods of his many wives and concubines! Solomon expanded the borders of Israel through peace treaties with the kings of many countries and principalities. He sealed those peace treaties by marrying the daughters of those rulers.

Solomon married 700 foreign princesses and took an additional 300 concubines into his harem! The man who inherited a kingdom that had been united as a nation under his father David, ignored the prime directive of Israel's God, Jehovah — *"Thou shalt have no gods before me"* (Ex. 20:3 KJV)! Marriage to foreigners was expressly forbidden by God! But the man whose first request of God had been for the wisdom to rule wisely, squandered that gift, and gave-in to his lust for sex and riches. Solomon sowed the seeds that ultimately destroyed the prosperity of his people and his kingdom when he abandoned the mandate that *Jehovah be the exclusive God of Israel.* [62] His toleration of the worship of pagan gods caused Israel to turn her back on the one true God! When he became old, his many foreign wives turned his heart away after other gods, for his heart was not wholly devoted to the Lord his God, as the heart of his father David had been (1st Kings 11:1-13). God had warned Solomon of the consequences of such behavior (1st Kings 9:6-9) but because of God's love of David, God did not punish Israel until after Solomon's death.

SOLOMON'S SON — REHOBOAM

When Solomon died, his arrogant son, Rehoboam, vowed to establish his authority by forcing an increased workload on *all* his people. This led to the rebellion of Jeroboam, who God raised up to lead a revolt of the 10 tribes of northern Israel against Rehoboam. Rehoboam prepared for war, but God sent an emissary to Rehoboam to tell him he must not fight, *for the Lord God had brought about the division of his kingdom!*

JEROBOAM — CIVIL WAR — & THE ASSYRIAN DESTRUCTION OF THE NORTH

After Jeroboam led the revolt, he severed all relationships with the two southern tribes of Judah and Benjamin! The kingdom that had been united by David, split into two kingdoms. The Southern Kingdom (under Rehoboam) was called the Kingdom of Judah. Jeroboam led the 10 tribes in the north of Israel to form the Kingdom of Northern Israel. Not wishing his citizens to make pilgrimages to Jerusalem to celebrate the four major religious feasts of Judaism (because an ecclesiastic allegiance to the religion of Judah would threaten his rule), Jeroboam abandoned the worship of Jehovah altogether and declared the god of the new Northern Kingdom of Israel would be the long forgotten *Golden Calf of Egypt.* He made two golden calves and placed one in a temple he built in Bethel (not far from Jerusalem). And the other was placed in a temple in the far north (in Dan). Jeroboam's fortress capital city of Shechem (also known as Sychar), was built on a mountain top, which was only about 40 miles north of Jerusalem. [63] Years later, Civil War broke out. The sad saga of that division is a lengthy complicated history that played out over several hundreds of years. Finally, because all the kings of the North had worshipped foreign gods, the Northern Kingdom of Israel was defeated by the Assyrians. In 722 BC they led their captives away to Nineveh in chains — with hooks in their noses!

---

[61] I Kings Chapters 2—10 and II Chronicles 7:19-22 and II Chronicles Chapters 8 & 9.
[62] I Kings Chapter 11
[63] I Kings Chapter 12

THE BABYLONIAN DESTRUCTION OF THE SOUTHERN KINGDOM

The Southern Kingdom lasted a little longer because eight of its kings had been faithful to Jehovah. However, because most of the kings of the Southern Kingdom had been evil and worshipped pagan gods, Jehovah sent the king of the Babylonians to conquer it. Nebuchadnezzar II victoriously entered Jerusalem after the Battle of Carchemish in 605 BC where he defeated an Assyrian-Egyptian coalition that had been arrayed against him and his allies. That is when the elite of Judah were taken captive to Babylon. Daniel, Shadrack, Meshack, and Abednego were among the captives taken.[64] Before Nebuchadnezzar returned to Babylon, he chose a puppet king to rule Jerusalem. However, after a few years, the vassal rebelled and formed an alliance with the Egyptians against the Babylonians. When Nebuchadnezzar learned of this, he returned with his army. In 586 BC, he completely destroyed the Southern Kingdom of Judah. Jerusalem and Solomon's magnificent Temple to God were razed to the ground.

Such is the sorry story of the corrupt apostate King Solomon, his arrogant foolish son, Rehoboam, and the ungrateful Jeroboam. The Israelites of David's divided kingdom abandoned Jehovah and worshiped foreign gods. Solomon's lament in the first chapter of Ecclesiastes is his acknowledgment of the utter stupidity of his *"vanity of vanities."*

INFANT SACRIFICE TO FALSE GODS

Solomon legalized the murder of innocent babies and children on the altars of pagan gods. After his death, his kingdom split, and innocent children were sacrificed on the altars to false gods in all the high places of both kingdoms for hundreds of years! Solomon caused Israel to commit "The Iniquity of the Amorites" (discussed near the end of Chapter 5: The Time Conundrum — in Book I).

WE HAVE DONE THE SAME THING! "BEAM ME UP SCOTTY!"

That cavalier utterance of an abortionist — while he was murdering a baby in the womb — would have been unimaginable when I was a young medical student in the early 1960s! The audio-video of that murder was actually aired on TV! Seeing the fetus struggle and then disappear into the suction-probe as the abortionist was flippantly saying: *"Beam me up Scotty,"* was the most horrific thing I have ever seen! Ever since Roe vs. Wade was passed in 1973, self-serving politicians have denied the sanctity of new life and have successfully campaigned on the reprehensible slogan of — *"A Woman's Right to Freedom of Choice."* This sounds like something good and venerable. But *Liberal Progressives* always hide their political goals in aspirational slogans. In reality, *"A Woman's Right to Freedom of Choice"* means women have the legal right to murder their unwanted babies — on demand! All legal protection of early innocent life has thus been stripped out of the legal code! In the past few years, it has come to mean — *Planned Parenthood can legally murder babies at any time during a pregnancy (including during the delivery of a full-term fetus) and sell the vital organs of the murdered fetus for additional profit!* These evil horrendous actions are sanctioned by the slogan of *"Freedom of Reproductive Rights,"* which is the key part of *"A Woman's Right to Freedom of Choice."* For the past 47 years, people in the United States of America have murdered more than

[64] The Ryrie Study Bible Introduction to the Book of Jeremiah and the Introduction to the Book of Daniel.

61 million innocent healthy babies! Vanity of Vanities![65] We must hear Solomon's laments and warnings. What we have done and are still doing is an evil, vile, abominable, wicked thing indeed! How long will God hold His wrath from us?

I know that was harsh. But "abortion on demand" is happening and suspecting it might someday be legally sanctioned is why I decided against becoming an Obstetrician. In my day, Obstetricians were the ones who usually performed abortions. There are times and circumstances when an abortion is necessary to save the mother's life, but if I were ever asked to abort an unwanted fetus, I knew I couldn't, because it would be something that would haunt me for the rest of my days.

I took the Oath of Hippocrates in 1966 when my Doctor of Medicine Degree was conferred on me. The oath I swore was the Traditional Hippocratic Oath. When I made that decision in 1966, I had no idea early innocent life would become so vulnerable to the political ambitions of politicians. I never thought:

- *The right to kill innocent babies would be championed by a major American Political Party—*
- *The Oath of Hippocrates would someday be "liberalized" to allow abortions on demand—*
- *And some American Medical Schools would abandon the Hippocratic Oath altogether.*
- *Nowadays, American Medical Schools encourage their students to form a committee for the purpose of writing an oath that satisfies the "moral compass" of their class!*
- ***I never imagined some doctors would spend their entire careers murdering innocent babies!***

Oh! Some of you object! You make a distinction between "fetus" and "baby?" Shame on you! A loving pregnant mother does not say: "I'm going to have a fetus!" She joyfully announces: "I'm going to have a baby!"

For hundreds of years, Israel murdered its innocent children—sacrificed them on their pagan altars to false gods! If we don't stop murdering our babies—if we continue going down this evil path—God will turn His back on us. I fear it is already too late. Since Roe vs. Wade was passed in 1973, the number of murdered babies had reached 61 million (in 2020)! That number is projected to reach 63 million in 2022!

63 million babies sacrificed on America's pagan altar to "Freedom of Choice" — since 1973! That number is growing every day. I believe America is no longer the home of the free (because of the brave). We are a nation that murders our unwanted children!

Some may consider this discussion of abortion is a departure from the central topic of this chapter: "Myth vs. Fact." **Not so! We murder our unwanted children! That is Fact!** For

---

[65] **More than 61 million babies killed in 47 years of legal abortion ...www.texasrighttolife.com>News>Abortion (2020)**

hundreds of years, Israel murdered its children in defiance of God's Commands: *"Thou shalt have no other gods before Me,"* and *"Thou shalt not murder!"* Moses warned them (Deut. 12:29-32, Lev. 18:3,21). They didn't listen, and God turned His back on them! It cost them their land and their national identity. That fact is just one of those "slippery slopes" of moral decay our nation has been slithering down for decades. We have been on that particular slippery slope for almost **half a century!**

THE CASE FOR ADOPTION

With certain exceptions that would legally allow abortion in cases such as those of incest, rape, or a pregnancy that threatens the life of the mother — certainly some middle ground can be found where the adoption of an unwanted newborn can be pre-arranged. Sources estimate there are about 2 million couples currently waiting to adopt in the USA, which means there are as many as 36 waiting families for every one child who is placed for adoption. Approximately 10% of women in the USA (6.1 million) have difficulty getting pregnant or staying pregnant. A 2002 study by the CDC showed approximately 56% of women who use fertility services consider adoption. According to the *Donaldson Adoption Institute*, 81.5 million Americans have considered adopting a child at one time in their lives. That's approximately 40% of all US adults — up from 36% in 1977.[66, 67] The truth is, there are people who want children who can't have them. If those babies that are being aborted, can be safely carried to term, and delivered, there are people who would be fulfilled and excitedly happy to adopt them! That is not a myth. Those are facts! That concludes my discussion of "the slippery slope" our nation is on. Now I want to get back to the discussion of the problems the SHBC has caused.

WHO WROTE GENESIS? WHO WROTE THE TORAH? — THE SHBC

Now I want to take a serious look at how Bible Criticism became a part of the curriculum of some Christian seminaries and why so many seminarians think the Biblical Creation Account is a myth. Sadly, I think the Schools of Bible Criticism have created a tangled muddle of deceptive confusions!

A large number of Protestant Christian seminaries in the western world teach a theory that claims Moses did not write the Torah. The proponents of this theory call themselves: *"The School of Higher Biblical Criticism,"* or "SHBC." The SHBC grew from an idea that began in France in the 17th century AD, which was based upon the study of the stylistic (or literary construction) of the Greek translations of the Torah the schools possessed. By the 19th century, the idea there are four distinctly different literary styles in the Torah had grown in popularity. The SHBC concluded there were four unknown authors of the Torah and at least two of them wrote the Genesis Creation *"story."* Later, other promoters of the SHBC concluded an unknown editor "redacted and reordered" the works of the other four unknown authors of the Torah. The theory suggests the work of the redactor is the reason the different literary styles in the Torah often blend one into another, since later writers did not discard the work of earlier writers, but simply inserted their views at various points in the texts of the translations the SHBC possessed. That is to say: The SHBC did not analyze the original Hebrew script of Moses. They say they

---

[66] How Many Couples are Waiting to Adopt? www.americanadoptions.com
[67] **The Changing Face of Adoption in the United States | Institute ... Aug 8, 2019**

based their analyses on the Pentateuch (which is a Greek translation of the Hebrew text of the Torah). If they analyzed the Greek Pentateuch, then they studied a text that was one step removed from the original Hebrew Torah. But if their analyses were based on a translation of the Greek text into their language (i.e., a translation from Greek into French or German), then they based their analyses on texts that were at least two steps removed from the original.

The proponents of the SHBC believe the 1st Chapter of Genesis was written 300 years after the 2nd Chapter. They think the first two chapters of Genesis are two different creation "stories," which were written by two different authors. The SHBC claims the 1st creation story in the Bible (Genesis 1:1—2:4a) was written last (in the 5th century BC) and is attributed to a Priestly writer who called God "*Elohim.*" They claim the 2nd creation story (Genesis 2:4b—25) — was written first (in the 8th century BC) and was written by a *"Yahwist writer"* who called God "YHWH."[68] This theory, which attempts to explain why there are two different names for God in the first two chapters of Genesis — appears to be a main-stream belief that is still taught in a number of Protestant Christian Seminaries today.

Two different authors, who have the same surname wrote the two books I have read that support this theory. The first book is: BRIDGES: *Reconnecting Science and Faith,* by Father Stephen Parker. Father Parker is an Episcopal Priest. He is a graduate of the College of William and Mary and the Berkeley Divinity School at Yale. He is also the scientist who has taught theology and astronomy for more than a decade to the senior class at the Salisbury School. I have met Father Parker and have dined with him. I think he is a mighty servant of God who has written an interesting, compelling book. I enjoyed reading his book.

The other book I read goes into a more detailed explanation of the theory of multiple Torah authors. That book is also a good read. Its author is Dr. Andrew Parker. His book is: THE GENESIS ENIGMA: *Why the Bible is Scientifically Accurate.* According to the cover page of his book: *"Dr. Andrew Parker is known by many as the scientist to best explain biology's Big Bang Theory of the diversity of life that emerged during the Cambrian period."* He is an honorary research fellow of Green Templeton College, Oxford University, and conducts research at the Natural History Museum in London. Dr. Andrew Parker has been named: *"One of the eight scientists for a New Century"—* selected by *the Royal Institute (London).* In his book, he states:

"With the myth of Mosaic authorship dispelled, we can begin to make use of that human history of the Near East. Using the text of the Pentateuch itself (*Parker's words, but my underlining*), we can deduce what type of person would want to write each passage. Then we can try to find them somewhere in the Bible itself."[69]

That's how this English academic expresses his "respect" for the oral tradition and written history of the Jewish people!

[68] Parker, Stephen: BRIDGES: Reconnecting Science and Faith. p.47-58, In Celebration of Biblical Evolution
[69] Parker, Andrew: THE GENESIS ENIGMA: Appendix—Who wrote Genesis? p. 232a

THE SHBC ATTACKS JUDAISM [70]

Dr. Andrew Parker's phrase: *"the text of the Pentateuch itself,"* is an admission the scholars of the SHBC based their claim (*"Moses did not write the Torah"*) — on their analysis of a Greek translation of the *Hebrew Torah*. Stated another way, the scholars of the SHBC <u>did not</u> analyze the *Hebrew text of the Torah* Moses wrote. They analyzed <u>a Greek translation</u> of the Torah.

In the last century, a sister school of *"The Higher Criticism,"* known as "*The Lower Criticism,"* has joined ranks with the SHBC. This school has used the *Septuagint* (i.e., the *Greek* translation of the *Hebrew Tanakh)*, to question the reliability of the *Tanakh* (i.e., the rest of the Hebrew Bible). Like the SHBC, the proponents of the school of *"The Lower Criticism"* (or SLBC) have also developed recensions based on variant translations they regard as more reliable than the traditional Hebrew Bible! Some later Jewish scholars have pointed out: These recensions have been accomplished by — *"Offering baseless emendations and conjectures that are without rational foundation."* [71]

THE OBJECTIONS OF JUDAISM TO THE SCHOOLS OF BIBLICAL CRITICISM

The Schools of the Higher and Lower Criticism attack two of traditional Judaism's most important beliefs and total commitments:

- God dictated the Torah to the man who wrote it — Moses.
- Therefore, the Torah is — *Divine*. [72]

The objections of Jewish traditionalists to the hypotheses of these Schools are so great that I would be remiss if I did not discuss what they say are their inaccuracies, prejudices, and bigotries. With the exception of my comments on Darwin's faulty science, what follows about the SHBC, the SLBC, and their key advocates, is taken from Rabbi Nathan Lopes Cardozo's article: On Bible Criticism and its Counterarguments, a Short History — 1995. [73]

A FRENCH PHYSICIAN, JEAN ASTRUC (1684-1766) —

is considered by many to be the real founder of classical Bible Criticism. He scorned the claim God spoke directly to Moses, as the Torah says. He argued Moses used two sources and ten fragments, which were written before his time. According to Astruc, Moses was not the author, but was a redactor of an earlier book of Genesis and part of the book of Exodus, and claims his primary sources referred to God as YHWH and Elohim.

JULIUS WELLHAUSEN (1844-1918) —

However, it was a German Lutheran Clergyman (Julius Wellhausen), who was also a professor of Theology and a Seminarian, who gave full impetus to the claim — Moses did not write the Torah. Wellhausen had several premises he wished to prove. He said:

---

[70] Article: *On Bible Criticism and its Counterarguments by Rabbi Nathan Lopes Cardozo; a Short History, 1995:* http://www.aishdas.org/toratemet/en_cardozo.html

[71] Ibid. *("Recensions:"* an editorial revision of an original literary work, based on critical examination of texts—in this case, translations of a text—i.e., copies of translated texts, which were not the original text!)

[72] Ibid.

[73] Article: *On Bible Criticism and its Counterarguments by Rabbi Nathan Lopes Cardozo; a Short History, 1995:* http://www.aishdas.org/toratemet/en_cardozo.html

- *"Some Jewish priests under Ezra's guidance redacted the Torah and the Book of Joshua in the time of the Second Temple"* (when small remnants of Jews returned to Jerusalem in the 5th century BC after Babylonian captivity).
- *"Their purpose was to perpetuate two myths:*
  - *Moses authored the Torah.*
  - *The Israelites participated in a central worship of their supposed god."*

Furthermore (according to Rabbi Cardozo), Wellhausen said—

- *"There never was a Tabernacle, and no revelation at Sinai ever took place."*
- *"If the so-called God of Israel ever existed, Moses must have considered him a local thunder god of Mount Sinai."*
- Wellhausen also said: *"The Torah was a complete forgery. It definitely was not a true verbal account of god's words to Moses and the people of Israel, for their god never existed!"* (The underlining is mine—O. David.)

So, Wellhausen claimed to know the mind of Moses! In his analysis of the Torah Commentaries, the only passages he considered authentic were those that fit his theory. All others, he contended, were forgeries. He went to great pains to point out what he considered corrupt vocabulary and internal inconsistencies in the texts he studied. He felt he needed to change the meaning of some of the words in the translations of the Torah he possessed — to make them fit his theory. He called his practice of changing the words of the translations he studied — *"conjectural emendation."* An emendation of a text is a correction or a revision of a text, which involves — *changing the words in the text!* It never disturbed him thousands of verses contradicted his theory. Instead, he contended: *"The unknown writers of the Torah were clever forgers who anticipated my theory, made false statements, and changed verses to refute my theory."* Thus, a 19th century German Lutheran Seminarian arrogantly tainted a Greek translation of the 3300-year-old Hebrew Torah! He made his own *"revised emendation"* of the Pentateuch by changing the words of the time-honored Greek text. His *"conjectural emendations"* produced a text that was *three* steps removed from the original! You can't say *"translation"* because he changed the meaning of the text!

Wellhausen arrogantly claimed the unknown writers of the 3300-year-old Hebrew Torah were clever forgers who anticipated the changes he would make 3300 years later! He contemptuously said they made false statements and changed verses to refute his anticipated theory! How can we trust His "imagined" revision? By his own admission, he conjectured his revisions by using assumptions, guesswork, imagination, speculations, and suppositions to formulate his hypotheses. He admitted his "conjectural emendations" were "imagined!"

It is no surprise he eventually suffered a crisis of his conscience, which caused him to resign his professorship in his Lutheran seminary and study Islam! I'll talk about that in The Epilogue (in Book III).

Nevertheless, Wellhausen's work was considered a masterpiece in his time, and most of his contemporaries and their students unquestionably accepted his work. He dominated his generation's Old Testament scholarship in Germany, England, and America. His disciples continued his work and claimed to discover more forgeries in the

Tanakh itself! Rabbi Cardozo claims the whole body of work of the SHBC and the SLBC eventually degenerated into an absurd redaction of the entire Tanakh. That is what I meant when I said I think: "The Schools of Biblical Criticism created — a tangled muddle of deceptive confusions."

DARWIN'S INFLUENCE

Why were Wellhausen's ideas so readily accepted, and why did the Schools of Bible Criticism gain so much traction? As it turns out, Charles Darwin's influence was a major factor. In Wellhausen's day, Darwin's "theory" of evolution was dominant. Darwin had won the day, and any discipline that accepted Darwin's theory was welcomed with open arms. Darwin's influence on Wellhausen was not widely known, but neither was it a secret. However, because of Wellhausen's academic status at the Seminary level, Wellhausen's influence, and rationalizations eventually began to impact the basic doctrines of orthodox Christianity, and was one of the factors, which led to a new movement in religious thought that has contributed to today's well-established philosophy of Religious Liberalism. Religious Liberalism attempts to reconcile pre-modern religious tradition with modernism.

Darwin's framework of evolution deeply influenced other Christians as well. The net result caused many to question and then to deny, all the supernatural events described in the Bible. The possibility of the existence of a supreme metaphysical force (i.e., God) conflicted with Darwin's premise of naturalism in evolution. After Darwin's book, "The Origin of Species" was published, anti-God people felt empowered. Religion and the Bible came under an attack. The Biblical Account of Creation must have been a fantasy, a cultural myth of a primitive people. Give thanks to Darwin for coming up with an alternative explanation that makes more sense. The stories of the fall of man, Noah's Flood, God's Covenants with Noah and Abraham, the Egyptian enslavement of the Israelites and their deliverance by God through Moses, were just that — "*stories*" — and were not to be taken seriously.

The New Testament must be equally ridiculed! The possibility of a Virgin Birth, the *myth* of a Son of God (one that could be killed, and then come back to life) — well, just how gullible can people be? "Liberal religionists," atheists, and anti-religious secularists jumped at the chance to re-interpret the Bible in a way that was considered to be "rational" and correlated with what was touted to be "the new *scientific* data." Thanks to Darwin, people began to think it more reasonable that everything developed through random chance and then progressed through natural selection. There was no longer a need for a god or any need for a code of behavior. Men could now be the masters of their own destiny.

If you want to vilify the Jewish people, begin by slandering their books (the Hebrew Torah and Tanakh.) If you wish to malign Christianity, you must first attack its books — the Old and New Testaments of the Judeo-Christian Bible. As you shall see, the Torah, the Tanakh, and the Judeo-Christian Bible are closely related.

ANTI-SEMITISM

Anti-semitism also played a role in the ascendancy of Darwinism and of Wellhausen's analysis of the Pentateuch. When Anti-Semitism became stronger in the immediate pre-Hitler days, many people felt the need to use the ideas of both men to give a final blow to the Jewish People, religion, and the Bible. When Friedrich Delitzch (1850-1922) delivered a lecture called *"Babel und Bibel,"* in which the Torah and Tanakh were considered devoid of any religious or moral value, Kaiser Wilhelm congratulated him for: *"Helping to dissipate the nimbus of the chosen people."*

If you want to vilify the Jews, you must first libel their holy book. *O. David*

REJECTION OF THE SHBC

However, the anti-Semites had their own critics. Solomon Schechter, who headed the Jewish Theological Seminary in its earlier and more Orthodox days exclaimed: *"Higher Criticism was no more than higher anti-Semitism."* According to the world-famous archaeologist *William F. Albright: "The Germans believed all things must either be German or valueless."* Albright also asked the question: *"How was it possible the scientific community accepted many of these theories without critical assessment, knowing many of the scholars of the School of Higher Biblical Criticism had shown their personal anti-Semitism completely overshadowed their intellectual honesty?"*

Special mention should also be made of Albright's archaeological discoveries. He convincingly demonstrated his archaeological research contradicted Wellhausen's view of Biblical history. Albright felt many of his archaeological discoveries destroyed the very foundations of Wellhausen's presumptions. Even in Wellhausen's day, other scholars raised objections against what they called: "Wellhausen's incredible guesswork and fantasies." In time it became clear the SHBC was developing into a cacophony of conflicting conjectures, which produced contradictory results. Over time, a paradigm-shift eventually concluded Wellhausen's type of literary criticism of the Torah was ineffective. This change in consensus opinion came from many disciplines.

In 1915, the Chancellor of England (the Earl of Halsbury) referred to the SHBC as: "Great rubbish!" Even the Irish historian, William Edward Hartpole Lecky, who was famous for his books and essays that expounded on the historical persecutions and excesses of the Roman Catholic and Protestant Christian Churches whenever they found themselves at the 'elbow of the arm of civil power' — pointed out: "Wellhausen's conjectures were contrived! They totally lacked hard evidence!"

DARWIN HAD A PROBLEM WITH HIS THEORY OF EVOLUTION.

As you shall see when you read Chapter 18 (in Book II), Darwin realized the fossil record in his day actually refuted his ideas of a slow gradual random chance development of life. So, he encouraged his supporters to continue to search for what he believed were the missing links in the fossil record, which (when found) would prove his theory. The lack of any missing-link fossil evidence eventually became known as: *"Darwin's Dilemma."*

To get around the fossil evidence against his theory, Darwin changed the direction of his own search. He put all his eggs into one basket and focused his attention on the results, which had been achieved by others in their selective breeding of only a few generations of domesticated animals. Impressed by the changes he saw; he speculated about what might be possible with selective breeding after tens of thousands of generations. Certainly (he mused), even greater changes could be possible — if given enough time. Surely (he reasoned), after millions of generations of selective breeding, it would be possible for an animal to change its "basic body plan," and morph into an entirely new and different type of animal with an entirely different basic body plan. [74] Of course, there was no way he could have known modern science would someday prove:

- The basic body plans of all animal life were established on the 'dawn' of the 5th Day of Creation! [75]
- They were established at the level of the Phyla of the animals—
- In the first 5 million years of the Cambrian Period—
- 530 million years ago!
- Darwin did not know; future discoveries of modern science would also prove — No new Phyla would ever appear in the fossil record after the early Cambrian Period! [76, 77, 78]

Unfortunately for us, those facts would not be discovered until long after Darwin's death. As it happened, Darwin imagined his scheme of evolution and believed his imaginary scheme could make it possible for life to climb his imaginary tree of evolution to produce the complexity and diversity of the life forms which were all around him. No fossil evidence of his tree of evolution has ever been found! [79]

Darwin failed to see the changes he observed were not changes in the basic-body-plans of the animals he observed. While the basic-body-plans of the phyla of animals he studied remained the same, the selective breeding he observed — caused changes in progeny, which were actually changes in the traits of the species of the animals that were bred.

All those changes in the traits of the animals bred, had occurred just as the Bible said evolution would occur — at the level of the species of animals — five levels below the level of the phyla of animals, which was the level where Darwin had speculated evolution would occur. Chapters 14-20 in Book II explain the history of Darwin's scheme of evolution and how what he thought happened differs from what the Bible says. Modern science now agrees with the Bible. In Chapter 18, Book II, you will discover — the Hebrew word English Bibles have translated as "after their kind" or "according to their kind" — is miyn. "Miyn" means "Species!" Those seven chapters in Book II explain why Darwinism is pseudoscience.

WHAT DARWIN DID NOT KNOW

The basic-body-plans of all animals were established at the level of the Phyla of all animal-life during the Cambrian Period on the 5th Day of Creation! Science has now proved it!

- The basic-body-plans of all animals living today suddenly and independently appeared on the dawn of the 5th Day of Creation — just as the Bible says!

---

[74] Schroeder The Science of God, Chapter 1, p. 9b
[75] In Book II I will explain why I think the Cambrian Period happened on the "Dawn" of the 5th Day of Creation.
[76] Schroeder The Science of God, Chapter 2, p. 30b
[77] Schroeder The Science of God, Chapter 4, p 69b
[78] Schroeder The Science of God, Chapter 6, p 88-89
[79] Schroeder The Science of God, Chapter 1, p 9c

- No new Phyla and therefore, no new basic-body-plans of any animal have occurred — not since their inception in the Cambrian Period on the 5th Day — not in Darwin's day — and certainly not since.
- Selective breeding has never caused any change in the basic-body-plan of any animal, and if history is any harbinger of the future, will never bring about the morphing of any animal into a new and different phylum (i.e., race, or tribe) of animals.
- Much like Wellhausen's ideas about the authors of the Torah, Darwin's ideas of evolution were all contrived!
- They were based on his imagination and his conjectures.
- People claim Darwin based his theory of evolution on science.
- In fact, true scientific investigation had little to do with it.
- As you shall see (in Book II), the Bible states evolution would occur at the level of the species!
- Modern science has now proved it!
- Modern Science has also proved the sequence of creation in the Bible is accurate.
- What the Bible says is what actually happened!
- The scientific discoveries of the last 85 years now show — there has been a convergence of agreement between Modern Science and the Bible.

THE FOSSIL RECORD HAS DESTROYED DARWIN'S THEORY.

After 165 years of searching (and still counting), and after the discovery of millions of additional fossils of ancient life forms (and still counting), today's fossil record is even more lethal to Darwin's theory than it was in his day. We now know modern science has disproved Darwin's ideas and has confirmed the type of evolution the Genesis Code in the Biblical Creation Account proclaimed — Evolution would occur at the level of the species of animals! However, this is something that is not widely known, and Darwin's theory is still being taught in our educational institutions as if it has been proved to be a law. Chapters 14-20 in Book II provide the evidence and make the case for these statements.

WHAT WILL FUTURE GENERATIONS THINK OF DARWIN & WELLHAUSEN?

The views of both men are still venerated and have had a tremendous impact on western society and Judeo-Christian beliefs. The influence of both men is still strong and widely felt. The adverse religious impacts of Darwinian theory and Wellhausen's religious conjectures, have also led many astray and away from a belief in God. Sadly, many in western societies have followed and are still following their siren calls.

Summary Points:
- Secular Society and some Theologians think the Genesis Account of Creation is a myth.
- Orthodox Jews and some Judeo-Christians disagree.
- The Bible says Moses authored the Torah.
- The SHBC claims Moses did not write the Torah.
- Orthodox Jews repudiate the SHBC because they believe God dictated the Torah to Moses.

- The SHBC has developed into a cacophony of conflicting conjectures, which have produced contradictory results.
- A paradigm-shift has now concluded Wellhausen's type of literary criticism of the Torah was illusory, and misleading.
- Darwinists have not accepted these conclusions, and some Protestant Christian Seminaries still teach Wellhausen's documentary hypotheses.
- It is not widely known Darwinism influenced Wellhausen.
- It is also not well known — Wellhausen suffered a crisis of his conscience, which caused him to resign his seminary professorship! He favored his conjectural analyses and gave up his faith! This will be discussed in the Epilogue of this series, which is in Book III.
- The fossil record has now disproven Darwinism, but this is not yet widely known. This will be discussed in Book II.
- In the last 49 years, more than 63 million babies have been murdered in the USA on the pagan altar of Freedom of Choice!
- Even if it were only 1, that 1 would have been too many!

"OUR ABBA FATHER"

The Fish Sign: ∝ *In Greek* ('ΙΧΘΥΣ i.e., ichthys = fish), *an acrostic for "Jesus Christ Son of God, Savior."* In the Introduction to this Chapter I talked about "Loving God" and "Fearing God." I recently heard a homily from Dr. Kurt Bjorklund, who is the senior pastor of the Orchard Hill Church on Brandt School Road in Wexford, Pennsylvania. He preached about Christ's instructions on how we should pray to God (Chapter Six—Matthew's Gospel). His sermon was such a clear explanation of the dichotomy of the attributes of the Christian God that I thought I should share his explanation of this difficult subject. The Diagram that follows is my rendition of the graphic he displayed during his homily (text and diagram by permission from Dr. Bjorklund).

THE LOVE OF GOD—THE ATTRIBUTES OF THE NEW TESTAMENT GOD (i.e., JESUS Christ)

Jesus said we should pray in private. When we address God, we should address Him as "our Father." Jesus said we should start our prayer with "Our Abba," which is the Greek familiar word for Father. The "Loving" attributes of Our Father are listed in the circle on the left. These are the attributes of a sentimental father. Our Father is "Immanent," meaning He is essential and internal (i.e., He dwells within us in the form of His Spirit, who dwells in all believers). He is "Familiar," meaning we are His children. Our Father is "Loving, approachable, and a bastion of safety."

THE FEARSOME ATTRIBUTES OF THE GOD OF THE HEBREWS: i.e., THE FEAR OF GOD

But when we say, "Hallowed Be Thy Name," we acknowledge God's holiness, His exalted sacredness, and His purity. These are the **YHWH-attributes of God**. The YHWH-attributes of God's holiness characterize His power (cf. Introduction—Part IX). They are the "Mystical" qualities of God. They are listed in the circle on the right. The mystical, fearful attributes of God are "Transcendent," meaning He is supernaturally supreme, excellent, unequaled, unmatched, heavenly, perfect, and divine. These attributes are "Mysterious, Terrifying, Unknowable, Dangerous (i.e., lethal to sin), and Fearsome."

Notice the two circles overlap. The overlap is where the Sentimental and Mystical Attributes of our Lord-God meet. If you were to bold the outlines of the overlap of the two circles, you would see the ancient Christian sign of the fish (mine—*O. David*). You would see: "Jesus Christ Son of God." You would see: "Our Savior."

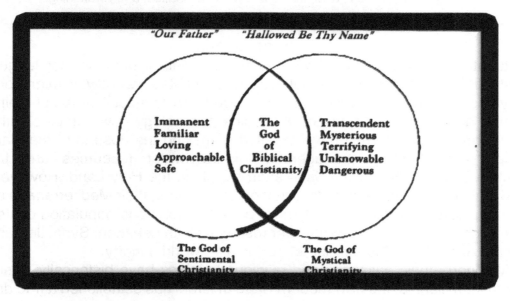

Our Loving Father said: *"Fear not, for I am with you. Be not dismayed, for I am your God. I will strengthen you. I will help you. I will uphold you with my victorious right hand."* Isaiah 41:10 RSV

INTRODUCTION—PART VII: A RENAISSANCE IN INDUSTRY, AGRICULTURE, RELIGION & SCIENCE, & AN INTRODUCTION TO: *"THE GENESIS CODE"*

Renaissance: a revival, a renewal, a reexamination, a re-awakening.

Pilate asked Jesus: *"What is truth?"* (John 18:38)

INTRODUCTION

It is fortunate the Jews of Israel have resurrected their ancient Hebrew language. The 1948 establishment of the new State of Israel has attracted a worldwide migration of Jews. Not only has their national identity and language been re-established, but their industry, agriculture, arts, sciences, medicine & medical technology now compete with Europe, Asia, and the Americas. They have excelled in making the deserts of their land bloom with their state-of-the-art management of freshwater resources and freshwater reclamation projects. Freshwater is in short supply in the Holy Land. However, Israelis are hard at work building several desalination plants along their Mediterranean coast with the goal of providing freshwater to Israel's desert regions and population centers. Israel shares its Jordan River Valley freshwater resources with Lebanon, Syria, Jordan, and the Palestinian Authority.[80] Modern Israel truly is a 1st world country.

Although ethnic animosity and religious tensions have historically existed in the Holy Land for millennia, the new modern State of Israel has established a true democratic government. All people who are living within Israel's borders, may become citizens of Israel, and elect their own representatives to the Knesset[81] if they accept the right of Israel to exist. The Arab population of Nazareth has done this. When I visited Israel in 2010, the population of Nazareth was ~ 70,000. In modern-day Nazareth, the descendants of Abraham & Hagar, and of Abraham & Keturah greatly outnumber the descendants of Abraham & Sarah. Nazareth and its surrounding regions of the Galilee are predominantly Arab now, and they have elected their own Arab representatives to the Knesset.[82]

A RENAISSANCE IN RELIGION

The new Israeli State has also fostered an intellectual renaissance that has resulted in an enlightenment of religious thought and interpretation, as religious scholars have probed the past and gained additional meaning and insights from ancient Hebrew manuscripts.

On Jan. 7, 2010, it was reported Professor Gershon Galil (at the University of Haifa), had deciphered what he believes to be the earliest known Hebrew writing. He found it on a three-thousand-year-old fragment of pottery that dates to the 10th century BC—i.e., to the time of David and Solomon. The Bible says, in the 4th year of his reign, King Solomon began to build the house of the Lord in Jerusalem (1st Kings 6:1). This verse also says Solomon did this 480 years after Moses led the Exodus of his people from Egypt! According to The Ryrie Study Bible, the 4th year of the reign of Solomon was

---

[80] Israel Proves the Desalination Era Is Here - Scientific American*https://www.scientificamerican.com › article › israel-proves-the-desalination...*

[81] Knesset: the elected legislative branch of the Israeli government. The Knesset passes all laws, elects the president, approves the cabinet, & supervises the work of the government through its committees.

[82] **The Status of Arabs in Israel https://www.jewishvirtuallibrary.org › the-status-of-arabs-in-israel.**

967 BC.[83] This would place the date of "the Exodus from Egypt" at 1447 BC (480 + 967 = 1447 BC). William F. Albright arrived at the same date for "The Exodus" through his archeological findings (cf. Chapter 26 in Book III). Professor Galil's discovery proves writing in the ancient Hebrew language existed hundreds of years before the dates prescribed in earlier research.[84]

Scholars tell us the original copies of the Old Testament were written on leather or papyrus from the time of Moses (circa 1450 BC, but others argue 1200 BC) — to the time of Malachi (circa 400 BC). Tragically, the originals were lost to antiquity.[85] Some believe the original manuscript of the Old Testament and the Ark of the Covenant disappeared around the time of Nebuchadnezzar's Babylonian conquest and destruction of Jerusalem, which occurred in 586 BC. Solomon's magnificent Temple to God in Jerusalem was destroyed at the same time.

The 1945 discovery of the Gnostic Gospels in the caves of Jabal al-Tarif near the town of Naj 'Jammadi in Upper Egypt sparked much controversy. (See Gnosticism commentary — Appendix V in Book III). On the other hand, the 1947 discovery of the Dead Sea Scrolls at Qumran has verified the accuracy of the Masoretic text of the Hebrew Bible, which was standardized and meticulously marked and counted by Jewish scholars between AD 600 and AD 950. The marking and counting were done to ensure future copies would be true to the ancient text. Before the discovery at Qumran, we did not possess copies of the Old Testament earlier than 895 AD. The Dead Sea Scrolls pushed that date back a thousand years and gave us a Hebrew text that dates from the 2nd to the 1st century BC of all but one of the books of the Old Testament — the Book of Esther

A 20TH CENTURY RENAISSANCE IN SCIENCE

We are fortunate the scientific discoveries of the past few decades in astronomy, paleontology, and high-energy physics have greatly enlightened us. These scientific discoveries have literally taken us to a better understanding of the beginning of time and the beginning of life on our planet. We have learned there was a time before which there was neither time, nor space, nor matter. And, the scientific discoveries, which have proved there was a sudden explosive development of life on our planet, have forced us to a reevaluation of the process and direction of evolution. [86] However, science can only take us so far. Nevertheless, within the professional scientific community, most scientists now understand the Bible is not about to be replaced with a slogan that can fit on the front of a T-shirt. Even the world-renowned Darwinist and Harvard paleontologist, Stephen Jay Gould, is on record for having written: "Science simply cannot adjudicate the issue of God's superintendence of nature." [87] This is why I disagree with Maimonides' belief that

---

[83] I Kings 6:1, the Ryrie Study Bible notes on I Kings 6:1, & the Ryrie Bible Introduction to the Book of Exodus.
[84] Article: Most Recent Ancient Hebrew Biblical Inscription Deciphered: by Prof. Gershon Galil of University of Haifa: Jan. 7, 2010, http://phys.org/news1821010334.html. The Ketef Hinnom Scrolls are in another style of Hebrew. They were discovered in 1997 and date to the 7th century BC! But this wasn't determined until their analysis was completed in 2023. See the last page of the Introduction—Part IX.
[85] The Ryrie Study Bible, © 1976, 1978 by The Moody Bible Institute of Chicago: Is Our Present Text Reliable? p. 1962
[86] Schroeder The Science of God Chapter 1 p. 18a
[87] Schroeder The Science of God Chapter 1 p. 18b

Science is the only path to knowing God. Only belief and faith in God can take us to those places that science can never go!

A CONVERGENCE OF AGREEMENT BETWEEN SCIENCE & RELIGION

Until the 1960s most scientists believed the universe had no beginning. Most believers believed it did. Many scientists also believed life on our planet (including mankind), arose gradually. Believers insisted all life was the result of the sudden creative acts of God because that was the message of the Bible. For centuries these opposing beliefs were irreconcilable. However, recent discoveries of modern science and a new wave of religious enlightenment and interpretation have shown an ever-increasing trend towards an agreement between the two disciplines. Opinions are now merging. The rapprochement in science started in physics and has slowly spread to biology. This reconciliation has now reached a majority of scientists. But reconciliation does not require every scientist to become a believer, nor does it require every believer to believe every aspect of modern science.

THE COSMOGONY OF NAHMANIDES & HIS "GENESIS CODE"

A rediscovery of the Cosmogony of Nahmanides is beginning to shed some light on religious thought as well. Nahmanides based his Cosmogony on his knowledge of the deeper meaning of the Hebrew script Moses wrote when he penned His Genesis Account of Creation. I have called his interpretation — *The Genesis Code.* Sadly, only a small number of people are aware of Nahmanides' Cosmogony. For society to realize science now agrees with Nahmanides' interpretation of the Bible's Creation Account, a critical mass of people must understand: The Hebrew text of the Torah is a text that carries a subtext within it — a subtext which Nahmanides interpreted. [88] His commentary on what happened at the moment of the beginning of God's creation reads like a modern-day physics textbook on the Big Bang Theory! I'll talk about that in Book I.

The flow of time and the exact sequence of the events from the Big Bang to the appearance of humankind are summarized in the thirty-one verses with which the Bible begins — i.e., the 1st Chapter of Genesis. The Bible uses only 31 verses and a few hundred words to poetically describe 15 ¾ billion earth-year-equivalents of cosmic history, [89](*) the subjects of which libraries of books have been written. For years I read the various English translations of the first two chapters of Genesis with a superficial and unlearned reading without gaining any significant understanding of the details of our origins. I have since learned those details were hidden in the original ancient Hebrew text. Because the details of our origins were hidden, Nahmanides and other ancient Jewish sages believed the various translations of the Torah (from the original Hebrew into other languages), have missed the deeper meaning of Moses' words.[90]

ATHEISTS & DARWINISTS WILL CRITICIZE THIS BOOK.

Religious fundamentalists, seminarians, liberals (both religious & secular), and some scientists will criticize it as well. However, careful examination will disclose: *Nothing in this book contradicts any of the basic tenets of Christian belief in Jesus Christ.* Christians should not fear any of the discoveries of science. If any scientific opinions have resulted

---

[88] Schroeder The Science of God Chapter 2 p. 20-21
[89](*) Cosmic Microwave Background Radiation data (often referred to as 'CBR') obtained in space by NASA in 2011 has reported an age of the Universe of 13.73 billion 'years.'—See Chapter 5 in Book I.
[90] Schroeder The Science of God Chapter 1 p. 18c

from bad science, the scientific method will eventually identify and eliminate them. Christians should understand the Bible needs no defense. But the Bible deserves our respect and challenges us to use not only our hearts, but also our minds to ponder its mysteries. The truth of the Word of God is indestructible and can handle all things!

IN 1897 THE POST-IMPRESSIONIST FRENCH ARTIST PAUL GAUGUIN CREATED A PAINTING HE INSCRIBED WITH THESE WORDS: "D'OU VENONS NOUS?" (Where do we come from?) "QUE SOMMES NOUS?" (What are we?) "OU ALLONS NOUS?" (Where are we going?) Science cannot and will never be able to answer these questions. Only Belief and Faith in God can take us to the places Science can never go! This book examines these questions and gives answers that come from the Judeo-Christian Bible. They are the lessons of Christian Belief and Faith.

- Where do we come from? ANSWER—We came from God! God made and created us!
- What are we? ANSWER—We are God's children!
- Where are we going? ANSWER—We are going to the eternal destiny we choose!
  - The "sheep of God" are going to The Good Shepherd (Jesus Christ), and our Loving Abba (God our Father) in Heaven.
  - The "goats" are going to God's Great White Throne Judgment! (See Matthew 25:31-46 & Revelations Chapters 19 & 20 — Our destiny is our free-will choice.)

SKEPTICS, WHO RIDICULE GOD'S WORD, ARE NOT AWARE THE GENESIS CODE EXISTS.

Knowing about the convergence of agreement between what modern science has discovered about our origins and what the Bible has stated for the last 3300 years is important when Christians are confronted with the pseudo-scientific claims non-believers make when they attack God's Word. We now know how to answer the skeptics. All their attempts to deny the existence of God, and to replace the Biblical Creation Account with their imaginary schemes of creation and development have failed. Their theories have now been disproved by the discoveries modern science has made in the last 85 years. The same body of scientific evidence has not only disproved Darwinism and Neo-Darwinian theory — but has also verified the accuracy of the Biblical Creation Account!

KNOWLEDGE OF THE GENESIS CODE IS NOT NECESSARY
for an understanding of Salvation. In this book, The Genesis Code discussion only applies to the first two Chapters of the Book of Genesis. When it comes to Salvation, no scholarly theory or special knowledge or interpretation is needed. The straightforward message of the Bible is crystal clear. The only pathway to Salvation is through complete belief, faith, trust, and commitment to Jesus Christ.

The Bible tells us Jesus was silent while the chief priests and the elders were accusing him. Pilate was amazed by His silence (Matt. 27:11-14)! Jesus finally broke His silence after Pilate asked if He was the King of the Jews (John 18:33). Jesus said: *"My Kingdom is not of this world"* … *"My kingdom is not of this realm" (John 18:36)*. Pilate replied: "So you are a king?" Jesus answered: *"You say correctly that I am a king. For this I have been born and for this I have come into the world, so that I may bear witness to the truth. Everyone who is of the truth hears My voice."* Pilate then asked Jesus: "What is truth?"

(John 18:37-38 NASB). Pilate could not discern the truth, even when *"The Truth"* was speaking to him!

Thomas saw and heard the truth from the risen Jesus Christ but doubted. When he touched Christ's wounds, he believed! Afterwards, Jesus said to him — *"Thomas because thou hast seen me, thou hast believed. Blessed are they that have not seen, and yet have believed"* (John 20:29 NASB).

BETWEEN THE COVERS OF THESE BOOKS, YOU WILL DISCOVER—

- Heaven is real! Heaven really does exist! The Laws of Relativity have changed the belief in a possible timeless existence from a theological claim to a scientifically possible physical reality! (Book I, & Book III — cf. Appendix III).
- There actually was a beginning! The first sentence of the Hebrew Bible states it. Modern Science has now proved it. This is an inconvenient truth atheists refuse to hear. (Book I)
- Both the Father and Jesus Christ are mentioned in the first verse of the ancient Hebrew Bible. The mention of the Father is in plain view. The reference to the Pre-incarnate Jesus Christ is hidden in the deeper meaning of the ancient Hebrew text. (Book I)
- The Pre-incarnate Jesus Christ was the First Wisdom of God, through whom God the Father created and made all that exists (Book I).
- God made everything from nothing (i.e., *Creation Ex Nihilo*—Introduction & Book I).
- Darkness was the original created thing. But its temperature, composition, and the space it now occupies have drastically changed since the beginning (Introduction & Book I).
- How the Universe, the Stars, our Sun, and our earth *may* have been created and made (Book II).
- How God *may* have made and evolved the life forms on our planet (Book II).
- Darwin was wrong. The evolutionary process described in the Bible differs from the type of evolution Darwin imagined (Introduction & Book II).
- Dinosaurs are mentioned in the Bible, but their Hebrew name is mistranslated in English Bibles (Book II).
- Cavemen are also mentioned in the Bible, but the Hebrew Bible and Modern Science define the word "*man*" differently (Book II).
- Did it take 15 ¾ billion earth-year-equivalents to create the universe and all that exists, or was it only six days? The answer to the Time Conundrum is discussed in Chapter 5 of Book I.
- Appendix I: The Duration of the Six Days of Creation (in current earth-year-equivalents), is explained in this Appendix to Book I.
- What the ancient Jewish sages thought God meant when He said:

  "I am Jehovah. There is no other. Besides Me there is no other God. I make light and create darkness. I make peace and create evil" Isa. 45:6-7 (The Interlinear Bible: Book II).

- Why a world-famous academic atheist has changed his mind and now believes in God (Book II).

- And, in Book III:
  - The 6th Day: "Man Made in His Image"
  - The 7th Day: The 1st Sabbath—Rest & Repose
  - (Gen.2: 4-6) Earth: From a Fiery Ball to a Toxic Water-World—a retrospective that tells us the 1st rain earth experienced was a colossal event that happened near the close of the 2nd Day of Creation.
  - Yuds—Lameds—Nefesh Haiyah—Neshama & Nephilim
  - The Garden of Eden
  - Adam Names the Animals: God Makes Adam's Helper
  - Appendix II: *"When the Fullness of Time Had Come"*
  - Appendix III: Heaven is "For Real," Heaven Really Does Exist
  - Appendix IV: "Made from Monkeys?"
  - Appendix V: Commentary on Agnosticism, Gnostics, & Gnosticism
  - Epilogue

❧
INTRODUCTION—PART VIII
SO MANY QUESTIONS! THE OTHER REASON I WROTE THIS BOOK!

"Teach thy tongue to say I do not know and Thou shalt progress." Maimonides

My failure to give the correct answer caused me to write this book. (O. David)

"WHAT IS DARKNESS?"

The question startled and stopped me. The person who asked that question was a member of the alto section of our Skidaway Island United Methodist Church (SIUMC) Choir. Everyone saw I was surprised—like a deer caught in the headlights of a car. I thought: Oh my! I've just started this Sunday School Class on the Old Testament and I don't know the answer to the first question!

My wife and I had been members of that Savannah, Georgia church for about a year when the Pastor discovered I was a certified Bethel Bible Series teacher. It wasn't a matter of inexperience that stopped me. Two decades earlier (when we lived in Yakima, Washington), I had completed the Bethel Bible Teacher-Certification Course. The Bethel Bible Series for congregants consists of 40 two-hour lessons — twenty on the Old Testament and twenty on the New. The people in my Yakima classes had registered for those courses, purchased the course material, and signed a pledge they would complete the course. However, this class in Georgia was different. They wanted the Bible to be our text. They wanted extemporaneous discussions of the Bethel lessons. Expository teaching was what they called it. We were starting our study with the Book of Genesis and suddenly, I felt vulnerable. They did not have the Bethel text before them and neither did I. It occurred to me, having the text of the course had provided a sense of security, but now I was on my own. I instantly thought of the old saying: "Fools rush in where angels fear to tread." They all had their Bibles open. We had just started reading and talking about the first chapter of Genesis. After I read Genesis 1:1, "In the beginning, God created the heavens and the earth," I paused—expecting someone might challenge two statements in the first verse of the Bible.
- There was a beginning.
- There is a God who created everything.

The class was silent. And I thought: Perhaps there are no skeptics in this class. Then I read Genesis 1:2 — *"And the earth was without form and void, and darkness was upon the face of the deep."* When I paused for the breath to continue, *the question* came—

"What is Darkness?"

The silence in that room was palpable. What stopped me was my ignorance. This was the first time anyone had asked *that* question. Perhaps the absence of any course material was the reason Val had asked that important question. Nothing interfered with her free association of thought. Prior to this I had always thought of darkness in terms of its religious connotation. Darkness is evil. Darkness is the absence of God and God's light. Darkness is the result of man's turning away from God.

My first concern was — *that* question, at *that* time, might lead to questions about Satan — and I wanted to direct the attention of the class to Jesus Christ. That is the way I had always taught the first three verses of Genesis. God the Father had already been mentioned in the first verse. I was about to read the first mention of the Holy Spirit in the second verse, and I had intended to reveal to the class what I thought was the first veiled reference to the Pre-incarnate Jesus Christ in Genesis 1:3 with the phrase: *"Then God said."* At that time, I thought *("Then God said")*, was the first reference in the Bible to *"the Word of God"* — which is Jesus Christ.

It is amazing how much can flash through your mind during a pregnant pause. I should have said: "I don't know." Instead, I answered: "Darkness is the absence of God's light" — and then quickly resumed reading verse 2 — *"And the Spirit of God was moving over the surface of the waters."* It was obvious Val was disappointed. Although darkness is the absence of God's light (in the religious sense), it suddenly occurred to me she already knew that and believed it. So why would she ask *that* question? Then it struck me. Did she want me to explain the *science* of darkness? I had never thought about the scientific definition of darkness before. Although she was not explicit, I sensed the class intuitively knew — the scientific definition of darkness was the thrust of her question. Everyone knew she had asked a serious question and had gotten an inadequate answer that trumpeted to the class — *he doesn't know!* Afterwards, I went home with a profound sense of failure. I felt I had: *"Darkened counsel by words without knowledge."* (cf. Introduction—Part V.) Little did I know it, but *that* question and my failure would lead me on a fascinating journey of my mind and heart, which would deepen my faith and give me a whole new perspective on the greatness of our Creator. Thank you, Val. I now firmly believe your question was inspired by the Holy Spirit.

THE TARGUM ONKELOS

Since then, I have come to believe the first veiled biblical reference to Jesus Christ is in the *Onkelos* translation of the first verse of the Bible — Genesis 1:1. (I will talk about that in Chapter 8 — Book I). Onkelos translated the Hebrew Torah (i.e., the five books of Moses) into Aramaic. Many believe Aramaic is the language Jesus Christ spoke. Scholars say the Onkelos translation is *the* version, which is closest to the meaning of the original ancient Hebrew text of the Torah.

THE BLACK OF SPACE

As it turns out, the scientific definition of darkness is — *Darkness is the Black of Space. Darkness may be the original created thing!* Today its temperature is an unimaginably cold -270 degrees Centigrade (2.73 degrees above absolute zero Kelvin) and it is getting ever colder with the passage of time. We would die an instant death if we were exposed to that temperature. However, there was a point in time, that point in the beginning when it was infinitely hot — so hot modern science cannot put a number on it. I have since learned the Hebrew word for darkness is *hoshek*. I had given a simple answer to the question, but as it turns out, the Hebrew concept of *hoshek* is not simple. It is incredibly complex. We'll introduce the concept of the *Black of Space* in Chapter 5 of Book I when we talk about the *Time Conundrum.* Then we'll expand the discussion in Chapters 7 and 8 of Book I when we discuss the deeper meaning conveyed by the Hebrew text of Gen. 1:2 and Gen. 1:3-5.

TWO JEWISH SAGES BELIEVED THE CREATION "STORY" IS NOT A "STORY!"

The Bethel Bible Series and other similar religious studies teach Moses was the author of the Book of Genesis and say Genesis is the first of the five books of Moses that comprise the Torah. Church related literature often claims Genesis is not a history of the universe or a history of man, but rather it is the history of the redemption of man. Religionists believe the thrust of the creation story is religious — not scientific. While the Book of Genesis does begin the Biblical history of the redemption of man, the idea that the thrust of the Creation "story" has nothing to do with science — is *not* true! As it turns out, and according to two ancient Jewish sages, nothing could be further from the truth. In their view, the "creation story" is *not a "story." It is science!* Maimonides and Nahmanides believed *Creation* actually happened the way Moses described it.

When one understands the deeper meaning of the Hebrew language Moses used when he wrote the Bible's Creation Account, one begins to understand — God told Moses *how* He *created and made* all things! If you continue with the pages that follow, you will understand — Modern Science now agrees with Moses! That is why I don't call the first two chapters of Genesis: The Creation *"Story."* Genesis One and Genesis Two are — *"The Biblical Account of Creation!"*

DR. GERALD L. SCHROEDER

I think Dr. Schroeder is the man who has best explained the controversies concerning the validity of the Genesis Creation Account and the authorship of the Torah. I'll mention him again in Chapter One of Book I, and I will quote him often throughout this entire book. His books have convinced me the Bible's Creation Account is correct. Regarding questions about our origins, his writings also show an increasing convergence of agreement between religion and science. The discoveries of scientists in the last 85 years show modern science now agrees with the Bible's Creation Account, which according to Jewish Tradition, was written by Moses 3,300 years ago (*Schroeder: The Science of God p. 22a*). Dr. Schroeder was born in the USA, and is a native of Long Island, New York. He now lives and works in Israel. He is a teacher at the Hebrew University in Jerusalem. Dr. Schroeder has entered the conversation with four unique qualifications.

- He is a scientist and a Nuclear Physicist who has a keen understanding of The Big Bang Theory.
- He is also an applied Jewish Theologian who is well versed on the commentaries of the ancient Jewish Sages.
- And he is conversant in the theology and opinions of ancient and modern Talmudic scholars.
- Furthermore, he is fluent in Hebrew — both written and spoken.

If you are a scientist, you are aware of the advances scientists have made in the last 85 years. However, if you are not familiar with the Bible you may not be aware — the discoveries of modern science (starting with the acceptance of Einstein's work on Relativity), have validated and confirmed the Bible's Creation Account. If you are not a scientist and have not read about the theological implications of the Bible's Creation Account, you may find what follows interesting. You might have your curiosity stimulated to the point you will begin to study the Bible. At the very least, you will understand the Bible is a serious book. I believe it is the greatest book ever written.

THIS BOOK IS A TUTORIAL

The tutorial style of writing enables students to understand complex concepts so thoroughly they can repeat them by rote. I have found this method of teaching enables students to literally own the information they study. The key to this kind of teaching is *repetition.* To teach scientific concepts efficiently, one must *repeat key concepts often.* When introducing new material, the teacher must review previously covered material — from different perspectives. This kind of teaching requires patience on the part of the teacher and the student. The reward of repetition is *retention and ownership* of the subject matter. *The Bible is also repetitious for the same reasons.*

DON'T READ THIS BOOK THE WAY YOU WOULD READ A NOVEL.
Read it one chapter at a time. Don't go to the next chapter until you have spent some time contemplating the chapter you just read. Keep a personal notebook. Write down the things you have learned. Also write down the things you question. Chances are those things will be talked about again in later chapters but approached from a different perspective. With each repetition, new information will be added that will give you some additional insight.

THIS BOOK RELATES EXTRAORDINARY EVENTS IN ORDINARY LANGUAGE.
Only one formula is mentioned, but it is a formula, which is well known to everyone —

$$E = mc^2$$

I define new terms and present historical, theological, and scientific concepts, events, and theories in plain language. The first mention of an historical event, a scientific fact, a new idea, or theory is simply stated. With each additional reference to the same subject, the simple introduction is repeated; but with each repetition something new and more complex is added. In this way the plot thickens. *Repetition* is the means by which we *grow* our understanding. Pretty soon the *unfamiliar* becomes *familiar* and can be explained to someone else using the lexicon, which has been so often repeated.

THE ADVICE OF AN ANCIENT JEWISH SAGE
Each subject in the Creation Account is introduced by the texts of English translations of the scriptures. Then the Hebrew words Moses used will be shown and the deeper meaning of the Hebrew text will be discussed. The deeper meanings of the Hebrew texts are *not* my invention. They are taken from the writings of ancient Hebrew sages as documented in Dr. Schroeder's books. **On 15 May 2022, Dr. Schroeder gave me permission to reference his books.** Therefore, I have placed the source references for the declarations my books make in a notes section at the bottom of the pages on which the statements are made. Direct quotes are indicated as such in the text. Sometimes my statements paraphrase the text of the reference material, but the reference is always given, and the author and source are always credited. I have carefully followed the advice of a 12th century Jewish sage — Moses Maimonides, who wrote:

"Whoever wishes to translate, and aims at rendering each word literally, and at the same time adheres slavishly to the order of the words and sentences in the original, will meet with much difficulty; his renderings will be faulty and untrustworthy. This is not the right method. The translator should first try to grasp the sense of the passage thoroughly and then state the author's intention with perfect clarity in the other language. This, however, cannot be done without changing the order of words, putting many words for

one, or vice versa, and adding or taking away words, so that the subject may be perfectly intelligible in the language into which he translates." [91]

I hope you can understand the difference between what Maimonides recommended and what Wellhausen did. Maimonides wanted translations to remain *true* to the meaning of the *original* texts. Wellhausen didn't work with the *original* Hebrew texts. Furthermore, he *changed* the meaning of his *translated* texts. He favored his *conjectural emendations over his faith.*

When *The Genesis Code* is applied — the Bible's account of creation can be compared with what modern science has discovered about our origins. After you have read Chapters 6, 7, and 8 in Book I, you will see the similarities between what the ancient Hebrew sages said about *the deeper meaning of the Hebrew text* of the Biblical Creation Account and *the current Standard Model of the Big Bang Theory.* When you understand the deeper meaning of the ancient divine Hebrew words God gave Moses, [92] you will understand the Biblical Creation Account explains the *how and the why* of our creation. It must be emphasized the ancient Hebrew sages believed Moses wrote down the words God dictated to him. They also believed those words carried a hidden meaning which they were able to decipher. Their interpretation of the deeper meaning is what I call *"The Genesis Code."* [93] Their knowledge of *The Genesis Code* enabled the ancient sages to formulate their Cosmogony.

Once you understand *The Genesis Code*, you will understand it explains what Dr. Andrew Parker referred to in the title of his book as — *"The Genesis Enigma."* He marveled the Bible's Creation Account and Modern Science agree. This book explains *why* they agree. *The Genesis Code* tells us: **God told Moses how He created everything!**

CHAOS TO ORDER

The word *"chaos"* appears time and again in the creation account. each creative act of God *starts with chaos* and *proceeds toward order.* This is the *opposite* of what would have happened if "natural development" had been led by Darwin's concept of — "random chance." No! God directed the development of all things! On each of the Six Days of Creation, the development of all things occurred through "Divine Intervention!" That is the message of the Bible!

If you do not believe in God, chances are your life may seem full of chaos. Do you sometimes feel your life is like a cork floating on an ocean in motion? Do you feel tossed to-and-fro without any sense of self-control? Have you been searching for some philosophy that gives you a sense of purpose? If any of this applies to you, start reading the Bible. The God who reveals Himself in the Bible can take your cork and form it into a seaworthy ship. His Holy Spirit will be your guide, your compass, your sail, your keel, your rudder, and your anchor. God will bring order out of your chaos. Just open your mind and heart and give God a chance!

---

[91] Sherwin B. Nuland, Maimonides, p. 147
[92] Sherwin B. Nuland, Maimonides, p. 136 (Maimonides believed: "The words of the Torah were dictated by God to Moses & are therefore not only infallible but divine.")
[93] Sherwin B. Nuland, Maimonides, p. 141 (Maimonides believed: "The biblical Moses himself wrote the Torah" — dictated to him by God.)

GOD MADE OUR BUILDING BLOCKS IN LIGHT! WE ARE MADE OF STARDUST!

Do the billions of brilliant lights in the night sky have anything to do with us? Actually, they do. In the chapters that follow, you will discover — Everything in our solar system, and the universe is composed of the debris from bygone stars! You will also understand the dust, dirt, and rocks of the earth are also the recycled debris of bygone stars. We, and everything in the universe have literally been made from the *stardust* of bygone stars! [94]

STAR DUST→FLOWER DUST—FROM THE MIND OF A FOUR-YEAR OLD!

Six years before the first edition of this book was published, [95] (while visiting my youngest daughter, her husband, and our four-year-old granddaughter Samy in Pittsburgh, PA), I told them I had started writing this book. At that time, I mentioned we are literally made of *stardust.* After a while, Christy and I started reminiscing about the time when we were involved in the YMCA *Y-Indian Princess Program* in Yakima, Washington.

The purpose of *Y-Indian Princess* is to provide an activity for daughters and dads to have some special *one-on-one time.* We joined a make-believe Indian Tribe at the YMCA. Our "tribe" picked a name for itself and decided on our motto. We called ourselves *"the Friendship Tribe."* Our motto was *"One for All & All for One."* We gave each other Indian names. My oldest daughter, Patricia, was also involved in *Y-Indian Princess.* We three were part of *the Friendship Tribe.* I designed the logo my wife sewed on our "tribal vests." The logo was *a pair of clasping hands* — as in the time-honored custom of shaking hands when people meet. One night each month the tribe gathered for fellowship. My daughters and I have many fond memories of our *Y-Indian Princess times.*

Patricia and Christy named me *Red Beaver* because I had red hair (at the time), and they thought I worked so hard. I named Christy *Laughing Eyes because* she was always cheerful and smiling. I named Patricia *Desert Flower* because she bloomed wherever we went. When we joined *Y-Indian Princess,* we lived in a vibrant community in the high desert plateau country of Central Washington State, nestled on the eastern slope of the Central Cascades, within the rain-shadow of that mountain range. With only 7 inches of annual rainfall, Yakima, WA depends on irrigation water from the snowpack in the mountains to support its huge agricultural production of apples, cherries, grapes, hops, mint, and sugar beets. Before we settled in Yakima, *Trish* had been moved a lot.

Patricia was born in Augsburg, Germany in March of 1968. That month was the 8th month of my 40-month active military tour of duty in the US Army. In Augsburg, I was a General Practice Doctor. My 1st assigned unit was an Artillery Battalion. I was their Battalion Surgeon.[96] In my 2nd year in Germany I was reassigned to an Infantry Battalion and became their Battalion Surgeon. When Trish was 2 years 8 months old, she moved with us to Birmingham, Alabama when I separated from the Army, became a civilian again, and became a 1st year General Surgery Resident. When she was almost 4 years old, she was moved a 2nd time when I changed to a Radiology Residency in Temple, Texas. When Trish was 5, she enrolled in a "Pre-School" Program in our neighborhood.

---

[94] Schroeder Genesis and the Big Bang Chapter 2 p 51 b

[95] That was when I was writing the 1st Edition. I am currently writing the 2nd Edition. Samy was 4 years old then. She will soon be 16 years old.

[96] A Battalion Surgeon in the US Army was a General Practice Doctor of Medicine (i.e., like a "Family Doctor"). That position was eliminated when the draft was suspended, and our Military Forces changed to voluntary service. When I served, all MDs and DOs who were in the Military were called "Surgeons."

When she was six, she entered the 1st grade of the Temple Elementary School. She was 7 years 10 months old when we moved to Oklahoma after I finished my Radiology Residency, took the American Board of Radiology examinations, became a Board-Certified Radiologist, and took a job with the Oklahoma City Clinic. When we moved to Oklahoma City, we rented a house and Trish enrolled in her 3rd school. After a few months we bought a house in another section of the city, which was in a different school district. So, she changed schools a 4th time. She was moved again when she was 8 years 3 months old. At that time, I moved my family to Yakima, Washington where I joined a private practice group of Radiologists and Trish changed schools a 5th time. By the time she was 8 years 3 months old, Trish had lived in two countries and 4 states — and had been a student in 5 different schools.

Returning now to the Stardust→Flower Dust Discussion — during my conversation with Christy, my granddaughter (Samy) was blissfully involved in her world of make-believe while she played nearby with her dolls. We had no idea she was listening. A few days later, Christy told us Samy announced she wanted to be a *Y-Indian Princess*. She also said she had picked her *Y-Indian Princess name.* Samy wanted to be called *Flower Dust!*

I thought: *Stardust→Flower Dust! From the mind of a four-year-old! Oh My!*
That was 12 years ago. I am now working on this rewrite of the manuscript.

THE JEWISH REBUTTAL OF EUROPEAN BIBLICAL CRITICISM

Now, after that "bit" of some of my personal history, I want to resume our discussion of the *Documentary Hypotheses of the European Schools of Biblical Criticism.* In my study of the history of *The School of Bible Criticism,* I have been greatly influenced by the reputations, scholarship, and opinions of Rabbi Chaim Heller, and Rabbi Nathan Lopes Cardozo.

RABBI CHAIM HELLER (1878-1960)

Rabbi Chaim Heller is widely known as one of the greatest Talmudic scholars of his time. He not only mastered the Oral Torah, but he also knew every extant ancient Bible translation in its original language — including those Bibles written in ancient Aramaic, Greek, Latin, and Syriac! In his 1911 publication: *"Untersuchungen ueber die Peschitta"* (i.e., "Investigations of the Common Syriac Version of the Bible"), *97 Rabbi Heller took issue with the theories of the Protestant European Schools of Higher and Lower Bible Criticism. Rabbi Heller concluded the differences from the Torah, which the SHBC and SLBC had *interpreted as "divergences"* — *were* actually *"variations"* in the different *translations* of the lectionaries these schools possessed! *The differences were due to the way their lectionaries were translated, and to the way the schools interpreted them.* He emphatically stated:

---

*97 Since the end of the 3rd Century AD, *"Die Peschitta"* has been the traditional Bible of Syriac-speaking Christians (who speak several different dialects of *Aramaic—the language Jesus Christ spoke*). *Die Peschitta* and *the Targum Onkelos* (a 1st Century AD Jewish translation of the *Hebrew Torah* into *Aramaic*), are important references for understanding *Mosaic Hebrew*, which is the language of the Dead Sea Scrolls (which were discovered in 1947 and date to the 1st Century BC). The more ancient Hebrew scriptures (i.e., older than the Dead Sea Scrolls), which were familiar to David and Solomon — disappeared after Nebuchadnezzar destroyed Jerusalem and Solomon's Temple in 586 BC. So, these 1st and 3rd Century AD Aramaic translations are important for understanding many ancient Hebrew words, the meaning of which had become obscure.

- "Every translation is a commentary, and the variations in the lectionaries the schools possessed, resulted from the various translators preferring one explanation of the Torah to another."
- Thus, the differences were —exegetical— (i.e., relating to the way they interpreted the texts they studied), rather than —textual— (i.e., relating to the way their lectionaries were written).
- Rabbi Heller emphasized the schools of bible criticism studied the Greek translations of the Torah & Tanakh they possessed (i.e., the Pentateuch & Septuagint).
- Furthermore, he showed all the differences they claimed — had come from the misapplication of one or more of the 32 Rules of Bible Interpretation enumerated by Rabbi Elazar ben Shimon.
- In his study, Rabbi Heller's arguments are unassailable because he gave examples of the mistakes these European schools made and showed how they misinterpreted and misapplied Rabbi ben Shimon's interpretive rules![98]

RABBI NATHAN LOPES CARDOZO CONTENDS—

"The struggle over the origin of the text of the Torah was, and is, not just an academic one. It is foremost a battle between divine authority and human autonomy. Modernity, starting with Spinoza (the first SHBC scholar), was looking for ways through which it could liberate itself from the biblical worldview and its far-reaching divine demands. Since it was this biblical text that made man submissive to divine authority, it was necessary to start an assault on the biblical text itself and strip it of its divine nature. The interplay between sociology and theology is a complex one, but what is clear is — what man will find and conclude is greatly dependent on the question of why he is looking. The Torah can be made to yield whatever meaning its interpreters like to assign it.

This fact is also of great importance in understanding what has happened within the Jewish community over the last two hundred years. To become part of the secular world, many Jews looked to bible criticism as a most forceful and welcome source of legitimization for the break with tradition. In reference to what Heinrich Heine [99] once called the portable fatherland of the Jew, the Torah was historicized, secularized, and fragmentized. It is hardly possible to ignore the fact that since the day when this fragmentation theory made inroads into the Jewish community, the Jewish People have lost much of their élan vital. It resulted in nontraditional forms of Judaism and eventually caused Jews to turn their backs on tradition altogether. The secularization of the Torah has led to secularization of the people" (a direct quote). [100]

Near the end of his article on counterarguments against the SHBC, Rabbi Cardozo wrote:

"Today honest Bible scholars no longer maintain the Torah is the result of different fragments edited and reedited. The Torah is now taken to be Mosaic in origin and content, and it has been acknowledged this tradition was well established in Pro-

---

[98] Article: On Bible Criticism and its Counterarguments by Rabbi Nathan Lopes Cardozo; a Short History—1995: http://www.aishdas.org/toratemet/en_cardozo.html
[99] Heinrich Heine: a 19th century German-Jewish poet and literary critic who converted from Judaism to Christianity.
[100] Ibid (Rabbi Cardozo's 1995 Article)

Mosaic times." [101]

THE JEWS OF MODERN-DAY ISRAEL ARE DIVIDED OVER RELIGION!

To comprehend Rabbi Cardozo's words, you need to understand — among the Jews in Israel who believe in Jehovah, religious convictions range from the ultra-liberal Jewish sects to the ultra-conservative Orthodox. Furthermore, some religious Jews have converted to Christianity and other religions, while others are self-directed secularists who are gnostics, agnostics, and atheists. This may be an oversimplification, but it seems to me, those Jews who welcomed *Bible Criticism* are somewhat like the character *Tevye (in Fiddler on the Roof)* — who asked God: *"Why couldn't you have chosen another people?"*

WHEN I RESEARCHED THE 'JEWISH' PART OF OUR JUDEO-CHRISTIAN TRADITION, I FOUND THE OTHER REASON I DECIDED TO WRITE THIS BOOK! I found how the ancient Jewish Sages and Talmudic Scholars interpreted the deeper meaning of the Hebrew text of the first two chapters of the Torah (i.e., the first two chapters of the Book of Genesis). What I found was — The Cosmogony of the Ancient Jewish Sages! When I learned the sages thought the Creation Account was science, I began to understand — Nahmanides' 13th century concepts of time, Galileo's 17th century concepts of time, and Einstein's 20th century concepts of time (i.e., Einstein's Laws of Relativity) — are all connected.

I realized the concepts of time described by Nahmanides, Galileo, and Einstein are all:
RELATIVE — RELEVANT —&— RELATED!
(This tenet will be explained in Book I)

Summary Points:
- There was a beginning.
- There is a God who created everything.
- Darkness is the Black of Space.
- Darkness is the original created thing!
- Two ancient Jewish sages believed the creation "story" is not a "story!"
- They believed it is science because God told Moses how He created and made all things.
- God made our building blocks in light!
- We are made of stardust!
- "Today honest Bible scholars no longer maintain the Torah is the result of different fragments edited and reedited. The Torah is now taken to be Mosaic in origin and content. It has now been acknowledged this tradition was well established in Pro-Mosaic times."
- (Pro-Mosaic times means: *During Moses' lifetime*). [102]

---

[101] Ibid (Rabbi Cardozo's 1995 Article)
[102] Ibid (Rabbi Cardozo's 1995 Article)

❧
INTRODUCTION—PART IX
JEWISH TRADITION

Hagar the Horrible: *"I'm through trying to talk philosophy with you, Lucky Eddie!"*
Lucky Eddie: *"Good! I have enough trouble when you speak Norwegian!"*

THIS BOOK IS SYMPATHETIC TO JEWISH TRADITION.

When the Schools of Bible Criticism focused on the two different names for God in Genesis One and Two, they decided two different unknown people wrote the first two chapters of Genesis. They also claimed a 3rd unknown person redacted the entire Torah. Jewish Tradition passionately disagrees! In the Part I Introduction, I mentioned Nahmanides believed God dictated the Torah to Moses. I also said Nahmanides thought God told Moses how He created, made, and has continued to make and form all that exists out of nothing — *Creation Ex Nihilo.* If one accepts his belief, then the differences between Genesis One and Genesis Two — are easily explained when one realizes God narrated the Creation Account to Moses using two different *perspectives* — God's perspective (in Genesis One), and Man's perspective (in Genesis Two) — and two different *time-reference-frames* — God's in Genesis One and Adam's in Genesis Two.

THERE ARE TWO DIFFERENT NARRATIVES IN GENESIS ONE.

The *1st Narrative in Genesis One* is told from *God's perspective of the Universe. The 2nd Narrative* in Genesis One is told from *God's perspective of the earth.* The two different narratives and perspectives in the 1st Chapter of Genesis are told in a sequence of six different time-reference-frames of *Six God-related days.* The Jewish sages believed the Six Days of God's Creation were very different from the days Adam experienced and we experience.

THERE IS A 3RD NARRATIVE IN GENESIS TWO.

The 3rd Narrative conveys an earthly perspective (i.e., ADAM'S PERSPECTIVE). Since Adam was made on the evening of the 6th Day, the 7th Day was Adam's first day. Therefore — the 1st Sabbath was Adam's first full day.

Maimonides believed — on the 1st Sabbath (*The 7th Day when God "rested"*), God *"got rid of"* all those billions of earth-year-equivalents *"the Six Days of the Ancient of Days"* represented and *reset* the clocks of the earth and the Universe! Just as He had reset the duration of the number of earth-year-equivalents that *each day of the six days of creation* represented and started that reset six previous times *at the beginning of each one of those six days of old* — at the beginning of the *1st Sabbath* (on the *7th Day*), Elohim reset the earth's clock one last time. He reset earth's clock to a new era of man's future time — an era of a new fixed rate of time-flow — *to the rate of time-flow Adam experienced on the 1st Sabbath.* Beginning with the 1st Sabbath (and for all future days after the 1st Sabbath), the earth's clock was reset to the same literal 24-hour day Adam experienced, and we experience today![103] These facts are touched on in Chapters 5 and 7 of Book I — Chapter 22 in Book II — and in Chapters 23, and 25 — in Book III. Chapter 25 explains how and why Maimonides decided this is what God had done.

---

[103] Schroeder: Genesis and the Big Bang Chapter 2 p 48-54

The Ancient Jewish Sages came to the realization of this concept through their understanding of the deeper meaning of the Hebrew language Moses used when he wrote the Biblical Creation Account. Furthermore, they also believed the Creation Account was fact — not fiction. They took it seriously and thought the first layer of meaning of the Mosaic Account has a religious significance. They believed the deeper meaning (*i.e., The Genesis Code*) — conveys an introduction to *The Science of God.* This book respects three traditional historic opinions of Judaism:

- God dictated the Torah to Moses.
- Moses wrote the words God dictated.
- The Torah is a serious document because it was — "Divinely Inspired."

אלוהים

How the Jews explained the different names for God in Genesis One and Genesis Two: In *The Interlinear Bible Old Testament* (a Hebrew to English Translation), the name of the Hebrew Creator-God in the 1st Chapter of Genesis is (אלוהים), which is transliterated in English as "*Elohim.*" *Elohim* tells Moses He created everything "*from nothing*" — i.e., CREATION EX NIHILO (cf. Chapters 3 and 4, Book I). In the rest of Genesis One, Elohim tells Moses what He did on each of the Six God-related Days of Creation. So, in the 1st Chapter of Genesis, Moses used only one name for God (אלוהים). The proper English Transliteration for (אלוהים) is "*Elohim.*" In all other English translations (אלוהים) is simply translated as "*God.*" (cf. Chapter 4, Book I, for the deeper meaning of "*Elohim.*")

IN THE 2ND CHAPTER OF GENESIS, GOD CHANGED HIS NAME.

When Elohim made and created the first man, the Jewish Sages believed God wanted to establish a close personal relationship with the crown of His creation — Adam. So, not only is the 2ND Chapter of Genesis told from a different perspective (Adam's), and a different time-reference-frame (the same 24-hour day Adam experienced, and we experience), but God also emphasized His close personal relationship with Adam by changing His name. But we don't see that new name for God (הוה) until we read Genesis 2:4. The Interlinear Bible transliterates (הוה) as "*YHWH.*" All other English Bibles translate (הוה) as — "*the LORD GOD.*"

הוה

(הוה) is a *Tetragrammaton,* which is entirely composed of consonants. This Tetragrammaton has no vowels and is intended to be *unpronounceable.* It is the most holy name for the supreme God of the Jews. In Genesis 4:26 (after Cain slew Able and after Adam and Eve came together again and Eve gave birth to Seth), the Bible says Seth's son Enos was born. The last part of that scripture says:

"At that time, people began to call on the name of 'YHWH.'"

This implies — when they called on the name of (הוה) they actually said a word that was centuries later transliterated into the English alphabet in English Bibles as — "*YHWH.*" However, the first few chapters of Genesis give us no clue as to what they actually said when they called on the name of *"YHWH."*

הוה-אלוהים

Then something different happened in Genesis 2:5, 2:7, 2:8, 2:9, and for all the rest of Chapter Two. In these verses we see God hyphenated His name and told Moses to write

His name as הוה-אלוהים. The Interlinear Bible transliterates (in English) this new hyphenated name for God as — *"Jehovah-Elohim."* Remember, English reads left to right →, and Hebrew reads right to left ←.

But, from the 9ᵗʰ Century Masoretic text and the 1ˢᵗ Century BC Dead Sea Scrolls, we have learned the hyphenated word that was added to (אלוהים) was the unpronounceable Tetragrammaton (הוה). So, the word Moses wrote for God's new hyphenated name in the 2ⁿᵈ Chapter of Genesis was הוה-אלוהים. Later, some Jewish Rabbis added some vowel sounds to this new most holy and fearsome name for the Hebrew God that was transliterated into English as "YHWH." *They added (e, o, a) to YHWH to form the word "YeHoWaH."*[104] They added YHWH to the Genesis One name for God (i.e., *Elohim*), to form the name — *"YHWH-ELOHIM"* — and they pronounced this hyphenated name — *YeHoWaH-ELOHIM.* Why did they think God would allow them to pronounce *"YeHoWaH?"*

THE DERIVATION OF YEHOWAH and JEHOVAH

When we go to The Hebrew and Chaldee Dictionary, which is in Strong's Exhaustive Concordance of the Bible, we find (אלוהים) is transliterated[105*] in English as *"Elohim,"* & (הוה) is transliterated in English as *"YeHoWaH."* The divine name *"YHWH"* for (הוה), which is called *"The Tetragrammaton,"* or *"Four Letters"* that represented this most holy name of God: has always been understood to possess fearsome power. The Jews believe the misuse of the name could bring destruction not only on its speaker, but also on the ones who were in the hearing of its pronunciation. So, the Jewish Rabbis believed that where *"YHWH"* was written in scripture it should not be pronounced — one should not even say the individual Hebrew letters that comprise this fearsome Tetragrammaton for the most holy name for God! This belief comes from the book of Exodus—

"Thou shalt not take the name of the Lord Thy God in vain." (Ex. 20:7)

So where did the transliterated word *"YeHoWaH"* come from? Answer — It comes from another word for God. That word is *'Adonai.*

אֲדֹנָי — *'ADONAI*

The 1ˢᵗ time the word *"Adonai"* appears in the Bible is in Genesis 15:2. In the 15ᵗʰ Chapter of Genesis, English Bibles say: *"¹...the word of **the LORD** came to Abram in a vision, saying, 'Do not fear, Abram, I am a shield to you. Your reward shall be very great.' ²And Abram said, "O **LORD GOD,** what wilt Thou give me since I am childless..."* (Genesis 15:1-2 NASB).

So, *English* translations of Gen. 15:1-2 don't help us understand how this helped the Jewish sages come up with a substitute name for (הוה), which they felt they could pronounce. However, look at what the Hebrew to English translation (in the Interlinear Bible) says in Genesis 15:1-2.

---

[104] In the Interlinear Bible, reference words for each Hebrew word are numbered. Each number corresponds to a transliterated English word for each Hebrew word that is in The Interlinear Bible. To find the corresponding transliterated English words, go to the Hebrew & Chaldee Dictionary that is in Strong's Exhaustive Concordance. The Interlinear Bible is a Hebrew to English translation of the Old Testament, & a Greek to English translation of the New Testament.
[105] (*) For an understanding of *"Transliterated"* texts, read the 1ˢᵗ page of Chapter 3 (in Book I).

*"¹...the word of **Jehovah** (which is the same as "YEHOWAH"—explained later) came to Abram in a vision, saying 'Do not fear, Abram: I am your shield, your reward will increase greatly.' ²And Abram said: '**LORD-JEHOVAH** what will you give to me since I am going childless...'"*

The Interlinear Bible prints a reference word number above each Hebrew word in the Old Testament. The reference number for the Hebrew word for *Lord* is *#136*. The reference word for *Jehovah (&/or Yehowah)* is *word #3068*. You can go to the Hebrew-Chaldee Dictionary in *Strong's Exhaustive Concordance* and find the number of the referenced words and discover the Hebrew words in the Biblical text, and their transliterated English equivalents as well as the meaning of the ancient Hebrew words. The transliterated Hebrew word for אֲדֹנָי (or "*Lord*" as English translations say) is *'Adonai.* The transliterated Hebrew word for הוה (which is— "*Jehovah*" — in the Interlinear Bible), is — "*YeHoWaH*" — in Strong's Hebrew-Chaldee Dictionary.

So, it was *Abram* who gave the Jewish Sages the answer to what they thought they could "*say out loud*" when they saw (הוה) in scripture. They took it to heart that Abram combined the Tetragrammaton *YHWH* and hyphenated it with another name for God "Adonai." When he "*spoke*" (i.e., "*Abram said*") *that hyphenated name to the Lord God Himself* in Gen. 15:1-2 — the sages got the idea they could take the vowel sounds in *Adonai* and put them *inside* "*YHWH*" to come up with a permitted pronounceable word (*YeHoWaH*) for this most sacred name for God. That is how — in the Hebrew to English translation of Genesis 15:1 (הוה) is transliterated as "*Yehowah.*" The Interlinear Bible prints the ancient Hebrew words above the English translation. So, when Moses wrote the name for God that Abram *spoke* in Gen. 15:2, he wrote:

אֲדֹנָי-הוה

YeHoWaH means: "*The Self-Existent or Eternal One.*" *'Adonai* is an emphatic form of *'Adoni,* which means: "*Lord, Master, Owner.*" Therefore, the written אֲדֹנָי-הוה = the spoken *Yehowah-Adonai,* which means: "*My Self-Existent Eternal Lord, Master, and Owner!*"

WHICH NAMES FOR GOD ARE PERMISSIBLE? WHICH ARE NOT?

When some devout Jews wish to print God's most holy name, they write *YeHoWaH* or *YaHWeH* (or *Yahweh*). They feel they can write these names in print forms ("which are not permanent") without causing offense. As I have just said, *Adonai* is another Hebrew name for God. *Adonai* is translated as "LORD" in English. Its Genesis Code meaning is: "*The Lord is our Master and our Owner.*" As just stated, the actual name, "*Adonai*" first appears in the Bible in Genesis 15:2 where it is hyphenated to *YHWH*. Abram addresses God as *YHWH-Adonai*.[106] But the Bible gives us no clue as to what Abram actually said when he pronounced "*YHWH!*" Several Jewish Sages concluded the word Abram probably said as a substitute for *YHWH was "YeHoWaH."*

SOME ENGLISH BIBLES USE A DIFFERENT SPELLING FOR YHWH.

In transliterated Hebrew to English versions of the Bible, 'Y' and 'J' are interchangeable. 'W' and 'V' are also interchangeable. Therefore, some English versions of the Bible render YHWH as JHVH. Both are unpronounceable Tetragrammatons for the most intimate, holy, and personal name for the God of Israel. Therefore, the permissible written form of

---

[106] The Interlinear Bible: Reference words 136 & 113 in Strong's Exhaustive Concordance—Hebrew/Chaldee Dictionary.

YeHoWaH (for YHWH) may also be spelled *JeHoVaH*. Undoubtedly the Hebrew word *YeHoWaH* will seem *unfamiliar* to many people. However, many Americans have heard of the transliterated Hebrew word — *Jehovah*. *Jehovah* (or *JeHoVaH*) is a less formal spelling of *YeHoWaH*. Both take their "e, o, and a" vowel sounds from *Adonai*. So, you see, the Interlinear Bible used the less formal spelling—**Jehovah.**

Thus, *YeHoWaH, JeHoVaH,* and *Yahweh* are the written substitutes for the most holy and venerated Hebrew name for the God of the Hebrews that some Jews feel they can write and say without causing offense to God. Hence, we get one of the most familiar written names for God: *Jehovah* — that is substituted for *JHVH*, which is the same as *Yehowah* — which is a substitute for *YHWH*.

We have been talking about the permissible written substitutes for the most holy, intimate, and personal names for God. However, some Jewish scholars *disagree* these substitute names are permitted when writing God's name! And other scholars say their pronunciation is also *prohibited*! Notice I have not attempted to explain what Jewish scholars mean when they say — *"print forms which are not permanent."*

> *If Lucky Eddie had trouble understanding Hagar when he was speaking "philosophy," imagine what he would have said if Hagar had been speaking Hebrew!*

I feel like I just finished the Saturday Edition of *The NY Times Crossword Puzzle!*

The European Schools in the 18th, 19th, and 20th centuries AD, who felt GENESIS TWO was written by a different author, called that author the *'Yahwist'* author, in recognition of the different name for God which is used in the Second Chapter of Genesis. *Yahwist* comes from *Yahweh* (which came from *YHWH* and *Adonai*).

NOW THIS IS WHAT I THINK.

This manuscript is divided into an Introduction & three books. The reason for this separate nine-part INTRODUCTION to the series has already been explained. The reason for the three additional books is because the Jewish sages thought God told Moses how He *created* and *made* everything using *two* different *perspectives* and *three* separate *narratives*. The three narratives can be explained as *three separate Acts in the same Play.* I have decided to discuss these three acts as three *'Tellings.'* Each *'Telling'* is a separate book. The word, *'Telling,'* honors the Jewish Oral tradition of the Torah, which pre-dated the written Mosaic text by ~ 2000 years. Nevertheless, the three *'Tellings'* should be read in sequence because (in this series), the complexity of *The Genesis Code* is sequentially explained (verse-by-verse) in sync with each verse of the Bible's Creation Account. So, the 1st Volume of the Series contains:

- THE INTRODUCTION AND BOOK I: THE 1ST TELLING covers Gen. 1:1-5 (Day One).
- BOOK II is THE 2ND TELLING — the which covers Gen. 1:6-25 (the 2nd-the 6th Day.)
- AND BOOK III is THE 3RD TELLING — Gen. 1:26-31 and all of Genesis TWO.

BOOK I IS THE 1ST TELLING (OR 1ST ACT) OF THE CREATION ACCOUNT.

The 1st Telling (Genesis 1:1-5) — is a general introductory statement, which informs us it was God who created everything in the beginning. It ends at the conclusion of *Day One.*

Thus, a time-reference-frame of *"Six God-related Days of Creation"* is introduced. Moses used the *cardinal* form for the name of the day Elohim called into being in the 1st Telling when He said — *"Let there be light."* He used the *cardinal* form (*Day One*), rather than the *ordinal* form (*the 1st Day*), to emphasize *Day One* was unique, because no other day preceded it. Many English translations do not make this distinction and refer to *"Day One"* as — *"the 1st Day."* As you shall see, there is a lot of information that lies beneath the surface of Moses' words. All eight chapters of Book I are devoted to the 1st Telling. The 1st Telling is told from God's perspective and is in a time-flow that relates to God and the universe (as a whole).

THE 2ND VOLUME IS BOOK II: THE 2ND TELLING (OR 2ND ACT) OF THE CREATION ACCOUNT.

In the 2nd Telling (Genesis 1:6-25), the account of the order of creation is continued in a time-reference-frame of an *ordinal* series for the remaining five days of Creation. Each day is like a separate scene in the play. On each day, God creates something new. Every day of creation ends with the same phrase: *"And there was evening and there was morning, Day One… the 2nd Day… the 3rd Day… etc."* Thus, *a timed sequence* of the Six Days of creation-events is introduced into the account. After *Day One,* the events of each new day build on the events of the preceding day. This is the reason the Bible uses *the ordinal form* for numbering the 5 days that follow *Day One.*

PERSPECTIVES REITERATED

The 1st Telling (Genesis 1:1-5) is BOOK I. The 1st Telling relates the story of *Day One* — from the perspective of *the universe at large*, which God created first. The perspective gradually shifts from the universe *to the earth* during the 2nd Telling (BOOK II — Gen. 1:6-25). In the 2nd Telling, it is as if God came to our earth after its rudimentary formation on the 3rd Day and stayed here on the 4th, 5th, and 6th Days of Creation — until His work of Creation was completed.

TIME-FLOW REITERATED

The Flow-of-Time in the first 25 verses of GENESIS ONE *is God-based.* This God-related time-flow covers the first five days and the majority of the 6th Day of Creation. Beginning with Genesis 1:26, when God *"made (asa) man in Our image,"* and for all the time in the Bible thereafter, *Time-Flow is related to Man,* and the chronology of the Bible and the flow-of-time on earth become one and the same. It was at this point that the common space-time-relationship between God and man was fixed. [107] (This particular point will be discussed in Chapter 25 — in Book III). The basics of the complexity of time-flow in GENESIS ONE AND GENESIS TWO will be covered in Chapter 5 of Book I. I refer to this complex time concept as the *"Time Conundrum."* These two scripture verses give us the hint that Time-Flow is *not* constant throughout the universe.

Psalms 90:4 "For a thousand years in thy sight are but as yesterday when it is past, and as a watch in the night."
II Peter 3:8 "…One day is with the Lord as a thousand years, and a thousand years as one day." (KJV).

When the Jewish sages compared Genesis 1:1 with Exodus 20:11, they concluded — *Different places throughout the universe have different time-flows.* How Moses phrased

---

[107] Schroeder Genesis and the Big Bang Chapter 2 p 52d

these two verses had special significance to them. The first part of Chapter 7 of Book I is devoted to that subject. Their understanding of the Hebrew language enabled them to probe the hidden depths of the meaning of Moses' words. The deeper meaning of Moses' words is something I refer to as: *"The Genesis Code."* They were able to decipher the code.

BOOK III IS THE 3RD TELLING (OR THE 3RD ACT) OF THE CREATION ACCOUNT.

The 3rd Telling begins with verse 26 of GENESIS ONE and continues through to the end of GENESIS TWO. This part of the Creation Account (Act 3 in the play) is told from the perspective of man. From the moment God *"created (barah) man in His own image"* (Gen. 1:27) by breathing *into his nostrils the breath of life"* (in the waning hours of the 6th Day in Gen. 2:7), the reference-frame of time-flow began to switch to the same 24-hour day-night cycle we experience today. Stated another way, on the 7th Day (see Chapter 25 in Book III), the 24-hour day-night cycle became the Time-Flow that is unique to our earth today. Time-flow switched to the same rate of time-flow Adam experienced, and we experience today. Once Adam was created, Time-Flow became Man-based because Adam & Eve were the finishing touches to God's creation of the earth. Everything necessary to ensure the continuance of the physical earth had been made. Before the *'making'* and *'creating'* of *'Man,'* Time was *'relative.'* It was related to God's creative activities throughout the universe. Time-Flow was God-based. The word *'relative'* gives you a hint of Einstein's discovery. But that is a concept, which will be developed in Chapter 5 of Book I.

INTELLIGENT DESIGN

The Bible makes the point — *Intelligent Design is the driving force of the Creation Narrative!* Yet, some people do not agree. In this nine-part Introduction, I have discussed several major historical conflicts of opinion over the questions of our origins.

- The conservative religious right and the liberal religious left have always been in conflict.
- Both religious groups have historically clashed with the claims of scientists in the past.
- Since most people do not know about the revelations of the Genesis Code interpretation of the Creation Account, they are not aware modern science now agrees with the Bible.
- And, if you think that is just the 'tip of the iceberg' you are right, because Atheists, Agnostics, Gnostics, Humanists, Darwinists, Neo-Darwinists, and other Secularists who have their own ideas about how we originated — have always opposed the Biblical Account of Creation and all religious groups!

Now, in the midst of all of this conflict, I am going to introduce even more mischief by beginning the discussion of *The Genesis Code,* which the Ancient Jewish Sages say is embedded in the Hebrew script of the first two chapters of Genesis. You will now be introduced to the Cosmogony of the Ancient Jewish Sages, which they derived from their understanding of the deeper meaning of Moses' words. Their interpretation of GENESIS ONE and GENESIS TWO is a fascinating saga I hope I can summarize for you in an interesting and understandable way. The revelations of *The Genesis Code* provide us with an expanded understanding of the greatness of our Creator. The deeper meaning of

Moses' words reveals an *Intelligent Design*, and *an all-pervading Wisdom that permeates all God's Creation*. The Bible's Genesis Creation Account describes a most serious and miraculous sequence of events, which modern science is just now beginning to understand. In the pages that follow you will see — Modern science now agrees with the Cosmogony of the Ancient Jewish Sages!

When you turn to the first page of Book I, you will begin your journey of discovery. When the curtain of Act I (The 1st Telling) is drawn back, you will be instantly transported to the moment of the beginning of *Eternity Present* (cf. Chapter 10: The 3rd Rock from the Sun — in Book II). *Eternity Present* marks the moment when time began! The Bible introduces *Man's journey into Eternity Present* with these words: **"In the Beginning..."**

Hold on to your hat.
This journey will astound you!

HOW TO STUDY THE THREE BOOKS OF THE GENESIS CODE:

1. Read the Paragraph Headings in each chapter.
2. Next, read the Summary Points (near the end of each chapter).
3. Go back to the beginning of the chapter and read straight through.
4. Keep a notebook. Write down any questions that "pop up" while you are reading.
5. Review the Summary Points again.
6. Keep track of any questions that remain. They may be answered in later chapters.
7. Keep an open mind.
8. Ponder your questions.
9. The Holy Spirit will guide you to what is right, just, and true.   *Soli Deo Gloria,*
                                                                              O. David

THE KETEF HINNOM SCROLLS

On May 5, 2023, I read of Professor Gabriel Barkay's discovery of The Ketef Hinnom Scrolls in 1979. They were written in a style of Hebrew (called Paleo-Hebrew), that is 500—600 years older than the style of Hebrew on the Dead Sea Scrolls. The Ketef Hinnom Scrolls were written on two tiny silver plates that were rolled into scrolls the size of cigarettes—intended to be worn as amulets around the neck. Their antiquity was not initially appreciated because it took several years of chemical treatment at the Israel Museum to carefully unroll the scrolls without damaging them. When unrolling was completed, the inscriptions were so tiny they could not be confidently read.

Then, near the turn of the century, advanced photo-analysis and computer enhanced techniques were developed at the University of Southern California that allowed researchers to read the Paleo-Hebrew letters on the scrolls. Scholars were startled to find preserved verses from Numbers 6:24-26, and Deuteronomy 7.

Paleo-Hebrew developed from an older script used in the Holy Land that is known as the "Proto-Canaanite" script. Paleo-Hebrew was used in Israel from ~1,000 BC – ~586 BC. Therefore, Paleo-Hebrew was used during the 1st Temple Period of Israel's history (i.e., Solomon's Temple). It is radically different from the Aramaic-influenced Jewish Bereshith Hebrew Square Script that was developed after the Babylonian Captivity when captive Judean Jews taken to Babylon in 586 BC by Nebuchadnezzar II were freed and returned to Judaea to rebuild Jerusalem and the Temple (i.e., the 2nd Temple).

Many of the Dead Sea Scrolls were written in the Aramaic-influenced Jewish Bereshith Hebrew Square Script and have been dated to the 1st century BC. In 586 BC, Nebuchadnezzar had razed Jerusalem and Solomon's Temple to the ground and had destroyed all copies of the Hebrew Bible that were found. The rebuilt Temple of Ezra's time is known as the 2nd Temple. The people wept because the 2nd Temple was only "a shadow" of Solomon's magnificent Temple. Captive Jews had stopped reading, writing, and speaking Hebrew because Nebuchadnezzar forbad it. He also outlawed the practice of Judaism and decreed the penalty of death to those who refused to worship Babylonian gods. 2nd Temple-Period Post-exilic Jews had to relearn the Hebrew language. They also developed a "new" Aramaic-influenced Jewish Bereshith Hebrew Square Script because Aramaic was the common language of the Holy Land when the captives returned. The Hebrew Square Script was the script Nahmanides used to derive his Hebrew Cosmogony. That is the reason I will discuss the Square Script in greater detail in Chapter 3 in Book I. In the Transliterated Hebrew to English text, the most holy name for God is 'YHWH.'

In the Aramaic-derived Post-exile Jewish Bereshith Hebrew Square Script, YHWH is written as יהוה. But in Paleo-Hebrew, it was written as .

The Ketef Hinnom scroll that pertains to Numbers 6:24-26 is the Aaronic Benediction. I will talk about Aaron's Benediction in the Epilogue in Book III. The Paleo-Hebrew text of Numbers 6:24-26 is almost identical in meaning to the Aramaic-derived Post-Exilic Jewish Hebrew Square Script text and is almost word for word the same as our Modern-day Biblical translations! For references, please look up "The Silver Ketef Hinnom Scrolls on the Internet.

The discussion of the various ancient scripts used in the Holy Land in the centuries before the birth of Christ, and during the 1st through 3rd centuries AD, is complicated by the turbulent history of what we refer to as "the Holy Land." So far as I know, the oldest "Hebrew" script was discovered on a shard of pottery by Professor Galil (University of Haifa) in 2008 that dates to the 10th century BC (i.e., 1,000 BC, the time of King David and Solomon). That inscription was written in a "Proto-Canaanite" script.

The Dead Sea Scrolls are younger than the two ancient Hebrew scripts above described. They date to the 1st century BC. Many of the Dead Seas Scrolls are written in the Aramaic influenced Jewish Be'reasheet Square Script of the 2nd Temple Period. Others were written in Paleo-Hebrew, and there are some that were written in Greek, and in "Cryptic A, B, and C Hebrew scripts" which use unusual signs to represent the Hebrew alphabet letters. Then there are also scrolls written in Jewish Palestinian Aramaic, Nabatean Aramaic, and "Koine" (a common dialect of the post-classical Hellenistic and Roman Periods). Just remember: Professor Galil's pottery inscriptions are from the 10th century BC – the Ketef Hinnom Scrolls are 6th century BC, and the Dead Sea Scrolls date to the 1st century BC.

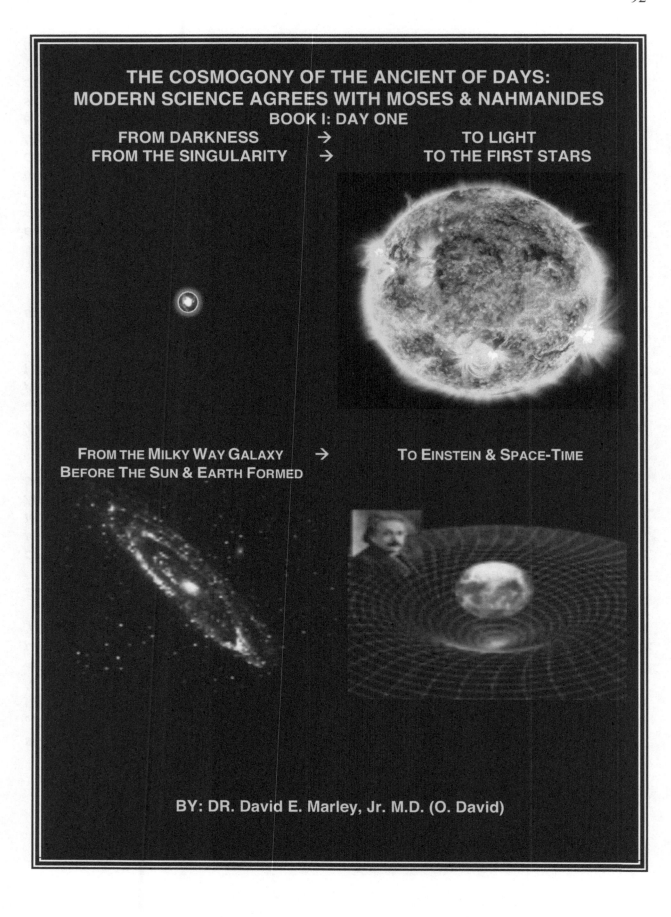

THE COSMOGONY OF THE ANCIENT OF DAYS:
MODERN SCIENCE AGREES WITH MOSES & NAHMANIDES
BOOK I: DAY ONE

FROM DARKNESS → TO LIGHT
FROM THE SINGULARITY → TO THE FIRST STARS

FROM THE MILKY WAY GALAXY → TO EINSTEIN & SPACE-TIME
BEFORE THE SUN & EARTH FORMED

BY: DR. David E. Marley, Jr. M.D. (O. David)

BOOK I:

- *EXPLAINS THE COSMOGONY OF NAHMANIDES,*
- *INTRODUCES NAHMANIDES' GENESIS CODE,*
- *EXPLAINS THE GENESIS TIME CONUNDRUM,*
- *CLARIFIES SEVERAL PUZZLING BIBLICAL PHRASES,*
- *AND REVEALS A CONVERGENCE OF AGREEMENT BETWEEN RELIGION & SCIENCE THAT HAS RECENTLY OCCURRED.*

❧

CONTENTS OF BOOK I

THE COSMOGONY OF THE ANCIENT OF DAYS:
MODERN SCIENCE AGREES WITH MOSES & NAHMANIDES
BOOK I: ACT I—THE 1ST TELLING

BOOK I: INDEX OF ILLUSTRATIONS, CHARTS, EXPLANATIONS & IMAGES

⚜ CHAPTER 1: THE GENESIS CODE

"Conflicts between science and religion result from misinterpretations of the Bible."
(Maimonides 12th Century AD)

"Science is not only the surest path to knowing God. It is the only path, and for that reason the Bible commences with a description of creation" (Maimonides 12th Century AD).
I disagree! [108*] **O. David**

"Study astronomy and physics if you desire to comprehend the relation between the world and God's management of it."
(Maimonides 12th Century AD)

"Everything that was transmitted to Moses by God was written in the Torah explicitly or by implication in the words and in the numerical value of the letters. The bent and crooked letters of the Hebrew language and the crownlets of the letters have special and specific meanings."
(Nahmanides 13th Century AD)

"IN THE BEGINNING"...

In English translations of the Bible, the opening phrase is — *"In the beginning..."* The Hebrew name for the First Book of Moses was originally *"Sefer Maaseh Bereshith,"*[109] which means, *"Book of Creation."* Translated into Greek, it becomes *"Genesis,"* which means *"Origins,"* because it gives an account of the creation of the world and the beginnings of life and society.[110] The first verse of the Bible emphatically states: *"In the beginning God created the heavens and the earth." (Genesis 1:1 NASB)*

MOSAIC AUTHORSHIP—JEWISH TRADITION & BELIEF

Jewish tradition ascribes these words to the great prophet *Moses* and credits him as the author of the written Torah. Torah means *Instruction*. The word refers to both the *written* Torah of Moses and to the *oral tradition* of the Torah, which began with Adam. *Torah* is the Hebrew name for the first five books of the 24-book Hebrew Tanakh. *Tanakh* is the name of the Hebrew Bible. Thus, the five books of Moses (i.e., the *Torah*), are the first five books in the Hebrew Bible.

THE PENTATEUCH

The five books of Moses are also known by another name. When the Torah was translated into Greek in the 2nd century BC, the *Greek* translation was called the *Pentateuch*. Pentateuch is *Greek* for *five-fold vessel, or five-volume book*. The Pentateuch became the first translation of the Hebrew Scriptures to be read by *Gentiles*. Therefore, the five books of Moses became the first five books in what would become *the Christian Old Testament*. Jewish historians believe Moses wrote the Torah in the 2nd millennium BC, perhaps as early as 1450 BC.[111] The Torah actually affirms Moses was its author.[112] Other Old Testament books testify Moses was the author of the Torah.[113]

[108*] **I do not agree. Science cannot prove God exists. Belief and Faith are the only pathways to knowing God.**

[109] *"Sefer Maaseh Bereshith,"* is a *transliterated* Hebrew-English text of the ancient Hebrew language. For an explanation of *transliterated texts*, see Chapter 3 in this book (Book I).

[110] The Pentateuch and Haftorahs: Edited by J. H. Hertz 2nd Edition, 1978, London Soncino Press, Introduction to the Book of Genesis. (See the Glossary in Book III for a definition of "Haftorahs.")

[111] The Ryrie Study Bible: Introduction to the Book of Genesis. p. 5

[112] Exod. 17:14; 24:4,7; 34:27; Num. 33:1-2; Deut. 31:9

[113] Josh. 1:7-8; 8:32; 22:5; 1st Kings 2:3; 2nd Kings 14:6; 21:8; Ezra 6:18; Dan. 9:11-13; Mal. 4:4

Five times in the New Testament, Moses is credited as the author of the Law.[114] None other than *the Son of God (Jesus Christ),* spoke four of the five New Testament references that credit Moses as being the author of the Law.

THERE WAS A BEGINNING—GOD CREATED ALL.

Approximately thirty-three hundred years ago, in the opening sentence of the Bible, the ancient text boldly declared there was:

- A beginning.
- There is a supreme deity called God.
- God created the heavens and the earth.

For centuries before Moses wrote the first words of *Genesis*, the Jewish people believed *in a beginning.* They believed in *a supreme deity who was the one true God.* They also believed *'the One True God'* was *the source* of everything that existed, exists, and will ever exist. These concepts have been passed down by an *oral tradition, which was originated by Adam,* approximately 5700 years ago. This oral tradition was written down for the first time *by Moses* in the first book of the Bible, so future generations could read the account of man's origins, how things came to be, and of God's interaction with man. For the next 3,000 years these concepts were accepted and were unchallenged.

GOD TALKED WITH MOSES.

The Gospel of Peter tells us: *"God inspired all scripture."* [115] The Book of Exodus informs us *God spoke face to face with Moses,* just as a man speaks to his friend.[116] God called Moses to the top of Mount Sinai and gave him *the Ten Commandments.* In the presence of Moses, God wrote the Ten Commandments on two tablets of stone — with His finger!

> *STOP! Think about how special that is! No human can understand the concept of creating the heavens and the earth. That is really "far out there!" But picking up a rock. That's something we can do. However, engraving that rock with your finger? Funny how holding a rock in your hand & touching it with your finger can give you an inkling of God's power! Just imagine the power that resides in God's finger!*

On one occasion Moses was on the mountain in conversation with God for forty days and forty nights (Exodus 24:18)! When he returned to the people, Moses gave them God's detailed instructions concerning God's rules for conduct and living.

THE TENT TABERNACLE & THE HOLY THINGS

God gave Moses the design of the tent tabernacle, the directions for making the articles to be placed within it, and the instructions for fashioning the garment of the high priest. God not only told Moses how the tabernacle articles and the high priest's garment should be made, but He specified the materials he should use, and ordered the specific placement of the each of the articles within the tabernacle. Exodus 25:9 says God told Moses to build the tent tabernacle: *"According to all that I am going to show you, as the pattern of the tabernacle and the pattern of all its furniture, just so you shall construct it."* (cf. Ex. 25:40.) God also told Moses the names of the craftsmen to employ — *Bezalel,* the son of Uri, the son of Hur, of the tribe of Judah; and *Oholiab,* the son of Ahisamach of the tribe of Dan. (See Exodus 31:2 & 6). Moses' writings also inform us God was a

---

[114] Matt. 19:8; Mark 12:26; John 5:46-47; 7:19; Rom. 10:5
[115] II Peter 1:20,21
[116] Exodus 33:9,11

constant presence among His people during the Exodus from Egypt, leading them in the form of *a pillar of cloud by day and a pillar of fire by night.*

> *Heb. 8:5 and 9:23-24 tell us the tent tabernacle Moses built was an exact copy of the Heavenly Tabernacle![117] However — we now know "The Tabernacle of God" that was among men and dwelled among them, so that they shall be His people, and God Himself shall be among them (Rev. 21:3)— was Jesus Christ, Who (at His 1st coming) became the sacrificial Lamb of God. Since the risen Jesus Christ is now with the Father in Heaven, there is no longer a temple in Heaven because — "The Lord God Almighty and the Lamb are (now) its temple (Rev.21:22)."*

THE NUANCES OF THE HEBREW LANGUAGE REVEAL A DEEPER MEANING.

When Moses wrote *the Creation Account*, his writing was simple. It was also succinct. He wrote in a way that could be easily understood by a host of ordinary people who had been enslaved in Egypt for 400 years. Today, many people believe English translations of the creation account are too plain, too basic, too uncomplicated. However, in the original Hebrew text, as in the layers of an onion, there are multiple layers of meaning. The outer layer of meaning is straightforward and immediately apparent. It is so simple critics have called it a mythical fairy tale, a fantasy. However, when you discern the deeper meaning of the Hebrew words, you reach the heart of the matter. The unique nuances of the Hebrew language allowed the ancient Jewish sages to *peel the onion* and glean the deeper meaning of the Hebrew description of *God's Account of His Creation.*

THE BIBLICAL CREATION ACCOUNT & THE BIG BANG THEORY ARE SIMILAR.

In the 1st two chapters of Genesis, when one compares the *sequence* of the scientific observations of modern-day cosmology and paleontology with the *sequence* of the events of each biblical day, the day-by-day match between the Bible and modern science is extraordinary.[118] This fact alone is strong evidence — *God inspired and directed Moses to write the Genesis Creation Account.*

THIS BOOK WILL FOLLOW THE CHRONOLOGY OF THE MOSAIC CREATION ACCOUNT.

My objective is to demonstrate — *the Biblical Account of Creation* and *The Big Bang Theory* are two descriptions (one ancient and one modern) of the same thing. You will see: *Modern science now agrees with Moses.*

DR. GERALD L. SCHROEDER

The premise — *"The Biblical Account of Creation and Modern Science are in Agreement"* — did not originate with me. I discovered it in the writings of Dr. Gerald L. Schroeder. Dr. Schroeder is *a nuclear physicist* who earned his Undergraduate and PhD degrees in Physics from the Massachusetts Institute of Technology. He is a renowned lecturer and adviser around the world. Dr. Schroeder is also an applied Jewish theologian who is now a resident of Jerusalem. He is on the faculty of The Hebrew University and presently teaches and works in laboratories at the Weizmann Institute, the Hebrew University, and the Volcani Research Institute in Israel. Hebrew is now his everyday language. His understanding of the deeper meaning of the Hebrew words Moses used in the Genesis Creation Account is solidly based on the way ancient sages of Judaism (men such as Maimonides, Nahmanides, Onkelos, and Rashi), interpreted Moses' words. His research

[117] Hebrews 8:5 & 9:23-24 (I like the way The Living Bible says it.)
[118] Schroeder The Science of God Chapter 4 p 66 c

has been reported in Newsweek, The Jerusalem Post, and numerous scholarly publications. ***Dr. Schroeder has given me his written permission to reference these three books (which you should read).***

- GENESIS AND THE BIG BANG: The Discovery of Harmony between Modern Science and the Bible. Dr. Gerald L. Schroeder, PhD, Bantam Books, New York, Toronto, London, Sydney, Auckland, © 1990
- THE SCIENCE OF GOD: The Convergence of Scientific and Biblical Wisdom. Dr. Gerald L. Schroeder, PhD. Broadway Books, New York, N.Y., © 1997
- THE HIDDEN FACE OF GOD: Science Reveals the Ultimate Truth. Dr. Gerald L. Schroeder, PhD. Touchstone books, Simon and Schuster, New York, N.Y., © 2001

TALMUDIC TRADITION

Talmudic tradition holds there was a time when all the knowledge revealed to Moses at Mount Sinai was still remembered, but unfortunately, much of that knowledge has been lost. Sages thereafter could only find hints of it by searching out the subtle meanings of the biblical text. Based on these hints they formed their concepts of the *space-time-continuum* that comprises the universe.[119]

The information was there all along, hidden in the nuances of Mosaic Hebrew. Sadly, the various translations of the Hebrew Bible miss the deeper meaning of the words Moses wrote. The Talmud metaphorically likens the translation of the Hebrew Bible into other languages: *as to a lion being locked in a cage — viewing all translations as misrepresentations of the original account — as damaging to the original as was the 586 BC Babylonian destruction of Solomon's Temple in Jerusalem.[120]*

Reggie White, an Evangelical Christian Minister and all-time great professional defensive end and member of the Pro-Football Hall of Fame, understood this. After his retirement from professional football, he began studying the Hebrew language, the Torah, and Torah-observant Messianic theology. He wanted to gain greater insight through studying the Hebrew script of the Hebrew Old Testament.[121]

THE OBJECTIVES OF THIS BOOK

In this book, we will first try to understand what Moses is talking about and discuss what ancient Jewish sages have interpreted his words to mean. Next, we will talk about the challenges posed by questioning individuals from the past to more recent times. Then, we will take a look at what modern science has revealed about each of these issues. You will see *all* the challenges to the Mosaic Creation Account have been dispelled by the discoveries modern science has made in the past eighty-five years. You will realize: *Science now agrees with, supports, and validates the Biblical Hebrew Account of Creation.*

THE JEWISH SAGES & THE GENESIS CODE

We will explore the deeper meaning of the Biblical narration of Moses as revealed to us by a 12th century Jewish sage, Rabbi Moses Maimonides (1135-1204 AD) — a 13th century Jewish sage, Rabbi Moses Nahmanides (1194-1270 AD) — and a 1st century

---

[119] Schroeder Genesis and the Big Bang Chapter 3 p 61 e & 62 a
[120] Schroeder The Science of God Chapter 5 p 77 a
[121] Article: Reggie White's search for Truth by Ben Rabizaden published Jan. 1, 2005, http://www.aish.com/ci/a/48943676.html

Roman nobleman, Onkelos (circa 35-120 AD), who moved to Jerusalem, converted to Judaism, and in the early part of the 2nd century, translated the Five Books of Moses into Aramaic (i.e., *The Targum Onkelos*, cir. 110 AD).[122](*) *Aramaic* is believed to be the language Jesus Christ spoke.[123] Aramaic is a Semitic language.(**) Of all the Semitic languages, Aramaic is the one closest to the ancient Hebrew Moses spoke and wrote. The two Rabbis just mentioned were named Moses. Moses and Elijah were the two most revered prophets of ancient Israel. They appeared with Jesus in His transfiguration (Matt. 17:1-9).

I have called the deeper meaning of the ancient Hebrew text — The Genesis Code. You will see — The Genesis Code and the scientific account of our origins are two mutually compatible descriptions of the same reality.

IN THE 12TH CENTURY AD, MOSES MAIMONIDES WROTE:

"Study astronomy and physics if you desire to comprehend the relation between the world and God's management of it."[124, 125] Maimonides taught: *"Conflicts between science and religion result from misinterpretations of the Bible."*[126] He said: *"Science is not only the surest path to knowing God, it is the only path, and for that reason the Bible commences with a description of creation."* [127] In his famous book, *The Guide for the Perplexed*, Maimonides instructed: *"We must form a conception of the existence of the Creator according to our capacities; this is, we must have a knowledge of metaphysics* (the Science of God), *which can only be acquired after the study of physics* (the Science of Nature); *for the science of physics* (the Science of Nature) *is closely connected with metaphysics* (the Science of God) *and must even precede it in the course of studies. Therefore, the Almighty commenced the Bible with the description of creation—that is with physical science."*

There was so much opposition by the church to his premise that an understanding of science could add to mankind's understanding of spirituality, that his book was burned by Jews and Christians alike.[128] **Nevertheless, I do not believe science is the surest and only pathway to God!** (CF. CHAPTER 2: THE PROBLEM OF GENESIS FOR SCIENTISTS WHO ARE AVID ATHEISTS.)

NAHMANIDES BELIEVED AND TAUGHT:

"A full understanding of the origins of the universe was contained in the Bible as received by Moses." [129] In the Introduction to his Commentary on Genesis, he stated: *"Everything that was transmitted to Moses by God was written in the Torah explicitly or by implication*

---

[122] Nissan Mindel: Onkelos - Jewish History - Chabad.org
http://www.chabad.org/library/article_cdo/aid/112286/jewish/Onkelos.html (*) Dates are disputed by some.
[123] Schroeder Genesis and the Big Bang Chapter 1 p 18b
(**) Semitic Languages: Languages spoken by Semites—a group of languages belonging to the Afro-Asiatic family and spoken in North Africa and Southwest Asia, including Hebrew, Arabic, Aramaic, Maltese, Amharic, and Sosaric. [Semites are the descendants of Shem, Noah's eldest son.]
[124] Schroeder The Science of God Chapter 3 p. 43 e
[125] Schroeder Genesis and the Big Bang Introduction p. 1 a
[126] Schroeder Genesis and the Big Bang Chapter 2: p. 27
[127] Schroeder The Science of God Chapter 1 p. 17
[128] Schroeder The Hidden Face of God Chapter 2 p 23 d & 24 a
[129] Schroeder Genesis and the Big Bang Chapter 1 p 19

in the words and in the numerical value of the letters. The bent and crooked letters of the Hebrew language and the crownlets of the letters had special and specific meanings." [130]

DR. SCHROEDER

As an example of Nahmanides' belief, let us consider the following example given us by Dr. Schroeder. In his book, *Genesis and the Big Bang.* Dr. Schroeder wrote:

"In our study of 'Genesis and the Big Bang,' it is essential to realize there are meanings to the Bible that are not apparent from a casual reading. The search to find meanings within the Bible that expand on the literal text has been a part of Western theology since its inception. These interpretations are based on more than merely the whim of the interpreter. There is a history and a basis to each insight brought forward by the scholars on which we are relying. The sense of these insights is carried by subtle variations in the grammar, by unusual patterns of letters, and even by nuances in the calligraphy of the Bible, the actual physical form of the text." [131]

Dr. Schroeder used the following example to demonstrate some of the subtleties found in the Bible. He chose this example not because it reveals profound secrets (although it does), but because laypersons and scholars alike can easily verify it.[132]

- The Torah Moses received from God is divided into five books: *Genesis, Exodus, Leviticus, Numbers, and Deuteronomy.* The ancient sages looked for the first time the Hebrew letter for 'T' (for Torah) appeared in the Hebrew text of Genesis. Then they counted out 49 letters from the 'T' and recorded the next letter (that is, they recorded the 50th letter). This process was repeated three times. The result was: *TORH*, the Hebrew word for *Torah*. When they did the same thing with *the Book of Exodus*, the result was the same: *TORH*.

- However, when they tried this formula for *Leviticus* (the middle book of the Torah), they got gibberish. Was there some other hidden message in Leviticus? So, they tried something else. They looked for the first letter of the four-letter explicit name for God (*JHVH*) and searched for the 1st appearance of the 1st letter ('J') in the Leviticus text. They then counted 7 letters, recorded the 7th letter, and repeated the procedure three times. The result was *JHVH* (for *Jehovah*). *Jehovah* is the *transliterated* English *equivalent* for *JHVH* that uses the Hebrew *consonants* of JHVH, and the *vowel sounds* of the Hebrew word *Adonai*, which English Bibles translate as *LORD*.

- Finally, they went to the last two books, *Numbers* and *Deuteronomy*, and repeated the formula, which had worked so well with Genesis and Exodus, using only one difference. They repeated the whole process *in reverse*. Once again, they found the word, *TORH. TORH* again appeared at the characteristic 49-letter spacing, *but backwards.* That is, it *faces* the *Jehovah* of *Leviticus*. They thus uncovered a hidden message within the five books of Moses — *Torah brackets God's name and always faces it.*[133]

130 Schroeder Genesis and The Big Bang Chapter 1 p 21 c
131 Schroeder Genesis and The Big Bang Appendix p 181 d & 182 b
132 Schroeder Genesis and The Big Bang Appendix p 182 b
133 Schroeder Genesis and The Big Bang Appendix p 182 c, 183 a

WHY SEARCH FOR TORH BY COUNTING 49 LETTERS IN GENESIS, EXODUS, NUMBERS, & DEUTERONOMY? Leviticus 23:15-16 commands Jews to count 49 days from the day of the *Feast of First Fruits* and celebrate the holiday of the *Feast of Weeks* on the next day (the 50th day). *The Feast of First Fruits is celebrated on the day after the Sabbath of the Passover. It is a pledge of the first fruits of the harvest to God.* The harvest begins 49 days after the *Passover* and is celebrated on the 50th day *after* the *Passover*. So, the Jewish *Feast of Weeks* celebrates the beginning of the harvest. *It also commemorates God's giving of the Law to Moses on Mt. Sinai.*[134] *That happened on the 50th day of the Exodus!* Chapter 25 in Book III revisits this subject. The end of this Chapter, "THE REST OF THE STORY" will explain why four Jewish feasts have special significance to Christians. After reading Chapter 25 (Book III), you will understand why *Christians started worshiping God on Sundays.*

WHY THE 7-LETTER COUNT TO SPELL GOD'S NAME IN THE BOOK OF LEVITICUS?

The number "7" occupies a special place in the Torah. The Sabbath is the 7th day of the week. The first Sabbath was the first day God made *holy by setting it apart.* It was the day God *rested* from His six days of work in His creation. *Devout Jews believe the observance of each Sabbath is a sign they are acknowledging God created the universe.*[135] (In Chapter 25 — Book III — the Sabbath is more fully discussed.)

NAHMANIDES' DESCRIPTION OF THE BEGINNING READS LIKE A MODERN-DAY PHYSICS TEXTBOOK. Later, when we talk about *the Big Bang Theory* description of the first picoseconds (trillionths of a second) of the beginning of the universe, you will discover, Nahmanides' description of the events of the beginning was eerily similar. He came to the same conclusions the Big Bang Theory has and described those first brief moments in a remarkably similar way. Nahmanides formulated his ideas in the 13th century AD. He did not have the benefit of the 19th and 20th century AD discoveries of modern science. How did he do this? He did it through his knowledge of the ancient Hebrew language, which helped him decipher *the deeper meaning of Moses' Genesis Creation Account.* Nahmanides and Maimonides were able to decipher — *"The Genesis Code."* We will discuss this in detail in Chapter 6 of this Book.

COGNITIVE DISSONANCE

Before we continue, I must call your attention to a technical term — "Cognitive Dissonance." Dr. Leon Festinger, a psychologist, coined the expression in 1956. Cognitive Dissonance means: "believing one thing while experiencing another."[136] Dr. Schroeder says cognitive dissonance is: "Humanity's inherent ability to ignore unpleasant facts helping us to retain the error of our ways."[137] I like to think of cognitive dissonance as — Our unique ability to ignore inconvenient facts that contradict our preconceived notions about the true nature of things. The church's burning of Maimonides books is a prime example of Cognitive Dissonance. In the next chapter, we'll discuss Einstein's greatest blunder, which is another example of Cognitive Dissonance.

[134] Schroeder Genesis and The Big Bang Appendix p 183 c
[135] Schroeder Genesis and The Big Bang Appendix p 182 c, 183 c
[136] Investor's Business Daily (Newspaper). An editorial: FEAR OF FLYING p A16, Monday, July 3, 2006
[137] Schroeder The Science of God Chapter 2 p 34

In the pages that follow — you will see: Cognitive Dissonance has been the primary obstacle that has separated religionists, scientists, and secularists from reaching an understanding and agreement as to the true nature of things. It seems we all have our individual prejudices and agendas, especially when it comes to believing or not believing in God, and in accepting or rejecting the notion — God created us and is the originator of all that exists. Cognitive Dissonance has not only separated mankind for centuries but has also prevented some brilliant scientists as well as religionists from making scientific and religious discoveries and conclusions which would otherwise have naturally flowed from their work. Our own Cognitive Dissonance is humankind's greatest barrier to understanding and enlightenment — because it blinds us.

Summary Points:

- The Hebrew name of the first book of Moses means: "Book of Creation." Translated into English, it becomes: "Genesis."
- Genesis means origins. Genesis also means source, coming into being.
- Moses wrote the Torah.
- The five books of the Torah are: Genesis, Exodus, Leviticus, Numbers, and Deuteronomy.
- The Greek translation of the Torah is called: "The Pentateuch," which means "five-volume book."
- The Torah comprises the first 5 books of the 24-book Hebrew Bible.
- The name of the Hebrew Bible is: "Tanakh."
- Torah means Instruction.
- Torah refers to the written Torah of Moses and the Oral Tradition of the Torah, which began with Adam.
- Jews, Christians, and Muslims believe there was a beginning. They also believe God created everything in the beginning.
- The interpretation of the ancient Mosaic text by Hebrew sages in the 12th and 13th centuries AD is referred to in this work as: The Genesis Code.
- The Genesis Code conveys a depth of knowledge that has been lost in our modern translations.
- In His Commentary on Genesis, Nahmanides wrote: "Everything that was transmitted to Moses by God was written in the Torah explicitly or by implication in the words and in the numerical value of the letters. The bent and crooked letters of the Hebrew language and the crownlets of the letters have special and specific meanings."
- The hidden message of the written word of the five books of Moses is: "Torah brackets God's name and always faces it."
- The Feast of First Fruits pledges the first fruits of the harvest will be given to God.
- The Feast of Weeks celebrates the beginning of the harvest and commemorates God's gift of the Torah to Moses at Mt. Sinai. This happened on the 50th day of the Exodus.
- Observance of the Sabbath is a sign acknowledging God created the universe.

- Nahmanides' description of the Beginning reads like a modern-day Physics textbook on the Big Bang Theory.
- This is because Nahmanides was able to decipher The Genesis Code.
- Modern scientific discoveries of the last 85 years support and validate the Genesis Account of Creation.
- Our own Cognitive Dissonance blinds us.

THE "REST OF THE STORY"

The Feast of [1]Unleavened Bread, the Feast of the [2]Passover, the Feast of [3]First Fruits, and the [4]Feast of Weeks (i.e., the Harvest), are the four feasts of the Jews, which have special significance to Christians.

1. The Feast of Unleavened Bread is associated with — The last Supper, Christ's Prayer in the Garden of Gethsemane, and the arrest and illegal night-trial of Jesus.
2. The Feast of the Passover is associated with — the Scourging, Crucifixion and Death of Jesus Christ.
3. The Feast of First Fruits is associated with — the Resurrection of Jesus Christ.
4. And the Feast of Weeks (also known as the Feast of the Harvest), celebrates the giving of the Law to Moses on Mt. Sinai. That happened on the 50th day of the Exodus from Egypt. Christians now call the Feast of the Harvest — "Pentecost" — which is Greek for "50th Day," because something special happened on the 50th day after Christ's crucifixion on the day of that particular 1st Feast of the Harvest that followed His crucifixion.
5. 40 days after His resurrection from the dead, while talking to His disciples on the Mt. of Olives, Jesus was taken up to Heaven. The disciples witnessed Christ's accention to Heaven. Two angels told the disciples Christ Jesus would return someday — "in the same way!"
6. Before He ascended to Heaven Christ told the disciples to return to the Upper Room and pray until "the Comforter" (i.e., The Holy Spirit) came.
7. That 1st Pentecost was ushered in on the 10th day after the Ascension of Jesus Christ to Heaven from the Mt. of Olives.
8. The Holy Spirit came to Earth on the 50th day after Christ arose from the dead. That 1st Pentecost marks the day the Christian Church was born.
9. So, the 1st Pentecost occurred on the Jewish Feast of the Harvest that occurred on the 50th day after Christ's crucifixion (cf. The Book of Acts).

The death and resurrection of Jesus Christ brought about God's New Covenant with man that replaces the Old Testament Dispensation of the Law. We no longer live under the Old Law. We now live under the new Dispensation of the Grace of Jesus Christ!

I suggest you skip ahead now, to the last few pages of Chapter 25 (in Book III). Start reading "WHY CHRISTIANS WORSHIP ON SUNDAY," and read to the end of the Chapter.

CHAPTER 2: THERE WAS A BEGINNING—A CREATION

"In the beginning God created the heavens and the earth." Gen. 1:1 (NASB)

THE BEGINNING OF—WHAT?

The opening sentence of the Bible makes several bold statements, which have caused great controversy and debate. Our English translations of Genesis 1:1 tell us there was a beginning, but do not say exactly what was begun. We are told an entity called God created. We are also told God created the heavens and the earth. The meaning of the earth seems straightforward. However, the heavens are a bit more problematical. Do 'the heavens' refer to the universe at large, or could there be a more restricted or proximate meaning, such as 'the atmosphere of our earth?' Perhaps 'the heavens' refer to something else? Maybe 'the heavens and the earth' refer to something more basic or fundamental, such as space and matter? If we can satisfy these questions, we are still left with: In the beginning of what? Could the answer be what God did? If so, then God created. Perhaps we are talking about His act of creation — creation itself? If that is the case, then we are talking about 'in the beginning of everything that exists and will exist.' In the next chapter we will talk about what the ancient Hebrew sages concluded. But, for now, let's decide the answer is implied. We must also consider, our ability to understand the first sentence in the Bible, may have something to do with our English translations.

There is another helpful hint our choice of the word, creation, may be correct. Let's take another look at the opening paragraph of the previous chapter, but this time I will underline some of the words.

In English translations of the Bible, Moses begins his account of creation with — *"In the beginning."* The Hebrew name for the first book of Moses was originally *Sefer Maaseh Bereshith* — which means — "Book of Creation." Translated into Greek, it becomes Genesis, meaning "origins," because it gives an account of the creation of the world and the beginnings of life and society. This first verse of the Bible emphatically states: *"In the beginning God created the heavens and the earth (Genesis 1:1)."* [138]

Now, read the two sentences formed by the underlined words (only the underlined words). The word [created] appears six times on this page, and the word [creation] appears ten times, two of which are in the underlined sentences. Perhaps that is a clue that "creation" is the right word for the implied object of — "In the Beginning." The ancient Hebrew text also tells us there was a CREATOR called God, and attributes creation to Him. Before this sentence, notice the word "CREATOR" appears only once (for there is only one "CREATOR" — God). In his book, THE HIDDEN FACE OF GOD, Dr. Schroeder informs us: *"Judaism, Christianity, and Islam all draw their understanding of creation from the opening chapters of the Book of Genesis. Genesis claims a single, eternal, omnipotent and incorporeal God created the universe."* [139]

So, in the first verse of the Bible, *four basic concepts* are boldly stated.

1) There was a beginning.

---

[138] The Pentateuch and Haftorahs Edited by J. H. Hertz 2nd Edition, 1978, London Soncino Press, Introduction to the Book of Genesis.
[139] Schroeder The Hidden Face of God Chapter 1 p 10 a

2) The beginning started with something which probably involved space and matter. For now, we'll consider we are talking about *"creation."*
3) The force and source of that creation was a supreme deity called God.
4) For now, let's consider what was created was the universe in general (i.e., the highest heavens), and our earth in particular.

THESE 4 BASIC MOSAIC CONCEPTS (IN GENESIS 1:1) HAVE BEEN CHALLENGED. Many people do not believe there was a beginning. They believe the universe is eternal — had no beginning — has always existed — and is in a steady unchanging state of existence from eternity to eternity. There are those who adamantly oppose the concept of any creation by a creator, and they challenge the concept of a God.

THE REBUTTAL

So, where do we begin the rebuttal? Let's start with a discussion of how man observed the world in which he found himself. What follows is an abbreviated synopsis of man's beliefs about the scheme of things based on his observations over time. From this review, we will see:

- Things are not always as they seem.
- What we think we perceive can lead to wrong conclusions.

Let us start our discussion with one of the most pre-eminent scientists and philosophers of all time — Aristotle.

*There once was a man, Aristotle. Who thought he knew a "lottle."[140] The movement of Sun from east to west, Taught him that his earth was best. So, he put that "fact" in his bottle. (*My Limerick — O. David)

ARISTOTLE & GEOCENTRISM

Aristotle (384-322 BC), a student of Plato, and teacher of Alexander the Great, thought his earth was the center of the universe.[141] To him, to us, and to all who have lived and all who will ever live on our planet, our sun appears to rise in the east and set in the west. Therefore, our sun must move around our earth — must orbit the earth.[142] Right? **Wrong!**

THE CHURCH SUPPORTED CONCEPT OF A GEO-CENTRIC EARTH WAS WRONG.

We now know our earth is not the center of the universe. Neither is our sun. But, for almost 2,000 years after Aristotle, that was the commonly held belief. The concept the earth is the center of everything in the universe fit in neatly with the theology of the early Christian Church.[143] In the Genesis Creation Account, man was the last creature God created. Man was made in the image of God, and God gave him dominion over all His creation (Gen. 1:26-28). Then, God brought every beast and bird to man to see what the man would call them (Gen. 2:19). The authorities of the early Christian church held fast to their belief — The pre-eminence of man in creation meant God had exalted man above all. It logically followed — man's home (the earth), should be at the center of all God created. However, trouble was ahead. The church sponsored concept of Aristotle's geo-centric position of the earth would inevitably be challenged by science.

---

[140] *"Lottle"* — Not a real word, but rhymes with *bottle*, & is intended to mean people think Aristotle knew *"a lot."*
[141] GREAT BOOKS of the WESTERN WORLD. Encyclopedia Britannica © 1952. #8. Vol. I. ARISTOTLE. Book II. On the Heavenly Bodies. p 357 (14 ii) & p 388 (296b [5][15][20][25] & 297a [5])
[142] Hawking A Briefer History of Time Chapter 2 p 8 b
[143] Schroeder The Science of God Chapter 1 p 8 b, c, d

COPERNICUS & HELIOCENTRISM

Nicolaus Copernicus (1473-1543 AD), a Polish astronomer, mathematician, physician, and a canon in the Roman Catholic Church, was born 100 years before the invention of the telescope. Looking at the heavens with his bare eyes, he agreed with Aristotle, who about 1,800 years earlier had concluded the earth was a sphere, because the shadow it casts on the moon during a lunar eclipse is always curved.[144] He also believed all celestial bodies in our solar system are spheres.[145] Copernicus concluded the earth is not the center of our solar system. The sun is.[146, 147] He is also credited with discovering earth orbits the sun once each year, and while doing so, the earth rotates on its axis, making one complete rotation every 24 hours. He believed the earth's rotation is responsible for our day-night cycle.[148] Copernicus kept his discoveries to himself until late in his life because he realized his discoveries would shake the very foundations of the theology of his day. The Church, claiming biblical truth, extended Genesis to include what it never did — a central positioning of the earth. The claim of the Church that the earth was geo-centric had nothing to do with the Bible.[149] It was the invention of a flawed philosophical religious doctrine. Until Copernicus, the world believed in the geo-centric or earth-centered scheme of the universe espoused by Aristotle. Some Christians still venerate the geo-centric doctrine of the early church. These Christians still consider modern science an enemy. Two Italian scientists who lived in the late 16th and early 17th centuries AD — Galileo and Bruno — embraced the Copernican theory. They suffered much personal injury at the hands of powerful church inquisitors.

BRUNO

Giordano Bruno went beyond Copernicus. He suggested space was boundless and the sun and its planets were but one of any number of similar systems. He thought there might be other inhabited worlds with rational beings, equal or possibly superior to us. For such "blasphemy" he was tried by The Inquisition. He was condemned and burned at the stake in 1600 AD![150]

GALILEO

Galileo Galilei was brought before The Inquisition in 1633 AD. Under the threat of torture and death, he was forced to his knees to renounce all belief in Copernican theories. Afterwards, he was sentenced to house arrest for the remainder of his days.[151, 152, 153] The tyranny of the Christian Church was the result of Cognitive Dissonance.

---

[144] GREAT BOOKS of the WESTERN WORLD: Encyclopedia Britannica © 1952. #8 Vol. I ARISTOTLE. Book II On the Heavenly Bodies. p 388 [5] and p. 389 [25]

[145] Article: When the Earth Moved: Copernicus and His Heliocentric System by Severyn Zoledziowski, http://info-poland.buffalo.edu/classroom/kopernik/copernicus.shtml

[146] Hawking A Briefer History of Time Chapter 2 p 10 b

[147] Schroeder The Science of God Chapter 1 p 8 a

[148] Article: When the Earth Moved: Copernicus and His Heliocentric System by Severyn Zoledziowski http://info-poland.buffalo.edu/classroom/kopernik/copernicus.shtml

[149] Schroeder The Science of God Chapter 1 p 8 b, c, d

[150] Article: Giordano Bruno (Italian Philosopher)-Britannica online http://www.britannica.com/EBchecked/topic/82258/Giordano-Bruno also Summary of the Trial Against Giordano Bruno http://asv.vatican.va/en/doc/1597.html

[151] Schroeder The Science of God Chapter 1 p 7 b

[152] Article: Summary of the Trial Against Giordano Bruno http://asv.vatican.va/en/doc/1597.html

[153] Hawkins A Briefer History of Time p 145-146

We now know for certain, as our earth orbits the sun; it is also spinning from west to east on its axis, completing a full rotation every 24 hours.[154] The rotation of our earth makes it appear to us our sun is revolving around us. Why? Because the *Newtonian Law of Inertia* makes it seem we are stationary.[155] So, things are not always as they seem.

THE KEPLER SPACE TELESCOPE

On March 6, 2009, at 10:49:57 PM EST, NASA launched a new space telescope, named "Kepler," which will replace the Hubble Space Telescope, which was our country's first telescope in space. The Hubble is our first large orbiting optical observatory built from 1978 to 1990 at a cost of $1.5 billion. NASA is concerned the Hubble's effective life is running out. The Kepler's mission is to search the Milky Way galaxy for planets similar to earth where liquid water and life might possibly exist.[156] Kepler was the German scientist who discovered planetary orbits are not circular. They are elliptical. The day after the Kepler telescope was launched, Robbin Meade, a news anchorwoman for CNN Headline News Channel was reading from her teleprompter. She said the new telescope had been launched the previous evening and was in orbit around the sun. She paused a moment to think about what she just read, and then exclaimed, "Wow, that really is something! How could it already be in orbit around the sun this soon?" The truth is — before NASA launched the new telescope, it was already orbiting the sun — even when it sat stationary on the launch pad. Why? Because our earth and everything in our solar system orbits the sun. The Kepler will remain for decades in orbit around our sun, weaving in and out of earth's orbital path as it "looks" far out in space as our solar system travels through the Milky Way. Things truly are not as they seem.

INERTIAL REFERENCE-FRAMES & UNACCELERATED SYSTEMS

If you really want to 'blow your mind,' modern science has discovered our earth is approximately 24,000 miles in circumference at the equator. Since it rotates on its axis once every 24 hours, the rotation of the earth causes all stationary objects on our equator, and people who are quietly sitting or resting — to move at a speed of 1,000 miles per hour![157] Next, consider the earth is orbiting the sun at the rate of 20 miles per second. That is 72,000 miles per hour![158] Finally, scientists tell us our entire solar system, including our earth and us, is rocketing through space around the center of our Milky Way Galaxy, at ten times that speed. That is 720,000 miles per hour![159] Yet, as we calmly go about our business on our planet, in our space-ship earth, we are not aware of any of this tremendous spinning, forward motion, and three-dimensional speed. Much the same as a passenger in an airplane flying along through a clear, cloudless, and tranquil sky is not aware of the 400-500 (or more) mph speed at which he is traveling, our **inertial reference-frame** within the atmosphere of our space-ship earth seems stable and motionless to us. This concept of **inertial reference-frames** was part of the principle of relativity first postulated by Galileo 300 years ago and updated by Einstein. It states: All the laws of physics (which are really no more than the laws of nature) are the same in all

[154] Schroeder The Science of God Chapter 3 p 44 a
[155] Schroeder Genesis and The Big Bang Chapter 2 p 41a
[156] Article: Kepler: home page http://kepler.nasa.gov/
[157] Schroeder The Science of God Chapter 3 p 44 b
[158] Schroeder The Science of God Chapter 3 p 44 c
[159] Schroeder The Science of God Chapter 3 p 44 c

unaccelerated systems — i.e., systems that have uniform straight-line motion. As long as we are within our inertial reference-frame (earth) we cannot use the laws of physics to determine earth's motion, because earth's motion has no effect on any dimensions we can measure within the frame.[160]

If we were on some other planet in our solar system, we could observe the earth moving, because we would be outside the inertial reference-frame of the earth. This is like saying the person in the airplane example is unaware of the speed of his flight, but another person on the ground is very much aware of the same airplane's speed since he is observing it from outside the inertial reference-frame of the airplane.

Unaccelerated systems are those systems, which have smooth uniform straight-line uninterrupted motion. The motion of a rocking chair is not smooth because it is intermittent and interrupted. We are very aware of our motion when we are rocking in a rocking chair because it is a good example of an interrupted accelerated system.

The key here is — the thing we call space (in the universe) in which our space-ship earth is traveling — is like a vacuum. Therefore, our flight is uninterrupted and seems uniform and smooth. Consequently, we are not aware of all the tremendous rotation and speed of our space-ship earth. All seems blissfully stable and secure to us as our earth [1]spins like a bullet — and [2]rockets along its orbit around the sun — while our solar system is [3]orbiting the center of our Milky Way Galaxy. All of this is happening at three different incredible speeds and with three separate directional motions! Indeed, things really are not as they seem!

THE VASTNESS OF THE UNIVERSE IS HARD TO COMPREHEND.

First, consider our Milky Way Galaxy travels through the universe at the speed of 2-million mph![161] If that is hard to imagine, think about this. A trip from earth to Andromeda (the closest galaxy to our Milky Way), would take 2 million light-years,[162] if our man-made spaceship could travel at the speed of light. That means 2 million years on earth would pass while our spaceship travels the 12 quadrillion miles (12×10^{18} miles) that separate us from Andromeda — if we could rocket along at a speed of approximately 670 million mph (actually 186,000 miles/sec. x 60 sec./min. x 60 min./hr. = 669,600,000 mph). At that speed (i.e., the speed of light) we would travel six trillion miles each earth-year and the total time that would pass on earth during the trip — would be two million years! This truly boggles our imagination and gives us some inkling of how small our tiny planet is in the grand scheme of God's universe.

In the next chapter we will talk about the different time-flow the earth would experience as opposed to the time-flow the travelers on the spaceship would experience during their theoretical trip to Andromeda. This will be something, which really will be astounding. I'll give you a hint now. It has something to do with the Laws of Relativity and the concept of *Eternity*.

AN ETERNAL, STEADY STATE, STATIC UNIVERSE? WITH NO BEGINNING AND, NO END? WHO SAID THAT? YEP! YOU GUESSED IT! ARISTOTLE! — AGAIN!

---

[160] Schroeder Genesis and the Big Bang Chapter 2 p 41 a, b
[161] Stephen Parker: Bridges—Reconnecting Science and Faith. p 96
[162] Schroeder The Science of God Chapter 9 p 128c

*"Nothing comes from nothing. Nothing ever could. So somewhere
in my youth or childhood. I must have done something good."*

Julie Andrews (who sang those lyrics in The Sound of Music movie), or the writer of that song, may have read Aristotle, who 2300 years ago, thinking that nothing comes from nothing, assumed nothing ever would or could. Therefore, Aristotle defined the universe as eternal, having no beginning and no end — being something, which has always existed in a static or steady state.[163] Right? **Wrong!**

Aristotle's concept of an eternal universe, with no beginning, stood in sharp contrast to the claim made a thousand years earlier in the opening sentence of the Hebrew Bible — *"In the beginning!"* [164] Jewish oral tradition is even older, tracing this belief to the first man, Adam. So, from the time of Aristotle, for the past 2300 years or so, and contrary to the claim of the Hebrew Bible, scientific theory believed the universe to be eternal — a belief that was based on Aristotle's error of interpretation of what he believed to be an unchanging stellar pattern of the heavens.[165, 166]

SCIENCE HAS PROVED THERE WAS A BEGINNING.

Even as recently as the 1960s, and in the face of mounting scientific evidence to the contrary, two thirds of leading U.S. scientists still believed in an Aristotelian static-steady-state-eternal universe![167, 168]

"Only in the past thirty years has science resolved the question. Based on data from telescopes and particle accelerators, the 3300-year-old Genesis 1:1 had been correct all along! There actually was a beginning!" [169]

This quote comes from Dr. Schroeder's book: The Science of God. That book was published in 1997. Since I am editing this paragraph in 2012, it has actually been 85 years since the Big Bang Theory was first proposed, and 47 years have come and gone since the most significant scientific proof of the validity of the Big Bang Theory was discovered. (See 'CBR' on the next page.)

WHEN WAS THE BIG BANG THEORY FIRST PROPOSED?

Father Georges Lemaitre, a Belgian cosmologist, physicist, and Roman Catholic Priest, is credited as being the Father of *the Big Bang Theory*. He wrote a paper in 1927 that provided a compelling solution to the equations of General Relativity for the case of an expanding universe, but his paper went *relatively unnoticed* (pun intended).

In 1929 (two years after Lemaitre's first paper), Edwin Hubble reported his 30-year study of the movement of the stars. Hubble's data showed the vast majority of stars were receding (i.e., moving away) from each other. His exhaustive study: with data, which had been accumulated over a period of three decades, provided a compelling case against the prevailing Aristotelian popular theory of an eternal, static, steady state, and unchanging universe. In other words— Hubble's data proved the universe is expanding! (We will talk more about Hubble's work in Chapter 9, in Book II).

---

[163] Schroeder The Science of God Chapter 1 p 6 b
[164] Schroeder The Science of God Chapter 1 p 6 b
[165] Hawking A Briefer History of Time Chapter 2 p 7 b & 8 a
[166] Schroeder The Science of God Chapter 2 p 22 b The Beginning of the Universe
[167] S. Bush, "How Cosmology Became a Science," Scientific American, Aug 1992
[168] Schroeder The Science of God Chapter 1 p 7 a
[169] Schroeder The Science of God Chapter 2 p 22 b—a direct quote of Dr. Schroeder.

ONE YEAR LATER (IN 1930), OTHER COSMOLOGISTS—

including Willem de Sitter, Albert Einstein, and the distinguished astronomer Arthur Eddington, concluded the models of a static, steady state, unchanging universe, which they had worked on for many years — were not satisfactory! When Lemaitre learned of this, he was greatly encouraged. As it turns out, Lemaitre had previously studied theoretical physics under Eddington's tutelage, and Eddington had regarded him to be "a very brilliant student who possessed great mathematical ability." Thus, it was at this point, Lemaitre called on his former mentor and drew Eddington's attention to his earlier work. Eddington at once called the attention of the other cosmologists to Lemaitre's 1927 paper and arranged for the publication of an English translation of Lemaitre's work. So it was, the English translation of Lemaitre's 1927 paper was republished "in Scientific Format" [170] (*) in 1931. This time, Lemaitre's theoretical calculations were taken seriously.

IN 1931, THE CONCEPT OF AN EXPANDING UNIVERSE WAS FINALLY ACCEPTED.

It was the combination of Lemaitre's republished 1927 paper — which presented a compelling solution to the equations of General Relativity, and strongly supported the case of an expanding universe — and Hubble's 1929 paper about his thirty-year study of 'star movement data,' (which supported Lemaitre's work), that convinced most astronomers the universe was indeed expanding.

So, in 1931 — the concept of an expanding universe was finally accepted. Hubble's thirty-year study of star-movement data revolutionized cosmology! Hubble proved the Universe is expanding.

LEMAITRE'S 1932 CONCEPT OF "AN EXPLOSION OF THE PRIMEVAL ATOM:"

A year later (1932), Lemaitre suggested, since the universe is continually expanding, it must have originated from a finite point. He reasoned it must have been smaller in the past. An extrapolation backward in time, he said, should lead to an epoch when all matter in the universe was packed together in an extremely dense state within a tiny, single finite point. Appealing to the new quantum theory of matter of the time, Lemaitre argued the physical universe was initially a simple particle — the primeval atom he called it — which disintegrated in an explosion— giving rise to space, time, and the expansion of the universe. Thus — in 1932 — The Big Bang Theory was born!

LEMAITRE & EINSTEIN

In 1933, Albert Einstein traveled with Lemaitre to California for a series of seminars. After Lemaitre explained his Big Bang Theory, Einstein stood, applauded, and said: "This is the most beautiful and satisfactory explanation of creation to which I have ever listened."

When Pope Pius XII claimed Lemaitre's new theory of the origin of the universe was a scientific validation of the Roman Catholic faith, Lemaitre was alarmed and pointed out to the Pope his idea was an unproved theory.

THE 1965 DISCOVERY OF CBR—THE "ECHO" OF THE BIG BANG:

In 1965, 38 years after Lemaitre had suggested his Big Bang Theory in his original 1927 paper, Arno Penzias and Robert Wilson of the Bell Laboratories published their discovery of Cosmic Microwave Background Radiation (CBR). CBR is the 'echo' of the Big Bang.

---

[170] (*) *"Scientific Format:"* There are specific rules for writing a scientific paper. These rules must be met before current-day editors of scientific publications will consider publishing a scientific study. The convention known as *"Scientific Format,"* ensures an efficient and consistent communication with the scientific community.

> *Shortly before his death, Lemaitre learned of Penzias' and Wilson's discovery. He was very pleased, because the discovery of CBR was the scientific evidence that proved Lemaitre's Big Bang Theory was correct! (I'll talk a bit more about CBR in Chapter 5 of this book). There is no question — today, the Big Bang Theory is the most creditable and most accepted theory of our beginning. The Big Bang Theory is now accepted by the vast majority of modern-day scientists as the true cause of the Beginning of the Universe ...[171, 172, 173, 174]*

THE PROBLEM OF GENESIS FOR SCIENTISTS WHO ARE AVID ATHEISTS—

and still support the Aristotelian concept of a steady-state static unchanging eternal universe, and still stubbornly deny the biblical claim of a beginning — is simply this: Science has now proved there actually was a beginning! Because 85 years have passed since the discovery of strong astronomical scientific evidence for an ever-expanding universe, and almost half a century has passed since the discovery of the proof there actually was a beginning (i.e., the discovery of CBR) — the majority of scientists now take the fact of a beginning as a given. In his book, The Science of God, Dr. Gerald Schroeder wrote:

> *"This shift in scientific opinion, after millennia of opposition, represents the most significant change science can ever make toward biblical philosophy. Evolution, dinosaurs, and cavemen are all trivial controversies when compared to the concept of a beginning. While the fact of a beginning does not scientifically confirm the existence of a beginner (God), it does open the doorway for that possibility." [175]*

Sadly, there are people who are either not aware modern science has confirmed the Biblical claim there was a beginning, or they are aware, but will not admit to the paradigm shift because of their own Cognitive Dissonance. To those who say the existence of God must be scientifically proved before they will believe it, the fact remains:

> **Proof of God's existence is something that is beyond man's capabilities.[176] The Science of man can never prove or disprove the existence of God. For mortals, the belief in God's existence is and will remain a matter of faith.[177] Now you can see why I disagreed with Maimonides' belief that the science of man is the only pathway to God.**

EINSTEIN'S GREATEST BLUNDER—1917—HIS COSMOLOGICAL EQUATION.

Scientific advances require proof and rest on discovered and established reproducible facts — not opinion. As scientific data accumulate, what tests to be true (i.e., is investigated and confirmed by the tests of other investigators), becomes accepted as a new, true scientific law. Even as great a scientist as Albert Einstein had to learn this lesson the hard way.

[171] Article: Georges Lemaitre, Father of the Big Bang
http://www.amnh.org/education/resources/rfl/web/essaybooks/cosmic/p_lemaitre.html
[172] Article: 'A Day Without Yesterday': Georges Lemaitre & the Big Bang by Mark Midbon
http://www.catholiceducation.org/articles/science/sc0022.html
[173] Article: Discovery of Cosmic Background Radiation: http://hyperphysics.phy-astr.gsu.edu/hbase/astro/penwil.html
[174] Article: Arno Penzias and Robert Wilson: Bell Labs, Holmdel, NJ http://hyperphysics.phy-astr.gsu.edu/hbase/astro/penwil.html
[175] Schroeder The Science of God Chapter 2 p 22 d
[176] Schroeder The Science of God Chapter 1 p 2 a
[177] Schroeder The Science of God Chapter 1 p 2 c

Several years before Einstein met Lemaitre (in 1917), Einstein and most scientists thought the universe was eternal, had no beginning, and was in an unchanging, static, steady state. As we have just said, Aristotle's idea of an unchanging universe prevailed. In that same year, using the laws of his own theory of General Relativity, which he had published two years earlier (in 1915), Einstein developed a series of equations with the intent of describing the condition of a static-state unchanging universe. So, fourteen years before Lemaitre's 1931 paper supported the idea of an expanding universe, Einstein made a major mistake. He was so influenced by Aristotle's prevailing idea of an unchanging universe that he feared his equations might lead to the conclusion that all the mass in the universe would bend space so much that it should have long ago folded in on itself and contracted and collapsed into a single dense blob. However, it seemed a given — the universe was spread out and did not seem to be contracting. Therefore, Einstein decided to insert an anti-gravity fudge factor in his calculations, which would mathematically 'prevent' the universe from collapsing. He called his fudge factor "The Cosmological Constant." His calculations became known as "Einstein's Cosmological Equation." He apparently did not see (without his Cosmological Constant), his calculations actually suggested the universe was dynamic — The universe had been constantly expanding!

The Universe is not static. It is Dynamic. It Is Expanding!

From 1912-1925, an astronomer at the Lowell Observatory in Flagstaff, Arizona (Vesto Slipher), published several papers reporting his astronomical data, which showed the universe is expanding.[178] Slipher's measurements rested completely on Einstein's own Theory of General Relativity and agreed with Einstein's untainted calculations — i.e., the solutions derived from Einstein's equations if one did not apply Einstein's Cosmological Constant.[179]

However, when Einstein read Slipher's papers, he had a problem. He so strongly believed in Aristotle's concept of an eternal, steady state, static universe that he refused to believe Slipher's data, and he stood by his fudge factor — his Cosmological Constant.

Einstein finally admitted his mistake in 1929 when Edwin Hubble reported his 30-year study, which showed distant galaxies were indeed moving away from the earth as well as from each other. The farther away they were, the faster they were moving. That discovery changed cosmology.[180] Hubble's agreement with Slipher changed Einstein's mind and caused him to write to his friend and fellow Nobel laureate, Max Born: "The denial of my own theory was the biggest blunder of my life." [181] Why? Because the accumulating data convinced Einstein that indeed day by day the universe was expanding. It was getting ever larger and larger.

Einstein realized--If one could make a movie of time, and then run the movie projector backward, the movie would eventually arrive at that point in time

[178] Article: Vesto Melvin Slipher (American astronomer) – Britannica …
http://www.britannica.com/EBchecked/topic/548821/Vesto-Melvin-Slipher
[179] Schroeder The Science of God Chapter 2 p 23 b
[180] Article: Expanding Universe http://archive.ncsa.illinois.edu/Cyberia/Cosmos/ExpandUni.html
[181] Schroeder The Science of God Chapter 2 p 23 b

> *(billions of years ago) when a tiny space inexplicably suddenly appeared. That tiny finite speck of space marked — "The Beginning of the Beginning!"* [182]

The statistical power of Hubble's three decades of accumulated data was so great, that Einstein was forced to change his mind. Hubble's data convinced Einstein that Aristotle had been wrong. Einstein had also been so enamored by Lemaitre's 1931 paper, that in 1933, he traveled to California with Lemaitre — so that he would be present for each of the seminars Lemaitre presented.

> *Later (in Chapters 3, 4, and 6 of this book), we will talk about a 13th century rabbi, Nahmanides, who would define the point marking the beginning as a tiny finite speck of space no bigger than the size of a grain of mustard. Modern day scientists supporting the most recent theory of our beginning would conclude the point marking the beginning was also a tiny finite speck of space. Lemaitre had called it the Primeval Atom. They called it the Singularity.*

EINSTEIN'S THEORY IS NOW A LAW.

At first, Einstein's concept of relativity appeared to be so highly speculative that it was referred to as a theory. Today, the accumulating scientific data from many other disciplines has proved beyond any shadow of a doubt that Einstein's Theory of Relativity is no longer a theory. During the past few decades, the relativity of time has been tested and verified thousands of times. Today, it is known as Einstein's Law of General and Specific Relativity.[183] Science has now proved Einstein discovered an overlooked law of nature.

EINSTEIN FAILED TO RECOGNIZE THE MOST IMPORTANT CONCLUSION OF HIS THEORY.

Before Slipper, Hubble, and Lemaitre published their work, Einstein could have followed his own discoveries and predicted the most important statement ever made relative to man and the universe. He could have been credited with the most significant change science can ever make toward biblical philosophy. There was a beginning! There was a creation! But he blew it! His own cognitive dissonance led him to refuse to give up his opinion in favor of his 'facts.'[184] He not only rejected Slipher's findings, but he deluded himself and others by conceiving and publishing his bogus cosmological equation. Once you have been published, it is hard to admit your error, and it is even harder to take it back. Because people who agree with you may not want to hear it.

Summary Points:

- The Bible is right. There was a beginning. Science has proved it.
- This proof is the most significant discovery science has ever made in regard to biblical philosophy.
- Aristotle was wrong. Our universe is not eternal.
- While the fact of a beginning cannot scientifically confirm the existence of a beginner (God), it does open the doorway for that possibility.
- A supreme deity we call God was the source and force of creation, but this can never be proved by science. This must remain a matter of belief and faith.

---

[182] Schroeder The Science of God Chapter 2 p 23 c
[183] Schroeder The Science of God Chapter 3 p. 47
[184] Schroeder The Science of God Chapter 2 p 23 c

- Judaism, Christianity, and Islam all draw their understanding of creation from the opening chapters of the Book of Genesis.
- Things are not always as they seem.
- What we think we perceive can lead to wrong conclusions.
- Aristotle was wrong. The earth is not the center of the universe. The sun does not orbit the earth.
- Copernicus was right. The sun is the center of our solar system. The earth orbits the sun.
- Einstein's Law of Relativity changed our understanding of our beginnings. Einstein could have been the one to discover the most important meaning of his own Law of Relativity — *There was a Beginning!* But his own cognitive dissonance blinded him.
- In the 13th century AD, Nahmanides (deciphering the Genesis Code), concluded the finite point marking the beginning of God's creation was a tiny speck of space no larger than a grain of mustard.
- Modern-day scientists supporting Father Lemaitre's Big Bang Theory of the Primeval Atom would come to the same conclusion but would call the chaotic speck of space the explosion created — *the Singularity.*

DON'T JUST BELIEVE IN GOD. BELIEVE GOD. BELIEVE GOD'S WORD, THE BIBLE.

Science has proved there was a beginning. The opening sentence of the 3300-year-old Hebrew Bible has been right all along. That same sentence says God created the heavens and the earth. If the first part of Genesis 1:1 is true — there was a beginning: it follows the rest of Genesis 1:1 is also true — God created! God is real. He is the Beginner — the Creator! He is The Source of all that was, is, and will forever be. We now know the universe is not eternal, but Jews, Christians, and Muslims believe God is! Christians have the certainty of their belief and the conviction of their faith in — **"the Great I AM"** (Exodus 3:14). The significance of the name God told Moses to call Him will be discussed in Chapter 10 (in Book II).

CHAPTER 3: FIRST WISDOM—INTELLIGENT DESIGN—ETERNITY

The First Wisdom of God, The Intelligent Design of God, The Hidden Face of God—Space, Matter, Time, Time-Reference-Frames, & Eternity → All are Relevant & Relative. (O. David)

ANCIENT VERSUS MODERN HEBREW TEXTS:

There are three distinctly different Hebrew texts — two ancient and one modern. The first three words of the Hebrew Torah look like this: .בְּרֵאשִׁית בָּרָא These Hebrew words read from right to left. The characters of that text are those of the ancient Post-exilic Hebrew Square Script alephbet of the 2nd Temple period. After WWII Jews returned to Palestine and reestablished Israel. They also resurrected their ancient Hebrew language.

The Modern Hebrew-to-English Transliterated Text of the Torah says: **"Be'reasheet barah."** This script is a transliterated Hebrew-to-English text that assigns each letter of the Hebrew alephbet to a letter in our English alphabet. Transliterated Hebrew texts are scripts, which translate the letters of the ancient Hebrew alephbet into the letters of the alphabets of modern-day languages. The name for the list of letters in the Greek language (*alphabet*) comes from the combination of its first two letters — the alpha and the beta. The first two letters of the Hebrew 'alphabet' are the aleph and the bet — therefore, '*alephbet*' is the transliterated Hebrew word for the ordered arrangement of the letters of the Hebrew language. Now study the illustration in the box below before proceeding any further. The arrows indicate the direction each text is written and read.

Genesis 1:1
Be'reasheet barah→ Elohim ←בָּרָא בְּרֵאשִׁית

[*Transliterated Hebrew-English Text*][→|←][*Jewish Bereshith Hebrew Square Script*]

In the Beginning of (?), God Created . . .English Translation

With First Wisdom, God Created . . . Onkelos Translation

THE FIRST HEBREW LETTER IN THE BIBLE LEADS US TO THE FIRST WISDOM OF GOD. *Be'reasheet barah* and בָּרָא בְּרֵאשִׁית are the first words of the first verse of the Hebrew Bible. *Be'reasheet barah* is written in the Transliterated Hebrew-English text, which reads as we do English, from left to right. The same meaning is conveyed by בְּרֵאשִׁית בָּרָא, but these words are ancient Jewish Bereshith Hebrew Square Script words — which read from right to left. *Be'* is a prefix meaning 'with.' בְּ is the same prefix as *be,'* and also means *'with,'* but בְּ is the first letter of the Post-Exilic Aramaic-influenced ancient Bereshith Hebrew Torah.[185] Both are known as the **"bet."** The *bet* is the second letter in the Hebrew alephbet. In the next chapter we'll see how Nahmanides, with his knowledge of The Genesis Code, gained insight and additional meaning from the shape of the בְּ (i.e., the **bet**). Nahmanides believed the *bet* is the first letter in the Hebrew Torah, because it is the letter that leads us to *the First Wisdom of God!* In the next chapter, I will also reveal the deeper meaning of a hidden message (using the *bet*) that Michelangelo painted into his

---

[185] Schroeder Genesis and the Big Bang Chapter 3 p 56 b

Jonah fresco in the Sistine Chapel. However, right now I want to present an interpretive concept introduced by Dr. Gerald L. Schroeder in his book, The Hidden Face of God.

THE KING JAMES VERSION & THE PROBLEM OF—'OF'

The King James Version of the Bible translated the opening Hebrew words of Genesis 1:1 as *"In the beginning."* According to Dr. Schroeder, *Be'reasheet* means *"In the beginning of,"* and should not be translated, "In the beginning." The difficulty with the preposition 'of' is — its object is absent from the sentence! Therefore, the King James translation merely drops it. This omission has caused "some" to believe the English translations of the first two chapters of Genesis have caused the entire English-speaking world (for the past 400 years) — to miss an important lesson of the Hebrew Bible's Creation Account.[186]

The 1st Edition of the King James Bible was published in 1611 AD. The King James Translation is based on the Latin Vulgate of St. Jerome and the Greek Septuagint. The Latin Vulgate of St. Jerome is the first Latin translation of the Hebrew Torah and Tanakh. St. Jerome wanted a translation of the Hebrew Torah and the rest of the Hebrew Old Testament in his native language. Believing the ancient Hebrew text would be more accurate than the Greek Septuagint; he translated the Hebrew Torah and Tanakh into Latin. He completed his Latin Vulgate in 405 AD.[187] The Greek Septuagint dates from 2,200 years ago. Therefore, the familiar opening phrase of the King James Bible, "In the beginning," is three translations downstream from the Aramaic-influenced Jewish Bereshith Hebrew script.[188] [Hebrew $>^1>$ Greek $>^2>$ Latin $>^3>$ English]

However, there is a translation that pre-dates the King James Bible by about 1,500 years. Since Aramaic is the closest neighboring historic language to the ancient Hebrew language, some claim the Aramaic translation of the Hebrew Torah more accurately conveys the meaning of the ancient Hebrew text. I'll talk about that next.

THE TARGUM ONKELOS (OR "UNKELUS")—THE ARAMAIC TRANSLATION OF THE TORAH:

Onkelos, a member of the Roman royal family and a convert to Judaism, translated the Five Books of Moses into Aramaic (cir. 110 AD). Aramaic was the common language of the Middle East for several centuries prior to and following the birth of Christ. Aramaic is also the language Jesus Christ spoke. Like Hebrew, it is a Semitic language. It is so close to Hebrew that it serves as a valuable linguistic cross-reference. By translating the Hebrew Torah into Aramaic, Onkelos provided definitions to many Hebrew words that had become obscure.[189]

THE FIRST MENTION OF THE FIRST WISDOM OF GOD COMES FROM THE TARGUM ONKELOS.

This 1,900-year-old Jerusalem Aramaic translation of Genesis sheds light on the meaning of the original Hebrew script. Be'reasheet is a compound word. The prefix be', means 'with.' However, according to Onkelos, Reasheet means — "First Wisdom." Therefore, instead of the familiar opening words of English translations of the Bible — *"In the*

---

186 Schroeder The Hidden Face of God Chapter 4 p 49 b
187 Vulgate I sacred text I Britannica.com htts://www.britannica.com/topic/Vulgate
188 Schroeder The Hidden Face of God Chapter 4 p 49 a
189 Schroeder Genesis and the Big Bang Chapter 1 p 18 b,c

beginning"— the Aramaic translation says: *"With First Wisdom God created the heavens and the earth."* [190]

GOD'S WISDOM

This First Wisdom concept of God's creation of the heavens and the earth is also expressed in other places in the Bible.

- *"Give thanks to the Lord...the God of gods...to Him who with wisdom made the heavens." (Psalms 136:1-5 NASB)*
- *"O Lord, how many are Thy works! In wisdom Thou hast made them all." (Psalms 104:24 NASB)*
- *"The Lord, by wisdom founded the earth. By understanding he established the heavens. By His knowledge the deeps were broken up, and the skies drip with dew." (Prov. 3:19-20 NASB)*

An often-quoted description of God's superior wisdom is found in Isaiah 55:8-9, which tells us, God's ways and thoughts (i.e., His actions and First Wisdom), are higher than ours: *"For My thoughts are not your thoughts. Neither are your ways My ways, declared the Lord. For as the heavens are higher than the earth, so are My ways higher than your ways, and My thoughts than your thoughts. Isa. 55:8-9 NASB."*

THE BEGINNING OF—WHAT?

The Answer goes back to Be'reasheet. So, now we have learned the King James Version dropped a preposition, and the Targum Onkelos says, "With First Wisdom God created." Does the absent object of the first sentence cause a problem? Yes. Why? Because, as we discussed in Chapter 2: The object of the preposition (which was dropped) — is implied. The problem posed is one of interpretation. Let's not be too critical of the King James Translation. The ancient Hebrew script did not clarify the question either. The ancient Hebrew sages had the same problem we do.

NAHMANIDES' CONCEPT OF THE BEGINNING OF THE UNIVERSE

In the year 1250 AD, Nahmanides described his concept of the beginning of the universe. With his understanding of the deeper meaning of the ancient Hebrew Creation Account, Nahmanides deduced:

- When God began creating the universe, it was so thin, it had no substance.
- The thin, substanceless entity He created in the beginning was the only physical creation to ever occur.
- All there would ever be, was concentrated within a tiny speck of space, which was the entire universe in the beginning.

This 700-year-old insight could be a quote from a modern-day physics textbook. In Nahmanides' view, as the universe expanded from the tiny space Elohim created in the beginning, the primordial substanceless substance within that tiny speck of space, changed into matter, as we know it. Nahmanides concluded: Biblical time started with the first appearance of true matter. The way he stated it was: *"Biblical time grabbed hold with the appearance of matter."* [191]

---

[190] Schroeder The Hidden Face of God Chapter 4 p 49 b,c
[191] Schroeder The Science of God Chapter 3 p 56 b

As we will later discuss: The time we experience is totally related to our material world. Einstein taught us this when he proposed his *Theory* of Relativity, which has now been proved to be — *The Law of Relativity*. Near the end of this chapter, I will talk about some interesting aspects of the Law of Relativity and what they tell us about time, time-reference-frames, time-flow, and the speed of light. You will see — it all has something to do with *Intelligent Design and Eternity*.

NAHMANIDES ON THE BEGINNING OF WHAT?

Nahmanides admitted his teachers also pondered the missing object of the preposition 'of.' In the beginning of what (?), they asked. In the beginning of *time* was their conclusion.[192] So, we have learned there are at least three different interpretations of the Hebrew word *be'reasheet*:

    (1.) 'With First Wisdom' (Onkelos).
    (2.) 'In the beginning' (King James Bible).
    (3.) And: 'In the beginning—of' (Nahmanides and Dr. Schroeder).

A POSSIBLE ANSWER TO THE BEGINNING OF WHAT?

Let's now re-examine Nahmanides' concept of the beginning of the Universe, which we just introduced.

> *In God's creation of the universe…His initial creation produced…an entity so thin it had no substance. … All there would ever be, was concentrated within a tiny speck of space, which was the entire extent of the universe — in the beginning…as the universe expanded…the primordial substanceless substance within that tiny speck of space…changed into matter…when matter appeared, time grabbed hold.*

As I look at this list, what stands out is: God's creation of the universe — produced — a thin entity — with no substance — concentrated in — a tiny speck of space — In the beginning. As the universe expanded — the entity with no substance — changed — into matter — and time grabbed hold. So, it seems the conclusions we reached in the previous chapter were pretty close to the mark.

- There was a beginning.
- *"The Beginning of"* — refers to the beginning of space, matter, & time.
- The source and force of the beginning was: *"The Strong One, The Almighty Supreme Leader — God."*
- What God specifically created was — space, matter, and time.
- In a more general sense, God created the universe at large and the earth in particular. Why the earth in particular? Because it is our home.

Our decision to call the object of—"of" — "*Creation*" — seems to be a good choice, because it is an all-inclusive term. In God's creation, God created Space, Matter, Time, the Universe at large, and our earth in particular. In short, God created everything that exists and will exist. Will exist? Yes, because God's creation goes on and on and on.

Now, with the Onkelos contribution to the Genesis Code, we are enlightened: *"With First Wisdom, the Lord God created the heavens and the earth"* — even if we still do not specifically know *how*, because God's thoughts and ways are higher than ours. Throughout the Bible, the superiority of the Wisdom of God is a recurring theme in

---

[192] Schroeder The Science of God Chapter 3 p 56 b

numerous passages of scripture. Now, let's look at what a wise King, Solomon, said about the origin of wisdom.

SOLOMON'S DISCOURSE ON THE ORIGIN OF WISDOM (PROVERBS 8:22-31 NASB):

"The Lord possessed me at the beginning of His way, before His works of old. From everlasting I was established from the beginning. From the earliest times of the earth, when there were no depths: I was brought forth. When there were no springs abounding with water before the mountains were settled. Before the hills I was brought forth: While He had not yet made the earth, and the fields, or the first dust of the world. When He established the heavens, I was there. When He inscribed a circle on the face of the deep; when He made firm the skies above; when the springs of the deep became fixed; when He set for the sea its boundary; so that the water should not transgress His command; when He marked out the foundations of the earth: Then I was beside Him as a master workman. And, I was daily His delight, rejoicing always before Him: Rejoicing in the world His earth, and having my delight in the sons of men."

The Ryrie Study Bible notes on this passage make the following points.

- *The "Me," in this scripture — is God's Wisdom. Wisdom comes from God.*
- *This passage shows Wisdom is older than creation and is fundamental to it.*
- *Wisdom assisted God as a master workman in His creation.*
- *Wisdom rejoiced in God's creation.*
- *From the earliest times of the earth, means the origins of the earth.*
- *Inscribed a circle, means the sky is a vaulted canopy over the earth.*
- *The face of the deep refers to the oceans.*[193]

Clear as mud? Once again, the Old Testament speaks to us in code! There is a deeper meaning of this scripture, which The Ryrie Study Bible missed. In Chapter 7 (of this book — Book I), and Chapter 10 (in Book II), you will discover, *"the face of the deep"* has a deeper meaning (pun intended) and does not only refer to the oceans. Later, in our discussion of *the 3rd Day* (in Book II), when God said: *"Let the dry land appear,"* you will learn — *"He inscribed a circle"* — has two meanings. In fact, after you have read the Genesis Code meaning of *Solomon's discourse on the origin of Wisdom* (Proverbs 8:22-31 — in Chapter 10 of Book II), you will understand the importance of *the sequences of creation*, which the first chapter of Genesis laid out.

SOLOMON, AN UNKNOWN PSALMIST, AND ONKELOS ALSO SAID:

- *"The Lord by wisdom founded the earth."* (Solomon — Prov. 3:19 NASB)
- A Psalmist wrote: *"With the Word of the Lord the heavens were made."* (Ps. 33:6 NASB)
- And, we have just discussed: *"In the beginning of (Creation), with First Wisdom, God created the heavens and the earth."* (Genesis 1:1 Onkelos Aramaic translation).

THE FIRST WISDOM OF GOD AND THE CREATION OF SPACE, MATTER & TIME:

Elohim's First Wisdom was the building block, the substrate, from which all the space, matter, and time of the universe were created. God's Wisdom is the interface between the *physics of the world* and the *metaphysics of creation*.[194] Since the physics of the world

---

[193] The Ryrie Study Bible: Notes on Prov.8: 22-31 p 949
[194] Schroeder The Hidden Face of God Chapter 5 p 88 b

is *the science of nature* and the metaphysics of creation is *the Science of God* (cf. Chapter 1/Maimonides), we can phrase this statement another way.

> *In the Onkelos translation of Genesis 1:1, "First Wisdom" Is the interface between the science of nature & the Science of God.*

We will add some additional complexity to this concept of *"The First Wisdom of God"* in Chapter 8 when the deeper meaning of the phrase: *"Then God said"* is discussed. When we reach that discussion (in Chapter 8 — of this Book), I will explain why I believe *The First Wisdom of God* in Genesis 1:1 was The Pre-incarnate Jesus Christ! However, before we go there, let's start building the foundation for our understanding of that essential concept.

ALL EXISTENCE EXPRESSES THE FIRST WISDOM OF GOD'S INTELLIGENT DESIGN.
ALL EXISTENCE IS THE HIDDEN FACE OF GOD.

Schroeder's book, *The Hidden Face of God*, is a masterful treatise on wisdom & existence. These two quotes from Dr. Schroeder are the essence of his book.

1. *"A single consciousness, an all-encompassing wisdom pervades the Universe. The discoveries of science, those that search the quantum nature of subatomic matter, those that explore the molecular complexity of biology, and those that probe the brain/mind interface, have moved us to the brink of a startling realization:* **All existence is the expression of God's Wisdom.** *In laboratories we experience God's Wisdom as information — first physically articulated as energy and then condensed into the form of matter.* [195](*) *Every particle, every being, from atom to human, appears to have within it a level of information — of conscious wisdom."* [196] (i.e., a finite fragment of God's First Wisdom — O. David).

2. **"Wisdom, information, an idea, is the link between the metaphysical Creator and the physical creation. First Wisdom is the Hidden Face of God."** [197]

INTELLIGENT DESIGN IS THE SINE QUA NON—OF THE FIRST WISDOM OF GOD.

As a lifelong Christian, and a physician, who walked the "Halls of Medicine" for forty years, I firmly believe this statement of David: *"For Thou didst form my inward parts; Thou didst weave me in my mother's womb. I will give thanks to Thee for I am fearfully and wonderfully made. Wonderful are Thy works, and my soul knows it very well (Psalm 139:13-14)."*

Many times, I have seen the evidence we are fearfully and wonderfully made. I have often witnessed the mighty hand of God in healing, and what I have learned about how the human body works, and how we are put together, has convinced me — **our bodies are the prima facie evidence of Intelligent Design.** Everything that exists is evidence that God's all-encompassing wisdom — *His First Wisdom* — does indeed *permeate and encompass* the Universe. Everywhere one looks: **The First Wisdom of God is manifest in His Intelligent Design!**

---

[195] (*) Energy & matter are two expressions of the same thing. This concept is introduced here & will be re-examined in Chapter Six.

[196] #1 above is a direct quote of Schroeder: *The Hidden Face of God Prologue xi* — with my parenthetical addition & my bolding.

[197] #2 above is a direct quote of Schroeder *The Hidden Face of God* taken from Chapter 4 p 49 c — with my bolding.

THE EVIDENCE OF INTELLIGENT DESIGN CAUSED A LIFE-LONG ATHEIST TO CHANGE HIS MIND & DECIDE THERE IS A GOD. Antony Flew (a preacher's son, and for fifty years, one of the world's foremost academic atheists) has recently renounced his former position and accepted the existence of God. For Flew, it is "the argument from design" that shows: *"The existence of God is probable!"* He has been impressed — by recent scientific developments, which suggest the universe is the product of Intelligent Design.

> *"It now seems to me that the findings of more than fifty years of DNA research have provided materials for a new and enormously powerful argument to design," explains Flew.*

Although Flew has not embraced Christianity (his father's faith), he now accepts the existence of God, saying he *"had to go where the evidence leads."* Flew also said Dr. Gerald L. Schroeder's book, *The Hidden Face of God,* and Roy Abraham Varghese's book, *The Wonder of the World: A Journey from Modern Science to the Mind of God,* are particularly impressive and played a major role in his change of mind.[198, 199]

⚜

SPACE, MATTER, TIME, & TIME-REFERENCE-FRAMES:
IT'S ALL RELEVANT & RELATIVE!

A turtle crawls into a police station and says: *"I've-been-mugged!"* The sergeant asks: *"By whom?"* The turtle replies: *"By a gang of snails!"* The Sergeant says: *"Tell me exactly what happened."* The turtle replies: *"I — don't — know! It — all — hap — pen — ed — soooooooo — f — a— s— t !"*

Although turtles and snails experience the same time-flow we do, I wonder if their perception of time-flow is different? Before Einstein, people thought *space, matter, and time* had fixed parameters, which never changed. For example:

- *Space*: An acre-foot of water is the same in Mississippi as it is in Minnesota.
- *Matter*: A pound in Victoria, Australia weighs the same as a pound in Victoria, B.C.
- *And Time:* A Belgrade minute is the same as a Brussels minute.

But Einstein said those things are only true — if they are '<u>in</u>' the same time-reference-frame.

ACCORDING TO EINSTEIN, TIME, MATTER, AND THE DIMENSIONS OF SPACE ARE EVER CHANGING AND ARE ALWAYS DEPENDENT UPON THE WAY IN WHICH THEY ARE OBSERVED.[200] He said:

"The same event, viewed from different time-reference-frames, will show different results that are specific for each time-reference-frame. It is all relative."

Uhmm — OK? What does that mean? The following example will help you understand this basic principle of The Law of Relativity. Let's look at how two people, in different time-reference-frames, perceive their speed of travel.

HOW OUR TIME-REFERENCE-FRAME INFLUENCES OUR PERCEPTION OF MOTION.

In the last chapter I talked about an example of a person on the ground watching an airplane flying through a clear, tranquil sky. Let's say that person is a man standing on

---

[198] Article: Antony Flew abandons Atheism—Former Atheist Believes in God
http://www.existence-of-god.com/flew-abandons-atheism.html
[199] Article: A review of 'How the World's Most Notorious Atheist Changed His Mind:'
http://anhonestdebate.com/2007/11/26/how-the-worlds-most-notorious-atheist-
[200] Schroeder The Science of God Chapter 10 p 162

the equator. So long as he is standing still, he thinks he is not moving. So, his perception of his speed of travel is zero mph. He is unaware he is actually spinning like a bullet at the rate of 1000 mph due to the rotation of the earth — and he is orbiting the sun at the rate of 72,000 mph due to earth's travel within its orbit around the sun — and at the same time, he is also rocketing along within our solar system as it orbits the center of the Milky Way Galaxy at the rate of 720,000 mph! His specific time-reference-frame controls his perception of all this motion.

The platform of his time-reference-frame is the inertial-reference-frame of a spaceship — the spaceship earth. Since he is standing still on the ground, he perceives he has no motion relative to the ground. Therefore, he is not aware of any motion because the platform on which he stands (i.e., the earth), is stable and is experiencing unaccelerated uninterrupted inertial motion as it travels through the vacuum of space at incredible speeds.

Like the man, we have all looked up and have seen the contrails of jet planes streaming overhead. All of us have followed the contrails to their origins and have seen airplanes jetting along as they produce their contrails. We know we are standing on the ground. We perceive we are motionless as we look up. We think we are not moving. But, since we are observing the airplanes from the ground, we are viewing them from an inertial time-reference-frame that is *outside of the* inertial time-reference-frames of the airplanes. Therefore, we are aware they are streaking along through earth's sky.

Now, suppose you are a woman who is on the airplane the man is watching. You and your airplane are also traveling through the space of the universe in the same spaceship the man is (i.e., the spaceship earth). However, for the duration of your flight (even though you will not perceive it), your speed of travel will be different from his. How? Let's see.

- Your airplane is flying from west to east at a speed of 500 mph.
- This means you are flying with the jet stream.
- This adds the speed of the jet stream to the speed of your airplane — meaning your airplane is traveling at 500+ mph. (The + represents the speed of the jet stream, which may vary at any specific point in time.)
- You are also traveling in the same direction the earth is rotating. This adds the rotational speed of the earth (1000 mph) to the speed of your airplane.
- Both are imperceptible to you because the sky is clear, cloudless, tranquil, and you are experiencing a smooth flight.
- Let's say you are reading a novel. You are focused on the novel, and you are not looking out of the window of your airplane. So, you will not be aware of the motion of other airplanes traveling in the opposite direction, or any landmarks you are flying over.
- Like the man on the ground, you are not aware of your speed of travel because you are experiencing the smooth unaccelerated uninterrupted inertial motion of the time-reference-frames of the earth and your airplane.
- Like the man on the ground, your perception of your speed is zero mph.
- And yet, you are also orbiting the sun, and rocketing along with the sun as our solar system orbits through the Milky Way Galaxy.

- All of this is happening simultaneously — at the same speeds as the man on the ground.
- What is the difference?
  - For the duration of your flight, you are rotating around the central axis of the earth at a combined speed of 1500+ mph (the rotation of the earth at 1000 mph, plus the speed of the airplane and the speed of the jet stream at 500+ mph).
  - That is 500+ mph faster than the man who is watching your airplane from the ground. Yet, all seems stable and motionless to you.

Who said: *"Women are not faster than men?"* (Silly, I know, but I couldn't resist it.)

I hope this example will help you understand: *Our time-reference-frame* determines *our perception* of the things we experience and the things we observe. That is why the same event (in this case an event involving the perception of the speed of an airplane), viewed from different time-reference-frames, will show *different results,* which are *specific* for *each time-reference-frame.*

In this example both travelers perceive they are motionless. The woman in the airplane is not focusing on any object outside of her time-reference-frame (i.e., her airplane). Therefore, she is not aware of any motion at all. However, the man on the ground is focused on an object that is outside of his time-reference-frame. He perceives the airplane is traveling faster than any other motion around him. *Both people are experiencing different time-flows.* However, *the difference* in their time-flow *is so infinitesimal* that humans *cannot perceive it.* Furthermore, the difference in the rates of time-flow of these two individuals is barely measurable. Since I have just mentioned time-flow, let's delve into that subject now.

ELECTROMAGNETIC RADIATION, RADIANT ENERGY, AND TIME-FLOW

Now let's talk about something which is even more astonishing. This subject has to do with the variations in *Time-Flow* that occur throughout the universe. However, the next example will involve differences in the rates of time-flow that are so vast, they will boggle your imagination! I will introduce the subject of *Time-Flow* here and will talk more about it in Chapter 5 (in this book). Now, hold on to your hat. This next example will explain how *the present* can turn into *Eternity*! However, the jump from the theological belief in a place where all existence is timeless (and therefore *Eternal*); to the realization that *an eternal existence is scientifically possible* — is so difficult to imagine — that I must first tell you the story of how man came to the realization of that theoretical possibility. This is a subject I am well acquainted with, because as a Radiologist, I used the *full spectrum of Electromagnetic radiant energies and ultra-sound and radio waves* in my practice of Diagnostic Radiology, Nuclear Medicine, and Irradiation Therapy. Those radiant energies and sound waves ranged from:

- The low energy soundwaves used in Diagnostic Ultra-Sound examinations—
- The low-energy x-rays used in Mammography—
- The variety of diagnostic & therapeutic radionuclides used in nuclear medicine—
- The intermediate energy x-rays used in Diagnostic Radiology x-ray films, angiography, and Computed Tomography (i.e., CT scans)—

- Magnetic Resonance Imaging (i.e., MRI scans), which pulsed radio waves through patients subjected to a magnetic field—
- To the high-energy penetrating Gamma Rays (γ) of Cobalt^{60} and Cesium^{137} & —
- The high-energy x-rays produced in an electron accelerator — when I treated patients with cancer.

TIME-FLOW VARIES THROUGHOUT THE UNIVERSE.

The study of Electromagnetic Radiation opened the doorway to our understanding that time-flow does indeed vary throughout the universe. The key to our understanding of electromagnetic radiation came from the study of the only form of electromagnetic radiation visible to humans — i.e., light. The man who enabled our understanding was Albert Einstein.

Albert Einstein's Theory of Relativity was so revolutionary that it completely changed our concepts of the universe and made sense of many seemingly contradictory observations of other scientists. It could be said, the trek to Einstein's understanding of the relationships between electromagnetic radiation, matter, time, time-flow, and the universe started with Johannes Kepler — in 1628!

KEPLER BELIEVED LIGHT HAS MASS AND EXERTS FORCE.

The comets that streak through our solar system are massive conglomerates of ice. Kepler observed the ice particles in the tails of comets were influenced by the Sun. When a comet is approaching the Sun, the tail of a comet trails behind it. But, when the comet passes and moves away from the Sun, its tail moves from the rear to the front of the comet and leads it! Kepler thought the change in the position of the comet's tail was the result of pressure exerted on it by the Sun. Since the tail is less dense than the main body of a comet, he thought solar radiation must blow the comet's tail away from the Sun. This was the first time anyone had suggested the radiant energy of light might also be associated with a mechanical pushing force.[201] Prior to Kepler, it had been assumed light was nothing more than substanceless energy. Kepler's observation was important because it meant light might also have some mass or weight.

JAMES CLERK MAXWELL—LIGHT TRAVELS AS WAVES MOVING AT A CONSTANT SPEED.

In 1864, and only a few months before the end of the American Civil War, James Clerk Maxwell suggested light and all other electromagnetic radiation moved through space as waves of energy — at a constant fixed speed.[202]

PLANCK'S QUANTA OF ENERGY AND QUANTUM MECHANICS

Thirty-six years later (in 1900), Max Planck got the idea that hot irons release their heat by shooting off hot particles of energy. He postulated these rapidly streaming tiny hot particles were actually radiant energy. He thought of them as particles or pellets, and he named them — *Quanta*. Thus, *the Theory of Quantum Mechanics was born*. So, Planck first thought the radiated energy of light behaved as particles do.

NICHOLS AND HULL PROVED KEPLER RIGHT.

In 1901, 273 years after Kepler (circa 1628), the pressure of radiant energy was actually measured by E. F. Nichols and G. F. Hull. They shined a powerful light on a mirror suspended in a vacuum and measured the deflection of the mirror caused by the

[201] Schroeder Genesis and the Big Bang Chapter 2 p 35
[202] Schroeder Genesis and the Big Bang Chapter 2 p 35-36

"pressure" of the light. Kepler was right. Light rays did exert "pressure." Therefore, light has both energy and mass![203]

LATER, PLANK BEGAN TO THINK MAXWELL WAS RIGHT—THE HOT QUANTA OF LIGHT MUST TRAVEL AS WAVES OF ENERGY. Plank observed — as an iron is heated — it first glows red. If heating is continued, the glow of the iron goes through a spectrum of color changes from red to white — the color of highest heat.[204] Therefore, Planck suggested the quanta emitted from a white-hot iron must have a greater amount of energy than those emitted by a red-hot iron. He had already suggested the quanta of heat coming off a hot iron behaved as particles do. Now, he began to think, the energy of an individual quantum of heated light was proportional to its frequency of vibration (a characteristic of a wave) — thus causing a quantum of light to move through space as if it were also a wave. Since it was also thought all radiation moved at the speed of light, Planck believed all quanta, irrespective of their energy, must also move at the speed of light.

THE PARTICLE-WAVE CONUNDRUM

The idea that Sunlight can influence the position of the tail of a moving comet gave birth to the idea that light waves can exert pressure and must therefore have some mass. The experiment, which measured the displacement of a mirror suspended in a vacuum by a powerful beam of light, definitely proved the theory — light waves do exert pressure and therefore — must have some mass. However, the idea that light has quanta (or particles) with mass, and yet acts as a wave caused a problem. Frequencies are associated with waves — not with particles. Additionally, the speed of light was thought to be always constant. But the idea that particles can have different energies implies the more energetic ones might have a greater pushing effect — a greater mass. If they were heavier, could that affect their speed? Wouldn't a greater weight slow them down? To this day, scientists are still searching for a cohesive theory, which will fully explain the phenomena of light and all radiant energy.[205]

ALBERT EINSTEIN, THE PHOTOELECTRIC EFFECT, & PHOTONS OF LIGHT

Einstein observed that light shining on certain metals created an electric current. A current of electricity is actually a flow of free electrons. But the electrons in metals are not free. They are 'bound' to the atoms of the metal. Therefore, Einstein suggested the light hitting the metals must have released some electrons from their electrical bonds to the metal's atoms and caused them to flow. He called this phenomenon the "photoelectric effect," and he began to think light was made up of units, which were composed of particles with mass (i.e., quanta), which travel through space as waves of energy. He called these units, "photons." Using Planck's theory of the quantum nature of light, Einstein postulated this photoelectric effect was the result of the photons of light colliding with the electrons in the metals. The mass of the quantum particles of the photons of light must have knocked some electrons out of their atomic orbits and caused them to flow in order to produce the electric current.

Einstein further postulated the photons of light (which travel at the speed of light) — have mass while they are in motion. But they lose their mass when they are stopped.

203 Schroeder Genesis and the Big Bang Chapter 2 p 35
204 Schroeder Genesis and the Big Bang Chapter 2 p 36
205 Schroeder Genesis and the Big Bang Chapter 2 p37

Therefore, a photon of light can act like a particle and a wave. While in motion, the photons of light can push things around, like the tail of a comet. Otherwise, light seems to act like a wave — having a frequency of vibration that is proportional to its energy. Thus, matter and energy appear to be intimately connected in this unique duality of the photons of light.[206] Einstein discovered this relationship and described it in his now famous equation: $E=mc^2$ where E is energy, m is matter (which has mass), and c is the speed of light. Einstein saw that matter and energy are intimately connected in the photons of light.[207]

> **This equation says energy and matter are two expressions of the same thing.**

MATTER FROM ENERGY AND ENERGY FROM MATTER

The primordial explosion that produced the beginning of the universe (i.e., The Big Bang) did not produce matter directly. It produced a pure, infinitely hot radiant energy of such a high level that matter was able to form from that energy. This transition is expressed by this equation. $E = mc^2$

The value of c^2 (the speed of light squared or multiplied by itself) is a huge number and implies even a tiny amount of matter contains a huge amount of energy, and therefore requires a huge amount of energy to form.[208] The amount of Energy in a lump of matter can be determined by multiplying the mass of the lump by the speed of light squared. The fact that both sides of an equation are equivalents tells us Energy can be transformed into Matter (with Mass), and Matter can be transformed into Energy. We will talk a bit more about this when we discuss what happened within the Singularity in The Beginning (See Chapter Six in this book).

THE CONUNDRUM OF THE SPEED OF LIGHT

However, what I want to emphasize here is — when something travels at the speed of light, the acceleration of an object at rest toward the speed of light, will increase its mass. The laws of physics tell us — if a man-made spaceship could be boosted to 90% of the speed of light, its mass would double. As it approaches the speed of light, its mass would increase precipitously. If it were to actually reach the speed of light, its mass would increase to infinity and so would the amount of energy required to move it to that point and maintain its speed.[209]

Man can build a spaceship. That spaceship will have a certain mass. But man has not yet discovered a source of energy that can boost the mass of a spaceship to infinity and maintain its travel at the speed of light. Man may never be able to build a vehicle that can travel at the speed of light. Oh, I suppose some brilliant physicists may have theorized a way to do this (through theoretical physics), but they haven't actually done it — *yet*.

The ability to travel faster than the speed of light has been imagined by people in the entertainment industry. In the movie Star Trek, when Captain Kirk gives the command to go to warp speed, his spaceship disappears in streaks of light! In the 1960s, I stood in a traffic island that was part of a pedestrian crosswalk in the middle of the Champs Elysees in Paris, France. I did that to take a timed exposure of the illuminated Arc de

206 Schroeder Genesis and the Big Bang Chapter 2 39-40
207 Schroeder Genesis and the Big Bang Chapter 2 p 40
208 Schroeder The Science of God Chapter 3 p 54-55 c
209 What if you traveled faster than the speed of light? By William Harris: www.science.howstuffworks.com

Triomphe at mid-night. What a magnificent sight that was! Traffic was heavy. I remember the sound and the wind from each car that buffeted me, as they sped by only a few feet away. However, the cars were not visible on the timed exposure. The film in my camera wasn't sensitive enough to record the presence of the cars in that low light environment. The only hint of their presence in my timed exposure was the streaks of light the film recorded. The cars moving toward me appeared as two continuous streaks of the white light, which came from their headlights. Those that were moving away from me were two streaks of red light, which came from their taillights.

Later, you will see the color Red (specifically, the "Red shift of light in space"), has a special significance and has greatly contributed to our understanding of the Universe.

So, the makers of Star Trek were able to demonstrate their concept of warp-speed in terms, which were meaningful because of our experiences with timed photography. However, the truth is — no one has found a way to travel at the speed of light — much less a way to travel at a rate that is greater than the speed of light! Later, in Chapter 7 of this book, and Chapter 9 (of Book II) when I talk about the Doppler Effect, you shall see how scientists have used the red shift of light from the stars in the universe to understand that the universe has been continuously expanding ever since that moment in Genesis 1:2c — "When the Spirit of God (i.e., 'The Wind' of God) hovered over the surface of the deep" — as some English Bibles say.

SUMMARY CONCLUSIONS ABOUT THE NATURE OF LIGHT:

Early on, scientists thought light was just a wave of energy. However, scientists have discovered light is composed of units. Einstein called those units **photons**. Science has found the photons of light have both **energy** (which travels in a wavelength with a frequency, which is proportional to their energy) — and **mass** (that science calls **particles** or **quanta**). Thus, the **photons of light** have a **dual nature**. They are particles (i.e., quanta), which have both mass and a vibrating energy. Einstein concluded that the photons of light are **quantum-particles**, which travel through space as waves of **energy**.

NAHMANIDES ON THE RELATIONSHIP BETWEEN TIME & MATTER

Nahmanides' insight that Biblical time grabbed hold with the appearance of matter was ingenious. Visible light rays, and invisible X-rays, Gamma rays, Alpha rays, Neutrinos, and all other forms of ionizing radiation — are forms of the broad spectrum of radiant energies we call electromagnetic radiation. Science has discovered electromagnetic radiation — i.e., all radiant energy — does not experience the flow of time. This is so important I must repeat it.

Radiant energy does not experience the flow of time!

What this means is: All forms of radiant energy, such as the light rays we can see, and all the invisible forms of electromagnetic radiation — **exist in a state in which time does not pass!** [210] Science has determined the fastest speed attainable in the universe is the speed of light. All forms of radiant energy travel at the speed of light. But light energy is the only radiant energy we can see. Science has discovered time-flow actually stops at the speed of light! [211] This is also so important: I must say it again.

---

[210] Schroeder The Science of God Chapter 3 p 56 c
[211] Schroeder The Science of God Chapter 10 p 162

> *Light travels at a speed, which stops Time-flow! Stated another way: If you could travel at the speed of light, no time would pass for you while you are traveling at the speed of light!*

A FLAWED EXPERIMENT

In 2011, a report by scientists at the CERN supercollider project in Switzerland revealed that one of the experiments they performed suggested neutrinos could travel faster than light! That suggestion made headline news and the famous TV and print-journalist, Charles Krauthammer, wrote a column about it. As it turned out, the experiment was flawed. The erroneous initial findings were the result of a faulty oscillator and a faulty fiber optic cable connection.[212] Once those faults were corrected, scientists concluded it is still true:

> *Nothing in the universe travels faster than light!* Unfortunately, the news of the flawed experiment did not make headline news.

WHEN TIME STANDS STILL

We are now getting close to understanding how scientists think the belief in an eternal existence is theoretically possible. People of faith believe God made it possible. So, what follows is not that important to those who have faith in God. I am only saying the following might be useful to believers if they are confronted by skeptics who deny the existence of God. I'm not saying this is how God did it! I'm just saying this is how God might have done it! The only constant in the entire universe is the speed of light. Science has discovered the speed of light through the vacuum of space is 186,000 miles per second! Einstein theorized and later experiments proved:

> *The faster one travels relative to another object; the slower time flows for a traveler relative to the flow of time measured by a stationary observer.*

This is part of the old Theory of Relativity again. This is also kind-of-like the previous example of the man on the earth and the woman on the airplane — except for the major difference that the speed-event in this example is infinitely greater. At the speed of light (the highest speed attainable in our universe), time ceases to flow altogether! The time of all events becomes compressed into the present, an unending now — an eternal now — i.e., Eternity! Thus, if we could somehow travel at the speed of light — time for us would stop!

> *During our journey at the speed of light, no time would pass for us!* [213]

So, in the example in the last chapter of a trip from earth to Andromeda, two million earth-years would have passed on earth during the trip — but for the people in the spaceship (traveling at the speed of light), time would have stopped, time would have stood still, and their time-flow would have been compressed into an unending now — an eternal now — a never ending Present! When they reach Andromeda, they will not have aged at all, not even by one trillionth of a second (i.e., not even a picosecond)! However, the speed of light travel is not attainable for us — not in our current state — for our bodies are confined to the time-reference-frame of our earth, which is controlled by all the physical laws of the universe.

---

[212] Article: Einstein can Rest Relatively Easy: by Jordan Cotler 3/20/2012: www.usnews.com/news/blogs
[213] Schroeder The Science of God Chapter 10 p 162

The photons of light, which are produced in the stars, travel great distances through the vast domains of space to reach us. During their flight, the photons of light increase their mass to infinity. At the same time, the energy of the wavelengths of light also increases to infinity. The relationship between the energy and mass of the photons of light change in such a way, that somehow the speed of light through the vacuum of space, is not diminished! It does not slow down! It remains constant![214]

> **This is the paradox of light. Man cannot figure out how to do this. *But God has! God "created" and "made" it that way!***

Almost every month, astronomers (i.e., the watchmen of our night skies) are detecting the arrival of the first photons of light from distant stars, which were born many billions of years ago — before the creation of our sun and the creation of our earth. Earth's astronomers are charting the locations of these 'new' stars in our night skies as soon as they are discovered. Those photons of light have been traveling for billions of years at the constant rate of 186,000 miles/second across the vast domains of space to reach us. They have remained intact during the billions of years they have journeyed to reach us, and those beams of light, which do not impact with our earth, will continue their journey after they have passed us. They will continue on their journey into infinity with their energy and their mass still intact and unabated.

> **So, the First Wisdom of God has created light photons that travel at a never-ending constant speed. They are the fastest things in the universe — so fast that their speed stops time-flow!**

As you will see (in Book II, Chapter 9), the sources of universal light (the stars) are not indestructible. They will eventually exhaust their supply of fuel and burn out. When they do, the light they make from their location in the night sky will go out. But the light rays they produced are infinite for as long as they travel through the vacuum of the space-time-continuum. During their journey, they will experience — a timeless existence so long as they continue onward in their journey through the vacuum of space. Those photons that illuminate each new distant point will cease to exist at the moment they illuminate something they hit when their motion is stopped.

ETERNITY — FROM A THEOLOGICAL CLAIM TO A PHYSICAL REALITY

The Bible says Heaven is eternal — i.e., a domain in which time does not pass — a domain where time stands still! Through our study of light, we now know the Laws of Relativity have changed the concept of a timeless existence from a theological claim into a possible physical reality.[215] This actually means — Heaven exists! "Heaven is for real!" (cf. Appendix III, in Book III). I wonder — Does the time-reference-frame of Heaven travel at the speed of light? I believe God will explain it to us when we arrive in Heaven where we will experience "Eternity Future" with Him (cf. Eternity Past, Eternity Present, & Eternity Future, in Chapter 10 of Book II). Nevertheless, we now know, the Laws of Relativity say: "Heaven is possible." But only God could have created it (O. David)!

Although we have been told about the Laws of Relativity, the concepts are something we have a great deal of trouble understanding. This is because, in our current state, the matter in our earthly bodies is intertwined with our God-breathed spirit and

[214] Schroeder Genesis and the Big Bang Chapter 2 p 34-44
[215] Schroeder The Science of God Chapter 10 p 162a

therefore all our existence within our earthly bodies is within the time-flow that is specifically related to our earth. What we experience is completely related to our material world. In the abstract, the concept that time grabbed hold when matter formed is something we can't touch or see or truly understand. The idea that time-flow stops at the speed of light, is something we cannot comprehend in our current state. But the relativistic physics of Einstein's Laws of Relativity say it is true.

> **And yet, generations of human experience _do_ testify to the truth of Nahmanides' time-matter-concept — because everybody knows — when the matter of our earthly bodies formed, earth-time grabbed hold of us, and our time on earth began!**

Summary Points:
- In the beginning of creation, with First Wisdom, God created, Space, Matter, Time, the universe at large, and our home — the earth. In short, in the beginning, God created everything that exists and will ever exist.
- God's thoughts and ways are higher than ours.
- Wisdom came from God and is older than creation — older than the heavens and the earth.
- Wisdom was God's master workman, assisting Him in His creation.
- In the beginning, God's First Wisdom was first articulated as energy, and later condensed into the form of matter.
- The universe is the product of Intelligent Design.
- Every particle, every being, from atom to Adam, appears to have within it a level of information, of conscious wisdom.
- Wisdom, information, an idea, is the link between the metaphysical Creator and the physical creation.
- The First Wisdom of God in the Onkelos translation of the Hebrew Bible is — the Hidden Face of God.
- At the speed of light, time-flow stops — there is no such thing as _'time.'_ At the speed of light, all existence is compressed into an unending present, which becomes _'an eternal now.'_
- The Laws of Relativity have changed the concept of timeless existence from a theological claim to a possible physical reality.[216] This is something the Bible has said about God for the past 3300 years.

THE CREATOR IS ETERNAL! LIGHT EXISTS IN A STATE IN WHICH TIME DOES NOT PASS! THE CREATOR CLOAKES HIMSELF IN THE ONLY THING HE CREATED WHICH IS ALSO "TIMELESS!"

ALL UNBELIEVERS SHOULD TAKE A SERIOUS LOOK AT THESE BIBLE VERSES.
- _"Bless the Lord O my soul! O Lord my God, Thou art very great. Thou art clothed with splendor and majesty, covering thyself with light as with a cloak: Stretching out heaven like a tent curtain. (Psalms 104:1-2 NASB)._
- In the English translation of the Aramaic Bible, Psalms 104:1-2 says: _"He is covered in light like a cloak. He has stretched out Heaven like a curtain."_

---

[216] Schroeder The Science of God Chapter 10 p 162a

131

How appropriate — "God, the Eternal One" (who exists in a state in which time does not pass), "cloaks Himself with Light," which He created to exist in a state in which time does not pass! This is how He must have appeared to Moses (cf. Ex. 33:18-23; 34:5-6 & 29-35).

Here is what I Timothy 6:16 (New International Version — NIV) says about God and light:

- *"He alone is immortal and dwells in unapproachable light. No one has ever seen Him, nor can anyone see Him."*
- In the New American Standard Bible (NASB), Job 9:8 says: *"He alone stretched out the heavens, and treads on the waves of the seas."*
- The NIV of Psalm 18:12 says: *"Out of the brightness of His presence clouds advanced, with hailstones and bolts of lightning."*
- The NIV of Isaiah 40:22 states: *"He sits enthroned above the circle of the earth…He stretches out the heavens like a canopy, and spreads them out like a tent to live in."*
- Isaiah 45:12 (NASB) declares: *"It is I who made the earth and created man upon it. I stretched out the heavens with My hands, and I ordained all their host."*
- And Matt. 17:2 proclaims: *"And He (Jesus), was transfigured before them, and His face shone like the sun, and His garments became white as light."*
- In Revelations 21:9-27 and 22:1-5 the Apostle John describes the "New Jerusalem." Verse 21:23 says: *"And the city has no need of the sun or of the moon to shine upon it, for the glory of God has illumined it, and its lamp is the Lamb."* In 22:5 he says: *"And there shall no longer be any night; and they shall not have need of the light of a lamp or the light of the sun, because the Lord God shall illumine them; and they shall reign forever and ever."*

We have seen the Laws of Relativity have changed our belief in the possibility of a timeless existence from a theological claim to a possible physical reality — but not something man can do — something only God can do! Believers should understand this means—

- ***Light and all radiant energies exist in a state in which time does not pass!***
- ***Heaven is real!***
- ***Nothing is impossible for God!***

✣
CHAPTER 4: ELOHIM—CREATION EX NIHILO—A GRAIN OF MUSTARD & DIVINE TZIMTZUM

"The 1st hint of the Trinity is in the 1st verse of the 1st Chapter of the 1st Book of the Bible." O. David

"The basic principle of Biblical Religion is 'Creation from Nothing!' " Maimonides

"Elohim created everything that exists from nothing." Nahmanides

ELOHIM

The third word in the Hebrew Bible is Elohim (also spelled Elokiim). The number three has special significance. In Judaism, it is the symbol of holiness. Elohim is the name Moses wrote for The Creator in the first verse of his first book of the Torah. This name for God is uniquely Hebrew. It is not found in any other Semitic language.[217, 218] Scholars tell us Elohim means "the strong one, the mighty leader, the supreme leader." Note the three-fold definition. They also tell us the form of the word is plural, greater than two, indicating plentitude of power and majesty — allowing for the New Testament revelation of the Doctrine of the Trinity.[219] English has two noun forms, singular and plural. However, Hebrew has three noun forms — singular (one), dual (two), and plural (greater than two).[220] Christians, and Jews who believe in the Jewish Jesus (Jeshua), believe the greater than two plurality of Elohim, is the first hint of the Trinity given in the Bible. This hint is given in the very name of God Moses used for the Creator. There it is, in the very first verse of the Bible. We'll talk about the Doctrine of the Trinity in Chapter 23 (in Book III). When we do, we'll also discuss Judaism's opposition to the doctrine, but right now, I want to concentrate on what Moses says God did in the beginning — Elohim CREATED!

CREATION EX NIHILO—CREATION FROM NOTHING

The second word in the Hebrew Bible is the word Moses used for created. That word is barah, which means, to create from nothing. Maimonides said: *"He who does not believe in this and thinks the heavens and the earth have existed forever denies the essential and basic principle of biblical religion."* [221]

Elohim's creation of all that exists from absolutely nothing is at the root of biblical faith. To create from nothing is something only Elohim can do. Aristotle obviously knew nothing about Elohim.

ASA & YASAR

In the first two chapters of Genesis, there are two other words Moses used for the creation activity of God. They are asa, which means, "to make from some pre-existing substance," and yasar, which means, "to form from some pre-existing substance."[222] Later, in our study of the Creation Account, we will see when God instructed Moses to use these

---

[217] Article: Hebrew Names of God: Copyright John J. Parsons www.hebrew4chrisrians.com/
[218] Article: Elohim: www.theopedia.com
[219] The Ryrie Study Bible: Note on Gen. 1:1
[220] Billy Graham The Holy Spirit Chapter 1 p 8 c
[221] Schroeder Genesis and the Big Bang Chapter 3 p. 62 d
[222] The Ryrie Study Bible: Notes on Gen 1:1 refer to Elohim's creative activity in Gen. 1:25 when He made (asa) the beasts of the earth (from the already created earth which He created from nothing), and in Gen. 2:7 when He formed (yasar) man from the dust of the ground (the dust having also been created from nothing).

words. However, in Genesis 1:1, the word Moses used for Elohim's creation of the heavens and the earth was — barah — meaning God's initial creation—was from nothing.

As has been previously stated, the precision of each ancient Hebrew word God inspired Moses to use when he wrote the creation account conveys the deeper meaning of the Biblical Account of God's Creation Activity. This defining quality of the Hebrew language is something I have already referred to as *"The Genesis Code."* We have just added four more words to its lexicon — Elohim, barah, asa, and yasar.

APPLYING THE GENESIS CODE TO GENESIS 1:1

The first three Hebrew words of Genesis are: Be'reasheet barah Elohim. English translations simply state: "In the beginning God created..." but the Genesis Code conveys the deeper meaning:

In the Beginning of Creation, with First Wisdom, the Strong One, The Supreme Leader, The Almighty God created the heavens and the earth from nothing (Gen. 1:1 The Genesis Code). *O. David*

Our modern language translations only convey the simple first layer of meaning of the Hebrew Bible and miss the mark by a wide margin. For this reason, many nonbelievers think the Biblical Account of Creation is a laughable, simple child's tale. They do not take it seriously. They treat it casually and dismiss it as a fantasy or myth. As we shall see, nothing could be further from the truth.

THE "BET"

In the previous chapter, I introduced a discussion of the significance of the first letter in the Hebrew Bible — the "Bet" — and said it leads us to "the First Wisdom of God." In this chapter, I want to talk about what two men discerned about the bet. One was a famous 15th Century sculptor and artist — Michelangelo, who was familiar with Kabbalah.[223] The other was a famous 13th Century Jewish Kabbalist — Nahmanides. We'll start with Michelangelo.

MICHELANGELO'S JONAH FRESCO OCCUPIES THE MOST PRESTIGIOUS SPOT IN THE CEILING OF THE SISTINE CHAPEL.[224] Placed directly above the altar, the Jonah fresco was the last fresco Michelangelo painted. It is also the largest and most imposing. Jonah appears to be three-dimensional! His legs dangle out of the ceiling over the altar. His head leans back and upward as though he is peering into the sky above the chapel. God commanded Jonah to go to the sinful pagan capital city of the Assyrian empire to deliver God's message of condemnation and His command for repentance. Jonah didn't want to go to Nineveh, and boarded a ship, which was sailing in the opposite direction. God caused a horrendous storm at sea, and a great fish swallowed him. Three days later, the fish regurgitated Jonah out onto a beach. Jonah then obeyed God and went to Nineveh to fulfill God's command. After one day of preaching, the Assyrians and their king repented! The message of the book of Jonah is: "Although God judges the world (both Jews and

---

[223] *Kabbalah*: the ancient Jewish tradition of *mystical interpretation of the Bible*, first transmitted orally and using esoteric methods (including ciphers) — it reached the height of its influence in the later Middle Ages and remains significant in *Hasidism* (which is a fundamentalist form of Judaism, that opposes the *rigid academicism of rabbinical Judaism*). Maimonides and Nahmanides were 12th and 13th Century Kabbalists.

[224] *The Sistine Secrets* by Benjamin Blech & Roy Doliner: *The Jonah panel:* Understanding the Hidden Messages: p. 226-232

Gentiles) — God does not want any nation or people to perish. That's why God sends us messengers to warn us we must turn from our sins."

THERE ARE THREE HIDDEN KABBALISTIC SECRETES IN MICHELANGELO'S JONAH FRESCO. According to the authors of the book: *The Sistine Secrets* by Benjamin Blech & Roy Doliner, the Sistine Chapel is full of covert Kabbalistic symbols, which Michelangelo painted into the ceiling frescos. The various nude figures convey hidden messages from the artist. From the positions of their extremities and fingers, to the positions of their bodies, one can imagine the outlines of the letters of the ancient Hebrew alephbet. In the Jonah fresco:

1. ***Jonah looks up toward God*** — not down to the altar where Pope Julius II sat during a service. Jonah (yo-NAH — in Hebrew) means: *"God will answer."* Jonah also means *"Dove."* In Christianity, the dove symbolizes the Holy Spirit. Michelangelo's message from Jonah's upward gaze is: *"The Holy Spirit was not present in the Sistine Chapel when Julius II was the Pope."*

Jonah's upward gaze (toward God) means:

225

The Holy Spirit was not present in the Sistine Chapel when Julius II was Pope.

2. ****Jonah's hands are contorted to form the bet*** (ב), **which means "house of God."** This was meant to convey — **we must allow God to find a home in our midst.** Christians believe our body should be a holy temple for God. We must keep our bodies free from sin. Michelangelo contorted Jonah's hands, turning them backward, to form the bet. The contortion creates a symbolic confusion of right and left. Michelangelo's secrete message is — *A nation that can't tell its right from its left is a nation that has blurred the line between right and wrong, good and evil, and is a nation that has gone astray.*[226] **Michelangelo thought Julius II and his uncle Sixtus IV (who commissioned the Sistine Chapel) were corrupt popes who served mammon rather than God (cf. Matt. 6:24).**

---

[225] Jonah Fresco image courtesy of: "Public Domain Images of the Sistine Chapel."
[226] I sometimes think this has happened to us.

Jonah's Hands form the Bet (ב)—"The House of God."

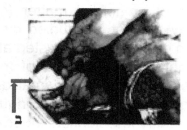

3. ***The great prophet's legs form the Hebrew letter, he'*** **(ה)**, for "*five*" — **symbolic of the Five Books of Moses,** which comprise the first 5 books of the Hebrew Bible and the Christian Old Testament Bible. The 5 books of Moses (*also known as the Torah*) are the original key to understanding our link to our Creator. **The Hebrew Torah is the common root between Judaism and Christianity.**

Jonah's Legs form the He' (ה)

The Torah is the common root between Judaism and Christianity.

NAHMANIDES AND HIS TINY GRAIN OF MUSTARD—THE SINGULARITY:

We have already seen, ancient Hebrew is read from right to left, and the opening words of the ancient Mosaic text of Gen. 1:1 look like this — בראשית ברא. In the Introduction to his Commentary on Genesis, Nahmanides deduced:

"Elohim created everything that exists from nothing."

He came to this conclusion from the meaning of the Hebrew word *barah*, and the shape of the first Hebrew letter in the Bible, the *bet*. To us, the bet (ב) looks like a backward written block letter "C." Since the bet is closed on three sides — above, below, and to the right (i.e., to the past) — Nahmanides concluded the events that preceded or led up to the beginning of creation, are beyond the reach of man's knowledge and discovery. However, since the bet is open to the left (i.e., to the future), he reasoned the events that followed the moment of the beginning of creation, could be and would eventually be discovered by man.[227]

MODERN SCIENCE AGREES WITH NAHMANIDES.

According to modern science, the most credible current theory of our beginning is The Big Bang Theory. Scientists who are currently working on the assumptions of The Big Bang Theory believe the moment of the Beginning involved the creation of a tiny Black-Fire speck-of-space, which was created by an immense explosion of unimaginable magnitude. Scientists have determined what was created in that minuscule speck-of-space was — an infinite amount of primordial matter. Scientists call that tiny Black-Fire

---

[227] Schroeder Genesis and the Big Bang Chapter 3 p. 56 b and p. 57 a

speck-of-space — The Singularity.[228] They have concluded: What preceded the appearance of infinite amounts of primordial matter (compacted into the tiny finite primeval space of the Singularity) cannot be studied by man — because none of the scientific laws, which now govern our existence, existed at that moment.[229]

The Singularity existed only for the briefest of moments (a few trillionths of a second), as a tiny speck-of-space of unimaginably small dimensions, containing infinitely high density, and an infinitely high temperature. The Singularity existed in such a state of extremes that science cannot quantify it. Scientists theorize the Singularity contained all the energy and the substrate from which everything in existence today — would be *made* and *formed*.

Nahmanides thought Elohim caused the greatest explosion in the history of the universe. His description of the tiny space the explosion created was his way of describing the tiniest speck-of-space he could imagine. He said it was: *"No larger than a grain of mustard."* He believed — *"At the instant of the beginning, all that is on and within the earth and all the heavens (in fact the entire universe), was somehow packed, compressed, squeezed into an extremely small chaotic speck-of-space that was no larger than a single grain of mustard."*[230]

If you take a single tiny mustard seed and hit it with a hammer, you will see just how small a "grain-of-mustard" is.

MODERN SCIENCE AGREES WITH NAHMANIDES.
- Agrees there was a beginning—
- Agrees about what was created at the moment of the beginning—
- Agrees man can never know what existed before the beginning—
- And agrees man would be able to discover what happened after the beginning.
- However, unlike Nahmanides, science has no clue as to what caused the Big Bang.[231]

TZIMTZUM & THE FIRST PICOSECONDS (TRILLIONTHS OF A SECOND) OF CREATION: Nahmanides believed the beginning moment of Creation was a Divine Act of Tzimtzum. Tzimtzum is a Divine contraction, a spiritual withdrawal of the Creator.[232] Tzimtzum is something only Elohim can do. The ancient sages deduced the concept of Divine Contraction, i.e., the spiritual withdrawal of the Infinite One (Elohim), from Isaiah 45:5-7:

"I am Jehovah, and there is none else: there is no God except Me...forming light and creating darkness; making peace and creating evil. I, Jehovah, do all these things. (The Interlinear Bible)

When the Infinite Source of Light contracts/withdraws — darkness is created. When the Infinite Source of Peace (shalom, from the root shalaim meaning whole, complete), withdraws — evil (which the ancient Hebrew sages defined as "a lack of perfection and completeness") — is created.

The ancient Jewish sages reasoned, the only act of Biblical Tzimtzum to ever occur, happened (in Genesis 1:1). When Elohim contracted, the physical complexity of

[228] Schroeder Genesis and the Big Bang Chapter 1 p. 24 d & Chapter 3 p. 66 a, b
[229] Schroeder Genesis and the Big Bang Chapter 3 p. 57—58 a
[230] Schroeder Genesis and the Big Bang Chapter 3 p. 65 b
[231] Schroeder Genesis and the Big Bang Chapter 3 p. 63 b,c,d
[232] Schroeder The Science of God Chapter 1 p. 16-17

the universe with its laws of nature emerged.[233] Before the moment in which Elohim created (in the eternity of Elohim), nothing existed but Elohim. Then, Elohim suddenly contracted. He removed a small part of His Infinite Unity and an explosion of extreme proportions occurred. This pulling back by the Eternal yielded the physical space for creation — for existence. At that moment, His contraction created an entity so thin it had no substance to it. It was the only physical creation to ever occur, and all there would ever be — was concentrated within that tiny speck of space. Nahmanides said it was about the size of a "Single Grain of Mustard." Father Lemaitre called it: "the Primeval Atom." Modern Science now calls it: "The Singularity." All agree: That speck of space was the entire universe when it first appeared! As the universe expanded from the size of that initial minuscule speck — the primordial substanceless substance, which filled that tiny speck of space, changed into matter, as we know it. Nahmanides said:

"With the first appearance of matter, time grabbed hold" [234]

Summary Points:

- Elohim is the first name for God in the Bible.
- Elohim is plural, greater than two, allowing for the New Testament revelation of the Trinity. The 2nd word in the Bible is *barah*. *Barah* means, *"to create from nothing."* Maimonides said: *"He who does not believe in this and thinks the heavens and the earth have existed forever denies the essential and basic principle of biblical religion."*[235]
- Nahmanides' agreed with Maimonides, and also concluded the deeper meaning of the Hebrew script of Genesis 1:1 tells us — *"In the beginning Elohim created all from nothing"* — (Creation Ex Nihilo).
- With his understanding of the Genesis Code meaning of *barah*, and from the shape of the first character (the *bet*, or ‫ב‬) of the first word of Genesis 1:1, Nahmanides concluded:
  - The bet is the first letter in the Hebrew Bible, because it is the letter that leads us to the First Wisdom of God!
  - Bet means: *"House of God."* We must allow God to find a home in our midst.
  - If we invite God into our earthly home, He will prepare a home for us in heaven.
  - The Bet is closed to the past — therefore, man can't discover what happened before the beginning.
  - The Bet is open to the future — therefore, man can discover what has happened after the moment of the beginning.
  - The cause of the beginning was a *Divine Tzimtzum*.
  - That act of Divine Tzimtzum involved a divine contraction/a spiritual withdrawal/ a pulling back by the Eternal.
  - Elohim's Tzimtzum caused the greatest explosion ever.
  - That explosion created an entity so thin it had no substance to it.

---

[233] Schroeder The Science of God Chapter 1 p. 16-17
[234] Schroeder The Science of God Chapter 3 p. 56 b
[235] Schroeder Genesis and the Big Bang Chapter 3 p. 62 d

- o This pulling back by the Eternal yielded the physical space for creation. The physical space Elohim created in the beginning was a tiny space the size of a grain of mustard.
- o That tiny grain of mustard-sized speck of space contained a primordial substanceless substance that was the primeval 'stuff' of all that ever would be created in the universe.
- o As the universe expanded, the primordial substanceless substance in the tiny grain of mustard-sized speck of space — changed into matter.
- o With the first appearance of matter — time grabbed hold.
- Michelangelo's painting of Jonah's *contorted* formation of the bet means: *"A sinful nation has lost its way — and can't tell right from wrong."*
- Modern Science doesn't know what caused the explosion in the beginning, and cannot attribute the beginning to God, or even prove God exists.
- However, science agrees with Nahmanides on all other points and calls the greatest explosion in all history, *The Big Bang.*
- Science now calls Nahmanides' *'grain of mustard,'* which was created by the Big Bang — *the Singularity.*
- Nahmanides' concept of *Elohim's Divine Tzimtzum* comes from the deeper meaning of the Hebrew word, *barah,* and his Genesis Code interpretation of Isaiah 45:5-7.

THE GENESIS CODE MEANING OF GENESIS 1:1

In the beginning of creation, by a minute degree of Spiritual Contraction (Tzimtzum), and with First Wisdom, The Strong One, The Supreme Leader, The Almighty God, Created the heavens and the earth from nothing.[236]

O.David

FROM ADAM TO NOAH — TO ABRAM — TO JOB — TO THE AMORITES — TO NINEVEH — TO THE CROSS: God walked with Adam and Eve in the Garden. Adam and Eve disobeyed God. Paradise was lost.

God reached out to Noah. Noah preached the Gospel to his neighbors, and warned of the coming flood, but they rejected his God. Noah built the Ark God commanded. The Flood caused a mass extinction of life. But Noah's family was saved, repopulated the world, and kept the Gospel of God alive.

God reached out to Abram, who responded. Abraham became the father of the Jews. They were known in the ancient world as: "The people of the Book." We have their "Bible," so we know their story. But we don't know the particulars of exactly how Abram came to know God. The Bible is not explicit about what happened before God spoke to Abram in Genesis 12:1. In a dream, God told Abram of the future enslavement of his people in Egypt for 400 years — "for the iniquity of the Amorites is not yet complete" (Genesis 15:12-16). When the iniquity of the Amorites was "complete," Abram's people would be delivered from slavery. We intuit God had been reaching out to the Amorites

[236] From now on, when you see the phrase: "The Genesis Code meaning" — the phrases that follow will be my rendition/interpretation, which is meant to convey the deeper meaning of the original Mosaic Hebrew text in Modern English. In the formulation of my interpretations, I have carefully and prayerfully followed the advice of Maimonides (See: THE ADVICE OF AN ANCIENT JEWISH SAGE: in INTRODUCTION—PART VIII).

just as He had reached out to Adam, Noah, and Abram. But, for 400 years the Amorites refused to listen to God.

We also don't know the story of how Job came to know God. We just know he was the priest of his family. We are not given Job's genealogy, but since he is not in the genealogy of Abram, we intuit he must have been a Gentile. Yet, "the God of the Jews" reached out to him and Job responded.

Talmudic rabbis felt the story of Jonah reminds us God judges the whole world — not just the Jews! No one can hide from God! Those who follow God must never give up on unbelievers because repentance is always possible. Furthermore, repentance is always accepted by God, even at the very last moment. God does not desire for any person or nation to perish. If they turn from their unbelief and repent, God will forgive all. Jonah was the one Old Testament prophet God chose to preach to the gentiles — i.e., the sins of Nineveh.

Finally, God gave Jesus Christ to the Jews as the ultimate sacrifice for the sins of the world. The Jewish Priests and Sanhedrin judged Him, demanded His death, and the Romans crucified Him. Christ's sacrifice was fulfilled. Christ's disciples spread the gospel to the Jews, and Paul preached the Gospel of Jesus Christ to the Gentiles. In these ways, the Gospel has been kept alive.

GOD HAS BEEN REACHING OUT TO THE ENTIRE WORLD (JEWS & GENTILES) SINCE ADAM.

CHAPTER 5: THE TIME CONUNDRUM: SIX DAYS OR 15 ¾ BILLION EARTH-YEARS?

"Ah! I think your Moses shall have been a fool!" (The King of Siam)

THE KING'S QUESTION

My favorite musical movie is the very popular 1956 Rodgers and Hammerstein production, *The King & I,* starring Yul Brynner (as the King of Siam), and Deborah Kerr (as Mrs. Anna), based on the novel, *Anna & The King of Siam* by Margaret Landon. My favorite scene begins in Anna's bedroom. She is peacefully sound asleep. In the wee morning hours, the King's servants awaken her with persistent knocking on her door. Mrs. Anna is informed the King has summoned her. She hurriedly dresses, and puts on a beautiful, modest, lacy-white gown. Her skirt is billowing outward, supported by the giant hoops beneath. Hurriedly entering the King's room, she finds him clothed in regal red accented with interweaves of gold. Not only is he barefoot, but he is also lying prone on the floor. Wearing an imposing pair of horn-rimmed glasses and peering at a gigantic open Bible, his majesty appears to be in deep, serious, studious contemplation of the text. As part of his charade, he ignores her; even though it is obvious he is aware of her presence. Finally, after a few moments, Anna speaks.

Anna: *"You sent for me your Majesty?"*
(There is a long silence because the King continues his charade of deep contemplation.)

Anna speaks again: *"Oooh. Your Maajesty is reeeading The Biiible."*
(Anna draws out her words to give emphasis.)

The King finally replies: *"Ah! I think your Moses shall have been a fool!"*

Anna: *"Moses?"*

The King: "moses, mo**oses, MOOSES!** *I think he shall have been a fool! Here it stands written by him. The world was created in six days! Now you know & I know it took many ages to create world! I think he shall have been a fool to have written this at all! What is — your — opinion?"*

Anna: *"Is that why your Majesty sent for me at this time of the night?"*

The King: *"That is not reason — but first I wish to discuss Moses. Now how can I ever to learn truth — if different English books — say different things?"*

Anna: *"Your Majesty, the Bible was not written by men of science, but by men of faith. It was their explanation of the miracle of creation, which is the same miracle whether it took six days or many centuries."*

The King rises and begins pacing around Anna. He suddenly stops, ponders for a second, and says: *"**I still think your Moses shall have been a fool!**"*

The King then sits and proceeds to dictate a letter to be sent to Mr. Lincoln of America, who is "very scientific ruler." He proposes sending several pairs of male elephants as a present, advising Mr. Lincoln they should be turned loose in the wilds of America to reproduce, so America may have its own supply of these magnificent beasts of burden.

Anna questions his proposal. *"Male elephants, your Majesty?"* (She says.)

This wonderfully delightful scene plays out with the King insisting Mrs. Anna's head never be higher than his. As he gradually lowers his head by slowly changing to a prone position, Anna is gradually forced to lie prone on the floor, all the while trying to manage her giant-hooped skirt as she writes the King's letter. While this is happening, the King continues to ignore her question about sending only male elephants to breed.

When he finally realizes his blunder, he suddenly springs to his feet, folds his arms over his chest, and in a loud voice, and with great bravado **the King says:**

"You fill in details. Etcetera! Etcetera! Etcetera! Good night!"

What a masterful musical! Truly wonderful, and immensely popular and successful! And Yul Brynner — what a magnificent performance! Only Yul Brynner — with his bald head, his bare feet, and his regal manner — could have pulled off the role of the King of Siam the way he did! He made me think: "If Yul Brynner really isn't the King of Siam — He should be!"

ONLY SIX DAYS?

The King of Siam's problem with the Genesis Creation Account is common to us all. The Genesis account gives God only six days to create the universe and everything in it, including the earth and us. Yet, current cosmology claims and indeed has proved it took 15 ¾ billion earth-year equivalents to accomplish the same thing. **From our earth**, the age of the universe has been measured using several independent methods, which include radioactive isotope dating, Doppler shifts in starlight, and a more recently discovered method that can determine the temperature of the Black of Space by measuring **C**osmic **M**icrowave **B**ackground **R**adiation (now known as **CBR**). Since the methods of these studies are totally unrelated, if an error had occurred in one measurement, one would not expect it to appear in the others. Yet the data taken from these diverse studies presents a strong and scientifically consistent argument for a very old earth and an even older universe.[237]

WHICH IS CORRECT—THE BIBLE OR COSMOLOGY?

Is it six days as Moses claims, or 15 ¾ billion earth-years, as cosmology argues? Strange as it seems, both are correct — literally![238] Six days of 24-hours each of 'God's Time' elapsed between 'The Beginning,' (that speck-of-time at the start of The Big Bang), and the appearance of mankind. Simultaneously it took some 15 ¾ billion earth-year equivalents (each year composed of 365 earth-day equivalents, each one of which literally contained twenty-four earth-hours), to get from 'The Big Bang' as astrophysicists call it, to mankind.[239] We are not talking about simple explanations such as calling each day of Genesis 2.5 billion years, so that 2.5 x 6 = 15 billion earth-years of cosmology. Neither is the consideration they are one and the same any attempt to change the functioning laws of nature.[240] Perhaps it is a good thing Mrs. Anna did not try to explain that conundrum to the King, even though it is doubtful she would have known the answer

[237] Schroeder Genesis and the Big Bang Chapter 2 p 28 a
[238] Schroeder Genesis and the Big Bang Chapter 2 p 29 b & d
[239] Schroeder Genesis and the Big Bang Chapter 2 p 29 b
[240] Schroeder Genesis and the Big Bang Chapter 2 p 29 b

in her day and time. The laughable example of the several pairs of male elephants for breeding purposes suggests — he is a character who is careless with his facts. The answer lies in what science refers to as 'Stretching Time,' and 'Time Dilation.' It has to do with time-flow and the specific reference-frame in which the flow of time is being measured.

GOD'S 'TIME' IS DIFFERENT.

So, how can six days be stretched to encompass 15 ¾ billion earth-years? Stated another way, how can 15 ¾ billion earth-years be squeezed into six days? The Bible gives us the hint this is possible.

"A thousand years in Your eyes are as a day that passes in the night."(Psalms 90:4 NASB)

"With the Lord, one day is as a thousand years and a thousand years as one day."
(II Peter 3:8 NASB)

These scriptures tell us God's perspective of time is different from ours. Deep within these scriptures is the truth — the six days of Genesis actually did contain the billions of earth-years of the cosmos — even while the days remained twenty-four-hour days. Long before the discoveries of modern science, ancient commentaries on the Torah definitively state, the Six Days of Genesis were twenty-four hours each, the total duration of which was the same as the six days of our workweek.[241] They also added: Those six twenty-four-hour-days contained all the secrets and ages of the universe.[242]

To understand the concept God's time-flow is different from ours requires us to consider, time-flow is not constant. That is, each of those distant stars in the night-sky has its own unique clock, each one different from the other, and each one different from the clock of our earth. Until Adam appeared on the 6th day, God alone was watching the clock, and that is key.[243] In Chapter 25 (in Book III), you will see — God reset the earth's clock on the 7th Day so — that very first Sabbath and all future earth-days would be different from The Six Days of Old.

THE UNIVERSE IS OLDER THAN THE EARTH.

In Chapter Seven, when Genesis 1:2 is discussed, you will see the Bible says: "The earth was not formed and was void." Yet, creation had already begun. Dr. Schroeder says:

"During the development of our universe and prior to the appearance of mankind, God had not yet established a close association with the earth. For the first one or two days of the six days of Genesis, the earth didn't even exist! Although Genesis 1:1 says: 'In the beginning God created the heavens and the earth,' the very next verse says, 'the earth was void and unformed.' The first verse of Genesis is a general statement meaning that in the beginning, a primeval substance was created, and from this substance the heavens and the earth would be made during the subsequent six days. This is explicitly stated later in Exodus 20:11, and 31:17: 'For six days God made the heavens and the earth.' From what were the heavens and the earth made during these six days? From the substance created in the beginning of those six days. Because there was no earth in the early universe, and no possibility of an intimate tie or a

---

241 Schroeder The Science of God Chapter 3 p 43 b, c
242 Schroeder The Science of God Chapter 3 p 43 c
243 Schroeder Genesis and the Big Bang Chapter 2 p 49 c

> *blending of the reference frames, there was no common calendar between God and the earth."* [244] *(A direct quote)*

EINSTEIN ON TIME-FLOW

The science of the concept that time-flow varies from place to place throughout the universe comes from Einstein's Laws of Relativity. Einstein demonstrated — when a single event is viewed from two separate frames-of-reference, a thousand or even a billion years in one frame-of-reference could indeed pass for one day in another. Einstein's Laws of Relativity tell us dimensions in space and the passage of time are not absolutes. Their measurements are an intimate function of the relationship between the observer and the observed. This is that old time-reference-frame concept again. To us, it seems incomprehensible that the flow of time, and dimensions in space, which are so constant in our daily lives, can actually change. However, they can, and they do.[245] It all depends upon the frame-of-reference.

TIME DILATION—SLOWING TIME-FLOW

Einstein discovered the rate at which time passes is not the same at all places in the universe. Each reference-frame in the universe (whether it is a star, a planet, an asteroid, or a comet), has its own unique time-flow. What are the primary determinants of time-flow? The gravity and the velocity of travel through space are the determining factors. The flow-of-time on a planet or a star with high-gravity or a high-velocity of travel — is slower than another planet or star that has a lower-gravity or lower-velocity of travel through space.[246] (Generally, the larger the planet, and the faster its orbital speed — the greater it's gravity.) This means the rate at which time passes (the rate of time-flow) is inversely proportional to the product of the gravity and orbital velocity of the reference-frame in which the flow-of-time is being measured. The ticks of a clock or the beats of a person's heart, which are recorded in a low-gravity, low-velocity system — become slower and farther apart when that clock or that person is transported to a high-gravity, high-velocity system. In the higher gravity-velocity environment, the rate at which time flows actually slows down! The phenomenon of slowing time-flow is called — Time Dilation.[247]

THE 'KEYSTONE KOPS' ANALOGY FOR TIME DILATION

Perhaps a theoretical example could be helpful. Suppose you were magically transported — say by one of those transporters on one of those Star-Trek spaceships — to a planet so large that its gravity alone, or the combination of its gravity and the velocity of its travel through space, slowed the flow-of-time by a factor of 350,000 relative to the earth's rate of time-flow. Theoretically, during the time three minutes would take on your new planet — two years would pass on earth.

Suppose you could, by looking through an immensely powerful telescope, be able to observe your family you left behind on earth. Their motion when they walked would look incredibly fast, perhaps even jerky — like those funny old movies that showed the Keystone Kops in motion.

[244] Schroeder Genesis and the Big Bang Chapter 2 p 49 d & 50 a
[245] Schroeder Genesis and the Big Bang Chapter 2 p 34 b
[246] Schroeder The Science of God Chapter 3 p 47 c
[247] Schroeder The Science of God Chapter 3 p 47 d

Now, after three minutes on that huge planet, suppose Dr. Spock energizes you again in his transporter and instantly returns you to the earth. Your family would have aged two years, but you would have aged only three minutes. Why? Because in this example, time-flow is slower on the larger planet by a factor of 350,000 relative to the earth's time-flow. Three minutes passed on the enormous planet where you were due to its higher-gravity and higher-velocity environment. During those three minutes — two years of time would have passed on the earth while you were away. The earth's lower-gravity and lower-velocity of travel through space would have caused earth's time-flow to be faster by a factor of 350,000 relative to the larger planet with the higher-gravity and higher-velocity.[248] Remember, the rate at which time passes (speed of time-flow) is inversely proportional to the gravity and velocity of the reference-frame in which the flow-of-time is being measured. It's part of Einstein's Laws of Relativity.

THERE ARE MANY AGES OF THE UNIVERSE.

Each planet, each star, in fact each location within the universe has its own gravity, its own velocity of travel through space, and therefore, its own unique light-wave frequency and its own unique rate of time-flow.[249] A complete understanding of this concept will be necessary for a full comprehension of what follows. Scientists have confirmed enough of these differences to understand this concept is valid for all points throughout the universe. Visible light originating from all the stars of the universe has the same physical properties. That is, the visible light coming to us from the stars in all points of the universe is the same entity, the same phenomenon, no matter where the star is located. In other words — light is light. However, the stars are the stellar clocks of the various locations within the universe because the wavelength of each star's light is unique due to the differences in each star's gravity and its velocity of travel within its orbit. Therefore, each stellar clock ticks at its own unique rate. The frequencies of light waves (i.e., the wave lengths of light) emanating from each star are the timepieces of the various locations of those stars within the universe. Since the wavelength of the light generated in each star is unique, there are as many places in the universe with its own unique time-flow as there are stars in the sky.[250]

STRETCHING LIGHT WAVES & SLOWING TIME-FLOW

To understand this phenomenon, let us consider the light that comes to us from our sun — our sunlight. Our sun is larger than our earth. Its speed of travel through space is also different. Its light is generated in a higher gravity-velocity environment than the lower gravity-velocity environment of our earth. Careful measurements of the wavelengths of sunlight which reach us have discovered the waves of sunlight are stretched by a factor of 2.12 parts-per-million relative to the light-waves that are generated here on earth (i.e., a fire, an electric light, or the chemically produced glow of a firefly). This stretching means the rate at which sunlight reaches us is lowered by a factor of 2.12 parts per million. For every million earth-seconds ticked off by earth-clocks, the sun's clock would lose 2.12 seconds relative to our earth-clocks. These 2.12 parts per million equals 67 seconds per earth-year, exactly the amount predicted by the Laws of Relativity.[251] Thus, we can see

[248] Schroeder The Science of God Chapter 3 p 48-49
[249] Schroeder The Science of God Chapter 3 p 49 d
[250] Schroeder The Science of God Chapter 3 p 50 a
[251] Schroeder The Science of God Chapter 3 p 50 b

there are any numbers of different ages for our universe, each being correct for the location at which the measurement is made. Theoretically, there could be other locations in the universe, which are so much larger than our earth, and with gravity-velocity parameters that are so much greater, where a clock could tick so slowly — that "a thousand years in Your eyes," as the Bible puts it, (or even a billion or more of our years) could pass, while their clocks recorded only — "a day." [252] This statement is also key to understanding what follows.

IF IT WERE ONLY THAT SIMPLE! STELLAR CLOCKS ARE NOT THE ANSWER!

Up to this point, the visible light we have been talking about is an excellent way to study the age of each light source in the universe. What we have been talking about so far are the Stellar-Clocks (i.e., the Star-Clocks) of the universe. They are accurate in telling us the age of each source of light. However, if we wish to have a full understanding of the complexities of time-flow throughout the universe, we need a clock that will measure the entire universe — a cosmic clock as it were — which would encompass the entire creation.

COSMIC MICROWAVE BACKGROUND RADIATION (CMBR OR CBR) — THE UNIVERSAL 'COSMIC' CLOCK: There is one source of radiant energy, which has been present since the beginning — since the creation of the universe. Arno Penzias and Robert Wilson discovered that source in 1965. They named it Cosmic Microwave Background Radiation, or CBR. CBR is the remnant, the echo as it were, of The Big Bang. It is ubiquitous. It fills the universe because it was caused by The Big Bang and was distributed throughout the universe as the universe expanded. As you shall later see (in Chapter 7), when we discuss when the Holy Spirit acted in Genesis 1:2c, The Holy Spirit initiated the expansion of the universe. (I want to say here that both the Hebrew and Greek words for "Spirit" also mean "Wind!" Therefore, the Holy Spirit can rightfully be called — "the Wind of God" in English — or a "Ruach Elohim" — in Hebrew.) The expansion, which the Wind of God initiated, was the moment cosmic radiant energy began to cool. CBR was infinitely hot in the beginning — so hot that science cannot put a number on it. However today, the expansion of the universe has cooled CBR so much that the current temperature of CBR is a frigid -270 degrees Centigrade (2.73° K above absolute zero ° Kelvin). CBR is now the accepted basis of so-called Cosmic Proper Time because it is the only parameter, **we can measure from the earth** that relates to the entire universe!

Our earth-made measurement of CBR is our Biblical clock of GENESIS ONE!

This is so important for us, I will have to remind you of this again, after I have discussed the two CBR measurements that have been recently made in space — by space probes.

> As you shall see, the CBR measurement **we have made from the earth** is still influenced by the gravity of the earth and its velocity of travel through space. This fact is of critical importance to us because **the measurement of CBR, which has been made from our radio-telescopes on earth — is the scientific proof that the Bible's Account of Creation is infallible!** We must also recognize, the measurement of

---

[252] Schroeder The Science of God Chapter 3 p 50 c

> *Cosmic Proper Time that we make from our earth does not replace the time-flow of each star in the universe. It augments it.[253]*

DARKNESS IS THE BLACK OF SPACE.

The physics of what scientists have learned from CBR is outside the scope of this book. For those of you who wish to delve into it, there are any number of textbooks on Astronomy and Cosmology that will explain it in a formulaic way. For our purposes, suffice it to say: The discovery and study of CBR has enabled scientists to determine the frequency and temperature of radiant energy in the universe at the actual moment primordial matter transformed into the first true matter! It is not a value extrapolated or estimated from conditions in the distant past or far out in space. It is measured right here on earth in the most advanced physics laboratories and corresponds to a temperature approximately a million-million times hotter than the current temperature of the Black of Space — which is now a frigid 2.73 degrees Kelvin.

> *At the moment true matter formed, Cosmic Microwave Background Radiant energy had a frequency and temperature, which was a million-million-times (10^{12} to 1) hotter than the CBR energy of today. This tells us the measurements we have made from our earth of the amount of stretching and cooling of CBR, which was initiated by the Holy Spirit, and caused the universe to expand — has slowed the universal cosmic-clock of the universe from its initial rate at the moment of the beginning, to its present-day rate by a factor of a million-million-to-one! This is a solid value in physics and is a true measurement that represents a correct value from the standpoint of our earth. It is a correct value from the time-flow reference-frame perspective of our earth.[254] This measurement reflects the influence of our earth's gravity, and its velocity of travel through our solar system. That is why measurements of the age of the universe, which have been made from our earth, and look backwards in time from the present, are expressed in terms of earth-year equivalents. From a practical viewpoint, from our perspective — using earth-based clocks running at a rate determined by the gravity-velocity environment of our earth — we measure a 15 ¾-billion earth-year age of the universe. That is the correct age of the universe from our local perspective. The Bible also adopts this perspective, but only for times after Adam.[255] This means the time-reference-frames of each of The Six Days of Creation were very different from the time-reference-frame of our earth today. Our current-day time-reference-frame was established the moment Adam was created. Because Elohim changed earth's time-flow when Adam was created — We now experience the same time-flow Adam did. This will be explained in Chapter 25 (in Book III).*

A NASA MEASUREMENT OF CBR MADE FROM SPACE

A different age of the Universe has been determined by measurements made in space by a NASA launched space probe, which provides us with a more universal representation of cosmic proper time. On November 21, 2011, using a space probe named the Wilkinson Microwave Anisotropy Probe (or WMAP): NASA reported the probe

---

[253] Schroeder The Science of God Chapter 3 p 53 b and Chapter 4 p 61 c
[254] Schroeder The Science of God Chapter 3 p 57 d, e and Chapter 4 p 61 c
[255] Schroeder The Science of God Chapter 3 p 58a

has mapped the Cosmic Microwave Background Radiation (or CBR) of the universe and produced the first fine-resolution 0.2-degree full-scale microwave map of the universal "sky." WMAP data has determined the age of the universe to be 13.73 billion years old, with a standard deviation of ± 137 million years.[256,257]

A MORE RECENT EUROPEAN SPACE PROBE MEASUREMENT

On 03/21/2013 an announcement from Paris reported a more recent measurement of the age of the universe, which has been determined from the European Planck Space Telescope, named for Max Planck, the German Theoretical Physicist who originated the Theory of Quantum Mechanics. The Europeans claim the Planck data is a bit more sensitive than NASA's WMAP data and reports the universe is 0.08 billion (i.e., 80 million) years older or 13.81 billion years old.[258] Although both space probes have reported data obtained from space, the Planck data suggests the cooling of the universe since *The Big Bang* has not been uniform, as previously thought. Some feel this raises the possibility *something* may have existed *before* our universe. Scientists will now puzzle over that question. Believers in God think we know the answer!

CBR MEASUREMENTS MADE BY SPACE PROBES, **ARE NOT IMPORTANT TO US!** From a theoretical viewpoint, the CBR measurements of time-flow that NASA and the European Space Agency (ESA) have made, serve as true universal cosmic clocks. But because their measurements were made in space, they are **not** influenced by the gravity and velocity of travel of any planet or star. Like our earth-influenced CBR measurement, space-probe measurements of CBR are also clocks that look backward in time to the moment of creation and reflect results that can be applied to the entire universe. However, so far as the earth and we are concerned, their fatal flaw is the so-called 'purity' of their measurements. They lack what I call "point-specific relevance to us." Those measurements that NASA and ESA have made in space have absolutely no specific relevance to us because they lack the time-flow influences that the speed of travel of our earth through the universe and its gravity exert on us. Let me now explain.

We now have two CBR ages of the universe determined from space that say the universe is 13.73 billion 'years' old (NASA—2011), and 13.81 billion 'years' old (ESA—2013). Although those space measurements express time in terms of years, 'those years' cannot really be considered equivalent to 'earth-years.' They are not affected by any earth-related factors because they were made in the vacuum of space.

However, we do have a CBR age of the universe that has been determined from telescopes made and located **on earth** that says the universe is 15 ¾ billion earth-years old. Does this mean that our 15 ¾ billion earth-year age of the universe is wrong?

No! The 15 ¾ billion earth-year age of the universe remains valid for us because it reflects our earth-oriented time-flow perspective. It truly reflects time in units of earth-years! Our 'earth-bound' CBR measurement has validity for us because it measures time-flow in the units of time we have all experienced — that is, in the same earth-year

[256] Article: Wilkinson Microwave Anisotropy Probe (WMAP)—NASA: http://map.gsfc.nasa.gov/
[257] Article: NASA's WMAP Project Completes Satellite Operations. http://www.nasa.gov/topics/universe/features/wmap-complete.html
[258] Article: Planck Space Probe Boosts Big Bang Theory—The Hindu: http://www.thehindu.com/sci- tech/science/planck-space-probe-boosts-big-bang-theory/article4534097.ece

> *units of time-flow the earth has experienced, and "man" has experienced since the moment Adam was created!*

Some will argue, the discrepancy between the space probe data and our earth-influenced data proves their claim The Big Bang Theory is wrong and supports their belief it was invented to discredit the Biblical Creation Account.

On the other hand, there is no question all three sets of data affirm the most startling first statement of the first verse of the Bible — **there was a beginning!** It can also be argued: All three measurements confirm the basic tenets of The Big Bang Theory, such as the immense explosion that started it all, and the sudden expansion that took place shortly thereafter, which Nahmanides and the Bible attributed to the Holy Spirit. So, there is no question our earth-bound measurements of CBR, and the space-probe-data corroborate:

- The universe is very old.
- Creation began with a massive explosion.
- That massive explosion created a tiny finite speck of infinitely chaotic space.
- Since the beginning of time the universe has been ever racing outward in an inertial expansion.

As we will discuss in the next chapter, an ancient Jewish sage, Nahmanides, described his concept of the beginning, which he formulated from his interpretation of the deeper meaning of the Mosaic Hebrew text of Genesis One. As you shall see, Nahmanides' description of the events of the beginning reads like a modern-day physics textbook description of The Big Bang Theory. Furthermore, when the WMAP and ESA data analysis is complete, we will know more about such matters as the density of the universe, the shape of the universe, and we will possibly know more about dark matter and dark energy.[259]

OUR EARTH-MADE MEASUREMENT OF CBR IS OUR BIBLICAL CLOCK OF THE 1ST CHAPTER OF GENESIS! The 15 ¾ billion earth-year CBR measurement of the age of the universe, which has been made from earth, is a more meaningful and relevant age of the universe for us than the 13.73-billion-year NASA-age or the 13.81-billion-year ESA-age of the universe determined from measurements made in space. Why? Consider that, regardless of who you believe wrote the Creation Account in our Bible — that account — was either written by a man (Moses), or some other men who were living on earth when it was written.

It is the earth's Creation Account. It is our story. Our planet earth is the only planet in the vastness of the entire universe to which the Creation Account in our Bible has any relevance.

> **THE BIBLE'S CREATION ACCOUNT IS OUR STORY — THE PROOF**
> *What proof do we have of this? Consider, Genesis One, Exodus 20:11, and Exodus 31:17 tell us God created the universe, our earth, and all that exists in Six Days. Now consider our earth-made CBR measurement tells us, since the first true matter formed, the radiant energy of the universe has been stretched by a factor of a million-million-to-one. Our earth-made CBR measurement is the only measurement of CBR that can give*

---

[259] The Wilkinson Microwave Anisotropy Probe: http://hyperphysics.phy-astr.gsu.edu/hbase/astro/wmap.html

us our million-million-to-one ratio in the perception of universal time-flow.[260] Unless another identical parallel universe exists somewhere, the statistical possibility is vanishingly small there could be any other location in the universe where a CBR measurement would yield the exact same result! Our million-million-to-one ratio in the perception of universal time-flow means:

- *While our earth-influenced cosmic clock records the passage of one minute of time-flow in the black void of space — The earth experiences the passage of a million-million-minutes!*
- **Now, here's the kick. When you divide our 15 ¾ billion earth-year age of the universe by the million-million-to-one ratio that our earth-bound CBR measurement gives us—**
- **The 15 ¾ billion earth-year age of the universe—**
- **Is reduced to the Six Days of Creation that are mentioned in Our Biblical Creation Account! [261]**
- **That is the 'proof of our pudding' so to speak!**
- *If you try dividing the space probe ages by the earth-influenced million-million-to-one ratio,*
- *You will get an erroneous number of days that will have nothing to do with our earth and therefore, nothing to do with our Bible's Creation Account!*
- **Now you can see how our earth-made measurement of CBR proves the accuracy of our Biblical Account of Creation!**

THE BIBLICAL CALENDAR: [262]

Two things about the description of time in the Bible can be deduced with certainty.

1. There are two distinct time-reference-frames in the Book of Genesis.
   - The first six days were very different from our current days and were in a time-flow that was God-based — each of those six days being 24-hours of God's time.
   - Time after Adam is earth-based and is the same 24 hours per day we experience today. Archaeology proves this. There are several archaeological discoveries in the post-Adam period that have been studied by methods, which have established age by isotopic radioactive decay. These very closely match the dates derived from the Biblical Calendar for the same events. Some of these are:
     o The Early Bronze Age,
     o The beginning of writing, and
     o The Battle of Jericho.
2. Elohim reset the clock of the earth the moment He made Adam. Adam's time, and all earth-time, thereafter, would be very different from the time-flow of the Six Days of Old. This will be fully explained in Chapter 25 (in Book III).

[260] Schroeder The Science of God Chapter 4 p 61 b
[261] Schroeder The Science of God Chapter 3 p 58 a,b,d
[262] Schroeder The Science of God Chapter 3 p 50d & 51a,b,c

DR. SCHROEDER SAYS there are no indications of any Biblical Time Dilation after Adam. He also said no possibility exists for Day One and most of the 2nd Day of creation to have a meaningful earth-based time-reference-frame we can relate to — because the earth did not exist for the first two of those six days.

The Duration of the Six Days of Genesis [263]
The Earth-Year Perspectives in this Chart Reflect CBR Earth-influenced data.

From God's (the Bible's) perspective looking forward in time from the start of Day One.	From the Earth's perspective looking backward in time from the Present.	Approximate years before Adam at the start of each day.
Day 1: 24 hrs God's-Time	8 billion earth-years	15 ¾ billion earth-years ago
2nd Day: 24 hrs God's-Time	4 billion earth-years	7 ¾ billion earth-years ago
3rd Day: 24 hrs God's-Time	2 billion earth-years	3 ¾ billion earth-years ago
4th Day: 24 hrs God's-Time	1 billion earth-years	1 ¾ billion earth-years ago
5th Day: 24 hrs God's-Time	½ billion earth-years	¾ billion earth-years ago
6th Day: 24 hrs God's-Time	¼ billion earth-years	¼ billion earth-years ago
Six 24 hr. days God's-Time	Total: 15 ¾ billion Earth-Yrs.	Days Before the Present

For those of you who want to know how the duration of each of the Six Days of Creation were calculated in terms of earth-years, see APPENDIX I (in this book).

Summary Points:
- The Bible says God created the Heavens and the earth in six days.
- Using different scientific methods (which we will refer to as 'earth-based clocks'), all running at a rate determined by the conditions of today's earth — science says creation required 15 ¾ billion earth-year equivalents to go from the Beginning to the creation of Adam. Man has been on earth only ~5,700 earth-years. Just a tiny "drop" in the bucket of earth-time.
- Both the Bible and Science are literally correct.
- The Six Days of Genesis actually did contain the billions of years of the cosmos. Each of those 'Six Days of the Ancient of Days' represented 24-hours of God-related time-flow. They were very different from what we experience today.
- That is because God's Time-Flow is different from ours.
- The stars (i.e., the stellar clocks) tell us time-flow varies throughout the universe.
- The universe is older than the earth.
- For the first one or two days of creation, the earth did not exist.
- God began forming the earth on the *2nd & 3rd Days* with His 1st separation of the waters.
- The Biblical Calendar is divided into two parts — the first six days of creation and the ~ 5,700 earth-years thereafter. Remember: The 7th Day of creation was the 1st 24-hour earth-day and was the beginning of our present-day time-flow, which started ~ 5,700 earth-years ago with Adam.

[263] Schroeder The Science of God Chapter 4 p 60 (Table) The Six Days of Genesis

- Cosmic Microwave Background Radiation (CBR) is the 'Cosmic' clock. It is a 'universal' clock that is tuned to the cosmic radiation present at the actual moment in the beginning when true matter formed.

- Today, using our measurements of CBR (made from earth), the CBR clock ticks a million-million-times more slowly than it did in the beginning. This is due to the million-million-to-one ratio of the stretching of the electromagnetic wave energies that were created in the Beginning, which was caused by the expansion of the universe and the concomitant cooling that resulted. Expansion, stretching, and cooling of the universe were all started by the Wind of God in Genesis 1:2c. This one-time phenomenon (the Wind of God, which was the Holy Spirit — the Holy Ghost — or the Ruach Elohim — in Hebrew), will be discussed in Chapter 7 in this book.

- From our local perspective (using earth-based clocks), the age of the universe has been determined by several independently different scientific methods to be 15 ¾ billion earth-years old.

- When one divides the 15 ¾-billion earth-year age of the universe by the earth-determined million-million-to-one ratio of CBR cooling that has occurred since the Beginning — those 15 ¾ billion earth-years are reduced to the Six GOD-based Days of Creation the Bible claims.

- Time before the creation of Adam is "God-based."

- Time after the creation of Adam is "earth based."

TWO ADDITIONAL EXAMPLES OF BIBLICAL TIME DILATION

Dr. Schroeder has stated there is no mention of any Biblical time dilation after Adam. However, there are at least two times I can think of when the Bible says God altered time-flow on earth after Adam. The 1st example was a judgment of God. The 2nd example was *a temporary stay* of a judgment of God.

THE 1ST EXAMPLE: GOD'S JUDGMENT OF "THE INIQUITY OF THE AMORITES" —

The first example of time dilation occurred when God decided: The iniquity of the Amorites had been completed. "Amorites" refers to all the Canaanites in Palestine, whose sins God had been tolerating. What happened? After the Exodus, and during Israel's conquest of Canaan, God commanded Joshua to destroy the Amorite coalition at the Battle of Gibeon in the valley of Aijalon. In answer to Joshua's public prayer God stopped the sun and moon for an entire day (Joshua 10:12-14)! God did this so that the Amorite forces could be destroyed. Why? Because in Abraham's time, God had been patient with the Amorites. He gave them 400 years to repent of their sins and change. But because they refused to do so, their time for judgment had come, and God used the Israelites under Joshua to execute that judgment. To gain some insight to this difficult, enigmatic story from Old Testament times, we need to review what happened in Abraham's time—more that 400 years earlier.

Chapter 14 of the book of Genesis tells the story of an earlier major war that took place during the lifetime of Abram that happened before God changed his name to Abraham. When that war broke out, Abram was living in Hebron by the oaks of Mamre ("the Amorite"), who lived west of the Dead Sea in the central highlands of southern

Canaan about halfway between Mount Moriah and Beer-sheba. Mt. Moriah was the place (in ~ 2,000 BC) that God sent Abraham to make a sacrifice offering of his son, Isaac.[264] It is also the site where (~ 1,000 years after Abraham's time) David built His City of David, which later became Jerusalem. Furthermore, Mt. Moriah is the place where (~ 1,000 years after David's time and ~ 2,000 years Before the Present), Jesus Christ was crucified. So, approximately 4,000 years Before the Present, Abram (the Hebrew)[265] was an ally of some Amorites who had given him permission to camp among them at a place that was a 3-day journey south of the "Land of Moriah."

Genesis 14 tells the story of four allied kings who lived in the north (in current-day Syria, Iraq, and Iran), who warred against five kings who lived in the Valley of Siddim, which was in the southernmost part of the Dead Sea Valley, in the land of Canaan. For 12 years, the kings in the Valley of Siddim had paid "tribute" (i.e., taxes) to Chedorlaomer, King of Elam — an area that was later Persia (i.e., Iran). But in the 13th year, they rebelled and refused to pay. In their war of retribution against those who rebelled, the four allied kings from the "north" also battled and defeated the Raphaim, the Zuzim, the Emim, the Horites, and the Amorites that they encountered along their route as they invaded south into the land of Canaan. The kings of the Dead Sea Valley were also defeated and Abram's nephew (Lot), and his family (who lived in Sodom) were enslaved and taken to an area that was just north of the land of Canaan.

Abram pursued Lot's captors with 318 men born into his household who were old enough to go to war. When he overtook them, he successfully conducted a surprise night-attack against Lot's captors, routed them, and pursued their fleeing armies to Hobath, north of Damascus (in current-day Syria). Abram recovered the loot that had been taken, and he freed Lot and all the people who had been captured and returned them to their homeland.

Upon his return from his defeat of Chedorlaomer and his allies, Abram was greeted by the King of Sodom in the King's Valley (also known as the Kidron Valley and/or the Valley of Shaveh). That valley separates Mt. Moriah from the Mount of Olives (where the Garden of Gethsemane is located). The King of Salem, Melchizedek ('the Priest of the Most High God'); who lived in his city on the southern slope of Mt. Moriah — served them bread and wine and invoked his blessings on Abram. Abram paid a tithe of 10% to Melchizedek and returned the rest of the recovered goods to the King of Sodom. Abram's military success made him an instant celebrity in the eyes his Amorite allies. Although Abram had been peacefully living among the Amorites in southern Canaan, his people were spiritually at risk because they were being exposed to Amorite pagan religious practices.

In Genesis 15: "a deep sleep, and a dream of terror, and darkness fell upon Abram." In his dream, God told Abram the day would come when his descendants would move to Egypt and be enslaved there "until the iniquity of the Amorites had been completed (Gen. 15:16)." But Egypt would be punished, and Abram's descendants would come away from Egypt with great wealth. The Genesis story of Joseph explains how (many years later),

---

[264] When Abraham demonstrated his determination to obey God, God stayed his hand and provided a substitute ram for sacrifice (as a type of Christ Jesus—cf. Gen. 22).

[265] A Ryrie Study Bible note on Gen. 14:13 says Abraham was the 1st person to be referred to as a *Hebrew* — an ethnic name derived from the name of his ancestor Eber (Gen. 11:14)

the Israelites moved to Egypt in a time of great famine. At first, they lived separately from the Egyptians in the region of the Nile delta and were protected by the Pharaoh that knew Joseph. But after the deaths of Joseph and his Pharaoh, things changed, and the Israelites were enslaved for 400 years — until the iniquities of the Amorites in Canaan had been completed. From what God said in Abram's dream, we discern God had been reaching out to the Amorites but had been rejected. God is long suffering and patient but will not hold his wrath forever. God had given the Amorites 400 years to change their ways and turn from their sins, but they refused to change. So, the question is: What were the iniquities of the Amorites? The answer is in Chapters 18-20 of the Book of Leviticus, where God says Israel shall not commit the sins of Egypt (where they were slaves) and Canaan (the land to which they were going Lev. 18:3). The iniquities of the Amorites in Canaan fell into 10 basic categories of sins — all forbidden by God.

- [1]Worshipping false gods and idols—
- [2]Marrying foreign wives who worshipped false gods—
- [3]Participating in the licentious religious sex-rites and sex-sins of the Amorites—
- [4]Sacrificing children to false Amorite/Canaanite Gods—
- [5]Defilement of oneself by consulting mediums, and wizards—
- [6]Telling lies, falsehoods, sowing dissention among brothers — [7]Cheating — [8]Coveting — [9]Envy — [10]Robbing & Thievery — all behaviors forbidden by God.

Do any of these forbidden sinful behaviors sound familiar to you today? Leviticus is especially harsh about sacrificing children. Burning children on a pagan altar of sacrifice, was a type of ancient Amorite/Canaanite abortion. It was the way they got rid of their unwanted children that were the result of their licentious sex behaviors.

The entire context of Joshua's invasion of Canaan in the Book of Joshua is one of God's judgments of the Amorites and Canaanites for all their iniquities. Much the same as God would later use the Assyrians and the Babylonians to inflict judgment on the Israelites of the Divided Kingdoms of Israel for their adopted Amorite-like behaviors — in Joshua's time, God used the tribes of Israel to drive the Amorites out of the Land of Canaan because of their iniquities. However, Israel failed to drive all the Amorites away. The Amorites and Canaanites were not innocent, nor were they ignorant of the God of Israel. They had heard about but rejected Israel's God.

I remember kneeling in the Garden of Gethsemane on my first visit to the Holy Land. That is the place where Jesus prayed for the cup to be removed from Him—"Yet not my will, but thine be done"—He prayed (Luke 22:42). Jesus was in such agony that He sweated blood! "Blood sweat" happens when extreme anxiety causes adrenalin levels to surge and rupture the capillaries in sweat glands. Modern Medicine calls it "hemohidrosis." God sent an angel to strengthen Jesus. I was overwhelmed by my thoughts of that night when my Lord Jesus was arrested in that Olive Grove by a cohort of Roman soldiers (300 to 600 soldiers). As I was kneeling at the foot of an ancient Olive tree, I looked up toward the West. There, across the Kidron Valley, which separates the Garden of Gethsemane from Jerusalem, I saw the Temple Mount, which stands on Mt. Moriah. The Temple Mount is crowned by the golden Dome of the Rock (Islam's 2nd most sacred site), and the dark Dome of the Al-Aqsa Mosque nearby (which is Islam's 3rd most sacred site). Muslims believe their Great Prophet Muhammad was transported from Islam's most sacred site (the Great Mosque of Mecca) to al-Aqsa during his night journey. Just below the façade of the Dome of the Rock I saw the Golden Gate of the Temple Mount through which Christ triumphantly entered the city on Palm Sunday — only 5 days before he was arrested. The Golden Gate is the only eastern-facing gate on the Temple Mount. It was sealed up by Muslims in 810 AD to prevent the Jewish Messiah from entering the city when He comes. The Crusaders reopened it in 1102 AD, but Saladin closed it again in 1187 AD. It was finally bricked up in 1541 AD by the Ottoman Sultan Suleiman.

Then I looked toward the left of the Temple Mount — to the southernmost slope of Mt. Moriah. There, I saw the ancient City of David (said by some to have been the site of Melchizedek's City of Salem, which David had captured from the Jebusites). My mind wandered to the story of David walking on the roof of his palace one spring night to look out on his capital city. David had sent his army commander to besiege Rabbah, but David stayed in Jerusalem. There, on a roof-top below his palace, he saw Bathsheba bathing, and David fell from grace. He committed adultery and murder.

Then my mind wandered to the story of Abraham's defeat of Chedorlaomer and his allies when he freed Lot and returned to the Kidron Valley to meet the king of Sodom and Melchizedek.

Next, I thought of the time when God commanded Abraham to take Isaac and journey to the Land of Moriah to make a burnt offering of Isaac. In a flash, my thoughts in the Garden went back to the last bricking up of the Golden Gate (almost 9 centuries ago) — to 2000 years ago when Jesus was arrested in the Garden — to 3000 years ago when David sinned with Bathsheba — to 4000 years ago when God stopped the sacrifice of Isaac. And then, my thoughts returned to 2000 years ago — when God allowed the sacrifice of His only begotten Son, Jesus Christ. All of that happened on the mountain that was arrayed before me — **Mount Moriah!**

On the next to last day in Jerusalem, we visited the ruins of the High Priest's house. That is where Jesus was taken in chains at midnight, after His arrest in the Garden. That is where the Sanhedrin held the illegal night-trial of Jesus. Suddenly, when I was standing on the back row of our group as our guide showed us the uncovered ruins of the food cellars of Caiaphas's house, I felt the touch of a hand on my shoulder! I felt it pulling me away from the group! As I turned around to see who was touching me, I saw no one! But my eye caught the sight of an old worn stone path behind us. I walked toward it. As the voice of our guide faded away, I found myself standing on that old stone path. Patches of grass had sprouted between the stones. I was standing on the southern slope of Mt. Moriah. To my left I could see the south wall of the Temple Mount with the Al-Aqsa Mosque looming above it. I looked down the path toward the east and saw the Mt. of Olives (across the Kidron Valley). I knew just around the Southeast corner of the Temple Mount wall (and hidden from my view), was the Garden of Gethsemane. At that moment I realized this was the path Jesus trod as He was taken in chains by that Cohort of Roman soldiers and the mob that accompanied them — from the Garden that night to His trial! That was the moment I felt closest to Jesus during that visit because I knew for certain Jesus walked on that very path! He *continued walking in God's plan all the way to the Cross where He died for you and for me on the next day. Then, on the 3rd day, He arose from the dead. 40 days later, He ascended back to Heaven from the Mt. of Olives, where He will return just as He went (Acts 1: 9-11), when He comes again to correct all wrongs and make all things new.*

On my last day in Jerusalem, we visited the Garden Tomb which is just outside the Damascus Gate. Looming above the Garden Tomb is an ancient rock quarry, more than 3000 years old, that looks like a skull (Golgotha)! Golgotha is located on the north saddle of Mount Moriah! As I gazed at that "skull" I knew that was the place where Christ was crucified! That, dear reader, is what the Land of Moriah means to me. I rejoice that the Bible tells us the Mount of Olives will be the place where the Messiah will come when He returns to earth again!

THE 2ND EXAMPLE OF TIME DILATION IN THE BIBLE —

involved a temporary stay of judgment for the Iniquity of the Kingdom of Judah. In Part VI of the Introduction, I talked about the apostasy of King Solomon that led to the Civil War that broke out after his death. That war split his kingdom into The Northern Kingdom of Israel, and The Southern Kingdom of Judah. All the kings of the North were evil and worshipped other gods. Of the 20 kings of the Southern Kingdom, only 8 were good and faithful to God. The other 12 were evil. The evil kings of both kingdoms worshipped pagan gods. They erected altars to them in the high places. The evil kings of Judah also profaned God's Jerusalem Temple by placing idols there. **Both kingdoms sacrificed children on the altars of their pagan gods!**

The 2nd example of Time Dilation after Adam happened during the reign of the good king Hezekiah, who was the 13th king of the Southern Kingdom of Judah. Hezekiah became king when he was 25. The Bible says: "He did good in the sight of the Lord." He restored the Temple in Jerusalem, cleansed it of all profane things, tore down all the idols in Judah, reinstituted the priesthood, and reestablished the Jewish holy days and celebrations to the Lord. Under his rule, Judah prospered, and the Lord God defended Judah against an Assyrian siege of Jerusalem after the Assyrians conquered the Northern Kingdom of Israel and took the ten tribes of the North in captivity to Assyria. When the king of Assyria besieged Jerusalem, the angel of the Lord struck 185,000 Assyrian soldiers dead. The Assyrian king retreated to Nineveh and was assassinated while he was worshipping in the temple of his pagan god (cf. Chapter 19:35-37 of II Kings).

After God delivered The Southern Kingdom of Judah from the Assyrian siege of Jerusalem, a day came when Hezekiah became mortally ill with a boil. The prophet Isaiah told him God said he would die. Hezekiah believed this meant he would be denied heaven and would go to Sheol (see Isaiah Chapter 38). So, he wept and prayed to the Lord to spare his life. God answered his prayer and told Isaiah to tell Hezekiah that He would add 15 years to his life. After that, because of the evil done by the kings of the Southern Kingdom, the Babylonians would conquer Judah and lead the tribes of Judah and Benjamin into slavery. So, we see God was patient: as He had been with the Amorites. But when the iniquity of the Southern Kingdom was complete, history records that God used the Babylonians to punish the iniquity of the Southern Kingdom of Judah.

Hezekiah took this promise as a good thing since the downfall of Judah would not happen in his lifetime. He asked God for a sign God's promise would come true. Isaiah gave Hezekiah a choice. At sunset, God would either cause the shadow of the earth to go up or down the western facing stairs of Ahaz ten stair-steps. Hezekiah chose for the shadow to go back down the stairs at sunset because that would be the opposite of what normally happened. On the day God gave His sign of cure, the Interlinear Bible Translation in Isaiah 38:7 makes it clear God caused the sun to reverse its setting (for a brief moment) and go back up. This caused the shadow of the earth to reverse its normal upward course as the sun set and go back down the stairs a distance of ten steps.

What was good for Hezekiah became bad for Judah. Hezekiah's evil son (Manasseh) was born in the third year of the additional 15 years God had given Hezekiah. Manasseh was the most evil of all of the kings of Judah. During his 55-year reign, he undid all the good his father had done. He reestablished idol worship, profaned the Temple, practiced witchcraft, used divination, dealt with mediums and spiritualists, and instituted infant sacrifices to foreign gods. He burned his son on the altar of Molech as a ritual sacrifice to that pagan god! The Bible says, 'Manasseh shed very much innocent blood until he had filled Jerusalem from one end to another.' (See II Kings, Chapters 18-21, II Chronicles, Chapters 29-33 & Isaiah, Chapters 36-39.)

Since Roe vs. Wade (January 22, 1973), we have murdered more than 61 million helpless innocent babies on our pagan altar of "Freedom of Choice (2020 data)!" [266,267] The slaughter of innocents continues (& is projected to reach 63 million procedural abortions in 2022[***]) because the politicians who support abortion on demand, claim abortion is a right. But they can't say it is an **unalienable** Right. Unlike the God-given unalienable Rights of Life, Liberty, and the pursuit of Happiness, **God (the giver of all life) has not given us the right to murder our children!**

"YOU HAVE SOWED THE WIND & REAPED THE WHIRLWIND."

Both kingdoms of a divided Israel abandoned God and sacrificed their children to false gods. And, both kingdoms were scattered to the winds. Like the ancient Amorites and Canaanites, ancient Israel "sowed the wind and reaped the whirlwind" (Hosea 8:7)! Hosea was a prophet to the Kingdom of Northern Israel in the 7th Century BC. Hosea warned the Northern Kingdom God would punish them for their worship of Baal (Hosea 2:13). In Hosea 4:11-19, he chastised them for turning their backs on Jehovah, worshipping foreign gods, participating in religious prostitution rites, and sacrificing children on the altars to Baal (Hos 9:13). In 722 BC Assyria conquered the Northern Kingdom and led its people away in chains to slavery in Assyria.

The Southern Kingdom lasted a bit longer because 8 of its kings had been good. Nevertheless, most of its kings had been evil, so 136 years after the fall of the Northern Kingdom (in 586 BC) God sanctioned the Babylonian destruction of Jerusalem and the fall of the Southern Kingdom of Judah. The conquest of Judah started in 605 BC. Judah

---

[266] & [265] Query 50 million abortions claim checks out. Query More than 61 million babies killed in 47 years of legal abortion.

(***) Query: ABORTION statistics https://nric.org › factsheets › FS01AbortionintheUS PDF (The 0 after FS is a NUMBER — IT'S ZERO —NOT THE LETTER "O"! That is important if you want to see the GUTTMACHER DATA!)

became a vassal state but rebelled. Nebuchadnezzar II returned in 586 BC and razed Jerusalem to the ground! I talked about that in Part VI of the Introduction.

WE HAVE DONE THE SAME THING.

A prominent member of the U.S. Senate who recently voted against legislation that would protect infants who survive botched abortions: stood on the steps of the Supreme Court and said to a crowd of rabid supporters of *"legal"* abortion:

"I want to tell you (he said the names of two conservative Supreme Court Justices). You have unleashed the whirlwind, and you will pay the price. You won't know what hit you if you go forward with these awful decisions."[268]

If Hosea could have heard that politician parody his words ("You have unleashed the whirlwind"), I think he would be surprised his words were used to defend the very law that (~ 2700 years after his time), legalized abortion on demand in our country. The ancient Amorites, Canaanites, and Israelites learned God will not withhold His wrath forever! "God hates hands that shed innocent blood" (Prov. 6:17c)! We must stop murdering our children. We must return to God. We must humble ourselves — change our ways — get on our knees — repent our sins — and beg for His forgiveness, His grace and loving kindness. **But our opposition to Roe vs. Wade must be peaceful. Judgment and vengeance belong to God alone!** (cf. Romans 12:19, Deut. 32:35, Ps. 94:1, I Thess.4:6, and Heb. 10:30)

The Jews of the Northern Kingdom of Israel disappeared from Biblical history after they were taken to Assyria in 722 BC. They were called "the Ten Lost Tribes of Israel" because they never returned to the Holy Land. After the fall of Assyria, they were dispersed throughout Asia-Minor, Greece, and Macedonia. That dispersion is known as "The Great Diaspora." Some of their descendants, in what is modern-day Turkey, Macedonia, and Greece, were visited by Paul when he preached to them in their synagogues during his missionary travels in the 1st century AD.
The Babylonian conquest of Judah under Nebuchadnezzar II caused the 2nd Diaspora of the Jews. Both Diasporas were judgments of God for the "iniquities" of the Northern and Southern Kingdoms of the Jews. However, after Babylon fell, a small remnant of Jews returned to Israel to rebuild Jerusalem and God's Temple. But the Southern Kingdom never regained its former glory.
There is much wisdom in the Book of Hosea. Hosea explains how the kingdom that was united under David, divided against itself after Solomon. It is the story of a people who: "Sowed the wind and reaped the whirlwind" (Hosea 8:7). Adopting the licentiousness of the Amorite way of life, they abandoned their God, and started worshipping the false gods of Canaan. They cultivated their animal natures and lived in

---

[268] I saw that speech on TV. However, I decided to withhold the Senator's name, but he made his speech on the steps of the Supreme Court, and every major national media TV channel showed it. Millions of Americans saw and heard him, and the text of his speech was made available for the public to read on a large number of web sites.

sin. I encourage you to read the Book of Hosea now. Read it and reflect on what has been happening to our country over the past 50 years (since the 1970s). It seems to me we are now a nation divided against itself. About half of us think our government can solve all our problems. Half of us live mostly in cities and want a government that redistributes wealth and decides who gets what, when, and where. They want an intrusive Federal Government that will control every aspect of our lives — from the cradle to the grave. That half has excluded God from our schools, demonstrates against freedom of conservative speech, defies laws that hinder their political goals, fosters abortion, reinterprets the constitution, and promotes government welfare.

The other half seems more closely tied to the land, and values the government established by our 18th Century Forefathers — a government that allows individual initiative, industry, philanthropy, charitable giving, and "the freedom of our God-given life (all life), liberty, and the pursuit of happiness." We are indeed a divided people.

There are people in our country who think man is wise and can build his own utopia — a utopia apart from God. Truth has suffered and is difficult to discern because moral boundaries and ethics are now blurred by lies. We are now a country that has strayed away from God. We don't know our right from our left, or good from evil. Our media that once prided itself on accurate truthful reporting, has changed. The majority of our media are championing the philosophy that man can solve all of his problems. They no longer simply report the news. They spin the news and are doing their utmost to shape and form public opinion so that all of us will conform to their vision of the future. A certain brand of "opinion" reigns. Truth has been abandoned. The freedom of self-determination is on trial, and the jury of public opinion is now tainted by the propaganda of biased reporting. The Marxists, Socialists, & Communists in our country wish to destroy our hard-won freedom and the democracy established by our forefathers.

Solomon's Book of Proverbs is full of Godly advice, and: "forms a library of instruction on how to live a godly-life and how to be assured of our reward in our life after death. Every facet of human relationships is mentioned, and the teaching of the book is applicable to all men everywhere (and in all times—my parenthetical emphasis)."[269] We must follow the dictates of our God-given gift of discernment to walk with God and do what is right, just, and true. That is the gift Solomon prayed for in the beginning but abandoned.

On the other hand, Solomon's Book of Ecclesiastes may have been written by the older Solomon, who was reflecting on the errors of his ways, after he abandoned his God. In the beginning and middle part of his Book of Ecclesiastes, Solomon reflects on the futility of human wisdom — the futility of the pursuit of pleasure and great wealth — the futility of materialism — the futility of political success — the futility of false worship — the futility of the wickedness of man's natural nature — the storms of old age — and the inevitability of judgment. All is vanity. From the outset, Solomon tells us a life lived without God is "The Vanity of all vanities." He concludes his book by saying God gives

---

[269] The Ryrie Study Bible Introduction to the Book of Proverbs (direct quotes).

order and peace to one's life. We must love God and love one another. He praises God and warns us there is no joy or enjoyment in a life without God. And yet, Solomon led Israel away from God!

The Book of Hosea also ends on a note of optimism. But ancient Israel ignored his advice and became the slaves of other human governments. The 14th Chapter of Hosea tells us God is the answer. Read the 14th Chapter of Hosea now and pray it is not too late for us. Otherwise, history teaches us our "Government of the people, by the people, and for the people" will pass away from the face of the earth. We the people, will be the instruments of our own undoing!

For several generations, our history has not been taught to our youth. Chapter 21 in Book II explains what has happened in our institutions of learning, and how that is responsible for the rot and internal decay that now threatens the future of our nation.

I never before considered the connection between "Time Dilation" and "The Iniquity of Abortion on Demand." But an atheist (who claims there is no such thing as "time"), challenged me to explain why he should think: "a silly myth about God stopping the Sun for a day so Joshua and his barbaric tribe would have time to commit genocide against a tribe of innocent people—could be justified." He said that "myth" was one reason he couldn't believe in the barbaric unjust God of the Hebrews. But God warned the Amorites judgment was coming, and God was patient. However, after 400 years, God used the Jews under Joshua to judge and vanquish the Amorites. God pronounced the same judgment against the Jews of Northern Israel (725 years) later, and the Jews of Judah (about 136 years after that), because they were also sacrificing their children to pagan gods. Because of their apostasy, the Jews lost their Holy Land and their national identity. Both kingdoms were carried away in chains to foreign lands. Because of the apostasy of their ancestors, Jews have not had a country of their own — free from foreign rule for centuries. It would be 2500 years before the new independent state of Israel was re-established. Now you know "The Rest of The Story."

For half a century we have been sacrificing our innocent babies on the pagan altar of "Freedom of Choice." How long will God withhold His judgment of us? (cf. Jeremiah Chapter 19)

❖
CHAPTER 6: The beginning of *"THE BEGINNING"*...

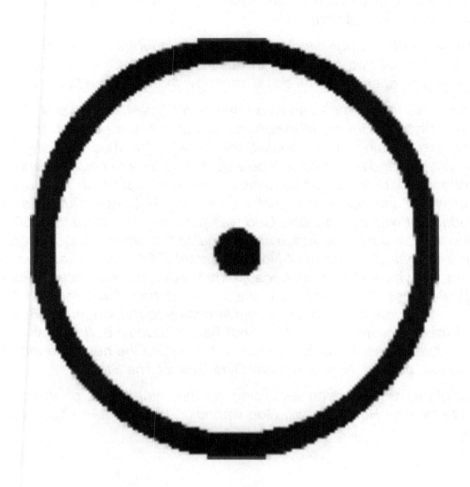

THE CIRCLE AND THE DOT
"HOW GREAT THOU ART!"

THE COSMOGONY OF NAHMANIDES — A GENERAL STATEMENT

In the year 1250 AD, Nahmanides described his concept of *"The Beginning,"* which he deduced from his knowledge of the deeper meaning of the ancient Hebrew script of the Biblical Account of Creation written by Moses. This chapter will examine what he said about *"The Beginning,"* and will compare his biblically derived cosmogony with what scientists are now saying. Today, the majority of scientists support the *"Standard Model of the Big Bang Theory."* When one considers *The Big Bang Theory* is based on the scientific discoveries of the last 85 years, it is truly astonishing that Nahmanides' 13th century cosmogony is remarkably similar. We will start the comparison with an explanation of THE CIRCLE AND THE DOT figure on the preceding page.

NAHMANIDES — THE CIRCLE AND THE DOT

Nahmanides thought *"THE BEGINNING"* started with an unimaginable extreme explosion that resulted from a minute spiritual contraction of the Creator. This contraction of the Creator is known in Hebrew Cosmogony as: *"Elohim's Tzimtzum."* So, now consider the Circle and the Dot figure on the previous page.

- *The Dot represents the tiny speck of space that was created by the Creator's Tzimtzum. Nahmanides said that tiny speck of space, was the entire Universe, when it was the size of "a Grain of Mustard" — at the beginning of 'THE BEGINNING.'"*
- *Nahmanides believed the Explosion that "created" the Dot, caused all within the Dot to be extremely dense, hot, and chaotic.*
- *According to Nahmanides, the Circle represents the circumference of the Universe when (shortly after the Beginning), an act of the Holy Spirit caused the Dot to expand to the size of "a Grapefruit."*
- *The expansion initiated some separation within the chaos of the Dot. The separation allowed some cooling.*
- *The cooling calmed the chaos within the Dot.*
- *Eventually, after the Universe attained the size of a Grapefruit, the separation and cooling brought more order to the chaos of the explosion that had caused the Beginning — thus making it possible for true matter to form.*
- *Nahmanides said: "The expansion of the Dot was the beginning of the transformation of primordial matter into true matter."*
- *As you shall see, Science now says: The sudden expansion of "the Dot" was the point at which theoretical quarks[270] and known electrons formed.*

SOME SPECIFICS ABOUT NAHMANIDES' CONCEPTS OF THE BEGINNING

According to Nahmanides, at the briefest instant following Elohim's Tzimtzum, all the matter of the universe was concentrated in a very small space ('the Dot'), no larger than a *"Grain of Mustard."* At this brief moment, matter was so thin, so intangible; it really wasn't matter, as we know it. It did not have real substance, and it did not have form. But it had the potential to become matter, as we know it. So, let's call this intangible pseudomatter — primordial matter.

---

[270] Schroeder Genesis and the Big Bang Chapter 3 p 66-67

THE SUDDEN EXPANSION OF THE GRAIN OF MUSTARD TO THE SIZE OF A GRAPEFRUIT:
What happened next? Nahmanides theorized this primordial matter suddenly expanded. From that initial concentration of the intangible primordial matter in its infinitely small space ('the Dot'), which was the universe at the moment of the beginning (i.e., Nahmanides' *"Grain of Mustard"*), the substanceless 'not matter' pseudomatter (primordial matter), which was within the Dot, suddenly expanded. This expansion, which was caused by the Holy Spirit, also caused the universe to expand with it.

THE HOLY SPIRIT INITIATED AN EXPANSION THAT ALLOWED TRUE MATTER TO FORM.
This expansion not only caused the grain of mustard to grow larger, but it also brought about a change in the primordial matter. It realized its potential and became matter, as we know it. From this ethereally thin primordial matter (i.e., pseudomatter with the potential to become), came everything that has existed, or will ever exist — was, is, and will ever be *formed*! [271] When matter formed, time grabbed hold — that is to say: *Time began!*[272]

LET'S LOOK AT WHAT MODERN SCIENCE SAYS ABOUT—"THE BEGINNING."
I need to start this *discussion with a brief explanation of "SCIENTIFIC NOTATION."* This *segment uses Scientific Notation* (or "SN") to express numbers, which range from the colossally large to the minutely small — so that they will be easier to compare and compute. If you are not familiar with "SN," you should read about it in a math textbook.[273] But, if you don't want to take time to do that, you might tussle with this explanation of mine.

Scientific Notation expresses numbers using the base of 10. For *large* numbers, where zeros are placed to the right of a digit (of the base 10), and the required number of zeros fill the space between the *base of 10 digit* and the decimal point (i.e., 1,000,000.), the zeros indicate an increasing magnitude of positive value.

EXAMPLE:
In "SN," you should write 1,000,000. —as— 1×10^6 (or you could write 1,000,000. — as: (10^6). The superscript "6" is "positive," and indicates the number of zeros that follow the "1." In reality, you are adding 6 zeros and are moving the decimal point to the right of the "digit 1" by placing the 6 zeros between the 1 and the decimal point. Therefore, if you want to express the number 2,000 in SN, you write it this way: $(2 \times 10^{3)}$. In like manner, 1×10^4 is the same as 10,000. So, to summarize: 1 is 10^0 $10 = 10^1$ $100 = 10^2$ $1,000 = 10^3$ $10,000 = 10^4$ $100,000 = 10^5$ and $1,000,000 = 10^6$ etc. And $15 = 1.5 \times 10^1$ $150 = 1.5 \times 10^2$ $1750 = 1.75 \times 10^3$ $20,000 = 2 \times 10^4$ and $2,000,000 = 2 \times 10^6$ etc.

So, for *large* numbers, place the decimal so there is one non-zero digit to the left of the decimal point. You then add the number of zeros to the right of the non-zero digit — that are needed to move the decimal point to the right. The number of zeros you need to add will be the exponent of the number 10 and will be written as a positive superscript to the base number of 10. Example: 60 million = $6. \times 10^7$ (but it is not necessary to write the decimal point after the 6. We simply understand $6 \times 10^7 = 60,000,000$.

[271] Schroeder Genesis and the Big Bang Chapter 3 p 65 a
[272] Schroeder The Science of God Chapter 3 p 56 b
[273] Or, you could go to the Internet, and Google https://www.mathisfun.com/numbers/scientific-notation.html.

For *small* numbers (which are less than 1), a minus sign indicates the number of digits that should be placed after the decimal point. For example: 10^{-3} stands for 0.001 (that is to say, the 1 requires two zeros to be placed after the decimal point before you write the 1. That is because you need to move the decimal point 3 places to the left of the non-zero digit. The $^{-3}$ superscript of the base 10 is written as a negative number (i.e., 10^{-3}).

EXAMPLE: $1 \div 1000 = 0.001$ (derived by dividing 1 by 1,000).

So, how do you express 0.001 in Scientific Notation? You place a decimal to the right of the digit "1" (i.e., 1.0). Then you move the decimal point 3 places to the left—

(i.e., . 0 0 1)
3←2←1

So, 1×10^{-3} or just 10^{-3} is the way you write 0.001 using Scientific Notation. When you read (THE EARLIEST TIME MATH CAN HANDLE), on the next page, you will see how useful *Scientific Notation* can be.

MODERN SCIENCE & THE BEGINNING

Modern Science now agrees with Nahmanides' concept of *"the Circle and the Dot."* Since Nahmanides thought the Universe started as a tiny dot and suddenly inflated to the size of a grapefruit, we might think of the circle as a sphere. Apparently, this was the concept considered by most 20th and 21st century scientists before NASA published its first WMAP space probe data in 2011 (cf. Chapter 5). Now, NASA says the WMAP data suggests the universe *is flat!*[274] For me, that is going to take a bit of '*getting used to.*' Perhaps we should now think of "*the circle*" as if it is a 3-dimensional *disk* or *egg,* rather than a sphere. Nevertheless, since I am using a two-dimensional circle to represent a three-dimensional 'egg-shaped' or 'disk-shaped' universe, there are two additional things wrong with *the Circle and the Dot figure.* First — the circle is too small. And second — the dot is much too large. It should be microscopic. However, I want to use the symbol of the Circle and the Dot (◎) to illustrate some complex and theoretical points about the origin of the universe. I like to think this Circle and Dot symbol represents —

ELOHIM'S BARAH AND OUR HURRAH!

So, the dot represents Nahmanides' *"Grain of Mustard,"* which is the same thing as *"the Singularity"* of Modern Science — and is also the same thing as Lemaitre's *"Primeval Atom."* As we shall later discuss, during the unimaginable temperature extremes within *the dot* that were produced by *The Big Bang explosion* (which was caused by *Elohim's Tzimtzum):* What was created — was almost instantaneously destroyed! The result was a rapid-state flux-and-flow of energy into matter — and matter back into energy! Most of what existed within the dot at the beginning and during the brief existence of *the dot* was *almost pure energy!* There was very little else.

MODERN SCIENCE AGREES.

The present universe is the result of *a Big Bang,* a massive explosive expansion from a single point. At this point, energy and matter first appeared. Science cannot explain what caused *The Big Bang.*

---

274 Article: Google—WMAP 9 Year Mission Results - Wilkinson Microwave Anisotropy Probe
https://wmap.gsfc.nasa.gov/news/

The Earliest Time Math can Handle

According to modern science, the conditions that existed prior to the appearance of energy and matter are not known and can never be known! But science now says we can attempt to describe the conditions that existed at a point in time that was close to, but *after* the start of the universe. When we use Scientific Notation (or SN for short) that point was at about 10^{-43} seconds *after* The Big Bang! 10^{-43} seconds can be written as: 0.0000000000000000000000000000000000000000001 seconds and is only a minute fraction of the time it takes for an eye-blink! When we write this incredibly small number in the conventional way, 42 zeros separate the decimal point (on the left) from the number 1 (on the right). Therefore, since the zeros appear to the *right* of the decimal point, each zero makes the amount of time that passed after The Big Bang become smaller. Another way of expressing this infinitesimally small number is: 0.1 x 10 to the minus million-million-million-million-million-million-millionths-power of a second. Folks, that's 7 groupings of one-millionth of a second, with each grouping of six zeros representing one-millionth of a second! Or we could write it as, $0.1 \times 10^{-7 \times 6 \text{ millionths} = -42 \text{ millionths of a second}}$, which is the same as writing it as: 1×10^{-43}. Or we could just simply write it as 10^{-43} seconds (for short). Anyway you want to express it, that is the earliest time the math which functions in our world can possibly handle.[275]

The Size of the Dot at the Moment of the Beginning

So, at 10^{-43} seconds, after The Big Bang, the universe was the size of a speck of dust (i.e., the dot in our circle drawing). At that moment, the dot was so small; it may have been below the resolution power of an electron microscope! This means, when Elohim underwent His spiritual contraction, (*His Tzimtzum*), He did not have to contract much at all! Now, 15 ¾ billion earth-year equivalents later, the universe has expanded so much there are no telescopes powerful enough to allow us to see its limits![276]

The Extreme Temperature of the Dot at the Moment of the Beginning:

At 10^{-43} seconds after The Big Bang, when all matter was concentrated into a core location the size of a speck of dust, the temperature was 10^{32} degrees Kelvin [277] (or 100 million-million-million-million-million °K.)

That is 100000000000000000000000000000000.00 degrees Kelvin![278] That is an incredibly huge number, since 32 zeros separate the 1 from the decimal point (i.e., 32 zeros are written *between* the 1 and the decimal point)! As a comparison, the temperature of the center of our Sun is much cooler. It is only 15 million (15,000,000) degrees Kelvin. That is a mere (sarcasm) 15×10^6 °K or 1.5×10^7 °K. [279] If they had known the center of our sun is "about" 85 million-million-million-million °K cooler than the Singularity — Shadrach, Meshach and Abednego might have said: *"It's cool in the center of that furnace, man!"* [280]* That is just my warped sense of humor (See the Fiery Furnace — in Daniel 3). The Bible says the heat of the Fiery Furnace burned away the ropes with which Shadrach,

---

[275] Schroeder Genesis and the Big Bang Chapter 3 p 62 d & 63 a & p 65 c
[276] Schroeder Genesis and the Big Bang Chapter 3 p 65 c, d
[277] Kelvin temperature scale: an extension of the degree Celsius scale down to *absolute zero*.
[278] 10^{32} degrees Kelvin can be written as: (100 000000 000000 000000 000000 000000). By adding spaces, so the zeros are grouped in millions, you can more easily see there are 5 groupings of 6 zeros, which follow the two zeros in one hundred. Now, it is easier to see: 5 x 6 = 30 zeros + the 2 zeros in 100 = 32 zeros, or 10^{32} °K for short.
[279] Schroeder Genesis and the Big Bang Chapter 3 p 65 d, e
[280]* 100 x 10^{30} minus 15 x 10^6 = 85 x 10^{24} or 85 million-million-million-million °K cooler than the Singularity!

Meshach and Abednego were bound, but not a single hair of their heads was burned. Their clothes were untouched by the flames and the stench of the fire was not upon them! Nebuchadnezzar saw a fourth man walking with them in the midst of those flames, *like a son of the gods*! Yet, the furnace had been heated 7 times greater than ever before and was so hot that the men who threw them into the fiery furnace perished!

> ***The Pre-Incarnate Jesus Christ Himself had shepherded Shadrach, Meshach, and Abednego through their fiery furnace experience! Jesus was with them and had saved them from those terrible flames!*** [281]

TIME ZERO—IS OUTSIDE OF PHYSICS AND MATHEMATICS.

The Physics & mathematics, which govern our world, cannot deal with times earlier than 10^{-43} seconds after the beginning. Prior to that time, the temperatures and densities of matter exceeded those, which can be described by the laws of nature that now govern everything we do. Because of this, cosmological theory cannot define the actual *time-zero* beginning of the universe in any dimensions, which would be meaningful to man. [282] Seven hundred years earlier, Nahmanides said we could never know what happened before the beginning. Science now agrees. Nahmanides got his intuition to make that statement from the shape of the *bet* and the deeper meaning of the Hebrew verb — *barah* (cf. Chapter 4).

THE SINGULARITY WAS EXTREMELY SMALL, DENSE, HOT, & CHAOTIC.

As the study of events following The Big Bang is extended mathematically to earlier times, the size of the universe shrinks toward zero. Inversely, the temperature, density, and chaos of the universe — increases toward infinity. Physicists think the actual instant of the beginning was the moment when an infinitely small point of space was packed with primordial matter, which was squeezed into an infinitely high density. The explosive interactions within that infinitely small point of space resulted in a condition of extreme chaos. Modern science has named that condition of infinities — the Singularity. As just stated, the Singularity cannot be treated by conventional mathematics. [283]

WHAT WAS MATTER LIKE IN THE BEGINNING?

Science agrees with Nahmanides. Within the Singularity, matter was not matter, as we know it. The high pressure and temperature in the core of the Singularity had reduced all matter to pure energy. The concept of matter, even the tiny theoretical fundamental particles called *quarks* (Nahmanides' substanceless substance which I referred to as primordial matter), has no meaning for the temperature, pressure, and special dimensions which are speculated to have existed at that very early time. There was exquisitely hot energy and very little else. All within was in a state of *extreme chaos*. However, after only a few *picoseconds* (i.e., a few trillionths of a second) after *the beginning of The Beginning,* within the initial core location of the Singularity, a sudden inflation occurred that forced *the energy-matter-continuum* outward — in all directions. The sudden inflation of the Singularity not only happened almost immediately after the beginning of the Big Bang, but it also happened infinitely faster than you can blink your eyelids! Science says the

[281] **H.A. Ironside's book: *"Daniel"* p. 32-33**
[282] Schroeder Genesis and the Big Bang Chapter 3 p 66a
[283] Schroeder Genesis and the Big Bang Chapter 3 p 66b

cause of this inflation is not known and cannot be determined.[284] (*Nahmanides said the Holy Spirit caused it.*)

EXPANSION OF THE 'DOT' INTO A CIRCLE THE SIZE OF A GRAPEFRUIT

Scientists now agree with Nahmanides and think the sudden expansion (and/or inflation) of the dot of the Singularity to the size of a grapefruit-sized circle — happened at 10^{-35} seconds after The Big Bang. This sudden expansion pushed back the boundaries of space. That force came from within the Singularity. There was no "*without.*" There was and is the universe and the space it occupies. According to science, the universe was and is the totality of all physical existence.[285] Now, before you read the next paragraph, I want to remind you, at 10^{-42} seconds *after* the Beginning (i.e., *after The Big Bang*), the temperature of the Singularity had been estimated to be about 10^{32} °K!

LOWERING OF PRESSURE AND COOLING—ALLOWED TRUE MATTER TO FORM.

As the inflation occurred, there was a lowering of pressure and temperature. By the time the universe had inflated to the size of an egg, more moderate temperatures were achieved, with cooling to about 1,000000000,000000000,000000000 degrees Kelvin (or one billion-billion-billion-degrees Kelvin). With SN we would write that temperature as, 10^{27} °K. The temperature had been 10^{32} °K. This cooling by a factor of 10^5 °K (or 100,000 °K) does not seem like much, but it was enough to start the process that led to *the formation of true matter*. Energy could now condense into the tiniest of particles — i.e., theoretical quarks and known electrons. This took place according to the equation expressed by Einstein ($E = mc^2$), where E is energy, m is matter [with mass], and c is the speed of light. Einstein's equation tells us energy and matter are different states of a single *Energy-matter-continuum.* *

Energy is matter in its intangible form. Matter is energy in its tangible form.[286]

As the inflation of the dot progressed out away from the core, pressures and temperatures continued to fall. Conditions became less harsh. The transition of energy to the more substantive forms of tangible matter continued. The material universe (as we understand it) came into being. The entire process is referred to as *The Big Bang*. Today, this process is so widely accepted by researchers currently active in cosmology that it is now referred to as: *The Standard Model of the Universe.* [287]

"DIVINE DIRECTION"—THE OPINION OF THE ANCIENT JEWISH SAGES:

At this moment do you have a sense of *déjà vu*? You should, because you can now see how similar the current scientific theory of the start of the universe is to the 13th century AD Cosmogony of Nahmanides.

- *How could he have theorized our origins resulted from a massive explosion that created the first tiny speck of space?*
- *What made him think the ethereal substance produced at the instant of the beginning (in that tiny space), was not real matter?*

[284] Schroeder Genesis and the Big Bang Chapter 3 p 66c
[285] Schroeder Genesis and the Big Bang Chapter 3 p 66d & Chapter 5 p 93a
[286] Schroeder Genesis and the Big Bang Chapter 3 p 67a
[287] Schroeder Genesis and the Big Bang Chapter 3 p 67b,c

- *How could he have suspected a sudden expansion of that tiny speck brought about not only the transition of primordial non-matter into real matter — but the time and the space for that expansion was also concurrently provided?*

Nahmanides gave us a hint when he posed and then answered his own question about *Divine direction* when he said: *"God knows all life, but the degree of Divine direction to an individual, depends on how close to God, he or she wants to be."*[288]

About fifty years earlier, Maimonides made the same observation in his book: *The Guide for the Perplexed.* Concerning this, Dr. Schroeder wrote that Maimonides said: *"Only the totally righteous have one-on-one Divine direction, and even that guidance may not ensure a life free of pain and suffering. For the rest of us, chance and accidents do occur. It's our choice as to where we, as individuals fall within that spectrum of behavior that stretches from intimate Divine direction to total random chance."* [289]

Nahmanides and Maimonides must have had a very close relationship with God. It is a matter of faith, but I believe God inspired them. Since science can never tell us anything about what existed before Elohim created, we must either think about that moment in theoretical terms, or we can cling to the explanation already given us by Nahmanides. That explanation involves his concept of *Divine Tzimtzum.* Elohim started His creation by an act of spiritual contraction. Prior to that, nothing else other than Elohim existed. Elohim filled all of Eternity. When Elohim contracted, all that he created became the size of a speck of dust. So, Elohim did not have to contract much at all. Now, after 15 ¾ billion earth-years have passed, the universe has expanded so much that man can never have the tools to see it all.

The seven major points of agreement between the Ancient Hebrew Cosmogony of Nahmanides and the current day Cosmogony of Modern Science are listed in the Table near the end of this chapter. But, before reading them, consider the following.

ELOHIM TRULY IS ALL-POWERFUL—ALMIGHTY.

The concept of Divine Tzimtzum as the cause of The Big Bang gives modern man a hint of the power of God. The tiniest contraction of His Holy Being resulted in the most powerful explosion there will ever be. It produced a tiny speck of space of unimaginably small dimensions. Yet, the extreme high temperatures generated were off any of the charts of today's physical universe and are unknowable to man. The density of the primordial matter within that tiny space was infinitely high — beyond any of our imaginings. Modern science has named that speck of infinities the Singularity. I have heard of the all-powerful God all my life, but the science of the beginning, which was created by the greatest scientist that ever was, is, and will ever be (God), puts a whole new perspective on the magnitude of His power for me. The Onkelos translation of Genesis 1:1 emphasizes the role of *Elohim's First Wisdom* in creation. (In the last chapter of this Book — Chapter 8 — I will explain why I believe Elohim's First Wisdom in creation *was the Pre-Incarnate Jesus Christ!)*

Yet, the most powerful attribute of this God of ours isn't the raw force He can generate. It is His love for us that really astonishes our imagination. He loves us so much: He gave His most precious possession to us — His Son, Jesus Christ. Jesus was given

---

[288] Schroeder The Hidden Face of God Chapter 11 p 177 a
[289] Schroeder The Hidden Face of God Chapter 11 p 177 b

to us as the example of how we should strive to be. Jesus gave His life for us as the one supreme sacrifice for all people of all time who believe in Him and accept the gift of His sacrifice (Heb. 10:10-14).

The people of ancient Israel, who lived under the power and tyranny of Egypt as slaves for four hundred years, had long since forgotten the freedom of the nomadic life their patriarchs had known. They only knew the hardships of forced labor, the few spartan comforts of their fleshpots, and the hovels, which were their shelters. Egyptian control was a constant presence in their lives. The one thing slave and ruler had in common in ancient Egypt was — force. The Egyptians used it. The Israelites experienced it. Egyptian hierarchy controlled every aspect of ancient Israel's existence by the merciless application of force. It was only the clear demonstration of the power of the God of Moses, which persuaded Pharaoh to release them. And it was the power of the miracles Moses performed in God's name that persuaded the Israelites to follow Moses as he led them forth into the stark wilderness of the Sinai desert.

Moses placed his trust in GOD'S LOVE—for God's Love
is God's Power to lead, and to provide.
"Now abide faith, hope, love, these three.
But the greatest of these is Love." (I Cor. 13:13)

The Old Testament emphasizes the power of the God of the Hebrews. In the Old Testament, He seems to be more about power and judgment than love. Yet, over time, in the Old Testament and especially in the New Testament, the full picture of the all-loving God emerges. You may ask why God revealed Himself to man in this way. The answer, perhaps, may be suggested in the stories of the many examples of human experience given to us in the Bible.

God always works with us where we are—not where we should be.

So, the next time you pray, consider: Oh, God, how great is your power! How marvelous is your creation! How magnanimous is your love! How magnificent is your gift of Jesus Christ! And the next time you sing How Great Thou Art — think of the CIRCLE & THE DOT.

HOW GREAT THOU ART

[VS. 1: THE UNIVERSE] O Lord My God; when I in awesome wonder; consider all — the worlds thy hands have made. I see the stars; I hear the rolling thunder; thy power throughout; the universe displayed.

[VS. 2: THE EARTH] When through the woods; and forest glades I wander; and hear the birds; sing sweetly in the trees. When I look down; from lofty mountain grandeur; and see the brook; and feel the gentle breeze.

[VS. 3: THE SACRIFICE OF CHRIST] And when I think; that God His Son not sparing; sent Him to die; I scarce can take it in. That on the cross; my burden gladly bearing; He bled and died; to take away my sin.

[VS. 4: THE 2ND COMING OF CHRIST] When Christ shall come; with shouts of acclamation; and take me home; what joy shall fill my heart. Then I shall bow; in humble adoration; and there proclaim; my God how great Thou art.

[CHORUS] Then sings my soul; my Savior God to Thee. How great Thou art. How great Thou art. Then sings my soul; my Savior God to Thee. How great Thou art. How great — Thou — Art!

SUMMARY POINTS:
HEBREW COSMOGONY & MODERN SCIENCE COSMOGONY COMPARISON CHART
Modern Science Now Agrees with Nahmanides' Interpretation of Moses.

I. Nahmanides' Hebrew Cosmogony	II. Modern Science Cosmology
1. There was a beginning.	1. There was a beginning.
2. There was a 'Beginner,' a Creator.	2. Science cannot disprove a 'Beginner.'
3. The beginning started with a spiritual Contraction of the Creator, Elohim (i.e., *Elohim's Tzimtzum*), which caused a massive explosion that created a tiny speck of space.	3. The beginning started with a Big Bang, a massive explosion from a single point, where all energy & matter appeared. Science cannot explain the cause of The Big Bang.
4. Events prior to the beginning can never be known or studied by man.	4. Events prior to the beginning can never be known or studied by man.
5. At the beginning *of the Beginning,* the Creator concentrated all the matter that would ever be created into a very small space no larger than a grain of mustard.	5. At the beginning *of the Beginning,* a very small space, a mathematically untenable microscopic Singularity inexplicably appeared.
6. The matter in the grain of mustard-sized speck of space was Ethereal: not true matter but had the Potential to become matter.	6. The Singularity contained the potential for all matter: quarks, free electrons, & the chaotic energy of a black fire.
7. The Holy Spirit caused an expansion that allowed the ethereal matter to become true matter. This allowed the universe to enlarge as it filled with matter. Time began when the first matter formed.	7. An unexplained inflation happened which suddenly expanded the universe. This allowed the formation of the first true matter. When the first true matter formed, Time began.

In the year 1250 AD Nahmanides used his intuition, his revelation from God, and his knowledge of *The Genesis Code* to describe a concept of the beginning, which is remarkably similar to the conclusions reached by the modern scientific advances and studies that have occurred over the last 85 years.[290] Everything points to a Supreme Central Intelligence — an all-pervading Wisdom — and a universe created by Intelligent Design. People of faith have believed this all along. Skeptics, who can get beyond their own *cognitive dissonance,* will be able to look at the data and change their minds — i.e., become believers in Jesus. **The Bible has been correct all along!**

THERE WAS A BEGINNING! THERE IS A CREATOR! THERE IS ONLY ONE GOD!
TO GOD BE ALL GLORY, LAUD, HONOR, AND POWER. AMEN.
O. David

---

[290] Article: Creation of a Cosmology: Big Bang Theory. http://ssscott.tripod.com/BigBang.html This article is an excellent historical review of the various contributors to the Big Bang Theory. Georges Lemaître, a Belgian Catholic priest, set down one of the first modern propositions of the Big Bang theory for the origin of the universe. It was in 1927 that he published his Hypothesis of the Primeval Atom, which was based on Einstein's work. 1927 is the date used for the 85-year figure given above, as I typed this paragraph in 2012.

❖
CHAPTER 7: BEFORE THE HEAVENS & EARTH WERE FORMED:
ALL WAS (I) WITHOUT FORM & VOID—THERE WAS ONLY
(II) DARKNESS—(III) DEEP—(IV) SPIRIT—&—(V) WATERS.

"When God initiated creation, He began creating (barah) before He made (asa) the heavens and the earth"—Ancient Talmud Scholars

'Et' means—'the'— Meaning there was One & Only One Creation.
The Ancient Talmud Scholars & Dr. Gerald L. Schroeder agree on this.

The writing of this chapter was especially difficult. The 1st writing took six weeks. Thoughts often came while sleeping. In a fog of sleepiness, I got up to write them down—then tried to make sense of them after daybreak. (O. David)

THE GENESIS CODE

The previous six chapters explained the concept of the Genesis Code and discussed how science has determined the universe is not eternal. The Bible had been right all along — there actually was a beginning! We also discussed the First Wisdom of God (i.e., His Intelligent Design), and wrestled with the mysteries of the Genesis time conundrum, which have brought us to understand science has proved the theological claim that Eternity exists — is actually a physical possibility. In Chapter Five, the Genesis Time Conundrum was explained, and we now understand the Biblical Six Days of Creation and the 15 ¾ billion earth-year equivalents of Creation which science claims, are two different expressions of the same thing — the amount of time Creation required. We have also explained — in the first two Chapters of Genesis the Creation Account is told three times over using two different perspectives — God's and man's. In the previous chapter, the similarities of the Cosmogony of Nahmanides and the Big Bang Theory were discussed. The former was the result of Nahmanides' 1250 AD interpretation of the deeper meaning of the ancient Biblical text. The latter is based on the scientific discoveries of the last 85 years. It is truly amazing the two accounts agree. **However, the world is not yet aware Moses' Biblical Account of Creation has now been validated by modern science.**

Ancient Talmud Scholars took special note of the mention of the heavens *before* the earth in Genesis 1:1. From the verbs *barah, asa,* and *yasar* they concluded, when God initiated creation, He began creating (*barah*) 'the stuff' from which He would first make (*asa*) the heavens, and then later form (*yasar*) the earth. They deduced this from a comparison of Genesis 1:1 with Exodus 20:11 and Exodus 31:17. In Genesis 1:1, they also took special note of *the repetition* of the simple two-letter Hebrew word *"et,"* which they interpreted as *"the."* Dr. Schroeder agrees!

Gen. 1:1 "In the Beginning God created (barah) 'et' (the) heavens & 'et' (the) earth."

From the repetition of *"et,"* they deduced there was one and only one creation. In the initial act of creation (i.e., Elohim's *barah*), the potential existed for all that will ever be. Everything that will ever be, was created by God's initial act. They deduced, in God's grand scheme, only time was needed to form the potential of creation into substantive matter. This was also revealed to them by the slight variation of the wording of Exodus 20:11 and Exodus 31:17, which they compared to Genesis 1:1.

Genesis 1:1 "In the Beginning, God created (barah) 'et' (the) heavens and 'et' (the) earth. Exodus 20:11 "For six days God made (asa) 'et' (the) heavens and 'et' (the) earth."

(The same words and phrasing are found in Ex. 31:17. Note the repetition of *'et'* in the Genesis and Exodus texts.)

From all this the ancient Talmud Scholars concluded, all was created in the beginning, but it would take Six Days of making after the moment of creation to make and to form the heavens and the earth. It would take Six Days in God's time-reference-frame and 15 ¾ billion earth-years in man's.[291] Dr. Schroeder

In Isaiah 48:13 [292] God said: *"My hand laid the foundation of the earth, and my right hand spanned the heavens; I call to them, and they stand together."* (This is just another scripture that confirms Genesis 1:1).

I now want to talk about how the Bible moves on from the general statement of the beginning (in Genesis 1:1), to some specifics that concern the status of the earth at the moment of the beginning. The specifics the Bible mentions involve the deeper meaning of several mysterious and puzzling phrases which are found in our English translations of Genesis 1:2.

* *"The earth was without form and void — Gen. 1:2a (KJV)*
* *And Darkness was upon the face of the deep — Gen. 1:2b (KJV)*
* *And the Spirit of God was moving over the surface of the waters." Gen. 1:2c and 1:2d (NASB)*

BEFORE THE HEAVENS & THE EARTH WERE FORMED ALL WAS: (I) WITHOUT FORM & VOID— THERE WAS ONLY — (II) DARKNESS — (III) DEEP — (IV) SPIRIT —&— (V) WATERS.

NOW, IS THE TIME TO EXPLAIN THE DEEPER MEANING OF GENESIS 1:2.

The second verse of Genesis takes us from *the Dot* to *the Circle*. It starts with the condition of the universe when it was a microscopic *"Dot"* (Gen. 1:2a,b) — and ends with an act of the Holy Spirit that caused the sudden expansion of *"the Dot"* to form *"the Circle."* Nahmanides said *"the Circle"* was about size of a *"grapefruit"* (cf. Genesis 1:2c,d and cf. Chapter 6). The timeline of Genesis 1:2 covers what God did immediately after He created *the Dot*. This act of God's Spirit began immediately after *the Big Bang*. In a flash (like the blast of a booster rocket in space), the action of God's Spirit took the universe from the first few picoseconds of the existence of *'the Dot'* (Genesis 1:2a,b) — to *'the Circle'* (Genesis 1:2c,d) — when *the first ingredients* (free electrons, protons, neutrons, and theoretical quarks), could begin to form what would later become *true matter*.[293,294] As you shall see, the first true matter that formed was *Hydrogen* and *Helium*. The beginning of the nucleosynthesis of the heavier elements would have to await God's formation of the first stars — an event that will be described in Genesis 1:3 (in Chapter 8 of this book). However, these events in Genesis 1:2 took place *before* the heavens with their first-order stars, and our solar system with its earth, were *made* and *formed*.

Genesis 1:2a,b describes the first picoseconds after the appearance of *"the dot."*

[291] Schroeder Genesis and the Big Bang Chapter 5 p 92 b, c
[292] Schroeder Genesis and the Big Bang Chapter 5 p 92 b, c
[293] Weinberg The First Three Minutes Chapter 1 p 8a and Chapter 5 p. 110 and 111
[294] Schroeder Genesis and the Big Bang Chapter 5 p. 87 e

"ᵃThe earth was without form and void. ᵇAnd Darkness was upon the Face of the Deep."

Genesis 1:2c,d describes what the Holy Spirit did after *"the Dot"* appeared.

"ᶜAnd the Spirit of God was moving over the ᵈsurface of the waters. (NASB)

LET US NOW EXAMINE: *"And, the earth was* — **(I) *WITHOUT FORM & VOID.*"**

THE UNIVERSE IS OLDER THAN THE EARTH.

We have seen there is an abundance of scientific evidence for a very old earth and an even older universe. Genesis 1:2 continues the general overall statement of creation, which was started in Genesis 1:1. This second verse of the Bible (Genesis 1:2a,b) opens with the specific condition of the earth at the moment Elohim began creating. The earth was not formed. All was void in that speck of space where the earth would ultimately appear. This translation of the original Hebrew is the first apparent meaning of Moses' words, and it is a fair and accurate translation of the most straightforward meaning of the Hebrew text. The specific mention of the earth in the Biblical Creation Account, tells us — the Creation Account is our story! Why? Because — of all the planets in our solar system, the earth is the only planet mentioned in the first two chapters of Genesis. Nahmanides and several other ancient Jewish sages also told us the Hebrew language of the Torah conveys a deeper meaning. We will now take a look at the Hebrew words Moses used in Genesis 1:2a,b that convey the deeper meaning of these verses.

Genesis 1:2a: "The earth was 'tohu' and 'bohu.'" (The Hebrew/English Interlinear Bible)

THE DEEPER MEANING of GENESIS 1:2a COMES THROUGH an ANALYSIS of "TOHU" &"BOHU."
In English translations of Genesis 1:2a, "tohu" is translated as "without form" (i.e., unformed).[295] The word, which is translated as "void," is "bohu." When we peel the onion, we learn the deeper meaning of tohu is "chaos." Since we are talking about "the Dot" (the Singularity), and since "the Dot" was extremely small, exceedingly hot, and infinitely dense — then the chaos of tohu was also extreme. Thus, the deeper Hebrew meaning of tohu is — "extreme chaos."

"Bohu" means, "filled with the building blocks of matter."[296] However, since no true matter could form within the Singularity, the deeper Hebrew meaning of bohu is — "filled with the ethereal building blocks of primordial pseudo-matter." [297]

When God started creating — the heavens and the earth did not exist. That is to say, the universe, and all that it contains did not exist! Specifically, as it pertains to us — *in the beginning of The Beginning* — our solar system did not exist. In the space where the heavens would *first* appear, and the earth *would later be formed* — *all was unformed and void.* In the beginning when God started creating: He started by creating the potential for all that will ever be.

When an important fact is introduced, the Bible often repeats the important point by immediately stating the same facts in another way. So, I say again — at the time God began creation — He did not start with the formation of the earth, or the heavens for that

---

[295] Schroeder The Science of God Chapter 3 p 57 b
[296] Schroeder The Science of God Chapter 3 p 57 b
[297] Schroeder The Science of God Chapter 3 p 57 b

matter. No. He started with the creation (*barah*) of the potential "stuff" from which He would later "make" (*asa*) and "form" (*yasar*) the heavens and the earth. Immediately after He began — all that would ever exist was in a microscopic "Dot-of-space" that was filled with the ethereal building blocks of primordial pseudo-matter. The nature of His creation at this point in time was one of extreme chaos — all of which he created from nothing — (*Creation Ex Nihilo*)!

APPLYING THE GENESIS CODE TO GENESIS 1:2a:

When the Genesis Code is deciphered, we see the deeper meaning of Genesis 1:2a is:

When Elohim began creating, and before He formed the heavens and the earth, His Tzimtzum created a primeval speck of space, ('the Dot') that was filled with the ethereal building blocks of primordial pseudo-matter. All that was within that primeval speck-of-space was in a state of extreme chaos.   O. David

FROM CHAOS TO ORDER

The only phrase in the Creation Account that is repeated at the end of each day of creation is: "*And evening and morning was day one...the 2ⁿᵈ day, the 3ʳᵈ day...etc. etc. etc.*"

The hidden meaning of this repeated phrase is — *on each day of the Six days of Old, God's creations proceeded from chaos to order.* I will briefly talk about this now but will more fully discuss it in the next chapter (Chapter 8) when we arrive at the first appearance of this biblical phrase. The first hint of the *hidden* meaning of this Biblical phrase was revealed to us when we learned *tohu* was *the extreme chaos*, which existed in the beginning within the Singularity (before anything else was formed). As you shall see, the sequence of God's creation always proceeds from chaos to order. On each of the Six Days of Creation, the work of the Creator forced an incremental degree of order upon of the extreme chaos of the beginning.

THE SINGULARITY CONTAINED PURE ENERGY & PRIMORDIAL PSEUDOMATTER.

At the beginning of the universe (when the Big Bang created the Singularity), the pressures and the temperatures produced by this 'mother of all explosions,' approached infinity. When the universe was created, it was infinitely small. All the energy there will ever be — was concentrated into that infinitesimally tiny primordial speck of space science has named — the Singularity. The energy within the Singularity was almost pure energy. But a tiny amount of something else was also present. The Singularity contained the full spectrum of electromagnetic radiant energy and a tiny amount of primordial pseudo matter — something that had the potential to become matter whenever the necessary conditions for its transformation into true matter existed. We know what electromagnetic radiation is. And we know the full spectrum of electromagnetic radiation included the photons of visible light. But exactly what was the composition of the Singularity's primordial pseudo matter? The answer is free electrons, and a tiny volume of protons, neutrons, and something called quarks. [298]

(II) THE DEEPER MEANING OF "DARKNESS"

"And Darkness (hoshek)— was upon the face of the deep." (Genesis 1:2b)

What is darkness? The simple and obvious answer is — the absence of light. True, but the simple answer is not the correct answer. The correct answer is a bit more complicated.

---

[298] Schroeder Genesis and the Big Bang Chapter 5 p. 88 e and 89 a

As we shall see, darkness is possibly *the* created substance of the universe. The creation of darkness has something to do with free electrons and photons.

FREE ELECTRONS

According to the glossary of Stephen Hawking's book, *A Briefer History of Time*, an electron is an extremely light particle with a negative electrical charge that is attached to and orbits the positively charged nucleus of an atom. [299] However, that definition doesn't apply to the kind of electrons God created in the beginning. Those electrons were *free* electrons. Free electrons are sort-of-like single males who are playing the field and have not yet become '*attached.*'

FREE ELECTRONS, PROTONS, & PHOTONS WERE INSIDE THE BLACK-FIRE OF THE BEGINNING.

In the Beginning, the Singularity that was produced by the Big Bang, was a tiny Black-Fire! That tiny Black-Fire-Space was infinitely hot in the Beginning! It was filled with extremely energetic — free electrons, free protons, free light-photons — as well as the full spectrum of all the electromagnetic radiant energies, which were produced by the mother of all explosions (i.e., *The Big Bang*) — *in the Beginning.*

Becoming attached to a free proton is something free electrons are designed to do. When they 'attach,' an atom of an element is formed. The simplest element is *Hydrogen.* Hydrogen is formed when one free electron is attracted to and attaches itself to one free proton — and *'sets up house'* by going into an orbit around that proton. When this happens, the proton becomes the nucleus of the element we call — *Hydrogen.* Because of its simple structure, Hydrogen was the first element — *the first matter that formed.*

However, within the Singularity, the conditions were so extreme that free electrons had no possibility of forming any attachments! Why? Because the extreme temperatures and pressures of *The Big Bang*, caused the velocities of the photons in the Singularity to be so great that they caused extremely violent collisions. Remember photons not only have wavelengths. *They also have mass.*

The infinitely small space in which all this energy driven soup was confined, guaranteed the violence, and resulted in total chaos. These photon-electron collisions were so frequent that every time a free electron tried to attach to a proton, it was hit by a photon, which would knock it out of its almost established orbit. At the same time, the photons were diverted by each collision. These collisions were so violent and so frequent that not only was Hydrogen prevented from forming but also — the photons (i.e., *visible light itself*) were literally locked within the initial mass of the universe. Therefore, inside the Singularity, and for a brief period of time after its creation, energy and pseudo-matter were in a continual state of flux and flow. Energy became pseudo-matter, and pseudo-matter was instantaneously destroyed and — reconverted back to energy. Since visible light was prevented from emerging from this flux and flow, *The Big Bang* literally produced

[299] Stephen Hawking A Briefer History of Time Glossary p 150

— *a black fire* — which was infinitely hot. All that was within that tiny black-fire speck-of-space was in a state of — tohu (i.e., *a state of extreme chaos*)![300],[301]

THE ANCIENT SAGES' INTERPRETATION OF DARKNESS (I.E., HOSHEK)

According to the ancient Jewish Sages, this darkness contained the source of energy that was to power the forces that led to life. This revelation came from Isaiah 45:7a:

"I (Elohim) form (yasar) light and create (barah) darkness (hoshek)." (KJV)

According to this verse, the first creation (i.e., "*barah*") was *darkness* — not light! The darkness was a black-fire — a type of energy that emitted no visible light. The surface and interior of the universe was black so long as the photons and free electrons in the Singularity were mixed in a chaotic confused turmoil of energetic collisions. So, the Bible tells us — <u>Darkness</u> *is a created, possibly <u>the first created</u> substance of the universe!*[302] As you shall see, for the 8-billion earth-year duration of *Day One,* the <u>color</u> of God's creation was — **BLACK!**

(III) DEEP: (I.E., THE DEEPER MEANING OF "TᴱHOM.")

Genesis 1:2b *"And Darkness (Hoshek) was upon—the face of the deep (the Tᵉhom')."*

We have just discussed that darkness (i.e., *the hoshek* that was *the black fire* produced by *The Big Bang*) was possibly *the first* created substance of the universe! Now we need to understand *where* the darkness was. *What and where was the face of the deep?* What does the *'face of the deep'* (or in some translations, the *'surface of the deep'*) mean?

THE DEEPER MEANING OF "TᴱHOM," (or 'the face of the deep,')—IS "CHAOS!"

Since Genesis 1:2a,b is describing the conditions within the Singularity, it is important to remember, the operative word for understanding the environment within the Singularity is — *Chaos.* The Hebrew word, which is translated as *'the deep'* is — **Tᵉhom.** So, darkness was upon *the face of the 'Tᵉhom.'*

Most English Bibles and the Pentateuch and Haftorahs edited by J. H. Hertz translate *tᵉhom* as *'the deep.'* The Hebrew word *"tᵉhom,"* is reference word # 8415 in *Strong's Exhaustive Concordance of the Bible. The Hebrew & Chaldee Dictionary* in Strong's Concordance defines *Tᵉhom* as — *an abyss* — or *a surging mass of subterranean water supply, deep place, or depth.* So, we can easily see why English translations of Genesis 1:2b accepted the simple straight-forward meaning of "the deep" and did not look below the *"surface of the face of the deep"* to discover the deeper meaning of *"the abyss."*

NOW LET'S LOOK FOR THE DEEPER MEANING. HERE'S WHERE IT GETS INTERESTING.

Tᵉhom is from the prime-root reference-word #1949 ("*huwm*"), which means — *to make an uproar or agitate greatly or destroy. Huwm* is from the prime-root reference-word #2000 ("*humam*") that means *to put in commotion, disturb, destroy, break, crush, trouble, and vex.* Putting the definitions of all three Hebrew words (*tehom/ huwm/ and humam*) together, we find the deeper meaning of /the face of the deep /the surface of the deep

---

[300] Schroeder Genesis and the Big Bang Chapter 5 p 87-90
[301] Schroeder The Science of God Chapter 3 p 57 b
[302] Schroeder Genesis and the Big Bang Chapter 5 p 90 a

and /the abyss is — *"to agitate greatly and to destroy, put in commotion, disturb, break, crush, trouble, and vex."*

Now, let's approach this *"agitating, crushing, destroying, vexing"* interpretation problem from another direction. The Hertz commentary on Genesis 1:2 in The Pentateuch and Haftorahs defines *t*ᵉ*hom* as *"the abyss."* The Webster New World Dictionary of the American Language defines *"abyss"* as *"the primeval great chaos or deep."* The Winston Dictionary defines abyss as *"the original chaos,"* an immeasurable space or depth, *"as of water."* The most prevalent translation, *'the deep,'* is a fair translation, but it doesn't match the context or the deeper meaning of *the black-fire of darkness, or the chaos of tohu* — which were responsible for the chaotic conditions within the Singularity. Also, we must keep in mind: The Singularity was a tiny, microscopic dot. So, the meaning of *the deep* cannot be construed to mean *a great depth of ocean waters,* as most modern translations infer for two reasons:

- 1st, the Singularity was immeasurable because it was infinitely small. No great depth of anything could have existed.
- 2nd, during the brief existence of the Singularity, and before it underwent a sudden expansion, the earth had not been formed and no water had been made.

As you shall see, the first water would be made in the stars, but at this moment in the Creation Account *on Day One,* no stars existed. The first stars would not be *"born"* until the very end of *Day One.* Since tehom is *the deep* in one definition, and tehom is *the abyss* in another. And since one of the definitions of the abyss is *the primeval great chaos,* and another definition of the abyss is *the original chaos:* then it stands to reason: *tehom = deep = abyss = to put in commotion/agitate greatly/destroy/break/crush/trouble/and vex.*

Is there one word that can adequately describe all of this turmoil? *Chaos* is the operative word for describing the conditions within the Singularity. *Chaos* fits the context best. Therefore, the Genesis Code meaning of *'t*ᵉ*hom'* must be — *"the primeval great chaos of the Beginning."*

So, the Genesis Code meaning of Gen. 1:2b is:

And Darkness was upon the face of the primeval great chaos of the Beginning. (O. David)

DR. SCHROEDER'S EXPLANATION OF 'THE DEEP'

Dr. Schroeder defines the deep as 'the primeval space created at the beginning.' [303] One of the Winston Dictionary definitions of abyss is 'an immeasurable space or depth.' However, in this case, within the microscopic dot that was the Singularity, that primeval speck-of-space was immeasurable, not because of some great depth but because it was so small — so infinitely small! So now we have two ancient Hebrew words in the 2nd verse of Genesis One — "tohu," and "tehom," which have something to do with — "Chaos." I look at the deeper meaning of these two words in this way. *Tohu* describes the extreme chaos of the violent interactions of the primordial *"soup"* that was *"boiling"* within the Singularity when it was created *in The Beginning. Tehom* describes the *"kettle"* in which the tohu was boiling. That *"black kettle"* was *"The Black-Fire of Darkness"* surrounding

---

[303] Schroeder Genesis and the Big Bang Chapter 5 p 93 b

the tohu within that tiny immeasurable space that *Elohim's Tzimtzum "created."* Both the *Kettle* and the *Soup* were *black*! As you shall see, *light* eventually emerged from the tohu, but the *Hoshek* (i.e., the Darkness, or *the Black-of-Space*) remains! Could *tehom* actually be something, which is still indefinable that Scientists now postulate is — "Dark Matter and Dark Energy?" ***Only God knows!***

APPLYING THE GENESIS CODE TO GENESIS 1:2 a,b:
(Genesis 1:2a,b describes what happened within the *'Dot'* at the beginning of THE BEGINNING.)

The Genesis Code Interpretation of Genesis 1:2a
When Elohim began creating, and before He formed the heavens and the earth, His Tzimtzum created a primeval speck of space, ('the Dot') that was filled with the ethereal building blocks of primordial pseudo-matter. All that was within that primeval speck-of-space was in a state of extreme chaos.

The Genesis Code Interpretation of Genesis 1:2b
The chaos of that primeval speck of space (the 'dot') was enveloped by the Darkness of a Black Fire. Thus, Darkness was upon the face of the primeval great chaos of the Beginning.   (O. David)

THE FIRST BLACK HOLE:
The chaos within the Singularity was so intense that the Singularity soon faced self-annihilation. If God did not act again, if He allowed things to continue according to His natural laws of nature, all would have eventually ground down to a halt. Why? Because: The Singularity was the very first *Black Hole!* Its gravitational vortex was so extreme; it would have pulled in on itself until it eventually disappeared. In that first spot of space following creation, all the primordial mass of the universal energy-matter-continuum was concentrated in a single point. When a vast amount of mass is in a small volume, the gravity generated by this mass can be so great that nothing can escape (not even light). Within a few trillionths of a second of its creation, the Singularity was threatened with self-destruction. What made this first black hole of the Singularity different from all future black holes was: *True matter* did not cause its gravitational attraction. *Primordial pseudomatter caused it*, because at this moment in time, true matter had not had a chance to form.

BLACK HOLES TODAY
Black holes were discovered a few decades ago. Matter, light, whatever comes near, is drawn into a black hole by its massive gravitational attraction. Black holes develop when a star dies. Stars die when their nuclear fuel is exhausted. Black holes typically form when a massive star, which is at least ten times greater than the mass of our sun — has used up its nuclear fuel. The cooling process, which follows, causes the core mass of the star to collapse toward the center of the collapse. As the core of the star collapses, the concentration of matter becomes so great that its gravity pulls all its mass along with its light photons, into the central vortex of the collapsing star. That is how black holes are born. Nothing escapes — not even light! All is darkness. All is black.[304]

---

[304] Schroeder Genesis and the Big Bang Chapter 5 p 93 c

Our sun was born late on the 2nd day of creation about 4.6 billion years ago.[305] Scientists estimate our sun burns 660 million tons of Hydrogen per second. It fuses this Hydrogen into Helium and energy. [306] Someday our sun will exhaust its supply of Hydrogen and burn out. But we should not worry about it — because scientists estimate our sun has enough fuel to last another five to six billion years![307] Furthermore, when our sun burns out, it would be most unusual for a black hole to form — because the mass of our sun is 1/10th the size of those stars which typically form black holes when they die. Some say, when our Sun dies, it will swell into a red giant, which will engulf Mercury and Venus, and reach the earth. When that happens, scientists say life on earth and our planet will end in fire. The Sun will then become a faintly visible planetary nebula (for about 10,000 years) and will then become a dying ember of a star, known as a white dwarf, that is only a little larger than the earth (6 billion years from now). [308]

Oh well, that is neither here nor there. But we should be aware of it, and you should know the apostle Peter prophesied the heavens and the earth would be destroyed by fire.

II Peter 3:2-7 NASB says: [2]"You should remember the words spoken beforehand by the holy prophets and the commandment of the Lord and Saviour spoken by your apostles. [3]Know this first of all, that [b]in the last days [c]mockers will come with their mocking [d]following after their own lusts, [4]and saying, [a]'Where is the promise of [b]His coming? For ever since the fathers [c]fell asleep, all continues just as it was [d]from the beginning of creation.' [5]For when they maintain this, it escapes their notice that [a]by the word of God the heavens existed long ago and the earth was [b]formed out of water and by water, [6]through which [a]the world at that time was [b]destroyed, being flooded with water. [7]But [a]the present heavens and earth by His word are being reserved for [b]fire, kept for [c]the day of judgment and destruction of ungodly men."

II Peter 3:10-13 NASB says: [10]"But [a]the Day of the Lord [b]will come like a thief, in which [c]the heavens [d]will pass away with a roar and the [e]elements will be destroyed with intense heat, and [f]the earth and its works will be burned up. [11]Since all these things are to be destroyed in this way, what sort of people ought you to be in holy conduct and godliness, [12]looking for and hastening the coming of the Day of God, on account of which [b]the heavens will be destroyed by burning and the [c]elements will melt with intense heat. [13]But according to His [a]promise we are looking for a [b]new heavens and a new earth, [c]in which righteousness dwells."

Can we be certain scientists are right about their 6-billion-years-from-now-prophecy? Who can say it will not happen sooner? So, scientists have theorized our earth will be destroyed in fire when our sun dies, and Saint Peter prophesied the earth will be destroyed by fire *on the Day of the Lord*. When will that happen? Only God the Father knows for certain *when* and *how* (cf. Matthew 24:35-44 **THE RAPTURE).** Believers in

[305] Schroeder The Science of God Chapter 4 p 68 a
[306] Schroeder The Science of God Chapter 9 p 128 d
[307] Hawkins A Briefer History of Time Chapter 8 p 75 c
[308] What will happen when our Sun dies? by Deborah Byrd & Eleanor Imster, May 11, 2018
What will happen when our sun dies? I Space I EarthSky
https://earthsky.org › space › what-will-happen-when-our-sun-dies

Jesus Christ should not worry about this. Why? Because we will not be here when the heavens and the earth are destroyed by fire. We will be with our Lord Jesus Christ, our Father God, and the Holy Spirit and all the heavenly hosts in the newly created heavens and earth *where righteousness dwells* — when *the old heavens and earth* are destroyed by fire.

FOR THE BRIEFEST MOMENT, JUST AFTER THE BEGINNING, THE SINGULARITY THREATENED TO BECOME A SUPER BLACK HOLE. Immediately following creation, when all primordial matter was concentrated at one point, conditions existed for a super black hole. Within the Singularity, not only was visible light trapped by the violent collisions which prevented the formation of true matter, but the high gravitational forces within that minuscule speck of space, also threatened. Indeed, Darkness was upon the face of the primeval great chaos of the Beginning. An outside force was needed to neutralize both restrictive processes.[309] So, let's turn our attention to what Elohim did next.

Pretty soon, within a few picoseconds of the beginning of creation, Elohim would change the environment into a new set of conditions, which would allow real matter to form. What did He do? It has something to do with *the Wind of God,* which is the same as *the Spirit of God,* or as some Christians say: *The Holy Ghost,* and other Christians say: *The Holy Spirit.* [310]

(IV) SPIRIT

GENESIS 1:2c "AND THE <u>SPIRIT OF GOD</u> WAS '<u>MERAHEFET</u>' (MOVING) *over the Surface of the Waters."*

If that primeval super black hole had persisted, all would have been lost. Creation would have pulled in on itself and vanished. However, The Holy Spirit intervened. At this crucial moment, the primeval great chaos of the Singularity, which was enveloped by the darkness of a black fire was literally moved by God's Spirit. *In Scripture (in both the original Hebrew language and the later Greek translations), the word for Spirit also means Wind.*[311] The Hebrew word for **moving** is *merahefet. Merahefet* also means **brooding or hovering.** So, the *Wind of God* **moved and brooded and hovered** over God's creation just as a hen broods over her eggs to hatch them and bring forth new life,[312] or as a bird hovers above its nested young feeding and protecting them.[313]

MAIMONIDES' EXPLANATION OF "THE WIND OF GOD"

In his commentary on Genesis 1:2c, Maimonides said *'The Wind of God'* has the meaning of *'Divine Inspiration,'* or *'God's Divine Will.'* So, *'The Wind of God'* was the force required to overcome the contracting self-destructive influence that threatened the Singularity at this moment. But, according to Maimonides, *'The Wind of God'* was also a *'Divine Act.'* God willed an expansion of the black-fire dot, at the precise moment when it was on the verge self-destruction, when the laws of nature threatened to turn it into a super black

---

[309] Schroeder Genesis and the Big Bang Chapter 5 p 93 d & 94 a, b
[310] Schroeder Genesis and the Big Bang Chapter 8 p 117 e
[311] Billy Graham the Holy Spirit Chapter 2 p 13
[312] Billy Graham the Holy Spirit Chapter 2 p 15
[313] Schroeder Genesis and the Big Bang Chapter 5 p 94 b

hole.[314] This term, *'Wind of God'* is used only once in Genesis. This expansion was a one-time phenomenon. One-time phenomena are rare in nature. However, both science and the Bible call on such a one-time phenomenon at this particular juncture. It was a *'Wind of God'* (in Greek), a *'Ruach Elokiim'* (in Hebrew), and *an inflationary epoch* (in scientific terminology). It was needed and it occurred. [315]

(V) WATERS

"The Spirit of God was 'merahefet' (hovering) over the Surface of the Waters."[316]

Why is water mentioned at this point in Gen. 1:2c? Dr. Schroeder explains it this way. *"Water is the common stuff from which the heavens, the earth and all that they contain would be produced."* [317]

Remember, St. Peter said: *"the earth was formed out of water & by water"* (II Peter 3:5b).

Schroeder's explanation sounds very similar to the interpretation of the Hebrew word *bohu*, which we have just discussed. However, when *the Wind of God* acted, the only nuclei that formed (at the moment of inflation) were the nuclei of the two lightest elements, Hydrogen and Helium. *Water* had not been formed because one of its two elements, *Oxygen*, had not yet been made. Water (H_2O) is formed when two Hydrogen nuclei unite with one nucleus of the heavier element, Oxygen. This union is called *"nucleosynthesis."* But *heavy nucleosynthesis* requires the temperature extremes that only exist in stars, and the stars had not yet been born. As we shall see, star birth will happen in Genesis 1:3, which will be discussed in the next chapter. Therefore, what we think of, as *'water'* really doesn't fit the context of the conditions within the Singularity, which was the only thing that existed when *the Wind of God* acted.

Perhaps this first mention of water at this early time makes sense *if* it is understood, the *'water'* of Genesis 1:2c and II Peter 3:5b *actually was bohu*, (i.e., the ethereal building blocks of primordial matter from which Elohim would form all that would later exist). In this sense, the *'water'* of Genesis 1:2c and II Peter 3:5b is different from the *'waters'* of Genesis 1:6 and thereafter. That is, it is different from what we think of as water. When we think of water, we are thinking of the life-nourishing compound so familiar and necessary to all life. However, in the time-reference-frame of Genesis 1:2c and II Peter 3:5b, the Bible is referring to when the Spirit of God moved over the surface of the "waters." This happened before the Hebrew term for water took on its present meaning. It began to take on its present meaning on the *3rd Day,* when *"the waters of the 3rd Day"* refer to the substance that filled the seas.

But, here, in Genesis 1:2c and II Peter 3:5b, the Bible is still discussing the events that took place on *Day One,* when the earth was *not formed and was void* — when all that existed — was *the Singularity*. At that time, the Biblical use of the term, *'water,' refers to*

---

[314] Schroeder Genesis and the Big Bang Chapter 5 p 94 b
[315] Schroeder Genesis and the Big Bang Chapter 5 p 94 c
[316] The Interlinear Bible: Hebrew, Greek, English (moving gently on the face of the waters)
[317] Schroeder Genesis and the Big Bang Chapter 5 p 93 b

the ethereal building blocks of primordial matter; the substance from which all the true matter of the universe would be formed![318]

It is important to remember, up to this point in our discussion; all this chaos is taking place within the confines of a microscopic speck of space represented by *the Dot* (the Singularity) that we talked about in Chapter Six. We must also remember, within *the Dot*, the *bohu* (which contained all the ethereal primordial building blocks of matter) was right there in the middle of all of the extreme chaos of *tohu.* However, it was precisely at this point that God's Spirit (*God's Wind*), caused a sudden change in *'the Dot',* which would bring forth an ever-increasing degree of '*order.*'

FROM THE DOT TO THE CIRCLE—SUDDEN INFLATION CAUSES TRUE MATTER TO FORM.

Just before the Wind of God caused the inflation/expansion of *'the Dot',* science tells us the diameter of the Singularity was 10^{-24} centimeters (cm). A centimeter (cm.) is 10 millimeters (mm.) which are just about this long [┄┄┄]. It takes 2.2 cm. to equal one inch. One tenth of a cm. (or 1 mm) is approximately this long [·]. So, all my illustrations of *'the Dot'* (which measured only 10^{-24} cm), are too big. The Singularity was so small that no man-made instrument, perhaps not even a powerful electron microscope, could have '*seen*' it. The theoretical computed size of the Singularity supposedly defines its diameter at 10^{-35} seconds after *the beginning of The Big Bang.* So, in less than a second after the beginning, 'The Wind of God,' acting for only a minuscule fraction of a second, caused an expansion of the universe at a rate far in excess of any rate prior to, or after, this episode. This caused the universe to almost instantly inflate to the size of a grapefruit *('the Circle'* in our example given in Chapter Six).[319]

THE CIRCUMPUNCT—THE SIGN OF ILLUMINATION: A UNIVERSAL SYMBOL FOR GOD:

'The Circle and the Dot' illustration introduced in Chapter Six is actually a primeval symbol which has had many different meanings throughout history. Alchemists used it as a symbol for gold. In ancient Egypt, it was the symbol for the sun god — *Ra.* Eastern philosophy treats it as a symbol of 'the Third Eye, the Divine Rose, and the Sign of Illumination.' Early mystics called it 'The Eye of God,' which is the origin of the 'All-seeing Eye' on the Great Seal of the United States. In modern astronomy, it is used as a solar symbol. It is known as *'the Circumpunct.'* The Circumpunct was the symbol of the Ancient Mysteries — one of its most esoteric being 'the Rose,' which was used as a symbol for perfection. In Freemasonry, it is the symbol of 'the Rose Cross' when it is placed on the center of a cross.[320]

In the words of one of the characters in Dan Brown's novel, *The Lost Symbol:* "The Circumpunct is a universal symbol for God. Throughout history it has been all things to

---

[318] Schroeder Genesis and the Big Bang Chapter 9 p 130b
[319] Schroeder Genesis and the Big Bang Chapter 5 p 93b
[320] Dan Brown The Lost Symbol, a novel Chapter 84 p 316 & Chapter 85 p 320

all people — it is the sun god Ra, alchemical gold, the sign of illumination, the all-seeing eye, the Singularity point in The Big Bang —The Great Architect of the Universe."[321]

THE INITIAL EFFECT OF INFLATION—THE FIRST TRUE MATTER FORMED & TIME BEGAN.
The inflation caused by the Wind of God created more space for the primordial matter to expand. This provided the separation needed to decrease the number of collisions of photons and free electrons. For the first time, free electrons were able to combine with protons. When the free electrons began to attach with protons, the first atom to form was the simplest and lightest element, Hydrogen. When that happened, *Time Began.* As time moved on, the number of formed and stable Hydrogen atoms increased. With the increase in the number of formed and stable Hydrogen atoms, the number of free electrons decreased. A smaller number of Helium atoms (the second lightest element) also formed. Gradually the number of violent particle collisions diminished. With the diminished number of collisions came a gradual reduction of temperature and a concomitant reduction of pressure. Finally, as more and more free electrons combined with the nuclei of Hydrogen and Helium, the number of collisions between the photons and free electrons diminished so much that the photons could *'range free"* within *the tohu of the Circle.* When this happened, visible light (individual photons) could separate from the black fire of the full spectrum of radiant energies first generated in the Singularity and break free to range into the darkness of the *infantile* universe. This first emergence of light that we are currently describing occurred *at the nuclear level.* It did not happen all at once but would require an epoch of time.

IT STILL TOOK SEVERAL HUNDRED-THOUSANDS OF YEARS AFTER THE DOT BECAME THE CIRCLE BEFORE LIGHT COULD EMERGE FROM THE DARKNESS ON THE NUCLEAR LEVEL.
Science has theorized it took several hundred-thousands of years of continued expansion, after the universe inflated to the size of a grapefruit, and the first atom of Hydrogen formed, and time began — for the extreme temperatures and the chaotic collisions of photons with matter — to diminish to a critical point. But during this time, the expansion of the universe, which was caused by the Holy Spirit, finally brought enough cooling for that critical event to occur. When the temperature fell below 3,000 degrees K, light separated from matter on the *nuclear* level, and began to emerge from the darkness of the black fire that was the Singularity in the beginning.[322]

However, *at the nuclear level,* the candlepower of the random emergence of individual photons was not sufficient to illuminate the universe as a whole. Both science and Hebrew theology agree the inflationary epoch did not instantly bring light to the universe at large. But something else would happen billions of years *after* light had emerged on the nuclear level, *which would illumine the entire universe.* That something else would merit its own special mention in the next pronouncement of God which is recorded in the Bible in Genesis 1:3 — *the first Biblical mention of light.[323]* This use of a separate phrase to mention the making of light on the universal level implies that it took more time.

---

[321] Dan Brown The Lost Symbol, a novel Chapter 126 p 468
[322] Schroeder Genesis and the Big Bang Chapter 5 p 88d
[323] Schroeder Genesis and the Big Bang Chapter 5 p 89 c

Nevertheless, when light first emerged *on the nuclear level,* the first true matter could start to coalesce. This matter, now consisting of approximately 75% Hydrogen and 25% Helium, could begin to cluster, and over the next several billion years; the clusters would grow large enough to form the first galaxies and stars. But life as we know it could not yet form. Life requires more than Hydrogen and Helium.[324] In the next chapter, when we discuss the birth of the first stars, we will see how Elohim brought forth the heavier elements which would eventually lead to life as we know it.

Here, in Genesis 1:2, we have been talking about the initiation of the inflationary epoch that brought about the formation of the first true matter, the beginning of Time, and the random emergence of individual photons of visible light at the nuclear level. In the next chapter we will discuss the events listed in Genesis 1:3-5, when Elohim formed the first stars. This was an event that took place in billions upon billions of gaseous clusters of Hydrogen and Helium throughout the universe. Those first stars would have so much candlepower and would produce so much light that God would give that universal event a name. As we shall see, He would call it — **DAY.**

Summary Points:

- God initiated only one act of creation — His *Tzimtzum*: His *barah.*
- With His act of Tzimtzum He created the substrate He would use to make (*asa*) and form (*yasar*) everything else.
- This substrate was *the black fire of darkness,* which the ancient sages believed contained the source of energy God would use to power the forces that led to life.
- God's one act of creation caused the appearance of a tiny speck of space the size of a microscopic dot — also called the grain of mustard (Nahmanides), the Primeval Atom (Father Lemaitre), and the Singularity (defined by modern science).
- The operative word for describing the conditions within The Singularity is *chaos.*
- Initially, the Singularity consisted of the energy of a black fire, which contained the full spectrum of radiant energy, and a tiny amount of primordial matter.
- The chaos and high gravity within 'The Singularity' caused a back-and-forth flux and flow of energy to primordial matter with an almost instantaneous reconversion to energy. This prevented true matter from forming and also prevented the emergence of visible light.
- The Singularity was *a black hole.* It was enveloped by *the darkness of its chaos.*
- In less than a second after the beginning, the Spirit of God (the Wind of God — The Holy Spirit) intervened and caused an inflation/expansion of The Singularity from a microscopic dot to the size of a grapefruit.
- The Spirit of God brought order to the chaos. This allowed the first true matter to form and Time to begin. Eventually, light would be able to separate from the darkness of the beginning and emerge into the universe. That is the subject of the next chapter.

---

[324] Schroeder Genesis and the Big Bang Chapter 5 p 90 b

APPLYING THE GENESIS CODE TO GENESIS 1:2.
GENESIS 1:2A &B DESCRIBE THE SINGULARITY (THE DOT) IN THE BEGINNING
GENESIS 1:2a

"ªThe earth was without form and void. (KJV)"

THE GENESIS CODE MEANING OF GENESIS 1:2a IS:

When Elohim began creating, and before He formed the heavens and the earth, His Tzimtzum created a primeval speck of space, ('the Dot') that was filled with the ethereal building blocks of primordial pseudo-matter. All that was within that primeval speck-of-space was in a state of extreme chaos.

GENESIS 1:2b

"ᵇAnd Darkness was upon the Face of the Deep. (KJV)"

THE GENESIS CODE MEANING OF GENESIS 1:2B IS:

The chaos of that primeval speck of space (the 'dot') was enveloped by the darkness of a Black-Fire. Thus, darkness was upon the face of the primeval great chaos of the Beginning.

GENESIS 1:2c,d

"ᶜAnd the Spirit of God ᵈmoved upon the face of the waters (KJV)."
IT IS AT THIS POINT IN THE BIBLICAL NARRATIVE THAT THE 'DOT' SUDDENLY BECOMES THE 'CIRCLE.'

THE GENESIS CODE MEANING OF GENESIS 1:2C,D IS:

Then the Wind of God hovered over that tiny black-fire speck-of-space (the 'dot'), and nurtured it, protected it, and made it suddenly swell and grow (into the 'circle'). O. David

✣
CHAPTER 8: LIGHT (DAY)—DARKNESS (NIGHT)—DAY ONE

"Then God said, let there be light; and there was light. "And God saw the light was good.
And God separated the light from the darkness. And God called the light day, and the darkness
He called night. And there was evening and there was morning, one day." Gen. 1:3-5 NASB

These verses bring us to the end of the *Day One* of creation. *"One Day"* spans the first five verses of the first chapter of Genesis. *"Day One"* was 24 hours in God's time-reference-frame and 8-billion earth-years in earth's time-reference-frame. *Day One* started 15 ¾ billion earth-years BA (before Adam) and ended 7 ¾ billion earth-years BA.

The main subjects of this chapter are LIGHT and DARKNESS. We will begin our discussion by considering the metaphysical (i.e., the *religious*) attributes of light and darkness (Part I). In Part II of this chapter, I will discuss the scientific (i.e., the *physical*) characteristics of light and darkness.

PART I: THE METAPHYSICAL ASPECTS OF LIGHT

This discussion of the metaphysical aspects of light will lead us to an understanding of the *"light" of Jesus Christ*. Our investigation of the *"light" of Jesus Christ* will involve an examination of:

- *The phrase "Then God said"—*
- *The religious concepts of Divine Direction, Divine Intervention, and Divine Punctuation—*
- *The meaning of the phrase, "The Word of God"—*
- *The connotation of "First Wisdom"—*
- *The import of Intelligent Design, and a consideration of — The connections between the biblical phrases: "Then God Said — The Word of God — and The First Wisdom of God."*
- *Lastly, we will discuss the doctrinal concepts of — Intelligent Design — the Hidden Face of God, and— the New Testament revelations of the Pre-incarnate Jesus Christ.*

These concepts must be contemplated before we discuss God's physical creation of light. That happened near the end of *Day One*. As you shall see, this will be an important discussion, because the crucial role the Pre-incarnate Jesus Christ played in God's Creation is hidden in the Mosaic account. After the connections between *"the Word of God"* and Jesus Christ have been clarified, you will have a newfound appreciation for the revelations of Jesus Christ that are in the 1st Chapter of the Gospel of John, the 1st Chapter of the Book of Colossians, and the 1st Chapter of the Book of Hebrews. You will see the Biblical revelation of Christ is progressive. He is hidden in the Old Testament. Only occasionally do we get hints of His existence in Old Testament scripture. However, He is openly revealed in the New Testament in the person of *the Incarnate Jesus.* As you shall see, He has been present all along.

THE LIGHT OF JESUS CHRIST—

Genesis 1:3 begins with these words: *"Then God Said."* This phrase is intimately associated with the Biblical concepts of: *Divine Direction, Divine Intervention, and Divine Punctuation.* A series of Divinely directed interventions of God caused the punctuated developments that happened on each Day of Creation. God did this with pronouncements of His Word. God literally spoke all things into existence!

Genesis 1:3 is the first time we encounter the phrase — *"Then God said."* After the beginning (in Genesis 1:1), and after the action of the Holy Spirit (in Genesis 1:2c), the phrase *("Then God said")* indicates each time the Creator imposed *'His Will'* on the natural flow of creation with acts of *Divine Direction through Divine Intervention.*

The first time *God imposed 'His Will'* was when He initiated the beginning in Genesis 1:1 by a minute spiritual contraction of His eternal being. The ancient Hebrew sages called *God's "First Divine Act of Intervention"* (i.e., the thing God did that started His Creation) —*"Elohim's Tzimtzum."* According to Hebrew Cosmogony, a sudden, minute spiritual contraction of the Creator's spiritual being caused the immense explosion that modern science now calls — *"The Big Bang."* This set-in motion a chain-reaction of chaotic events, which if left unchecked, would have eventually led to the formation of *a black hole.* If that had happened, the creation process would have gravitated to a fatal end. This was discussed in Chapter 7. Another act of Divine Intervention was needed to prevent an inevitable black-hole destruction of *'the Dot.'* So, Elohim intervened a second time.

The second time Elohim imposed 'His Will' on Creation was when *His Spirit hovered over the surface of the chaos* (in Genesis 1:2c) and *initiated a sudden expansion of 'the dot'* to the size of a *'Grapefruit'* — (Nahmanides' description of Elohim's second act of Divine Intervention). Thus, Elohim initiated an expansion of the universe — *which led to the formation of the first matter.* The universe has been expanding ever since. This was also discussed in the previous chapter.

"THEN GOD SAID" — DESIGNATES ABRUPT, PUNCTUATED, SUDDEN CHANGES.

In the 1st Chapter of Genesis, after the Holy Spirit initiated the expansion of the universe, all other expressions of *Elohim's Will* are announced by the biblical phrase — *"Then God said."* In the New American Standard Bible or NASB, this phrase appears nine times in the first chapter of Genesis. *"God said"* appears 10 times! Every time the Creator spoke, He imposed *'His Will'* on His Creation through *Divine Intervention.* Each time God spoke *'His Will,'* abrupt and sudden punctuated changes in the sequences of creation occurred. This is an extremely important concept. Since Darwin's time, the accumulated fossil data of the past 165 years *have proved Darwin's theory wrong!* [325] The ten-fold declarations of abrupt and sudden punctuated change in the first chapter of Genesis stand in stark contrast to *Darwin's imagined idea of slow random gradual change,* which (for generations), has been preached by Darwinists.[326, 327] Beginning with Genesis 1:3 and continuing through Genesis 1:31, these *Divine punctuations* in the development of the world are evident from *the tenfold repetition* of —*"God said."*[328] For God to say something *is for Him to do it.* The Bible teaches — *There is power in God's Word.*

---

[325] The 1st Edition of Darwin's book was published in 1859. Since I am editing this chapter in 2024, 165 years have passed since Darwin's book was 1st published. During the past 165 years the accumulating fossil evidence shouts out to the world: *"Darwin was wrong!"*

[326] Schroeder The Science of God Chapter 2 p 28 b,c,d & p 29 a,b

[327] Schroeder The Science of God Chapter 2 p 29 c—33 a

[328] Schroeder Genesis and the Big Bang Chapter 10 p 158 b

"GOD SAID," IS THE FIGURATIVE EQUIVALENT OF "GOD WILLED."

(Hebrews 11:3) *"By faith we understand the worlds were prepared by His Word, so that what is seen was not made out of things which are visible."* [When I read this scripture I not only think about the universe, but I also think about atomic structure and the subatomic "world," i.e., quarks, protons, neutrinos, electrons, neutrons, atoms, elements, and molecules.]

(II Peter 3:5) *"By the Word of God the heavens existed long ago, and the earth was formed out of water and by water."*

(Psalms 148:1-5) *"Let the heavens, the heights, all His angels, all His hosts, sun and moon, all stars of light, the highest heavens, and the waters that are above the heavens praise the name of the Lord, for He commanded, and they were created."*

(John 1:1) *"In the beginning was the Word, and the Word was with God, and the Word was God."*

(Isaiah 40:5, 8) *"The glory of the Lord will be revealed, and all flesh will see it together; for the mouth of the Lord has spoken it...For the Word of our God is eternal and stands forever."*

The Psalmist drew upon Genesis 1:3 — *"Then God said"* when he wrote Psalms 33:6 — *"By the Word of the Lord were the heavens made."*

These are just a few verses of scripture that declare there is power in the Word of God. The commentary on Genesis 1:3 in The Pentateuch and Haftorahs (which was based on Psalms 33:6), makes the following point about the phrase — *'Then God said*: *"One of the names for God in later Jewish literature is — 'He who spake' and the world came into existence."*

On each of the *Six Days of Creation,* the phrase *"Then God said,"* marks every time when *the spoken Word of God* directed the processes of creation. Each one of the pronouncements of God that follow the phrase, *"God said,"* must be taken as the figurative equivalent of — *"God Willed."*

THE CONNOTATION OF FIRST WISDOM (ALL-ENCOMPASSING WISDOM)

In Chapter 3 we discussed the concept — all existence is the expression of an all-encompassing wisdom, which pervades the Universe. In science laboratories we experience this all-encompassing wisdom as information first physically articulated as energy and then condensed into the form of matter. In Chapter 6 we said: *"Energy and matter are two expressions of the same thing."* Every particle, every being, from atom to Adam, appears to have within it a level of information — a level of conscious wisdom.[329] This reminds us of the words of the Onkelos translation of Genesis 1:1: *"With First Wisdom, Elohim, the Almighty God, created the heavens and the earth from nothing."*

INTELLIGENT DESIGN, CONSCIOUS WISDOM, & DIVINE PUNCTUATIONS ARE ATTRIBUTES OF 1ST WISDOM. The self-evident *Intelligent Design* we see in every created thing is an expression of the *Conscious Wisdom of God.* The Onkelos Aramaic translation of the Hebrew Scriptures is the first Biblical declaration of the *First Wisdom of God* that

---

[329] Schroeder The Hidden Face of God Prologue xi, & Chapter 3 p 49 c

engineered the *Intelligent Design,* which permeates all God's creation. In the first chapter of Genesis, the hallmarks of Intelligent Design are *the abrupt and sudden changes,* which occur on each day of creation that immediately follow the tenfold repetitions of the phrase: *"God Said".* On each day, the abrupt and sudden changes that follow each spoken command of the Creator *mark the Divine Punctuations,* which represent each and every time *Elohim imposed His Will on the sequences of creation with pronouncements of His Word.* Thus, the Conscious Wisdom of God (*that is self-evident in Intelligent Design*) is an expression of *The First Wisdom of God.* The spoken Word of God and the written Word of God are also expressions of *The First Wisdom of God* — the former audible and perceptible to God's appointed men and women throughout history — and the latter, recorded and archived in the Bible.

IN THE OLD TESTAMENT, JESUS CHRIST IS THE HIDDEN FACE OF GOD.

Then God Said — The Word of God — The First Wisdom of God — and — The Intelligent Design of God: are all attributes of the *Hidden Face of God.* The following discussion should convince you — In the Old Testament, *the Pre-incarnate Jesus Christ is the Hidden Face of God!* In Chapter 3, the concept of *the Hidden Face of God* was introduced when we discussed this quote: *"Wisdom, information, an idea, is the link between the metaphysical Creator and the physical creation. It is the Hidden Face of God."* [330]

The opening verse of the Onkelos Aramaic translation of Genesis 1:1 tells us *"With 1st Wisdom, God created the heavens and the earth."* We have discovered *Jesus Christ is the 1st Wisdom of God.* Thus, in all our English translations of the Bible, Jesus Christ is the Hidden Face of God in the Old Testament. He is not openly revealed. Instead, we are given hints of His existence throughout The Old Testament. He was openly revealed to us in The New Testament when He was sent to earth to save man. There is an often-quoted concept:

> *"The New Testament is in The Old Testament, concealed."*
> *"The Old Testament is in the New Testament, revealed."*

The revelations of the Genesis Code have confirmed this means: *Jesus Christ is in the Old Testament, concealed. Jesus Christ is in the New Testament, revealed.*

The apostle Paul testified to this in Hebrews 1:1-2 NASB, when he said: *"God has in these last days spoken to us by His Son, whom he has appointed heir of all things, and through whom also He made the worlds."*

Paul also proclaimed the Supremacy of the Son of God in Colossians 1:15 when he said: *"He* (i.e., Jesus Christ) *is the image of the invisible God, the first born of all creation."*

The invisible God is just another way of saying — the unseen God or the Hidden Face of God. The Living Bible says it best. In Col. 1:15-19, the Living Bible says: *"Christ is the exact likeness of the unseen God. He existed before God made anything at all, and in fact, Christ Himself is the Creator who made everything in heaven and earth, the things we can see and the things we can't; the spirit world with its kings and kingdoms, its rulers, and authorities; were all made by Christ for His own use and glory. He was before all else began and it is His power that holds everything together. He is the Head of the body made up of his people* (that is, his church), *which He began; and He is the Leader of all those*

---

[330] Schroeder The Hidden Face of God Chapter 4 p 49 c

who arise from the dead, so that He is first in everything; for God wanted all of Himself to be in His Son."

In the KJV of John 1:1-5, the apostle tells us: *"In the beginning was the Word, and the Word was with God, and the Word was God. The same was in the beginning with God. All things were made by Him, and without Him was not anything made that was made. In Him was life, and the life was the light of men. And the light shineth in the darkness and the darkness comprehended it not."*

In the 1st Chapter of his Gospel, John told us God sent John the Baptist to proclaim Jesus Christ was the light — the true light — that God sent to everyone who might believe. **Those who receive Him** would be given the right to become children of God. Then, the apostle John told us John the Baptist said this about Jesus Christ: *"The Word* (i.e., Jesus Christ) *that was God became flesh and dwelt among us, full of truth and grace as the only Son of the Father...This was He of whom I said, He who comes after me has a higher rank than I, for He existed before me...For the Law was given through Moses...Grace and truth were realized through Jesus Christ...No man has seen God at any time; but the only begotten God* (Jesus Christ), *who is in the bosom of the Father, He* (Jesus Christ) *has explained Him." (John 1:14-18 NASB)*

Thus, it was John the Baptist who witnessed to us, the Word that was with God in the beginning, was the Pre-incarnate Jesus Christ. We can therefore conclude:

- In the Onkelos Aramaic Translation of Gen.1:1, Jesus Christ is hidden in the *"With First Wisdom of God"* phrase.
- Jesus is not named in all other English translations of Gen. 1:1, but we have learned:
    - ✓ All existence is the expression of the all-encompassing First Wisdom of God.
    - ✓ Intelligent Design permeates all of God's creation.
    - ✓ The First Wisdom of God engineered the Intelligent Design that is so evident.
    - ✓ The 10-fold repetitions of the phrase *"God said,"* in Genesis One, refers to the Spoken Word of God.
    - ✓ The Spoken Word of God is The First Wisdom of God.
    - ✓ And "In the beginning," The First Wisdom of God was the Pre-incarnate Jesus Christ.

Thus, it was through the Pre-incarnate Jesus Christ that God created everything!

In Col. 2:2-3 NASB, the apostle Paul may have said it best: *"We now have the full knowledge of God's mystery of Christ. In Christ all the treasures of wisdom and knowledge are hidden."* This is the true meaning of the 1st Chapter of the Gospel of John. Jesus Christ is hidden in the Hebrew script of the first verse of the Old Testament (i.e., *"In the Beginning, with First Wisdom, God created the heavens and the earth."*) Nevertheless, the Pre-incarnate Jesus Christ was there, and was the active force in creation. The deeper meaning of Moses' words in the Onkelos translation of Genesis One — reveals His presence and His role to us. Now, with this information, and the testimony of John the Baptist, Christians now know:

- Jesus Christ was God's instrument in creation.

- He was and is the link between the metaphysical Creator and God's physical creation.
- Jesus Christ links us to God.
- He is our pathway to God!

THE LIGHT OF JESUS CHANGED SAUL.

Before we leave our discussion of the metaphysical aspects of light, I want to tell you what happened to a man named Saul. This tale is told by Saul in Acts 9:3-23. It is also told in Acts 22:1-16 and is conveyed a third time in the 26th Chapter of Acts. But I need to tell you a little bit about Saul before I relate the story.

Saul of Tarsus was a Jew who was also a Roman Citizen. His Latin (Roman) name was Paul. He lived in the time of Jesus, but there is no biblical mention of any personal meeting between the two men. On the night Jesus was arrested in the Garden of Gethsemane, He was chained and brought to the house of the High Priest where He was illegally tried before the Sanhedrin. His trial was an illegal showcase — *a Kangaroo Court* — because the High Priest had predetermined the verdict, and His trial was held at night! (*Jewish Law prohibited nighttime trials!*) I suspect Saul may have been present at Christ's night trial because I believe Saul was a member of the Sanhedrin. Paul persecuted Christians (cf. Gal. 1:13-14, & Acts 22:20), and He "voted" against them in trials (cf. Acts 26:10-11where he says: "*I cast my vote against the Christian saints.*")

After Jesus arose from the dead and ascended to Heaven, Christians were actively pursued and persecuted by the Jewish authorities. Saul was a big part of that. He held the coats of the people who stoned Stephen. After the martyrdom of Stephen, Saul made it his business to travel throughout the region arresting and persecuting members of the early Christian Church. Now, let's take a look at the Bible's account of how the literal *light of Jesus* brought Saul to his knees, stopped his persecution of Christians, converted him to Jesus Christ, and completely changed his life.

While on his way to Damascus to persecute the Christians there, a light from heaven suddenly flashed around Saul. When Saul fell to the ground, he heard a voice saying: "*Saul, Saul, why are you persecuting Me?*" Saul replied: 'Who art thou Lord?' The voice then said: "*I am Jesus whom you are persecuting. But rise and enter the city, and it shall be told you what you must do.*" The story in the 9th Chapter of Acts goes on to say the men who traveled with Saul stood speechless because they heard the voice but saw no one. Years later, when Saul was defending himself and speaking to a mob of angry Jerusalem Jews who wanted to kill him, he said: "*And those who were with me beheld the light but did not understand the voice of the One who was speaking to me.*" Acts 9:8 says: "*And Saul got up from the ground and though his eyes were open, he could see nothing. And leading him by the hand, they brought him into Damascus.*" Much later, when he told king Agrippa his story (cf. the 26th Chapter of Acts), Paul said: "*the light of Jesus Christ was brighter than the sun and caused my whole party to fall to the ground!*"

These scriptures tell us Jesus appeared and spoke to *Saul* in the form of a flashing light from heaven that blinded him. The men with Saul certainly understood Saul was blind after Jesus spoke, because they had to lead him by his hand into Damascus (Acts 9:8). When the Lord sent Ananias to cure him, something like scales fell from his eyes (cf. Acts 9:18). In this case, the light of Jesus Christ blinded Saul! That experience changed his life. After Saul regained his sight, he became a disciple of Jesus Christ and started using his Roman name (*Paul*). He became the missionary to the Jews and Gentiles of Asia Minor and Europe, and preached the Gospel of Jesus Christ throughout Turkey, Macedonia, Greece, and Rome. Paul became *the apostle to the Gentiles*. He founded many Christian Churches along the trade routes that connected Europe to Asia Minor.

Saul's metaphysical encounter with Jesus Christ had a physical (*scales over his eyes and blindness*) and a metaphysical effect on Saul (*conversion to Jesus Christ*). Afterwards he was a changed man. No longer motivated by judgment and hate (*as the man known as Saul was*), he started using his Roman name (*Paul*), and devoted his life to preaching the Gospel of Christ *to the Gentiles*.

CONCLUSION TO PART I: THE METAPHYSICAL ASPECTS OF LIGHT

The Pre-incarnate Jesus Christ was the First Wisdom with which Elohim created the heavens and the earth from nothing. In the Old Testament, Jesus Christ is the Hidden Face of God! Are you still not convinced? Read the 8th Chapter of John. Beginning with verse 12, notice how many times Jesus uses the words *"I am."* The Jews challenged Him after Jesus said: *"Truly, truly, I say to you, if anyone keeps My word, he shall never see death"* (vs. 51). This discourse ends with Jesus telling them: *"Before Abraham was born, 'I AM'"* (John 8:58). Jesus used the same name Jehovah used when Moses asked God his name (cf. Exodus 3:14). The significance of this name for God — *"I AM"* — will be discussed in Chapter 10 (in Book II).

PART II: THE PHYSICAL CHARACTERISTICS OF LIGHT (i.e, THE SCIENCE OF LIGHT)

We will now talk about God's physical creation of Light. He called it — *"DAY."* This discussion will require an examination of:

- The Biblical command: *"Let there be light"*—
- Electromagnetic Radiation (i.e., full-spectrum *'light'*)—
- How God made the first Galaxies and Stars—
- The Biblical phrase: *"The light was good"*—
- God's separation of light from the darkness of the Beginning:
  - The science of the separation of day from night—
  - An understanding that day and night cycles occur throughout the universe (i.e., they are not the sole purview of the earth)—
  - The religious connotations of "day" and "night"—
  - An examination of the importance of other separation concepts in the history of Israel—
- The naming of light and darkness—
- The Genesis Code meaning of *"evening and morning"*—
- And the significance of the *"cardinal numbering of the day"* when light appeared.

FROM DARKNESS TO LIGHT

In the beginning, God *created Hoshek* (Darkness*).* His creation began with the sudden appearance of a black-fire dot. All that was within that black-fire dot, was in an extreme state of turmoil — extreme chaos. Light was locked in. Light was trapped. From the moment of the beginning and for the next 8-billion earth-years of *"Day One"* darkness prevailed, and *black* was the color of God's creation. However, all would instantly change when God spoke His first word to His creation in Genesis 1:3-4b.

*"Then—**God said**—let there be light, and there was light (Gen. 1:3).*
And God saw that the light was good (Gen. 1:4a).
And God separated the light from the darkness." (Gen. 1:4b—NASB).

It took eons of time from the expansion of the universe to the size of a grapefruit before visible light could come forth (i.e., light with a wave frequency we can see). But God created light the moment He initiated *The Big Bang.* The light of Genesis 1:3 existed prior to the divine separation of light from darkness (described in Genesis 1:4b). The Talmud and modern cosmology both acknowledge: *The first light produced by Elohim's Tzimtzum* (i.e., *The Big Bang*), was of a nature so powerful, it would *not* have been visible to humans. *The Big Bang explosion* produced *a black fire.* Science has taught us the black fire of that early period was in the energy range of gamma rays. Gamma rays are so energetic, they will penetrate a considerable thickness of lead shielding. Their energy is far in excess of the energy of the light rays that are visible to the eye. The energy of gamma rays is also many times greater than the x-rays that are used in diagnostic studies such as CT scans, chest x-rays, and mammograms. Gamma rays are so destructive that they are one of the forms of high-energy electromagnetic radiation I used when I treated patients with cancer.

As the expansion initiated by the Holy Spirit continued to cause separation and cooling, the thermal energy of all of the electromagnetic radiant energies in the universe eventually fell to 3000 degrees Kelvin. It took several hundred thousand years for this to happen.[331] However, before visible light could come forth, stable matter started forming the moment inflation started. *Hydrogen* was the first matter to form. *Helium* was next. As cooling continued, more and more electrons became bound to the nuclei of hydrogen and helium. As greater numbers of stable atoms of hydrogen and helium formed throughout the expanding universe, the number of collisions between the free electrons and the photons of light diminished to the point that the photons of the visible range of light broke free and emerged into the universe. Both scientifically and theologically, when this happened, light became the light we can see, and the darkness (i.e., the *hoshek)* remained dark because it was composed of the powerful black-fire radiant energies we cannot see.[332] Thus, *Hoshek — was — the Black-of-Space.*

In the beginning (within the Singularity) *the Black-of-Space* was unimaginably hot — so hot science cannot put a number on it. Today, after 15 ¾ billion earth-years of expansion and cooling, *Hoshek* (i.e., the Black-of-Space) still contains the radiant energies we cannot see. However, it is now made up of something we call *Cosmic Microwave Background Radiation* or 'CBR' and, to a lesser extent something else as yet indefinable that science calls *dark matter,* and *dark energy,* which fill the whole of an expanded universe that is estimated to be an incredible 156 billion light-years across![333] During the estimated 15 ¾ billion earth-years that have passed since the beginning, the

[331] Schroeder Genesis and the Big Bang Chapter 5 p 88 d
[332] Schroeder Genesis and the Big Bang Chapter 5 p 89 c
[333] Article: Space.com—Universe Measured: We're 156 Billion Light-Years Wide; by Robert Roy Britt: http://www.space.com/scienceastronomy/mystery_monday_040524.html

continuing expansion-inflation of the universe has cooled *the Black-of-Space* to an incredible 3 degrees above *absolute zero* (2.73 ° Kelvin, or -270 ° Centigrade)! Furthermore, this *deep freeze of space* is moment-by-moment growing ever colder with each incremental degree of the continuing expansion of the universe.[334]

ELECTRO-MAGNETIC RADIATION—FULL SPECTRUM 'LIGHT'

Now is the time to add an additional layer of complexity to several concepts that have been introduced in preceding chapters. As stated, visible light is only a part of the broader spectrum of wave energies and frequencies scientists refer to as electromagnetic radiation. There is a wide range of photon energies within the spectrum of electromagnetic radiation, which vary from the weak microwaves in our small microwave ovens, to the powerful gamma rays used in medical treatments for cancer, or the gamma rays that emanate from our sun. However, within only a few trillionths of a second after the beginning, the Holy Spirit initiated a series of events, which would eventually lead to the freeing of visible light from matter when He caused the Singularity to suddenly expand. After the Holy Spirit acted, a few individual light rays began to emerge from the darkness of the beginning and range free into the ever-expanding universe.[335]

The point of this explanation is: *Visible light was part of the broad spectrum of the black-fire radiant energies produced in the beginning.* However, the light that we can see was initially locked in by the violent electron-photon collisions that were continuously occurring within the confines of the Singularity during its brief existence.

In the last chapter we said the ancient Jewish sages believed the sudden expansion of the universe from the dot to the grapefruit was the result of the direct action of God's Spirit. We have mentioned that event was the second time the Creator imposed *His Will* on the otherwise natural flow of the events of His creation. Today, scientists speculate this sudden expansion happened at 10^{-35} seconds *after The Big Bang*. At that moment, Elohim's Spirit willed an expansion of the universe at a rate far greater than any rate prior to or following that event.[336] At that moment, the ingredients of *the first true matter* started to form but were still locked within the chaotic flux and flow of *energy-to-matter-to-energy.*

Dr. Steven Weinberg (winner of the 1979 Nobel Prize for Physics) believes, 3 minutes and 46 seconds after the Singularity had suddenly expanded to the size of a small circle; enough cooling would have occurred so that the universe would be on the verge of the first nucleosynthesis. However, another 700,000 years of additional expansion and cooling would be necessary for the temperature to drop to 3,000 degrees Kelvin — the point where the electrons and the nuclei of hydrogen and helium (which had been violently colliding within the Singularity), could begin to form stable atoms, so that — visible light could break free at the *nuclear* level, *and emerge into the universe.*[337, 338] I wish to emphasize this first freeing of light occurred at *the nuclear level.* But, if any of us could have observed this phenomenon, this random emergence of a few individual photons from the darkness of the universe would *not* have made much of an impression.

---

[334] Schroeder The Science of God Chapter 4 p 61c,d
[335] Schroeder Genesis and the Big Bang Chapter 5 p 89 b
[336] Schroeder Genesis and the Big Bang Chapter 5 p 93a
[337] Steven Weinberg The First Three Minutes Chapter 5 p 110b & 112b,c
[338] Schroeder Genesis and the Big Bang Chapter 5 p 88 d

The amount of luminescence (of each individual photon of visible light) might have been just about as impressive — as the brief glow of a firefly on a dark summer night.

So, the next time you witness *the ephemeral "fireworks" of fireflies* on a dark summer night, think of Genesis 1:2c and just imagine that *the Holy Spirit is moving over the chaos of the deep — "In the Beginning."*

Several billions of earth-years would pass between the event described in Gen. 1:2c when the moving of The Spirit of God over the surface of the waters caused a few photons of light *to break free on the nuclear level* — and the events described in Gen. 1:3-5, when the first stars were born *and light broke free on the universal level.*[339] We'll discuss what science believes happened during that eon when we talk next about how Elohim made the first galaxies and stars.

WHEN ELOHIM MADE THE FIRST GALAXIES AND STARS

Genesis 1:3 is the first Biblical pronouncement of the emergence of light on the universal scale.

This verse introduces the moment Elohim ignited the billions upon billions of clusters of Hydrogen (H2—*a diatomic gas*) and Helium *gas* (He—*a monoatomic gas*), which had developed in the universe after the expansion of the Singularity before Elohim commanded: *"Let there be light."* Those stars were what scientists refer to as 1st order stars, which were massive giant stars that were several orders of magnitude larger than our sun, many of which were short lived and died in a supernova explosion. Our sun was not part of that process. Our sun would be born from the fiery death of one of those giant 1st or 2nd order stars. It would take billions of years from the first appearance of light on the universal scale before our sun would be "born." The scientific explanation of how we now think God ignited the stars is fascinating.

HOW THE FIRST GALAXIES AND STARS WERE BORN FROM CLUSTERS OF THE FIRST TWO ELEMENTS. After the universe expanded to the point where cooling to 3000 degrees Kelvin was achieved, the first matter that formed, began to fill the universe with billions of clusters of the two lightest elements. *Hydrogen* (the lightest element) was the first atom to form. It is also the simplest and most abundant element in the universe. The nucleus of an atom of Hydrogen has one proton. Protons carry a positive (+) electrical charge. A single electron, which carries a negative (−) charge, is attracted by the proton, attaches to it, and orbits the proton. When the electron attaches to the proton, the proton becomes the nucleus of the simplest atom there is: (*Hydrogen*). The second lightest element, *Helium*, has a nucleus that contains two protons and two neutrons. Neutrons are electrically neutral. Two electrons attach to the two protons and orbit the nucleus of an atom of Helium. The concentration of these two elements within the expanded universe is approximately 75% Hydrogen and 25% Helium.[340]

WEAKENING OF GRAVITATIONAL ATTRACTION

At the moment light first broke free (*at the nuclear level*), the universe was devoid of the more complex and heavier elements, which would be necessary to form life. True matter started to form, but the composition of this matter was only hydrogen, helium, photons, and neutrinos. The heavier elements would have to be synthesized, but a problem soon

---

[339] Schroeder Genesis and the Big Bang Chapter 5 p 95
[340] Schroeder Genesis and the Big Bang Chapter 5 p 90 b

developed. As the size of the universe enlarged beyond the size of a grapefruit, the expansion-inflation of the universe caused such a separation of the elements that the gravity throughout the enlarging universe was weakened. The *gravitational attraction* was so reduced that heavier nuclei could not form.[341](*) However, the formation of trillions of the first two 'lightweight' atoms of hydrogen and helium continued unabated.

IGNITING THE NUCLEAR FURNACES OF THE UNIVERSE — THE IMPORTANCE OF CLUSTERS:
Stars were needed before heavy element synthesis could begin. This would happen, but it would be a slow process requiring a lot of time. I have just explained how gravity had been weakened by the expansion-inflation that occurred. However, I did not say gravity was *"dead."* As additional eons passed, (even though the universe was continually enlarging), the weak gravitational attraction between the lightweight elements of hydrogen and helium was enough to begin the clustering of some of these lightweight elements, which were in close proximity. *Clustering was a key event.* As these clusters slowly enlarged, their increasing mass resulted in a greater gravitational pull. The eventual result was the formation of billions upon billions of enlarging *clusters of hydrogen and helium gas* throughout the expanding universe.[342]

GENESIS 1:3 *"THEN GOD SAID, LET THERE BE LIGHT, AND THERE WAS LIGHT."*
The increasing gravitational forces caused core pressures to rise. This rise in core pressure began to squeeze the hydrogen and helium nuclei together. Finally, a critical pressure was reached. The first nuclear furnaces to illumine the darkness of space with light were ignited by the fusion of trillions upon trillions *of the nuclei of Hydrogen and Helium gas* within those clusters of these first two elements. At the end of the 8-billion earth-year-equivalents of *Day One,* the 1st order stars of the universe were born.[343] Heavier element synthesis could now begin.

NEWLY FORMED HEAVY ELEMENTS WERE INITIALLY LOCKED WITHIN THE STARS.
Thus, the first matter of the universe clustered and then ignited as the universe continued to grow in size as it formed its first stars and galaxies on *Day One.* How long it took is anyone's guess, but we know it took several billions of earth-years after the first clusters of hydrogen and helium began to form. Well into *the 2nd Day of creation,* the newly formed heavier elements were still locked within the 1st order stars, which had formed at the end of *Day One.*[344] Something else was needed to bring about a release of those elements so that even heavier elements could come into being. That something else was *the death of the 1st order stars!* Since they have just been "born," so-to-speak, I will wait until the next chapter to talk about their death. That will be a subject for discussion when we talk about what happened on *the 2nd Day* (in Chapter 9, in Book II).

GENESIS 1:4A "THEN GOD SAW THAT THE LIGHT WAS GOOD."
The direct, simple, and straightforward meaning of *"the light was good"* is — God was pleased with the result of His formation of light. The light He formed fulfilled His will for the good of man.

---

[341] Schroeder Genesis and the Big Bang Chapter 5 p 90 b. (*) Gravity involves more than the simple electrical attraction of protons & electrons. The phenomenon of *Gravitational Attraction* is poorly understood.
[342] Schroeder *Genesis and the Big Bang* Chapter 5 p 90 c
[343] Schroeder *Genesis and the Big Bang* Chapter 5 p 90 c
[344] Schroeder *Genesis and the Big Bang* Chapter 5 p 91 b,c

"IT WAS GOOD," SIGNALS BOTH SATISFACTION AND COMPLETENESS.

In the first chapter of Genesis, the recurring Biblical phrase *"It Was Good,"* appears near the end of each account of *the Six Days of Creation.* Onkelos thought this phrase signaled when a work of creation was completed, durable, and satisfied the Lord.

THE BIBLICAL DESCRIPTION OF "THE DIVISION OF THE WATERS" IS A TWO-STEP PROCESS, WHICH OCCURRED ON TWO SEPARATE DAYS OF CREATION.

On *the 2nd Day,* God separated the waters *"above"* from those *"below"* when He made the *"firmament"* (which God called *"Heaven"* — Genesis 1:8). On the *3rd Day,* He separated *the waters below* (i.e., the waters on the earth), by causing the earth's *"dry land"* to appear (Genesis 1:9-10). Thus, the division of the waters occurred in two separate phases on two separate days. At the end of *the 2nd Day,* the phrase *"it was good,"* does *not* appear. But at the end of *the 3rd Day,* it *reappears* — signaling God was pleased with both separations of the waters He made. We will talk about the separation of the waters in more detail in Chapters 9 and 10 in Book II.

In the first 30 verses of the Bible, Onkelos translated *"it was good"* — literally. No deeper meaning was interpreted. However, on the *6th Day,* at the completion of all God's labor, the Hebrew text added one word to the otherwise straightforward statement of, *"it was good."* This caused Onkelos to search for a deeper meaning. We'll talk about his different interpretation of (*'it was very good'*) in Chapter 24 (in Book III), when we come to Genesis 1:31.[345]

COMMENTARY ON 'IT WAS GOOD' (GENESIS 1:4A):

The Pentateuch & Haftorahs note on *"it was good"* refers the reader to page 193 of that book — to Note A. This note is very detailed and lengthy. The parts I quote verbatim (not necessarily in the order of their appearance in my commentary) will be indicated by quotation marks. The rest will be my understanding of this commentary, which I will convey to you through paraphrasing. (For the definition of Haftorahs[346], see the footnote below.)

PARAPHRASE (#1)—THE PENTATEUCH & HAFTORAHS COMMENTARY ON, 'IT WAS GOOD:'

The first two chapters of the Book of Genesis go to the heart of the ancient Hebrew Cosmogony. Unlike all "the gods" in other ancient cultures, the Hebrew God is a kind and benevolent God who creates all to be good for the benefit of the last creature He created — man. He brings order out of the chaos of *The Beginning* to create for man a utopian home for his abode. That is the Creator's *Divine Intent*, and He carries it through. So, with every detail of His creation, and before He proceeds to His next act of creation, the Hebrew God looks at each stage of His creation to insure it is complete and fulfills His will for the ultimate good of man.

VERBATIM: (#1)

"In contrast, we find all other ancient cosmogonies, whether it be the Babylonian, or the Phoenician, the Greek, or the Roman, alike unrelievedly wild, cruel, even foul. Thus, the Assyro-Babylonian mythology tells how, before what we call earth or heaven had come

---

[345] Schroeder *Genesis and the Big Bang* Chapter 6 p 103 d,e

[346] **Haftorahs:** A series of selections from the books of the Prophets of the Hebrew Bible (the Tanakh) that is publically read in Synagogue worship. It is linked to the Torah reading that precedes it. The Haftorahs reading follows the Torah reading in worship on each Sabbath and on Jewish festivals and fast days. Also spelled: Haftarah, Haftoroh, and Haphtara.

into being, there existed a primeval watery chaos — Tiamat — out of which the gods were evolved."

PARAPHRASE (#2)—

In the Assyro-Babylonian cosmogonies, several contesting deities warred among themselves causing great carnage and the deaths of some gods as they struggled for control. There are some deities with names, which are found in the Hebrew Cosmogony — names like "*Abyss*" and "*Chaos.*" The earth, the heavens, the sun, moon, plants, animals, and man, are grotesquely created through lust, murder, mayhem, and carnage. The winner of the war of the gods is Marduk. Marduk kills Tiamat. He crushes her skull and cleaves her carcass in two. He fixed one half of her carcass on high to form a firmament to support the waters above it.

VERBATIM: (#2)—

"Many moderns feign to believe that this is the source from which Genesis One is taken. But a thorough-going Bible critic like the late Sir Godfrey Rolles Driver (Magdalen College, Oxford) *admits: 'It is incredible that the monotheistic author of Genesis One could have borrowed any detail however slight, from the polytheistic epic of the conflict of Marduk and Tiamat. When neighboring peoples deified the sun, moon and stars, or worshipped stocks and stone and beasts, the sacred river Nile, the crocodiles that swam in its waters, and the very beetles that swarmed along its banks, the opening page of scripture proclaims in language of majestic simplicity that the universe and all that therein is, are the product of one supreme directing Intelligence; of an eternal, spiritual Being, prior to them and independent of them. Judaism holds that the world was called into existence at the Will of the One, Almighty, and All-good God. Nowhere does this fundamental conviction of Israel's faith find clearer expression than in Genesis One.' "* [347]

CONCLUSION OF THE DISCUSSION OF "IT WAS GOOD:"

The *"it was good"* phrase repeated so often in the first chapter of Genesis — was made by the One, the Only, Almighty, and All-good God of the Hebrews, when He viewed each of His creations at their completion and declared them to be good, a fulfillment of His will for good, and something which would be useful, beneficial, and good for mankind.

WE WILL NOW CLOSE THIS CHAPTER WITH DISCUSSIONS OF:

- The separation of light from darkness.
- The scientific connotation of the separation of light from darkness.
- Nahmanides' explanation of Day-Night Cycles on earth.
- Day and night cycles throughout the universe.
- The religious connotations of the separation of light from darkness.
- Other separation concepts in the history of Israel.
- The names God gave to the separate entities of light and darkness.
- And the phrase — *"And there was evening and there was morning, Day One."*

THE SEPARATION OF THE LIGHT FROM THE DARKNESS:

"And God separated the light from the darkness (Gen. 1:4b)."

"And God called the light day, and the darkness He called night (Gen. 1:5a)."

---

[347] The Pentateuch and Haftorahs Edited by J. H. Hertz p. 193

THE SCIENTIFIC CONNOTATION OF THE SEPARATION OF THE LIGHT FROM THE DARKNESS. The significance of the Hebrew concept of *"separation"* has scientific and religious implications. In Genesis 1:4b—1:5a, the first layer of meaning comes from the science of the separation of the light from the darkness of the Beginning.

In the beginning (Gen. 1:1) light was trapped within the chaos of the darkness. The black fire that engulfed the Singularity was the first entity created by God! In Genesis 1:2c, after God's Spirit caused the universe to suddenly expand from the size of a microscopic dot to the size of a grapefruit, the first small amounts of true matter formed and a few individual photons of light broke free. This *first freeing* of a few random photons of visible light happened on *the nuclear level.* It would have been no more impressive than the brief glow of a few fireflies on a dark summer night.

For eight billion earth-years, clusters of hydrogen and helium gas formed within the black- of-space as the universe was expanding. Then, in Genesis 1:3, *light suddenly broke free.* This freeing of light happened on the *universal level.* At that moment, the first stars were "born" when billions upon billions of clusters of hydrogen and helium gas spontaneously ignited. We are not talking about fireflies in Genesis 1:3! We are now talking about *real candlepower!* The accumulative candlepower of all those stars flooded the universe with light. There was so much illumination that Elohim named that event. He called it ***"Day!"*** Yet, *hoshek* (the darkness of the universe) remained. Elohim called it ***"Night!"*** (See Genesis 1:5a.)

NAHMANIDES EXPLANATION OF DAY-NIGHT CYCLES

Nahmanides said: *"On the earth both evening and morning are always present. There are on the earth at every moment ever changing places where it is morning and in the places opposite them it is evening."*

This view required an understanding that the earth is a rotating sphere. This comprehension of the illumination of the sun's light on a rotating spherical earth in a time of history when the vast majority of people felt the earth was flat, and sailors were fearful of sailing off the edge of the world is truly remarkable and is evidence that Nahmanides had an advanced and well-developed understanding of the phenomena that produce the day-night cycles on earth.[348]

DAY AND NIGHT CYCLES THROUGHOUT THE UNIVERSE:

Some have wondered about this mention of the terms *Day* and *Night* on *Day One*; before the earth and the sun were made. For years I also wondered about this. However, I now realize the reason for my wondering stemmed from my provincial thinking — my earth-oriented mindset.

At billions upon billions of places throughout the universe, *before* the sun and the earth were made, day and night cycles began the moment the first galactic and universal stellar systems were formed! Day and night cycles are not the sole dominion of the earth! *Every* celestial ball spins like a bullet and orbits its own star — its own source of heat, light, and day. The night (i.e., the *hoshek* or darkness) has always been there since the beginning, and recaptures that half of all planets, which is their dark side when they spin toward it — away from the light of the stars of their solar systems. Metaphorically speaking, history teaches us we do the same thing. People and nations too — are

[348] Schroeder *Genesis and the Big Bang* Chapter 6 p 96 c and 97 a

continuously spinning from our dark side — to God's light — then, to our dark side again — and from our dark side back toward God's light of Jesus Christ. This is the struggle we experience in our daily lives — the struggle against *"our carnal flesh"* — our struggle *against our human nature* (cf. Romans 8:1-16). However, unlike the planets in space, we can break our cyclical behavior. But we can't do this on our own. We need the help of the Holy Spirit to stop our "spinning." With the Holy Spirit's help, we can say "**NO**" to our dark side. We can choose to walk and live in God's light.

THE RELIGIOUS CONNOTATION OF THE SEPARATION OF LIGHT AND DARKNESS:

The religious significance of light and darkness involves the Hebrew spiritual concept of *Tzimtzum*. Tzimtzum is *a Divine Act of God*. According to Hebrew Cosmogony, it was the spiritual withdrawal of God that began creation. The ancient Jewish sages believed this concept was conveyed by Isaiah 45:6-7 (KJV): *"I am Jehovah... there is none else; There is no God beside Me...I form light and create darkness. I make peace and create evil."*

English translations of this scripture tell us God told Isaiah: *"I form light and create darkness."* We can now understand the significance of the difference. Elohim *formed* the light from the darkness He *created* in the beginning. In the scientific sense, the ancient sages believed — *darkness was the original created thing.* They interpreted this to mean a minute spiritual withdrawal (or contraction) of God *created* the black-fire speck-of-space, which was the universe in the beginning. We have already talked about this. We have also explained: Science believes it has now discovered *the how,* of how God *formed* and *made* light. But, for me and perhaps for you, there is a problem with the last part of this scripture.

"I make peace and create evil." (???)

The idea our loving *God makes peace* doesn't surprise us. It fits with everything the Bible teaches us about God. But — *"I create **evil** ?"* That statement causes us — pain! Why would our loving God say such a thing? Is Isaiah telling us light symbolizes peace? Is he saying darkness represents evil? Is he saying: When our Creator created darkness — He actually created evil? Why would our loving God do such a thing?

THE JEWISH SAGES' COMMENTARY ON "PEACE" AND "EVIL"

The ancient Jewish Sages intuited a different meaning when they searched for the religious connotation of these words. They did not simply think light represented good and darkness represented evil — as English translations of Isaiah 45:6-7 imply. Their interpretation went much deeper.

Their concept of *"peace,"* in Isaiah 45:6-7, comes from the meaning of the Hebrew word, *"shalom"* — from the root *"shalaim"* — meaning *"wholeness or completeness."* Their understanding of the word English Bibles translate as *"evil,"* came from what they discerned would be the result of — *"A withdrawal of the shalom that the presence of the Infinite represented."* If the spiritual presence of God causes one to experience *the peace of God*, which comes from an awareness of one's *wholeness and completeness* when in God's presence: Then a loss of God's presence would result in the loss of that feeling of wholeness and completeness — a loss of contact with the peace of perfection that is God!

So it is, we see this scripture does *not* mean God created evil in the way most moderns interpret evil to mean.[349]

On a personal level we can say it means: *If we do not have God in our lives, we are not whole — we are not complete. We have shut ourselves away from God's light. And we cannot experience God's peace. In a very real modern-day sense, we have made ourselves — an easy prey for doing evil. It all has something to do with our God-given free will. It is our choice!*

This helps me understand why I *feel* bad when I *do* bad. When I am doing "bad," I have to turn my back on God to do it. When I turn my back on God, I shut myself away from God's light, and I cannot experience God's peace. When I am doing bad, The Holy Spirit convicts me. He chides me through my conscience. This causes me turn away *from my willingness to do bad.* When I turn once again toward God, confess my bad, and ask for forgiveness, God forgives and accepts me back into His light. That is when my sense of wholeness and completeness returns, and I am once again at peace with God and The Holy Spirit.

THE RELIGIONS THAT HATE FORGET WHY GOD GAVE US FREE WILL.

The religions that preach hate are *not* doing God's work. We can identify those religions by what they say and do. They say the people who don't believe as they do are "heretics" and "infidels." Their prescription for infidels and heretics who refuse to convert to their beliefs has always been persecution, torture, and a painful death. Historically, all three of the major monotheistic religions have had zealots who committed hate crimes in the name of the God they claim to worship. The following examples come to mind.

- The Jews of the Northern and Southern Kingdoms of Israel who waged Civil war against eachother for several hundreds of years (after the death of King Solomon)—
- The evil Jewish Kings of both the Northern and Southern Kingdoms, who turned their backs on the God of the Exodus (Jehovah), and worshipped and sacrificed their children to foreign gods—
- The European Roman Catholic Christian Crusaders, who waged war on Muslims in the Holy Land in eight major campaigns between 1096 AD and 1291 AD—
- The Roman Catholic Inquisitions in Medieval Europe, in which people were judged and burned at the stake for being "heretics" and "infidels"—
- The persecutions, tortures, murders, and religious wars of Protestants in Europe after they separated from the Roman Catholic Church—
- The Moorish conquest of western Europe in the 8th Century—
- And the actions of *Radical Islamists in modern times*. These seven examples come to mind.

CAREFUL HERE. I DID NOT SAY — "TRADITIONAL ISLAM."

- Traditional Muslims follow the teachings of the Islamic prophet and messenger Muhammad (Sunnah). They preach and practice peace! Traditional Muslims believe God (Allah) is eternal, transcendent, and absolutely one. Allah is incomparable, self-sustaining and neither begets nor was begotten. They believe Islam is the complete and universal version of a primordial faith that has been

---

[349] Schroeder *The Science of God* Chapter 1 p 17 a

revealed before through many prophets including Abraham, Ismael, Isaac, Moses, and Jesus. They believe these previous messages and revelations have been partially changed or corrupted over time, and that the Quran (that came from God's most revered prophet—Muhammad) is the final unaltered revelation from Allah.

- The Muslims I personally know are "Traditional Islamists." They are some of the best, honest, honorable, upright, and friendly people I have ever known. I have great admiration and respect for them because of the peace they practice in their daily lives and because of the good they do. To them, the historical Jesus Christ of Nazareth was one of the prophets of Allah. Although they do not believe he was the Son of God, I can still find common ground with them. I will always extend my hand of loving friendship to Traditional Muslims.

- To those Christians who would accuse me of being a hypocrite for saying this, I say—I know God can and will handle all the religious differences the mind of mortal man can conceive. Furthermore, I place my trust in Jesus. Jesus will handle my "hypocrisy." This I absolutely know — ***God and Jesus look at our love for eachother.***

NO! I SAID — RADICAL ISLAMISTS" —

- Because throughout their history and continuing to the present, Radical Islamists preach and practice — *"Death to all Infidels!"* To all of you *"progressives"* out there who object to the term ("Radical Islamists") and claim those who use the term are *"Islamophobics"* — I say: **Your Cognitive Dissonance has blinded you!** Heaven help you! If you come under their thumb, you will not like it! For those who wish to read an interesting article about *radical Islamic terrorism* and its affinity in form and spirit to the radical Western ideologies that produced the terrors of *Hitlerian Germany and the Stalinist Soviet Union*, I refer you to the article written by Scott Philip Segrest: *"Radical Islam and Modern Ideology."*[350]

CONVERSION THROUGH COERCION—

What part of *free will* do those who hate not understand? God values *free will* so much that He gave it to us — all the while knowing His gift would someday cost Him the mortal life of His Son, Jesus Christ! Because of our prejudices, and with our judgments of others: We, who claim to be the people of the One True God (i.e., peaceful Jews, peaceful Christians, and peaceful Traditional Muslims), have been hurting eachother and God, ever since He made us! Oh, how I wish we could learn to love one another, and treat *all people*, as we would want to be treated.

THE GOD OF ALL CREATION IS A LOVING, PEACEFUL GOD.

Zealots don't know or forget — God is Love! Arguably, some have said: Peace loving Muslims, Christians, Jews, and all others who believe God is Love — worship the same God, although they may call Him different names. All of us who believe *"God is love,"* must try to practice the love and peace of God. As you will see when you read Appendix III (in Book III), and *"The Choice We Face"* (in the Epilogue — also in Book III) — **God looks at our love!**

---

[350] https://sites01.lsu.edu/faculty/voegelin/wp-content/uploads/sites/80/2015/09/Scott-Segrest1.pdf

OTHER SEPARATION EVENTS IN ISRAEL'S HISTORY

In the third chapter of Genesis, we discover man can separate himself from God, as Adam and Eve did when they disobeyed God's command and were so ashamed, they hid from Him (Gen. 3:8). If you hide from God, there is no chance He will be intimate with you. On this, Nahmanides said: *"God knows all life, but the degree of Divine direction to an individual person depends on that person's individual choice of how close to God he or she wishes to be."* [351]

The degree of our closeness to God is a matter of *our free will. It is a matter of our choice.* In Genesis 12, God commands Abraham (then named Abram) to leave Mesopotamia and go to a land God would show him. God commands this so that Abraham would separate himself from the pagan influences of the society in which he was born. Later, in the Biblical narrative of Genesis, we see separation within families (Abraham from Lot and Jacob from Esau). We know Abraham and Jacob remained faithful to God. Lot and Esau were exposed to pagan influences and turned from God. There was also the separation of the infant nation of Israel from their pagan neighbors in the Holy Land, and in Egypt as well. As part of His command to avoid pagan influences, God fostered the concept of marriage within the tribe. In Exodus 19:6, God commanded Moses to tell Israel: ***"You shall be to Me a kingdom of priests and a holy nation."***

HOLY—SEPARATE—SET APART

The Hebrew word for holy is "*kodesh.*" *Kodesh* means, "separate," and "set apart." The modern connotation of "holy" misses the mark, relating the word to being worthy of adoration.[352] Spiritual separation from worldly lusts and unjust practices is also an important Christian concept. Christ commanded us to be *in* the world, but not *of* it.[353] Thus, this first mention of "*separation*" (in Genesis 1:4b) has far flung religious implications for the nation of Israel and Christians as well. We'll talk more about "*kodesh*" in Chapters 25 and 28 (in Book III).

GEN. 1:5B: "AND THERE WAS EVENING ('EREV') AND THERE WAS MORNING ('BOKER'), Day One." This is a strange phrase because we think each day begins with morning and ends with evening. Our concept of the sequence of the day and night cycle is reversed in this scripture. However, the straightforward, simple meaning of this phrase can be easily understood if we are made aware of the Jewish concept of the beginning of a day. The Jewish definition of "*a day,*" comes from Leviticus 23:32. This scripture tells the Jews when *The Day of Atonement* (the holiday the Jews call Yom Kipper) will begin and end. *"It shall be for you as a Sabbath of solemn rest...from evening to evening you shall celebrate your Sabbath" Lev. 23:32."*

The holiday begins with evening and extends to the beginning of the following evening. [354] Thus, this language construct for the average person goes no deeper than the Jewish concept of — "a day." The sages had to dig to uncover the deeper meaning.

[351] Schroeder *The Hidden Face of God* Chapter 11 p 177 a
[352] Schroeder *The Science of God* Chapter 5 p 77 a
[353] *The Ryrie Study Bible* note on John 17:15 states: Christ does not teach withdrawal from the world, but that Christians should be in the world but not of it—vs.14-16.
[354] Schroeder *Genesis and the Big Bang* Chapter 6 p 96 a

THE DEEPER MEANING OF THE PHRASE: "THERE WAS EVENING AND THERE WAS MORNING."
This phrase is repeated at the conclusion of each day of creation. This six-fold repetition calls attention to the phrase. It adds an emphasis, the meaning of which was elusive to early Bible scholars. Why repeat the phrase? Nahmanides, backed by Onkelos, provided a brilliant insight into the language of Moses with his interpretation, which is solidly based on an understanding of the deeper meaning of the Hebrew language.

EVENING = EREV = CHAOS

The Hebrew word for evening is "*erev.*" The root of *erev* means mixed-up, stirred together, disorderly, chaos. Evening is followed by darkness. As the light fades, our vision becomes progressively impaired. Today, when evening comes with its darkness, we simply turn on a light. However, before electricity, before the wide range of lights we can now call to our command, imagine what descending darkness would have meant to the ancient Hebrew. The outlines of objects would have become blurred, mixed-up, and disorderly as night fell. Continued activity without some illuminating source would have resulted in chaos.

MORNING = BOKER = ORDERLY

The Hebrew word for morning is "*boker.*" It has the *opposite* meaning of "*erev.*" Boker means discernible, distinguishable, and orderly. Morning brings the first light. As the dawn rises, objects become more and more distinct. Human activity can be conducted with the order that clear vision provides.

NAHMANIDES—

decided the text is telling us something crucial about the flow of matter in the universe — something that can only happen to a subsystem contained within and yet is still in contact with a larger system. The phenomenon was so important that it was identified six times in the Biblical Creation account — as the flow from evening to morning. We are being told: *On each day of God's creation, there was a systematic flow from each evening's darkness (i.e., the persistent disorder of the initial act of creation, which in the Beginning, initiated the chaos of the black-fire dot) → to the progressive ordering of each new morning's light (i.e., the incremental ordered harmonious cosmos, which resulted from God's creative activity on each of the Six Days of Creation).*[355]

GENESIS 1:5B. "And there was evening and there was morning, DAY ONE."

Day One has a special meaning of its own. We measure the age of the universe to be 15 ¾ billion earth-year-equivalents. When we state its age in billions of "earth-years," we are talking about an earth-based time-reference-frame, which is looking backward from the present to the past. However, the Bible's perspective is God's perspective. God looks forward from the beginning. As we have stated before, the Bible's perspective is a God-based time-reference-frame. We learn this from the biblical text, which calls the first day of creation, *"Day One"* — instead of — "the 1st day." Moses used the absolute <u>cardinal form</u> — *"Day One"* — because it was viewing time from the beginning of time looking forward toward the future — a perspective from which there was no other time for comparison.[356] Remember Nahmanides said: **"When the first matter formed, time grabbed hold."** [357] By this he meant Biblical time started on *"Day One,"* the moment the

[355] Schroeder *Genesis and the Big Bang* Chapter 6 p 96-98
[356] Schroeder *The Science of God* Chapter 4 p 65 b, c
[357] Schroeder *The Science of God* Chapter 4 p 65 b

first matter formed. For the days of creation which follow, the <u>ordinal</u> <u>form</u> of numbering is used: the 2nd day, the 3rd day, etc., because each additional day of creation is a time-reference-frame which is based on *Day One* of Genesis[358]

APPLYING THE GENESIS CODE TO GENESIS 1:3-5

Gen. 1:3 NASB "Then god said, let there be light, and there was light."
The Genesis Code: *Next, by His Word, God formed the Light out of the Darkness.*
Gen. 1:4a NASB "Then God saw that the light was good."
The Genesis Code: *When God examined the Light, He was satisfied, called it good, and determined it was complete, and fulfilled His Will for the benefit of man.*
Gen. 1:4b NASB "And God separated the light from the darkness."
The Genesis Code: *Then God willed the Light to separate from the Darkness.*
Gen. 1:5a NASB "And God called the light day, and the darkness He called night."
The Genesis Code: *God named the Light "Day," and He named the Darkness, "Night."*
Gen. 1:5b NASB "And there was evening and there was morning, Day One."
The Genesis Code: *At the end of His Work on Day One, God was pleased the Light He separated from the chaos of the Darkness of the Beginning—calmed the Darkness and brought forth a degree of Order.*

DAY ONE

Day#	Start of Day	End of Day	Bible's Description	Scientific Description
One	15 ¾ billion earth-years Before Adam. Adam was created in ~3700 BC or ~5700 earth-yrs. Before the Present.	7 ¾ billion earth-years Before Adam (B.A.)	Universe created. Light separates from the Darkness of the Beginning. (Gen. 1:1-5)	The Big Bang marks the Creation of the universe. Light breaks free as Electrons bond to atomic nuclei. Stars & Galaxies start to form.

Day one lasted 8 billion earth-years. [B.A. means 'before Adam.']

Summary Points:
The first time God imposed His Will was when He initiated Creation with His Tzimtzum.
God's Tzimtzum caused the Big Bang.
The second time God imposed His Will on Creation was when He Willed His Holy Spirit to hover over the chaos of the Singularity. (Gen. 1:2c)
Each additional time God imposed His Will on Creation is marked with the Biblical phrase: "Then God said."
For God to say something is for Him to do it.
Each time God spoke, a new work was done.
God's Word is all-powerful.
With First Wisdom, God created.
First Wisdom is the Word of God.
The Word of God Is Jesus Christ.

---

[358] Schroeder *The Science of God* Chapter 4 p 67

Jesus Christ is the image of the invisible God, the first born of creation.

In the Old Testament the Pre-incarnate Jesus Christ is the Hidden Face of God.

The deeper meaning of this statement for Christians is Jesus Christ is in the Old Testament, concealed. He is in the New Testament, revealed.

The Pre-incarnate Jesus Christ was in the beginning with God.

The Pre-incarnate Jesus Christ was the First Wisdom of God.

Through Him were made all things that were made.

Jesus Christ is our link (our pathway), to God the Father. *"In Him was life, and the life was the light of men* (John 1:4)!"

In the beginning, full spectrum light was created by ELOHIM'S TZIMTZUM. However, it was so powerful it would not have been visible to humans. It was a black-fire dot-of-space (i.e., the Singularity), which was so chaotic that visible light was locked in.

The light that was formed in Genesis 1:3 with God's pronouncement of "Let there be light," was visible light.

At the nuclear level, Light emerged from the darkness of the chaos of the Singularity when The Holy Spirit's stirring of the chaos within the Singularity caused it to expand and the first true matter to form. (Gen. 1:2c)

At the universal level, it was released by the nuclear fusion within the billions of first order stars that God formed and ignited within the cores of billions of galactic clusters of hydrogen & helium, which He fashioned throughout the universe on Day One. (Gen. 1:3)

Each star became a factory for producing the heavy elements of the universe that (in our corner of the universe) would be used by God to form our Sun, our earth, and Life, as we know it.

The *"It was good"* phrase (repeated so often in Genesis 1), was made by the One and Only Almighty and All-good God of the Hebrews when He viewed the completion of each of His creations and declared them to be good, a fulfillment of His Will for good, and something, which would be beneficial and good for mankind.

Separation has both a scientific and a religious significance.

From the scientific perspective, the first separation in creation occurred between light and darkness.

Darkness was the first substance God created.

The Singularity was a Black-Fire Dot of Extreme Chaos.

On the Universal level, visible Light (with a candlepower sufficient to illumine the universe) emerged when the core pressures within the billions of clusters of hydrogen and helium gas reached the ignition level. At that point, the H and He nuclei underwent fusion, and the first Stars were born.

God's naming of "Day" and "Night" signaled the completion of His work on "Day One," and His ownership and approval of His work.

In a religious sense:

God's Light is the spiritual presence of God in our lives

Darkness is — the absence of God in our lives.

The presence or absence of God in a person's life is a matter of that person's free will —his or her free choice.

It is a matter of how close to God a person chooses to be.

When one applies The Genesis Code to the repeated phrase: *"And there was evening and there was morning,"* one understands: Each act of God on the six days of creation brought about a degree of order out of creation's initial chaos.

Man's perspective of time looks backward from the present to the Beginning.

The Lord God is Eternal — that is, He has always existed. He has no beginning and no end. Everything about God's existence is in the perspective of an eternal, never ending NOW. However, so far as the creation account is concerned, God's time-perspective looks forward from the moment of the Beginning to the present.

The phrase, *"Day One,"* conveys the deeper meaning that the Bible's perspective of time in the six days of creation is God's perspective. God looks forward in time from the moment of the Beginning to the present. Although God knows the date, God is also looking forward to the time of the Second Coming of Christ. (Pun intended.)

We must all do our part to help bring about Christ's return by going into the world in the name of the Father, Son, and Holy Spirit, teaching the world to observe all that Christ commanded. (Matt. 28:19-20).

THE HIDDEN FACE OF GOD IS 1ST REVEALED IN THE GENESIS 5 GENEALOGY.

We often skim over the 5th Chapter of Genesis because, at first glance, it is a boring list of the genealogy of Adam to Noah. However, when scholars looked for the deeper meaning of the Hebrew names of the 10 men listed, they were astounded by what they discovered. Their study of the *original roots of the Hebrew names* in the Adam to Noah Genealogy disclosed God's first Biblical revelation of the Gospel of Jesus Christ.

Hebrew Name:	English Meaning:	The Hidden Meaning:
Adam	*Man*	*"Man is appointed mortal sorrow,*
Seth	*Appointed*	*But, the Blessed God shall come*
Enos	*Mortal*	*down teaching that His death shall*
Kenan	*Sorrow*	*bring the despairing rest."*
Mahalalel	*Blessed God*	
Jared	*Shall come down*	*'The Blessed God who came down*
Enoch	*Teaching*	teaching *was Jesus Christ.*
Methuselah	*His death shall bring.*	
Lamech	*the Despairing*	This is the Gospel hidden in the Genesis
Noah	*Rest*	5 Genealogy of Adam to Noah.

The Bible is the product of God's supernatural engineering. It is an integrated message system consisting of 66 books, penned by 40 authors over thousands of years. Here, we find the first message of the Gospel of Christ, *hidden* in the Genealogy of the 5th Chapter of Genesis. God had already laid out His plan for the redemption of man from the original sin committed in the Garden of Eden by Eve and Adam. The history of man started in the Garden of Eden. In the last chapter of the last book of the New Testament (The Book of Revelation), the Bible comes full circle. *In heaven* we again find *The Tree of Life*—the same tree that stood in the center of the Garden of Eden—now freely available to all believers—*because they have been granted entry into God's Eternity Future.*

(Ref: Chuck Missler: Internet Article: Your questions answered: Meanings of the Names in the 5th chapter of Genesis).

The Genesis Code—Day One & The Standard Model of the Big Bang

The Genesis Code and Day One: Gen.1:1 correlates to (1.) of the Big Bang Theory. Gen.1:2 correlates to (2.) of the Big Bang Theory. Gen.1:3-5 correlates to (3.) of the Big Bang Theory.	Standard Model of The Big Bang Theory: The scientific correlate to the Biblical narrative of Creation in Genesis 1:1-5.
(1) Creation of 'the dot'/the Singularity (Gen1:1) *In the Beginning of creation, by a minute degree of Spiritual Contraction (Tzimtzum), & with First Wisdom, The Strong One, The Supreme Leader, The Almighty God created the heavens and the earth from nothing.* (Nahmanides believed Elohim's Tzimtzum caused an immense explosion, which initiated the beginning by creating a tiny speck of space that was infinitely small, hot, and chaotic.)	(1) All Existence started with an immense explosion, that science has named: The Big Bang. The Big Bang created an infinitely small speck of space, the Singularity. The Singularity was composed of almost pure energy and a tiny amount of primordial pseudo-matter, which was in a continual chaotic state of flux and flow. The cause of this explosion is unknown.
(2) From the Singularity (i.e., 'the Dot') / to the Universe (i.e., 'the Circle'): (Gen.1:2a) *When Elohim began creating, and before He formed the heavens and the earth, His Tzimtzum created a primeval speck of space, ('the Dot') that was filled with the ethereal building blocks of primordial pseudo-matter. All that was within that primeval speck-of-space was in a state of extreme chaos. (Gen.1:2b) The chaos of that primeval speck of space was enveloped by the darkness of a Black Fire. Thus, darkness was upon the face of the primeval great chaos of the Beginning. (Gen. 1:2c,d) Then The Wind of God Hovered over that tiny black-fire speck-of-space (the 'dot') and nurtured it, protected it, & made It swell & grow* (into the 'Circle').	(2) The Singularity was a violent black fire that had the potential to produce all matter. The excessive gravitational pull within the Singularity created a black hole that threatened its existence. Suddenly, an expansion inexplicably occurred which caused the separation needed for true matter to form. In the 'Blink of a Geological Eye,' The Singularity expanded from a microscopic dot to the size of a grapefruit. Science cannot explain what caused the sudden expansion of the Singularity. (Nahmanides believed the sudden expansion was caused by God's Spirit—The Wind of God, or a "Ruach Elohim"—in Hebrew).
(3) Gen.1:3-5. (From Darkness to Light): *Next, by His Word, God formed the Light out of the Darkness. When God examined the Light, He was satisfied, called it good, and determined it was complete, and it fulfilled His Will for the benefit of man. Then God willed the Light to separate from the Darkness. God named the Light "Day," and He named the Darkness, "Night." At the end of His Work on Day One, God was pleased the Light He separated from the chaos of the Darkness of the Beginning—calmed the Darkness and brought forth a degree of Order.*	(3) After the expansion, the chaos subsided so that visible light could separate from matter & emerge. The matter consisted of 75% Hydrogen (H) & 25% Helium (He). But the expansion had caused so much cooling that no heavy element synthesis could occur. Over eons the cumulative effect of gravity caused these 1st two elements to gather into billions of gaseous clusters of (H) & (He) gas throughout the continually expanding universe. When core pressures reached a critical point, clusters of (H) & (He) ignited & formed the first stars. Heavy element synthesis could begin. Light permeated all corners of the universe as star birth & star death caused a cycle of production of the elements that would be needed to form life.

APPENDIX I: HOW THE EARTH-YEAR PERSPECTIVES OF THE SIX DAYS OF GENESIS WERE CALCULATED[359]

The Earth-Year Perspectives in this Chart Reflect CBR "Earth influenced Data" (or EID).

Duration of Each Day from God's Perspective Looking forward in time from the Start of Day One.	Duration of Each Day from the Earth's Perspective Looking backward in time From the present.	Approximate years before Adam at the start of Each day.
Day One 24 hrs of God's Time	8 billion earth-years	15 ¾ billion earth-years ago
2nd Day 24 hrs of God's Time	4 billion earth-years	7 ¾ billion earth-years ago
3rd Day 24 hrs of God's Time	2 billion earth-years	3 ¾ billion earth-years ago
4th Day 24 hrs of God's Time	1 billion earth-years	1 ¾ billion earth-years ago
5th Day 24 hrs of God's Time	½ billion earth-years	¾ billion earth-years ago
6th Day 24 hrs of God's Time	¼ billion earth-years	¼ billion earth-years ago
6-24-hr-days God's Time	Total: 15 ¾ billion Earth-Years	Days Before the Present

These Earth-year-equivalents for each "Day" of Creation were determined from Radio Telescopes located on the Earth. Therefore, this data is influenced by Earth's gravity and its orbital speed-of-travel around our Sun. Thus, this chart contains "EID."

This chart requires some explanation. I promised you only one equation ($E=mc^2$), but perhaps I may be forgiven if I tell you — the equations in this appendix are for those who have quantitative minds and have no problems with equations. If equations 'turn you off,' you might want to skip the following explanation.

In this chart — while each of the 6 days of Genesis One are listed as 24 hours of God's Time — the earth's perspective of each day is given in earth-years, which are exactly the same as those that Adam experienced, and we experience today. The earth-year length of each of the succeeding six days of creation is half again as long as the day that preceded it. The number of earth-years in each of the days of creation in Genesis One is calculated according to the following equation:

$$A = A_0\, e^{-Lt}$$

Where: **A** is earth-time — i.e., the number of earth-years contained in each Genesis Creation-Day during the six-day period of creation. **A₀** is the ratio of CBR (Cosmic Microwave Background Radiation) temperature then (10.9×10^{12} degrees Kelvin in the beginning), to now (2.73 Kelvin in our present). **L** is the natural log of 2 (written *ln 2*) & equals 0.693 divided by the half period — for each Genesis Day. And **t** is time in Genesis Days (with **t** increasing from zero to 6).

An understanding of **e** in the equation requires an appreciation of the concept of a narrowing of the perspective that each day of creation represents, as the focus of the Genesis Creation Narrative progressively narrows from the generalities of the scope of the universe at large to the more narrow focus of the specifics of each succeeding day of creation. Each day of the Genesis Creation Account exponentially represents fewer earth-years as perceived from our earthly vantage point. However, the biblical relationship for

---

time is *not* an artificial ten-based logarithmic scale that is commonly used in graphing data that range over many orders of magnitude, and which are displayed on a logarithmic graph. Instead, the Genesis Creation Account has chosen a base that occurs throughout the universe: A base of *scientific notation* that is known in mathematics as — *the natural log of e*.

The graceful curve of the Nautilus seashell occurs in nature more often than any other shape. Its lines trace out an exponential spiral where each successive swirl becomes wider by a fixed mathematical factor. Nature shows this beautifully displayed graceful succession of swirls in the curves of animal tusks, the distribution of the seeds of a sunflower, and the location and spread of the stars in the spiral galaxies of the universe at large — our own Milky Way Galaxy included. Jakob Bernoulli formulated the shape of this curve in the mathematical terms of polar coordinates:

$$r = e^{aH}$$

Where *r* is the distance from the x-y intersection on a graph (i.e., the origin, *0*); **a** is a constant; and *H* is the angle between the line of origin *Or* and the x-axis. As *H* increases in value, *r* spirals out from its origin.

The negative of this equation:

$$r = e^{-aH}$$

mathematically describes the relationships of the spiral in the other direction as the spirals travel toward their origin in a swirling vortex that has no end, and always moves closer to, but never reaches the origin.

Just as the value of *pi* or *π* (3.14159…) is basic to descriptions of all circles (i.e., π times the diameter of a circle equals its circumference), so *the natural log of e* is basic to all spirals. Actually, a circle can be seen as a special case of a spiral where the rate of growth is zero. The natural log of *e* appears throughout nature and mathematics.

In order to learn the duration of each Genesis Day as viewed from earth's perspective of time, one must integrate the equation thus:

Integral of $A = (-A_0 / L)\, e^{-Lt}$

and solve the integrated equation for each of the 6 days. Since the units are days, one must convert the earth-days to earth-years by dividing by 365. The result gives the data in the preceding Table.

One must take the calculated duration of each of the six days of creation and add them together to obtain a prediction of the age of the universe. The sum of the six days equals 15.75 billion earth-years. Thus, the age of the universe as determined by earth-influenced measurements is 15 ¾ billion earth-years.

———————————

THIS CONCLUDES BOOK I: ACT ONE: THE 1ST TELLING OF THE GENESIS CREATION ACCOUNT. From the Beginning to the end of Day One covers a period of time, which is the equivalent of 8 billion earth-years. The narrative in Genesis 1:1-5 is told From God's Perspective — In God's Time-Flow.

THERE ARE TWO MORE BOOKS IN THIS SERIES. BOOK II: IS ACT TWO OF THE CREATION ACCOUNT. IT COVERS THE 2ND TELLING, WHICH TELLS THE TALE OF THE 2ND THROUGH THE 6TH DAYS OF CREATION. The Biblical Account of the 2nd Telling is told in Genesis 1:6-25. In Book II, God's Perspective shifts from the universe to the earth on the 3rd Day. The 2nd Telling is told in a Time-Flow of five God-related Days. If we were to express those last five Days of Creation in earth-years, they would have been the equivalent of 7 ¾ billion earth-years.

BOOK III IS ACT THREE: THE 3RD TELLING — FROM THE END OF THE 6TH DAY TO THE END OF THE 7TH DAY. This account is told in Genesis 1:26 — Genesis 2:25. The 3rd Telling is told from Adam's Perspective, and in Adam's Time-Flow of a literal 24 hour-Day. *"Adam's time"* was the same as our time — i.e., identical to our current days. Therefore, the duration of *the very 1st Sabbath* (i.e., the 7th Day, was literally 24-hours — the same amount of time-flow that we experience as *"a day"*). This will be explained in Book III.

Soli Deo Gloria,
O. David

THE COSMOGONY OF THE ANCIENT OF DAYS:
MODERN SCIENCE AGREES WITH MOSES & NAHMANIDES
BOOK II: THE 2ND — THE 6TH DAY OF CREATION

ON THE 2ND DAY, EARTH CHANGED

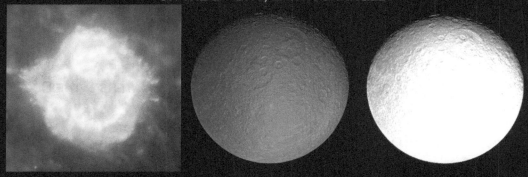

FROM A **FIERY BALL** IN **SPACE** (2ND DAY) → **A TOXIC WATER-WORLD** (3RD DAY) → **A SNOW-BALL EARTH** (4TH DAY)

LATE ON THE 4TH DAY, OUR LIFE-FRIENDLY BLUE PLANET WAS BORN

DINOSAURS, MAN-LIKE HOMINIDS, AND MAN ON THE 6TH DAY

By: Dr. David E. Marley, Jr. MD (O. David)

Book II is a tutorial on the earth sciences.

CONTENTS OF BOOK II

THE COSMOGONY OF THE ANCIENT OF DAYS:
MODERN SCIENCE AGREES WITH MOSES & NAHMANIDES
BOOK II: ACT II—THE 2ND TELLING

CHARTS & IMAGES:

CHAPTER 9: THE 2ND DAY—GOD'S 1ST SEPARATION OF THE WATERS & THE BEGINNING OF THE EARTH.

By the Word of God, the heavens existed long ago, and the Earth was formed out of water and by water.
II Peter 3:5

Praise God in His sanctuary; Praise Him in His mighty expanse. Ps. 150:1

And God called the expanse Heaven. Gen. 1:8

Praise God from the Heavens. Praise God from the Highest Heavens, and the waters that are above the Heavens. Ps. 148:1,4

Praise God from the Earth. Ps. 148:7

"From the fact that the Sun appeared on the 4th Day, we learn that during the first three days, the Holy One used to create and destroy worlds.   *Rabbi Abahu, 5th Century AD*

And the LORD GOD of hosts, the One who touches the land so that it melts.   *Amos 9:5*

THE 2ND DAY OF CREATION LASTED 4 BILLION EARTH-YEARS.

2nd Day: 24hrs. of God's Time	Lasted 4 billion years	Started 7 ¾ billion yrs. BA
God's Time Perspective	Earth's Time Perspective	Earth-years before Adam[1]

[1] Schroeder *The Science of God* (Table) Chapter 4 p 67

Genesis 1:6-8 [6]*Then God said, let there be an expanse in the midst of the waters, and let it separate the waters from the waters. (Some translations use firmament for expanse.) [7]And God made the expanse and separated the waters which were below, from the waters which were above the expanse; and it was so. [8]**And God called the expanse heaven.** And there was evening and there was morning, a Second Day.* (NASB)

This scripture tells us what God did on the *2nd Day*. He created an expanse in the midst of the waters. His purpose was to separate the waters *above* from the waters *below*. **Then, He named that expanse. God called it "*Heaven.*"** Plain as day? No! Once again, the Bible speaks to us in code. We now have a new list of questions to ponder.

In this chapter, we'll talk about *Four Questions, Two Perspectives & a Perplexing Mystery.*

1. What is the expanse God called Heaven?
   A. The religious meaning of Heaven.
   B. The scientific meaning of Heaven — Nahmanides on the Mystery of Heaven.
2. What is water? An Introduction to Water.
3. What are the waters above Heaven? They are the waters in deep space—in The "Highest Heavens,"(i.e., above the Earth's Heaven)—a Universal Perspective.
4. What are the waters below Heaven? They are our waters on Earth—Perspective of the Earth.
5. During the Bible's discussion of the 2nd Day of Creation, the perspective of the Creation Account begins to Focus on the Earth.
6. The Vision of Amos (an Earthly perspective) will be introduced.
7. Then, this chapter will conclude with a Perplexing Mystery—Volcanism and Earth's 1st Rain.

1. <u>WHAT IS THE EXPANSE GOD CALLED HEAVEN?</u>

The Psalmist wrote: *Praise God in His sanctuary; Praise Him in His mighty expanse. Ps. 150:1 (NASB)*

A. THE RELIGIOUS MEANING OF HEAVEN—THE ABODE OF GOD

Two thousand years ago, as the disciples watched Jesus being lifted up in the sky from the Mount of Olives, *a cloud received Him out of their sight.* As He was ascending, they were intently gazing into the sky. When He disappeared in *the* cloud that received Him, they suddenly became aware two angels (in white clothing) were standing beside them. The angles asked: *"Men of Galilee, why do you stand looking into the sky? This Jesus, who has been taken up from you into heaven, will come* (again) *in just the same way as you have watched Him go into heaven (Acts 1:9-11)."* This account in the first chapter of Acts is vitally important to all Christians because it gives us important information about heaven, and it promises Christ will come again. Let us now consider what the Bible says about *Heaven*.

THE CLOUD THAT RECEIVED JESUS WHEN HE ASCENDED FROM MT. OLIVET

Psalm 150:1 tells us God's sanctuary is His mighty expanse. Genesis 1:8 tells us God called (named) His mighty expanse "*Heaven*." The disciples knew, when Christ was transfigured, God had spoken from a bright cloud. Peter, James, and John witnessed it. From the cloud God said:

"This is My beloved Son with whom I am well pleased. Listen to Him" (Matt. 17:1-21; Mark 9:2-7; & II Peter 1:16-18).

From their childhood, the disciples had heard the stories of the Exodus when God led the children of Israel through the wilderness of Sinai in a Pillar of Cloud by day and a Pillar of Fire by night. They heard about the many instances when God appeared to His people cloaked in a cloud.

In His first advent, God sent Jesus to earth to show us how to live. Jesus also came to atone for our sins by becoming the sacrificial Lamb of God. At the moment of His ascension, Christ had completed His first mission to the earth, and He was returning to Heaven to be with His Father. The disciples understood the cloud that received Jesus when He ascended from the Mount of Olives was God the Father. The disciples believed God had cloaked Himself in a cloud to receive His wounded Son and escort Him back to Heaven. These verses also tell us He promised to return again to earth (His 2nd Advent) — in the same way.

HEAVEN IS GOD'S ABODE.

In the Introduction, I mentioned the Heavens have long been considered the abode of the gods. Christians know Heaven is the abode of the One True God. The Bible is full of religious statements about Heaven. However, there is a lot of mystery in these statements. For example, when the apostle Paul spoke of a man who was caught up to *the 3rd Heaven* (II Cor. 12:2), Paul was referring to himself.

In II Chron. 2:6, after Solomon built his magnificent Temple to God, he wrote: *"But who is able to build a house for Him? The Heavens and the Highest Heavens cannot contain Him."*

In Revelation 19:11, the apostle John wrote several mystical statements about Heaven. In regard to the promised Second Advent of Christ he wrote:

- *"And I saw Heaven opened; and behold, a white horse, and He who sat upon it is called faithful and true; and in righteousness He judges and wages war."*
- In Revelations 11:14, John had already written: *"And the armies which are in Heaven, clothed in fine linen, white and clean were following Him on white horses."*
- In Rev. 19:17-18, he also wrote: *"And I saw an angel standing in the sun; and he cried out with a loud voice saying to all the birds which fly in midheaven, come, assemble before the great supper of God in order that you may eat the flesh of kings."* (This is part of the description of the Battle of Armageddon.)
- Furthermore, John wrote: *"And I saw a New Heaven and a new earth; for the first Heaven and the first Earth passed away, and there is no longer any sea. And I saw the holy city, the New Jerusalem, coming down out of Heaven from God, made ready as a bride adorned for her husband"* (Rev. 21:1-2)

Eight hundred years earlier, when he talked about the future Millennial Kingdom, Isaiah said God said:

- *"For behold, I create (barah) a New Heavens and a New Earth. But be glad and rejoice forever in what I create; for behold I create Jerusalem for rejoicing and her people for gladness"* (Isaiah 65:17-18).
- Isaiah also wrote: *"Thus says the Lord, Heaven is My throne, and the Earth is My footstool"* (Isaiah 66:1).

Although the phrase, the birds which fly in midheaven, clearly refers to the sky of our Earth, there is much mystery in the other verses concerning the meaning of Heaven — the Highest Heavens — the 3rd Heaven — the armies in Heaven — a New Heaven — a New Earth — the passing away of the First Heaven and the First Earth — and the New Jerusalem coming down out of Heaven from God. For Christians, these mystical terms have special meanings. For example, Christians understand Paul's *3rd Heaven* is the abode of God and their future home. There is no doubt when the Bible is referring to Heaven in its metaphysical sense (as it is in these statements), it is emphasizing the religious connotation of Heaven. However, *the 3rd Heaven* is a real place. For Christians, the metaphysical is just as real as the physical, because it represents their future reality — their eternal life after death. However, since the main premise of this book is — *the language of the Creation Account is science* — we will now turn our attention to the scientific meaning of Heaven.

B. THE SCIENTIFIC MEANING OF HEAVEN—NAHMANIDES ON THE MYSTERY OF HEAVEN

Let's start with a statement of Nahmanides. In referring to Genesis 1:8, Nahmanides said—

"The Heaven God formed on the 2nd Day initially intercepted the light that existed from Day One."

He was not willing to comment further on the composition of Heaven, because he considered it one of the deep mysteries of the Bible. So, we are on our own when we ponder his concepts of Heaven.[360]

PSALM 148 GIVES US THE ANSWER.

There are two inspired writers in the Old Testament, who use the same words when they talk about Heaven. I think this helps us understand and distinguish the deeper meaning of Heaven. The first writer is Solomon who introduces a distinction regarding Heaven. The second writer is an unknown psalmist who clarifies Solomon's distinction. In II Chronicles 2:6, Solomon makes reference to two Heavens — *the Heavens* and *the Highest Heavens.* What is Solomon talking about? Is there a difference? The writer of Psalms 148 not only refers to the two Heavens (using Solomon's exact words), but he also defines the words for us and clarifies their meaning. Psalms 148 is a Creation Psalm, a psalm of praise to the Lord. It can be divided into two parts.

"PRAISE THE LORD FROM THE HEAVENS" — PSALMS 148:1-6

The 1st six verses of Psalms 148 mention those entities from the Heavens that should praise God.

1"PRAISE THE LORD! Praise the Lord ªfrom the Heavens; Praise Him in the ᵇheights! 2Praise Him, ªall His angels; Praise Him, ᵇall His hosts! 3Praise Him, sun and moon; Praise Him, all stars of light! 4Praise Him, ªHighest Heavens, and the ᵇwaters that are above the Heavens! 5Let them praise the name of the Lord, for ªHe commanded and they were created. 6He has also ªestablished them forever and ever. He has made a ᵇdecree, which will not pass away" Psalms 148:1-6.

These first six verses of Psalms 148 are focused on things that are *in and from the Heavens.* The Psalmist first says to praise the Lord — *from the Heavens.* He next says to praise Him — *in the heights*. Then he mentions angels, the hosts of the Lord, the sun and moon, all stars of light, the Highest Heavens, and the waters that are above the Heavens. Note the *plurality* of *the Heavens* and *the Highest Heavens.* By this inference, we can say these verses are talking about *the universe at large.* The plural form of the Heavens, angels, hosts, the Highest Heavens, and the waters above the Heavens, tells us (*in each case*) the psalmist is writing about *more than one entity.* When he mentioned the stars, he clearly wrote *all* the stars. He also mentions *two Heavens—the Heavens* and *the Highest Heavens.* So, it can be logically inferred *the expanse God called Heaven in Genesis 1:8* is composed of two *different* Heavens: *the Heavens* and *the Highest Heavens.*

"PRAISE GOD FROM THE EARTH." — PSALMS 148: 7-14

Verses 7-14 talk about those entities — *from the Earth* — *that should praise God.* All of the things that should praise the Lord are things that are — *on the Earth.* The psalmist mentions sea monsters, all deeps, fire and hail, snow, and clouds; stormy wind, mountains, and all hills; fruit trees and all cedars; beasts and cattle; creeping things and winged fowl; Kings of the Earth and all peoples; Princes and all judges of the Earth, both young men and virgins; old men and children. The references to the Earth's *hail, snow, clouds, and stormy wind*, are entities that come from or are generated in *the Earth's*

[360] Schroeder *Genesis and the Big Bang* Chapter 9 p. 130 *c*

atmosphere. So, the latter part of Psalm 148 <u>*focuses specifically on our Earth, and its*</u> <u>*atmosphere*</u> — *its sky*. With this revelation, we can ask two informed questions.

- *What if —the Highest Heavens—* means deep space; *the universe at large* (i.e., all of those stars and galaxies out there)?
- *What if —the Heavens—* refers to the *atmospheres* of *all* of the individual planets of the universe *in general (from God's perspective)*, and *the atmosphere of our Earth, in particular (from man's perspective)?*

WHAT WE SEE WHEN WE LOOK UP

Perhaps it would be helpful to change our focus from the philosophical to the experiential—i.e., from what has been written about the mystery of the Heavens and the Highest Heavens to what we actually experience when we look up. What we see when we look up depends upon *when* in our day-night cycle we look. This analogy is from man's perspective.

"LIE TO ME"

There was an interesting TV series called *"Lie to Me."* The main character had a unique deception-detecting skill. He could study a person's reactions and tell when he was lying. In his institute he had a small cubicle set up as a conference room. It had walls made of *a special type of glass*. It had powerful overhead lights. This small room was located in the center of a larger room equipped with cameras and recording equipment so that the reactions and responses of a suspect in the small cubicle could be recorded. When they placed the suspect in the cubicle, the overhead lights were always turned on bright. The outer room was darker. The small lights of the workstations and the audio-video equipment could not be discerned from the inner cubicle when its lights were on. From the suspect's perspective, it seemed he was in a small room *with solid walls*. He could not see anything taking place in the larger darker room. He was not aware of its existence. At some point in the interview, the bright lights in the cubicle were turned *off*. After the suspect's eyes adjusted to the darkness, he became aware the walls of his cubicle were made of glass, because he could now see into the larger, surrounding room. It always shocked the suspect to learn his interview (which he thought had been conducted in private), had been observed and recorded by others. When the audio-video recording of the interview was shown, and the telltale signs of lying were explained, the evidence was so overwhelming that *all* liars confessed.

A SIMILAR THING HAPPENS TO US—WHEN WE LOOK UP.

When our sun is brightly shining, it is as if we are in that small special glass-walled cubicle with the overhead bright lights turned fully on. What we seemingly see is our *solid* walls, earth's blue sky with its clouds. We can see the contrails of overflying aircraft, the birds flying in *midheaven*, and sometimes we can see our moon. If it is raining and stormy, everything is gray and dreary, and we can see the lightning flashes and hear the thunder. But the rain and the clouds obstruct our view. What we see — seems very *local* to us. Except for our Moon, on clear sunny days, everything we see in our sky seems to be related to the atmosphere of our earth. We literally see heaven — *our heaven in the singular*. Even if we are looking through a powerful telescope, it would be difficult to see *the Highest Heavens* (in the plural) — i.e., all those other planets in our solar system with their individual atmospheres, some of which contain rings. What we see is *our heaven, our sky* — i.e., *the atmosphere of our earth.* Our solar system and the rest of the universe are still "out there" surrounding us, but we cannot see beyond our "sky" because of the overwhelming brightness of our sun.

However, on a clear night when we look up (while the other side of our terrestrial ball is shielding us from the direct brightness of our sun), we are like the subject in the small cubicle when the bright overhead lights are turned off. After our eyes have adjusted to the dark, we can see what is beyond the *cubicle* of our planet's atmosphere. We see the planets in our solar system, and we can see the vastness of the universe with all of its billions upon billions of stars. We see *"the larger darker room"* that has been surrounding us all the time. We see the universe. We literally see *the Highest Heavens.* We can gaze into the deepness of space and wonder about the vastness of the universe at large.

THE DEEP MYSTERY NAHMANIDES WOULD NOT DISCUSS — THE DEEPER MEANING OF HEAVEN.

Armed with this perspective, let us now consider that the deeper meaning of *'Heaven'* (*on the 2nd Day of Creation*) — refers to *both* the formation of *the universe at large* and the *beginning* of the formation *of the atmospheres of the individual planets of the universe.* Specifically in regard to the planet earth, we are talking about *the beginning of the formation of the primordial core of our earth, its moon, and its primordial atmosphere* (after ¾ths of the time span of *the 2nd Day* had passed). Why mention our earth on the *2nd Day*? Because modern science has discovered — earth *most probably* started to form during the last billion years of the estimated 4-billion-year span of *the 2nd Day.* God did not name this terrestrial ball on which we live until the *3rd Day* when He completed the separation of the waters that He started on the *2nd Day.* As we shall see in the next chapter, on the *3rd Day* He caused another separation of the waters when He said:

"Let the waters below the Heavens be gathered into one place, and let the dry land appear" (Genesis 1:9).

It was at this point on the *3rd Day* (*when the dry land appeared*) that God named our planet — *Earth* (Genesis 1:10). However, during the last epoch of the *2nd Day*, conditions within our solar system would have favored the formation of Earth's core. Following that, Earth would have begun to grow until it had achieved enough mass to spin itself into a sphere, which (*at the end of the 2nd Day*), would become completely covered by *the waters below.* The waters that are *above the Heavens* (i.e., *in the Highest Heavens*) will also be discussed later in this chapter. For the next few paragraphs let us *speculate* about *what may have happened.*

WHAT MAY HAVE HAPPENED.

In Chapter 8 of Book I, we discussed how the first galaxies, and the 1st order stars of the universe *may* have been formed. Remember the premise — *By repetition we learn.* Repetition followed by the introduction of something new is the way we grow our understanding. A brief summary is provided as a review. After this review, *something new* will be added.

- It all began (*In the Beginning*) when God created *the dot.*
- Then, *The Wind of God* acted, and the dot *suddenly inflated* to the size of a *grapefruit.*

- As the grapefruit continued to expand, the first *true matter* (hydrogen and helium) formed, and *time grabbed hold* (time began).
- Over time, as the concentration of hydrogen and helium increased, billions upon billions of *clusters* of *Hydrogen & Helium gas* formed in the expanding universe.
- These clusters would become the nuclear fuel of future stars.
- At the end of the 8 billion earth-years of *Day One,* the core temperatures and pressures within the clusters reached the *point of ignition,* and the *H & He fused.*
- This fusion released tremendous amounts of *energy* and *light broke free.*
- When light broke free, the *first stars were born*, and the universe was filled with billions upon billions of brilliant points of light.
- At this point *God was satisfied,* called His work *good,* and named this segment of time — *Day One.* Thus, the stage was set for *the 2nd Day.*

NAHMANIDES: ON SOMETHING NEW

According to Nahmanides, *at the end of Day One, God named the expanse* that *intercepted the light,* which had escaped *the darkness of the beginning.* God called it — *Heaven.* Therefore, since it was the universe that had been illuminated, God's concept of *Heaven was — the universe at large.* During the *2nd Day*, when God divided the waters in the universe, He was simultaneously starting the formation of the first planets with their atmospheres, and He was continuing to form those things, which are in the deep space of the universe that are outside the atmospheres of the individual planets. At *the beginning of the 2nd Day*, the earth, and its atmosphere (i.e., the earth's "*Heaven*") had *not* been formed. Although the first stars had formed, light had escaped, and the synthesis of elements heavier than hydrogen and helium had begun; those elements were still locked within the first order stars. Something else was needed before our sun, our earth, and all the heavier elements that would be needed to bring forth life, could form. That something else, which was needed was *the explosive deaths of the 1st order stars.*

THE EXPLOSIVE DEATHS OF THE 1ST ORDER STARS—

probably began to occur early in the 4 billion earth-year time-reference-frame the Bible refers to as *the 2nd Day*. Scientists estimate the *2nd Day* started about 7 ¾ billion years *before Adam (BA)* and ended about 3 ¾ billion years *BA*.[361] Genesis 1:6-8 tells us it was in the 4 billion earth-year time-reference-frame of the *2nd Day of Creation* that *the heavenly firmament / or expanse, formed* (i.e., the 2nd and 3rd order stars and their planets, comets, and all of the other accoutrements of space). When the *2nd Day* ended, the universe would have been about 12 billion years old. Science tells us our Sun is a 3rd order star that is located in the main spiral of the Milky Way Galaxy. Our sun formed about 4.6 billion years BA.[362] So, according to modern science, our Sun was "*born"* late on the *2nd Day*, when the universe was about 11.15 billion years old.[363] The age of the universe (15.75 billion years), minus the age of our Sun (4.6 billion years) = 11.15 billion years.

NOW LET'S FOCUS ON OUR OWN BACK YARD—OUR GALAXY—THE MILKY WAY.

---

[361] Schroeder *The Science of God* Chapter 4 p. 67 (The Six Days of Genesis Time Chart) & also p 68*a*
[362] Schroeder *The Science of God* Chapter 4 p. 68 *a*
[363] Schroeder *The Science of God* Chapter 9 p. 128 *d*

We have learned the *oldest stars of the Milky Way* are found in globular clusters, *outside* of the main spiral disk of the Milky Way. They are barely visible to unaided vision.[364] From our vantage point, the heavens we see are almost totally composed of *the Milky Way's main spiral disk.*[365]

THE MILKY WAY—A HUGE SPLASH OF 'MILK' IN THE NIGHT SKY.

This image courtesy of: www.rpi.edu/dept/phys/Astro/astrophotos.html by permission.

THE MILKY WAY—OUR VIEW OF THE HIGHEST HEAVENS [366]

Following the beginning, and under the influence of the *Wind of God* (Gen.1:2), the universe raced outward in inertial expansion. After the 8 billion years of *Day One*, and during the *2nd Day of Creation*, *a massive galactic nebula* containing enough gases and dust to form a hundred billion stars — flattened into a massive spiral-like galactic disk 80,000-100,000 light years in diameter and 6,000 light years thick. It's our home in the universe — one out of a hundred billion galaxies we now know constitute the universe at large.[367] For centuries mankind has called this phenomenon —*the Milky Way*— because, on a clear night, when we get away from all of the ambient light of our cities and towns, we gaze upward and see *this huge splash of milk* stretching from horizon to horizon across the black fabric of the night sky. The Crow Indians call it *"the Hanging Road to the Beyond-Country."* They believe it is the path they will take to the Spirit World after death.[368]

DR. EDWIN HUBBLE

Up until the 1920s (AD), mankind thought the Milky Way was the entire universe. But, in the 1920s a man named Edwin Hubble peered deeper into the universe than anyone since Galileo could have imagined. In the mountains above Los Angeles, at the Mt. Wilson Observatory,[369] Dr. Hubble saw something in his powerful telescope that destroyed Einstein's cosmological constant and altered our image of the universe. Prior to Hubble, not only did mankind think the Milky Way was the entire universe but, most scientists, including Einstein (who had rejected Vesto Slipher's earlier reports), thought the universe was static, unchanging, and eternal — had always existed and had no beginning or end. Aristotle's concept of the universe prevailed.

---

[364] Schroeder *The Science of God* Chapter 4 p. 67 and 68 *a, b*

[365] Schroeder *The Science of God* Chapter 4 p. 68 *b*

[366] Schroeder *The Science of God* Chapter 9 p 128*c*

[367] Schroeder *The Science of God* Chapter 9 p 128 *c*

[368] Johnson *Hell is Empty* (a Sheriff Longmire novel) Chapter 13 p. 226

[369] Article: *Hubble's Guide to the Expanding Universe* by Christen Brownlee: http://www.pnas.org/site/misc/classics2.shtml

With the most sophisticated telescope of his day, Dr. Hubble learned our sun was only *one star among billions* within the Milky Way Galaxy. He also learned the Milky Way Galaxy was *not all* there is. Prior to Dr. Hubble, we had no good way to measure how far away things were from us. Dr. Hubble solved that problem. He reasoned the brightest stars in the night sky were most likely the ones which were nearest us. Conversely, the dimmest stars were farther away. This makes sense when you think about it. However, Dr. Hubble didn't just reason this. His conclusions were based on solid physics principles.

DR. JOSEPH VON FRAUNHOFER

In the early 1800s, an optician in Munich, Dr. Joseph von Fraunhofer, noticed — When a thin sliver of sunlight passes through a prism (a crystal), the spectrum produced by the prism was crossed by hundreds of thin black lines. These lines were also noticed in the sunlight reflected from our Moon, and in the light of other stars. They resulted from the selective absorption of specific light frequencies as the light of each star traveled from the star's surface through the cooler gases in the star's outer atmosphere.[370]

SIR WILLIAM HUGGINS

In 1868, Sir William Huggins realized the absorption spectra of the light of different stars showed that the locations of their spectral lines demonstrated *slight displacement* from star to star. Sir William concluded this displacement was a *Doppler Effect resulting from the motion of each star relative to the earth.*[371]

CHANGES IN THE WAVE LENGTHS OF SOUND AND LIGHT: THE DOPPLER EFFECT

In the 1940s, when I was a child in the small rural town of Brundidge in southeast Alabama, we lived near a railroad track. At night, when I heard the whistle of *"the night train,"* I would often run outside to see it pass. I called it *"the Silver-Bullet Chicago Express,"* because people said it traveled from Chicago to Panama City Beach, Florida. Panama City Beach and the Gulf of Mexico are about 125 miles due south of my hometown. That train was different from the smoky coal-fired work-horse steam engines of that day. It was a luxurious, fast, sleek, silver- and red-painted diesel-electric passenger train. My-Oh-My! It was magnificent! That train didn't slow down even one little *"tid-bit"* when it *"blew"* through tiny Brundidge, Alabama two nights each week. The folks from Chicago had fun things to do in Panama City Beach and were in a hurry to get there!

The *light* on its engine grew *brighter* as the train came toward me. The *sound emitted by the train* and *the sound of its whistle grew louder.* Science tells us these changes are the result of the *compression* of the sound and light waves coming from a moving object that is approaching us. As the train sped toward me, the distance its sound and light traveled to reach me was reduced. The pitch of the train whistle rose, and the loudness of its sound increased. The brightness of its light also increased because the wave lengths of its sound and light were being *progressively compressed* with each incremental decrease of distance between me and the train as it rapidly approached. The *compression shortened* the wave lengths of the train's light and sound and *increased* the frequency of each wave of sound and light. This caused the rise in the pitch of its sound and the increase in the brightness of its light. Science calls this *the Doppler Effect*, named

---

[370] Schroeder *Genesis and the Big Bang* Chapter 4 p. 72 *b* and 73 *a*
[371] Schroeder *Genesis and the Big Bang* Chapter 4 p. 73 *b*

for J.C. Doppler, a professor of mathematics in Prague — the man who first described the phenomenon in 1842.[372]

When the train passed by me, I had to brace myself, because that 72,000-pound diesel engine shook the ground, and the wind from the passing train was something fierce. The danger of being near that behemoth was exciting to a small country boy like me. The pitch of its whistle and the loudness of the sound of its wheels on the tracks would crescendo to a deafening peak — but then immediately decrescendo the very moment the train passed me by. As the distance between the train and me increased while it continued on its way, this lowering of pitch and softening of its sound would fade away until the calm of the night eventually returned, and I could once again hear the natural sounds of the night — i.e., the croaking of the frogs and the chirping of the crickets. When the excitement of the *"the Silver-Bullet Chicago Express"* was over and the relative quiet of my country-life returned, I always found myself imagining the fun those city-folk were going to have when they got to Panama City Beach, Florida and began to frolic in the warm pristine waters of the Gulf of Mexico and sunbathe on its white sandy beaches. Oh My!

When I was much later introduced to the significance of the Doppler Effect in a physics class, I learned the fading sound of the train's motion and whistle was the result of the *stretching and lengthening* of the sound waves coming from the train — caused by the ever-increasing distance between us. The rear lights on the caboose of the train also grew dimmer with each incremental increase in distance. The light waves were undergoing a similar stretching, which was the result of the same phenomenon we now call *the Doppler Effect*. For those of you who are less acquainted with trains, the example of an automobile or a Harley Davidson motorcycle approaching you and then passing you might give a more vivid mental picture of *the Doppler Effect* based on your own personal experience. Even today, when I hear *the Doppler Effect*, I often flash back to the wonderment of my childhood experiences of *"the Silver-Bullet Chicago Express."*

HOW DOES THE DOPPLER EFFECT HELP US UNDERSTAND THE UNIVERSE?

We can actually measure the changes in sound on what we call a *decibel scale*. The changes in light frequency can also be measured by *changes in the color* of the light waves when they are passed through a prism. The instrument used for this measurement is called a *spectrometer*. Light waves emanating from an *approaching* object are *compressed* and are seen through a spectrometer as a change in color toward the *blue* end of the spectrum. Light waves that are traveling away *stretch out* and shift toward the *red end* of the spectrum. Therefore, the *light from stars*, which are approaching us undergoes a shift towards the *blue end* of the spectrum, and the light from stars that are going *away* from us (i.e., *receding* from us) undergoes a shift towards the *red end* of the spectrum.[373,374]

The valves of my cornet have short springs in them. I learned I could make the valves move faster if I *stretched* the springs *a little bit*. After stretching them, the *allegro tempos*

---

[372] Schroeder *Genesis and the Big Bang* Chapter 4 p 71 *c*-72
[373] Schroeder *The Science of God* Chapter 3 p 55 Figure 2.
[374] Schroeder *Genesis and the Big Bang* Chapter 4 p 72 and 73

were easier to play *up to tempo* because the valves were more lively—more responsive. In fact, my performances of *allegro vivace* and *presto* tempos became *spectacular* — or so I thought. That childhood experience with valve-springs helped me understand something that is important when it comes to understanding how *the Doppler Effect* helps us measure *distances in space.* Think of a wave of light as if it were a spring. If you hold a short spring between your fingers and pinch it, you shorten the length of the spring. Pinching the spring (i.e., *compressing* it) shortens the spring by decreasing the distance between each spiral. It also raises the "*peaks*" and deepens the "*valleys*" of the spirals of the spring. The spirals of the spring are analogous to *the wave frequencies* — i.e., the peaks and valleys of each wave of light, and sound. Pinching a *spring-wave* of light causes it to be *compressed.* This causes a *blue shift* in its light spectrum. That is what happens to light from stars *approaching* us.

On the other hand, if you pull the ends of a spring *apart* with your fingers, you are *stretching* the spring. Stretching a *spring-wave* of light *lengthens* it, lowers the peaks and valleys of each wave, and increases the distance between each peak and valley of a wave of light. This causes a *red shift* in its spectrum. That is what happens to the light from stars *moving away* from us.

HUBBLE USED THE DOPPLER EFFECT TO DETERMINE DISTANCES IN SPACE.

Since the advent of telescopes, astronomers have been probing outer space, but they had no good measure of how far away things were. Hubble solved that problem by coming up with something he called **The Standard Candle** — a star of known brightness. If you know how bright a star is *relative to another star*, you can measure how far away it is. The *dimmer* a star is, the *farther away* it is from us. Conversely, the *brighter* a star is, the *closer* it is to us. Just as the train's light in the above example gets brighter and brighter as it approaches us, and dimmer and dimmer as it recedes from us, the same physics applies to stars, which are approaching and those that are receding from us.

Those stars that are *approaching* us show a progressive shift of their light toward the *blue* end of the spectrum. Stars that are *moving away* from us (receding) show a progressive *red shift* in their spectra. I know this is repetitious, but by now the concept should be indelibly imprinted. If you have trouble remembering which shift is *red* and which is blue, just remember the examples of the train and the car. The lights on the *rear end of the caboose* of a train are *red*—just like the *taillights of a car.* As the caboose travels away from us, the *red* lights on its rear grow dimmer and dimmer. Remember *red for rear lights.* Remember *red shift* for stars *moving away* from us. Now you've got it.

HUBBLE & HUMASON MEASURED THE BEHAVIOR OF GALAXIES.

This discovery alone would have been enough to ensure Hubble's place in the *Astronomer's Hall of Fame.* But Hubble took another step. He also measured the *behavior* of the galaxies. In the early 1900s, Hubble and his spectroscopist, Milton Humason, spent *three decades* measuring distances to other galaxies and the shift in the spectra of light emitted by the stars of those galaxies. **In 1929,** he concluded the *majority* of galaxies are moving *away* from us. Not just moving away from us, but also moving away from our Milky Way Galaxy. And he also showed they are *moving away from each other.* He did this by *quantitating* their Doppler shifts of light. *Most stars and galaxies* showed a *red shift* in the spectra of their light. In other words, Hubble's discoveries, and exhaustive measurements (over a 30-year period), which were based on sound Doppler-effect physics principles showed us —*the universe is expanding*— *getting bigger with every second.* Since those discoveries, Hubble's results have been verified by others. Those astronomers who have continued Hubble's work have also confirmed there is a consistent distribution of the relative velocities among the majority of the galaxies. Almost *all* are *moving away* from a common universal center at speeds proportional to their distance from that center. The farther away a galaxy is, the faster it is moving away. Because we are also within a moving galaxy, we cannot locate the center of universe.[375]

HUBBLE'S "STANDARD CANDLE" & THE ANDROMEDA NEBULA

Hubble found one of these *Standard Candles* within a swirl of stars called the *Andromeda Nebula*. Before Hubble, astronomers thought *Andromeda* was just a bit of star dust <u>inside</u> the Milky Way Galaxy. When Hubble calculated the distance, he realized the Andromeda Nebula is *2 million light years away!* [376] On the night he made that discovery our concept of the extent of the universe was instantly changed! Hubble realized Andromeda was *another galaxy* — one that is <u>outside of,</u> but *just like* the Milky Way. So, in that instant, on that night, the universe went from being just our Milky Way Galaxy, which is about 100,000 light years across, to becoming this *unfathomable universe* that is billions of light years across!

THERE ACTUALLY WAS A BEGINNING!

Hubble's Data was the 1st proof the Bible & Lemaitre were right! When Einstein learned of Edwin Hubble's discoveries, he journeyed to Mt. Wilson to meet with Hubble. It was there that Einstein told Hubble what he also told his friend and fellow Nobel laureate Max Born — His Cosmological Equation was the biggest blunder of his life![377,378] Hubble's data convinced Einstein of that part of the *"motion-picture of time"* that he initially refused to see. When one reverses the data, one eventually comes to that point in the past when the universe was a single point — i.e., *the Singularity* of modern science, Lemaitre's *"primeval atom,"* or what Nahmanides called —"the *Dot*," which (in Nahmanides' mind) was a speck of space no larger than a grain of mustard.

---

*Here was the 1st discovered scientific proof there actually was a beginning! Mankind would have to wait another 36 years for the discovery of the 2nd important scientific proof of a beginning. That happened in 1965 when Arno Penzias and Robert Wilson discovered the echo of the Big Bang, which is Cosmic Microwave Background Radiation (i.e., CBR—cf. Chapter 5 in Book I). CBR is the scientific proof that the Bible's Creation Account is infallible—(**i.e., the Biblical Creation Account is "Our Story."**)*

It was in 1929 that Edwin Hubble's three decades of astronomical data convinced Albert Einstein the opening statement of the ancient Hebrew Bible had been correct all along! But almost no one else noticed, because 1929 was the year of *the Great Depression*! It takes a great man to admit he is wrong. But Einstein thought Hubble's data was irrefutable, so he retracted his *Cosmological Equation* that he had purposefully designed

---

[375] Schroeder *Genesis and the Big Bang* Chapter 4 p. 73 *c, d*

[376] Schroeder *The Science of God* Chapter 9 p 128*c*

[377] Schroeder *The Science of God* Chapter 2 p 23 *b*

[378] Article: *Edwin Hubble Biography* from Nick Greene:
http://space.about.com/od/astronomerbiographies/a/edwinhubble.html

to support his preconceived concept of an eternal steady-state static universe with no beginning. Dr. Schroeder has written:

> *"Einstein could have been credited with the most significant change science can ever make toward biblical philosophy. Evolution, dinosaurs, cavemen are all trivial controversies when compared to the concept of a beginning. While a beginning does not confirm the existence of a Beginner (God), it does open the way for that possibility."*[379]

EXPLOSIVE STAR-DEATH BRINGS NEW SYNTHESIS.

The energy produced by the fusion of *Hydrogen & Helium* within the core of a huge star will not only form heavier elements, but the outward flow of energy will also support the outer layers of the star. When the nuclear fuel of a star is consumed, the release of energy ceases. When this happens, gravity will cause the star to collapse. The collapse of the center of those stars that are at least ten times the size of our sun, will result in the formation of *a black hole*. However, in all other stars (even large supernovae that are less than ten times the size of our sun); when the collapse occurs, the inward plunge of the entire mass of the star toward its core will release a burst of energy that rebounds from its center *as a massive shock wave*. This *explosive* shock wave will carry with it all of the rocks, the heavy elements, and the lighter gases away from the center of the dying star — literally spewing them out into surrounding space. All of this debris will eventually form the cores of new planets. The heavy rocky matter will eventually accrete into *terrestrial* planets, which will form *near the center* of the new nebula. The *lighter gases* will be flung *farther out* from the center of the dead star, and eventually form *Giant Gas planets.*

Scientists believe the primordial core of our earth was formed in this way. All of the expelled matter attracts other *H & He* nuclei from the surrounding space. Thus, the cycle of cluster formation begins anew. *However, the larger clusters of H & He gas will gravitate more tightly together and because of their greater gravity, they will move toward the center of the dead star. These are the clusters that will eventually ignite to form a new star.*

On the other hand, the smaller clusters of gas and those widely dispersed *free molecules* of *H & He,* which have *not* yet *clustered* — will be flung father out by the rebounding shock wave. Over eons of additional time, all of these elements will recycle the matter in space and form new stellar systems. In the process, new stars of all sizes are born. The larger ones will be capable of heavy element nucleosynthesis.

The process of birth, life, death, and the recycling of the elements of dead stars continues to this day. Science tells us there will be no end to this process. Theology agrees — *all of God's creation will continue unless God acts to terminate it.* Thus, all of the elements that now exist in the universe have been made (*asa*) and are still being formed (*yasar*) by God. We are all *made of recycled stardust.* There is no other way, consistent with our understanding of cosmological processes, to account for the abundance of elements heavier than helium in our universe.[380]

The formation of the elements of our solar system took many billions of years in the universe-based reference-frame of time. In God's time-reference-frame it took into the *3rd*

---

[379] Schroeder *The Science of God* Chapter 2 p 22 *d (A direct quote of Dr. Schroeder.)*
[380] Schroeder *Genesis and The Big Bang* Chapter 5 p 91 *c*

Day. All of this time the universe was expanding. By the time the universe was ready for our solar system (with its supply of life-essential heavy elements and light), it was already very big and very old.[381]

THE TEACHINGS OF AN ANCIENT HEBREW SAGE

A fifth century AD Hebrew sage, Rabbi Abahu, said:

"From the fact that the Sun appeared on the 4th Day, we learned during the first three days, the Holy One created and destroyed worlds."

It is astounding he would come to this conclusion because his only source for study was the text of the ancient Hebrew Bible.[382] The science that is so convincing to us today would not be discovered for another sixteen centuries!

2. WHAT IS WATER? AN INTRODUCTION TO WATER.

"Know this first of all, that in the last days mockers will come with their mocking following after their own lusts, and saying, 'Where is the promise of His coming? For ever since the fathers fell asleep, all continues just as it was from the beginning of creation.' For when they maintain this — **it escapes their notice that by the Word of God the heavens existed long ago and the earth was formed out of water and by water, through which the world at that time was destroyed being flooded with water.** *But the present heavens and earth by His word are being reserved for fire, kept for the day of judgment and destruction of ungodly men" (II Peter 3:3-7)*

I gave you the entire introductory quote of St. Peter's *"Design of the Future,"* because it emphasizes *the essential role God gave to water when He created the heavens and the earth.* I highlighted this role, but I did not want to simply quote the importance of water — without giving you the full context of *St. Peter's statement.*

We have already discussed *when* the first two and most abundant elements in the universe formed (i.e., *hydrogen and helium* — see Chapter 7 & Chapter 8 in Book I). We also mentioned that the other elements which are heavier and more complex than hydrogen and helium were formed in the nuclear furnaces of the stars. You see, the nuclear furnaces of the stars — *are the forges God uses to fuse things together.* Now, let's do a little chemistry so that we can gain some understanding of how God makes and forms things.

- *If three atoms of helium* are fused together, *carbon* is produced. This is vitally important, because in the next chapter, you will discover — *carbon is essential for life.* Why? Because *all* life forms are *"carbon-based."*
- If *four atoms of helium* are fused together, *oxygen* is produced.[383]
- If *two atoms of hydrogen and one of oxygen* are fused together, *the essential life-giving elixir —water—* is produced.[384] We write the union of this compound as — H_2O.
- This is the mechanism whereby the Master Chemist of the Universe (God) makes and forms all elements and compounds.

---

[381] Schroeder *Genesis and the Big Bang* Chapter 5 p 91 *d*

[382] Schroeder *Genesis and the Big Bang* Chapter 5 p 91 *e*

[383] Parker *The Genesis Enigma* Chapter 2 p 42 *b, c*

[384] Schroeder *The Science of God* Chapter 8 p 120*c*

IT IS BELIEVED THE FIRST WATER GOD MADE—

was formed in the billions upon billions of large 1st order stars that God ignited on Day One (which were larger than our sun)—in what Nahmanides considered to be the universe at large. The foregoing is actually a bit more complicated than this. For brevity, I did not discuss the necessary intermediate formations of some isotopes which have extremely brief half-lives. Nevertheless, starting with iron, *all nucleosynthesis of elements, molecules, and compounds heavier than hydrogen, helium, deuterium, lithium, beryllium, and boron—is believed to have happened in the nuclear furnaces of the early stars. Therefore, it is believed the first water to be made was made in the stars. It was also in this way that all ninety-two naturally formed elements were formed and made through the process of star-birth, star-life, star-death, and the rebirth-of-new-stars. So, it is out of the nuclear furnaces of the stars — out of light— that all matter heavier than iron is produced.*

The exceptions to this mechanism of nucleosynthesis are hydrogen, helium, deuterium, lithium, beryllium, and boron. The last four of these 'lightweight' elements are produced in deep space by cosmic radiation. These "lightweight" elements do not require star-fusion to form. Furthermore, they burn up too quickly by the fusion reactions that occur in stars. Therefore, they cannot form in the stars. They are formed in deep space by the cosmic radiation emitted by the stars. They have a smaller mass and a smaller number of electrical charges than Hydrogen and Helium. Therefore, because their nuclei have less binding energy, it takes less velocity and lower temperatures to force the fusion of their nuclei together than the reactions that produce Hydrogen and Helium in deep space. [385]

Perhaps the reason *Day One* lasted 8 billion earth-years, is because it took that long for all of the hydrogen and helium in the universe to form the billions of *clusters* that finally gravitated together so tightly that their core pressures eventually reached the pressure required for the H and He molecules to spontaneously ignite to produce the first stars. None of the 1st hydrogen and 1st helium in the universe was produced in the nuclear furnaces of the stars.[386]

Remember — the two most abundant elements in the universe (hydrogen and helium), began forming *after the Singularity* suddenly appeared and then was instantly inflated by *the Wind of God* to the size of a *grapefruit*. This happened *before* the first stars were born. Please also understand: *All of the heavier elements, molecules, and compounds — are produced in the stars — **including those that are essential for life**.* It wasn't until after the stars were born that deuterium, lithium, beryllium, and boron could be produced in space by cosmic radiation and survive. Now, indelibly imprint this statement into your memory.

Without light, life as we know it would not have been possible.*[387]*

GOD IS LIGHT AND LIFE!

---

[385] Beryllium and Boron: More Cosmic Connections with Fusion

[386] Is my body really made up of star stuff? - NASA StarChild

[387] Parker *The Genesis Enigma* Chapter 2 p 42 *c, d, e*

Man needs to understand — *God is "Light."* In the book of 1st John, the apostle said: *"This is the message we have heard from Him and announce to you, that God is Light, and in Him there is no darkness at all...if we walk in the light...the blood of Jesus His Son cleanses us from all sin. (1st John 1: verses 5-7 NASB)."* By this John literally meant — God is light— in every sense of the word! He created *light* to dispel *the darkness and chaos, which were in the beginning.* Then he created the *lights* in the highest heavens — (i.e., the sun, moon, and stars). And He created, made, and formed all that exists (**including life itself**) — *out of light!* Jesus said: *"I am the way, the truth, and the life"* (John 14:6). He also said: *"The Father and I are One"* (John 10:30).

Our God is our light and the source of all life. In Him alone — there is no death! In Him alone — There is life eternal! Yes, <u>JESUS CHRIST is light and life</u>, however He is also — So Much More (Now read the Gospel of John Chapter 1: verses1-5. This scripture is about "The Word," who is Jesus Christ)!

3. <u>What are the waters above heaven?</u>

Some think 'the waters above' refers to the waters in Earth's atmosphere.
The Ryrie Study Bible commentary on Gen. 1:7 interprets *"the waters above heaven* as the suspension of a vast body of water in vapor form over the earth, making a canopy that caused conditions on the early earth to initially resemble a greenhouse. This may have accounted for the longevity of humans in the early accounts of Genesis and for the tremendous amounts of water in the great flood in the time of Noah" (according to the Ryrie Study Bible notes).

We now know this interpretation — is not correct.

Understanding the sources of earth's water is a lesson in geophysics. For decades after it was learned our earth was once molten, it had been assumed the water of the earth's oceans came from the condensation of *steam* held in a primeval cloud that surrounded the molten earth. However, it would have been necessary for the upper surface of such a cloud to have been hot enough to maintain the water in its vapor form and at the same time close enough to the earth's surface so the earth's gravitational force would keep the water vapor from escaping into space. These requirements severely limit the maximum possible size of such a cloud. In the early 1950s calculations were made, which showed the amount of water such a cloud could hold would have been only a tiny fraction of the one billion, four hundred million (1,400,000,000) cubic kilometers of water that are contained in earth's oceans today. Therefore, the geophysical constraints on the size of such a vapor cloud invalidate this proposed explanation.[388]

It also seems counterintuitive to think the expanse God called heaven in Genesis 1:8 could refer *only* to the earth's atmosphere. Our planet is only a tiny speck in the vastness of the universe. From the perspective of the universe at large, what God called *heaven* in Genesis 1:8 refers to *the entire expanse* of the universe. However, from *man's perspective*, I concede it may be appropriate to consider *the mighty expanse over the immediate vicinity of the earth* (in the singular) *as our earth's atmosphere.* It all depends on whose perspective we are referring — God's or man's.

WHAT ARE THE WATERS ABOVE HEAVEN?

---

[388] Schroeder *Genesis and the Big Bang* Chapter 8 p 125d-126a

ANSWER: THEY ARE THE WATERS IN DEEP SPACE.

The first Biblical mention of *the waters above the expanse,* which God called *heaven* (in the singular), is in Genesis 1:7.

7 "And God made the expanse (—that God called "heaven" in Gen.1:8—) and separated the waters, which were below from the waters which were above the expanse; and it was so."

THE WATERS ABOVE THE EXPANSE — ARE AGAIN MENTIONED IN PSALM 148.

"Praise Him, highest heavens, and the waters that are above the heavens!" ... "Let the waters that are above the heavens (i.e., above the expanse) *praise the name of the Lord. For He commanded and they were created." Psalm 148:4b*

We have already concluded *the heavens* (in Psalm 148) refers to the atmospheres of the planets in the universe in general (from the perspective of the universe as a whole); *and the atmosphere of the earth (in particular)* with its moon (from man's perspective). *The highest heavens* refers to everything else in deep space which is outside of the atmospheres of the planets. Therefore, it is concluded — *the waters that are above the heavens* refers to the waters that are in deep space. This interpretation will become more meaningful and convincing as we continue the discussion of how our Solar System may have formed.

HOW OUR SOLAR SYSTEM MAY HAVE FORMED. THE GENERATION OF A MOLECULAR CLOUD.
On the 2nd Day, within the main spiral of the Milky Way Galaxy and 2/3rds of the way out from its center, a large 2nd order star (a supernova) burned out. After burning brightly for billions of years it finally exhausted its supply of hydrogen and helium. Under the influence of its own gravity, the structure of this now dead star, which had lost the out-flowing support of the heat produced in its core, started to collapse toward its center.[389] The rebounding shock wave from its center was so strong that the products of its nuclear synthesis, were spewed out into the surrounding space. The result was a massive molecular cloud composed of icy gases, ice-coated dust sized particles, ice-coated minerals, ice-coated rock, and all the heavy elements of nuclear synthesis that contained all the building blocks which would be necessary to form our solar system, our planet earth, and life. This massive molecular cloud was the offspring of a previous supernova that had undergone a similar cycle of birth and death.[390] That supernova had originated from one of the billions upon billions of clusters of H & He that had made up the grapefruit-sized universe, which in turn had been born from the inflation of that primeval "dot of black-fire-space" created by Elohim's Tzimtzum. This sequence of events, consisting of star-birth, star-life, star-death, and star-rebirth; is part of the recycling and regeneration that Elohim commands as He continues to make and form new stellar systems in His ever-expanding universe. In a metaphorical and metaphysical sense, we undergo the same process. We are born, we live, we die, and we are re-born—the sheep among us (i.e., those who believe in Jesus Christ), are re-born in heaven. The goats—(who reject Jesus), are re-born in hell.

---

[389] Schroeder *Genesis and the Big Bang* Chapter 8 p 116 *d*
[390] Schroeder *Genesis and the Big Bang* Chapter 8 p 117 *a*

COUNTER-BALANCING FORCES CONCENTRATE MATTER & FORM A NEW CENTER.

As the strong forces of the gravity between the components of the molecular cloud increased, the cloud began to once again collapse towards its center. However, at the same time, the increased gravitational forces between its components caused an ever-increasing rate of spin of the cloud. The rate of spin began to accelerate just as an ice skater increases her rate of spin when she moves her arms toward the central mass of her body. The accelerating rate of spin produced a centrifugal force which counterbalanced the collapsing central force of gravity. This counterbalance, which resulted from an accelerating rate of spin of the molecular cloud, prevented the formation of a black hole. Thus, the majority of the matter in the cloud and the clusters of hydrogen and helium gases from the surrounding space concentrated towards the now cold center of the cloud. This cold center would eventually become the point where our sun (a smaller 3rd order star) would form, and its hydrogen and helium gases would be compressed and ignite.[391]

AS DEBRIS ACCRETES, THE MOLECULAR CLOUD FLATTENS INTO A DISK SHAPE.

Because of its accelerating rate of spin, the cloud began to flatten, becoming more and more disk shaped as the result of these forces. The particles of ice-coated rock and ice coated particles not drawn into the cloud's center were able to grow, forming larger agglomerates of matter that scientists now call *planetesimals.* These planetesimals would eventually become the primordial cores of the future terrestrial planets in our solar system through a violent process of collisions that science calls *accretion.*[392] Our earth was one of those.

But before the molecular cloud's core pressure reached the critical point of ignition — the temperature of the disk had become incredibly cold in the aftermath of the death of its most recent supernova. The water and other gases that had been formed in the nuclear furnace of the now dead 2nd order star had frozen 'rock hard' after coating the other rocks and minerals in the cloud.

Except for the possibility of other undiscovered planets in the universe, which may have been uniquely fashioned and positioned in relation to their stars as our earth was, we think all other surface water throughout the universe exists in the deep freeze of space as — ice. For this reason, the waters above the heavens, may refer to the vast amounts of ice in the form of icy comets, and ice-coated particles of dust, rock, asteroids, and minerals, and perhaps as snow and ice in the polar regions of the terrestrial planets in the vast reaches of outer space. It is also possible that other terrestrial planets in the universe may have some subterranean water. Our earth is the only planet in our solar system that we currently know of where water exists in all three of its forms—

1) Ice,
2) Vapor (or Steam), and life giving—
3) Liquid water.

We will talk more about *accretion* as we discuss the formation of the primordial core of our earth when we later examine the meaning of "*the waters below heaven.*"

[391] Schroeder *Genesis and the Big Bang* Chapter 8 p 117 *a*
[392] Article: How Stars Form-STARBASE: www.ph.surrey.ac.uk/astrophysics/files/how_stars_form.html

4. WHAT ARE THE WATERS BELOW HEAVEN? THEY ARE OUR WATERS ON EARTH.

"And the LORD GOD of hosts, the One who touches the land so that it melts; the One who builds His upper chambers in the heavens (i.e., the highest heavens), *and has founded His vaulted dome over the earth* (i.e., the heaven, which is the atmosphere of earth) — *He who calls for the waters of the sea and pours them out on the face of the earth* (a reference to the waters below heaven) — *The LORD is His name." Amos 9:5-6*

CIRCUMSTELLAR DISKS FORM NEW SOLAR NEBULAE.

With the first mention of the phrase, *"the waters below" (Gen. 1:7),* the Biblical narrative *begins to shift focus* from the universe at large *to our solar system* and to those forces which would eventually initiate the formation of our planet earth, its moon, and earth's atmosphere. From this point onward in the Biblical narrative of the first chapter of Genesis, the *focus progressively shifts to the planet earth,* which God made and formed to be the womb, the cradle, and the home of the creature He intended to be the principal and dominant focus of all His creation — *man.* Because the Biblical narrative in Gen. 1:7 begins to focus on the earth, from this moment onward, when we see the term — *heaven*— we will consider it to refer to *the atmosphere of our earth.* The only exception will be when the Biblical text clearly indicates the Bible is talking about heaven in *its metaphysical sense.* For the same reason, we will consider the phrase — *the waters below* — to refer to the *waters on our planet earth.*

A NEW SOLAR NEBULA (OUR SUN) WAS BORN.

4.6 billion years ago (*years before Adam*); about 850 million years before the end of the 2nd *Day,** when the universe was about 11.15 billion years old; and shortly after the Milky Way had formed; something of colossal importance to us happened. Our Sun was born. At a point estimated to be 30,000 light years from the center of the Milky Way, and just north of the central plane of the Milky Way; a seminal event occurred within a small molecular cloud that had resulted from the death of a previous 2nd *order supernova* that existed in this location. An increasing rate of spin of the molecular cloud produced a centrifugal force which was balanced by the collapsing central force of gravity. This attracted most of the *heavy matter* and *the largest gaseous clusters* in the cloud toward *its center.* Under the influence of gravity, the core pressures, and temperatures *in the large clusters of H & He gas* in the center of the cloud slowly increased to the point that *stellar fusion occurred.* When that happened, the hydrogen and helium gases in its center re-ignited, and our Sun was born.[393] Once the core of a molecular cloud has ignited, its disk-shaped debris-field can be properly renamed a *circumstellar disk.* Like our Sun was at its birth, most of the stars in our Milky Way Galaxy are surrounded by such disks of debris and hydrogen and helium gas that we now call — *circumstellar disks.* The circumstellar disk that became our solar system consisted of a new hot dense center (our Sun) and its surrounding flattened swirling circumstellar disk-shaped debris-field. Thus, this disk formed *a new Solar Nebula.* The stage was now set for the forming of the *planets* in our solar system.

---

* *15.75 billion yrs. (-) 4.6 billion yrs. = 11.15 billion yrs. after The Beginning, our Sun was born. Stated another way, 12 billion years (Day 1 & 2) (-) 11.15 billion yrs. = 0.85 billion yrs. or 850 million yrs. before the end of the 2nd Day — our Sun was born.*

[393] Schroeder *The Science of God* Chapter 9 p 128 *d*

ACCRETION FORMED OUR SOLAR SYSTEM

Because of gravity, the debris-field within of our new solar nebula, which contained the ice-coated dust, ice-coated rocks, and ice-coated minerals began to move. These small collections of solid matter began colliding and merging. As stated, this process was an extremely violent process science calls *accretion*. The accreting agglomerates of rocky debris formed larger bodies. These larger bodies eventually became *planetesimals* with sizes up to a few kilometers across. These planetesimals grew to the point that their increasing gravitational pull influenced the motions of other planetesimals. This increased the frequency of collisions. The increased frequency of impacts caused the larger planetesimals to grow even more rapidly. As planetesimals began to collide and fuse with other planetesimals, *planetary embryos* formed and became the *cores* of our solar system's *terrestrial planets.* Over millions of years, the process of collision and accretion continued until, within the inner region of our solar nebula, the debris-field that resulted from the death of the preceding supernova *cleared*, leaving only four large bodies. These large bodies were *Mercury, Venus, Earth, and Mars.* They are the *Terrestrial Planets* in our *inner* solar system.

THE GIANT GAS PLANETS

Before our Sun was born, the centrifugal spin of the newly forming molecular cloud had caused some of the lighter gases to be flung farther out from the center of the molecular disk. That is to say, not all of the Hydrogen and Helium had been collected near the center of the molecular cloud. After our Sun ignited, a solar wind (which will be later described), literally *blew* some of the lighter gases even farther out from its center. Those planets that formed farther out from the center of the disk were enriched with these lighter more *volatile gases*, especially hydrogen and helium. For example, the largest planet in our solar system, Jupiter, has such a massive amount of hydrogen that its atmospheric pressure is 3,000 times that of the earth! That amount of pressure would instantly crush our delicate bodies flat.[394]

Just outside of the orbit of Mars (the fourth terrestrial planet from our sun), lies a remnant of the original stellar debris-field. This remnant of debris lies in a neutral zone of gravitational pull located between the competing gravitational forces of Mars and Jupiter. It is composed of the smaller bits of mineral-rock that were not pulled into impact with the larger terrestrial planets. This residual debris-field comprises *the main asteroid belt* that separates the *terrestrial planets* from the larger *giant gas planets* that formed from the lightest gases which were flung farther out into space by the shock wave of a dying supernova, and the solar wind that came along after our Sun ignited. I call these giant gas planets *Jason, but I spell it—"J-SUN,"* for *Jupiter, Saturn, Uranus, and Neptune.*[395] Tiny *Pluto* is not a gas giant. It is much farther out. How to classify Pluto has been a bit of a puzzle.

---

[394] Schroeder *Genesis and the Big Bang* Chapter 8 p 117 *c*
[395] Article: Gas Giants *www.solstation.com/stars/jovians.html*

SCHEMATIC OF OUR SOLAR SYSTEM

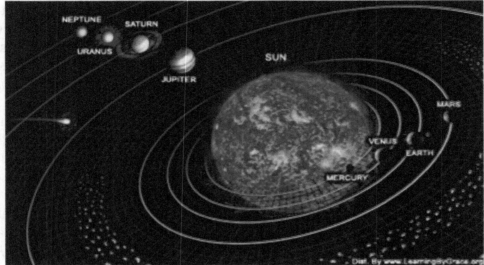

The outer *giant gas* planets are pictured on the left of the diagram. Jupiter is just outside the main *asteroid belt*. Saturn (with its rings), Uranus, Neptune, and the much smaller Pluto (not shown) are farther out, in the order listed. The four *terrestrial* planets are inside the asteroid belt. The smallest and closest to the Sun is Mercury. Next is Venus. The earth, with its moon, is pictured next, and Mars (just outside the orbit of the earth) is the nearest of the terrestrial planets to the asteroid belt. A comet (left) streaks through the solar system. Free Solar System Image by permission: www.LearningByGrace.org

CONTROVERSY OVER PLUTO

Since its discovery in 1930 and until 2006, Pluto was considered a planet. But in 2005, Caltech researcher Mike Brown announced he had discovered a new object in our solar system, which was more distant, and larger than Pluto. This new object has been named *Eris*. The International Astronomical Union met in Prague in 2006 to make a final decision. They decided a planet must fulfill three criteria:

- It must orbit its star (in this case, our sun).
- It must have enough mass to spin and pull itself into a spherical shape.
- It must have accreted *all* the other debris in its orbit through impact collisions.

Pluto satisfies the first two criteria. However, while the rest of the planets have essentially cleared their debris fields out completely, Pluto has not cleared out its surrounding debris field. As I write this, Pluto has only a fraction of the mass of the rest of the debris in its orbit. Pluto does have moons, but even with the mass of its moons, Pluto still doesn't dominate its orbit. Because of this, *Pluto, Eris,* and the Asteroid *Ceres* have been given the new designation of *"dwarf planets"*.[396] Although Pluto is too small to be called a planet, it is one of the larger members of what is called the *Kuiper belt*.

THE KUIPER BELT—BEYOND THE GAS GIANTS, & T-TAURI SOLAR WINDS & COMETS—

Some lightweight (nongaseous) planetesimals that have not had enough time to accrete into planets populate *the Kuiper belt*. Pluto is one of these. Someday, if Pluto accretes the lightweight solid planetesimals in its orbit to the degree that it becomes the dominant

---

[396] Search for: Why is Pluto no longer a planet?

body in its orbit, it will qualify for the designation of — *planet*. In the grand scheme of things, that will happen. All it will take is more *"Pluto-time."* Meanwhile, there is something else, which is even farther out than the Kuiper belt that is still considered to be part of our solar system. That something has been named the *Oort cloud*.

THE OORT CLOUD—

is composed mostly of comets made of ice and dust materials from the original nebula of our solar system carried into the outer reaches of our solar system by a fierce solar wind called the *T-Tauri phase* of the development of our sun. The orbits of these icy comets, like *Halley's Comet*, periodically cause them to streak through our solar system. When they get near the sun, they heat up and release a long tail of dust and gas.

T-TAURI SOLAR WINDS

Shortly after a new star is "born," it can expel vast amounts of its matter in one explosive burst that creates a fierce solar wind. I have just mentioned this phenomenon that has been named *the T-Tauri phase of a star*. When this happened with our sun, chances are it produced a solar wind so fierce that it blew all residual interplanetary gases into the outer space of our solar system — i.e., those parts of our solar system that are beyond our asteroid belt. The atmospheres of the early terrestrial planets would have also been whisked away as well. However, in the case of the earth, this did not happen. Earth's atmosphere is ideal for us. It contains a life-giving breath of 20% oxygen and 80% nitrogen. *So, the timing* of the T-Tauri phase of our sun *was just right for the earth.*

• ***Earth could have been a planet without any Water!*** *If the T-tauri solar wind had happened too early (before the aggregation of the matter that formed our planet), the water-ice that coated the debris of rock and minerals in the orbit of our primordial earth: would have evaporated and been lost to space. We would have been a planet without any water and therefore, a planet without life!*

• ***Earth could have lost its Atmosphere!*** *If the T-tauri solar wind had happened too late, i.e., after the earth's atmosphere formed, it would have whisked away our atmosphere! Earth would have been a planet without surface water and without an atmosphere that supports life!*

• ***The T-Tauri solar wind came at just the right time.*** *It happened after the agglomeration of our planetary matter and before the major volcanic out-gassing that started the formation of our life-giving oceans and atmosphere!* [397]

5. FOCUS ON EARTH

Now that we have a basic understanding of planet building and how our solar system may have formed and matured, we can turn our attention to how scientists think our earth began to form, and examine the deeper meaning of the phrase, *"the waters below heaven,"* as it applies to our earth.

The Bible says: *"The Lord God touched the earth so that it melted."* (Amos 9: 5-6)

This scripture is part of a series of visions of God's coming judgment of Israel. In one of Amos' visions, he tells the Israelites — Who it was that sent him to warn them. He tells them it was *"the LORD GOD, The One* who *touches the land so that it melts."* Among the

[397] Schroeder *Genesis and the Big Bang* Chapter 8 p 122 *b-e* & p 123 *a*

truly remarkable things about the Bible is the fact that scripture can simultaneously refer to past, current, and future events. Warnings and prophesies in scripture can have *more than one time-space-continuum application.* When God started forming our earth, He touched the land so that it melted. Modern science tells us this is exactly what happened! When Elohim began forming the earth, its surface became an "ocean on fire," and stayed that way through a continuous relentless bombardment that lasted for hundreds of millions of years as earth slowly increased its mass and size through the impact-accretion of countless bombarding meteorites.

EARTH FORMED AS A FIERY BALL IN SPACE: THE EARTH WAS "BORN" IN THE FIRES OF IMPACT-ACCRETION.

Accretion is a violent, chaotic process. Each day of Elohim's creation proceeded from chaos to order. The *planetary embryo* that grew in the *'womb of space'* to eventually become the planet earth, was *'grown'* in extreme violence and chaos. Science informs us each accretion resulted from the explosive impacts that came from earth's collisions with the smaller debris in its orbital path — as the earth's *planetary embryo* orbited through its almost circular path around our sun. In this way, our planet was born in fire. ***It formed as a fiery ball in space!***

According to the History Channel program, *"How the Earth Was Made,"* the man who first proposed this theory of the hellish origins of the earth was the Victorian scientist *Lord Kelvin.*[398] We have already mentioned *the Kelvin temperature scale* that bears his name. Kelvin was a British expert in thermodynamics. He is credited with the idea the earth was formed by collisions from countless meteors (asteroids or comets entering earth's atmosphere). The meteors were the debris, which had been spewed out from the dying supernova[399] that preceded the formation of our sun. The continuous bombardment that began about 4.5 billion years ago (BA) caused the surface of the earth to be an ocean of molten rock miles deep. It is estimated earth's surface temperature exceeded 8,000 degrees Fahrenheit, similar to the surface temperature of our sun. During this hellish epoch, huge meteorites rained down in a relentless bombardment that lasted several hundred million years! It ended when the vast majority of the planetary debris in earth's orbital pathway was cleared out by impact-accretion as it was incorporated into earth's mass.

Since then, Kelvin believed the earth has been slowly cooling down. The fires of our planets' interior (visible in the volcanic eruptions of today), suggested to him our planet had once been completely molten. In his time however, Kelvin was not aware of a key source of heat in the core of our earth that prevented the earth from cooling at the rate he predicted. That source of continuing heat in the core of our earth was later discovered to be *radioactivity.*

EARTH'S CORE—

is an incredibly hot solid iron sphere the size of our Moon — that is surrounded by a churning 'sea' of molten liquid iron, nickel, and rock! Some of the deepest mines on earth

---

[398] The History Channel: *How the Earth Was Made: Part I..*
[399] Supernova—Merriam-Webster definition: the explosion of a star in which the star may reach a maximum intrinsic luminosity one billion times that of the sun.

are in South Africa. If you tour a South African diamond mine (or a gold mine), you will quickly discover it is air-conditioned. South African mines have to be, or they could not be worked. By the time you would have descended one kilometer (0.6 of a mile) in the mine, you would have discovered air-conditioning is required to make the mine habitable. Compared to the average radius of the earth (3,959 miles mean radius at the equator),[400] these mines penetrate just the narrowest film of earth's surface. This is because the core of our earth is incredibly hot. Scientists tell us at 300 km. (about 180 miles) below the surface of the earth, the temperature exceeds 1,500 degrees Centigrade. At earth's center, the core temperature is about 4,200 degrees Centigrade![401] This heat (that melted the young earth), came from two sources:

(1) The *kinetic energy* from the early meteorite impacts that caused the accretions of the first planetesimals that formed the earth, and—

(2) The *decay of radioactive nuclides* contained within those early accreting meteorites.

The *kinetic energy* was a one-time contribution to our thermal balance. *The radioactivity* is a continuing but decreasing phenomenon.[402] Because of the decrease in radioactivity over time, and the fact that the frequency of meteorite impacts has almost completely ceased (as the majority of the debris in earth's orbit has been cleared), the surface of the earth has cooled enough to allow a *solid surface crust* to form. But the fact that the earth's core remains incredibly hot, and its mantle is molten is extremely important for our protection.

EARTH'S MAGNETIC FIELD PROTECTS US FROM THE LETHAL EFFECTS OF COSMIC RADIATION. How earth's magnetic field is generated has everything to do with the makeup of earth's core, its mantle, and the *motion* of the *mantle around* the *core*. The immense pressure on the iron core keeps it in its solid form. We know this from studying how seismic waves from earthquakes travel through the earth.[403*] However, the motion of the churning 'sea' of molten liquid iron, nickel, and rock that surrounds the mass of earth's radioactive solid iron core *results* from the *rotating spin* of our planet. It is this *motion* that *generates the magnetic field* around our planet, which diverts the major portion of the cosmic radiation that reaches our outer atmosphere. If this cosmic radiation were not deflected, earth's surface would be continually bathed by lethal ionization — *lethal to all forms of life.*[404]

Since Kelvin we have learned the radioactive particles of uranium, thorium, and potassium are in huge abundance in the core of our planet. The heat produced from the decay of these particles has kept our core extremely hot for the estimated 4.5-billion-year history of earth. In the 20th century, science found a way to use radioactive particles to determine the age of the planet more accurately.

---

[400] Article: Radius of the Earth: http://www.universetoday.com/26629/radius-of-the-earth/
[401] Schroeder *Genesis and the Big Bang* Chapter 8 p. 125*a*
[402] Schroeder *Genesis and the Big Bang* Chapter 8 p. 125*b*
[403*] Article: *The Truth about Earth's core:* by Paul Preuss of Science Beat, Berkley Lab 5/12/2003 http://www.lbl.gov/Science-Articles/Archive/Phys-earth-core.html **For many years, scientists have compared the seismographic recordings of volcanic eruptions from numerous locations the world over. Changes in the way sound waves travel through the earth (and various known materials) have allowed scientists to infer the nature, composition, temperature, and the dimensions of earth's core.**
[404] Schroeder *Genesis and the Big Bang* Chapter 8 p. 125*c*

ARTHUR HOLMES & RADIOACTIVE ISOTOPE DATING

In 1911, Arthur Holmes, a 21-year-old gifted geology student, used radioactivity to revolutionize our understanding of the age of the earth. After Holmes, geologists would talk in the terms of *billions*, not millions of years. The basis of Holmes' radioactive dating is the principle of *radioactive decay*. For example, *radioactive* Uranium-238 *decays to lead* over a period of *billions* of years. The **half-life of U-238 is 4.5 billion years.**[405,406] By measuring *the ratios of U-238 to lead in crystals trapped in ancient rocks*, Holmes accurately calculated their age. The accumulating data of this method now measures the age of the earth to be approximately 4.5 billion years. For the first time, scientists had a method for measuring the age of the different rocks on our planet. After Holmes' discovery, we can now look deep into the past and tell the earth's history.[407]

EARTH'S 2ND RADICAL CHANGE—FROM A FIERY BALL IN SPACE—TO A WATER WORLD:

We now think that 4.4 billion years ago (before Adam); about 650 million years before the end of the *2nd Day* when the earth was about 100 million years old; meteors still crashed into the planet, but the number of impacts per unit time declined as the debris in earth's orbit began to clear. This caused a gradual cooling of earth's mantle and allowed most of the earth's surface to solidify into a crust of dark volcanic rock. Even at this early stage — *water was forming on earth's surface.*[408]

THE SIGNIFICANCE OF ZIRCON CRYSTALS

No rocks have survived this most early period, but tiny crystals of *zircon* did. *Uranium carrying zircon* is one of the crystals that *help date the earth*. Zircon crystals are *only* found in erupted magma rocks. They form deep within the earth's semi-liquid molten mantle when subterranean water mixes with super-heated rock deep within the earth causing the rock to melt and boil up to erupt through surface vents. These crystals contain *the* evidence that water molecules had once been trapped within the zircon.[409]

HOW WATER CAME TO EARTH'S SURFACE AND HOW VOLCANISM FORMED EARTH'S ATMOSPHERE.

One theory seems most plausible. As the earth cooled, the volcanic activity in the earth's subsurface semi-liquid mantle of molten rock caused cracks in the surface rocks of earth's crust. For eons of time, *volcanism* caused a continuous spewing out of tons of carbon dioxide, sulfur dioxide, and copious volumes of super-heated vaporized water molecules in the form of *steam*.[410] Where did the water and these chemicals originally come from? The answer is — *from outer space*. The material that accreted to form earth's mass contained the ice-coated building blocks that Elohim had made and formed in the nuclear furnaces of the stars of the universe. A *colossal* volume of water had been brought into the body of the earth in the *water-rich* asteroids and comets which peppered the earth

[405] Article: Radioactive Half-Life (cont'd): NDT Resource Center
http://www.ndt-ed.org/EducationResources/HighSchool/Radiography/halflife2.html
[406] Article: Query 'Exploring possibilities-Canadian Nuclear Association.' Then select Article with the same title. Next, click 'What is Radiation?' Under the index that will appear on the left, look under 'Nuclear Decay' and select 'Half-Life.'
[407] Article: Rocky Road: Arthur Holmes. *http://www.strangescience.net/holmes.html*
[408] The History Channel: *How the Earth Was Made: Part I*
[409] Article: Precocious Earth http://science.nasa.gov/headlines/y2001/ast17jan_1.html
[410] Article: Volcanic Gases and Their Effects **volcanoes**.usgs.gov/hazards/gas/**index**.php

during the accretion process. Some pieces of ancient meteorites, the material from which the earth itself formed, contain about 5% water. Scientists believe it was the water in objects like these that provided the source of earth's water, oceans, and atmosphere. Since zircon crystals formed deep within the earth's molten mantle, they are *the evidence* that *our planet's water arrived from outer space*, carried to earth by the billions upon billions of meteors that impacted our fiery ball as the mass of our earth formed. That's how Elohim began separating the waters above from the waters below. [411]

The Bible says on the *2ⁿᵈ Day* Elohim created the heavens to separate the waters *above* the heavens from the waters *below* the heavens. So, the Bible states there was water in the deep of space. *The waters in the highest heavens* — was the ice that coated the rocky asteroid-debris and the ice in the comets in the deep of space. The water within and coating the heavy rocky debris, which had been spewed out into space from the dying supernova that preceded our sun, came from *the meteors* that impacted with our earth and *accreted* to form our planet. In specific regard to the earth, since the Bible says the waters above heaven were separated from the waters below heaven on the *2ⁿᵈ Day*, it would have been necessary for the earth's core and mass to start forming during the *2ⁿᵈ Day* so that there would be a *domicile* for the waters God separated from the waters above and placed below — *"the heaven (in the singular) of the earth."*

VOLCANIC OUT-GASSING POLLUTES EARTH'S PRIMORDIAL ATMOSPHERE.

So, 4.1 billion years before Adam; about 350 million years before the end of the *2ⁿᵈ Day*, when the earth was about 400 million years old; an epoch of volcanic eruptions unleashed the products of volcanism into the earth's early atmosphere and caused massive lava flows to envelope earth's thin surface crust. The continuous volcanic eruptions and the cooling lava beds unleashed immense volumes of *steam*, which rose to join the carbon dioxide, sulfur dioxide, and other noxious gases, ashes, and silicates of volcanism that continuously spewed forth for millions of years into the young earth's atmosphere. The earth was blanketed by a thick, dark poisonous cloud. Dr. Schroeder simply called this an epoch of *volcanic eruptions*. Science has labeled it an epoch of *volcanic out-gassing*.[412,413] Does the Bible give us any hints that this happened? We have already mentioned the vision of Amos.

2. THE VISION OF AMOS: (AMOS 9:5-6)

"And the LORD GOD of hosts, the One who touches the land so that it melts." (v.5)

This verse can be interpreted as a reference to the moment God began creating the primordial fiery ball of the earth through the impact-accretion of matter on the 2ⁿᵈ Day of Creation. Since scripture may have more than one time-space-continuum application, it can also apply to the volcanic eruptions throughout earth's history and to the future destruction of the heavens and earth by fire on "The Day of the Lord" as prophesied in II Peter 3:7; 10; & 12; after which The Lord God will create a new heaven, a new earth and a new Jerusalem—II Peter 3:13; Rev. 21:1-2; & Isa 65:17-18.

---

[411] The History Channel: *How the Earth Was Made: Part I*
[412] Schroeder *Genesis and the Big Bang* Chapter 8 p. 122 *e*—123 *a*
[413] The History Channel: *How the Earth Was Made: Part I*

"6a The One who builds His upper chambers in the heavens,"

> *His "upper chambers in the heavens" refers to the deep space of the universe (at large) where Elohim placed the waters above the heavens — that is, the waters which are outside of the waters He placed below. The waters below are, in general, the waters He placed on various planets throughout the universe. From man's perspective, the waters below are those waters Elohim placed on our earth.*

"6b And has founded His vaulted dome over the earth,"

> *The vaulted dome is "the atmosphere of the earth." The next statement specifically mentions those waters below, which He placed on the earth.*

"6c He who calls for the waters of the sea and pours them out on the face of the earth.
6d The LORD is His name."

> *We have not yet introduced the epoch of relentless rain that formed the oceans. I will give you a hint in the next paragraph but will wait until we discuss Genesis 2:4-6 in Book III to reveal "the mystery."*

7. A PERPLEXING MYSTERY—THE ENIGMA OF GENESIS 2:4-6.

I will mention this mystery here to tweak your curiosity, because Genesis 2:4-6 is a part of *the 3rd Telling of the Genesis Creation Account* and thus appears in the Second Chapter of Genesis. I mention this scripture now (out of sync with where this particular account of the *2nd Day of Creation* actually appears in the First Chapter of Genesis), because it is a retrospective of something that happened on the *2nd Day of Creation but was not discussed in the Bible until the 3rd Telling of the Creation Account.* Genesis 2:4-6 gives us important information about how our earth got its first atmosphere and oceans. I will discuss Genesis 2:4-6 in detail in Chapter 26 (which is in Book III). But I will tell you now — the deeper meaning of this enigmatic scripture tells us *when the earth got **its first rain.*** The next paragraph gives you some insight into how volcanism caused it.

VOLCANISM CAUSED AN EPOCH OF UNRELENTING RAIN THAT FORMED EARTH'S 1ST OCEANS & ATMOSPHERE.

As huge quantities of volcanically produced *steam* were vented onto and above the earth's cooling surface, colossal amounts of super-heated water vapor rose to join the carbon dioxide and other gases and products of volcanism in the early atmosphere of the earth 4.1 billion years ago (before Adam).[414] So, when the earth was only about 400 million years old, (about 350 million years before the end of the *2nd Day*), this condensing water would trigger the first and greatest down-pour of rain the earth would ever see. This "drenching of the earth" was either equal to or perhaps even greater than God's unleashing of the waters that caused Noah's Flood! Scientists believe it rained continuously from thunderstorms for a hundred million years! The result would be *a water-world!* At the end of this deluge, our fiery planet was converted from *a fiery ball in space* into *a planet that was submerged under a great depth of ocean water!*[415] We will talk

---

[414] Schroeder *Genesis and the Big Bang* Chapter 8 p. 122 *e* & 126 *b, c*
[415] Article: Earth in the Beginning by Tim Appenzeller, National Geographic Magazine Dec. 2006
Search: Early Earth Article, Hadean Information, Earth History Facts
http://science.nationalgeographic.com/science/space/solar-system/early-earth.html

about this again in Chapter 26 (in Book III). More detail will be added at that time. I will give you a hint now. There are two Hebrew words in Genesis 2:6, that have been mistranslated in all the English translations of the Bible. The first word was mistranslated as "*a mist,*" or "*vapor.*" The deeper meaning of that Hebrew word is "*steam*" (in English). The second Hebrew word has been mistranslated as "*watered.*" The deeper English meaning of that Hebrew word is "*drowned.*"

LET'S NOW CONTINUE THE DISCUSSION OF HOW THE EARTH'S FIRST OCEANS AND ATMOSPHERE WERE TOXIC.

4 billion years ago (before Adam); about 250 million years before the end of the *2nd Day,* when the universe was 11 ¾ billion years old, and the earth was about 500 million years old; its surface was a vast ocean. Its monstrous seas were iron rich, making them an olive-green color. Carbon dioxide, sulfur dioxide, other noxious gases, and the silicate products of volcanism still filled earth's atmosphere so thickly that the skies appeared purple red. The dense atmosphere produced enough pressure to crush a human body flat. It was also incredibly hot, with temperatures exceeding 200 degrees Fahrenheit. *This toxic water-world* would remain for another ½ billion years. But further dramatic changes were on their way. Renewed volcanic activity would trigger the construction of the first continents by creating an entirely new kind of rock. On the *3rd Day of Creation,* earth's land masses would appear, and earth would become a *granite planet.*

HOW OUR MOON MAY HAVE FORMED 4 BILLION YEARS AGO:[416] THE COLLISIONAL EJECTION THEORY.

Early in the formation of the earth, about 4 billion years before Adam, a Mars sized planet is believed to have impacted with the earth. The impact was believed to have been a glancing blow. Nevertheless, the impact caused vaporization, melting, and the throwing off of debris from the impactor and the earth's outer surface layer into the space around the immediate vicinity of the earth, creating an encircling ring of debris. Scientists postulate the debris ring accreted to form our moon, possibly within a few hundred thousand years. They also think our moon was closer to the earth when it began forming — orbiting it once every few days. The heat from the accreting particles caused the moon to at least partially melt, creating a lunar magma ocean. However, due to its smaller size, the moon cooled more rapidly than the earth.[417]

THE CONCLUSION OF THE 2ND DAY

Elohim did not pronounce His work '*good*' at the end of the *2nd Day.* The Jewish sages think He withheld this statement because the work of the separation of the waters was *incomplete* and *would not be completed until the 3rd Day.*[418] The usual pronouncement of "*there was evening & morning, another day,*" does appear — thus signifying Elohim had imposed an additional degree of order on the prevailing chaos of the beginning.[419]

---

[416]Article: Precocious earth   http://science.nasa.gov/headlines/y2001/ast17jan_1.html
[417]Article: The Collisional Ejection Theory
http://www.windows.ucar.edu/tour/link=/earth/moon/collision_ejection_theory.html
[418] Schroeder *Genesis and the Big Bang* Chapter 6 p 103 *d*
[419] Schroeder *Genesis and the Big Bang* Chapter 6 p 103 *c*

THE 2ND DAY OF GENESIS[420] LASTED 4-BILLION EARTH YEARS.

Day #	Start of Day 2	End of Day 2	Bible's Description	Scientific Description
Two	7¾ billion yrs. Before Adam	3¾ billion yrs. Before Adam	God made an expanse He named Heaven to separate the waters above from the waters above.	The Disk of Milky Way forms. Our Sun, a main sequence star forms. Primordial earth & its moon form.

Summary Points:

1. On the *2nd Day,* God made an *expanse* (*firmament*) He named *heaven*.
2. He made the expanse to separate the waters *above* from the waters *below*.
3. This was His first separation of the waters.
4. The term *heaven* has both religious and scientific connotations.
5. In the *religious sense*, *heaven is the abode of God.* This is the mystical sense of heaven. The Apostle Paul called it *the 3rd Heaven.*
6. In the *scientific sense*, the *heaven* of Genesis 1:8 refers to the *universe*.
7. For reasons discussed, it is supposed the deeper meaning of heaven (in the scientific sense) refers both to the formation of the universe at large and the beginning of the formation of the atmospheres of all of the planets in the universe.
8. In the scientific sense, the phrases—*the heavens,* and *the highest heavens*—used by Solomon and the author of Psalm 148, are interpreted to mean:
    * The heavens = the atmospheres of the individual planets in general, and the atmosphere of the earth and its moon in particular (a reference to man's perspective).
    * The highest heavens = everything else in deep space which is outside of the atmospheres of the planets.
9. Water is the life-giving elixir made from the union of two atoms of hydrogen and one atom of oxygen.
10. The first water made was formed by God in the stars.
11. The *"waters above heaven"* refers to the water that exists in *"the highest heavens,"* that is, *in deep space.* In deep space most water is believed to exist in its solid form — the ice that exists in comets and coats asteroids. Water is still made in stars that are larger than our sun.
12. The *"waters below the heavens"* refers to the waters that exist on the planets of the universe (in general).
13. So far as *man* is concerned, *"the waters below heaven"* refers to *the water that exists on our planet earth.* So far as we currently know, earth is the only place in our solar system where water exists in all three of its forms: as a solid (ice), as a gas (steam or vapor), and in its life-giving liquid form. (*Steam is superheated vapor.*)

420 Schroeder *The Science of God* Chapter 4 p 67

14. A colossal volume of water had been brought into the body of the earth in the water-rich asteroids and meteors that peppered the earth during the accretion process. The *zircon crystals* that formed deep within the earth's molten mantle (and are found in abundance in lava flows), *are the evidence that our planet's water arrived from outer space.* Water was carried to our earth by the billions upon billions of meteors, which impacted our fiery ball as the mass of our earth formed.[421]

15. For reasons discussed, it is believed the earth, and its atmosphere began to form late on the *2nd Day* to provide the platform for establishing the waters below the heavens.

16. The conclusion of the *2nd Day* is *the only time* in His creation that God did not pronounce His work *'good.'* The ancient sages reasoned the pronouncement of *'good'* was withheld by God because the work of the separation of the waters was not completed until the end of *the 3rd Day.* At that point, God pronounced the work good, complete, and named the newly formed planet — *earth.*

17. The Bible does however make the customary statement at the end of the *2nd Day*: *"There was evening and there was morning, a second day."* This statement indicates — at the end of the *2nd Day*, God was pleased there had been a satisfactory progression *from the chaos of the beginning toward order.*

GOD BROUGHT FORTH WATER FROM ROCK.

The Bible tells of two times during the Exodus when God instructed Moses to bring forth water from rock. The first is recorded in Exodus 17:1-7 and occurred at a place called *Rephidim.* There was no water and the people complained. God told Moses to *strike* the rock. When he did, fresh water came forth. This happened before the Israelites arrived at Mt. Sinai, where the law was given. The second incident occurred after the people refused to obey God's command to conquer the land of Canaan (i.e., *the Holy Land*). As punishment, God turned them back into *the Wilderness of Zin* (arguably on the Sinai Peninsula, or on the east side of the Gulf of Aqaba opposite the Sinai Desert in what is now a part of Saudi Arabia). At *Kadesh/Meribah*, they again complained of a lack of water. This time, God instructed Moses to *speak to the rock before the people that it may give forth its waters.* But Moses had been provoked by the people (Psalm 106:32-33). Because of his frustration and anger at the people, instead of *speaking* to the rock, he disobeyed God and *struck* the rock *two* times. Again, water rushed from the rock and satisfied the people's thirst. This is recorded in Numbers 20:1-13. The impression upon the people was that *Moses had provided the water, not God.* For his disobedience God punished Moses by not allowing him to enter the Holy Land. Skeptics believe these accounts are myth. However, *science confirms there is water in all rocks, but only a tiny amount of water is in each rock.* The water in all rocks came from outer space (the waters above). *The miracle is — the amount of water in that one rock was sufficient for the people's needs. Once again, the Bible has been proved correct. All things are possible with God!*

---

[421] The History Channel: *How the Earth Was Made: Part I*

OUR 'GOLDILOCKS PLANET' & ITS 'IDEAL' SUN

Scientists tell us our Sun is only an average size star. Its core temperature is not hot enough to have manufactured the heavy elements it contains. They say those heavy elements were made within the much larger star that pre-existed our Sun, which was in close proximity to that spot of space in the Milky Way Galaxy which would later become our solar system. Larger stars, which are several times hotter than our Sun have a shorter lifespan because they consume their supply of hydrogen and helium at a much faster rate. In the case of the larger 1st or 2nd order star that preceded our Sun—when it '*died,*' its '*life*' ended in a supernova explosion that spewed out its heavy elements into its surrounding space. Those elements were later incorporated into our Sun and the terrestrial planets of our solar system when they were '*born*' through the mechanisms that were described earlier in this chapter. *The average size of our Sun is extremely important to us. Average size stars have a much longer lifespan and allow enough time for their planets to cool and mature.* It so happens our earth is '*just the right distance*' from our '*just right*' Sun to allow the conditions that nurture the life forms on our planet. Because Elohim formed our planet in the way He did, we have all the right conditions and all the elements (including the heavy elements formed in a pre-existing supernova) that were necessary for our earth to become and continue to be a life-giving planet. That is why some astronomers have called our earth—*the Goldilocks Planet.* It is — '*just right for life.*'[422]

ELOHIM CONTINUES TO MAKE AND DESTROY 'WORLDS.'

Now, we have a better understanding of the chaos that formed the universe, our solar system, and our planet earth. What God had begun on a micro-scale of chaos within the Singularity, He continued on the macro-scale of chaos in the continually expanding universe. Today, scientists gaze into the universe with their powerful telescopes, some of which they have placed in space, and they see everywhere the evidence that Elohim continues to make and destroy '*worlds.*' In the next chapter and from that point onward, the Biblical Creation Account focuses on the earth and the changes that Elohim brought forth to make it — the ideal home for man.

[422] Stephen Parker *Bridges-Reconnecting Science and Faith:* p. 100-101

❖
CHAPTER 10: THE 3ᴿᴰ DAY & THE 3ᴿᴰ ROCK FROM THE SUN

SUMMARY REVIEW OF THE 2ND DAY

A brief summary of the *2nd Day* will help to solidify the key events that provided the foundation for the development of the *3rd Day* when Elohim completed the separation of the waters.

When Earth Formed (4.5 billion years ago), it started as a Fiery Ball in Space.

- Modern science has theorized 4.5 billion years ago (about 11 ¼ billion years after the beginning,[423] and about 3 ¼ billion years after the start of the *2nd Day of Creation*),[424] the earth began to form from the impact-accretions of countless meteors.

The Meteors that Formed the Earth came from a Dying Supernova.

- Those meteors were the debris that was orbiting the center of what would become our solar system. They had been spewed forth by a massive rebounding shock wave. That shock wave had been created by the 'death' of a supernova that was a 2ⁿᵈ order star, which had been 'born' on the 'dawn' of the *2nd Day* but met its end only a few billion years later in the 'afternoon' of the *2nd Day*. It had been the nuclear furnace, which produced the building blocks of our solar system — the rocky matter, gases, elements, and compounds heavier than the hydrogen and helium that Elohim had made and formed after *His Holy Spirit* had expanded the Singularity on *Day One.*

Earth is one of Our Solar System's Four Terrestrial (Rocky) Planets.

- Our planet is one of the four fiery balls composed of the heavy rock-matter of our young solar system, which science has named *the terrestrial planets*. The four terrestrial planets are *Mercury, Venus, Earth, and Mars*. They are listed in the order of their distance from the Sun. Mercury is the closest to the Sun. Earth is the third farthest from the Sun — literally the *3rd Rock from the Sun.*

Earth's Hot Iron Core Surrounded by a Mantle of Molten Liquid Rock.

- At the end of the *2nd Day*, about 3 ¾ billion years ago (Before Adam was created),[425] and approximately 12 billion years after the beginning,[426] when the earth was about 750 million years old[427] — our planet had an incredibly hot solid radioactive iron core approximately the size of its moon, which was surrounded by a molten mantle of liquid rock and nickel that was miles deep.

Water was Trapped within the Molten Liquid-Rock Mantle of the Earth.

- There were colossal quantities of vaporized water trapped within the mantle of the earth (in its super-heated vapor form — i.e., *steam*). All of this water had arrived from outer space as part of the billions upon billions of meteors that had built up the mass of the earth by impact-accretion.

As Impact-Accretion Slowed, Cooling Began & a Surface Crust Formed.

---

[423] (15.75 − 4.5 = 11.25)
[424] (11.25 - 8 = 3.25)
[425] (15.75 − 12 = 3.75)
[426] (8 + 4 = 12 billion years)
[427] (12 − 11.25 = 0.75 billion, or 750 million)

- As the debris-field in earth's orbit was slowly cleared through impact-accretion, the mass of the earth grew even as the frequency of impacts gradually lessened. Cooling resulted. This allowed the formation of a thin brittle surface crust.

Volcanic Outgassing produced a Toxic Water-World & an Opaque Atmosphere.

- The last phase of earth's development on the *2nd Day* involved earth's first epoch of volcanic outgassing that lasted approximately 100 million years! The products of volcanism within earth's molten liquid mantle were first carried onto earth's surface and then into its atmosphere. In this way, the products of volcanism not only changed the earth's surface crust but also formed the earth's *primordial*[428] atmosphere. For 100-million-years, an unremitting epoch of the early earth's 1st volcanic outgassing produced earth's primordial opaque, poisonous, atmosphere, and caused a *continuous downpour* of rain that formed earth's first primordial toxic ocean. Thus, after Elohim *made* the earth out of the chaos of fire, He next transformed it into *a toxic water-world.*

A Toxic Water-World with a Poisonous Opaque Atmosphere

- At the end of the 2nd Day, earth's terrestrial mass was completely submerged in an ocean of olive-green deadly iron-rich water that was in turn, encapsulated by a dark, hot, poisonous purple-red atmosphere, which was so opaque that *if* there could have been a creature on it with the capability of sight, it would not have been able to see the billions upon billions of brilliant points of light from the stars of the surrounding universe. As you shall see, the light of our sun would not be able to reach the earth's *primeval*[429] surface until the earth's primordial atmosphere had been cleared of trillions upon trillions of tons of volcanic debris. That didn't happen until the *4th Day!* Meanwhile, storms with massive waves raged over the surface of earth's toxic waters.

Nahmanides:

- As we discussed in Book I — In the 12th century after Christ, Nahmanides studied the Mosaic Hebrew of the 1st Chapter of "Genesis" and wrote his cosmogony. Nine centuries later, Modern Science "caught up."

Now we are ready for something new — *the 3rd Day, the 3rd Rock from the Sun, and Elohim's 2nd Separation of the Waters below the Heavens.* On the 3rd Day, earth changed once again and became a *Granite Planet* when its continents "*separated the waters below,*" and earth's 1st life forms suddenly appeared.

THE 3RD DAY LASTED 2 BILLION EARTH-YEARS: EARTH'S TIME PERSPECTIVE.[430]

The *3rd Day*: 24hrs of God's Time	Started 3 ¾ Billion yrs. BA	Ended 1 ¾ Billion years BA
God's Time Perspective	Earth-years *Before Adam*	Earth's Time Perspective

---

[428] *Primordial*: "i.e., *first formed*, giving origin to something derived or developed."
[429] *Primeval*: "the earliest ages in the history of the world — i.e., raw and elementary."
[430] Schroeder The Science of God Chapter 4 (Table) p 67

THE 3ʳᴰ DAY AND THE 'WATERS BELOW.'

⁹ *"Then God said, ᵃ 'Let the waters below the heavens be gathered into one place and let ᵇthe dry land appear;' and it was so. Genesis 1:9 NASB ¹⁰And God called the dry land earth, and the ᵃgathering of the waters He called seas. And God saw that it was good." Genesis 1:10 NASB*

THE 3ʳᴰ DAY AND THE FIRST LIFE ON EARTH

¹¹ *"Then God said, 'Let the earth sprout ᵃvegetation, plants yielding seed, and fruit trees bearing fruit after their kind; with seed in them, on the Earth;' and it was so." Genesis 1:11 NASB¹² "And the Earth brought forth vegetation, plants yielding seed after their kind, and trees bearing fruit, with seed in them, after their kind; and God saw that it was good." Genesis 1:12 NASB*

THE CONCLUSION OF THE 3ʳᴰ DAY.

¹³ *"And there was evening and there was morning, a 3ʳᵈ Day." Genesis 1:13 NASB*

ON THE 3ʳᴰ DAY, THE CREATION PERSPECTIVE SHIFTS FROM THE UNIVERSE TO THE EARTH.

The Universe is about 11.25 billion years older than the Earth.[431]* As stated in the Introduction, the Genesis 1:1-8 perspective of the first two days of the creation narrative relates to the universe, which Elohim created first. But in Genesis 1:9-13, the perspective of the Creation Account shifts to the Earth after God gathered *the waters below into one place* (in Genesis 1:9), and then God *"called the dry land earth"* (in Genesis 1:10). With the advent of the *3ʳᵈ Day of Creation*, the perspective of the Creation narrative shifts from the universe at large to the 3ʳᵈ Rock from the Sun, when Elohim named our planet *"Earth."* Since God named our planet on the *3ʳᵈ Day,* we will (from now on), refer to our planet by its name and I will try to remember to spell it with a capital 'E' as befits a proper name.

ELOHIM PERFORMED TWO MAJOR ACTS OF CREATION ON THE 3ʳᴰ DAY.

As we have said, when the *3ʳᵈ Day* began, the Earth was completely submerged in water. Then, Elohim formed the 2ⁿᵈ separation of the waters below the heavens by commanding the dry land to appear. The Bible says Elohim made the first life on the Earth when He commanded the Earth to bring forth vegetation. He then named this new creation, *"Earth."* The Bible tells us God declared both of His *3ʳᵈ Day* creations *"good."* The Biblical phrase: *"And God saw that it was good,"* signifies His satisfaction with the work — the work was a fulfillment of *His Will for good* and represented something that would be good for mankind (see Chapter 8: in Book I: "IT WAS GOOD"). The *3ʳᵈ Day* closes with the now familiar Biblical statement: *"And there was evening and there was morning, a 3ʳᵈ Day"* — signifying Elohim's activities on the *3ʳᵈ Day* had imposed another act of order on the primordial chaos of the beginning.

THE BIBLE & SCIENCE AGREE — ON THE 3ʳᴰ DAY, LIFE-FRIENDLY LIQUID WATER AND EARTH'S 1ˢᵀ LIFE-FORMS SUDDENLY APPEARED.

The Bible — The Biblical account of the *3ʳᵈ Day* mentions the first liquid water on Earth as the oceans and dry land appear (Genesis 1:9). This is followed by *plant life* (Genesis 1:11). Though a simple reading of the text implies all types of plants appeared (*"after their kind"*) on the *3ʳᵈ Day, Kabala* (i.e., the Jewish tradition from which the ancient Sages derived their interpretations of the *Hebrew Tanakh*) claims: *"There was no special day assigned for this command for vegetation alone since it is not a unique work."*

Of all the events listed for *the Six Days of Creation*, this is *the only one* the Jewish sages claim *was not limited to a particular Day.* They believe *the development of the Earth's*

---

[431] * Age of Universe 15.75 (-) Age of the Earth 4.5 = 11.25 Billion Years or 11 Billion 250 Million Earth-Years.

forests and flora happened over an extended period of time. It started on the *3rd Day,* but continued through the *4th, 5th, and 6th Days of Creation.*[432]

Science — The dawn of the *3rd Day* marked the close of the *2nd Day* epoch during which the Earth had been bombarded by a rain of meteors so intense as to have made the start and the survival of life highly improbable. Modern science tells us this rain of meteors ceased 3.8 billion years Before Adam. As the Earth cooled, liquid water *suddenly appeared!* Science also says the appearance of liquid water was followed *almost immediately* by the first forms of life, i.e., *single-cell bacteria*, and an unclassified life-form known as *the Archaea!*[433] These first life-forms were *microscopic*. Contrary to the prevailing popular scientific opinion since the 19th century, new fossil data demonstrate the Earth's first plant life also appeared immediately after liquid water and not billions of years later as some have claimed![434] The first plant life on Earth suddenly appeared on the 3rd Day of Creation. It was simple and was also microscopic (i.e., invisible to the naked eye).

I.   SCIENCE EXPLAINS THE 2ND SEPARATION OF THE WATERS—THE WATERS BELOW.

Now let us examine what modern science has to say about *how the waters below* were gathered into one place so that *the dry land could appear.*

A.   FROM A BALL OF FIRE TO A WATER WORLD—EARTH'S 2ND RADICAL CHANGE

This discussion takes us back to an event that started late on the *2nd Day* and continued into the *3rd Day.* Some of the oldest rocks on Earth are *lava-rocks* that have been found in the stream beds of a region in South Africa. Billions of years ago, these stream beds were on the ocean floor. Scientists believe these unique rocks give us the clue that late on the *2nd Day,* our planet was completely submerged in water. These primeval lava-rocks are called *Pillow rocks* because their rounded shape looks somewhat like a pillow.

B.   PILLOW-SHAPED LAVA-ROCKS

The oldest Pillow lava-rocks are 3.5 billion years old. This means they actually formed early on the *3rd Day* of creation. Although they contain no fossils, they are the second oldest evidence we have that the fiery ball of the early Earth evolved into a water-world. For a period of time, the Earth was completely covered by water. The oceans dominated. Scientists believe the unique shape of pillow-rocks tells the story. These ancient Pillow lava-rocks formed 3.5 billion years ago (Before Adam) under great depths of ocean water when magma was extruded from the depths of the molten mantle of liquid volcanic rock surrounding Earth's core. The volcanic pressures beneath forced the magma upwards through the cracks that volcanic pressure created in the crust of Earth's sub-aquatic surface. Back then, the early Earth's rocky surface became the ocean floor. When the Earth's surface was completely submerged in ocean water, the Earth became a "water-world." Today as then, this unique pillow-shape is most commonly formed when extruded magma (i.e., *lava*) cools and solidifies under deep ocean water.

Today, the only places new pillow-shaped lava-rocks are created on Earth are:
*   In the ocean depths off the coast of Hawaii—

---

[432] Schroeder *The Science of God* Chapter 4 p 68 c
[433] Schroeder *The Science of God* Chapter 6 p 86 b
[434] Schroeder *The Science of God* Chapter 4 p 68 b

- In recently discovered mid-oceanic ridges where active volcanic vents erupt through the ocean floor—and
- In lava-flows that come from sub-glacial volcanoes.[435]

With the exception of the Earth's oldest *Sedimentary rocks* (3.8 billion years old), most rocks found from the period 3.5 billion years ago (corresponding to the *3rd Day of Creation*), have been *pillow lava-rocks*. By one billion years into the history of Earth's existence, water had taken over. But geologists believe it had already been around for a very long time.[436]

The primeval Earth's first lava-flows extruded onto the Earth's surface, cooled there, and produced *Basaltic lava-rocks*. Thus, the Earth's first surface rocks were *basalt*. Then, after a continuous epoch of volcanism created the early Earth's first toxic atmosphere and oceans, and the Earth's surface was covered by great depths of water, the lava-flows that continued to extrude onto the ocean floor — became *Pillow-lava rocks*. Pillow-lava rocks are also *Basalt*.

C. FROM A WATER-WORLD TO A GRANITE PLANET—EARTH'S 2ND EPOCH OF VOLCANISM

Modern science theorizes 3.4 billion years BA, the Earth was just over a billion years old. The opaque purple-red primordial toxic atmosphere had already been formed on the *2nd Day* by the first volcanic outgassing the Earth would experience, and the 100-million-year continuous epoch of rain that followed created the primordial lethal olive-green iron-rich oceans that dominated at this time. However, everything was about to change again. Another epoch of volcanism on the *3rd Day* would soon begin under the oceans, that would form a new tougher kind of rock, which would give birth to Earth's first continents. These new rocks would be very special. A few billion years later, mankind would name this new kind of rock — *Granite*.

D. HOW THE EARTH FORMED ITS FIRST GRANITE.

Unlike the 1st epoch of volcanic outgassing, which vented into Earth's atmosphere, this 2nd epoch of renewed volcanism (on the *3rd Day*), fractured the submerged crust of the Earth that was now on the ocean floor. Ocean water plunged into the cracks and poured into the molten magma beneath. The water superheated the magma and produced *steam*. When the magma began to rise, the steam boiled up ahead of the magma, and created subsurface cavities or chambers within the Earth's molten liquid-rock mantle. These subsurface cavities are called *plutons*. The magma then rose and intruded into the plutons and cooled there.

Since cooling happened in subsurface chambers, the cooling occurred over a much longer period of time than is typically required for magma that extrudes onto the Earth's surface, or the magma that flows directly through the submerged crust of the Earth and onto the ocean floor. The rapid cooling of those early lava-flows had produced basaltic lava-rock. But the prolonged cooling of the lava in subsurface cavities (i.e., plutons) that had been created within the molten mantle-layer after the Earth became a water-world, promoted a much larger, tighter, and more cohesive structure of the minerals

---

[435]Article: Dive and Discover: Hot Topics: Lava Flows
http://www.divediscover.whoi.edu/hottopics/lavaflows.html
[436] The History Channel: How the Earth was Made: Part I

and crystals within the new type of lava-rock from that which was produced in the more rapidly cooling basaltic rock that was extruded onto Earth's surface early on the 2nd Day — or the pillow lava-rocks that formed on the ocean floor early on the 3rd Day. The tighter crystalline matrix of granite is responsible for its increased toughness and durability. Thus, the mixture of superheated water and mantle-magma produced an entirely new kind of rock. Shortly thereafter, also on the 3rd Day, through a process that science has named plate tectonics, granite eventually rose from the depths to form the first true continental crust. (The science of plate tectonics will be discussed in Chapter 12 in this book). This new kind of rock would eventually form the "heart, or core," of the Earth's continents. With this renewed volcanic activity that now was occurring under the sea, granite eventually began to appear everywhere.[437]

E. THREE KINDS OF ROCK FROM VOLCANIC ACTIVITY HAVE BEEN MENTIONED.
The first epoch of volcanic outgassing (on the 2nd Day of creation) produced basaltic rock. Basalt is the typical extruded rock that results from surface rupture and volcanic venting onto the Earth's surface, exposing the extruded rock to the Earth's atmosphere.

The second epoch of volcanic outgassing (on the 3rd Day) occurred beneath the oceans and produced at least two new kinds of rock: (1) Granite, which formed in subsurface/sub-oceanic chambers (i.e., plutons and fissures), and (2) Pillow lava rocks, which formed on the ocean floor when the volcanic venting occurred directly into the oceans. Basaltic rocks, pillow lava rocks, and granite are all igneous rocks. Igneous is Latin for fire or fiery. Igneous rocks are those rocks that form under conditions of intense heat and are produced by the solidification of volcanic magma.

Why did the volcanism on the 3rd Day sometimes produce pillow lava-rocks on the floor of the ocean, and at other times produced granite in large cavities below the floor of the ocean? Perhaps a pressure differential was involved. On the 3rd Day, when the upward pressures of volcanism exceeded the downward pressure of the ocean, pillow rocks formed on the ocean floor near volcanic vents. However, there may have been times when volcanic activity was less active, and the downward pressure of the ocean depths exceeded the upward volcanic pressure. At those times, ocean water entered the molten mantle layer through cracks in the ocean floor and boiled up as steam to form plutons in the mantle layer, ahead of the next volcanic eruption. This simplified explanation has emphasized the importance of whether volcanic venting occurred, and where it occurred. However, the subject is more complicated. Many other factors such as the chemical composition of the magma, the presence or absence of water and various gases, as well as the location and type of venting are also major determinants. There are a host of variable factors that determine which kind of igneous rock a volcanic eruption produces.[438] We know for example that today; volcanic activity continues to produce a great variety of different kinds of igneous rock.

F.   WHY GRANITE IS SO UNIQUE AND IMPORTANT
Granite is unique and important because it differs from basalt in three very essential ways.
- Granite has a much *lower density* than basalt. The difference in density between granite and basalt is greater than the difference in density between water and air.

---

[437] The History Channel: How the Earth was Made: Part I
[438] Article: Igneous Rocks http://www.tulane.edu/~sanelson/geol111/igneous.html

- Although basalt is heavier and denser than granite, *granite is a much harder rock than basalt!* Strange as it may seem, the greater density of basalt does not mean that it is more durable than granite. Just as steel is harder and more durable than iron, granite is a harder and more durable rock than basalt.
- *Granite is lighter than basalt.* Because of its lower density, granite is lighter than basalt. It literally floats on the molten liquid mantle of the Earth, but it is tough enough to withstand the erosive power of the oceans. Granite is typical of the continents — tough, but at the same time, lighter and more buoyant.

For these reasons, granite is a better material for the nexus or core of the continents that Elohim brought forth on the 3rd Day when He commanded the dry land to appear.[439]

II.   FIRST LIFE—THE VIEW OF MODERN SCIENCE

While the Bible talks about *macroscopic* plants being the first life forms, modern science claims the first life on our planet was *microscopic* life. Why doesn't the Bible mention microscopic life? A plausible explanation will be offered in the following discussion.

THE FIRST MICROSCOPIC LIFE & OXYGEN—THE SCIENTIFIC EXPLANATION

The first time the Biblical creation account mentions life is in Genesis 1:11-12.

[11]"Then God said, Let the Earth sprout (dasha) tender sprouts (deshe), the plant seeding seed, the fruit tree producing fruit according to its kind whichever seed is in it on the Earth. And it was so. [12]And the Earth bore tender sprouts, the plant seeding seed according to its kind, and the fruit tree producing fruit according to its kind, whichever seed is in it. And God saw that it was good." (From The Interlinear Bible: *Hebrew, Greek, and English*)

For the next two billion years, through the mechanism of plate tectonics, slowly but surely the granetoid protocontinents grew larger. On different parts of the globe granite crusts appeared that would one day form the hearts of the major land masses. The dominance of the oceans was over. The continents had arrived.

Elohim's separation of the waters below by causing the dry land to appear would change more than just the appearance of the planet. Two and a half billion years ago (BA), the shallow coastlines began to bring life to what would become a sunlit surface and help trigger the production of oxygen. Modern science has theorized that almost since the arrival of the first oceans, primitive single-celled life forms had appeared deep beneath the waves, living off the heat seeping between deep volcanic fissures. Science claims as soon as the Earth cooled and liquid water appeared, the first forms of microscopic life almost immediately appeared. According to science, these forms of microscopic life were *cyanobacteria* and *photosynthetic algae*.[440] Both take CO_2 (carbon dioxide — a product of volcanism) and convert it to life-giving O_2 (free oxygen). For many years the cyanobacteria and the algae pumped free oxygen into the toxic iron-rich oceans. However, scientists now believe — while the cyanobacteria and single-cell blue-green algae may have been the first oxygen producers, another oxygen producing entity almost simultaneously developed in the shallow coastal waters of Earth's emerging continents. *This new entity would for a time, become the major early producer of oxygen on our planet.* That entity was and is the *stromatolite*. Was and is? Yes, because this primeval entity can still be found in the shallow waters of some of today's coastal bays!

---

[439] The History Channel: How the Earth Was Made: Part I
[440] Schroeder *The Science of God* Chapter 4 (Table) p 67

THE TRANSFORMATION OF THE EARTH TO A BLUE PLANET—STROMATOLITES & O_2 [441]

In Western Australia a multitude of stromatolites fill the coastal ocean shallows of a place named *Shark Bay*. Stromatolites live off sunlight and fill the atmosphere with oxygen. Not only do stromatolites produce oxygen, but a byproduct of their metabolism is rock. It wasn't until the 1950s that the importance of Shark Bay was realized. Scientists discovered the stromatolites were coated with a covering *of slimy algae*. Scientists also found that stromatolites were made up of very thin layers of *cyanobacteria* that had built up slowly (layer by layer and year after year), as they used *light* energy to gain their food. So, *stromatolites are mounded rocky structures* that are covered with a coating of *photosynthetic cyanobacteria* and *photosynthetic blue-green algae*.

Therefore, *stromatolites combine the oxygen producing capacities of photosynthetic algae and cyanobacteria!* 2.5 billion years BA (*late on the 3rd Day*), all beaches on Earth resembled Shark Bay. Stromatolites were global. As stromatolites filled the shallows, they began to fill the oceans with oxygen. Over a period of 2 billion years, countless generations of stromatolites pumped out over 20 million billion (20 x 10^{6+9} or 20 x 10^{15}) tons of oxygen. At first, the oxygen dissolved into the oceans where it oxidized and rusted out immense quantities of iron. But eventually it would also fill the atmosphere and transform the planet. The Earth's very appearance was dramatically altered. As the oxygen content of the oceans increased and the iron oxidized and precipitated onto the ocean floor, the color of the oceans gradually changed from olive-green to blue. As the oceans filled to their capacity for absorbing the oxygen, the oxygen that was being produced by the stromatolites began to move on into the atmosphere. Life giving oxygen flooded the atmosphere and diluted the thick atmospheric carbon dioxide until eventually the atmosphere was cleared of its CO_2. In this way, Earth's atmosphere was eventually filled with breathable air.

SCIENTISTS BELIEVE WE GOT OUR PRESENT ATMOSPHERE 1.5 BILLION YEARS AGO.

Early on the *4th Day of Creation*, after nearly 2 billion years of oxygenation, our blue planet was born. According to science, what was started during the *3rd Day* was finally completed early on the *4th Day of Creation*. On the dawn of the *4th Day of Creation (approximately 1.5 billion years ago)*, the Earth got its blue oceans and its blue sky — life friendly creations of God. Relics of this great transformative period survive today in the colossal layers of iron-rich sediment, which were originally deposited on the floors of the ancient oceans. These so-called *'banded-iron' sediment-formations* are scattered throughout all areas of the globe. Although these banded-iron formations formed in the ocean depths, many have now been lifted to the surface through a process of continent building that science calls *'plate tectonics.'* These iron deposits are vital for today's economies. *They are the major source of all the iron mined today!* In the 1950s and 1960s, tons of iron were strip-mined from a considerable number of farm acres, owned by a prominent citizen of my hometown.[442] I now understand that Brundidge, Alabama, Pike County, Alabama, all of the United States of America, and all of the continents of the Earth — had once been completely submerged beneath a toxic iron-rich ocean that *"drowned"* the early earth at the end of the 2nd Day of Creation. 3 ¾ billion years ago, at the end of the 2nd Day of

---

[441] The History Channel: How the Earth was Made: Part I
[442] https://thediggings.com/usa/alabama

Creation, volcanic outgassing had transformed the fiery ball of our early earth into a toxic water-world!

THE 1ST MACROSCOPIC-LIFE: PLANTS YIELDING SEED & TREES BEARING FRUIT.

These forms of early life were actually the 2nd life-forms to appear on Earth. According to science, the second forms of life that appeared on Earth were what the Bible calls *plants yielding seed and the trees bearing fruit* (i.e., the vegetation mentioned in Genesis 1:11-12). These plants appeared on the land God brought forth when He separated the waters below the heavens. Why are these forms of *macroscopic* life mentioned as the first life-forms in the Bible? Was it because they are forms of life which would be meaningful and easily understood by ancient man? This seems reasonable, because we now know *bacteria* would not be discovered by man until the invention of *the first workable compound microscope* (~ the mid-1600s AD). That happened approximately 5400-5300 years after Adam was created, and ~ 3100 years after Moses wrote the Torah.[443]

DR. SCHROEDER THINKS:

"Because the Bible talks in the language of man, it consistently deals with aspects of life as they are directly sensible to humans. It is, for example, due to this human orientation that laws of biblically permitted and restricted foods (Lev. 11) discuss only forms of life visible to the unaided eye. Crustaceans are among the animals prohibited from consumption. Yet a glass of water or a leaf of lettuce need not be examined by the microscope to learn if a microcrustacean might be present. Because it would have been unrealistic to expect a mass of newly freed slaves 3,300 years ago at Sinai to grasp the meaning of bacteria and microalgae, it makes sense the biblical record of life starts with that which is visible."[444]

We now know the first visible life (i.e., *macroscopic* life) appeared on the *5th Day*. We also know *Earth's first visible plants* also appeared on the *5th Day*. All life before that was *microscopic*—i.e., invisible to the naked eye — *plants included*. I have already mentioned that Jewish tradition (*Kabala*) holds there was no special day assigned for the command for vegetation alone because it was not a unique work.

Nevertheless, land-based plants are now the major source of renewal for the life supporting oxygen of our planet's atmosphere. Plants take the carbon dioxide that is generated on the Earth and through the miraculous process of photosynthesis they use the energy of sunlight to convert it into oxygen.[445] High levels of CO_2 are poison to us. But for plants, CO_2 is food! Plants take the CO_2 that volcanism, forest fires, and Earth's life-forms make, and give us back the oxygen we need — to breath and live.

So, if you are concerned about atmospheric CO_2 concentrations — follow Israel's example. We could make our deserts bloom (cf. Introduction—Part VII: A Renaissance in Industry, Agriculture, Religion & Science). **We need to fund the research that is necessary to make *"Clean Energy"* affordable. In the meantime — We should stop fighting the efforts that keep our country energy-independent and focus on fresh-**

---

[443] Article: Antony van Leeuwenhoek http://www.ucmp.berkeley.edu/history/leeuwenhoek.html (Leeuwenhoek's description of living bacteria ~1650AD/ So—Moses wrote the Torah ~ 1450BC/ and Creation of Adam ~ 3700BC/ Therefore— 3700 + 1650AD = 5350 years after Adam, and 1450 BC + 1650AD = ~3100 years after Moses wrote the Torah—microscopes became good enough to allow men to examine the 1st microscopic forms of life.)

[444] Schroeder *Genesis and the Big Bang* Chapter 9 p 129 c

[445] Schroeder *Genesis and the Big Bang* Chapter 8 p 124 c

water reclamation projects. We need to plant more trees and other plants. We could feed the world!

Following the oxygenation of Earth's oceans and atmosphere, the Earth became more recognizable — more similar to today's planet, but before it would become the planet that we know today, a new cycle of cataclysmic events would take place.[446] Over the next billion years deep movements would wrench apart the Earth's crust, and the life (which had just begun), would face it toughest test yet — but that is a subject for *another "Day."*

FALSE PRESUMPTIONS

In the Introduction to this series, I mentioned some of the conflicts that have historically occurred between science and religion. I also mentioned there is a history of misunderstanding based on errors of interpretation. Sadly, both the advocates of science, and those who base their understanding of Earth-sciences on their religious interpretation of scripture — are hampered and often mislead by their own *Cognitive Dissonance.*

SOME OF THE MISREPRESENTATIONS WE DISCUSSED WERE:

- The Age of the Earth—
- Spatial Dimensions and the Flow of Time—
- The origin of Earth's ocean waters from the condensation of a primeval cloud that once surrounded our molten Earth—
- Aristotle's belief in a Geo-Centric position of the Earth — and,
- Aristotle's premise that — *Nothing comes from Nothing.*

These are just a few of the examples of faulty platforms of thought that science has recently corrected. Now, I am going to tackle another false presumption that is still believed by the majority of people. They accept it as true science even though new evidence brought to light over the last 85 years has proved that what is currently so ingrained in the majority of our institutions of learning about *how life originated* — is actually *pseudoscience!*

What follows will cause some of you a great deal of discomfort. You may refuse to believe it because you may already have a vested interest in the opposite point of view. Your own cognitive dissonance may initially cause you to reject the most recently published findings and conclusions of modern science concerning *the origins of life,* or *what some refer to as the source of life.* So, what is this particular faulty platform of thought that has, since 1859, caused secular academia to belittle, mock, and reject the Biblical Account of Creation? It has everything to do with an Englishman, who was born on the same day as Abraham Lincoln (February 12, 1809). This Englishman was the son of a prominent medical doctor. He was baptized in the Anglican Church but attended services in the Unitarian Church with his mother. He began his study of medicine at Edinburgh, but soon discovered he was not *"cut out"* to be a doctor. He then transferred to Cambridge (Christ's Church College) in 1828 to train for the ministry. While at Cambridge, he befriended a biology professor (John Stevens Henslow), and became interested in zoology and geography. Under the influence of Henslow and others at Cambridge, *he changed course again* (pun intended), and eventually became the

---

[446] The History Channel: How the Earth Was Made: Part I

naturalist that took ship on the H.M.S. Beagle for a protracted voyage to South America and the Galapagos Islands. *That man was Charles Darwin.[447,448,449,450]*

WRONG SCIENCE THEORY ON THE ORIGINS OF LIFE.

A. Darwin's Ideas of how life started—agreed with *the Abiogenic Origin of Life Theories of his Time.* Slowly, beginning in 1859 with the publishing of Darwin's book, steadily gaining popular approval in the late 19th and early 20th centuries, and until the mid-1970s; the accepted '*wisdom'* concerning the origins of Life was that Life started from—

- *Random-chance-reactions among primeval atoms of chemicals—*
- *over eons of time—*
- *gradually combining one chance-occurrence with others—*
- *until self-replication; and*
- *mutations — produced the first biological cell.[451]*

In a letter to Joseph Dalton Hooker on February 1, 1871, Charles Darwin addressed the question of the origin of life. Darwin suggested life could have possibly originated from abiogenic reactions among naturally occurring chemicals in warm ponds to eventually, over time produce a protein compound, which over additional time might undergo more complex changes that would eventually lead to life.[452]

B. GEORGE WALD

In the mid-20th century George Wald, a Harvard University biology professor, a Nobel laureate, and a proponent of Darwin's theory; made the following statement which was published in the August 1954 issue of the journal *Scientific American*: *"However improbable we regard this event (the start of all life), or any of the steps which it involves, given enough time it will almost certainly happen at least once. And for life as we know it...once may be enough. Time is in fact the hero of the plot. The time with which we have to deal is of the order of two billion years. What we regard as impossible on the basis of human experience is meaningless here: Given so much time the impossible becomes the possible, the possible probable, and the probable virtually certain. One has only to wait. Time itself performs miracles."[453,454]*

Why did Wald think the amount of time available for life to evolve was two billion years? Because he believed two billion years had passed between the first appearance of liquid water on Earth and the first appearance of life.[455] Right? **WRONG!**

First, we know Wald's belief in a two-billion-year hiatus between the first appearance of liquid water on Earth and the first appearance of life was wrong. We have already shown science now claims as the early Earth cooled after the impact-accretion

447 Article: Charles Darwin: Naturalist www.lucidcafe.com/library/96 feb/ darwin.html
448 Article: The Scientist: Charles Darwin www.blupete.com/literature/Biographies/Science/Darwin.html
449 Article: Rocky Road: Charles Darwin www.strangescience.net/darwin.html
450 Article: About Darwin www.aboutdarwin.com/darwin/darwin_01.html
451 Schroeder *The Hidden Face of God* Chapter 4 p 50b
452 Article: Darwin's Pond Probability: http://www.darwinthenandnow.com/tag/abiogenesis/ Also: Why Abiogenesis is Impossible: Article by Jerry Bergman, PhD; © 1999 Creation Research Society: First published in CRSQ—Creation Research Society Quarterly, Vol. 36, No. 4, March 2000: http://www.trueorigin.org/abio.asp
453 G. Wald, The Origin of Life, Scientific American, August 1954
454 Schroeder *The Science of God* Chapter 6 p 83a
455 Schroeder *The Science of God* Chapter 6 p 84 b

phase of Earth's history ceased, liquid water suddenly appeared. The first forms of life, bacteria and photosynthetic algae followed almost immediately — no billions of years were required.

Second, twenty-five years after Wald's statement was published, it was proved to be so wrong that in 1979, *Scientific American* reprinted it in a special publication titled *"Life: Origin and Evolution."* Only this time it appeared as a retraction! Dr. Schroeder stated in his book: The Science of God: *"I have seen no other retraction by a journal of a Nobel Laureate's writings. The retraction was unequivocal."* [456]

Let's review the history of why *Scientific American* jumped on Wald's bandwagon in 1954 and then, why it published its retraction in 1979. This story starts with a graduate student in Illinois.

C. STANLEY MILLER

Wald's statement was influenced by an experiment performed by a graduate student at the University of Chicago in 1953. Stanley Miller had produced amino acids (building blocks of life) by a series of *random chance* chemical reactions. Miller took a glass flask, created a vacuum in it, and filled it with the gases believed to have been present in Earth's *atmosphere* 3.8 billion years ago. 3.8 billion years ago was 11.95 billion years after *the Beginning*, and 0.05 billion (i.e., 50 million) years before the end of the *2nd Day of Creation* (which ended 12 billion years after *the Beginning*). Miller filled his glass flask with ammonia, methane, hydrogen, and water vapor, because they are the products of the volcanism which was so dominant at that time.

Miller then simulated lightning by passing charged electrical sparks through the walls of the flask. He was careful to exclude any *free oxygen* in the flask because it appeared on Earth about two billion years *later* (near the dawn of the *4th Day* of Creation) and would not have been present in Earth's atmosphere during the time Miller was attempting to simulate in his flask. Miller believed the electrical sparks produced *random chance* chemical reactions among the gases.

After two days, a reddish slime appeared on the interior walls of the flask. The slime was found to contain amino acids. It was known amino acids are the building blocks of proteins, and proteins are the building blocks of life. So, Miller concluded:

- *Since-if,* *random chance* chemical reactions in this experiment could produce amino acids in just two days.
- *Then-if,* given two billion years of *random chance* reactions throughout the Earth's vast atmosphere—
- *Then-surely* the first forms of life must have been the product of similar *random chance* chemical reactions during the epoch he simulated in his flask.[457]

I call this form of faulty reasoning *"Sitisams."* This acronym stands for —

"Since-if, Then if, Serial Assumption Mistakes."

I will talk about Darwin's *"Sitisams"* when I discuss his Theory of Evolution in **Chapter 17: HOW LIFE ORIGINATED—DARWIN VS. MODERN SCIENCE.**

[456] Schroeder *The Science of God* Chapter 6 p 84d
[457] Schroeder *The Science of God* Chapter 6 p 84a,b,c

When Wald looked at Miller's experiment, he agreed with Miller's conclusions. Wald had already *erroneously* claimed two billion years had passed between the appearance of liquid water on Earth and the appearance of the first simple forms of life. Now, he made another major mistake. He took two facts that were known to be true, and concluded they were related. He then made two assumptions that 25 years later, would be proved to be false.

What were the two true facts Wald considered?

(1) *Random chance chemical reactions* over two days produced amino acids. (True)

(2) Amino acids are the building blocks of proteins. (True)

How did Wald conclude the two true facts were related? He *assumed* the amino acids produced by the '*random chance*' chemical reactions in Miller's experiment would (over time), eventually combine to produce proteins. (Not so. This *assumption* was Wald's 2nd big mistake.)

What were his two additional assumptions that 25 years later — were proved false?

(1) The proteins *he assumed* would eventually be produced —

(2) Would turn into the first true life forms on Earth — if given additional eons of time.

The News Media jumped on this. It was immediately reported Miller had proved Darwin's Evolutionary Theory of the Origin of Life. Life had *randomly* started by *chance*. Or had it?

Twenty-five years later, with the crystal clear '*vision*' of the '*retrospectroscope*' we can see that Wald's 'facts' were:

> **True — True — But unrelated. Furthermore, his two additional assumptions — were false.**

D.   WHAT WAS MISSED?

1. Was it true that amino acids had been produced in two days in an experiment that simulated what was thought to have been the atmospheric conditions of the Earth 3.8 billion years before the present? Yes. Most would agree this statement was true.

2. Was it true that the amino acids had been produced by *random chance reactions*? This statement is *controversial*. Some claim the reactions were *neither* random, *nor* by chance.[458]

3. Was it true amino acids are building blocks of proteins? Yes. This was true.

4. Were the amino acids produced alive? **No!**

The chemicals in the experiment and the amino acids that resulted were *not* alive. They were inorganic compounds. To date, modern science cannot explain exactly how life formed. Science has discovered the compounds that direct organic cell reproduction — but science is clueless as to their origins.

"The machinery for organic cell reproduction is found in the genetic material DNA (deoxyribonucleic acid) and RNA (ribonucleic acid). We haven't a clue as to its origins, but it appears that it works in a manner consistent with the laws of physical chemistry. The DNA and RNA select from the pool of organic and inorganic compounds within a cell, those molecules that fit into the genetic-code material. While the DNA and RNA deal with

---

[458] Schroeder *Genesis and the Big Bang* Chapter 7 p 107a

the organization of complex molecules such as amino acids, qualitatively these acts of reproduction are as unintellectual as the growth of an inorganic mineral" — a quote from Schroeder.[459]

5. Was the assumption true that, given enough time, proteins would result from the combination of the amino acids thus produced? **No**! That assumption was quite a stretch. No proteins (alive or otherwise) were produced in Miller's experiment. And, as we shall see, even the two billion years Wald erroneously claimed were available for the *random chance* development of life would not have been enough time for Miller's amino acids to form proteins, or for life to come forth from these reactions. This will be discussed when we introduce the work of Professor Harold Morowitz — in this chapter.

E.   **WRONG SCIENCE THEORY ON THE ORIGINS OF LIFE SUMMARY:**

- Miller's experiment produced amino acids.
- There is disagreement about the chemical reactions in the experiment. Some scientists say they were not truly *random*, and neither were they — *by chance*.
- True, amino acids are building blocks of proteins, and proteins are basic components of all life forms.
- However, the amino acids produced in Miller's experiment were *not* alive and *no* proteins (*alive or otherwise*), were produced.
- Wald's assumption — that Miller's experiment would eventually produce life — was an erroneous assumption.
- As we shall see, the amount of time Wald thought available for the formation of life was also a false assumption.

Unfortunately, Wald concluded — *Surely life must have originated in this way.* When Wald, a famous Nobel laureate, interpreted the data in this way, the speculative jump from the production of amino acids — to life was easy to make for those who ascribed to the Darwinian concept of evolution. The lesson to be learned here is:

> *The trend of thought in this controversial study of life's origins was based on poorly researched science that was wrongly presented as fact by a reputable noted and influential personality who should have known better!*

By 1948 Wald was a full professor at Harvard. He was also one of the pioneering researchers in the biochemistry of vision. For that research he had already received the Nobel Prize. When Wald made such a claim regarding the significance of Miller's experiment, it was assumed by one and all that he knew what he was talking about — that it was a certainty that *random chance events* can and did lead to life. It was thus accepted by *all* — that evolutionary forces, guided solely by the laws of nature, *led from the first microbe to man.* However, Wald's skills in mathematics seem to be less than his skills in biology, and it was the mathematics of probability that would first question the validity of his assumptions.

III.   **THE FIRST CHALLENGE TO WALD'S ASSUMPTIONS CAME FROM A MATHEMATICIAN.**

In 1968, *Professor Harold Morowitz*, a physicist at Yale University, published his book: *Energy Flow in Biology.* He and other physicists and mathematicians had become

---

[459] Schroeder *Genesis and the Big Bang* Chapter 7 p 106c

concerned about the casualness with which some scientists studying the origins of life were assuming unlikely events must have occurred. He felt these scientists were making assumptions without any attempt to rigorously investigate the *probability* of such events. Morowitz presented computations of the time required for *random chance chemical reactions* to form a bacterium — not an organism as complex as a human, not even a flower; *just a simple, single-celled bacterium.* Basing his calculations on optimistically rapid rates of reactions, the calculated time for the bacterium to form exceeds not only the 4.5-billion-year age of the Earth, but also the entire 15 ¾ billion-year age of the universe! *"The likelihood of random processes producing life from a primordial bath of chemicals is even less likely than that of your shaking an omelet and having the yolk and the white separate back into the original form of the egg,"* he claimed.[460]

However, the assumption that *random chance* was the mechanism responsible for the source of life — that life came forth by *accident* rather than through *Divine Intervention and Intelligent Design* — planted by such a distinguished personality as Wald — remains with the general public even though *Scientific American* later acknowledged Wald had erred and printed a retraction 25 years later. Twenty-five years is a long time for an error to go uncorrected. When the first scientific discovery came along that proved Darwin, Wald, and Miller wrong — almost no one noticed. Even though *Scientific American printed a retraction of Wald's article*, people still think Darwin's Theory is correct.

A. WALD'S ASSUMPTIONS ABOUT MILLER'S EXPERIMENT LACKED SCIENTIFIC PROOF.

Assumptions were made, which were not, and have not been backed by fact. Darwin made a similar error when he proposed his theory about evolution in his book: *The Origin of Species.* This will be more fully discussed when we introduce the creation events that Elohim accomplished on the *5th Day of Creation* (in Chapters 13 and 14 of this book). However, at the time Darwin proposed his theory, the lack of evidentiary proof did not dismay him. He had not been perturbed by the missing links in the fossil record discovered in his lifetime. On no less than seven occasions in his seminal book *The Origin of Species,* he implored his readers *to ignore* the evidence of the fossil record as a refutation of his concept of evolution and to *"use imagination to fill in its gaps."* The fossil records' leaps and bounds, he claimed, were the result of its being *incomplete.*[461] Darwin's thesis of gradual evolution claims *"Natura Non Facit Saltum"* (<u>Nature Does Not Make Jumps</u>)! The millions of fossils discovered since Darwin's time, have proved that statement is clearly *false.*[462]

Nevertheless, after Darwin published the first book of his theory (in 1859), Darwinists have searched (in vain) for evidence in the fossil record for the transitional forms of life that would prove Darwin's theory of the evolution of life from the simple to the complex — from one Phylum of animals into another — and from that first complex ancestor into today's plethora of complex forms. Conversely, in his book, *The Science of God,* Dr. Schroeder said: *"In the entire fossil record with its millions of specimens, no midway transitional fossil has been found at the basic levels of phylum or class; no trace of an*

---

[460] Schroeder *Genesis and the Big Bang* Chapter 7 p 110f—p 111a
[461] Schroeder *The Science of God* Chapter 2 p 31b
[462] Schroeder *The Science of God* Chapter 1 p 10a

animal that was half predecessor and half successor.[463] Darwin would have been much closer to the truth had he written "Natura Solum Facit Saltum" (Nature Only Makes Jumps)." [464]

> **As we shall see, when you read Chapters 17 and 18 in this book, scientists now know — the millions of fossils that have been discovered since Darwin first published his book (165 years ago) absolutely refute Darwin's Theory.**

Once faulty science has been generally accepted, it is hard for the public to recognize the truth when it is finally discovered. Regrettably, the general public is still convinced Darwin, Wald, and others were right. In fact, when we examine the *5th and 6th Days of Creation,* you shall see — The people who still support the speculative assumptions of Darwin and Wald compounded their error by concluding—

Given additional epochs of time, those same simple life-forms could evolve into the plethora of complex life-forms we have today.

B. WHAT CAUSED 'SCIENTIFIC AMERICAN' TO MAKE ITS RETRACTION?

The answer has something to do with a man with an exotic name who used a sophisticated technology to study a special kind of ancient rock that we have not yet mentioned. He found the scientific proof that Darwin and Wald and the other proponents of the *Random Chance Origin of Life Theory* were wrong. Strange as it seems, Darwin's and Wald's views would ultimately be proved to be wrong by the fossil record itself.

The more complete present-day fossil record of the earliest life-forms actually shows—

- Neither the 4.5-billion-year age of the Earth nor the 15 ¾ billion-year age of the universe were necessary for the development of life.
- Since 1979, articles based on the premise that life originated from random chance chemical reactions over billions of years are no longer accepted by reputable scientific journals.[465]
- It was also discovered the *Random Chance Development of Life Theory* could not have produced even the simplest form of life in the 15 ¾ billion-year period of the existence of the universe.[466]
- Instead, science *has now proved* the Earth's first life forms *suddenly appeared* immediately after liquid water appeared on Earth — not billions of years later.[467]
- We have learned once again, *the Bible is correct — Life appeared immediately with the first appearance of liquid water on Earth — just as the Biblical account of the events of the 3rd Day of Creation said, and just as modern science has now proved.*

So, what was the scientific proof that was discovered twenty-five years after *Scientific American* printed its article about Wald's claims about *The Origin of Life*? What was the proof that caused that journal to print *a retraction* of its article?

---

[463] Schroeder *The Science of God* Chapter 6 p 95b
[464] Schroeder *The Science of God* Chapter 1 p 10a
[465] Schroeder *The Science of God* Chapter 6 p 85c
[466] Schroeder *Genesis and the Big Bang* Chapter 7 p 111a
[467] Schroeder *The Science of God* Chapter 4 p 68b

C. THE MAN WITH AN EXOTIC NAME; HIS SOPHISTICATED INSTRUMENT; & THE SPECIAL ROCK HE EXAMINED.

Scientific American withdrew its article 25 years after it had been written because the research performed by another Harvard professor proved Wald wrong. That man was a paleontologist — *Elso Barghoorn*. In the 1970s *Professor Barghoorn* reasoned correctly that if one were looking for scientific evidence that the first forms of life were single-cell bacteria and algae, the evidence would be small — perhaps *submicroscopic in size*. So, he decided he would need a special instrument to search for the evidence he sought to prove his thesis. That instrument was *the electron microscope*, a tool capable of examining minute structures that are so small as to be imperceptible to microscopes that probe images using visible light.

SEDIMENTARY ROCK

The special rock he examined was sedimentary rock. Why sedimentary rock? Because, if evidence of early life on Earth were to be found, some basic conditions must be satisfied that would favor its development.

FIRST: THE FIERY EARTH HAD TO COOL.

Our Earth (which was born in fire) had to cool to a temperature range that allowed *liquid water to form* and *aqueous chemical reactions to occur.*[468] The cooling of the Earth's crust occurred 4.5 billion years ago — about 750 million years before the end of the *2nd Day* of creation.[469] From that time onward, liquid water could have been available.

SECOND: LIQUID WATER IS NECESSARY FOR SEDIMENTARY ROCK TO FORM.

If we are searching for the fossil evidence of the earliest life, then we need conditions in which fossils can form. An organism lying among large rocks will not develop into a fossil. Fossils can be formed and preserved only in rock that has *weathered, sedimented*, and then *resolidified* after the sediment has encased the life-forms that will be *fossilized*. That will happen when the sediment "settles" and resolidifies.[470] The active ingredient necessary for this whole process is liquid water. When the surface of certain types of rock is exposed to liquid water for long periods of time, the rock will eventually soften and erode to form a soft layer of material that becomes suspended in the liquid water. When that happens, the suspended material can be transported by the liquid water to another "down-hill" site. When the flow of the water reaches a site where the flow is stopped, the soft suspended material will settle and deposit there. The settled material is called *"sediment."* Over time, the sediment builds up. Life-forms that are trapped in the layers of oxygen-poor sediment die and over additional periods of time, *fossilize*. So, *liquid water* is the necessary factor for the weathering, erosion, transportation, and sedimentation of the material of large preexisting rocks. If life-forms are trapped and buried in the process, they are preserved when the sediment resolidifies to form *sedimentary rock*. Therefore, Barghoorn thought the oldest known sedimentary rocks should provide the evidence for the earliest presence of abundant liquid water and also for the micro-fossil evidence of the Earth's first life-forms.[471]

---

[468] Schroeder *Genesis and the Big Bang* Chapter 7 p 111d
[469] Schroeder *Genesis and the Big Bang* Chapter 7 p 111d
[470] Schroeder *Genesis and the Big Bang* Chapter 7 p 111d & 112a
[471] Schroeder *Genesis and the Big Bang* Chapter 7 p 112a

In other words, if the *microfossils of single-cell bacteria and algae* could be found in the earliest known sedimentary rocks, this could be the proof of the earliest life-forms for which science had been searching. Why is liquid water so important to the origin of life? Because Barghoorn knew *all life on Earth is water-based.*[472] Barghoorn thought 3.8 billion years before the present might have been the earliest time life could have appeared on Earth.[473] So that is where he began his search.

THE OLDEST SEDIMENTARY ROCKS SHOWED CARBON, BUT NO LIFE.

Earth's oldest sedimentary rocks have been found in the southern *African Shield*, and in the *Canadian Shield* in North America. In geology the term, "Shield," refers to a broad flat area of exposed *Precambrian basement-rock* that lies at the center of each continent. The oldest sedimentary rocks on Earth are 3.8 billion years old. This means *liquid water* was present on Earth at least 50 million years before the end of the *2nd Day of Creation.* But *no signs of life were found* in the 3.8-billion-year-old sedimentary rocks. Instead, Earth's oldest sedimentary rocks showed deposits that were representative of *organic carbon.* Although no life had been found, this was still a very important discovery. Why? *Because life as we know it is also carbon based.* Carbon is *the only element* that can form the long, complex chains necessary for the presence of life. It is also *the steppingstone* for the production of the 86 natural elements heavier than carbon.[474] So, both *carbon and non-toxic liquid water* are necessary for life to develop.

THE OLDEST SEDIMENTARY ROCKS WITH EVIDENCE OF LIFE ARE 3.3 BILLION YEARS OLD.

In the midst of the African Shield, there is a chert rock (a brittle microcrystalline quartz) that is 3.3 billion years old. This chert rock has been named "*the Fig Tree Formation.*"

> *It was in the sediments of the Fig Tree Formation that the microscopic fossils of the Earth's earliest life-forms (spherical and rod-shaped single celled bacteria and algae) were discovered by Barghoorn when he examined samples of that unique rock with an electron microscope.*

Since science has determined the *3rd Day* started 3.75 billion years *Before Adam*, and Earth's first life-forms ***suddenly appeared*** 3.3 billion years ago after the *3rd Day* began:

WE CAN NOW SAY THE EARTH'S 1ST LIFE FORMS SUDDENLY APPEARED 3.3 BILLION YEARS AGO EARLY ON THE "MORNING" OF THE 3RD DAY OF CREATION!

3.75 billion (-) 3.3 billion = 0.450 billion (*or 450 million*) years after the start of the 3rd Day.

That was practically at *the 'Dawn' of the 3rd Day.* In the grand scheme of things that was only 500 million years after the oldest sedimentary rocks *proved* liquid water first appeared on Earth "*on the evening*" of the *2nd Day*, 3.8 billion years "Before Adam."

[3.8 billion minus 3.3 billion = 0.5 billion *or 500 million years!*]

So it is that Barghoorn discovered the evidence of carbon in 3.8-billion-year-old sedimentary rocks, and he also discovered the micro-fossils of the first forms of life on Earth in 3.3-billion-year-old sedimentary rocks! Now the evidence had been found that the first life on Earth *suddenly developed* 500 million years *after* the first appearance of

---

[472] Schroeder *The Science of God* Chapter 6 p 86b
[473] Schroeder *Genesis and the Big Bang* Chapter 7 p 111d
[474] Schroeder *The Science of God* Chapter 2 p 27b

liquid water on Earth! In paleontology, 500 million years is like — "*a blink of the Geologic Eye!*" With that perspective in mind, we can say the time that has passed since Adam was created (i.e., ~ 5700 years ago) is almost the same thing as "*the present!*" Biblically speaking, 5700 years ago is like: "*One day is as a thousand years and a thousand years as One Day*" (II Peter 3:8) — or "*as a watch that passes in the night*" (Psalm 90:4)!

500 million years compared to the 4.5-billion-year history of the existence of the Earth — is considered almost immediate development in the minds of paleontologists, thus proving — life suddenly developed immediately after liquid water made its first appearance on Earth. Not only did Barghoorn prove *Life first appeared on Earth* 3.3 billion years ago (at the dawn of the *3rd Day*), but he also discovered the microfossils in *the Fig Tree Formation that prove:*

• *The first microscopic life on Earth was identical in every respect (including size and scale), to the same organisms that are found in present-day aquatic environments!* [475]
• *During the 3.3 billion years of their existence, these organisms have not evolved into any forms of higher or more complex life!*
• *Life literally sprang forth in only a fraction of the time Wald had thought necessary. As soon as the conditions on Earth arose for life to exist — life appeared. No billions of years were required!* [476]

D. GOODBYE TO THE RANDOM CHANCE CHEMICAL REACTION ORIGIN OF LIFE ASSUMPTIONS!

Thus, the earliest evidence of life on earth dates to 3.3 billion years before the present (*on the 3rd Day*) — only 500 million years after the appearance of the Earth's first liquid water. At this relatively young age, several life-forms had already formed. So, it is we see there were three major consequences of Barghoorn's and Morowitz's work.

- Miller and Wald's "*Random-Chance Chemical-Reaction Origin-of-Life Theory*" — *was shattered!* The mathematics of Morowitz had already shown it is statistically impossible that random-chance events could have produced life in such a relatively short time of two billion years. Furthermore, Morowitz's calculations also showed neither the 4.5-billion-year age of the Earth nor the 15 ¾ billion-year age of the universe would have been enough time for life to form by random-chance chemical-reactions!

- Elso Barghoorn discovered what *the sequences of the Biblical Creation Account* has said all along — Life, the most organized system of atoms known in the universe — *popped into being in the blink of a geological eye!* [477] **Sudden developments are the hallmarks of Elohim's creations. We now know slow-gradual-change and random-events did not do the forming of early life.**[478,479,480]

[475] Schroeder *Genesis and the Big Bang* Chapter 7 p 112b
[476] Schroeder *The Science of God* Chapter 6 p 86b & 87a
[477] Schroeder *The Hidden Face of God* Chapter 4 p 51c
[478] Schroeder *Genesis and the Big Bang* Chapter 7 p 112b
[479] Schroeder *The Science of God* Chapter 6 p 85c
[480] Schroeder *The Hidden Face of God* Chapter 4 p 51c

- And just how did Barghoorn's discoveries affect the scientific world? Twenty-five years after Wald's statement had been published; **Scientific American retracted its article,** because <u>Elso Barghoorn had **unequivocally proved George Wald wrong**</u>! _**Since then, all articles that claim life originated by random-chance chemical-reactions are rejected by reputable Scientific Journals!**_ [481]

E.   SCIENCE STILL DOESN'T KNOW HOW LIFE BEGAN.

It is essential to understand — science has not provided explanations for the two principal starting points in our lives:

    (1) The start of the universe, and

    (2) The start of life itself.

As we have previously discussed, when we try to describe the conditions at that crucial interface between total nothingness and the start of our universe, we are confronted with a point in space having infinitely high density, infinitely small dimensions, and infinitely high temperatures that cannot be handled mathematically in the dimensions of length, width, height, temperature, time, or any of the physical dimensions that now limit our experience. _The Singularity,_ as we now call it, was outside of the dimensions that govern our existence. Nevertheless, the fact is — an untenable Singularity existed in real-time at the instant of the Big Bang.[482] In his discussion of the failure of science to answer the question of the origins of life, Dr. Schroeder's analysis is so cogent that I will now quote directly from his book, _Genesis and the Big Bang._

> _"The answers provided by science for life's origins are no more satisfying than those provided for the origin of the universe. Since the conference on Macro-Evolution was held in Chicago in 1980, there has been a total reevaluation of life's origins and development. In regard to the Darwinian Theory of Evolution, the world-famous paleontologist of the American Museum of Natural History, Dr. Niles Eldredge, unequivocally declared: 'The pattern_* [fossil record**] _that we were told to find for the last 120 years_ [since Darwin] _does not exist.'_
>
> _There is now overwhelmingly strong evidence, both statistical and paleontological, that life could not have been started on Earth by a series of random chance chemical reactions. Today's best mathematical estimates state there simply was not enough time for random reactions to get life going as fast as the fossil record shows that it did. The reactions were either directed by some—_
>
>   _(1) as of yet unknown physical force or_
>
>   _(2) a metaphysical guide; or_
>
>   _(3) life arrived here from elsewhere. But the 'elsewhere' answer merely pushes the start of life into an even more unlikely time constraint._
>
> _For decades, many scientists have presented the misconception that there are rational explanations for the origins of the universe, life, and mankind. The shortcomings of the popular theories were merely swept under the rug to avoid confusing the issues. The knowledge that scientists do not have these explanations has now been coupled by the awareness of the fossil record's failure to confirm Darwin's or any other theory of the_

---

[481] Schroeder _The Science of God_ Chapter 6 p 85c

[482] Schroeder _Genesis and the Big Bang_ Chapter 1 p 24e

gradual evolution of life. The demonstration of these misconceptions has brought many scientists and laypersons to an uncomfortable realization. The problems of our origins, problems that most of us would have preferred to consider solved by experts who should know the answers, in fact have not been solved and are not about to be solved, at least by the purely scientific methods used to date."[483*, 484**]

IV.   THE 'WISDOM OF MAN' HAS FAILED!

The wisdom of man has consistently failed to solve the questions concerning the origins of the universe, life, and mankind. When I contemplate this fact and think about the wisdom of man in comparison to the Wisdom of God, I can't help but recall the biblical account of Pharaoh's magicians trying to match the miracles God performed through Moses (Exodus Chapters 5-12). To people of faith, the answer to the mysteries of our physical existence is so simple. It has been there all along. Sadly, the book that contains the answers sits in plain sight on the shelves of many homes throughout our land — collecting dust — because so many people are too caught up in the struggles and pleasures of our secular world to give it the place of importance it should occupy in our homes.

CONCERNING THE ORIGINS OF THE UNIVERSE, LIFE, & MANKIND.

The answer is — there was a metaphysical guide. That guide was and is the Judeo-Christian God. In Genesis One his name is Elohim. The answer is in the very first verse of the bible — the book of books. The answer is — Elohim is the source! He is the author of all life and all existence.

THE GENESIS CODE MEANING OF SOLOMON'S DISSERTATION ON WISDOM: 'ETERNITY PAST. ETERNITY PRESENT, & ETERNITY FUTURE': Now that we have an understanding of the hidden meaning of the Mosaic account of *Elohim's Works of Old* (during the first three days of Creation), we can begin to understand other cryptic scriptures that make reference to the same time period.

The revelations of *the Genesis Code* make it possible for us to uncover the mysterious meanings of *Solomon's Dissertation on Wisdom* that is found in Proverbs 8:22-31. It is believed Solomon wrote this dissertation around 950 BC[485] — several billion years after the events it describes, and according to Jewish tradition, about 500 years after Moses wrote the words of the *Genesis Creation Account* — assuming a date around 1450-1410 BC for the Exodus and allowing for the 40 years of wandering of the tribes in the *Wilderness* after the people refused God's command to conquer and occupy Canaan.[486] God punished them for their disobedience by turning them back into the wilderness. They refused because of their fear of the *"men of great size"* (i.e., the Nephilim), who lived in fortified cities. These Nephilim (also known as the sons of Anak) were giants. We will mention them again in Chapters 23 and 27 (in Book III), when we talk about who the ancient Jewish sages thought these "animals" were. Yes, God turned them back into the Wilderness because of their lack of faith in God. Only two people survived that experience — Joshua, and Caleb. They were the only ones who were willing

---

483* Schroeder *Genesis and the Big Bang* Chapter 1 p 25 b,c [Eldredge says "pattern" in this quote.]

484** Schroeder *The Science of God* Chapter 1 p 10 a [Eldredge says "fossil record" in this quote.]

485 The Ryrie Study Bible p 937

486 The Ryrie Study Bible p 91

to obey God's command to conquer Canaan. All who refused to obey God — perished during the 40 years of wandering in the Wilderness! Forty years later, Joshua and Caleb led their children in the conquest of Canaan — after all who refused God's command had died. (See Numbers 14:26-45 and Deut. 1:19-46.) In the last Chapter, I talked about '*The Water from Rock incident' when Moses disobeyed God by striking the rock instead of speaking to it.* Out of his anger at the people, he struck the rock. When he struck the rock, the Israelites thought Moses had brought forth the water, not God. Because Moses disobeyed, God denied Moses' entry into the Holy Land. I think that is one of the saddest stories in the Bible.

Moses would have had ample time to write the Torah (i.e., the 5 books of Moses) during the forty years of Israel's punishment and wandering in the desert. However, no manuscript of the Torah that dates to this period has yet been found. This is not surprising. The exact location of Mt. Sinai (also called Mt. Horeb) has not been factually determined. There are about two dozen candidates for its location and nearly half a dozen for the location of the Red Sea crossing; where the Bible says God parted the waters for Israel's escape and then closed them to destroy the pursuing Egyptian army.[487]

SOLOMON'S WORDS ABOUT THE ORIGIN OF WISDOM. PROVERBS 8:22-31

I. **"Eternity Past:" From before the beginning to the Singularity.**

   (v.22a) *The Lord possessed me at the beginning of His way,*
   (v.22b) *Before His works of old.*
   (v.23a) *From everlasting I was established,*
   (v.23b) *From the earliest times of the earth.*
   (v.24a) *When there were no depths I was brought forth,*
   (v.24b) *When there were no springs abounding with water.*
   (v.25a) *Before the mountains were settled,*
   (v.25b) *Before the hills I was brought forth.*
   (v.26a) *While He had not yet made the earth and the fields,*
   (v.26b) *Nor the first dust of the world.*

II. **"Eternity Present:" from the beginning to the end of time.**

   (v.27a) *When He established the heavens, I was there.*
   (v.27b) *When He inscribed a circle on the face of the deep.*

III. **On the 2nd—4th Days of Creation in Eternity Present When the Earth was Established.**

   (v.28a) *When He made firm the skies above,*
   (v.28b) *When the springs of the deep became fixed.*
   (v.29a) *When He set for the sea its boundary,*
   (v.29b) *So that the water should not transgress His command.*
   (v.29c) *When He marked out the foundations of the earth.*

IV. **The Conclusion:**

   (v.30) *Then I was beside Him as a master workman.*
          And I was daily His delight,
          Rejoicing always before Him,

---

[487] Bruce Feiler Walking the Bible: Book I God of Our Fathers: Chapter 1. p. 40 b

(v.31)   *Rejoicing in the world, His earth,*
And having my delight in the sons of men." Proverbs 8:22-31

Now let's apply what we have learned from the Genesis Code to these words of Solomon. These words remind us of the Onkelos translation of Gen. 1:1 — *"With First Wisdom, Elohim created the heavens and the earth."*

In Solomon's dissertation it is important to understand these words are spoken by Wisdom. The Wisdom that is speaking to us is *"First Wisdom." First Wisdom is the Wisdom of God.* In Chapter Eight (Book I), I talked about my belief that *the First Wisdom* in the Onkelos translation of Genesis 1:1 *is the first reference in the Bible to Jesus Christ* (i.e., *the Preincarnate Jesus Christ*). These verses are easily divided into three specific time-reference-frames:

- "Eternity Past" [*before time began*]: from before the Beginning to the Singularity.
- "Eternity Present:" from the Beginning to the End of Time, and
- A Specific Point in "Eternity Present:" On *the 2nd, 3rd,* and *4th Days of Creation* when the Earth was established. The last two verses are a conclusion. We will now discuss each in turn.

I. "Eternity Past:" From before the beginning to the Singularity.

[22a] *"The Lord possessed me at the beginning of His way,* [b]*before His works of old."*

> *These words refer to the Eternity of Elohim before the beginning. Here, we are talking about the Eternity of God that existed before time began. When Moses asked God how he should reply to the sons of Israel when they ask the name of the one who sent him: God replied, "I AM WHO I AM — You shall say to the sons of Israel, 'I AM' has sent me to you" (Exodus 3:13-14)."*
>
> *The concept that the Hebrew God is "The Eternal One," Who exists in a state that is referred to as "The Eternal Now;" comes from the explicit venerated and unpronounceable four-letter name for God — YHWH (also spelled JHVH), in Genesis 2:4 and Exodus 3:14. This name for God is so holy that devout Jews will not attempt to speak it. YHWH is translated in most of our English Bibles as "The LORD GOD." Every time you see "The LORD GOD" in your Bible, realize this name for God is so reverential, so holy, that devout Jews, out of deep respect, will not say it out loud. In Hebrew, the spelling of the allowable pronounceable form, YeHoWaH, includes the letters of the verb "to be" in its three tenses. Those vowels are also found in "Adonai." I talked about that in the Part IX Introduction to Book I. So, from the conjugation of the verb "to be," from the very name God called Himself (I was, I AM, I will be), we understand that God is Eternal — He was, He is, He will be — always, and with no beginning for God and no end for God.* [488] *For our purposes (i.e., our perspective and time-flow), I have chosen to label the Eternity of God that existed before the Beginning as "Eternity Past." That is because before the beginning of all we know, only God existed. It was a time when only God was — "I WAS."*
>
> *When man tries to comprehend God, man must realize our creator is outside of all the dimensions that govern man's physical existence. Specifically, as pertains to this*

[488] Schroeder The Science of God Chapter 10 p 161f

discussion, God is outside of time: not just man's time, but outside of the time-flow that exists throughout the universe. In trying to come to grips with this concept, we must understand we are dealing with two frames of reference: one within and one outside of the flow of time. Man is within the flow of time that is specific for his location in the universe — the Earth. We discussed this concept in Book I: Chapter 5: The Time Conundrum. For God the Creator, who is outside of time; a flow of events has no meaning. There is no future in the sense of what will eventually happen. The future and the past are in the present. An "Eternal Now" pervades, which contains all the time-flows in the universe, and all of Eternity (which is outside of all time-flows). For God, there is no linear progression of time such as man experiences. Just as the flow of time stops at the speed of light (cf. Chapter 3), for God — all is — simultaneous.[489] The time-flow of all events becomes an "Unending Now;" an "Eternal Now" — "a never-ending Present! "All is compressed into "the Present." Hence, when Moses asked God His name in Exodus 3, God replied using the present tense of the verb "to be"— "I AM." So, when we try to define "God's Eternal Now" in terms we can understand, we can choose to divide the Eternity of God into three parts. As you will see, all parts apply to God, but only two of the three parts of Eternity will apply to us. And — they apply to all men and women, past, present, and future.

- *We can label the Eternity of God that existed before time began, that is, before the Big Bang that produced the Singularity — **"Eternity Past."***
- *We can label the block of time that encompasses the beginning of the universe to its end as — **"Eternity Present."***
- *And we can refer to all future time in the Eternity of God after the end of the universe and the world, as — **"Eternity Future."***

__"Eternity Past"__ obviously can only be applied to God.
__"Eternity Present"__ includes all people ever born and ever to be born of man and woman.
__"Eternity Future"__ also applies to all people. However, the Bible teaches, and Christians believe there are two very different "Eternity Futures" — Heaven and Hell.

This is what I think my Dad was going to say to his Sunday School Class on that Sunday Morning in 1985 when his heart suddenly stopped beating and he fell to the floor dead — after saying — "This morning we are going to talk about 'Eternity Past, Eternity Present, and Eternity Future.'" I think God had intended to take him home (painlessly) while he was doing what he loved best — teaching God's Word. But CPR was given him by a member of his class. The next two days were precarious because he had a dangerous arrhythmia that could not be controlled with medication. So, he was airlifted by jet to the University of Alabama Medical School Hospital, in Birmingham (my alma mater in fact), and died once again (this time in pain) after his coronary artery bypass surgery failed to save his life. I do not blame anyone for his death. All who treated my Dad had the best intentions and did their best. What was done to prolong his life gave me a chance to fly to Alabama from my home in Washington State, so that I could be

[489] Schroeder The Science of God Chapter 10 p 161e

with him those last few days. On the day he passed, my father told me: "Son there isn't anything that can happen to me that my Lord Jesus and I can't handle together."

Now that the three divisions of time in Solomon's dissertation on Wisdom have been defined and explained, let us now proceed with the discussion of the insights the Genesis Code discloses about the ancient Hebrew description of Elohim's Creation.

²²ᵃ *"The Lord possessed me at the beginning of His way, ᵇbefore His works of old."*

"The beginning of His way" (v.22a) refers to God's Creation. "The Lord possessed me at the beginning of His way," tells us God possessed Wisdom before He started creating. The phrase: "His works of old," (v.22b) refers specifically to the works Elohim did during the Six Days of Creation. Since the Bible says "the beginning of His way was before His works of old," First Wisdom is telling us the Lord possessed Wisdom before He started creating and also at the moment He started creating. Combining the two, we understand Wisdom is talking about the actual moment when Elohim began creating all that exists and will exist. Specifically, Wisdom is talking about the moment the Singularity was created: i.e., the moment of the Beginning — the moment of the Big Bang.

²³ᵃ *"From everlasting I was established,"*

Verse 23a means: the Wisdom of God existed with God in "Eternity Past." God's Wisdom has no beginning and no end. Like God, God's Wisdom is eternal and is outside of Time. I believe Jesus Christ is the personification of the First Wisdom with which Elohim created in the beginning. Jesus Christ was with Elohim in the beginning. It was the Preincarnate Jesus Christ who was the First Wisdom of God through whom all of Creation was Created, Made, and Formed.

The Singularity—The moment of the beginning.
²³ᵇ *"From the earliest times of the earth"—* may refer to:

- *The instant of the Beginning within the Singularity, when the ethereal primordial stuff from which all matter and all existence would form — or it may refer to—*
- *the moment the core of the earth began to form during the last phase of the 2ⁿᵈ Day when the debris-field in the orbital path of the primeval earth first began to clear by impact-accretion.*

However, this second possibility is believed to be less likely because the events described in verse 24 — center on the Singularity and happened before the earth was made. The events in verses 24-26 refer to the making of the earth and would happen billions of earth-years after the Beginning (i.e., the Beginning of His Way). Nevertheless, this phrase ("From the earliest times of the earth"), prepares us for a coming time-reference-frame shift from "Eternity Past" to "Eternity Present."

²⁴ᵃ *"When there were no depths I was brought forth."*
²⁴ᵇ *"When there were no springs abounding with water."*

The phrases (v.24a) "When there were no depths I was brought forth" and "When there were no springs abounding with water" (v. 24b) — definitely refer to the time of the existence of the Singularity. At that instant there was no water, and the Singularity was so infinitely small that there were no depths of anything.

[25a]Before the mountains were settled, [b]Before the hills I was brought forth. [26a]While He had not yet made the earth and the fields, [26b]Nor the first dust of the world."

Verses 25 and 26 add emphasis to this interpretation. The time to which Wisdom is referring in these opening phrases is the moment of the existence of the Singularity. All confirm Wisdom is talking about the moment in time that science calls — "the Singularity."

II. "Eternity Present:" from the beginning to the end of time.

[27a] "When He established the heavens, I was there.
[27b] When He inscribed a circle on the face of the deep (the tehom)."

Notice: these phrases are placed in the middle of Wisdom's soliloquy. This placement suggests the probability of more than one time-reference-frame meaning.

The 1st Time-Reference-Frame Interpretation of "The Face of the Deep" (i.e., the Tehom):

We have already discussed the first meaning of the face of the Deep in Chapter 7 when the meaning of the Hebrew word, "tehom," was discussed. Tehom has been casually interpreted in our English Bibles as "the deep." The ancient Hebrew meaning of tehom is "the primeval great chaos." It was concluded in that discussion the word "tehom" refers to the primeval great chaos of the Beginning within the speck-of-space Elohim created by His spiritual contraction — His Tzimtzum. That speck-of-space He created in the beginning was the entire universe when it was infinitely small and there were no great depths of anything. At that moment, the universe had not expanded, and Elohim had not yet made the earth. This was at the beginning of "His works of old." Science has named that speck of space "the Singularity"— what we have also referred to as "the dot," and what Nahmanides compared to "a speck of space no larger than a grain of mustard.'" Therefore, the first meaning of "He inscribed a circle on the face of the deep" refers to the moment of the existence of the Singularity. At the very Beginning, the Singularity was an infinitely tiny speck of "black-fire-space", and "the face of the deep" was the primeval great chaos of the Beginning. The "deep" of the Singularity was "immeasurable" because it was infinitely small. The only thing that existed at the instant of the Beginning was the primeval great chaos within the infinitely tiny Singularity.

The 2nd Time-Reference-Frame Interpretation of "The Face of the Deep" is — The Universe at Large.

A second interpretation of "the face of the deep" can be understood by the first appearance of this phrase in our English Bibles: Genesis 1:2—"And the earth was formless and void, and darkness was over the face of the deep; and the Spirit of God was moving over the surface of the waters." At this point in time, the universe was dark because light had not yet emerged. Then, the Singularity suddenly expanded under the influence of "the Wind of God" (i.e., the Holy Spirit—on Day One). "The Wind of God" or "Ruach Elohim" (in Hebrew) caused a sudden expansion of the Singularity, which grew to be immeasurably large (by the 2nd and 3rd Days). At this juncture, the "inscription of a circle" in Solomon's dissertation can be interpreted to be a reference to the establishment of the Earth — a work that began on the 2nd Day with the first separation of the waters above from those below. This separation of the waters was completed on the 3rd Day by the emergence of the dry land to separate the waters below. At this point, "the circle" that was inscribed — was the Earth, at the very moment that Elohim started forming it late on the 2nd Day. And the "face of the deep" on which the circle was inscribed, was the infinitely large universe within which He established the Earth. In this second meaning, "deep" really does mean deep. It was immeasurable because, by that time, the universe was so large.

Thus, "the inscription of a circle on the face of the deep" has two meanings:

- In the first, the circle is the Singularity, and the face of the deep is the chaos within the Singularity at the moment of the beginning; (i.e., at the earliest moment on Day One).
- In the second, the circle is the Earth **(cf. Isaiah 40:22 KJV, MLB, LB, & RSV)**, and the face of the deep is the universe at large, late on the 2nd Day, when Elohim started forming the primeval earth.

III. On the Day in Eternity Present When the Earth was Established.

28a "When He made firm the skies above, bWhen the springs of the deep became fixed, 29aWhen He set for the sea its boundary, bSo that the water should not transgress His command. cWhen He marked out the foundations of the earth;"

These verses clearly refer to the 3rd and 4th Days of Creation when the Earth became a life-friendly planet.

"He made firm the skies above" refers to the transparent oxygen-rich atmosphere of the Earth that was achieved on the 4th Day. "When the springs of the deep became fixed" refers to the Earth's vast subterranean quantities of liquid water. "When He set for the sea its boundary, so that the water should not transgress His command" is a reference to the moment in the 3rd Day when Elohim separated the waters below by commanding the dry land to come forth — i.e., when He established the first continents so that the vegetation could begin to flourish. It also refers to His transformation of the toxic iron-rich olive-green ocean at the end of the 2nd Day and to Earth's blue oxygen-rich life friendly seas on the 4th Day. "When He marked out the foundations of the earth" is a reference to the 3rd and 4th Days when He completed Earth's radioactive iron core, its surrounding mantle of molten liquid rock, its relatively thin layer of cooled rocky surface crust, its life-giving oceans, and its life-friendly atmosphere. These are the foundations of the Earth.

IV. THE CONCLUSION

30"Then I was beside Him as a master workman; And I was daily His delight, rejoicing always before Him, 31Rejoicing in the world, His earth, and having my delight in the sons of men" (Proverbs 8:22-31).

272

> *Hopefully, the foregoing explanation of the deeper meaning of Proverbs 8:22-31 makes sense in view of our newfound understanding of the Genesis Account of the first four days of Creation revealed to us by the Genesis Code. Now I wish to point out these last verses concerning the origin of Wisdom fit perfectly with the New Testament revelations of the pre-incarnate Jesus Christ that refer to His work in the beginning with the Father and The Holy Spirit. After reading these scriptures, it should become clear why I believe God's Wisdom (what Onkelos refers to as First Wisdom), which was beside the Creator as a master workman in the beginning was actually the pre-incarnate Son of God, Who in His first advent, came to Earth in the form of man. I am convinced this First Wisdom of the Old Testament was personified in the Godman of the New Testament that we know as Jesus Christ. In the New Testament He is known by many names. One of these names is "The Word." The nine-fold repetition of the phrase: "Then God said," which announces and punctuates each creation in the first Chapter of Genesis — is a reminder that Jesus Christ, who is First Wisdom, was beside Elohim as a master workman in all of Elohim's works of old.*
>
> *Therefore, we see, during the Six Days of Creation, the Pre-Incarnate Jesus Christ was beside the Father as a Master Workman. Jesus Christ was also daily the Father's delight and rejoiced always before Him, rejoiced in the earth, and was delighted in the creation of man and in the sons of men. We have already discussed these concepts in Chapter 8 when we talked about the Light of Jesus Christ. I just wanted to point out that we find the same theme again in Solomon's dissertation on Wisdom in his book of Proverbs.*

THE BIBLE WAS WRITTEN FOR ALL PEOPLE IN ETERNITY PRESENT.

Once we understand the deeper meaning of the original Hebrew language of Genesis One, we can begin to understand other scriptures in the Bible that touch on some of the aspects of God's Creation. Here, Solomon's words are a perfect fit to what modern science theorizes actually happened. There is an incredible continuity to the Holy Scriptures. The Bible was written by many Spirit-chosen people, over several hundreds of years. Yet, the message is consistent. The various writers of the Bible may not have understood the full implications of the words they were inspired to write, but their ancient words would convey an appropriate meaning to the people of their times and a deeper level of meaning to future men and women enlightened by future scientific discoveries. This is further evidence that God's revelation of Himself to man is *progressive*, and to the truth of Peter's statement that *all scripture is inspired by God* (II Peter 1:20-21). This is just another example of how God works with us where we are — at each one's level of enlightenment and understanding. Remember, from the meaning of the Hebrew verb *barah*, and the shape of the first letter of the Bible (*the bet*), the 13th century AD Rabbi and sage (Nahmanides) said man would be able to discover those things that happened after the Beginning, but those things that preceded the Beginning would be beyond man's capability to investigate and understand.

CHART: THE 3ᴿᴰ DAY OF GENESIS[490] LASTED 2-BILLION EARTH YEARS

Day #	Beginning of the 3rd Day	End of the 3rd Day	Bible's Description	Scientific Description
3	3 ¾ billion yrs. Before Adam	1 ¾ Billion yrs. Before Adam	Oceans & dry land appear. 1st life (plants) appear. Kabala claims this was only the start of plant life.	Liquid water appeared on Earth late on the 2nd Day 3.8 billion years ago. On the 3rd Day the Earth cooled and the 1st forms of life: bacteria and photosynthetic algae followed almost immediately (3.3 billion years ago). On the 3rd Day Earth also became a granite-planet as the 1st continents formed. The planet began changing on the 3rd Day from a toxic water-world with a poisonous opaque atmosphere (at the end of the 2nd Day) to a life-friendly planet with blue, oxygen-rich oceans and a clear blue oxygen-rich atmosphere. This change was completed on the 4th Day.

Summary Points:
- Beginning 15 ¾ Billion years Before the Present, the Genesis time-reference-frame of the first two days of creation relates to the universe, which was formed first.
- The Earth began forming about 4 ½ billion years Before Adam (late on the 2nd Day of Creation) by the impact-accretion of the debris within its orbital path around the sun.
- This debris-field was composed of the heavy rock-matter coated with its water-ice that had been spewed out from the center of a preceding dying supernova.
- On the 3rd Day of Creation, about 3 ¾ billion years before Adam, the Genesis time-reference-frame shifts from the universe at large to the Earth.
- Earth is one of the four planets in our solar system that is composed of the heavy rock-matter just mentioned. It is literally the 3rd rock from the sun.
- On the 3rd Day, Elohim performed two major acts of creation:
  - He commanded the dry land to appear, and
  - He commanded the dry land (of the Earth) to bring forth vegetation.
- Science states, late during the eon of the 2nd Day the Earth started as a fiery-ball, which resulted from an epoch of impact-accretion of a relentless bombardment of meteors. Near the end of the 2nd Day, Earth's first epoch of volcanic out gassing changed our Earth into *a toxic water-world with a toxic opaque atmosphere.*

---

[490] Schroeder The Science of God Chapter 4 (Table) p 67

- Science claims during the eon of the *3rd Day,* Earth's toxic water-world had begun to change into *a life-friendly blue granite planet* which resulted from two major changes:
  - A 2nd epoch of volcanism ruptured portions of the submerged sub-oceanic crust of the primeval Earth and formed a new kind of rock — *granite. Granite* would become the nexus of the Earth's first continents when it was lifted to the surface on the *3rd Day* (in Genesis 1:9) through a mechanism known as *plate tectonics.*
  - With the appearance of liquid-water on Earth, microscopic life appeared almost immediately. 3.3-billion-year-old *sedimentary rocks* contain the microscopic fossils of the first life on Earth — *simple single-celled bacteria, cyanobacteria, and photosynthetic single-cell algae.*
- Science believes *the cyanobacteria and photosynthetic algae,* which were discovered on *Stromatolites* in the coastal shallows of Shark Bay in Australia — were responsible for producing Earth's oxygen-rich blue oceans and blue atmosphere because they pumped out 20×10^{15} tons of free oxygen into the oceans. Then when the oceans were saturated with O_2 — the O_2 rose into and filled the Earth's atmosphere.
- The free oxygen in the oceans oxidized the quantities of iron in the oceans, which were then precipitated onto the ocean floor. These banded-iron formations are the source of the Earth's continental iron deposits, having been lifted up to the surface by plate tectonics when the continents formed on the *3rd Day.*
- *Kabala* claims — even though the Bible mentions plants as the first forms of life on Earth that appeared on the *3rd Day* — *there was no special day assigned for the command for vegetation alone since it is not a unique work.* Of all the events listed for *the Six Days of Creation,* vegetation is the only one Jewish tradition says occurred over an extended period not limited to a particular day.
- Microscopic life is not mentioned in the Bible. This is because the Bible talks in the language of man. It therefore deals with the aspects of life as they are directly sensible to humans. It would have been unrealistic to expect the ancient Israelites (3300 years ago at Sinai) to grasp the meaning of bacteria and microalgae. For this reason, it makes sense that the biblical record of life starts with what is visible to the unaided eye.
- Science cannot explain the start of the universe or the start of life itself.
- *Darwin's Abiogenic Random-Chance Chemical Reaction Theory of the Origin of Life* has been proved wrong by the discoveries of Elso Barghoorn.
- Regrettably, the general public still thinks the origin-of-life theory of Darwin (that Wald supported), is correct, even though Barghoorn found the microfossil record that proved Darwin wrong; and Morowitz proved the *assumptions* of the random-chance chemical-reactions theory of life were *statistically impossible.* Scientific journals have published the data that have proved Darwin and Wald wrong. But, the false theories of the origin-of-life are still taught in most institutions, and Darwinists still mock the Bible's claims of creation by an all-powerful and all-loving God.

- The answer concerning who created the universe, all that exists, and who was the originator of all life is simple for Jews, Christians, and Muslims. The answer is what the Hebrew Bible has claimed all along. The answer is God![491]

THE HOLY NAME OF JESUS CHRIST WAS NOT SPOKEN ALOUD BY ANGLICANS IN COLONIAL AMERICA.

When the most sacred Hebrew name for God, YHWH, was discussed, we mentioned devout Jews, out of deep respect and reverence, will not say that name for God out loud. In colonial America, there was the same historical reverential concern for the sacred name of Jesus Christ. This came from the Anglican tradition. To George Washington and to Anglican Christians in America in the 18th century, *Jesus* was a sacred name that had to be guarded and kept holy. This was in accordance with the 3rd of the Ten Commandments given to Moses by God — *"Thou shalt not take the name of the Lord your God in vain"* (Exodus 20:7). Thus, in the commonplace activities of 18th century Anglican Americans — such as farming, military action, business, and politics — the holy name of *Jesus Christ* would not normally be spoken aloud, outside of a worship setting. Out of deep respect for His holiness, colonial Anglicans avoided saying the name of Jesus in common parlance. For example, when George Washington referred to Jesus Christ outside of worship, he preferred to do so using *honorifics*, which were customary for his era. When speaking or writing of Jesus Christ, Washington often referred to Him as:

- *'Our gracious Redeemer,'*
- *'The Divine Author of our blessed Religion,'*
- *'The Great Lord and Ruler of Nations,'*
- *'The Judge of the Hearts of Men,'*
- *'The Divine Author of Life and Felicity,'*
- *'The Lord and Giver of all Victory, to Pardon our Manifold Sins,'* and
- *'The Giver of All Life.'*

These are just a few of Washington's many reverential terms for Jesus Christ that he used in common speech and correspondence. One of the most remarkable examples of his reverence for the sanctity of Christ's name was when he declared his feelings had been continually wounded by the profanity and swearing of the soldiers under his command. In his General Orders of July 29, 1779, he declared:

> *"Many and pointed orders have been issued against that unmeaning and abominable custom of swearing, notwithstanding which, with much regret the General observes that it prevails, if possible, more than ever; His feelings are continually wounded by the oaths and imprecations of the soldiers whenever he is in hearing of them. The Name of that Being, from whose bountiful goodness we are permitted to exist and enjoy the comforts of life is incessantly imprecated and profaned in a manner as wanton as it is shocking. For the sake therefore of religion, decency and order, the General hopes, and trusts that officers of every rank will use their influence and authority to check a vice, which is unprofitable as it is wicked and shameful. If officers would make it an*

---

[491] Schroeder The Hidden Face of God Chapter 1 p 10 a

> invariable rule to reprimand, and if that does not do, punish soldiers for offenses of this kind, it could not fail of having the desired effect."[492]

Thus, we see colonial Anglican Americans venerated the sacred name of JESUS in the same way the Jews reverenced the hallowed name of YHWH. They believed our Lord, Jesus Christ, spoke the truth two thousand years ago on that day in the portico of Solomon's temple, at the Feast of Dedication in Jerusalem, when He told the Jews: *"I and the Father are One." (John 10:30)*

THE INDIAN PROPHECY:

George Washington believed his life was protected by *Divine Providence*. In Peter A. Lillback's book: *George Washington's Sacred Fire* (p. 160-165), during the French and Indian War (in 1755), and in the Battle of the Monongahela near current-day Pittsburgh, Pennsylvania (in which General Braddock was killed), Washington's tunic was pierced four times by bullets, and the two horses he was riding were shot from under him. Yet, Washington was not hurt! He was the only officer in Braddock's force who was not killed or wounded! The British-Colonial army lost 714 men! The French and Indians lost 3 officers and 30 men!

Fifteen years later, while Washington was visiting lands ceded to him by the colonial government of Virginia for services rendered in the French and Indian War — along the banks of the Kanawha River in current-day West Virginia — Washington had an encounter with the Indian chief who opposed him in that battle. The tall shaman reverentially approached the hero of the Battle of the Monongahela, and (after an extended period of silence) spoke these words recorded for posterity by Washington's friend and personal physician, Dr. James Craik, preserving what has become known as the Indian Prophecy.

"I am a chief and ruler over my tribes. My influence extends to the waters of the great lakes and to the far blue mountains. I have traveled a long and weary path that I might see the young warrior of the great battle. It was on the day when the white man's blood mixed with the streams of our forests that I first beheld this chief: I called to my young men and said, mark yon tall and daring warrior? He is not of the red-coat tribe — he hath an Indian's wisdom, and his warriors fight as we do — himself alone exposed. Quick, let your aim be certain and he dies. Our rifles were leveled, rifles which, but for you, knew not how to miss — 'twas all in vain, a power mightier far than we, shielded him from harm. He cannot die in battle ... Listen! The Great Spirit protects that man and guides his destinies. He will become the chief of nations, and a people yet unborn will hail him as the founder of a mighty empire!"

Through the seven long years of the *War for Independence*, Washington exposed himself many times. Yet, he was never wounded! God protected him!

[492] Lillback George Washington's Sacred Fire Chapter 3: Did Washington Avoid the Name of Jesus Christ? p 55-57/p.160-165

CHAPTER 11: THE 4ᵗʰ DAY & THE "*ME'ORAHS*"

14 "And God said, let there be lights in the firmament of the heaven to divide the day from the night. And let them be for signs, and for seasons, and for days, and years:

15 And let them be for lights in the firmament of the heaven to give light upon the earth: and it was so.

16 And God made two great lights: the greater light to rule the day, and the lesser light to rule the night. He made the stars also.

17 And God set them in the firmament of the heaven to give light upon the earth.

18 And to rule over the day and over the night, and to divide the light from the darkness. And God saw that **it was good.**

19 And the evening and the morning were the fourth day (Genesis 1:14-19 The King James Bible)."

Elohim intended the Sun, Moon, and stars to give light to the Earth, and divide the light from the darkness. They were also to be to be used as *"signs for seasons, and for telling days and years* (Gen. 1:14-15)." English translations of the Bible *imply* the Sun, Moon, and stars were created on the *4ᵗʰ Day* (Genesis 1:16-18). However, according to modern science, the Sun, Moon, and stars were made *before* the *4ᵗʰ Day*, but would *not* have been visible (from the Earth) until the *4ᵗʰ Day*. Is Modern Science right? Is the Bible wrong? Or is this apparent conflict between the Bible and Science the result of a misinterpretation of the Bible?

As you shall see, the conflict between the Bible and Science concerning the *4ᵗʰ Day* comes from the *mistranslation* of *one* ancient Hebrew word. That word is — *"Me'orah."* English translations of the Bible mistranslate *"Me'orah"* as — *"light."* So far as I know, The Interlinear Bible quoted below, is the only exception to this statement.

THE 4ᵀʰ DAY OF CREATION

The *4ᵗʰ Day:* 24hrs. of God's Time	Started 1 ¾ Billion years ago	Ended ¾ Billion years ago
God's Time Perspective	Earth-years Before Adam	Earth-years Before Adam

The 4ᵗʰ Day lasted 1 Billion Earth-years: Earth's Time Perspective. [493]

THIS IS WHAT THE INTERLINEAR BIBLE (TIB) SAYS ABOUT THE *4ᵀʰ DAY.*

Gen. 1:14 "And God said, 'Let (me'orahs) luminaries be in the expanse of the heavens, to divide between the day and the night. And let them be for signs and for seasons, and for days and years.

Gen. 1:15 And let them be for (me'orahs) luminaries in the expanse of the heavens, to give ('owr) light to the earth.' And it was so.

Gen. 1:16 And God made the two great (me'orahs) luminaries: the great (me'orah) luminary to rule the day, and the small (me'orah) luminary and the stars to rule the night.

[493] Schroeder *The Science of God* Chapter 4 (Table) p 67

Gen. 1:17 And God set them in the expanse of the heavens, to give ('owr) light to the earth.

Gen. 1:18 And to rule over the day and over the night; and to divide between the ('owr) light and the darkness. And God saw that it was good.

Gen. 1:19 And there was evening and there was morning the 4th Day." (Gen. 1:14-19 — TIB)

ENGLISH TRANSLATIONS MISTRANSLATE THE HEBREW OF GENESIS OF 1:14-19. The scriptural quotes you have just read are taken from The Interlinear Bible — *Hebrew, Greek, English* — 2nd Edition © 1986 by Jay P. Green, Sr. The Interlinear Bible translates the Hebrew of the Old Testament Torah & Tanakh, and the New Testament Greek — into English. The transliterated Hebrew-to-English word (*me'orah*) means *"luminary."* The transliterated Hebrew-to-English word (*'owr*) means *"light."* The King James Bible (KJ), the Modern Language Bible (MLB), the Living Bible (LB), the Revised Standard Bible Version (RSV), and the New American Standard Bible (NASB)—(*all of them*)—mistranslate *me'orah(s)* as *light(s).* They correctly translate *'owr* as *light.* The *'two great luminaries'* mentioned in Gen. 1:16 of The Interlinear Bible are called *'the greater light'* and *'the lesser light'* in the KJ, the RSV, and the NASB. The LB calls them the *'sun'* and the *'moon.'* Only the MLB uses the word *'luminaries'* in Gen. 1:16 but, then reverts to *'a greater light'* and *'a lesser light'* in the same verse. Therefore, these English translations, miss the mark *by a mile!* The following discussion will reveal *why* this is a *major mistranslation* of the original Hebrew.

WHAT DID ELOHIM DO ON THE 4TH DAY?

The *4th Day of Creation* was the point when Elohim completed something He started on the *3rd Day.* It *all* has to do with the changes He brought about in the Earth's oceans and atmosphere after He made them late on the *2nd Day.* Specifically, it has something to do with the Earth's life-essential gas — *Oxygen.*

THE OXYGENATION OF EARTH'S OCEANS & ATMOSPHERE

The primordial atmosphere of the early Earth was initially *opaque.* Scientific data indicates it was during the *4th Day* that Earth got its present *transparent,* life-friendly, oxygen-rich oceans and atmosphere, and our *Blue Planet* was *"born."* By the end of the *4th Day,* the presence of abundant volumes of *oxygen* in our oceans and atmosphere changed our planet from a primordial raging hostile planet to one that could accept and nurture the fragile life-forms we are.

WHAT DOES 'OPAQUE' MEAN?

Prior to the *3rd Day,* the iron-rich oceans were *toxic,* and the purplish-red poisonous primordial atmosphere of the Earth, was *opaque.* When we say *opaque,* we mean the *visible light* emitted by our Sun *could not penetrate* the primordial (i.e., *'first formed'*) atmosphere of the primeval Earth — (i.e., *the earliest stage of the history of the atmosphere of the primitive Earth*). However, other forms of radiant energy could. These are all *'invisible'* forms of radiant energy from the Sun and other radiant sources of energy in the universe. Since we cannot *see* these spectra of energy, we *might* refer to them as *dark energy* — since they have been present from the beginning and were major components of *'the black fire'* of the Singularity that *locked in* the photons of *light* that we can see. However, the truth is, no one really knows exactly what so-called *"dark energy"* actually is! Scientists now say it comprises about 68% of the universe, and it affects the expansion of the universe. But other than that, they say *dark energy* is a complete mystery![494] So, please forgive what I am next going to say if it is out of touch with what you consider *dark energy* to be.

INFRARED RADIANT ENERGY & 'THE GREENHOUSE EFFECT'

We now know the surface of the Earth and the clouds in Earth's atmosphere absorb some (but not all) of the *visible light rays,* and some of the full spectrum of the *invisible electromagnetic radiant energies* that come to our Earth from our Sun and outer space. *The full spectrum of electromagnetic radiant energies emitted by our Sun* (from the highest to the lowest frequencies), is composed of gamma-rays, X-rays, ultraviolet light, and infrared radiation. It also includes — *visible light.* With the exception of *visible light,* all other electromagnetic radiant energies (including the radiant energy of radioactive isotopes) have wave-length frequencies that are invisible to us. Infrared radiation (*i.e., infrared light*), is one of those energies that is invisible to our eyes, but we can feel it as heat, because it interacts with our bodies by exciting our molecules, thus generating heat. Electromagnetic radiant energies of all wavelengths will heat the surfaces that absorb them. But infrared radiation is the most common radiant energy we absorb. We absorb infrared energy and then we emit its heat. That is why our bodies (and all animal bodies) glow when viewed through an infrared detector.

The gases in Earth's atmosphere — such as *carbon dioxide, sulfur hexafluoride, methane, chlorofluorocarbons, and nitrous oxide* — also reflect some of the infrared energy and electromagnetic radiant energies that come into our atmosphere — in all directions. Most of it is reflected away from the earth. This is fortunate, because some of the invisible spectra of electromagnetic radiant energy that enters our atmosphere are lethal to life.[495] Modern science has learned the infrared energy that is absorbed, is the radiant energy that is primarily responsible for something scientists call: *"the greenhouse effect."* Thus, *the greenhouse effect* keeps the atmosphere and surface of the Earth much warmer than *if* the infrared absorbers were absent from our atmosphere.[496] CO_2 (and the other infrared absorbing gases in our atmosphere) perform an essential life-friendly service that helps make life on our planet possible.

FROM OPAQUE TO TRANSLUCENT TO TRANSPARENT—ON THE 3RD & 4TH DAYS:

Late on the *2nd Day,* as Earth's first age of volcanism began to subside, the volcanic ash and silicates in the early Earth's primordial atmosphere began to slowly settle on the Earth below. With the aid of the first oxygen-producing microscopic *living bacteria* and microscopic *single-celled algae (*that were in *'full bloom'* on the *3rd Day*), Earth's primordial opaque toxic atmosphere slowly began to change. On the *3rd Day* Earth's atmosphere gradually became less *opaque* and more *translucent,* allowing visible light to diffusely pass through. Finally, by the *4th Day,* the transformation from an *opaque* atmosphere (*on*

---

[494] Dark Energy, Dark Matter I Science Mission Directorate
https://science.nasa.gov/astrophysics/focus-areas/what-is-dark-energy
[495] Earth's Magnetic Field shields us from most of the lethal ionizing cosmic radiant energies (*cf. Chapter 9 in this book*).
[496] Article: The Greenhouse Effect May 7, 2009, ... www.physicalgeography.net/fundamentals/7h.html

the *2ⁿᵈ Day*), to a *translucent* atmosphere (*on the 3ʳᵈ Day*), to a *transparent* atmosphere (*on the 4ᵗʰ Day*), was completed.

ME'ORAH (LUMINARY)

When Moses wrote Gen. 1:14-16, he talked about *'luminaries'* in the expanse of the heavens. Unfortunately, the Hebrew word English translations of the Bible interpret as *'light(s),'* should have been translated as *'luminary(ies).'* The ancient Hebrew text does not say *'light(s)'* appeared on the *4ᵗʰ Day!* The ancient text says *'me'orah(s),'* appeared on the 4ᵗʰ Day. *Me'orah* means *'a luminous body, or luminary.'* [497] The Talmud Scholars interpreted Genesis 1:14-16 to mean: "The luminous bodies *appeared* in the heavens on the 4ᵗʰ Day" (cf. THE CONCLUSIONS OF THE TALMUD on this page).

The *first light* mentioned in the Hebrew Bible was spoken into existence by God on *Day One* (Gen. 1:3). In Genesis 1:14-16, the word Moses wrote (that means *'luminaries'),* tells us the events of the *4ᵗʰ Day* are told *from the perspective of the Earth*. We have already said that the perspective of the Creation Account shifted from the universe to the Earth the moment God named the dry land *'Earth'* (Gen. 1:9-10). That happened on the *3ʳᵈ Day* (cf. Chapter 10: *The 3ʳᵈ Rock from the Sun*). We now know this separation of the waters into seas was the result of the lifting up of the ocean floor by the forces in the molten mantle of the Earth — something that modern science has named *'Plate Tectonics.'* Plate Tectonics is the mechanism by which Elohim *'makes'* and still *'forms'* the emerging land masses on our planet. We will talk about Plate Tectonics in the next chapter. The events of the *3ʳᵈ* through the *6ᵗʰ Days* are in a *God-based time-flow* but are told from a *perspective that relates to the Earth.*[498]

THE CART BEFORE THE HORSE?

The Bible tells us Elohim created plants on the *3ʳᵈ Day*. He caused them *'to sprout'* on the just created land masses. So, English translations of the Bible *tell us plants* appeared on the Earth on the *3ʳᵈ Day* (Gen. 1:11) and *imply that lights appeared* in the expanse of the heavens on the *4ᵗʰ Day* (Gen.1:14-18). Since light is essential for the growth of plants, and also provides the energy for photosynthesis in plants, it would seem the Bible should mention the appearance of *light* on Earth *before* it talks about *the appearance of plants*. Is the Bible guilty of putting the cart before the horse? No! Moses did not say *'Lights!'* [499]

WHEN WERE THE LUMINARIES MADE & SET IN THE EXPANSE?

English translations of the Bible do not say *when* God made earth's two great luminaries or *when* He set them in the expanse. English translations *imply* the *"greater and lesser lights and the stars"* were made and set in the expanse of the universe on the *4ᵗʰ Day*. However, it did not happen that way.

THE CONCLUSIONS OF THE TALMUD.

In Chapter 9, we mentioned Rabbi Abahu said the Sun *'appeared'* on the *4ᵗʰ Day*. Notice he did not say the Sun was *'created'* on the *4ᵗʰ Day*. The scholars of the Talmud teach: the Sun, Moon, and stars were established *before* the 4ᵗʰ Day, *but did not become visible*

---

[497] For the Hebrew word in Gen. 1:14 that English Bibles translate as 'light, 'The Interlinear Bible refers the reader to word #3974 in Strong's Exhaustive Concordance of the Bible. In the Hebrew & Chaldee Dictionary (which is in Strong's Concordance), the referenced transliterated Hebrew word #3974 is —me'orah— meaning a luminous body, or luminary.
[498] The New American Standard Bible (NASB): Genesis. 1:9,10.
[499] Schroeder *Genesis and the Big Bang* Chapter 9 p 130*b,c*

until the 4ᵗʰ Day.[500] The reason the Talmud scholars believed this is because Moses wrote *'luminaries'* instead of *'lights.'* They felt the ancient Hebrew text was telling us the heavenly bodies that illuminated the Earth *pre-existed* the Earth, but for some reason, they did not become visible from the Earth until the *4ᵗʰ Day.*

MODERN SCIENCE AGREES WITH THE TALMUD.

We now know our Earth and our Moon started forming in the "evening" of the *2ⁿᵈ Day.* But we think our Moon is younger than our Earth. Scientists believe our Moon was probably formed by debris thrown outward from the Earth when another equally large celestial body collided with the Earth as it was forming late on the *2ⁿᵈ Day.*

The Sun and many of the stars are older than the Earth. They *pre-existed* the Earth, but they would not have been visible from the Earth on the *2ⁿᵈ and 3ʳᵈ Days* because Earth's primordial atmosphere was toxic and opaque. The reason the heavenly bodies that illumine the Earth became so clearly visible on the *4ᵗʰ Day* was because of the transformation of Earth's atmosphere that occurred on the *3ʳᵈ and 4ᵗʰ Days.* By the end of the *4ᵗʰ Day,* Earth's atmosphere became so *transparent* that the Sun, Moon, and stars could have been seen from the Earth. The transparency of the Earth's atmosphere that developed on the *4ᵗʰ Day* was the direct result of *the photosynthesis of free oxygen.*

PHOTOSYNTHESIS WAS A KEY EVENT.

The primeval *microscopic* plant-life that suddenly appeared on the *3ʳᵈ Day* was a *key event* that helped *clear* the Earth's atmosphere through the process of *photosynthesis.* Photosynthesis in bacteria, algae, and stromatolites, drastically reduced the volcanically produced concentrations of carbon dioxide, nitrogen compounds, hydrogen sulfide, and other noxious volcanic gases in the atmosphere. Through the miracle of photosynthesis, atmospheric *carbon dioxide* was *converted* into *free-oxygen* and *cellular material.* By the *4ᵗʰ Day,* the Sun and those stars that developed before the Earth formed, could have also been seen from the Earth *if* there had been any creatures on the Earth that had the capability of sight. However, the first creatures with sight would not appear on the Earth until the *5ᵗʰ Day.*

ONLY FROM THE EARTH CAN OUR MOON BE SEEN AS A 'GREAT LUMINARY.'

Genesis 1:14-19 describes the events of the 4ᵗʰ Day from the viewpoint of the Earth. This is made *clear* (pardon the pun) by the reference to *the Moon* as one of the two great luminaries. Genesis 1:16 says God made two great luminaries. The Sun is the great luminary that rules our solar system's day. The Moon is the small luminary (that along with the stars), rules our night. Although the Moon is smaller than the Earth and minuscule compared to the Sun, the Earth is the only celestial body in the universe that is close enough to its Moon *'to see'* our Moon as a *'great luminary.'*[501] We know the Moon is not a true source of light because it is not a star. But from the viewpoint of our Earth, it is obvious our Moon is the smaller of the two great luminaries in our solar system. Our Moon *reflects* the light from the Sun onto the *'night side'* of the rotating Earth. Like the mirror that the doctor wears on his forehead which reflects the source of light in the examining room into his patient's throat, the Moon reflects the light of the Sun onto the dark side of the Earth's surface at night.

---

[500] Schroeder *The Science of God* Chapter 4 p 68d—69a
[501] Schroeder The Science of God Chapter 4 p 68d—69a

We have just added another layer of explanation to two seemingly contradictory statements about the 3rd and 4th Days of Creation that are in our English translations of the Hebrew Bible.

Now, let's try to clarify the confusion our English translations of the Bible have created.

(1)   DAY& NIGHT CYCLES BEGAN BEFORE OUR SUN & EARTH WERE MADE.

The Bible says God made light on *Day One.* When He did that, He named the light *'day'* and He named the darkness *'night.'* This happened on *Day One,* before our Sun and Earth formed. We might ask, how could there have been day and night cycles before our Sun and Earth formed? The fact that the Bible first mentions day and night cycles on *Day One* tells us many stars and planets in the universe preceded our Sun and our Earth. They formed on *Day One!* These planets formed after the deaths of some of the 1st order stars in the universe had ignited and then later burned out on *Day One* after exhausting their supply of hydrogen and helium. On *Day One* and the *2nd Day*, the universe contained a number of celestial *'balls'* (i.e., planets), which were spinning on their axes in space and orbiting their individual stars long before our Sun, Earth, Moon, and our Solar System were made (*cf. Nahmanides' Explanation of Day-Night Cycles in Chapter 8 of Book I*).

(2)   PLANTS BECAME THE MAJOR SOURCE OF OXYGEN ON THE 5TH DAY.

In Chapter 10 we discussed the most plausible reason the Bible doesn't talk about the microscopic life that appeared on the *3rd and 4th Days of Creation*. The ancient Hebrews in Moses' time would not have understood microscopic life. We also mentioned Jewish tradition suggests God's making of plants was not limited to a single day. The Sun, and Moon were made and formed on the *2nd Day* but would *not* have been visible from the Earth until the *4th Day* because Earth's primordial atmosphere was *opaque*. Now we see the mistranslation of one Hebrew word clarifies the confusion English translations have caused by mentioning plants on the *3rd Day,* before they mention the Sun, Moon, and stars on the *4th Day*. The fact that Moses used the Hebrew word that means *'luminaries'* to describe the events of the *4th Day* — clarifies this Biblical riddle. Scientists now think the photosynthesizing microscopic bacteria and plants of the *3rd and 4th Days* were responsible for making the oxygen that cleared our oceans and atmosphere. The earth's oceans and atmosphere became life-friendly on the *4th Day*. When Earth's atmosphere became *transparent*, visible light could reach Earth's surface, and those microscopic photosynthesizing organisms kicked into "overdrive." Then, when visible plants (i.e., macroscopic plants) began to appear on the *5th Day*, photosynthesis took off like a rocket!

THE FIRST LIFE FORMS ON EARTH DID NOT NEED OXYGEN TO THRIVE.

There is *'hard'* evidence (pun intended) of when the first simple life-forms appeared. And there is also *'hard'* evidence they preceded the appearance of more complex forms of life. That evidence is indelibly stamped into the *fossil record*. It is from the fossil record that scientists can date the transformation of our Earth's biosphere from one that was without oxygen to our present oxygen-rich atmosphere.

EARTH'S 1ST LIFE-FORMS THE PROKARYOTES — DID NOT NEED OXYGEN.

The oldest evidence of life on Earth are the micro-fossils of the first bacteria that formed. They did not have any cellular nuclei. These are the microscopic fossils of the life-forms that Professor Barghoorn discovered (with his electron microscope) in the 3.3-billion-year-old rocks of the *Fig Tree Formation*. Those microscopic fossils date to the "dawn" of the *3rd Day*. These bacteria are classified as *'prokaryotes.'* The word *'karyo'* is from the Greek, *'karyon,'* meaning *'a nut, a kernel, or a nucleus.'* In this case — it means *'nucleus.'* *'Pro'* (Latin and Greek), is a prefix signifying *'before or in front of'* and, in the word *prokaryote* is meant to be interpreted as — *'before nuclei.'* Therefore, a prokaryotic bacterium is an organism *that has no nucleus.* Its genetic material is not bound within a central membrane. These prokaryotic bacteria were *very primitive* microorganisms and were the *first forms of biological non-plant life. The majority of prokaryotes are single-cell bacteria.*[502] They still exist, but after eons of time, more advanced nucleus-containing *bacteria — the 'eukaryotes' —* appeared.

EUKARYOTES NEED OXYGEN.

The prefix, *'eu,'* is from the Greek, meaning *'good, well, or true.'* When placed before the word *'karyote,'* the meaning is: *'true kernel.'* More specifically, the word —*Eukaryote*— refers to living micro-organisms whose cells contain a nucleus that houses the majority of the cell's DNA. The 1st eukaryotes were also *micro*scopic single-celled organisms. Multicellular eukaryotes soon followed (most of which were *macro*scopic). They appeared on the *5th Day*. These eukaryotes are the basis of all higher-level complex life-forms. All life forms larger than one-celled organisms are classified as multicellular eukaryotic life.[503]

This is an oversimplified explanation of the two different life forms. However, it is enough of a differentiation to suit our current purpose — that of explaining the basis of the different metabolic pathways of these two early life-forms. The difference has to do with whether *oxygen is* or *is not* used. One thrived in an *anoxic (without oxygen)* environment, and the other required the presence of free molecular oxygen to gain energy from its food.

SINGLE-CELL (PROKARYOTIC) CYANOBACTERIA & THE 1ST PRODUCTION OF FREE OXYGEN

For this discussion, I need to go back to those *prokaryotes* that developed in the time-reference-frame of the *3rd Day*. As mentioned in Chapter 10, the first production of free-oxygen on Earth began early on the *3rd Day* in some of the Earth's earliest oxygen-producing prokaryotes — *the Cyanobacteria.* These simple primeval microorganisms also thrived in the noxious *anoxic* volcanic environment of that period. These nucleus-free *prokaryotic bacteria* and their slightly earlier single-cell bacterial relatives (i.e., the primordial single-cell bacteria that did *not* produce oxygen and developed slightly earlier on the *3rd Day*) — remained the sole representatives of life on Earth for the next 2.5 billion years — well into the *4th Day*.[504] They remained the *only* life-forms on Earth for the 2.5 billion years that followed their first appearance. Cyanobacteria have a blue-green photosynthetic pigment. They were originally thought to be in the family of the *Cyanophyta* and were first classified as *blue-green algae* (i.e., microscopic single-cell "*plants*"). Some people still refer to cyanobacteria as blue-green algae. *'Phyta'* is the plural form of *'phyto'* which comes from the Greek *'phyton.'* Phyton means *'plant.'* *'Cyano'* comes from the Greek *'kyanos,'* and means *'blue.'* So, the word — *Cyanophyta* — literally means: *'blue*

---

[502]Schroeder Genesis and the Big Bang Chapter 9 p 131c
[503] Schroeder *The Science of God* Chapter 4 p 70a
[504]Schroeder *Genesis and the Big Bang* Chapter 1 p 14b

plants.' *Cyanophyta* were originally classified as *plants* and were commonly referred to as *'blue-green algae.'* They have now been *reclassified* as a specific form of *bacteria*, hence the name — *Cyanobacteria.* Cyanobacteria are *prokaryotes* (i.e., single-cell microorganisms *without nuclei*). Most Scientists believe they suddenly appeared 3.3 billion years ago. But a few argue they are even older and *evolved* somewhere between 4.0 and 3.5 billion years ago.[505] The reclassification of things is one of the confusing things about the scientific method. When new knowledge is gained, it becomes necessary to update the old classifications that have been discovered to be erroneous.

THE FIRST EUKARYOTIC OXYGEN-PRODUCING PHOTOSYNTHETIC ORGANISMS

Late on the *3rd Day, photosynthesis started in single-cell algae.* This led to a *gradual change* in Earth's atmosphere *from opaque to translucent.* We are still talking about *micro*scopic forms of life. But now we are talking about the *earliest true photosynthetic plants.* However, those *single-celled algae* were *eukaryotes* which were organisms whose cells contained nuclei. They were more advanced higher order living organisms, which suddenly appeared in massive numbers and became global in their distribution at the juncture of the 3rd and 4th *Days.* The older *single-cell prokaryotic bacteria* (i.e., the photosynthetic cyanobacteria) and their slightly older non-oxygen producing single-cell prokaryotic bacterial relatives (that some scientists argue were the 1st life-forms on Earth), appeared on the "dawn" of the *3rd Day.* But these more advanced eukaryotic single-celled algae oxygen-producers, which appeared on the *3rd Day* were *late comers.*

STROMATOLITES WERE COVERED WITH PHOTOSYNTHETIC PROKARYOTES & EUKARYOTES.

As more dry-land appeared (on the *3rd Day*), and the more advanced eukaryotic plant-life began to thrive on the emerging continents, a new entity appeared in the shallow waters of the early Earth's newly formed coastal bays. That new entity was the *"stromatolite."* Stromatolites also appeared late on the *3rd Day* and built into massive numbers by the *4th Day.* They were rocky mounded structures that were coated with very thin layers of *the older photosynthetic cyanobacteria.* But they were also covered with *the newer eukaryotic photosynthetic blue-green algae.*

At the juncture of the *3rd and 4th Days,* stromatolites became global in distribution. We have already talked about stromatolites in Chapter 10: *The 3rd Rock from the Sun.* *Stromatolites* began to appear in shallow coastal bays throughout the globe. At that point, *the stromatolites and the early simple land-based single-cell eukaryotic plants* began to produce *massive quantities of free oxygen.*

Slowly but surely, the concentrations of free oxygen began to rise in Earth's oceans and atmosphere. During the *4th Day* (with the further cooling of the Earth), and the continued conversion of atmospheric carbon dioxide to free oxygen through the miracle of photosynthesis — the concentration of Earth's atmospheric oxygen finally reached the point where the Earth's formerly *translucent* atmosphere became *transparent.* By the *4th Day,* eukaryotes dominated.[506]

METABOLIC PATHWAYS IN ANOXIC VERSUS OXYGEN-RICH ENVIRONMENTS

It should not be surprising the first simple life-forms used (and still use) a metabolic pathway that is different from later, more complicated life-forms.

---

[505]Article: Photosynthetic Microorganisms: www.novelguide.com/a/discover/wmi_02_00444.html
[506]Schroeder *The Science of God* Chapter 4 p 69*g*

THE PRIMORDIAL PROKARYOTES USED FERMENTATION TO METABOLIZE THEIR FOOD.

The first primitive bacteria (the prokaryotes that thrived in the anoxic heat of volcanic vents), obtained their energy for life through the process of the *fermentation* of existing organic material.

Fermentation does not require oxygen. It is an anoxic chemical process that reduces larger organic molecules into smaller fragments. Therefore, the first primitive bacteria (which had no cellular nuclei) thrived in the primordial atmosphere of the Earth that was completely devoid of free oxygen.

The primeval cyanobacteria that appeared later and which have already been mentioned, are also an example of prokaryotic life. But they are *photosynthetic* prokaryotes *that produce oxygen.* Nevertheless, they also thrived in the anoxic atmosphere of the early Earth. However, they may be the first producers of oxygen on our planet. Therefore, they are an extremely important link in the chain-of-life that led to the development of higher order organisms, some of which also produced oxygen.

The process of fermentation still occurs today. We benefit from it when we use it to make the wine we enjoy. The fermentation that occurs in the anoxic environment of the barrels in which wine is placed, converts the sugars of the grapes into alcohol. We also benefit from it in the production of milkfat in the anoxic environment of a dairy cow's rumen.[507]

EUKARYOTES & 'RESPIRATION'—A MORE ENERGY-EFFICIENT PROCESS

More advanced Eukaryotic nucleus-containing bacterial cells live in an oxygen-rich environment and obtain their energy from a two-step process known as *'respiration.'* In respiration, the first step of metabolism is the same as in fermentation. But, in the second step, *eukaryotes* oxidize the products of fermentation. That is to say, they take the products of fermentation, combine them with free oxygen, and *combust* them to produce the by-products of water and carbon dioxide. This combustion in the second step gives the eukaryotes almost *twenty times* more energy from their digested organic material than can be obtained by the fermentation of the same food.[508]

The 'fermentation' process was developed when the biosphere of the early Earth was devoid of any free oxygen. However, with the advent of abundant photosynthetic life, and the subsequent availability of free oxygen, the *'respiration'* of organic matter became possible. The respiration process was then annexed onto the existing fermentation pathway of cells. It was so efficient that it became the dominant metabolic pathway for life. In Elohim's ordering of nature, it seems nothing is ever wasted. The first metabolic pathway (fermentation) is still retained. In some cases, it is the only metabolic pathway that is necessary. However, in others, it is still the first step, but nature proceeds to the next phase that occurs in respiration. Respiration *oxidizes* and *combusts* the products of fermentation and thus multiplies the amount of energy that is released by a factor of twenty-fold.[509]

[507] Schroeder *Genesis and the Big Bang* Chapter 9 p 131*d*
[508] Schroeder *Genesis and the Big Bang* Chapter 9 p 131*e*—132*a*
[509] Schroeder *Genesis and the Big Bang* Chapter 9 p 131e—132a

URANIUM

When the concentration of oxygen reached 1% in Earth's biosphere, it left its imprint on the geological record by causing *oxidation reactions* that could *not* have occurred previously. The presence of the oxygen-rich compounds of uranium — *for example, UO_2 {Uranium-Dioxide} and U_3O_8 {Triuranium-Octoxide}* — in sediments less than 2 billion years old and the absence of oxygen-rich uranium compounds in older sediments — tells us *free oxygen* became available at about 2 billion years *Before Adam*. Two billion years *Before Adam* was 13.75 billion (*15.75 – 2 = 13.75*) years *after the Beginning* (i.e., during the *3rd Day of Creation*).[510] Therefore, we now know the production of free oxygen reached this concentration *late* on the *3rd Day*. With the continued production of oxygen, its concentration in the atmosphere began to rise. By the end of the *4th Day*, Earth's atmosphere was so rich in free oxygen (O_2), and so poor in carbon dioxide (CO_2) and the other noxious products of volcanism that it was completely *transparent*. So, at the end of the *4th Day*, the Sun, Moon, and stars could be seen for the first time from the Earth. Future creatures that would be formed on the *5th Day* would be able to see the luminaries and the stars. And some of those that would be formed on the *6th Day* would be able to use the luminaries and the stars to tell *"the times and the seasons and distinguish day from night."*[511]

IRON DEPOSITS

Iron in marine deposits provides another clue to the oxygenation of Earth's atmosphere. The oxidized form of iron (Ferric Oxide or Fe_2O_3) first appeared as the rusty rock strata[512] that accounts for much of the world's minable iron reserves. I also talked about that in the previous chapter. Radioactive dating of these iron deposits indicates their formation and burial occurred during a span of several hundred million years, slightly over 2 billion years ago (*during the 3rd Day of Creation*).

At this time, in addition to the fossil evidence of the presence of single-celled cyanobacteria and single-celled algae, the fossil record also indicates there was an abundance of oxygen-producing eukaryotic life as well (i.e., the microscopic blue-green algae, stromatolites, and land-based plants).

So, we now see how important light is to the pathways that led to life. The Sun and the stars provide the energy for photosynthesis (the catalyst as it were), so that without the visible spectrum of sunlight, the small quantities of oxygen produced by cyanobacteria and single-celled algae *alone* could not have formed sufficient oxygen to cause the changes that occurred on the *3rd and 4th Days of Creation*.

No, the production of *free oxygen* ramped up *big-time* when light began to penetrate the Earth's atmosphere as the opaque products of volcanism in Earth's primordial atmosphere were slowly cleared. When that happened, the higher-order eukaryotic life-forms (the blue-green algae, land-based plants, and stromatolites) could

---

[510] *Age of the universe (15.75 billion yrs.) minus 2 billion yrs. = 13.75 billion yrs. after the Beginning was when free oxygen appeared in Earth's atmosphere. Day One (8) billion yrs. + 2nd Day (4) billion yrs. + 3rd Day (2) billion yrs. is,,, 8+4+2=14 billion years after the Big Bang was when the 3rd Day ended. Therefore, 14 - 13.75 billion years after the Beginning was 0.25 billion (or 250 million) years before the end of the 3rd Day; That's when oxidation reactions 1st began to occur.* Therefore, the production of free oxygen started causing oxidation reactions *late* on the *3rd Day*.

[511] Schroeder *Genesis and the Big Bang* Chapter 9 p 132*b*

[512] Rust is hydrated Iron III Oxide, or $Fe_2O_3 \times H_2O$.

join in with the single-celled cyanobacteria and single-celled algae by contributing their photosynthesis of oxygen in a major way. We now know it was the availability of *free oxygen* that allowed the development of life-forms larger than single-cell bacteria and single-cell algae, and also produced the ultraviolet-absorbing ozone layer (O_3) that would allow the future population of the oceans and the dry-land of Earth's continents — on the *5th and 6th Days of Creation.*[513]

SUMMARY OF THE FOSSIL EVIDENCE OF THE EARLIEST LIFE FORMS ON EARTH

- We can now see yet another example of how Elohim set in motion a chain of events in His creation that was guided by His will and intervention.[514] The Biblical account announces the sudden appearance of life on the newly formed and forming Earth. This is something modern science confirms. We now know the simplest, earliest microscopic life-forms on earth (the *Prokaryotes*), were definitely present in massive numbers by 3.3 billion years ago, early on the *3rd Day.* They were the *only* life-forms on Earth for the next 2.5 billion years![515]

- Later — on the *3rd Day*, the first multi-cellular life-forms entered the fossil record. By the *4th Day* multicellular life dominated. That is to say, the *4th Day* marked the dominance of "*Eukaryotic*" life. All life-forms larger than one-celled organisms are *eukaryotes.*[516] Prior to this, single-cell prokaryotes dominated, even though a smaller number of single-cell eukaryotes existed.[517] This transition from single-celled dominance to multi-celled dominant life required the genetic material of living cells to be moved from the cytoplasm and basement membranes — to the nuclei of the younger more advanced and higher-order multicellular life-forms that science classifies as *eukaryotes*. It also required the development of an oxygen-rich atmosphere to replace the primordial[518] *anoxic* energy-inefficient atmosphere of the primeval[519] Earth.[520]

- We also know this transition began to occur (2.5 billion years Before Adam) during the *3rd Day* and was completed during the *4th Day*.[521] By the end of the *4th Day*, Elohim had *made* and *formed* the Earth to the point where it contained all of the necessary ingredients that would be required for the work He would accomplish on the *5th Day*.

- The Biblical account of the *4th Day* ends with the familiar biblical statements of: "*God saw that it was good,*" and "*there was evening and there was morning, the 4th day*" (Genesis 1:18-19).

---

[513]Schroeder *Genesis and the Big Bang* Chapter 9 p 130-133

[514]Schroeder *Genesis and the Big Bang* Chapter 9 p 144*a*

[515]Schroeder *Genesis and the Big Bang* Chapter 1 p 14*b*

[516]Schroeder *The Science of God* Chapter 4 p 70*a*

[517]Schroeder *The Science of God* Chapter 4 p 69*g*

[518]Primordial (*first formed*)

[519]Primeval (*an early stage in evolution*).

[520]Schroeder *Genesis and the Big Bang* Chapter 9 p 144*b,c*

[521]Schroeder *Genesis and the Big Bang* Chapter 9 p 144*c*

THE 4TH DAY OF CREATION[522] LASTED 1-BILLION EARTH YEARS.

Day #	Start of Day 4	End of Day 4	Bible's Description	Scientific Description
4	1 ¾ Billion yrs. Before Adam	¾ Billion yrs. Before Adam	Sun, Moon, & stars become visible in the heavens. Gen. 1:14-19 & (Talmud Hagigah 12a)	The Earth's atmosphere becomes transparent. Photosynthesis produces an Oxygen-rich atmosphere.

Summary Points:

- Our Sun was formed 4.6 billion years ago at "dusk" on the *2nd Day of Creation*.
- Our Earth started forming 4.5 billion years ago during the "night" of the *2nd Day of Creation*.
- Our Moon is younger than the Earth. It formed "near midnight" on *the 2nd Day*.
- The Luminaries are the Sun, the Moon, and of the stars in the universe.
- The Sun and the stars were formed before the Earth but could not have been seen from the Earth before the *4th* Day because Earth's Primordial (*first-formed*) atmosphere (which formed *on the 2nd Day*) *was opaque*. On the *3rd Day*, Earth's *evolving* primeval atmosphere *became translucent*. Finally, on the *4th Day*, Earth's life-friendly *transparent* atmosphere was "*born*."
- Since the Earth is the only place in the entire universe from which our Moon can be perceived as one of the two *great luminaries*, the mention of the Moon as "*the small luminary...to rule the night*" in Gen. 1:16 confirms the Bible's description of the events of the *4th Day* is from *the perspective of the Earth*.
- As already stated in the Introduction—Part IX: *Jewish Tradition*, the flow-of-time in the first 25 verses of Genesis Chapter 1 is God-based.
- However, beginning with verse 9 and continuing through to the end of Genesis Chapter 1, it is as if Elohim came to the Earth, and stayed here while He *made* and *formed* things on the *3rd, 4th, 5th, and 6th Days of Creation*. That is to say: Elohim used an '*Earth-oriented-perspective*' when He talked to Moses about the creations He brought forth on the Earth during those *last 4 Days of Creation*.
- On the *4th Day of Creation*, Earth got its life-friendly biosphere.

So, if you were to climb into a time-machine and travel backward in time to about 900 million years *Before Adam*, you would be traveling back to the evening of the *4th Day of Creation* (cf. the Chart at the end of Chapter 12: *The Island that Sailed North*). Chances are — when you stepped out of your time machine and took your first breath of fresh air — you would have breathed in one of the Earth's first untainted puffs of *free oxygen*. But don't stay too long. The Earth was still a very hostile and dangerous place.

---

[522]Schroeder *The Science of God* Chapter 4 p 67

In the next chapter we will talk about how the worst *Ice Age* the Earth has ever seen had just ended, and a renewed epoch of volcanism was about to begin that would split asunder the Earth's first giant supercontinent — *Rodinia*. However, with the break-up of Rodinia (near the end of the *4ᵗʰ Day*), our life-friendly blue planet would be '*born*,' and one of the Earth's *many epochs of global warming* would return to the planet that was '*born-in-fire.*' That particular epoch of global warming would lead the way to the Earth's first *explosion* of **visible** animal and plant life-forms that occurred in the early part of the *5ᵗʰ Day* — a *Period of Geologic-Time* scientists refer to as — *"The Cambrian Period."* Many of those *dangerous* animal life-forms would become *the progenitors of all* the Earth's modern-day animals.

As you shall see, our current-day epoch of global warming (*that began near the end of the 6ᵗʰ Day*) was the catalyst that led to the development of our current-day civilizations!

CHAPTER 12: THE ISLAND THAT SAILED NORTH

When Korah rebelled against Moses. God caused the Earth to open up and swallow him,
his supporters, and all who rebelled against Moses. Numbers 16

The Lord descended upon Mt. Sinai in fire.
It smoked like a furnace, and the whole mountain quaked violently. Exodus 19:18 NASB

"And the Lord God...The One who touches the land so that it melts..." Amos 9:5 NASB

THIS CHAPTER IS ABOUT HOW EARTH'S VOLCANISM CHANGES OUR PLANET.
THERE ARE THREE MAJOR TOPICS FOR DISCUSSION:
I. An Introduction to The Science of Plate Tectonics.
II. The Existence & Destruction of two Supercontinents in Earth's History.
III. The Modern Scientific Categorization of Time: The Geologic Timetable.

INTRODUCTION

Since this chapter will involve a general discussion of what modern science has learned concerning events in Earth's history that took place on *the 4th, 5th, and 6th Days of Creation*, and will introduce the names of segments of Earth-time scientists have categorized and placed in a Geologic Timetable; it will be useful to see how the Geologic Timetable relates to the Six Biblical Days of Creation. The Geologic Timetable will be shown and explained in the last part of this chapter after we have completed a very basic and simplified introduction to the science of Plate Tectonics. The discussion of the time segments of the Earth's history will also be very basic. My goal is to give the reader an overview of the *'forest'* that is so full of information about the abundance of life that developed on our planet — without becoming *'bogged down'* by examining *'each leaf.'* By doing this, you will see how similar the saga of modern science is to the account the Bible presents for the last two days of creation. Now that we are narrowing our focus to the last two days, I believe you will see the sequence of the development of the Earth and its varied life-forms (that science has recently confirmed) is virtually the same as the sequence the Bible has proclaimed for the past 3,300 years! Moses gave us that sequence in the first chapter of Genesis.

We'll start with charts that will seem familiar because we have already used the same format when we discussed the first 4 days of creation. The charts below detail the start and end of the Biblical blocks of time the Bible labels as *the 4th, 5th, and 6th Days of Creation*. In each chart, the phrase: *'24 hrs. of God's Time,'* reminds us, each day of creation was 24 hours, a Biblical concept that looks at Universal Time-Flow *from God's perspective.* God's time-flow during the *Six Days of Creation*, which Proverbs 8:22 refers to as *"His Works of Old,"* views time-flow from *The Beginning looking forward*. The rest of each chart looks at Time from the Earth's perspective — which concerns the time-flow that is unique to our planet. *Earth's Time Perspective looks backward in time.* Earth's Time Perspective looks at the events of each day of creation in terms of the blocks of time that occurred *before Adam was made and created*.

THE 4TH DAY

The 4th Day: 24hrs of God's Time	Started 1 ¾ Billion years ago	Ended ¾ Billion years ago
God's Time Perspective	Earth-years Before Adam	Earth-years Before Adam

The *4th Day* lasted 1 Billion Earth-years: Earth's Time Perspective. [523] The *4th Day* started 1,750,000,000 years BA & ended 750,000,000 years Before Adam.

THE 5TH DAY

The 5th Day: 24hrs of God's Time	Started ¾ Billion years ago	Ended ¼ Billion years ago
God's Time Perspective	Earth-years Before Adam	Earth-years Before Adam

The *5th Day* lasted ½ Billion (500 million) Earth-years: Earth's Time Perspective.[524] The 5th Day started 750,000,000 years BA & ended 250,000,000 years Before Adam.

THE 6TH DAY

The 6th Day: 24 hrs of God' Time	Started ¼ Billion years ago	Ended 5,700 years BP
God's Time Perspective	Earth-years Before Adam	Ended with Adam

The *6th Day of Creation* lasted approximately ¼ Billion (250 million) Earth-years.[525] The *6th Day* started 250,000,000 years BA. It ended with the 1st man, Adam (5,700 years *Before the Present*). Adam is believed to be the 1st Homo sapiens Elohim *made & created*.

In this discussion, it will be useful to refer to these three charts. We'll start with the incredible geologic story of an island in the Pacific Northwest — Vancouver Island. Elohim started forming and making Vancouver Island near the equator of our planet during the *5th Day of Creation*. He then '*sailed*' it North and East to its present location.

I.   THE SCIENCE OF PLATE TECTONICS

VANCOUVER ISLAND, B.C. — THE ISLAND THAT 'SAILED' NORTH AND EAST.

It was a beautiful day in the fall of 1977 when we drove onto the ferry in Seattle, Washington. Our destination was Vancouver Island, British Columbia. We had moved to the Pacific Northwest the preceding year and my parents, who lived in Alabama, were with us. This trip to Vancouver Island would be the first time any of us had set foot on that magical island. It was also the first time my parents had visited Washington State. The cars were neatly lined up for an orderly entry onto the ferry. People were friendly and in a good mood. The brisk fall weather did not bother true Northwesterners. But I was cold. The invigorating crystal-clear air provided a stellar view of snowcapped Mt. Rainier to the southeast. The mountain loomed large over Seattle. Mt. Rainier appeared so close it seemed you could touch it. To the northeast, Mt. Baker and the other snowcapped peaks

523 Schroeder The Science of God Chapter 4 (Table) p 67
524 Schroeder The Science of God Chapter 4 (Table) p 67
525 Schroeder The Science of God Chapter 4 (Table) p 67

of the North Cascades were also visible, and to the west — we had a clear view of Mt. Olympus, on the Olympic Peninsula just across Pudget Sound from Seattle — also snowcapped. The water of Pudget Sound was calm and reflected the azure blue of a cloudless sky. Seagulls were everywhere, their distinct cries easily heard above the din of the harbor and the city. Numerous ferries to other points west, north, and south of Seattle, and a number of sailboats plied those pristine waters. People were enjoying a most pleasant but cold fall day. After driving onto the ferry, we left our car and climbed to the upper passenger decks where we bought sandwiches, warm cocoa, and hot coffee, and settled into comfortable seats. We enjoyed our lunch as we marveled at the beautiful vistas of Pudget Sound while our ferry sailed north. Time flies when you are enjoying yourself. In no time at all, it seemed, we sailed into the harbor of Victoria, B.C. — on the south end of Vancouver Island.

BEAUTIFUL VICTORIA

Victoria is unique. Some areas exude a European ambiance. It is a modern city that preserves the atmosphere of some of the best of the 'old world.' We treated my parents to afternoon tea at the Empress Hotel; an experience my wife, daughters, and mother especially enjoyed. We also toured the city and surrounding neighborhoods. Like all areas along the coastal regions of the Pacific Northwest, the vegetation was lush and beautiful. The private homes were immaculate, and the landscaping was spectacular. It seemed everyone had received from 'The Almighty' the gift of a green thumb. After a very pleasant evening in Victoria, the next morning we boarded a tour bus for a trip to Butchart Gardens — one of the most beautiful gardens in the world. On that tour bus our guide talked about the geological history of Vancouver Island. The sun was streaming in the nearby window. It was so warm that I became sleepy. However, I will never forget something the tour guide said. It seemed so preposterous that it instantly cleared my fog of sleepiness. He told us Vancouver Island was initially formed near the equator. Then, over eons of time, it 'sailed north and east' to its present location, where it formed the northern boundary of the waterway that connects Pudget Sound and the Georgia Strait to the Pacific Ocean! Millions of years later, that connecting waterway would be named — *the Strait of Juan de Fuca*,[526] for the Greek Captain and navigator who sailed with a Spanish expedition in 1592. He was seeking the fabled *Strait of Anián*.[527] The Strait of Anián was an imagined mythical narrow strait, which in antiquity was believed to separate Asia from the Americas.

Has this astounding tale of an island that sailed northeast tweaked your interest? Are you asking yourself: 'How could this have happened?' The answer has to do with something that we have already mentioned: *'Plate Tectonics.'* Plate Tectonics is the study of the Earth's crust. It is the study of the mechanism and results of large-scale movements of the Earth's crust that produce Earth's Mountain ranges and extensive fault systems. Plate Tectonics is the name of the theory that ascribes continental drift, volcanic and seismic activity, and the formation of mountain-belts, to moving plates of the Earth's crust that float on the Earth's semi-liquid molten mantle rocks. I'll use the fascinating geological history of Vancouver Island as an introduction to the subject. Next, we'll talk a bit about

---

[526] Article: **Sudden Abrupt Changes in Creation** —World Atlas: http://www.worldatlas.com/aatlas/infopage/juandefuca.html
[527] Article: The Strait of Anián: the Northwest Passage: http://www.corvalliscommunitypages.com/Americas/hudsonbay_canada/anan.html

the geological history of Washington State and use that example to segue to a discussion of the formation of two giant supercontinents that existed at separate times in Earth's geological history. Modern science believes they formed and then separated at two different times during the last three days of creation.

THE GEOLOGICAL HISTORY OF VANCOUVER ISLAND.[528]

The rock that makes up most of Vancouver Island originated near the equator in the southwestern Pacific Ocean between 420 and 380 million years ago — in the middle of the Paleozoic Era,[529] *on the 5th Day of Creation* (cf. the Chart at the end of this Chapter). The explosive volcanic birth of the island took place in part of what was a piece of the Earth's crust that scientists call a *'terrane'* that they have named *'Wrangellia.'* A terrane is a section of the Earth's crust that is defined by clear fault-lines and structural properties that distinguish it from adjacent terranes. *Tectonic plates* are larger than terranes. Tectonic plates consist of several terranes that have fused together to form a larger plate. The heat energy of Earth's molten mantle may sometimes cause a terrane to break away from a plate and attach to another plate. Thus, tectonic plates may display a variety of different geological structural properties that represent the different terranes of which they are composed. Wrangellia is a mountainous terrane, which encompasses southeast Alaska, the Queen Charlotte Islands, and portions of the Pacific Northwest Costal Mountains.

The foundation of Vancouver Island was first formed by undersea granite lava-rock. Later, the calcified shells of innumerable marine animals layered on the original granite foundation and eventually became limestone. Propelled by forces deep within the molten mantle layer of the Earth, Wrangellia slowly drifted to the northeast from its original location near the equator to its current location in the northern hemisphere at the entrance to what became *Pudget Sound.* About 100 million years ago (during the Cretaceous Period on *the 6th Day of Creation*), Wrangellia ended its millions-of-years voyage (*for the time being*), when it collided with and fused to the North American Continental Plate. Slow tremendous forces caused some regions to fold and buckle into mountain ranges, while other regions crumbled and eroded.

TWO OTHER TERRANES COLLIDED WITH VANCOUVER ISLAND AND BECAME PART OF ITS MASS. About 48 million years ago (*also during the 6th Day*), two smaller pieces of the Earth's crust, the *Pacific Rim terrane,* and the *Crescent terrane*, collided and joined with the southern part of Vancouver Island. That part of the island (where the city of Victoria is located), is made up of granite and gneiss rock (*i.e., metamorphic rock*), which is thought to have formed from magma that originated deep within the Earth's molten mantle. When the collision occurred, the volcanically formed part of Vancouver Island was uplifted. The granite foundation of present-day Victoria was exposed during the collision-uplift that occurred 48 million years ago. That happened in the Eocene Epoch of the Tertiary Period during the *6th Day of Creation*.

---

[528] Article: Geological History of Vancouver Island:
Query—"Geological History of Vancouver Island-Capital Regional District"
[529] The Geological nomenclature will be explained in this chapter.

GRANITE IS HARDER, LIGHTER, AND MORE BUOYANT THAN BASALT.

When we discussed how granite forms, we said it is a much tougher, but lighter and more buoyant rock than basalt. The foundation of the Earth's continental plates is granite. We have just described how a granite terrane 'floated' north and east from its birthplace (like a ship), on the molten subsurface mantle of the Earth to its present-day location. The journey took millions of years. But it occurred, nevertheless. Vancouver Island is not the only part of the Earth that originated at another point on our globe and then (over *Epochs* of time), moved somewhere else. In fact, all land masses on Earth have done this. Not only have the terranes and tectonic plates of the Earth traveled to other points, but they have been in constant motion since their formation and are still moving and are ever changing. To gain a better understanding of the motion of the continents, we need to travel farther back in time. We need to go back to the *4th Day of Creation*. The *4th Day* started 1 ¾ billion Earth-years ago, before Elohim made and formed the 1st man— Adam.

THE 4TH DAY AND PLATE TECTONICS[530]

When the oxygenation of Earth's atmosphere was completed, the Earth would more closely resemble the *'Blue Planet'* we know today. This happened late on the 4th Day (900 million years ago), during the Neoproterozoic Eon. However, before this happened, a new cycle of cataclysmic events occurred. In the early "*morning*" of the 4th Day (~1.6 billion years ago and for the next several million years), deep movements within the Earth's molten mantle wrenched Earth's surface crust apart, and the Earth's 1st giant supercontinent (*Rodinia*) formed. After Rodinia formed — the life that had just begun in the oceans faced its toughest test.

THE ANALOGY OF THE HEN'S EGG

To better understand what followed, let us consider the composition of a hen's egg. The analogy of the hen's egg will help us understand the *Theory of Plate Tectonics*. A hen's egg has a yellow yolk in its center. This yolk is surrounded by a generous semi-liquid layer called the egg white. The egg white is mostly made up of albumin (a protein), and water. The outer protective layer of the egg is a thin, hard, fragile shell that is composed of the mineral calcium.

The yellow egg yolk is analogous to the hot central core of the Earth. The egg white represents the ocean of molten rock in the mantle that surrounds the Earth's core. The thickness of Earth's mantle is greater than the diameter of Earth's core. Finally, the eggshell represents the Earth's surface crust. Like an eggshell, the Earth's crust, when compared to the mantle and core, is relatively thin and fragile. Subject the eggshell to pressure and it cracks. Now, imagine for a moment that the egg yolk and the layer of semi-liquid egg white are extremely hot, like the Earth's core and mantle. Remember, the Earth's molten mantle-rock is full of super-heated water which came from outer space. The water was brought to the Earth by the countless numbers of meteors, which were part of the debris that had been deposited in the orbital pathway of the Earth after the death of the 2nd order supernova, which had preceded the formation of our sun. Each one of the meteors that collided with the early Earth, contributed to its mass, and contained some water. The tremendous internal fires of the Earth and the steam thus produced have (over eons), caused numerous fractures of the Earth's thin surface crust that have caused

---

[530] Documentary: The History Channel: How the Earth Was Made: Part I.

the Earth's surface to resemble the irregular pieces of *a jigsaw puzzle*. These irregular pieces are *the Earth's tectonic plates*, the foundations of which *are mostly granite*. They literally *float* on Earth's molten mantle-rock layer. Earth's tectonic plates are always in constant motion because they are propelled by the energy of the Earth's internal heat and volcanism. Large portions of these tectonic plates are submerged beneath Earth's Oceans. Other portions have been lifted up by forces which will next be described. The crust of the submerged oceanic tectonic plates is heavier and thinner (about 4-5 miles thick), than the surface crust of Earth's continental land-mass tectonic plates, which vary in thickness from about 21 to 30 miles.[531] The Earth's continental landmasses comprise about 30% of the Earth's surface. The Oceans cover the remaining 70%.[532]

PLATE TECTONICS[533]

As late as the early 20th century, scientists thought the continents were *fixed*. However, *identical freshwater fossils* were found on both the *western* coasts of Europe and Africa, and on the *eastern* coastlines of the Americas, which would pose a challenge for scientists to explain. Scientists the world over realized these identical species of ancient fresh-water life would not have been able to swim the vast salty waters of the *Atlantic Ocean* — that now separate the western and eastern burial grounds of their fossilized remains. They have also determined these fossils were not the only fossils discovered that demonstrate a bizarre intercontinental distribution. How could this be? At first, scientists were stumped. At first, no one came up with a plausible explanation. Then in 1912, a new theory was proposed by the German scientist, *Alfred Wegener,*[534] that would eventually develop into today's *Theory of Plate Tectonics*. Wegener theorized the Earth's continents were initially in close contact when they developed, but then were slowly moved apart over billions of years by forces that originated deep within the Earth's molten rocky mantle.

ENTER THE U.S. NAVY[535]

A great deal of credit goes to the U.S. Navy. Thanks to maps of the ocean floor which have resulted from immense volumes of sounding data gathered by the U.S. Navy during years of study, it has been discovered the Earth's crust *is not a solid continuum*. The Earth's crust is made up of large plates that are in continuous motion. About twelve plates, which contain combinations of continents and ocean basins, have moved around on the Earth's surface through much of geologic time.[536]

THE CONTINENTAL COASTLINES NOW FIT TOGETHER LIKE A JIGSAW PUZZLE.

We now know today's continents used to be in close proximity. In the very distant past, they actually fit together. Then over eons of time, they drifted apart. Scientists now have the data, which shows that deep beneath the Earth's surface crust, mobile molten mantle-rock is in a continuous cycle of circular motion that is driven by the convection currents of heat generated deep within our planet. Where these currents rise, a rift forms and the

---

[531] Article: The Restless Earth: a Geologic Primer- Burke Museum
Query—"The Restless Earth: a Geologic Primer—Burke Museum of"
[532] Article: Inside the Earth—Enchanted Learning Software:
http://www.enchantedlearning.com/subjects/astronomy/planets/earth/Inside.shtml
[533] Documentary: The History Channel: How the Earth Was Made: Part I.
[534] Article: The Himalayas - Geology - Formation of the Himalayas-ThinkQuest: from
library.thinkquest.org/10131/geology.html
[535] The History Channel: How the Earth Was Made: Part I.
[536] Article: The Interior of the Earth: by Eugene C. Robertson: http://pubs.usgs.gov/gip/interior/

Earth's surface plates are pushed apart. New crust is created on the ocean floor through volcanic activity within Earth's molten mantle layer that fills in these new suboceanic gaps that are created by the rifts. The continents of the Earth are made up of tough but light slabs of granite that literally float on top of Earth's molten mantle magma.

THE TECTONIC CYCLE

In the rift-zones of the Earth's suboceanic tectonic plates, volcanic lava bubbles up and the newly produced suboceanic rock slowly moves the Earth's tectonic plates. On the opposite side of the volcanically active rift-zone, *an equally dynamic process balances* the new production of surface crust. The opposite side of the moving plate is driven under the adjacent edge of another plate. This creates a zone of *subduction* where the opposite edge of the plate is driven downward into the Earth's mantle where the plate rock that was formerly on the surface is melted, destroyed, and recycled into the Earth's molten mantle-rock. This is how the Earth's Mountain ranges are formed. Much like fresh-fallen snow is *buckled up* by the edge of a snow-shovel forming parallel ridges as it is pushed along, the part of the next plate that is adjacent to the subduction zone *is lifted up and buckled into ridges.* This is how the *'spine of mountains'* that parallels the western coastlines of North and South America formed.

In the same way, and over millions of years, the subduction of the northern edge of the *Indian* tectonic plate is being forced beneath the southern edge of the *Eurasian* tectonic plate as the northern movement of the Indian plate causes it to collide with and dive beneath the Eurasian plate. At the same time, at the subduction zone, the buckled southern edge of the Eurasian plate *is being lifted up to form the Himalayas.* [537]

Thus, we see science has discovered — on one edge of each tectonic plate (i.e., the rift-zone edge), new crust is created on the ocean-floor through volcanic activity within the Earth's mantle layer. This volcanically produced new rock fills in the suboceanic gaps and pushes the rift edges of the tectonic plates apart.

On the opposite side of each plate (the subduction zone), the ever-moving plate is driven underneath the adjacent plate with which it is colliding. That part of the plate is driven down into the depths of the Earth's molten mantle layer and is liquefied by Earth's internal fires and recycled into new molten mantle material. It has just been explained that subduction is also the mechanism through which Earth's Mountain ranges are created. If it were not for this recycling part of the tectonic cycle, the diameter of the Earth would be ever expanding. However, the forces that create new rock along the expanding suboceanic rift-edge of each tectonic plate — and the forces that destroy old rock at the subduction edge of each plate — are so nearly equal that the diameter of our globe has essentially remained the same during the 4-plus billion-year age of the Earth! Therefore, we see there is a continuous recycling of the continents which involves a destruction of the old and a reforming of the new. The whole process causes only a few centimeters of movement of the tectonic plates each year, but that is enough movement to account for the very dramatic changes our globe has undergone over the billions of years of its existence. This mechanism caused Vancouver Island to sail northeast with its terrane

---

[537] Article: The **Himalayas** - Geology - **Formation** of the **Himalayas**-ThinkQuest: from library.thinkquest.org/10131/geology.html

from the place of its birth to its current location. For as the ocean plates move, so do the continents. Now you can see — *we all live on ships.*

II.   TWO GIANT SUPERCONTINENTS IN EARTH'S HISTORY
RODINIA: THE 1ST GIANT SUPERCONTINENT.[538]

'*Rodinia'* is from a Russian word meaning "*homeland.* It is believed ~1.6—1.0 billion years ago (during the *4th Day* — which began 1 Billion 750 million years ago and ended 750 million years ago); the first emerging continental crusts were pushed together by plate-tectonic motions until they formed one landmass — a giant supercontinent. Scientists have named Earth's first supercontinent — *Rodinia.* Its exact size and configuration are unknown and are the subject of much debate, but the rocks of ancestral North America are believed to have formed its core. Current-day Canada and the USA are believed to have formed the heart of this first supercontinent. Supposedly, it was a desolate place — a barren continent, like today's Sahara Desert. *Speaking of desolate, every time I drove through the Great Salt Lake Basin in Utah, I thought about Rodinia*

RODINIA: A HOSTILE, BARREN PLACE

When Rodinia formed, most of what became the western portion of North America was believed to be a vast flood plain. Geologists found evidence there were thick strata of sand and silt deposited there. They theorized most of the landscape of what eventually became western North America was a rusty-red color. Perhaps this was the result of the oxidization of the banded-iron deposits that formed when the Earth became a water-world on the *2nd Day.* On the *3rd Day*, landmasses had been lifted up above the surface of the waters through the mechanism of plate tectonics. Finally, on the *4th Day*, this prehistoric flood-plain became part of Rodinia when Earth's early landmasses fused into Earth's first giant supercontinent.

WHEN EARTH HAD ONE CONTINENT, ONE HOSTILE OCEAN & SCANT OXYGEN.

Scientists believe when atmospheric oxygen levels were slowly increasing at this early date, the atmosphere still contained less than 5% of Earth's current oxygen levels and lacked the protective ozone layer that shields the Earth from intense ultraviolent radiation today. There was only one great planetary ocean at that time, which spawned violent storms over its vast expanse. Nothing protected Rodinia's landscape from the storms at sea, so great destruction was wrought over the low-lying supercontinent by periodic massive tidal waves. Within this bleak and hostile world, the first rocks of Washington State formed in the primordial heartland of Rodinia more than a billion years ago — *during the Mesoproterozoic Eon — early on the 4th Day of Creation.*

THE BELT SUPERGROUP AND STROMATOLITES

During the *4th Day of Creation* when Rodinia formed, another very distinctive group of primordial sedimentary rocks were formed in another giant basin that is part of what is now British Columbia, Alberta, Montana, Idaho, and Washington State. These special rocks are now called the *'Belt Supergroup,'* named for the small town of Belt, Montana which is nearby. The 'Belt-rocks' are multicolored sandstone, siltstone, and limestone,

---

[538] Article: Query— *"Northwest Origins - Burke Museum of Natural History and Culture"* to access the article by Townsend and Figge concerning Northwest Origins and An Introduction to the Geologic History of Washington State. Then click on *"The Dance of the Giant Continents: Washington's Earliest History."*

which are noted for their beautifully preserved sedimentary features. These include mud-cracks and ripple-marks. However, their most important and significant feature is their abundant remarkably preserved fossilized evidence of 'stromatolites' — cabbage-shaped fossils left by the action of *cyanobacteria* and *blue-green single-cell algae*. We have already mentioned stromatolites in Chapter 10 when their significance in the manufacture of oxygen was discussed. Stromatolites first appeared during the *3rd Day of Creation* (~ 2.5 billion years ago during the *Paleoproterozoic Eon*) and were very important in the transformation of Earth's atmosphere to a transparent oxygen-rich life-friendly atmosphere near the end of the *4th Day*. Here, the *Belt Supergroup* has preserved the fossilized evidence of their existence well into the *4th Day*. Today, living functional stromatolites can still be found in the shallow waters of *Shark Bay* in Australia (cf. Chapter 10). In Washington State, the Belt-rocks are exposed extensively in the eastern *Okanogan Highlands*, an area that I visited frequently when I lived in central Washington State. At the time, I did not realize the significance of the geology of the area. The *Belt Supergroup* also makes up most of the spectacular mountains of *Glacier National Park in Montana*.

IN ANTIQUITY, THE BELT SUPERGROUP REACHED ASTONISHING HEIGHTS.

The Belt-rocks are astonishingly thick. Geologists tell us in antiquity they accumulated to an altitude of 50,000 feet near the Washington-Idaho state line, dwarfing current-day Mt. Everest in the Himalayas! The first time I drove I-90 through the Belt-rocks on the Washington/Idaho border, I was compelled to stop frequently to enjoy the magnificent views of the Belt-Supergroup valleys, cliffs, and peaks. However, the Belt-Mountains thin rather rapidly as one travels east towards central Montana. The tectonic rupture that is believed to have split Rodinia apart (also during the *4th Day*), abruptly truncated the giant basin in which the *Belt Supergroup* sediments accumulated. The missing western margin of the Belt-basin today — is now thought to be either part of Australia or Asia.

SNOWBALL EARTH: THE GREATEST ICE AGE THE EARTH HAS EVER SEEN
(*cf. the end-of-chapter Chart*).

Somewhere between 900 million and 750 million years ago (during the *4th Day*), *Earth's greatest Ice Age* was spawned. The formation of Rodinia had triggered the biggest freeze the Earth has ever seen! The position of Rodinia blocked the water currents that brought warm water from the equator to the poles. Without this heat, the poles froze, and the ice reflected the sun's rays away from the Earth. Scientists believe ice and snow covered the entire Earth to great depths. The oceans were covered in a sheet of ice almost a mile thick! Some scientists call this time — the *'Cryogenian Period.'* This was when the Earth morphed *from a water-world into* a *"Giant Snowball."* When Rodinia caused the sudden development of the Earth's most extensive Ice Age, all the microscopic continental plant-life that had developed on the emerging continents on the *3rd Day,* was snuffed out — *in the blink of a geological eye!* The only life remaining on *"Snowball-Earth"* was the marine algae and bacteria. However, they became trapped beneath mile-thick sheets of sea ice and were suddenly in total darkness. Surface temperatures fell below minus 40 degrees Fahrenheit! Except for marine algae and bacteria, all other life was driven to extinction! The whole planet was dying![539]

---

[539] Documentary: The History Channel: How the Earth was Made: Part I

OUR EARTH HAS EXPERIENCED MORE THAN ONE ICE AGE.

Scientists tell us the Earth has undergone more than one Ice Age. Each Ice Age brought about mass extinctions of life. The formation of Rodinia on the *4th Day of Creation* is believed to have caused the greatest ice age the Earth has ever seen. But now is not the time to discuss the Earth's Ice Ages. We will defer that discussion to Chapter 22: *The 6th Day: Modern Land-Animals, Mammals, & Man-like Hominids.* For now, we will continue the discussion of the science of plate tectonics and the *'Dance of the Giant Continents'* —i.e., the movements of the *'ships'* on which we live.

THE DEATH KNELL OF RODINIA

Near the end of the *4th Day of Creation*, a renewed epoch of active volcanism began. Beneath the ice of the *'Snowball'* that Rodinia had caused the Earth to become, vast volcanic eruptions began splitting Rodinia apart, bringing the *Cryogenian Period* to an end, and finally rupturing the supercontinent. So far as geologic events are concerned, the breakup of Rodinia occurred rather suddenly. Carbon dioxide released by the volcanic eruptions produced a temporary greenhouse-effect. The ice sheets drew back. Shallow seas opened up, and stromatolites (fed by the increased levels of the atmospheric volcanically produced CO_2 pollution), rapidly converted the CO_2 into atmospheric oxygen. Thus, oxygen levels increased and late on the *4th Day*, our Earth got its present transparent, life-friendly, oxygen-rich oceans and atmosphere. With the break-up of Rodinia (at the end of the *4th Day*), our *'Blue Planet'* was born. When oxygen levels rose and warmer temperatures developed, primitive organisms became more complex and more dangerous. Scientists believe the rapid 'evolution' of the visible macroscopic primitive life-forms that occurred on the *5th Day of Creation*, was triggered by the break-up of Rodinia. They believe this brought an end to the *Cryogenian Period* as the circulation of warm equatorial waters toward the Earth's polar regions resumed. All agree the explosion of the first *visible macroscopic* plants and animals that occurred during the subsequent *Ediacaran* and *Cambrian Periods*, of the *late 4th Day* and the early *5th Day* (respectively) were triggered by the break-up of Rodinia. Thus, the catalyst to the explosive development of *complex macroscopic* (**visible**) life-forms on the *5th Day* was **Global Warming,** which was brought about by a renewed epoch of volcanism.

THE END OF RODINIA

As stated, scientists think the end of Rodinia began about 750 million years ago (at the close of the *4th Day* and the early *'dawn'* of the *5th Day of Creation*), in what is now east-central Washington State. The Earth's first giant supercontinent eventually fell victim to the fires within the Earth's interior. The slow buildup of heat beneath Rodinia caused its crust to dome, stretch, and weaken. When the breaking-point was reached, the giant supercontinent began to rupture along a rift-line near the current-day town of Pullman, Washington. At just a few centimeters a year, the breakup was a slow process, but over millions of years, the increments began to add up. Scientists theorize that perhaps ten million years after the crust began to dome and stretch, the waters of the ocean flowed into a newly formed rift-valley.

A MODERN-DAY RIFT-VALLEY GIVES US INSIGHT.

The original rift-valley that split Rodinia apart was probably similar to the modern-day rift-valley that runs between Israel, Jordan, Saudi Arabia, and Northeast Africa. Geologists have named this rift-valley — *The Afro-Syrian Rift.* The northern part of this rift-valley starts in Northern Israel at the Sea of Galilee. As it extends to the south, it separates Israel from current-day Jordan. We call that part of this modern-day continental rift, *the Jordan River Valley* — so named in Biblical times, although it is much older than Adam — the Earth's first "*man.*" As the Jordan River flows southward out of the Sea of Galilee, it eventually flows into the Dead Sea — shortly after it passes below the ancient city of Jericho (which is situated a few miles west of and above the Jordan River's western shoreline). The shores of the Dead Sea are 1,292 feet below sea level. The Dead Sea shoreline is the lowest point of land on the face of our planet! As the rift-valley continues south beyond the terminus of the Dead Sea, it runs through the Gulf of Aqaba, which separates Saudi Arabia from the Sinai Peninsula. From the Gulf, the rift-valley continues southwestward through the bed of the Red Sea and on into Northeast Africa through Ethiopia, Somalia, Kenya, Uganda, Lake Victoria, and Mozambique. This southern part of the Afro-Syrian Rift-Valley is slowly tearing Africa apart. Eventually, millions of years from now, as the southern part of the rift deepens and widens, the waters of the Red Sea and the Gulf of Aden will rush in and create a new gulf or sea as Somalia breaks away from Africa to form a new Somali tectonic plate.

JESUS CHRIST

I have visited Israel on two occasions in recent years. In northern Israel, the Sea of Galilee (which is located in the northern part of the rift-valley that is on the dividing line between two continents — Africa and Asia), was the place *Jesus Christ* spent most of His time during His ministry. There, He gathered his disciples, and He performed many of His healing miracles. It was on the shores of that inland lake where He preached the Sermon on the Mount (Matthew: Chapters 5, 6, & 7). The New Testament says multitudes followed Him wherever He went. Later, on two separate occasions; and with only a few loaves of bread and a few fish — He fed the crowds who had assembled to hear His teachings and be healed by Him (Matthew: Chapters 14 and 15). Our Lord lived among the people of Galilee and ministered to their physical and spiritual needs. The shores of that freshwater lake have special significance to Christians for these reasons. As I stood on those sacred shores I thought of Christ. I tried to imagine what I might have witnessed and felt if I had been there in *His time*. Later, when I visited Jericho, Qumran, Ein Gedi, Masada, and the western shoreline of the Dead Sea (located farther to the south), I began to imagine what the landscape might have looked like 2,000 years ago — *during the time of Christ.* Two thousand years ago seems like a long time. However, when one considers our Earth is about 4.5 billion years old, the two thousand years that have passed since our Lord walked on this Earth is only a tiny fraction of Earth's history — *not even the slightest 'blink of the geological eye.'* We impatiently anticipate and wait for His promised return. But, when we reflect on the age of our planet, we can begin to appreciate the meaning of Psalms 90:4 and II Peter 3:8.

- *"For a thousand years in Thy sight are like yesterday when it passes by, or as a watch in the night."* (Psalms 90:4)
- *"But do not let this one fact escape your notice, beloved, that with the Lord one day is as a thousand years, and a thousand years as one day."* (II Peter 3:8)

THE RIFT THAT TORE RODINIA APART BECAME THE PANTHALASSIC OCEAN.
As the rift in Rodinia continued to grow it eventually formed a vast ocean Science has named the *Panthalassic Ocean*. Panthalassic is Greek for *all seas*. Geologists tell us the Panthalassic Ocean separated the Americas, Siberia, and Scandinavia from Antarctica, Australia, and the rest of the eastern hemisphere.

After the break along the rift, the new coastline of ancestral North America ran through what is today Eastern Washington State, near modern-day Pullman, Washington. The authors of the article, *'The Dance of the Giant Continents,*[540] Catherine L. Townsend and John T. Figge, made a comment about Pullman which I thought was funny. After they said the new coastline developed near current-day Pullman, they wrote: *"...confirming the long-standing suspicion that Pullman was always a stone's throw from the end of the world."* Townsend and Figge are affiliated with the University of Washington and the Burke Museum of Natural History and Culture, which is on the campus of the University of Washington in Seattle near Pudget Sound. Therefore, the University of Washington is located in western Washington State. For those who may not know, *Washington State University is in Pullman, Washington,* which is a few hundred miles to the east of the University of Washington, not very far from the Idaho border. The two schools are archrivals. Each year, their football teams — the *Huskies* of the University of Washington, and the *Cougars* of Washington State University — clash in an event called *the Apple Cup*. The game is alternately played in the stadiums of each school. I know of a — *"no greater rivalry"*— between two great universities. So, in this article written by Townsend and Figge, we have two *Huskies* saying the *Cougars* are located *"a stone's throw from the end of the world!"* I wonder if they stopped for a moment to consider *where* that comment left Seattle and the University of Washington? At the moment in time of which they were writing, the spot on our globe that would millions of years later *become* Seattle, might have been a part of the ocean floor, perhaps near the equator — *literally beyond the end of the world and covered by a great depth of ocean water.* Their humorous comment is somewhat like — ***The Pot calling the Kettle — "Black."***

THE PACIFIC NORTHWEST COASTLINE—AT THE END OF THE 4TH DAY.[541]
Approximately 750 million years ago, the western portion of the rift that developed near current-day Pullman, pushed both halves of Rodinia apart; separating what is today Eastern Washington State from Antarctica, Australia, and Northern China. As the rift zone split Rodinia apart, the Panthalassic Ocean flowed into it and became ever wider as the suboceanic western edge of the rift produced the new oceanic crust that drove the two halves of Rodinia farther and farther apart. However, the eastern edge of the rift-zone was the part of the rift that became part of Eastern Washington State. That eastern edge of the rift was the *passive* part of the new continental margin. Today, that passive part of the new continental margin, is called — *the Okanogan Highlands*.

As the western most half of Rodinia sailed away under the tectonic influence of its active rift-zone — for the next 400 million years the eastern part of the rift-line in Eastern Washington State remained tectonically quiescent. During this period, if any man had

---

[540]Article: Query— *"Northwest Origins - Burke Museum of Natural History and Culture"* to access the article by Townsend and Figge concerning Northwest Origins and An Introduction to the Geologic History of Washington State. Then click on *"The Dance of the Giant Continents: Washington's Earliest History."*
[541] *"The Dance of the Giant Continents: Washington's Earliest History."*

been around, he could have stood on the ground near current-day Pullman and peering west would have seen nothing but empty ocean. During my many visits to the Okanogan Highlands when I lived in Washington State, I had no idea the land upon which I stood was once the broken edge of Earth's first ancient giant supercontinent — *Rodinia*.

THE 5TH DAY BEGAN WITH THE EXPLOSION OF EARTH'S 1ST VISIBLE LIFE FORMS.

750 million years ago, as the Pacific Northwest passed through the *Paleozoic Era*, it witnessed a veritable explosion of life. [542]

- In the ocean off its shores, *the first visible animals appeared* in the fossil record of the *Cambrian Period* about 570—505 million years ago. (Cf. the Chart at the end of this chapter.)
- The *first fish* appeared in the *Ordovician* Period (about 505—438 million years ago).
- The *first visible plants* invaded the land in the *Silurian Period* (about 438—408 million years ago).
- The *first amphibians* showed up in the *Devonian Period* (408—360 million years ago).
- And *the first true reptiles* came forth during the *Carboniferous Period* (360—286 million years ago).

All of these periods Earth-scientists have named — fall within the period the Bible calls the *5th Day*. Notice the sequence of the appearance of these various forms of life:

- Fish
- Land plants
- Amphibians
- Reptiles

This explosion of numerous and varied distinctive life-forms suddenly appeared on Earth on the *5th Day of Creation*, beginning at the point in Earth-time scientists have named — *the Cambrian Period.*

A BAVARIAN VILLAGE IN THE MIDDLE OF THE CASCADE MOUNTAINS OF WASHINGTON STATE

Somewhere around the *Devonian Period* of the 5th Day (about 408—360 million years ago), a major change occurred along the continental margin in eastern Washington State. The oceanic plate, previously fixed to the continental margin, plunged underneath the continent along a new subduction zone. This ended a 400 million year-history as a passive continental margin. Along the coastline in Eastern Washington State and British Columbia, the newly subducting plate gave rise to a *volcanic arc* which *developed inland*, intruding *granite-type plutons* into the much older *continental sediments* and *basaltic lava-flows* which had been accumulating for over a billion years.

Leavenworth is a quaint little town in the Cascade Mountains of Washington State. This small tourist attraction is modeled after a typical Bavarian mountain-village. When I was in the US Army and stationed in Augsburg, Germany — I often skied in the nearby Bavarian Alps, which were only 100 kilometers (60 miles) south of Augsburg. Six years later, when I visited Leavenworth, Washington (which is near Yakima, Washington where I lived and practiced Medicine), it felt so familiar. The surrounding terrain is *alpine*!

---

[542] Ibid

Leavenworth is nestled into the slope of nearby *Mt. Stuart*. Mt. Stuart is the tallest non-volcanic peak (9,415 feet above sea level), in the Cascade Range of Washington State. Mt. Stuart and the mountains near Leavenworth are granite plutons that intruded into the Cascade Range, which is mostly volcanic basalt. Some have claimed that Mt. Stuart is the largest exposed mass of granite in the lower 48 states of the USA.[543] So not only does Leavenworth *look like* an alpine Bavarian village, *but the terrain that surrounds Leavenworth looks like the German Bavarian Alps* — which are part of the Central Alps in Europe. The Central European Alps are mainly composed of crystalline rock (granite and gneiss), or of slate.[544] Leavenworth, Washington reminded me of the Bavarian town of Oberammergau in the Alps of Southern Germany. Mount Stuart reminded me of the *Zugspitze* near Garmisch-Partenkirchen (Germany's tallest mountain — 9,718 feet) where I often snow-skied. Although the German side of the Zugspitze is mostly compact limestone, the Austrian side of the Zugspitze is mostly granite.[545]

PANGAEA—EARTH'S 2ND SUPERCONTINENT

Scientists have concluded the continental fragments that separated and moved apart during the breakup of Rodinia slowly began to come back together again during the latter half of the *Paleozoic Era*. By the *Permian Period* (286—245 million years ago) during the *'twilight* and *evening'* of the *5th Day* & the *'dawn'* of the *6th Day of Creation*), the supercontinent cycle had come full circle again. This newly formed supercontinent has been named *Pangaea*, a Greek name meaning — *all lands*.

PANGAEA CAUSED ANOTHER MASSIVE EXTINCTION OF LIFE.

Many scientists say the assembly of Pangaea caused the Permian-Triassic Extinction (which happened in the *Permian Period on the 5th Day* after Pangaea formed). Scientists say Pangaea caused large-scale climatic chaos and the collapse of many ecosystems, both on land and in the oceans. At this time, most of North America again became a desert. Some say these drastic climatic reverses at least contributed to a great mass extinction that occurred early on the *6th Day of Creation* (245 million years ago) — at the end of the *Permian Period*. No one questions the fact that literally 90% of all species of life went extinct. All agree the Permian-Triassic Extinction was the largest extinction event in the history of life on Earth! But the ultimate cause of that extinction remains controversial and is still a subject of much debate. A growing number of geochemists and paleontologists are *now* suggesting *the Permian-Triassic extinction* (at the juncture of the 5th and 6th Days) followed a major impact by an asteroid that completely disrupted Earth's ecosystem.

Another asteroid impact may have also caused the extinction of the *Dinosaurs*. That occurred much later — on the *6th Day,* 70 million years ago, during the *Cretaceous Period,* which was the last period of the *Mesozoic Era.*

Nevertheless, Pangaea persisted over much of the Permian and Triassic periods (286-208 million years ago), a span of about 78 million years. During this period, the

---

[543] **Mount Stuart. pages uoregon.edu (**Some make this claim for Stone Mountain, Georgia)

[544]Limestone Alps – Wikipedia en.wikipedia.org › wiki › Limestone_Alps

[545] Hanging out at the top of Germany, 3 of 4 I Fotoeins Fotografie fotoeins.com > 2011/11/29>

western coastline of North America curved through western Idaho. Sediment-mud, silt, sand, and calcium carbonate accumulated in thick layers beneath the shallow seas along the continental shelf of Eastern Washington State.

We have just stated the construction of Pangaea left much of present North America as a windswept desert. Does the *'desert part'* give you a sense of déjà vu? No wonder, because when Rodinia assembled, the same thing happened. Pangaea's windswept desert, coupled with the widespread extinction of life on both land and in the seas, presented a bleak picture. However, conditions improved drastically in the *Triassic Period*, and life recovered to a significant degree. From the survivors of the *Permian-Triassic Extinction,* life gave rise to the first true *Dinosaurs* and *the earliest mammals*. On the ancient supercontinent of Pangaea, things were finally starting to look better.

However, it seems all things on this Earth eventually come to an end. This tectonically quiet, comfortable arrangement in the Pacific Northwest ended a little more than 200 million years ago, as Pangaea also began to break apart.

THE BREAKUP OF PANGAEA

Pangaea also eventually fell victim to the destructive forces of Earth's internal heat. Like Rodinia before it, about 205 million years ago (during the *6th Day of Creation*), rift zones developed in Pangaea and Earth's second giant supercontinent began to tear apart to form *the Atlantic Ocean*. A rift-zone developed between what became the modern eastern and western hemispheres, which became a spreading center that progressively pushed the two hemispheres apart. As Pangaea broke apart, North America was forced to drift westward at the same rate that the Atlantic Ocean was expanding. The westward drift of the North American continent had perhaps its most dramatic effect on the Pacific Northwest. The western coastline had been passive since the breakup of Rodinia, but the new tectonic activity began to affect the western edge of the continent as the *Pacific Ocean Basin* began to subduct the newly created North American continent's western shoreline. Volcanic islands, active subduction zones, and new violent volcanic arcs developed as Pangaea broke apart.

THE ATLANTIC OCEAN EXPANDS WHILE THE PACIFIC OCEAN SHRINKS.

Today the Atlantic Ocean is still expanding, slowly growing larger and larger each year. At the same time, the Pacific Ocean is proportionately becoming smaller. At the rate of only a few centimeters a year this phenomenon is not noticeable. However, eons from now, scientists say it will gain the attention of generations in the distant future — that is, unless mankind causes his own destruction by some other means or unless some other destructive act of nature intervenes. Maybe someday, because of the continued widening of the Atlantic Ocean and the shrinking of the Pacific Ocean, airfares from New York to Tokyo may be only a small fraction of the cost of an airfare from New York to London or Paris. However, scientists have made another prediction. Some believe that a third supercontinent will form someday which will bring about unpredictable, but dire consequences for our planet. For each time in the Earth's past that a supercontinent has formed, Ice Ages and massive extinctions of life-forms have occurred.

THE DIFFERENT ORIENTATIONS OF RODINIA & PANGAEA [546]

Although the orientation of Rodinia remains a subject of major debate, and the configuration of Rodinia is unknown, most geologists believe the majority of the mass of Earth's 1st giant supercontinent may have been located *south* of the equator. However, there seems to be a consensus that the east coast of present-day North America was most probably adjacent to western South America, and the west coast of North America was probably in continuity with what is Australia and Antarctica today.

For the most part, scientists agree the orientation of Earth's second supercontinent, Pangaea was quite similar to the orientation of today's land-masses — that is, the north-south orientation was about the same. Today, the majority of our planet's landmasses are oriented north of the equator. When Pangaea pulled apart, the separation created the coastlines of today's continents, but their drift apart was mostly in an East-West direction.

Though it is claimed by most that Earth has experienced the formation and break-up of two supercontinents in its history, according to an article from Washington Education, the Burke Museum, entitled — *The Dynamic Earth: A Geologic Primer:* "There is growing evidence even older supercontinents may have predated Rodinia in Earth's history." [547]

III.   THE GEOLOGIC TIMETABLE — A CATEGORIZATION OF EARTH-TIME:

For the last few pages, I have been using strange sounding names to refer to segments of Earth-time as if they are terms that are a part of everyone's vocabulary. Now is the time to talk a bit about these terms, how they came about, and why scientists use these terms to refer to specific events in Earth's history.

Have you ever noticed how prominent the rocks are in almost all the movies of the old West? Some rocks are big. Others are massive, especially those on the Utah/Arizona border in a place called Monument Valley. The rocks the Cowboys and the Indians ride around and hide behind are ubiquitous. Their sizes, shapes, colors, and orientations are extremely variable. Why are rocks so prominently featured in the old Western Movies? Perhaps because, in a lot of the arid areas of the Western United States and Mexico where many of the old western films were made, there are numerous scenes in which there are so few trees. However, if you think about it and if you begin to take note, you will notice rocks are prominently present in almost all movies and in nearly all locations. That is because our planet is a rocky planet, one of the four rocky or terrestrial planets that formed in our solar system. Rocks are prominent because they are the *'building blocks'* of Earth's land masses. Written on and within the rocks of our planet is the history of how the Earth formed. There are other tales written there as well. The rocks of our planet also contain the stories of the rise and fall of whole ecosystems, animals, and other forms of life that existed and then passed away during the different ages of the development of the Earth. Each layer of rock tells its own story. The very deepest layers

---

[546] Article: Dance of the Giant Continents by Catherine L. Townsend and John T. Figge
  www.washington.edu/burkemuseum/geo_history_wa/Dance%2...
[547] Article: The Dynamic Earth: A Geologic Primer—
http.//www.washington.edu/burkemuseum/geo_history_wa/The%20Restless%20Earth%20v.2.0.html

are the oldest. Each succeeding layer closer to the surface represents a younger and more recent age.

Over the past 200 years Geologists have worked to categorize and order the major geologic events in the Earth's history. In the 1800s they began developing a scheme of time based on the history of life that is recorded in the fossil record, which is found in the different layers or strata of rock that comprise the Earth's surface crust. They have used the changes in the fossil record to mark and define major significant divisions of Earth-time, such as the mass extinction of some life forms and the development of new ones.

In the 1950s, the evolving science of *Geochronology* used the decay rates of certain radioactive isotopes to assign specific ages to the geologic timescale (or *Timetable*). Thus, *the Geologic Timetable* of significant events in Earth's history is and will continue to be *'a work in progress'* — something that is influenced by, and changes with each new discovery.

The Geologic Timetable that is on the next page may already be antiquated by new discoveries of unpublished data, or by published discoveries of which I am not aware. However, this table of events may seem familiar to those of you who are already schooled in this subject. There is no doubt some of you will dismiss it as too antiquated to be taken seriously since there are more recent charts which refer to the same blocks of time by different names. However, I feel it is significant to this discussion because it clearly illustrates an essential historical point — *continuing research builds new platforms on the foundations of old platforms of thought and discovery.* The chart that follows is therefore an important benchmark in the history of scientific research and discovery. The following discussion will explain how scientific opinion about the age of our planet is progressing. Our understanding of the *'ages'* of development of the life-forms on our planet — is still evolving.

If you find the rest of this chapter confusing or too laborious you may want to skip it — although I hope you won't because of its scientific importance. If you are a scientist who researches and teaches these subjects, you may be critical of my discussion of *Geologic Time*. Should this be the case, please remember I am trying to introduce complex material in a logical way to people who may have only a passing acquaintance with this subject.

When scientists configured *the Geologic Timetable*, they divided *Earth-Time* into the broad categories of: *Age, Eon, Era, Period, and Epoch.* Time at the top of the table is the most recent. At the bottom of the scale, the record of *Geologic Time* begins 4.55 billion years ago with the formation of the Earth. So, when reading any *Geologic Timetable*, it is best *to start at the bottom of the chart* and *read toward the top.* Science has labeled the block of time that marked the beginning point of the Earth: *the 'Precambrian Age.'* The Precambrian *Age* is further subdivided into the *'Hadean,'* the *'Archean,* and the *'Proterozoic Eons.'*

Now, take a little time to study and familiarize yourself with the following chart of the Geologic Timetable before proceeding any further.

GEOLOGIC TIME SCALE

EON	ERA	PERIOD		EPOCH	Age
Phanerozoic	Cenozoic	Quaternary		Holocene	Present
					0.01
				Pleistocene	
					1.6
		Tertiary	Neogene	Pliocene	
					5.3
				Miocene	
					23.7
			Paleogene	Oligocene	
					36.6
				Eocene	
					57.8
				Paleocene	
					66.4
	Mesozoic	Cretaceous			144
		Jurassic			208
		Triassic			245
	Paleozoic	Permian			286
		Pennsylvanian			320
		Mississippian			360
		Devonian			408
		Silurian			438
		Ordovician			505
		Cambrian			570
Precambrian	Proterozoic				2500
	Archean				3800
	Hadean				4550

Age in millions of years before present

The Pennsylvanian & Mississippian Periods are Collectively called "THE CARBONIFEROUS" PERIOD.

This *Geologic Timetable* is still widely used in North America. (*Image: Geological Society of America*)[548, (*)] Time in this chart is in millions of years. **The Precambrian Age** (*began with the Hadean Eon* 4,550 million years ago (which can be written: 4,550 x 10^6 years, or 4.55 x 10^9 years, which is the same as 4.55 billion years ago). Then, *Earth's 1st life forms suddenly appeared on the "dawn of the 3rd Day of Creation in the Archean Eon.* **However, those 1st life forms were microscopic (i.e., invisible to unaided vision)!**

THE PRECAMBRIAN AGE

Let us start our discussion at the bottom of the Geologic Time Scale and work our way to the top. **Geologists have named the earliest block of Earth-time — *the Precambrian Age.*** According to the calculations of geologists, *the Precambrian Age* began 4.55 billion years ago and ended 570 million years ago.

According to the Geologic Time Scale of our Earth, *the Precambrian Age* covers the vast majority of the time of the existence of the Earth. It covers all but about the last 570 million years of the Earth's history. Stated another way, the Precambrian Age covers the first 3.98 billion years of Earth's existence, which is about 87% of Earth's history. [This calculation assumes the Earth is indeed 4.55 billion years old. Therefore, 4.55 billion (-) 0.570 billion = 3.98 billion years: and 3.98/4.55 x 100 = 87.47 %]. Since the Biblical *2nd Day of Creation* is believed to have begun 7.75 billion years ago and ended 3.75 billion years ago, we see that the Geologic Time Scale starts near the end of the *2nd Biblical Day of Creation.* Therefore, The Geologic Time Scale does not include the 8 billion years of *Day One of Creation* or the first 3.2 billion years of the *2nd Day of Creation* [7.75 billion minus 4.55 billion = 3.2 billion]. In other words, the Geologic Time Scale begins 11.2 billion years *after the Beginn*ing. This statement assumes the moment of the Beginning occurred 15.75 billion years ago [15.75 billion (-) 4.55 billion = 11.2 billion years]. **Thus, science has shown something the Bible has claimed all along. For the 11.2 billion years that followed the Big Bang in the Beginning — 'the Earth was without form and void' (Genesis 1:2a)! That is to say — At The Beginning and for the next 11.2 billion years of the existence of the Universe, the Earth did not exist!**

WHY NAME THE 1ST AGE OF TIME—'PRECAMBRIAN?'

Many of the names in the Geologic Timetable relate to the modern geographic areas on our globe where fossil discoveries have been made. The first segment of time in the table that has been labeled as a *'Period'* of time, occurred in the *Paleozoic Era* and has been named: the *'Cambrian Period.'* The Cambrian Period began 570 million years ago. Since the *5th Day of Creation* is believed to have started 750 million years ago and ended 250 million years ago, we can see that *the Cambrian Period* refers to a block of Earth-time that occurred during the *'morning'* of the *5th Day of Creation.* Cambrian refers to *Cambria,* which comes from the Celt word *'cymru'* for *Wales.* Therefore, the word *'Cambrian'* pertains to modern-day Wales, which was called *Cambria* in ancient times.

---

[548] Article: Query: *"Northwest Origins—Burke Museum of Natural History and Culture"* to access the article by Townsend and Figge about Northwest Origins and an Introduction to the Geologic History of Washington State. Then click on *"The Restless Earth: A Geologic Primer."*

(*) This Timetable lists 570 million years ago as the starting point of the Cambrian Period. Others claim the *Cambrian Period* began 540-543 million years ago.

When Charles Darwin wrote his book: *The Origin of Species*, the commonly held opinion of paleontologists of his time was: the oldest animal fossils on Earth were the *trilobites* and *brachiopods* that were found in rock-strata now known to be about 540 million years old (the *5th Day of Creation*). Because the fossils were found in Wales (*ancient Cambria*), they called this *the Cambrian Period*.[549] Many paleontologists of Darwin's time believed simpler forms of life must have existed before this but left no fossils because they were invertebrates (i.e., *had no skeletons*). Some believed the Cambrian fossils represented the moment of God's creation of the first animals, or the first deposits of the Biblical Flood of Noah's time. Darwin said:

> *"The difficulty of assigning any good reason for the absence*
> *of vast piles of strata rich in fossils beneath the Cambrian*
> *system is very great."*

Nevertheless, he hoped such fossils would someday be found because he also wrote:

> *"Only a small portion of the world is known with accuracy."*[550]

It is important to note the fossils that were discovered in Wales were *macroscopic* fossils. That is, they were so large that they **were visible** — i.e., they could be seen with normal, unaided vision. They were believed to be the remains of the Earth's first animal life-forms.

THE LAYERS OF ROCK WE CAN STUDY FORM THE THIN SURFACE CRUST OF THE EARTH.

The scientists of Darwin's time rightly deduced the development of the Earth occurred in layers or strata. They also correctly concluded the deepest layers were the earliest layers to form. When one considers this concept of the layered development of the Earth, it is understood — the molten mantle of the Earth (upon which the surface crust floats) formed before the Earth's surface crust cooled. Furthermore, the incredibly hot central solid iron core of the Earth is even older than Earth's mantle and surface crust. The layers of rock in the Earth's surface crust that are *below* the Cambrian layer are indeed much thicker and older than those *above* the Cambrian layer. Therefore, these deeper, older strata were named '*Pre-Cambrian strata*,' and the time that they formed is called '*The Pre-Cambrian Age*.'

DARWIN'S DILEMMA

Darwin and the paleontologists of his time puzzled over the lack of any evidence of life in those layers of rock that were deeper and earlier than the Cambrian layer. Darwin called this puzzle his '*dilemma*.' Since his time, this puzzle has been referred to as **'*Darwin's Dilemma.*'** Darwin realized — if his theory of evolution were true, there had to be swarms of earlier life-forms that preceded the sudden appearance of the many and completely different life-forms that had been discovered in the Cambrian layer. He hoped someday the evidence of earlier life-forms in Pre-Cambrian strata would be discovered. He also hoped those "*pending*" discoveries would prove his theory of — *slow smooth transitional evolution*. He realized the lack of any evidence of slow gradual development, and transitional life-forms in Pre-Cambrian strata, threatened his theory. He decided the lack of any such evidence could be due to the delicate nature of such life. The molten heat in

[549] Article: Introduction to the Vendian Period: from — http://www.ucmp.berkeley.edu/vendian/vendian.html
[550] Article: Introduction to the Vendian Period: from — http://www.ucmp.berkeley.edu/vendian/vendian.html

the Earth's mantle could have destroyed the evidence of the gradualism that must have occurred when the deeper strata formed.[551,552]

NEW DISCOVERIES IN THE 20TH CENTURY PUSHED BACK THE FOSSIL HISTORY OF LIFE.
In Chapter 10: *The 3rd Day and the 3rd Rock from the Sun,* we talked about Professor Barghoorn and his discovery of the *microfossils* of life-forms that date to 3.3 billion years *Before the Present* (BP). As Darwin had hoped, Barghoorn's discoveries *have found the evidence of earlier life-forms* — earlier than those that lived in the Cambrian Period. Science has learned Earth's first life-forms were **microscopic — *i.e., invisible to normal sight*.** These discoveries have solved 'Darwin's Dilemma,' **but have not confirmed his theory of evolution!** Since then, evidence of earlier life has also been discovered in Pre-Cambrian strata in Australia, Canada, China, and other locations throughout our globe.

We now know the *Cambrian* rock stratum in Wales (discovered in Darwin's Day) with its **visible** fossils of ancient animal life — had formed on the *5th Day of Creation.* However, the Cambrian stratum was not the earliest rock stratum on Earth that contained fossilized evidence of early life. Therefore, we see since Darwin's time, the fossil history of life on Earth has been pushed back from the Cambrian Period (which is the first Period in the **Phanerozoic Eon,** which means **"the Eon of the visible animals"**), into the *Precambrian Age* when life-forms were **not visible to the naked eye.** Scientists have discovered *the oldest Pre-Cambrian stratum,* dates back to 4.55 billion years Before the Present! *The oldest Cambrian stratum* dates to only 570 million years *Before the Present!* Since the Precambrian Age started 4.55 billion years ago, it began late on the *2nd Day of Creation.* New discoveries have pushed back the fossil history of *liquid water* from the *5th Day* into the *2nd Day of Creation* and *the earliest life-forms to the dawn of the 3rd Day!* **These discoveries were made after Darwin died!**

THE PRECAMBRIAN AGE ENCOMPASSES: THE HADEAN, ARCHEAN, & PROTEROZOIC EONS.

- *The Hadean Eon:* (4.55-3.8 billion years ago: corresponds to the *2nd Day of Creation*). *Hadean* comes from the word, *Hades* — relating to a hellish time in the geologic history of the Earth. The Hadean period relates to the time when the Earth formed in the fires of a continuous meteorite bombardment over millions of years. Thus, Earth was "born" as a fiery ball in space on the *2nd Day of Creation.* During the Hadean Eon—

  ✓ Our Solar System formed.
  ✓ The Earth formed. Matter aggregated into Planetesimals and then into Planets.
  ✓ Comets, Asteroids, and Giant Gas Planets formed from the remaining material.

- *The Archean Eon:* (3.8-2.5 billion years ago: mostly relates to the *3rd Day*). It started 50 million years before the end of the *2nd Day* and ended 75 million years before the end of the *3rd Day. Archean* comes from the Greek, *Archaios* (also spelled *Archean*), for 'ancient' or 'beginning,' and is a term used to designate the earliest known rocks. Archean also refers to one of the earliest known life-forms. Modern science has discovered there were and are a class of the earliest life-forms

[551] Article: Darwin's Dilemma: http://www.darwinsdilemma.org/darwins-dilemma.php
[552] Article: Deepening Darwin's Dilemma: by Jonathan Wells; Discovery Institute; Sep. 16, 2009, http://www.discovery.org/a/12471

that thrived and still thrive in the hellish environs of the fires of volcanism. Scientists call these life forms: *the Archaea*. We briefly mentioned these early life-forms in Chapter 10, when we discussed the Earth's first simple life-forms. Dr. Barghoorn reported the fossil data that proved the Archaea appeared 3.3 billion years ago (on the *dawn* of the *3rd Day of Creation*). The Archaea still thrive near and in suboceanic volcanic vents.

✓ During the Archean Eon (*late 2nd and early 3rd Days of Creation*) the Earth's surface crust cooled and Earth's 1st continents formed when Elohim completed the separation of the waters below by commanding the dry land to appear on the *3rd Day*.

✓ The appearance of Earth's earliest micro-fossil evidence of life occurred around 3.3 billion years ago in the form of the Earth's 1st Prokaryocytes which, in addition to the Archaea were:

✓ The 1st simple single-celled bacteria, cyanobacteria (1st classified as algae, but now reclassified as bacteria), and the 1st true simple single-celled algae that appeared 3.3 billion years ago on the *3rd Day*. The cyanobacteria and algae were the active principles of the Stromatolites that produced the majority of the Earth's 1st oxygen. (See Chapter 10.)

✓ A few scientists claim the cyanobacteria and Archea appeared even earlier — late, on the *2nd Day*.

• *The Proterozoic Eon:* (2.5-0.57 billion years ago: spans the *3rd, 4th, & 5th Days of Creation*). The Proterozoic Eon followed the Archean Eon and preceded the Phanerozoic Eon (cf. The Geologic Time Scale Chart). The meaning of *Proterozoic* can be discovered through the following process of analysis. We have to start with the root word, *zo*, which is the same as *zoo*. *Zoo* comes from *zoion* which is Greek for animal. The word, *zoo*, is properly changed to *zo* if it is used in a word where it is written before a vowel—in this case, *i*, as in *ic*. *Ic* is an English suffix that is taken from the French (*ique*), or from the Latin (*icus*), or from the Greek (*ikos*). All three are suffixes used to form adjectives meaning: 'having to do with, characteristic of, having the nature of, caused by, like, or consisting of.' The prefix *pro* comes from the Latin word *pro* which means, 'before, forward, or for.' Therefore, the word *Proterozoic* means *'before life-forms that were animal-like.'*

Some scientists have proposed the Proterozoic Eon should be divided into three categories. Within these categories some have named subsegments they call: Vendian, Edicaran, Tonian, and Cryogenian. Still others have proposed the Proterozoic Eon be called the Cryptozoic Eon because some fossils of this time are difficult to examine. Cryptozoic means the secret or hidden animal. If you want to investigate why some scientists have proposed these changes, be my guest. Such is the nature of the clarification or the confusion of progress. The term, cryptozoic, seems to have fallen by the wayside and is no longer used to refer to the Proterozoic Eon. Nevertheless, the classification debate still rages. Someday, scientists will sort it all out and a consensus of opinion will be reached.

Nevertheless, most agree it was Elso Barghoorn who discovered the microscopic evidence of the Earth's earliest life in the Fig Tree Formation.

Barghoorn pushed back our knowledge of the Earth's 1st life to 3.3 billion years before the present: into the Archean Eon; the middle period of the Precambrian Age. Barghoorn's discoveries confirmed Darwin's expectations that someday evidence of earlier life forms than those of the Cambrian Period might be found in older rock strata but, unlike the macroscopic Cambrian life; Pre-Cambrian life was microscopic — not visible.[553] [*Just remember the Archean-Proterozoic Eons (cf. The Geologic Time Scale Chart) of the Pre-Cambrian Age are the eons in which the appearance of the simplest types of life, and widespread glaciations and mountain formations, as well as the laying down of iron and copper deposits, occurred.*]

SOME GEOLOGIC TIMETABLES REPLACE THE PROTEROZOIC EON WITH THREE SUBDIVISIONS (THE PALEO-, MESO-, AND THE NEO-PROTEROZOIC EONS).

- *The Proterozoic Eon* (2.5 billion-543 million years ago—from the 3rd Day into the 5th Day of Creation)

Starting at the bottom of this chart (oldest time) and proceeding to the top (most recent time) we have —

THE DIVISIONS OF THE PROTEROZOIC EON

Neoproterozoic	900-543 Million years Before the Present	Stromatolites began to decline & Eukaryotes became more prevalent. (On The 4th & 5th Days of Creation)
Mesoproterozoic	1.6 Billion-900 Million Yrs. Before the Present	Oxygen levels increased in the atmosphere, reducing ammonia & methane levels. (On The 4th Day)
Paleoproterozoic (START HERE)	2.5-1.6 Billion years Before the Present	Continent formation began on the 3rd Day of Creation. (*explanation follows)

- *Paleoproterozoic Eon:* (from 2.5 billion to 1.6 billion years ago) During the 3rd Day of Creation. *Paleo* means ancient / primitive / historically early. *Protero* means before. *Zoic* means animal-like. Therefore, *Paleoproterozoic* refers to the Eon before the 1st primitive or ancient animal-like life forms developed. It was during this Eon the 1st continents formed (on the 3rd Day).

    ✓ (*) Others say the 1st continents rose in the late Archean Eon, (which ended in the early part of the 3rd Day).

- *Mesoproterozoic Eon:* (from 1.6 billion to 900 million years ago) On the 4th Day of Creation. *Meso* is Greek for middle. So, the Mesoproterozoic Eon refers to a middle period of time in Earth's history before the 1st ancient animal-like life forms appeared.

    ✓ During this period, oxygen levels in the atmosphere increased,
    ✓ And atmospheric ammonia and methane levels declined.
    ✓ Rodinia formed.

---

[553] Article: Introduction to the Vendian Period: from—http://www.ucmp.berkeley.edu/vendian/vendian.html

- *Neoproterozoic Eon:* (from 900 to 543 million years ago) The late 4th and early 5th Days of Creation. *Neo* is Latin for new or recent; therefore, the Neoproterozoic Eon refers to the most recent ancient period before the 1st primitive visible animal-like life forms appeared (Cambrian period).

  ✓ Stromatolites began to decline,
  ✓ Rodinia broke apart.
  ✓ Eukaryotes became more prevalent.

This Chart Maps the Timeline of the Pre-Cambrian Age by Dividing the Proterozoic Eon of the Geologic Time Scale into Early, Middle, & Late Divisions that are called: the Paleo- Meso- & Neoproterozoic Eons.

THE DIVISIONS OF PRE-CAMBRIAN TIME:[1]

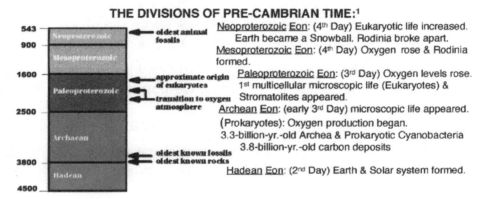

Remember: Start reading this chart at the bottom & read to the top.

REFRENCE ARTICLE: The Precambrian: http://www.ucmp.berkeley.edu/precambrian/precambrian.html

THE PRE-CAMBRIAN AGE COMPRISES 87% OF EARTH'S HISTORY. DURING THIS AGE:

1. The Earth and our Solar System formed.
2. Earth started as a hellish fiery ball; changed into a toxic water world; became a snowball in space; & finally changed into the life-friendly blue planet of today as—
3. Earth's oceans and atmosphere formed.
4. The 1st microscopic forms of single-cell life appeared (Prokaryotes).
5. The 1st tectonic plates formed, and the 1st continents rose.
6. And just before the end of the Pre-Cambrian Age, the Earth's 1st multicellular microscopic life forms (Eukaryotes) appeared.
7. All life in the Precambrian Age was Microscopic — not visible to the naked eye.

THE REST OF THE GEOLOGIC TIMETABLE FALLS UNDER THE PHANEROZOIC AGE (CF. CHART ON THE LAST PAGE OF THIS CHAPTER).

I HAVE RENAMED THE PHANEROZOIC EON— THE PHANEROZOIC AGE.

THE PHANEROZOIC AGE is the **present** Age of geologic time. It began 570 million years ago and extends to the present. Thus, the Phanerozoic Age began on the 5th Day of Creation and continues through the 6th Day of Creation and into our present *Age.*

Phaneros is Greek for **visible**. When combined with *zoic*, it means, **visible animals.** Its major divisions are the Paleozoic, Mesozoic, and Cenozoic Eras.

Even though I can't see you, I suspect that your eyes have 'glazed over', and your eyelids closed long ago as the result of all this tedious minutia. So, for the rest of the Geologic Timetable discussion, I am going to *'cut to the chase,'* and use as few words as possible to list the major events.

- **The Paleozoic Era:** (570-245 million years ago: the 5th Day of Creation). *Paleozoic* means ancient or primitive animal-like life. The periods of the Paleozoic Era are divided as follows:

  - *The Cambrian Period:* (from 570 to 505 million years ago). We have already talked about the origin of the term 'Cambrian.' However, we will expand the discussion of what occurred in the Cambrian Period in the next chapter when we examine what the Bible says about the 5th Day. Visible life forms suddenly appeared. The Cambrian period is characterized by—[554]

    - ✓ The 1st simple marine animal & plant life as shown by the 1st large (visible) fossils found in Wales, Cumberland, and later in the Burgess shale of Canada.
    - ✓ Major animal groups began to appear in this period.

  - *The Ordovician Period:* (from 505 to 438 million years ago). *Ordovician*—a Roman name for an ancient Celtic tribe in Wales. The rocks in Wales of the Ordovician Period are characterized by—

    - ✓ An abundance of the 1st fish & marine plants, &
    - ✓ By deposits of limestone, lead, & zinc in rock strata.

  - *The Silurian Period:* (from 438 to 408 million years ago). *Silurian* — comes from the Silures: an ancient warlike tribe of southeastern Wales conquered by the Romans about 80 A.D. The rocks of this Geologic Period are characterized by—

    - ✓ The 1st land-plants, &
    - ✓ The 1st land-animals; scorpions, and wingless insects.
    - ✓ Extensive coral reefs developed.
    - ✓ Also, glacial ice began to melt; causing sea levels to rise.

  - *The Devonian Period:* (from 408 to 360 million years ago). Named *Devonian* because its rocks were 1st studied in Devonshire, in southwestern England Characterized by the appearance of:

    - ✓ The 1st amphibians (including the Dinosaur ancestors), and
    - ✓ The dominance of fish

  - *The Mississippian Period:* (from 360 to 320 million years ago). The 1st period of the Paleozoic era in North America. Characterized by:

[554] Article: The Dance of the Giant Continents: An Explosion of life in the Paleozoic Era: by Townsend & Figge httpj://www.washington.edu/burkemuseum/gio_history_wa/Dance%20of%20the%20Biant%20Continents.html

✓ The 1ˢᵗ appearance of reptiles, & the 1ˢᵗ winged insects.

- *The Pennsylvanian Period:* (from 320 to 286 million years ago). The 2ⁿᵈ period of the Paleozoic Era in North America. Characterized by:

  ✓ The formation of coal deposits.

- *And the Permian Period:* (from 286 to 245 million years ago). Named after *Perm*, a former province of Russia. The fossils 1ˢᵗ found in Perm & in similar strata elsewhere are characterized by:

  ✓ Increased reptile life. Geologists also tell us—
  ✓ The Appalachian ranges in North America formed, and there was—
  ✓ A marked advance of glaciers, especially in the Southern Hemisphere.
  ✓ Earth's 2ⁿᵈ Giant Supercontinent, Pangaea, began to form.

o **The Mesozoic Era:** (245-66.4 million years ago: the 6ᵗʰ Day of Creation). *Mesozoic* means middle animal. Scientists have named the Era that followed the Paleozoic Era and preceded the Cenozoic Era, the Mesozoic Era. It has been divided into three major periods: the Triassic, the Jurassic, and the Cretaceous. All three were dominated by giant reptiles.

- *The Triassic Period.* (From 245-208 million years ago). *Triassic* means *three*. Named for a threefold division of the rocky strata at its type locality discovered in central Germany. Refers to the oldest i.e., the 1ˢᵗ period of the Mesozoic Era, characterized by:

  ✓ The dominance of reptiles, and the
  ✓ Appearance of primitive tropical trees with palm-like & fern-like foliage.

Earth's 2ⁿᵈ Giant Supercontinent (Pangaea) started forming late on the 5ᵗʰ Day of Creation, during the Permian Period. The final consolidation of Pangaea happened early during the 6ᵗʰ Day at the juncture of the Triassic and Jurassic Periods. Almost as soon as it had formed, Pangaea began to break apart. The breakup of Pangaea in the Middle Jurassic period led to the origin of the Central Atlantic Ocean basin. Thus, the Triassic-Jurassic Juncture in the early part of the 6ᵗʰ Day of Creation marks the beginning of a new cycle of ocean-basin opening, through continental extension, and oceanic closing along subducting oceanic tectonic plates and continental margins. This phase of the Earth's tectonic plate history was marked by Late Triassic–Early Jurassic rifting and Middle Jurassic to Holocene drifting of surface tectonic plates. [555]

- *The Jurassic Period.* (From 208-144 million years ago). *Jurassic* comes from the Jura Mountains (between France and Switzerland) which exhibit a certain type of limestone. Characterized by:

  ✓ The dominance of dinosaurs.

[555] Article: http://www.answers.com/topic/triassic-period#ixzz1ApfgZUiw   McGraw-Hill Science & Technology Encyclopedia:Triassic:

- *The Cretaceous Period.* (From 144-66.4 million years ago). From the Greek *creta*, for chalk. Characterized by:

  ✓ The dying out of toothed birds (such as the Archeopteryx — cf. Chapter 22).
  ✓ The dying out of dinosaurs.
  ✓ The development of the 1st mammals.
  ✓ The development of flowering plants and,
  ✓ The deposit of chalk beds.

- **The Cenozoic Era:** (66.4 *million years ago to the present:* the 6th Day of Creation). *Cenozoic* means new or recent animal life and designates the geological era which follows the Mesozoic Era and extends to the present. The Cenozoic Era is characterized by the development and dominance of mammals. The Cenozoic Era is further divided into the 'Tertiary and Quaternary Periods.'

  - *The Tertiary Period:* (from 66.4-1.6 million years ago). *Tertiary* means third and designates the 1st period of the Cenozoic Era or its system of rocks. This period is further divided into the Paleogene and Neogene systems.

    A. **The Paleogene System** is subdivided into the Paleocene, Eocene, and Oligocene Epochs.

    ➤ *The Paleocene Epoch:* (from 66.4-57.8 million years ago). *Paleocene* means recent-ancient. Paleocene is the geologic name assigned to layers of rock with certain distinctive characteristics and distinguishing fossils that are positioned between two strata, one deeper (older) and another nearer the surface (younger) which have other fossils and characteristics. The Paleocene layer contains the fossils of the Earth's — 1st giant mammals.

    ➤ *The Eocene Epoch:* (from 57.8-36.6 million years ago). *Eocene* means new-dawn, and designates the earliest time of the Tertiary Period in the Cenozoic Era when:

      ✓ Mammals became the dominant animals.
      ✓ Also, the fossils of the earliest grasses are found in this layer of rock.

    ➤ *The Oligocene Epoch:* (from 36.6-23.7 million years ago). *Oligocene* means small-recent and designates the 2nd Epoch of the Tertiary Period in the Cenozoic Era characterized by the development of the:

      ✓ Higher mammals which were much smaller than the giant mammals of the Paleocene Epoch.

B. **The Neogene System** (23.7-1.6 million years ago) is subdivided into the Miocene, & Pliocene Epochs. The rocks of the Neogene System show —

✓ Considerable development of mammals and birds. (The fossils of most other forms showed very little change).
✓ A time in which some continental movements occurred. (The most significant being the connection of North and South America which happened in the late Pliocene Epoch).
✓ Also, climates cooled during the Neogene culminating in the continental glaciation that occurred in the Quaternary Period that followed.[556]

The Neogene System is further subdivided into the Miocene and Pliocene Epochs.

➤ *The Miocene Epoch:* (From 23.7-5.3 million years ago). *Miocene* means less new. Characterized by:

✓ The building of mountain ranges in Europe, Asia, and South America.
✓ The development of larger mammals than those in the Oligocene Epoch.
✓ And the appearance of the earliest hominids (a primate belonging to a family: Chimps, gorillas, humans, and orangutans make up the family Hominidae).

➤ *The Pliocene Epoch:* (from 5.3-1.6 million years ago). *Pliocene* means "more new." By the beginning of the Pliocene Epoch, the outlines of North America were almost the same as today. During this epoch, the mountain ranges of North America formed (the Cascades, Rockies, and Sierra Nevada). The Appalachians are older, having formed in the Paleozoic Era. The Colorado Plateau was uplifted. There was also activity in the mountains of Alaska and in the Great Basin ranges of Nevada and Utah.

In Europe the Pliocene Sea covered small portions of the northwest part of the European continent, as well as a large area around the present Mediterranean Sea. A number of volcanoes were active, among them Vesuvius and Etna. Considerable mountain building occurred in Europe as well, including the folding and up-thrusting of the Alps. The climate of the Pliocene was markedly cooler and drier than that of the Miocene and foreshadowed the glacial climates of the Pleistocene epoch. The life of the Pliocene was very similar to today.[557] Thus, the Pliocene Epoch is characterized by —

[556] Article: http://www.answers.com/topic/neogene#ixzz1ArO17HXv : Neogene
[557] Article: http://www.infoplease.com/ce6/sci/A0839380.html#ixzz1ArAdfzhW: Pliocene epoch

    ✓ The development of modern plants and animals.
    ✓ By the increased size of mammals.
    ✓ By global climatic cooling that led to the Ice Ages of the Pleistocene Epoch,
    ✓ And by the formation of mountain ranges in western portions of North and South America, and on the European continent.

- *The Quaternary Period*: (1.6 million years ago to the present).
  1. The Pleistocene Epoch (from 1.6 million—10,000 B.C. ~12,000 years ago). *Pleistocene* means most new. This epoch was characterized by—
  2. The rise and recession of massive continental ice sheets of the Earth's most recent Ice Age,
  3. And the appearance of the Earth's earliest humans (Homo sapiens). (**)
  4. The huge ice sheets that had developed over the northern and western parts of North America and most of Scandinavia were at their maximum geographic extent about 18,000 years ago, during the Pleistocene Epoch. However, they were in full retreat by 14,000 years before the present.[558]

  > *The Holocene Epoch* (from 10,000 years BC to the present). *Holocene* means "whole-recent." The Holocene epoch thus designates the most recent epoch of geologic time. The Holocene Epoch began at the end of the last Ice Age about 10,000 B.C. (~12,000 years ago). The early phase of the Holocene was geologically the most eventful. The landscape near the margins of the glaciers was unstable and very dynamic. As the Pleistocene ice sheets melted, enormous volumes of water, stored as glacier ice for many thousands of years, returned to the oceans via "meltwater" rivers and streams.
  >
  > As the ice sheets shrank, sea levels rose an average of 426 feet, drowning the continental margins and closing many land-bridges, including the land-bridge across the Bering Strait between Asia and North America that had enabled humans to migrate to the Americas. The great weight of the massive glaciers had caused a marked degree of depression of the Earth's surface crust. As the ice sheets waned, the Earth's crust again rose, rebounding from the release of the weight of thousands of meters of glacier ice, creating uplifted shoreline features and sediments. Parts of the Hudson Bay and Scandinavia were uplifted several hundred meters. Maximum uplift occurred in the early Holocene, but uplift continues even today although at much slower pace.
  >
  > **Most importantly, the Holocene Epoch has been characterized by Global Warming. An epoch of Global Warming that began 12,000 years ago is the seminal cause of**

---

[558] Article: http://www.answers.com/topic/pleistocene#ixzz1AqwzmlTc: Pleistocene

the development of human civilization, and the complex agricultural, industrial, and technological societies of today.[559]

Summary Points:

- The purpose of this chapter has been to highlight some of the major things science has discovered about the changes the Earth went through during the last *Three Days of Creation.*

- What modern science says about when life appeared on the Earth and what changes it underwent as the Earth changed has also been examined in the most basic and summary way in order to present 'The Big Picture' without becoming bogged down in endless detail.

- The attempt to catalogue these events and changes has proved to be a daunting task.

- Some of you may feel this chapter contains too many details. However, there is a fine balance between too many facts and not enough.

- No doubt, some (and perhaps much) controversy may result over some of the events that are cataloged. For example, some published articles disagree about which period of the Paleozoic Era the Appalachian Mountains formed.

- The voyage of discovery that science is on will change what we think we know as new discoveries are made and scientists who have differing opinions eventually reach a consensus. That is how science works.

- The next few chapters will look at what the Bible says about the 5th and 6th Days of Creation.

- Hopefully, after you have grasped the basic information of this chapter, you will see that modern science agrees with the Bible about the sequences of development of the Earth and its life-forms.

- The Bible doesn't say anything about geology. Perhaps this is because it was written for all men in all times and the first people for whom the Bible was written would have been mystified by what we now think is common knowledge about how our planet evolved.

- The main topics of this chapter are:

  - ✓ Plate Tectonics,
  - ✓ Two Supercontinents in Earth's history,
  - ✓ And The Geologic Timetable.

- I have made a Table that compares the times in the Geologic Timetable to the Biblical Six Days of Creation. It appears on the last page of this chapter. My table maybe the only one of its kind in existence. So far as I know, no one else has attempted this. The format is mine. It is not drawn 'to scale.' The main events and life-forms that modern science says appeared in each eon, period and epoch are included.

---

[559] Article: http://www.answers.com/topic/holocene#ixzz1AqwzmlTc: Holocene
(**) Science and the Bible define 'man' differently. This will be discussed when we reach the 6th day.

- When you look at the last chart in this chapter it is extremely important that you understand the following salient points.

  - ✓ **There are only two "Ages" in <u>my</u> Geologic Timetable**, the Precambrian & the Phanerozoic Ages.
  - ✓ **I renamed the Phanerozoic Eon — "The Phanerozoic Age," and thus divided Geologic Time into (1) the Age of Invisible Life (i.e., The Precambrian Age) and (2) the Age of Visible Life (i.e., The Phanerozoic Age).**
  - ✓ All life in the **Precambrian Age was microscopic** (invisible to unaided vision).
  - ✓ No animal life existed in the Precambrian Age. **This is something Darwin did not know.**
  - ✓ When Animals first appeared (in the Phanerozoic Age), **they were the first visible forms of life!**
  - ✓ **Phanerozoic means 'visible animals.'**
  - ✓ The Cambrian fossils that were discovered in Darwin's "day" were the earliest visible life-forms that appeared on the Earth.
  - ✓ The Cambrian Period is the point in Geologic Time when the Phanerozoic Age began.
  - ✓ The Bible only mentions the making and forming of visible life.
  - ✓ Visible life-forms would have been the only life-forms that Biblical man would have understood.
  - ✓ The first visible life-forms mentioned in the Bible were made on the 5th Day. On this, the Bible and science agree.
  - ✓ **Darwin was not aware the 1st life on Earth was microscopic.**
  - ✓ **Earth's 1st microscopic life-forms were discovered by Professor Barghoorn almost a century after Darwin died.**

I created the Chart on the next page. It compares the Geologic Timetable to the Biblical Six Days of Creation. Please Note: The Holocene Epoch (the Epoch in which Adam lived and we live) started approximately 12,000 years ago, or 10,000 BC. That point in time is noted in the time column as "0.01" and was $0.01 \times 10^6 = 10,000$ years BC (Before Christ). So it is that the Holocene Epoch (the epoch in which we live), began 10,000 years Before the birth of Jesus Christ.

AGE	EON	ERA	PERIOD	EPOCH and LIFE		LIFE	Time	6 DAYS of CREATION
P H A N E R O Z O I C A G E		C E N O Z O I C	Quaternary Period	Holocene: Bow & Arrow		Humans	~0.01	Adam—Present
				Pleistocene Man-like Hominids: Flake/Blade-Tools		Atlatl	~1.6	6th Day
			Tertiary Period	Pliocene Modern animals & Core/Flake-Tools/ Hand-ax		plants appear	~5.3	
				Miocene Earliest Hominids			~23.7	
				Oligocene Higher mammals			~36.6	
				Eocene Mammals dominate			~57.8	
				Paleocene 1st Giant Mammals				
		M E S O Z O I C	Cretaceous	1st Mammals & Trees (Dinosaurs & toothed birds Die out)		Meteor Impact?	~66.4	
			Jurassic	1st birds / Dinosaurs dominate		Pangaea ends	~144	
			Triassic	Reptiles dominate. Pangaea starts breaking up		Permian-Triassic Extinction	~208	
		P A L E O Z O I C	Permian	Reptiles increase		Pangaea forms	~250	5TH Day
			Pennsylvanian	Coal deposits			~286	
			Mississippian	Reptiles & 1st winged insects			~320	
			Devonian	1st Amphibians & earliest known Dinosaurs			~360	
			Silurian	1st Land Plants, Animals & Wingless insects			~408	
			Ordovician	1st Fish			~438	
			Cambrian	1st appearance of VISIBLE animals in the fossil record— The Cambrian Explosion of Life.		Global Warming After Rodinia broke up	~505 ~543	
P R E C A M B R I A N A G E			Neoproterozoic Eon [Rodinia breaks up: Ediacaran Fauna Appear. The Cryogenian Age (Snowball Earth)			Eukaryotes Dominate	~570	Late 4th & Early 5th Day
			Mesoproterozoic Eon (Oxygen levels rise to today's levels : Rodinia forms)			Eukaryotes	~900	4th Day
			Paleoproterozoic Eon (continent formation continues: Stromatolites caused Oxygen levels to rise)			Eukaryotes	~1600	3rd Day
			Archean Eon (1st continents form) & Earth's 1st Life Forms → Prokaryotes & Archea (Early 3rd Day)			Cyanobacteria & Archea	~2500 ~3800	Late 2nd & Early 3rd Day
			Hadean Eon [Hellish] (Earth & our Solar System Form)				~4550	End 3.75 Billion yrs. ago Late 2nd Day

⇑

*~Time is not to scale.
Time in Millions of Years.

2nd Day
Start 7.75 Billion yrs. ago

Genesis 1:3 Then God said, 'Let there be light,' and there was light.
Genesis 1:2 (c) And the Spirit (Wind) of God was hovering over the face of the waters.
Genesis 1:2 (b) And Darkness was upon the face of the deep.
Genesis 1:2 (a) And the Earth was without form and void.
(The Beginning/The Singularity) Genesis 1:1 In the beginning God created the heavens and the earth

End 7.75 Billion yrs. ago
Day One
Start 15.75 Billion yrs. ago

START HERE AND READ TO THE TOP.

❖
CHAPTER 13: THE 5TH DAY
Life with a Living Soul

"Conflicts between science and the Bible arise from either a lack of scientific knowledge, or a defective understanding of the Bible" (Maimonides 12th Century A.D.)[560] *Sometimes — Both! (O. David)*

INTRODUCTION

We are going to talk about two examples that illustrate the truth of this statement that was made by one of the most prestigious and influential Jewish sages of all times. Until recently, there have been two conflicts between Science and the Bible that concern the 5th Day of Creation.

The first came from *a mistranslation of one Hebrew word.* That mistranslation has persisted in *all* the English translations of the Bible since the publication of the King James Version in 1611 AD. The ancient Hebrew word for *'winged insects'* was at some time *mistranslated* as *'birds.'* Thus, English translations of the Bible erroneously say God created birds on the 5th Day of Creation. Scientific discoveries have revealed birds were created on the 6th Day.

The second mistake involves *both* a *mistranslation* of the original Hebrew *and a lack of scientific knowledge.* The words that were mistranslated were *'taninim gedolim.'* Once the true meaning of *'taninim gedolim'* was discovered, *a conflict with science was uncovered.* That conflict has only recently been resolved. The argument has been recently made that the *'taninim gedolim'* refer to the *progenitors* of the terrible GIANT reptiles that appeared on the 6th Day that we now call — *"Dinosaurs."* Science has discovered *the progenitors of the Dinosaurs* were in fact *created on the 5th Day.*

The truth of the matter is — English translators of the Bible had no idea what type of animal the Hebrew Torah was talking about in Genesis 1:21. When we get to the discussion of that verse, you will see various English translations name seven different animals — from whales to alligators and from jackals to dragons! Science has *proved* the Dinosaurs first appeared in the *Triassic Period, on the 6th Day of Creation.*[561] The Dinosaurs were *terrible GIANT reptiles.* But scientists now believe they evolved from a smaller *progenitor* that appeared on the 5th Day of Creation. Just recently, the correct translation of the Hebrew Torah has brought about a convergence of agreement between Science and the Bible. So, the conflict which resulted from *a mistranslation of two Hebrew words, and a lack of scientific knowledge,* now seems to have been resolved. As it turns out, very recent scientific discoveries have now placed *the origin* of the *progenitors of the Dinosaurs* squarely in the middle of the 5th Day of Creation. The most recent discovery was published in October of 2010.

So, a mistranslation of one Hebrew word in English Bibles has led people to *incorrectly* believe birds were created on the 5th Day (while science has discovered *"winged insects"—not birds*—were created on the 5th Day). And the true meaning of

---

[560] Schroeder The Science of God Chapter 1 p 3
[561] Articles: USGS—1st Dinosaurs: Eoraptor: http://pubs.usgs.gov/gip/dinosaurs/when.html & http://www.newscientist.com/article/dn9927-faq-dinosaurs.html : FAQ: Dinosaurs

'taninim gedolim' still remains a mystery to most translators of English versions of the Torah.

OUTLINE FOR THIS CHAPTER

I.   A comparison of an English translation of the 5th Day with the Hebrew-English translation of the Interlinear Bible.
II.   General comments.
III.   Commentary on *'Then (And) God said.'*
IV.   Discussion of Genesis 1:20.
V.   Discussion of Genesis 1:21.
VI.   Remarks concerning Genesis 1:22 and 1:23.

So now, let's get to it.

THE 5TH DAY

The 5th Day: 24hrs of God's Time	Started ¾ Billion years ago	Ended ¼ Billion years ago
God's Time Perspective	Earth-years before Adam	Earth-years before Adam

The 5th Day lasted ½ Billion (500 Million) Earth-years: Earth's Time Perspective. [562]

I.   A COMPARISON OF THE NEW AMERICAN STANDARD BIBLE VERSION OF THE 5TH DAY WITH THE HEBREW-ENGLISH TRANSLATION OF THE INTERLINEAR BIBLE.

The following is the Biblical account of the events of the 5th Day: (*from the NASB*[563])

> [20]*"Then God said, 'Let the waters <u>teem</u> with <u>swarms</u> of living creatures, and let <u>birds</u> fly above the earth in the open expanse of the heavens.' (Gen. 1:20)*

> [21]*And God created <u>the great sea monsters</u>, and every living creature that moves, with which the waters <u>swarmed</u> after their kind, and every <u>winged</u> <u>bird</u> after its kind; and God saw that it was good. (Gen. 1:21)*

> [22]*And God blessed them, saying, "Be fruitful and multiply, and fill the waters in the seas, and let <u>birds</u> multiply on the earth." (Gen. 1:22)*
> [23]*And there was evening and there was morning, a 5th Day."*
> *(Gen. 1:23)*

Now let's look at what *the Interlinear Bible* says about the 5th Day of Creation. (The Interlinear Bible translates the Hebrew text of the Old Testament into our modern-day English vernacular.) Unlike the King James Version of the Bible, the Interlinear Bible translation of the Old Testament is not based on the Latin Vulgate of St. Jerome or the

---

[562] Schroeder The Science of God Chapter 4 (Table) p 67
[563] NASB—New American Standard Bible

Septuagint. In the Interlinear Bible, the Hebrew text of the Old Testament is the *Masoretic*[564] text.

> [20]*"And God said: 'Let the waters <u>swarm</u> with the <u>swarmers</u>, having a <u>soul</u> of life; and let the <u>birds</u> fly over the Earth, on the face of the expanse of the heavens.' (Gen. 1:20)*
>
> [21]*And God created <u>the great sea animals</u>, and all that creeps, <u>having a living soul</u>, which <u>swarmed</u> the waters according to its kind, and every <u>bird</u> <u>with</u> <u>wing</u> according to its kind. And God saw that it was good. (Gen. 1:21)*
>
> [22]*And God blessed them saying, 'Be fruitful and multiply, and fill the waters in the seas, and let <u>birds</u> multiply on the Earth.'*
> *(Gen. 1:22)*
> [23]*And there was evening and there was morning, a 5th Day."*
> *(Gen. 1:23)*
> (The underlining in both versions is mine.)

By now you have noticed both translations mention *'birds'* and *'great sea monsters/sea animals.'* This appears to contradict what I said in the Introduction to this Chapter. That is because, (*unfortunately*) *the Interlinear Bible makes the same mistake other English translations of the Bible make.* I beg your patience on this point for right now. The following discussion will clarify.

II.   **GENERAL COMMENTS**

In four short verses on the 5th Day, the Bible says The Creator created the Earth's first visible animal life-forms. He started creating life in the *waters*, where He caused *'swarmers with a soul of life to swarm.'* Then He continued His creation of life with life-forms that could *fly* over the Earth in Earth's sky.

In Chapter One of Genesis, Biblical *Time-before-Adam is so highly compressed* that the Bible simply does not take the time to describe exactly what happened or provide any detail of the sequence of creation that caused life to advance from the simple to the complex — except in the broadest of terms. The Bible only lists some broad categories of the life-forms Elohim created on the 5th and 6th Days of Creation. The only exceptions to this are the specific mention of cattle and Adam on the 6th Day. The Bible is so eager, so fervent to get on with the mention of Elohim's penultimate creation on the 6th Day (the first man, Adam), and the story of mankind[565] that the second of these rapid-fire biblical statements of the creation of life on the 5th Day adds only three cursory and quasi-enigmatic details about the kinds of life He created on that day. He created:

- The great sea animals (monsters),
- All that creeps (every living creature that moves),
- And all those that fly.

---

[564] *Masoretic*: of the Masora, i.e., all of the accumulated Jewish tradition concerning the correct Hebrew text of the Old Testament.
[565] Schroeder The Science of God Chapter 4 p 32 d & 33 a

The *'after their kind, or according to their kind'* statements tell us (on the 5th Day), Elohim created *large groups* (basic categories) of animals on the Earth that could *swarm* in the waters and *fly* in the sky. These brief statements do not provide any specifics or details and leave much to our imagination. From *'man'* onward (i.e., from Gen. 1:26 through the rest of the Old Testament, and through all of the New Testament), biblical time is *time as we know it.* It is no longer compressed.[566] However, since the ancient Hebrew language contains multiple layers of meaning, *the Genesis Code* will help us gain a deeper and more complete understanding of what Elohim did on the 5th Day.

With the information modern science has added to this tale of our origins, which were discussed in the preceding chapter, you will be able to see the events of the 5th Day (that are sequenced in the Bible), precisely coincide with the chain of events modern science has cataloged in the Geologic Timetable. When you read the following discussion, you will find it helpful to frequently refer to the Geologic Timetable at the end of the last chapter.

Let us continue this discussion with an examination of each verse of the Bible's account of the 5th Day in the order of its appearance.

III.   COMMENTARY ON "THEN (AND) GOD SAID."

This commentary has already been covered in Chapter 8. Please refer to Chapter 8 (in Book I).

The discussion of *"Then God said,"* begins with the discussion of *"The Light of Jesus Christ, in Chapter 8 of Book I."* The phrase *"Then God said"* in the 1st chapter of the Book of Genesis signals the *abrupt sudden punctuated Divine developments God commanded on each and every "Day" of Creation by pronouncements of His spoken Word.*

DISCUSSION OF GENESIS 1:20

THIS IS WHAT GEN. 1:20 SAYS IN THE NEW AMERICAN STANDARD BIBLE (NASB) TRANSLATION.

*20Then God said, "Let the waters <u>teem</u> with <u>swarms</u> of living
creatures, & let <u>birds</u> fly above the earth in the open expanse
of the heavens.*

THIS WHAT GEN. 1:20 SAYS IN THE INTERLINEAR BIBLE (TIB) TRANSLATION.
*20 And God said, "Let the waters <u>swarm</u> with the <u>swarmers</u>, **having
a <u>soul</u> of life**; and let the <u>birds</u> fly over the Earth, on the face of the
expanse of the heavens."*

So, where does all of the creative activity on the 5th Day occur? It occurs in two places — in Earth's waters and in Earth's sky. And exactly what occurs? There is a sudden appearance of visible living creatures — *first* in the waters, and *second* in the sky. In the *New American Standard Bible*, the English word *teem* is an intransitive verb that means: *"to be full of an extremely large number of people, animals, or things in a place."* Since the Bible does not mention people until the 6th Day, we know the living creatures created on the 5th Day are living animal life-forms (exclusive of people), that <u>teemed</u> in <u>swarms</u> in Earth's <u>waters</u>, and <u>flew</u> in <u>swarms</u> in Earth's <u>sky</u>.

---

[566] Schroeder The Science of God Chapter 4 p 33 a

Now, let's take a look at the *Interlinear Bible English translation* of the ancient Hebrew script. Just to give you an idea of how one uses the Interlinear Bible, I will explain the process of how one derives, *'Let the waters swarm with the swarmers,'* from the ancient Hebrew words. The Interlinear Bible takes the *Jewish Bereshit Hebrew text* (see illustration in Chapter 3) and prints the English meaning *below* each *Bereshit Hebrew* word. *Above* each Hebrew word a *number* is printed. To find *the Jewish-English transliterated equivalent* of each *Hebrew* word, one can look up that number in the *Hebrew & Chaldee Dictionary* that is part of *Strong's Exhaustive Concordance of the Bible*. In this way one can discover not only the transliterated Hebrew word, but also the deeper and expanded dictionary meanings of each *Hebrew* word.

It is important to take the ancient Hebrew script and convert it *into the Jewish-English transliterated equivalent* for three reasons. *First*, the transliterated words use the English alphabet. *Second,* we can read the transliterated text from left to right (i.e., the same direction we read the English language), and *third*, we can type the transliterated Jewish-English script on our computers and typewriters. This makes it easier for us to read and transcribe the words even if their proper pronunciation may remain a mystery.

The translation of the Hebrew into English in the Interlinear Bible for Genesis 1:20 says, "Let the waters (*mayim*) swarm (*sharah*) with swarmers (*sherets*)—taken from (*sharats*)." *Mayim, sharah* and *sherets/sharats* are the Jewish-English *transliterated* words for the original ancient Hebrew script of the key words in the first phrase of Genesis 1:20. In the preceding sentence I placed *one* English equivalent next to *mayim, sharah, and sherets/sharats*. The word *sharah* has a number of possible meanings, some of which are to wiggle, *swarm*, abound, breed, bring forth, increase abundantly, creep and move. Creeping brings forth the vision of moving along with the body close to the ground, moving slowly, slithering, or crawling stealthily. *Sharah* is commonly translated as — *to swarm*. The word *sherets* is most often taken to mean *an active mass of minute animals, creeping things, or moving creatures or tiny moving animals.* Hence the English translation in the Interlinear Bible says, *'Let the waters swarm with swarmers.'* This is the last time I will explain *the process*. From now on, the transliterated Hebrew word will simply be spelled out without boring you with the process one has to go through to find the transliterated Hebrew words.

The word *swarm* is also an *intransitive verb* which can refer to a gathering of a mass of life-forms that literally *over-run everything*. English dictionary definitions of *swarm* and *swarmers* say the words can refer to large groups of *water insects* or large groups *of animal-life that move in a confused or disorderly manner*. So, we can imagine the Bible is saying — an infinite variety of aquatic animals, fish, amphibians, and other creatures such as worms, reptiles, and water insects were created and flourished in the Earth's waters on the 5th Day. *A swarm of swarmers* can also apply to masses of infinite varieties of flying insects *in the Earth's sky* (such as bees or gnats and other flying insects such as dragonflies, etcetera). *Intransitive verbs do not take a direct object*. The lack of a direct object is an indication *all* the life-forms brought forth on the 5th Day were *in a great abundance* and *in a large variety*. This interpretation agrees with one of the meanings of the Hebrew words *sherets/*and *sharats* — *"Small or tiny life-forms that breed and increase abundantly."*

THE "SOUL OF LIFE" IN GEN. 1:20 (THE INTERLINEAR BIBLE)

*"...**having a soul** (i.e., a Nefesh) **of life...**"*

ONCE AGAIN, THE GENESIS CODE REVEALS A DEEPER MEANING OF THE ANCIENT HEBREW SCRIPT.

This small detail (**sarcasm**), that the animals created on the 5th Day had a *soul*, is omitted from other English translations of the Bible. However, *the concept that animals have a soul is extremely important.* The Hebrew word for *soul* that the Torah uses in Gen. 1:20 is *'nefesh.'* Hebrew has two words for soul — *nefesh* and *neshama*. Both are *Divine Gifts of God*. The *nefesh is the soul of animal life.* Elohim placed this soul of animal life (this *nefesh*), in *all animals, including man*. It is a bit of *divinity* Elohim placed in *all* living animals. *The second Divine creation*, the *neshama*, is mentioned later, on the 6th Day, when Elohim created *the first man* (the first human) in Genesis 1:26. *The neshama is unique to humankind.* Humans have both the *nefesh* and the *neshama*. According to ancient Hebrew belief, the mention of the neshama *only in relation to Adam* (who was the next to last creation of Elohim on the 6th Day), means — all other animals have *only the nefesh.*[567] We'll talk more about *the neshama* and how it differs from *the nefesh* when we discuss the *creation of Adam* on the 6th Day. I will talk about that in Chapter 23: *The 6th Day—Man "Made" in "His Image,"* in Book III.

THE "BIRD" CONUNDRUM
20 *"And let the birds ('oaf') fly over the Earth"*...(Gen. 1:20)
21 *"and every bird ('oaf') with wing according to its kind"*...(Gen. 1:21)
22 *"and let birds ('oaf') multiply on the Earth"*...(Gen. 1:22)

According to Dr. Schroeder, English translations of Genesis 1:20-22 mistranslate the ancient Hebrew word, *'oaf'* (also spelled *oof*, and *ofe*).[568] English Bibles translate that word as: *"a bird that flieth, or a flying fowl."* Dr. Schroeder says *Oaf* actually means: *"a winged animal."* [569] Sadly, the Interlinear Bible also fails to make this distinction. Dr. Schroeder says: *"The Hebrew word for bird is not oaf."* According to Dr. Schroeder: *"The Hebrew word for 'bird' is 'tsepoor.'"* [570] We get this from *the Flood-Story* in the 7th Chapter of Genesis (i.e., the flood for which Noah had been building his ark). Genesis 7:13-15 describes Noah loading his Ark with animals.

> 13"*In this same day Noah and Shem and Ham and Japheth, the sons of Noah, and Noah's wife and the three wives of his sons with them, went into the ark.*

14*They, and every animal after its kind, and every beast after its kind, and every creeping thing that creeps on the earth after its kind; and every fowl after its kind, every bird ('**tsepoor, or tsippor'**) of every wing. And they went into Noah and to the ark, two and two of all flesh, in which is the breath of life (Gen. 7:13-14, The Interlinear Bible)."*

---

567 Schroeder The Science of God Chapter 9 p 139 e
568 Schroeder The Science of God Chapter 6 p 94 b,c.
569 Schroeder The Science of God Chapter 6 p 94b
570 Schroeder The Science of God Chapter 6 p 94 b

According to Dr. Schroeder, in this scripture, *the Hebrew word the Interlinear Bible correctly translates (*in this case*) as 'bird' is not 'oaf' — it is 'tsepoor.'* Tsepoor can also be spelled other ways.[571] In this scripture, English translations of the Bible (including the Interlinear Bible) *correctly* translate the Hebrew word 'tsepoor' as *'bird.'* According to Dr. Gerald L. Schroeder, current scientific theory holds that the first appearance of life-forms *that had wings were **not** birds. Factually, the fossil data shows the first winged-life forms were water insects which originated about 330 million years ago.*[572,573,574] 330 million years ago falls within the time frame of the 5th Day of Creation and relates to *the Mississippian period of the Paleozoic Era* when small reptiles and the 1st winged insects appeared (cf. the Chart at the end of the last Chapter). The 1st reptiles appeared slightly earlier, in the Devonian Period (408—360 million years ago) and are thought to be the progenitors of the Dinosaurs that appeared in the Jurassic Period (208—144 million years ago), on the 6th Day.

THE 1ST INSECTS ON EARTH WERE WINGLESS & APPEARED NEAR THE MIDDLE OF THE 5TH DAY OF CREATION.

According to Dr. David A. Kendall,[575] *the oldest insect fossils (*discovered so far*) are tiny imprints of *wingless insects* found in sandstone rocks of the *mid-Devonian Period* (which are 380 million years old — on the 5th Day). Dr. Kendall also says these earliest fossils closely resemble modern springtails (*Collembola*), but even by this time, they show most of the specialized evolutionary features that characterize the present-day members of this insect order (e.g., *the reflexed 'tail' used for jumping*). It is Dr. Kendall's opinion this would suggest the insect-stock from which they arose must have *already* been very old in *Devonian times. He thinks the first primitive wingless insects probably appeared much earlier, at least in the Silurian Period, around 410-440 million years ago.*[576] The Silurian Period was that part of the 5th Day of Creation when the 1st wingless insects, macroscopic land-plants, and land-animals (larger than the animals of the Cambrian Period) appeared.

WINGED INSECTS APPEARED LATER.

As just stated, Earth's 1st insects were the wingless insects that appeared somewhere between 410-380 million years ago in the Silurian/Devonian Periods of the 5th Day. Dr. Schroeder states there is no fossil evidence of any life-form with *primitive wings* prior to the appearance of *the fully developed winged insects* 330 million years ago. The fossil record tells us there was *an abrupt and sudden leap* from wingless insects to winged insects that had a wingspan of 30 centimeters as soon as they appeared. Since about 2.2 cm. equals one inch, 30 cm. translates to a wingspan of 13.6 inches! According to Dr. Schroeder, *'that is quite a mosquito.'*[577] Dr. Kendall's article shows a picture of a huge archaic dragonfly-like insect named the *Meganeura* whose fossils show a wingspan that measures 70 cm! That's a wingspan of 31.8 inches! Now, that is quite a dragonfly! Its picture in Kendall's article is a drawing that was reconstructed from fossils found in rocks

---

[571] The Interlinear Bible & The Hebrew & Chaldee Dictionary in Strong's Exhaustive Concordance of the Bible.

[572] Schroeder: The Science of God Chapter 6 p 94 b

[573] J. Kaiser, "A new Theory of the Insect Wing Origins," *Science* 266:363, 1994

[574] J. Marden and M. Kramer, "Surface Skimming Stoneflies: A Possible Intermediate Stage in Flight Evolution," *Science 266:427, 1994*

[575] Article Query—"Insects & Other Arthropods" Select & click on "Insect Fossils." Articles by David Kendall Phd

[576] Article: Insect Fossils: by David A. Kendall, BSc, PhD, © 2010 http://www.kendalluk.com/fossil.html

[577] Schroeder The Science of God Chapter 6 p 94 c

of *the Carboniferous period* that are about 320 million years old.[578] 320 million years ago corresponds to the beginning of *the Pennsylvanian Period* of the *Paleozoic Era.* The *Carboniferous period* of the Paleozoic Era is another name applied to the time span 360-286 million years ago. (See the 'Geologic Time Scale' in Chapter 12 and my Chart at the end of Chapter 12). The Carboniferous encompasses *both the Mississippian and the Pennsylvanian Periods* when great forests and swamps abounded that nature later turned into enormous coal deposits.

WINGED BIRDS DEVELOPED ON THE 6TH DAY OF CREATION.

Dr. Schroeder's knowledge of the ancient Hebrew language helps to clear up an apparent discrepancy between what most English versions of the Bible (*including the Interlinear Bible*) say happened on the 5th Day by claiming that winged birds appeared at that time. The fossil record shows *winged birds appeared in the Mesozoic Era* (specifically in the *Jurassic Period*), which started 208 million years ago and ended 144 million years ago. The Jurassic Period corresponds to a time that occurred early on the 6th Day of Creation and is the period when dinosaurs dominated. Many scientists believe the *Archaeopteryx* is the earliest undisputed bird.[579] Some claim the few fossils of the archaeopteryx that have been discovered suggest this animal is a cross between a reptile and a bird that dates to the Jurassic Period. It may have been a poor flier but fly it did. We will talk about the Archaeopteryx when we reach the scriptures that talk about the 6th Day of Creation (in Chapter 22: *The 6th Day—Modern Land Animals, Mammals, & Man-Like Hominids—* at the end of this Book—i.e., Book II).

So, the use of the word *'bird'* in the Interlinear Bible and other English translations of Gen. 1:20, 21, & 22 is a *mistranslation* of the Hebrew word *'oaf.'* The *oaf were not birds. They were flying insects.* God created the flying insects during *the Mississippian Period of the Paleozoic Era (on the 5th Day).*[580] According to science, *flying birds were not created until the Jurassic Period of the Mesozoic Era*[581,582] *(on the 6th Day).* On this, both science and *the Genesis Code* agree. *The Jurassic Period was when the 1st Birds appeared, and the Dinosaurs dominated.* (cf. with my Chart at the end of Chapter 12).

The mistranslation of the Hebrew word (*oaf*) in English Bibles is a good example of Maimonides' claim in the 12th century AD, that "*Conflicts between science and the Bible arise from either a lack of scientific knowledge or a defective understanding of the Bible.*"[583] In this case, because *oaf* was mistranslated as *birds,* the conflict on this point was due to a mistaken understanding of the Bible.

IV.   DISCUSSION OF GENESIS 1:21

[21]*"And God created <u>the great sea animals</u>, and all that creeps." Gen. 1:21*
Some skeptics of the truth of the Bible ask a simple question: *Why aren't Dinosaurs mentioned in the Bible?* Actually, they are. The word *—Dinosaur—* was coined by Sir

---

[578] Article: Insect Fossils: by David A. Kendall, BSc, PhD, © 2010 http://www.kendalluk.com/fossil.html
[579] Schroeder The Science of God Chapter 6 p 95 c and d
[580] Article: Geologic Time—Enchanted Learning.com http://www.enchantedlearning.com/subjects/Geologictime.html
[581] Article: Geologic Time—Enchanted Learning.com http://www.enchantedlearning.com/subjects/Geologictime.html
[582] Article: Truth in Science: Did Birds Evolve from Dinosaurs? By Dr. Marc Surtees
http://www.truthinscience.org.uk/site/content/view/231/65/
[583] Schroeder The Science of God Chapter 1 p 3

Richard Owen in 1841.[584] He combined the Greek word — *'deinos,'* which means *'terrible'* with another Greek word — *'sauros'*— that means *'lizard.'* *'Saur'* is a variant of *'saurus,'* *'sauro,'* or *'sauria.'* He said: *"The Dinosauria were 'terrible lizards.'"* Sir Richard also established the London Natural History Museum in 1881.

So, *"Dinosaur"* is a coined English word that is a composite of two Greek words that mean *'Terrible Lizard.'*[585] The word, *dinosaur,* doesn't appear in the ancient Hebrew script written by Moses, because Moses wrote the Torah in Hebrew. However, Moses used a term that has the same meaning of Sir Richard's word — *Dinosaur.* How do we know this? Let's take a look at four specific verses of scripture, one from Genesis, and three from the Book of Exodus. In Genesis 1:21 the Bible tells us the 5th Day of Creation was *the day* God created (*barah*) the basis for all animal life.[586] The Hebrew text of Gen. 1:21 mentions the *'taninim gedolim.'* They were one of the categories of animals God created on the 5th Day. As you shall see, the word *'category'* is extremely important in this discussion. Dr. Schroeder says: *"If you pick up five different English translations of the Bible, you are likely to find at least five different translations of 'taninim gedolim'"* —

- *Whales,*
- *Alligators,*
- *Sea monsters, the great sea animals, sea serpents,*
- *Jackals, and even*
- *Dragons.*[587]

The correct translation of *'Gedolim'* is easy. Gedolim means **'BIG.'** So, the first *category* of animals mentioned in Genesis 1:21 are the **'BIG TANINIM.'** The meaning of *'taninim'* is more obscure and takes a bit of detective work to uncover. Since the narrative in Exodus is interesting, we'll try to uncover the deeper meaning of *'taninim'* by concentrating on an historical account of something Moses wrote — *something that happened to him.*

GOD TALKED TO MOSES ON MT. HOREB.[588]

The story begins in the 3rd Chapter of Exodus. One day while Moses was pasturing a flock on the slopes of Mt. Horeb (the mountain of God), an Angel of the Lord appeared to him in a blazing fire in the midst of a burning bush that was *not* consumed by the fire.[589] Moses went to investigate this phenomenon. When he did, he encountered God. God called to him from the midst of the burning bush. God identified Himself to Moses as *the God of Abraham, Isaac, and Jacob.* It was in this encounter that God gave Moses a mission that changed his life. God told him to return to Egypt and tell Pharaoh to — *"Let My people go!"* Well now — that caused a problem for Moses. Moses did not want to go! For 40 years, Moses had been a fugitive from Egypt because he had killed an Egyptian who had been beating a Hebrew. Forty years earlier, when Pharaoh found out Moses had

[584] Sir Richard Owen: The man who invented the Dinosaur – BBC by: Tom Mullen www.bbc.com > news > uk-england-lancashire-31623397.
[585] Schroeder The Science of God Epilogue—Well, What about Dinosaurs? p 191 a
[586] Schroeder The Science of God Epilogue—Well, What about Dinosaurs? p 193 b
[587] Schroeder The Science of God Epilogue—Well, What about Dinosaurs? p 193 & 194
[588] In scripture, Mt. Horeb and Mt. Sinai are thought to be the same mountain. —Ref. The Ryrie Bible note on Exodus 3:1
[589] Exodus, Chapter 3. The Angel of the Lord was a theophany — in this case, God Himself!

killed an Egyptian, he tried to kill Moses. That is why Moses fled Egypt and settled in the austere desert-land of Midian.[590]

Moses first objected by telling God he was not worthy to go on this mission. To this, God replied — He would be with him. Moses next asked: *"What should I say to the people of Israel when they ask who sent me?"* God said he should say: *"I AM WHO I AM has sent me."* Then, in the 4th Chapter of Exodus Moses again objected by asking what he should do if the people and Pharaoh did not believe God had sent him. That is when God told Moses He would give him three miracles to perform for Pharaoh. These miracles would convince Pharaoh Moses was indeed God's messenger. It was the *first* of these *three sign-miracles* that gives us — *the deeper meaning of 'taninim.'* This sign-miracle has to do with a miraculous and frightening transformation of Moses' shepherd-staff.

THE STAFF BECOMES A 'NAHASH,' (A SNAKE). EX. 4:3

In Exodus 4:3 God demonstrated to Moses the first sign-miracle God would give him to perform before Pharaoh. God told Moses to throw his shepherd's staff on the ground. When Moses threw his staff on the ground, it became a *'nahash'* — a snake. Moses was frightened and fled from the snake. Then, in Exodus 4:4, God told Moses to pick the snake up by its tail. When he did, it became a shepherd's staff again. I don't think I could have done that! I'm certainly not as brave or trusting as Moses. But then again, what would I have done if God had actually said that to me?

THE STAFF BECOMES A 'TANEEN.' EX. 7:9,10

Now, let's fast forward to the scene in Exodus when Moses and Aaron are before Pharaoh and this sign-miracle was actually performed. In Exodus 7:9 God said to Moses:

> *"When Pharaoh speaks to you saying, 'Work a miracle,' you shall say to Aaron, 'take your staff and throw it down before Pharaoh, that it may become a taneen.'*

In Exodus 7:10, in Pharaoh's presence, and after Pharaoh asked them to *'work a miracle,'* Moses and Aaron did as the Lord commanded. When Aaron threw his staff down before Pharaoh it became *'a taneen'* (also spelled—taninim, tanniyn, tanneen, tanneem, and tanniym). Tanniym, taneen, and tanneem are the plural forms of taninim — the word that appears in Genesis 1:21.[591]

WHEN LATER SPEAKING TO MOSES, GOD CALLS THE STAFF A 'NAHASH.' EX. 7:14-16

In the meantime, Pharaoh is being stubborn and won't let the people go. So, God speaks to Moses and says:

[14]"...Pharaoh's heart is stubborn; he refuses to let the people go. [vs.15]Go to Pharaoh in the morning as he is going out to the water, and station yourself to meet him on the bank of the Nile; and you shall take in your hand the staff that was turned into a 'nahash,' (footnote 592) *[16]and you will say to him, 'The Lord, the God of the Hebrews, sent me to you, saying 'Let My people go, that they may serve Me in the wilderness.' But behold you have not listened until now."*

---

590 Exodus, Chapter 2
591 The Interlinear Bible & The Hebrew & Chaldee Dictionary in Strong's Exhaustive Concordance of the Bible.
592 The Interlinear Bible & The Hebrew & Chaldee Dictionary in Strong's Exhaustive Concordance of the Bible.

This is when God told Moses to warn Pharaoh the Nile River would turn to blood — i.e., the 1st of 10 Plagues.

NOW CONTEMPLATE WHAT THE BIBLE TELLS US ABOUT THE SIGN-MIRACLE OF MOSES' STAFF.

- In Ex. 4:3 the staff became a *nahash*, a snake, when it was thrown to the ground on Mt. Horeb.
- In Ex. 7:9, 10 the staff became a *taneen* when thrown to the ground in front of Pharaoh.
- In Ex. 7:14-16 God said the staff had become a *nahash*, a snake, when it had been thrown to the ground in front of Pharaoh.

Now the obvious questions are:
(1) Why did the staff become a *taneen* when it was thrown to the ground before Pharaoh when it *had become a nahash* the 1st time God told Moses to throw it to the ground on Mt. Horeb?
(2) And (in Ex. 7:14-16) why did God say to Moses — in his next encounter with Pharaoh on the bank of the Nile he should take with him the staff that had become a *nahash* when it was thrown to the ground before Pharaoh? This is especially puzzling because in the actual encounter with Pharaoh the Bible says the staff had become a *taneen* on that particular occasion.

When God said the staff had become a *nahash* when the miracle was performed before Pharaoh and the Bible had previously recorded it had become a *taneen* instead, is extremely important. This indicates — the Bible is telling us something about these two Hebrew words. The Bible is telling us these two words are *related*. And I mean — *"intimately related!"*

THE RIDDLE SOLVED

Dr. Schroeder calls our attention to the fact — no specific animals are named in the first chapter of the Genesis Creation Account. *Man,* and *cattle* are the only exceptions to this rule. The Bible refers to the creatures and animals that were made on the 5th and 6th Days only in the broadest of terms or categories of living things. (For this explanation, the word *"category,"* is an important word to keep in mind). Later, in two of the Exodus accounts, the specific name of an animal is mentioned. That animal is a *snake,* (Ex. 4:3 and Ex. 7:14-16). *Snakes* are a specific *species* of animals that belong to the *phylum* of animals that science has classified as *Reptiles*. Therefore, the name '*taneen*' (Ex. 7:9-10), which is the plural form of '*taninim*' (Gen. 1:21) must be the name of *the basic category* or *large group* (i.e., *or phylum*) of animals to which snakes belong. Since Gen. 1:21 defines the category of animals by calling them '*taninim gedolim,*' the Bible is telling us the proper modern-day meaning should be — '*BIG REPTILES.*' The *Dinosaurs* were the GIANT '*BIG REPTILES*' that dominated early on the 6th Day (i.e., the English meaning of their *Hebrew name*). And they were also '*TERRIBLE LIZARDS*' (the Greek meaning of the English name that Sir Richard Owen coined for them by combining two *Greek words* — *"deinos"* (for terrible), and *"sauria"* (for lizards). So, *Dinosaurs* are mentioned in the Bible, *but the Bible uses their Hebrew name.*[593]

IS THE BIBLE REALLY IMPLYING DINOSAURS WERE CREATED ON THE 5TH DAY?

Dr. Schroeder's academic analysis of the Hebrew linguistics of the Bible is certainly impressive. But is it correct? Until recently, conventional scientific wisdom placed the evolution of dinosaurs in the late *Triassic Period* somewhere around 230 million years ago. That would have been early on the 6th Day of Creation. Conventional scientific wisdom also held that the dinosaurs dominated *the Jurassic Period* (also on the 6th Day: 208—144 million years ago) but had become extinct (died out) sometime during *the Cretaceous Period* (also on the *6th Day:* 144—66.4 million years ago). So, is science right? Is the Bible wrong? Or is Dr. Schroeder's analysis a misinterpretation of the Bible?

THE EARLIEST DINOSAURS LIVED IN THE DEVONIAN PERIOD—ON THE 5TH DAY.

Recent discoveries (in the last decade) have caused scientists *to believe* the first dinosaurs evolved from the *archosaurs,* the *'ruling lizards'* that shared the earth with other families of early reptiles, 250 million years ago in *the late Permian Period of the Paleozoic Era.*[594] According to the Geologic Timetable, the Permian Period was the last period of the Paleozoic Era and extended from 286—245 million years ago (the last part of the 5th Day of Creation). Then additional discoveries caused some scientists to accept a date of 385—380 million years ago as the earliest date for Dinosaurs.[595] However, an even more recent discovery of *fossilized dinosaur footprints* in Poland's Holy Cross Mountains has pushed the known existence of those beasts back to 397 million years ago. If confirmed, this discovery will prompt some revision in the evolutionary consensus.[596] (**) Both 380 million years ago and 397 million years ago would place the existence of *the earliest known dinosaur* to the *Devonian Period of the Paleozoic Era*, which, according to the Geologic Timetable extended from 408-360 million years ago. Folks those dates of 380 and 397 million years ago are right *'smack-kadab'* in the middle of the 5th Day of Creation!

There is an ongoing debate between scientists as to exactly what type of animal actually represents *the earliest known dinosaur, and what kinds of fossils can be accepted as representing the earliest known dinosaurs.* There is no question that the *archosaurs* were the *'ruling lizards'* that shared the earth with other families of early reptiles in the late Permian Period (the 5th Day). And, that the Dinosaurs of the 6th Day evolved from them also seems to be generally accepted. But, whether or not they qualify as an *early dinosaur* is a point of current-day debate. Someday, and perhaps with the evidence of new *as yet undiscovered older fossils*, a consensus will be reached that establishes the very first Dinosaurs were indeed created sometime on the 5th Day. The question seems to be

---

[593] Schroeder The Science of God Epilogue: Well, What about Dinosaurs? p. 193 and 194.

[594] Article: The Great Archosaur Lineage: Crocodiles, dinosaurs, pterosaurs, and many other beasties! http://www.ucmp.berkeley.edu/diapsids/archosauria.html

[595] Article: Query— "The First Tetrapods—The Story of Tetrapod Evolution:" http://dinosaurs.about.com/od/otherprehistoriclife/a/tetrapods.html Article by Bob Strauss

[596] Article: The First Tetrapods—The Story of Tetrapod Evolution: by Bob Strauss http://dinosaurs.about.com/od/otherprehistoriclife/a/tetrapods.html (**) Here is a quote from this article: 'Scientists once agreed that the earliest tetrapods...dated from about 385 to 380 million years ago. That has all changed with the recent discovery, in Poland, of tetrapod track marks dating to 397 million years ago, which has had the effect of "dialing back" the entire evolutionary calendar by a whopping 12 million years. If confirmed, this discovery will prompt some revision in the evolutionary consensus (as well as this article).'

whether or not the *archosaurs* were true Dinosaurs. Nevertheless, no one seems to question they were — *Terrible Big Lizards.* Dr. Schroeder's analysis *seems to be correct.* God did in fact create the big terrible lizards (the *'taninim gedolim'*), on the 5th Day after all. Nevertheless, the fossil evidence tells us they did not become dominant, and they did not morph into the terrible giants *that we all think of* as Dinosaurs until the Jurassic Period of the Mesozoic Era, which was the Period in the 6th Day of Creation (from 208—144 million years ago), when the Giant Dinosaurs dominated. Some of those giants were *true tetrapods* and others were predominately *bipedal* because they had dwarfed upper 'legs.' (By the way: **Archosaurs are members of a subclass of marine reptiles that includes Crocodiles.**)

V.   REMARKS CONCERNING GENESIS 1:22 AND 1:23

We now know *the Genesis Code* has revealed the proper English translation of these two verses is:

[22]And God blessed them saying, "Be fruitful and multiply, and let all the families of all the swarmers fill the oceans and let all the families of swarming, flying insects multiply on the Earth, and swarm through the Earth's sky (Gen. 1:22). [23]And at the end of the 5th Day God was pleased with the additional degree of order He had imposed on the initial chaos of the beginning of His creation (Gen. 1:23).

Verse 23 is that familiar statement that appears at the end of each Day of Creation. It means — the Creator's creative activity on the 5th Day imposed an additional degree of order upon the *'face of the chaos of the beginning.'* Thus ends the Biblical account of the 5th Day of Creation.

THE 5TH DAY OF GENESIS[597] LASTED 500 MILLION EARTH YEARS

Day #	Start of Day 5	End of Day 5	Bible's Description	Scientific Description
Five	750 Million yrs. Before Adam	250 Million yrs. Before Adam	1st animal life swarms in the waters; followed by reptiles & winged animals (Gen.1:20-23	1st multicellular animals— waters swarm with animal life having the basic body plans of all future animals; winged insects appear.

Summary Points:

- The Interlinear Bible and other English translations of the Bible that mention the creation of birds and fowls on the 5th Day — mistranslate the Hebrew word, 'oaf.'
- The 'oaf' were large, winged insects.
- Birds were not created on the 5th Day. But all sorts of large, winged insects were. On this, both modern science and the Genesis Code agree.
- Birds were created on the 6th Day.

---

[597] Schroeder The Science of God Chapter 4 (Table) p 67

- English translations of the Bible that translate 'taninim gedolim' as whales, alligators, sea monsters, great sea animals, and or dragons — are also mistranslations of the Hebrew text.
- The Genesis Code tells us the *'taninim gedolim'* were *'big reptiles.'* They were the *'terrible lizards'* (i.e., *the Greek meaning* of the English "coined" word that *'Dinosaur'* describes).
- It used to be thought the dinosaurs evolved on the 6th Day of Creation. It is true they became dominant on the 6th Day and also suddenly disappeared from the fossil record on the 6th Day.
- However, newly discovered data suggests the earliest known Dinosaurs, (the big terrible lizard-like reptilian ancestors of the terrible GIANT lizards of the Jurassic Period on the 6th Day), were actually created on the 5th Day. I am confident when a scientific consensus is reached, we will see (once again), the 3,300-year-old Hebrew Bible has been right on this point all along.
- The Genesis Code tells us all animals, including man, have an animal soul, the Nefesh. When we study the 6th Day, we will discover the Bible says man also has a Divine gift the other animals do not have. That gift is the *Neshama* — the Hebrew word for the *'God breathed soul that is unique to humans.'*
- The Bible tells us — in addition to the abundant varieties of flying insects and the terrible big reptiles that suddenly appeared on the 5th Day, the waters of the Earth also 'swarmed' with an infinite variety of other visible animal life-forms. In the next chapter, we will talk about what modern science has learned about these other life-forms that were *'made'* on the 5th Day.

APPLYING THE GENESIS CODE TO GEN. 1:20-23:

Gen. 1:20 Then God said: "Let the waters swarm with swarmers, having the living soul of animal life; and let the winged insects fly and swarm in the Earth's sky."

Gen. 1:21 And God created the big reptiles, and all the families of all the animals that creep and swarm in the waters and in the air, according to their kind. And God gave all of them the living animal soul. When God examined the results of His creations on the 5th Day He was satisfied and determined the results were complete and would ultimately fulfill His will for the benefit of man.

Gen. 1:22 And God blessed them saying, "Be fruitful and multiply, and let all the families of all the swarmers fill the oceans and let all the families of swarming, flying insects multiply on the Earth, and swarm through the Earth's sky."

Gen. 1:23 At the end of the 5th Day God was pleased with the additional degree of order He had imposed on the initial chaos of the beginning of His creation.

CHAPTER 14: THE 5ᵀᴴ DAY, THE CAMBRIAN EXPLOSION OF VISIBLE ANIMAL LIFE, & CHARLES DOOLITTLE WALCOTT

The Cambrian Fossils, which were discovered in the Burgess Pass in NW Canada, are the most important paleontological discovery of all time. They are *the* scientific evidence that *destroyed* Darwin's idea of *gradualism* in evolution. I will talk about them and the man who discovered them in this chapter. O. David

In the next few chapters, you will read the stories of three important people who have prominently figured in man's efforts to answer the questions about our origins. Those people are Charles Doolittle Walcott, Stephen Jay Gould, and Charles Darwin.

- This chapter will concentrate on the discoveries and accomplishments of Charles Doolittle Walcott.
- Chapter 15 will tell the story of Stephen Jay Gould and his criticisms of Walcott.
- Chapter 16 will be about Charles Darwin — the Man.
- Chapter 17 will present Darwin's ideas about the origin of life and contrast his ideas with what modern science has discovered.
- Chapter 18 will present Darwin's ideas about evolution and compare his ideas with what the Bible says. You will see modern science has now proved — it all happened the way the Bible said.
- Chapter 19 will be a discussion about how life evolved in antiquity as opposed to modern times.
- Chapter 20 will examine the tenets of the Big Bang Theory and the Cosmogony of the Ancient Jewish Sages. You will see how two ancient Jewish Sages and Modern Scientific discoveries have reached the same conclusions. Chapter 20 will end with a discussion of the possibility of *'a tie that binds.'*
- Then Chapter 21 will explore the agenda of Darwinists.
- After we have done all of this we can resume (in Chapter 22) the discussion of the Biblical Account of what happened on the 6ᵗʰ day.

In previous chapters we presented the scientific evidence that proved the first life-forms on Earth were the *microscopic organisms* that *suddenly appeared* on the 3ʳᵈ Day. For the past 3,300 years the first Chapter of Genesis has presented to us its account of *the origin of life on Earth*.

- Immediately after Liquid water appeared on Earth,
- Life appeared.

Both happened early on the 3ʳᵈ Day of Creation. So, the Bible correctly tells us — the timing of the origin of life on our planet was at the appearance of liquid water on the 3ʳᵈ Day. The Bible also has given us the mechanism for life's origins — *"the earth brought forth life"* (Gen. 1:11).[598(*)] That is to say, the Earth had within it the special properties needed to bring about the beginning of life. But the Bible does not mention *microscopic*

---

[598] Schroeder The Science of God Chapter 2 p. 29a (*) Gen.1:11—mentions tender sprouts (vegetation) as the 1ˢᵗ life (on the 3ʳᵈ Day). Even though the Bible mentions 'plants' as the 1ˢᵗ & only forms of life on earth that appeared on the 3ʳᵈ Day, Kabala claims there was no special day assigned for vegetation alone, since it was not a unique work. The Bible doesn't mention the microscopic life that science says occurred on the 3ʳᵈ Day. (See discussion in Chapter 10.)

life. Perhaps the reason the Bible doesn't mention microscopic life is because the ancient Hebrews (for whom the Bible was originally written) would not have understood it.

Modern science has discovered two other important facts that close ranks with the Bible.
(1) There was a beginning to our universe.
(2) Life started *abruptly and rapidly* on Earth. [599] There was no slow random chance development.

In this chapter I will talk about the time when the first *visible* animal life-forms (*i.e., the 1st macroscopic life-forms*) — appeared on our planet. According to the Bible, *they appeared on the 5th Day of Creation* (before *man* was made on the 6th Day). It is believed the reason the Bible doesn't give specific details about the types of visible life that suddenly appeared on the 5th Day is because the ancient Hebrew would not have understood those life-forms. Those life-forms had a very different appearance from the life that was on our planet when God made Adam at the end of the 6th Day. The Bible simply informs us — *the waters and the air swarmed with swarmers on the 5th Day.* Perhaps the reason the life-forms of the 5th Day are mentioned in the Bible in general terms only — is because the Bible was *also* written for '*all- people-in-all-times*,' and Elohim knew later generations would eventually discover and understand the remarkable life-forms He created on the 5th Day. This chapter will tell the extraordinary story of *how* those remarkable forms of ancient life were discovered in the early part of the 20th century. But understanding those life-forms? That is something we are just now beginning to do. Before you continue with this chapter look at the chart: '*The Geologic Timetable Compared to the Six Days of Creation*' at the end of Chapter 12. Notice under the column labeled '*Age*' that the timeline of the Earth is divided into *Two Ages:*

- THE PRECAMBRIAN AGE: the Age of invisible life—(i.e., microscopic life),
- THE PHANEROZOIC AGE: the Age of visible life—(i.e., macroscopic life).

'Phanerozoic' means '*visible animals.*' *The Phanerozoic Age* started with the beginning of the Paleozoic Era. 'Paleozoic' means '*ancient or primitive animal-like life.*' As the chart shows, *the first visible animals on Earth appeared early on the 5th Day during the Cambrian Period.*

Prior to the *Cambrian Period of the Phanerozoic Age* (i.e., in the *PRECAMBRIAN AGE*), all life on Earth was microscopic (i.e., *invisible* to the naked eye). Therefore, the first life that appeared on Earth was *microscopic life.* Stated another way — *All life that appeared during the Precambrian Age was not visible to the naked eye. Visible animals appeared on the 5th Day.* **This discovery was made after Darwin died and was something he did not know.** The Precambrian microscopic life was single-cell algae, bacteria, Archaea, and protozoans — *but there were no animals until the 5th Day.*

Since the life-forms on the 5th Day were very different from those we know today, we must ask: Did they contribute anything to modern-day life? *Did at least some* of the animals and plants *known to us today come from* some of those first visible animals and plants *that suddenly appeared* on the 5th Day? The answer is: Yes. Obviously, many people agree. However, what most people generally accept is the answer to the question

---

[599] Schroeder *The Science of God* Chapter 2 p. 29b

— has been historically influenced more by what Charles Darwin thought than by what the deeper meaning of the ancient Hebrew Biblical scripture said. That is understandable because the existence of *The Genesis Code* was not generally known in Darwin's day. Today, most people do not know *The Genesis Code* exists.

In this chapter we will talk about the most important Paleontological discovery of our time, the man who made it, what he did after his discovery, and how and perhaps why it was buried in the basement archives of the Smithsonian Institution in Washington, DC for eighty years! The reason this discovery is so important is because I will be presenting the scientific proof that:

- *The Earth's first visible animals and plants suddenly appeared in the first phase of the Cambrian Period!*
- *When they appeared, they were fully developed!*
- *They did not gradually evolve in the way Darwin had imagined!*
- *They literally exploded upon the scene in the first five million years of the early Cambrian Period!*

When you have finished this chapter, you will see — for the past 3,300 years *The Genesis Code* that has been hidden in the ancient Hebrew Torah for centuries — has been saying all along what modern science has only recently discovered about the 5ᵗʰ Day of Creation. In the next chapter we will also examine the criticisms a later generation of Darwinists would scornfully heap upon the man who discovered the fossil evidence of the Cambrian Explosion of life.

CHARLES DOOLITTLE WALCOTT

Now is the time to turn our attention to what some have called the most important discovery of all time. It has everything to do with one of America's foremost scientists, a world-renowned paleontologist who became the world's first expert on the explosion of the multicellular life-forms that *suddenly* and *abruptly appeared* in the first five million years of the Cambrian Period.[600] As a personal friend of three Presidents of the United States, this man had enormous political influence.[601] For years he had been the director of the Smithsonian Institution in Washington, DC — the largest organization in the world of museums and curators in his day. For this reason, he also had tremendous professional influence.[602] We are talking about *Charles Doolittle Walcott* (1850-1927). He made an incredibly important discovery. However, when one pronounces his middle name (*Doolittle*), the sound of his middle name reminds us of two other English words — "*do little.*" This is ironic because all his contemporaries thought: "*He was the man who did so much!*" However, a younger generation of paleontologists would critically claim — for some private reason he never explained — *Walcott did very little about it!* The story of what he did and what some say he later failed to do is most intriguing.

THE BURGESS PASS AND ITS BURIED TREASURE

The story of Walcott's most important discovery begins in the Burgess Pass of Western Canada. However, before continuing with Walcott's story, let's start with the geologic history of that spot on the Earth where Walcott made his discovery. For this story we must

---

[600] Schroeder, The Science of God, Chapter 2, p. 35e
[601] Schroeder, The Science of God, Chapter 2, p. 37c
[602] Schroeder, The Science of God, Chapter 2, p. 37b

travel back in time to a point *early on the 5th Day of Creation at the beginning of the Cambrian Period.*[603]

THE CAMBRIAN WORLD: This map shows the Earth as scientists think it was in the Cambrian Period. The Cambrian Period is the 1st Period of the Phanerozoic Age when the 1st visible animals and plants appeared. The Phanerozoic Age is the age of visible (macroscopic) plants and animals (cf. the Chart at the end of Chapter 12.) Green areas on this map represent continents. To those of you men [*] who have a form of colorblindness that prevents you from seeing some shades of green and red — the continents will look yellow — as they do to me. My wife says the continents are yellow-green (in this image), and Mountain ranges are in red. (But the red looks orange to me.) Dark blue denotes deep ocean. The submerged shallow continental shelfs are colored light blue. (Scientists think Earth's current continents were arranged as depicted by the dotted intracontinental lines.) The location of the Burgess Pass fauna (discovered by Charles Doolittle Walcott in 1909) is indicated by a star that is superimposed on the submerged shallow continental shelf of the continent *Laurentia* (western North America). Notice North America and Canada are located south of the equator. Also notice that the continents are mostly located in the southern hemisphere![604]

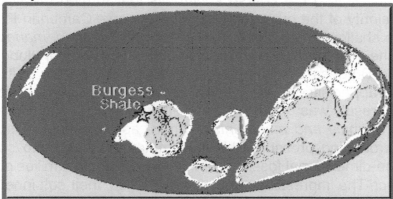

This image is from: "**The Burgess Shale - (UCMP), Berkeley** ucmp.berkeley.edu › cambrian › burgess"

Approximately 560 million years ago, on the spot where Walcott made his discovery (in 1909), there was a layer of *fine mud* on the top of a stepped continental shelf, which was submerged beneath the shallow waters of a tropical sea near the equator. A limestone reef marked the edge of the shallowest part of this continental shelf. Beyond the upper edge of the reef the bank abruptly fell away to a depth of 200 meters to the floor of the shelf. Just how far was this drop of 200 meters? Since one meter is 1.0936 yards, think

---

[603] Schroeder, The Science of God, Chapter 2, p. 34c and 34d

[*] **Deuteranopia – Red-Green Color Blindness –** *Deuteranopia* is a form of red-green deficiency that mostly affects men. It is the most common type of "color blindness." My deuteranopia gave me an advantage in Radiology. My grayscale is enhanced above "normal," and my extreme near-sightedness gave me a "built-in magnifying glass!" This enabled me to detect tiny cancers that color advantaged people with normal vision have difficulty seeing. For me, tiny breast and lung cancers (many of which were curable) were easy to see. I believe God built me to be a Radiologist.

[604] **The Burgess Shale - (UCMP), Berkeley** ucmp.berkeley.edu › cambrian › burgess

of 200 meters as a distance that is about 19 yards longer than two football fields.[605] Paleontologists have called this unique shallow tropical sea — *the Burgess Shallows*.

THE BURGESS SHALLOWS TEEMED WITH LIFE.

The Burgess shallows *'swarmed with swarmers.'* Life was there in abundance. The temperate sunbathed waters teemed with a plethora of marine animals and plants. Soil from the contiguous continental shoreline continuously washed down and refurbished the shallow sea with the essential nutrients that the marine animal and plant-life needed to flourish.[606]

At regular intervals the accumulated weight of the mud and the excreted products of marine animal-life would increase beyond that which the reef could support. Every time that happened, the sediment at the edge of the reef broke loose and raced down the steep bank to the floor of the shallow shelf that was 200 meters below. Consequently, the *fine* silt-like mudflow *gently swept up* all life-forms in its path and carried them down to the floor of the shelf, entombing them in layers of oxygen-poor mud and silt.[607]

THE MUD-SILT OF THE BURGESS SHALLOWS WAS UNIQUE.

Usually, only the hard tissues of fossilized animals such as their bone and teeth survive the burial process. However, the *fineness* of the mud-silt of the Burgess Shallows was extremely important. Unlike the *coarse sediments* that formed the Cambrian strata in Wales and the majority of the other more common *coarse* Cambrian Period continental soil-slides into the shallow tropical seas that entombed, *crushed, mangled,* and in some cases *destroyed* their-life forms in countless other locations on our globe; *the fineness* of the mud-silt in the Burgess Shallows burial ground captured the soft outer and inner tissues of the entrapped life-forms — *intact!* It also —*infiltrated*— the animal's inner organs! The final result was — the anoxic environment in the Burgess shallows— *preserved whole animals and plants intact!* Then, as the layers of successive slides increased the surrounding pressure, the mud metamorphosed into shale rock[608] that contained the three-dimensional fossils of a multitude of whole families of marine animals and plants — *intact!* The impressions of their soft tissues, their soft inner organs, as well as the skeletons of those forms that had bony parts — *were perfectly preserved!* Both vertebrates (animals that had vertebrae and spinal cords and bony endoskeletons), and non-vertebrates (those animals that were truly soft-bodied, and those which had exoskeletons but did not have vertebrae or spinal cords), were equally preserved alike. *A unique and complete history of the Earth's first macroscopic animal and plant life- forms lay recorded in stone!* [609]

ALL THE WHILE, THE BURGESS SHALLOWS WERE IN MOTION—SAILING NORTH.

Yet, this burial ground was not a tranquil resting place. Although *the Burgess Shallows* were part of a terrane that originated near the equator; all the while that its animals and plants were flourishing, dying, and being entombed and fossilized; the Burgess Shallows terrane had been 'sailing' North, away from the equator, at the rate of a few centimeters

---

[605] Schroeder, The Science of God, Chapter 2, p. 34d
[606] Schroeder, The Science of God, Chapter 2, p. 34e
[607] Schroeder, The Science of God, Chapter 2, p. 34e and 35a
[608] Shale [shayl] a dark fine-grained sedimentary rock composed of layers of compressed clay, silt, or mud.
[609] Schroeder, The Science of God, Chapter 2, p. 35b

each year — sailing toward the colder climes of the North. A few centimeters each year does not seem like much, but it was enough to have changed the topographical features of our globe many times over since the beginning of the Cambrian Period of the Paleozoic Era — some 570 million years ago. This continental shelf with its entombed fossilized treasures was destined to become a portion of the mountainous regions of Western Canada. Millions of years passed during its voyage. But then, one day not too long ago (in terms of geologic time), its *'ship'* collided with the main North American Continental Plate. A portion of its borders *dived beneath the North American Plate and was carried down* (with its treasure) into the depths of the molten mantle layer of the Earth to be lost forever.[610]

However, fortunately for us — a portion also carrying a treasure-trove of fossilized animal and plant remains — was *buckled up* by the collision and lifted to great heights to become part of the rugged mountains that border the Western coast of North America. This particular ridge would become the *Burgess Pass* in Western Canada.[611]

THE BURGESS PASS WOULD UNDERGO 4 OTHER REMARKABLE CHANGES BEFORE WALCOTT WENT THERE.

Before Walcott set his feet on the Burgess Pass in 1909, millennia would pass during which four other acts of nature would occur.

1) *First*, after being lifted by the mechanisms of plate tectonics — in the millennia that followed the uplift, the valuable shale rock was once again *buried* under multiple layers of topsoil, which formed from the life cycles of innumerable and younger continental plants and animals that flourished and died in the area.

2) *Next*, the topsoil was *completely covered* under the tons of snow and ice of the Earth's many Ice Ages that followed.

3) *Then*, beginning about 12,000 years ago (~10,000 BC) at the start of the epoch in which we live (*the Holocene Epoch*), the glacial ice plowed its way south and *bulldozed* the topsoil away from the valuable shale. In doing so, the glacial ice came to rest on top of the Burgess Pass shale.

4) *Finally*, when our current cycle of global warming began in the early *Holocene*, as the glaciers began to melt and recede from the area, *the geologically valuable shale*, which had been *buried* for millions of years *was once again exposed*.

Thus, it was that nature buried, then lifted up, then reburied the valuable shale only to uncover it one last time as if it were some pirate's treasure-trove waiting for a skillful adventurer to make its discovery known.[612]

THE MAN WHO DID SO MUCH.

Charles Doolittle Walcott must have been the kind of person who would have said his vocation was also his avocation. In the summer of 1909 this rugged adventurer spent his summer holiday packing by horse in the Canadian Rockies. The scenery in the mountains of British Columbia was spectacular. Magnificent mountain peaks surrounded lush fertile valleys thousands of feet below. At the moment he made his unparalleled discovery he was standing on the shale-rock of a mountain saddle-ridge that connects Mt. Wapta and

[610] Schroeder, The Science of God, Chapter 2, p. 35c
[611] Schroeder, The Science of God, Chapter 2, p. 35d
[612] Schroeder, The Science of God, Chapter 2 p. 36a

Mt. Field near the Burgess Pass. From the height of this ridge the crystal-clear water of the mountain streams coursing through the luxuriant mountain valleys below must have appeared as glistening ribbons of reflected sunlight. However, Walcott wasn't focused on any of this. With his practiced geologist's eye, he was attracted to the shale on the saddle between the two mountain peaks. He bent over and picked up one of the many pieces of shale. Looking intently at the fine ridges on one of its edges, he gave the rock a gentle tap with his specially designed geologist's field-hammer, and like a practiced sculptor or an experienced diamond cutter, he expertly broke the rock in two. The result was beyond any of his expectations. There, within the rock was the three-dimensional fossilized imprint of a *CRUSTACEAN!* [613] (*)

A CRUSTACEAN! HOW COULD THIS BE?

According to the prevailing view of the majority of paleontologists of Walcott's time, the shale of the Burgess Pass was *too old* to contain a fossil *as complex* as the specimen he had uncovered. He had bought into the prevailing 20th Century school of thought that believed 550 million years ago (i.e., *in the very early Cambrian Period)* — the only life on Earth was the most simple of forms.[614]

ABRUPT, SUDDEN, PUNCTUATED DEVELOPMENT, INTELLIGENT DESIGN, & DIVINE INTERVENTION!

Walcott instantly recognized his own personal dilemma.

- There could be no way the popular assumptions about evolution originated by Darwin could have advanced life from the one-celled microscopic invisible protozoans of the Pre-Cambrian Age — to the complexity of this macroscopic visible crustacean in the short time span of the first five million years of the Cambrian Period — during which the Cambrian Explosion of life occurred!
- There simply had not been enough time for that to have happened! It was just 1909, but well into the 1970s, the 19th Century ideas of Charles Darwin — which were still vigorously defended by the majority of succeeding generations of Orthodox Darwinists and Neo-Darwinists [615] (*) — *assumed* a period of time *in excess of 100 million years* would have been necessary for *the-basic-body-plans* of any advanced life-forms to evolve from the simplicity of the microscopic protozoans of Pre-Cambrian life! [616]
- Walcott had to come to grips with the simple fact that he had discovered a truly remarkable three-dimensional fossil *of a complex life-form that suddenly appeared, fully developed, in a remarkably short timeframe. The fossilized specimen that he held in his hand had suddenly appeared in the first 5 million years of the earliest part of the Cambrian period! Who on Earth would have believed this?*

[613] Schroeder The Science of God Chapter 2 p. 36b (*) **Crustacean:** an invertebrate animal with several pairs of jointed legs, a hard protective outer shell, two pairs of antennae, and eyes at the end of stalks. Lobsters, crabs, shrimp, crayfish, water flees, barnacles, & wood lice are crustaceans. Subphylum: *Crustacea.*
[614] Schroeder The Science of God Chapter 2 p 36b
[615] (*) **Neo-Darwinists:** A Theory of Evolution that starts with Darwin's ideas of gradualism & natural selection but also includes the science of modern population genetics and recognizes other new scientific discoveries.
[616] Schroeder, The Science of God, Chapter 2, p. 36b

Walcott picked up another piece of shale, which yielded yet another fossil of completely developed complex life. Sample after succeeding sample yielded a remarkable variety of equally eccentric animal fossils. He meticulously recorded each fossil in his journal, and over the next decade he returned to the area each year to collect more samples. In all, Walcott collected and shipped more than 60,000 of these fossilized specimens to his Smithsonian Institution![617]

WALCOTT HAD BELIEVED IN A 'GOD-DIRECTED' ORDER OF GRADUAL EVOLUTION.

Walcott was no Neo-Darwinist. Walcott believed in God — **and so did Charles Darwin, as we shall later see!** Walcott may have known that Darwin believed in God — that is, if he had read Darwin's book from cover to cover. Why cover to cover? We'll get to that in the next chapter when we discuss Stephen Jay Gould's *misquote* of Darwin in the last paragraph of Darwin's book "*The Origin of Species*." But, for right now, I want to talk about Charles Doolittle Walcott.

Walcott also believed in Darwin's concept of *gradualism*. That is understandable because the majority of the paleontologists of his time championed Darwin's original assumption of *gradualism* in evolution. But Walcott differed from the Classical (Orthodox) Darwinists and the Neo-Darwinists in that he believed in **a God-directed gradual evolution** — a form of evolutionary belief that saw the Creator of all things working through nature, gradually changing the early simple forms of life into the modern complexity that we have today.[618]

As we shall later see, Darwin, who was baptized in the Anglican Church and raised in the Unitarian Church by his mother, was a tormented man who struggled with the concept that evolution is a *God-directed process*. [619] But, not until Walcott held these remarkable specimens in his hands had anything in his belief system contradicted his belief of gradualism in a God-directed scheme of evolution. He still believed *"God did it"* — that God created and formed everything. But it was the evidence of *sudden, abrupt change*, and of *punctuated development* that he held in his hands, which *upset Walcott's apple cart* — so to speak.[620]

Specimen after specimen reaffirmed the Genesis Code revealed Biblical concepts of Intelligent Design, Divine Intervention, and God's institution of abrupt, sudden, punctuated development in all things that we have emphasized so much in preceding chapters.

The ancient Jewish sages noted the ten-fold repetition of the phrase *'Then God said'* that punctuated each act of God's creative activity in Genesis One. They concluded from that phrase and the narrative, which followed each and every time it appeared in Genesis One — that **Intelligent Design, Divine Intervention, and Abrupt, Sudden, Punctuated Changes** were the direct results of God's own labor on each and every one of those *'Six Days of Old'* (see Chapter 8 under the discussion of Gen. 1:3 — *"Then God Said"*). But these Biblical concepts that had been written down centuries before by Maimonides, Nahmanides, and the other Jewish sages who were able to understand the deeper

---

[617] Schroeder, The Science of God, Chapter 2, p. 36c
[618] Schroeder The Science of God Chapter 2 p. 38a
[619] Article: About Darwin.com—Who was Darwin? www.aboutdarwin.com/darwin/whowas.html
[620] Schroeder The Science of God Chapter 2 p. 38a

meaning of the Hebrew text of Genesis One — were certainly not commonly known in Walcott's day. Neither are they widely known in our day.

WALCOTT REALIZED THE IMPORTANCE OF THE BURGESS PASS FOSSILS.
They are the irrefutable evidence that Proved Darwin Wrong!

There is no question Walcott realized the importance of his discoveries. The numerous fossils he collected are evidence of this.[621] There is no escaping the fact they display the basic anatomies (i.e., *the basic-body-plans*) of all animals alive today. Walcott's 60,000 fossilized specimens reveal extraordinary facts. Immortalized in stone, these fossils show the **sudden, punctuated, simultaneous, independent, and separate development** — in the brief timespan of the first 5 million years of the Cambrian Period — of animal life forms that had:

- Heads, eyes, mouths, and gills—
- Jointed limbs and intestines—
- Sponges and worms—
- Insects—
- Fish—
- Vertebrates and Invertebrates—
- And soft-bodied and hard-bodied animals.
- These life-forms displayed all the phyla (i.e., the basic-body-plans) of animals that exist today.
- The 60,000 fossils he collected during his summer excursions of discovery in the Burgess Shale over the next 10 years would be found to represent some 34 phyla,[622] 70 genera and 130 separate species! [623,624] **(#)-(##)-(###),** & 625

"There had been no gradual evolution of simple phyla such as sponges into the more complex phyla of worms and then into other life forms such as insects. According to these fossils, at the most fundamental level of animal life (**the phylum, i.e., the basic-body-plan**), *the dogma of Orthodox Darwinian evolution, that the simple had evolved into the more complex, that invertebrates had evolved into vertebrates over 100-200 million years — was fantasy not fact!"* [626*] **(A direct quote from Dr. Schroeder)**

[621] Schroeder The Science of God Chapter 2 p. 36d
[622] Schroeder The Science of God Chapter 7 p. 102a,d
[623] Schroeder The Science of God Chapter 2 p. 36e
[624] (#) **Phylum** (fi'lem). n. [pl. Phyla from the Greek 'a phylon', race, or tribe;] one of the large, basic, fundamental divisions of the plant or animal kingdom, such as the basic-body-plans that characterize a 'race' of animals or plants. (##) **Genera** (plural form of L. genus) a kind. Genus—in biology, a classification of plants or animals with common distinguishing characteristics. A 'genus' is a main subdivision or a family of animals or plants and includes one or more 'species.' The genus name is capitalized (e.g., 'Homo sapiens', the scientific name for man). (###) **Species** (from L. specere, to look at—pl. species) a Sub-family—in biology, a group of animals or plants, usually constituting a subdivision next smaller than a genus, having certain common characteristics which clearly distinguish it from other groups, and which are ordinarily inherited.
[625] [Pdf] Charles Doolittle Walcott - National Academy of ... www.nasonline.org/publications/biographical-memoirs/memoir-pdfs/walcott-charles.... National Academy of Sciences. Charles Doolittle Walcott. 1850—1927. A Biographical Memoir by ELLIS L. YOCHELSON.
[626*] Schroeder, The Science of God, Chapter 2, p. 36e & 37a **(A direct quote from Schroeder's book.)**

In fact, the existence of these fossils destroyed all five pillars of Darwin's classical assumptions about the origin of life on Earth (this will be discussed in Chapter 17). They also prove Darwin's assumptions about the gradual and transitional development of new and different complex phyla of animals (with all their divisions of subphyla, classes, orders, genera, and species) from older different and more simple phyla — Did not occur as Darwin had imagined! These fossils were the indisputable proof that multiple complex independent and separate phyla of animals had suddenly and simultaneously appeared, fully developed, in the extremely brief early part of the Cambrian period. The simple fact is — the existence of these fossils proved the Bible right and proved Darwin wrong!

CRITICS SAY: THE MAN WHO DID SO MUCH, DID VERY LITTLE WITH HIS DISCOVERY.

Some say, after a decade of collecting and studying his fossils, Walcott then reburied them! They say he effectively reburied them in the drawers of the Smithsonian Institution by failing to publish his findings in any meaningful way. That is, he failed to publish his findings in any widely read and influential scientific journals. Furthermore, they say he did not complete the study of his extensive collection. According to his critics he did make a rather modest disclosure of his findings and analyses in a publication that had an extremely limited circulation — the *Smithsonian Miscellaneous Collections.*

(As you shall see in the next Chapter, Walcott did receive worldwide recognition for the work he did, and the scientists of his time were very much impressed by the papers he published. The numerous honorary doctorate degrees he received from prestigious Universities the world over are evidence of this.)

Nevertheless, eight decades after his death, a younger generation of scientists would claim it was inexplicable that Walcott did nothing else. According to them, the net result was that the world would have to wait a long time for the news of his astonishing discovery. Why? They say we will never truly know. Eighty years would pass before they were rediscovered by a graduate student, *Simon Conway Morris.* It was Morris who eventually played a key role in the interpretation of these fossils.[627] The credit goes to Morris for cataloguing all 60,000 of Walcott's fossils. Still, the fact remains — Walcott's critics claim he could have used his professional and political influence *to shout out* the news of his significant find. He could have hired an army of graduate students and *cracked his whip*, so to speak, to complete the study of his Cambrian fossils and then make known to the world the findings of his treasure-trove. Instead, (according to his critics), he sealed his lips and never spoke of them again.

The fact remains — we now know Walcott's fossils revealed that all sorts of complex life had suddenly appeared, fully developed on our planet in the short time frame of the early Cambrian Period, and not the way that, ever since Darwin and even today, most academics imagine. Furthermore, this fact was obvious the minute Walcott published his first paper in *the Miscellaneous Smithsonian Collections.*

---

[627] Schroeder, The Science of God, Chapter 2, p. 37b and 37e

Summary Points:
- The first life-forms on Earth appeared immediately after liquid water appeared on the 3rd Day.
- The first life on Earth was *invisible*. It was the *microscopic* forms of Pre-Cambrian life that were discussed in Chapters 10, 11, and 12.
- The first visible forms of life suddenly "*exploded*" upon the scene in the early phase of the Cambrian Period at the beginning of the 5th Day.
- Those forms of life were fully developed when they first appeared.
- They were discovered by Charles Doolittle Walcott when he explored the Burgess Pass in the Canadian Rockies.
- **The Burgess Pass fossils are the scientific evidence that refutes all of Darwin's conjectures. They are the evidence that proves the Genesis Creation Account correct.**

CHAPTER 15: STEPHEN J. GOULD CRITICIZED CHARLES DOOLITTLE WALCOTT.

The conflict between people who believe God created us & directed our evolution & those who don't, can be explained by examining the beliefs of Gould, Walcott, & Darwin. That is what I want to do in this chapter & the next. This chapter will focus on Gould & Walcott. The next chapter will focus on Darwin. O.David

Eight decades after Walcott died, a younger generation of scientists criticized Walcott for failing to conduct a complete analysis of the fossils he discovered and collected. They claimed he failed to "follow-through." They also criticized the work he did.

Darwin published the first edition of his book on *The Origin of Species* in 1859. Since then, the accumulated data of 165 years of scientific inquiry *has now disproved every one of Darwin's ideas about how life originated,* and *most of his ideas about how life evolved*[628] and yet, secularists, academics, and the media still treat his ideas as if they are a proven law![629] We must ask ourselves why? Why do they ignore the evidence that overwhelmingly refutes Darwin's ideas? Are they ignorant of what has happened, or are they just ignoring the science that is so convincing? Is the problem *their own cognitive dissonance* or *do they cling to Darwin's ideas because they must if they are to continue pursuing their political agenda of societal change?* Perhaps the answer can be found through an examination of one of the most influential evolutionists of our time. Let us now turn our attention to the words of *Stephen Jay Gould.*

MUCH OF THE BEHAVIOR OF PRESENT-DAY DARWINISTS CAN BE EXPLAINED BY THE BELIEFS, THE COGNITIVE DISSONANCE, AND THE INFLUENCE OF STEPHEN JAY GOULD.

The following discussion will help us understand why Gould did what he did. Gould misquoted his hero, Darwin. But, before we talk about that, you will see Gould had some unkind things to say about Walcott. Gould claimed:

- *Walcott erroneously 'shoehorned' all the Burgess fossils by classifying them into groups of known modern-day animals in order to maintain his belief in God's gradual methods.*[630] *This is ironic because Gould — like Darwin, and Walcott — also initially believed in gradualism in evolution. However (as you shall see), Gould did not believe in God. Furthermore (in Chapter 21), you will see Gould changed his mind and abandoned Darwin's idea of —* "Gradualism!"

- *Next, Gould said —* "Walcott misinterpreted the Burgess fossils in a comprehensive and thoroughly consistent manner."[631]

- *Finally, Gould claimed the reason Walcott made these mistakes is because —* "Walcott's belief in God kept him from realizing the significance of his find."[632]

Let's examine each of these attacks on Walcott.

---

[628] Schroeder *The Science of God* Chapter 2 p 39 *b&c*
[629] Schroeder *The Science of God* Chapter 2 p *39d,e* & p 40
[630] Schroeder *The Science of God* Chapter 2 p 38*b*
[631] Gould, *Wonderful Life: The Burgess Shale & the Nature of History.* Preface & Acknowledgements
[632] Schroeder, *The Science of God,* Chapter 2, p. 38*a*

GOULD CLAIMED WALCOTT MISCLASSIFIED AND MISINTERPRETED THE BURGESS FOSSILS.
Darwinists have claimed Walcott did not *'follow through,'* and they have puzzled why? In 1989 the Book *Wonderful Life: The Burgess Shale & the Nature of History* was published. The author was one of the world's most influential and published advocates of the modern-day modifications of Darwinian and Neo-Darwinian theory. That man was *Stephen Jay Gould* (1941–2002), a renowned professor at Harvard University. In his book Gould said, after Walcott made his discovery—

> *"Walcott proceeded to misinterpret the fossils in a comprehensive and thoroughly consistent manner."*

Why? Gould claimed the reason Walcott failed to follow through — *"arose from his conventional view of life."* Gould said Walcott *'shoehorned'* every last burgess animal into a modern group, viewing the fauna collectively as a set of primitive or ancestral versions of later, improved forms *"in order to maintain his belief in God's gradual methods."*[633] In response to this charge Dr. Schroeder asked the question:

> *"If Walcott thought Burgess was just a variation of the same old stuff, why his extraordinary effort to collect so many fossils and then keep them for himself?"*[634]

IN DEFENSE OF WALCOTT

Shoehorned! Really? We now know the varieties of animals on our planet are confined to 34 phyla,[635] which define the basic-body-plans of all animal life today — of which there are approximately thirty million species.[636] The Cambrian explosion produced *more than* the 34 phyla that exist today, but the other plans failed to fulfill the requirements for survival.[637] Stated another way:

None of the "other plans" fit into any of the classifications of today's animals because they did not survive! They became extinct!

Yet, the fact remains — Walcott never finished a complete study of the archive he collected. Why? We don't know for certain because he never explained — but consider this.

Walcott first went to the Burgess Pass in 1909. Eighteen years later, he died. During the first ten years of those last eighteen years of his life, he spent each summer busily collecting his 60,000 fossil specimens. Just think of the time and devoted work that required. Although he did not know it, at the time he stopped collecting fossils, he had only eight more years to live. When one of Walcott's biographers (Ellis L. Yochelson) studied Walcott's work and publications, he wrote:

"In terms of sheer volume, he definitely was one of the most productive paleontological writers in America. At the time of his death, he had contributed 70% of all published

[633] Gould, *Wonderful Life: The Burgess Shale & the Nature of History.* Preface & Acknowledgements.
[634] Schroeder, *The Science of God,* Chapter 2, p. 38*b*
[635] The number of animal phyla varies between 30 and 40, depending on who you read.
[636] Schroeder, *The Science of God,* Chapter 7, p. 102*d*–103*a*
[637] Schroeder, *The Science of God,* Chapter 7, p. 102*a*

information on the Pre-Cambrian and Cambrian of North America; half written during his years with the Smithsonian.'[638]

When he considered the state of knowledge of the primordial terrain in America in the time Walcott began his study (i.e., the field conditions under which he worked, and the area he covered) — Yochelson thought Walcott's achievements were simply astounding. Yochelson wrote:

"His work has been, if not criticized, at least negated by some subsequent workers as being more or less compilation:"

Yochelson believed Walcott's critics were much too harsh in their indictments. Yochelson wrote his biography of Walcott in 1967. That was 22 years before Gould criticized Walcott in his book. Yochelson continued:

"In so far as generalization may be made about his published work, specimens are well prepared, fossil illustrations are fine. Descriptions are clear and species' names closely follow the practices of nomenclature prevailing during his lifetime. Walcott's Cambrian work is basic — no other term applies. It must be noted that, by its nature, paleontology is an additive field, perhaps more so than almost any other major discipline of science. It is always subject to continuous revision as new collections and scientific personnel permit. That the observed range of some fossils has been modified, that new genera have been named, and that new stratigraphic formations have been defined — in no way detracts from Walcott's pioneer accomplishments." [639]

Yochelson said the facts are:
* Walcott published five full volumes of *Smithsonian Miscellaneous Collections* and aggregates which report his Burgess Shale findings and analysis.
* His published writings cover nearly 2500 pages — not including his accompanying plates of photographs![640]
* His accompanying plates of photographs[641] are extensive!
* People who admire the man think his publications were an impressive volume of work, all of which he accomplished during the last eight years of his life.
* There is no doubt he made a good decision to classify the animals he believed to be early representatives of the phyla with which he was familiar (i.e., our modern-day animals).
* That he did not try to classify those varieties which did not seem to fit was also a good decision.
* He left them alone for some future thought.

[638] Article: *Charles Doolittle Walcott (1850-1927): A Biographical Memoir* by Ellis L. Yochelson © 1967 the National Academy of Sciences, Washington, D.C. http://www.nap.edu/html/biomens/cwalcott.pdf
[639] Article: *Charles Doolittle Walcott (1850-1927): A Biographical Memoir* by Ellis L. Yochelson © 1967 the National Academy of Sciences, Washington, D.C. http://www.nap.edu/html/biomens/cwalcott.pdf
[640] Article: *Charles Doolittle Walcott (1850-1927): A Biographical Memoir* by Ellis L. Yochelson © 1967 the National Academy of Sciences, Washington, D.C. http://www.nap.edu/html/biomems/cwalcott.pdf
[641] **Photographic glass-plates** preceded photographic film as a capture medium in photography and were still used in some communities up until the late 20th century. They were thin plates of glass that were coated with light-sensitive silver salts.

- Perhaps it is true Walcott made some mistakes of classification.
- Certainly, it is true, in the final analysis, he didn't get around to classifying all of the fossils collected.
- But the work he did has been called '*laudable*' by other modern-day paleontologists who take a kinder and gentler view of Walcott's accomplishments.

For example, here are perhaps the finest words of tribute ever written about Walcott. They were written after his death in 1927. They come from his long-time friend and fellow geologist, *Whitman Cross*. Cross wrote to his friend *W.C. Broeger*, who was an eminent Norwegian geologist:

"His (Walcott's) *own work is, of course, far from finished. It would have been so, no matter how long he had lived. How can great research, with ever-growing material and new developments, be completed? But assistants will be able to prepare much more of the results for publication. I have never known a man whose life was so dominantly one of intellectual work, with real recreation playing so small a part. He did not know how to play. He saw so many things to do and had so many opportunities which he could not refuse to accept. It is quite remarkable to see a man with no college education — the lack of which was at times evident — rise to the head of a learned profession and receive the highest academic honors from universities and societies the world over. His ability and accomplishments could not be passed over."*[642]

SPECULATIONS ON WHY WALCOTT HAD SO LITTLE FORMAL EDUCATION

Walcott was born into a family of some note. His grandfather, Benjamin Stuart Walcott, had moved from Rhode Island in 1822 and became one of the leading manufacturers in central New York State. His father (also Charles Doolittle Walcott), a man of unusual energy, was well established in business, and held an influential and leading place in his community. Unfortunately, he died at the age of thirty-four, leaving a wife and four children, the youngest of whom was the two-year-old Charles Doolittle Walcott. The early death of his father caused considerable economic hardship. That explains why he did not complete his education. It was an economic necessity for Walcott to enter the work force as soon as possible.

In addition to the death of his father when he was two years old, there was also another minor little thing (sarcasm) which may have interfered with Walcott's education — the American Civil War. Walcott was born in 1850. In April 1861 (when he was 11 years old), the Civil War broke out. It lasted until April 1865. When the war ended, he was 15. We know Walcott began his education in the public school system of Utica, New York (in 1858), at the age of eight — six years after the death of his father. That was three years before the outbreak of the Civil War. From there he went to the Utica Academy. Three years after the end of the Civil War he left the Utica Academy but did not graduate. The year was 1868. During four years of his ten-year school experience, the fate of our nation hung in the balance. Those four years of great uncertainty came precisely in the middle of his formal schooling. What kind of distraction and hardship do you think that might have been?

---

[642]Article: *Charles Doolittle Walcott 1850-1927—A Biographical Memoir* by Ellis L. Yochelson: © 1967 National Academy of sciences, Washington, D.C. p. 513-514 http://www.nap.edu/html/biomems/cwalcott.pdf

At the age of 18, Walcott entered the work force, all the while searching for an interest that might become a vocation. He soon developed an interest in geology. When he was 21, he took a job as a farm laborer on the *William P. Rust* farm at Trenton Falls, New York. He arranged with Mr. Rust to do a certain amount of farm labor for his room and board and reserved the remainder of his time for doing geological study and field work on the rocky strata of the Rust farm. By this time, he had truly become intrigued with geology and had decided he wanted to be a geologist. This rather unusual arrangement lasted for five years. During the early part of his stay on the Rust farm (in 1872), Walcott married *Lura Ann Rust*, the youngest of eight children in the Rust family. But only sixteen months after their wedding Lura Ann died! He later married Helena Breese Stevens in 1888. They had four children.

Now, if one is interested in geology or any number of other fields, one is expected to attend institutions of higher learning and earn a qualifying degree. However, in Walcott's day, the lack of a certified academic degree did not stand in the way of an enterprising and industrious individual who was willing to self-educate himself and do the work that would earn the recognition of others. Although Walcott's education was without any certification (i.e., not even a high school diploma), it is obvious the man never stopped learning.

WALCOTT WAS AWARDED 12 HONORARY DOCTORATE DEGREES.

In the final analysis, many prestigious academic institutions did recognize his accomplishments.

- He received three Medals of Honor from foreign geological societies and the Hayden Medal from the Academy of Natural Sciences of Philadelphia.
- He was also awarded 8 honorary LL.D. degrees, 2 honorary D.Sc. degrees, 1 honorary Ph.D. degree and a Doctor Honoris Causa.
- One of his D.Sc. degrees came from Cambridge and was conferred on him during the celebration of the Semicentennial of the publication of Darwin's *Origin of Species.*
- His Ph.D. degree was bestowed on him by the University of Oslo during the 100th anniversary celebration of that prestigious university.[643]

I suspect many current-day academics may be privately envious of the sheer numbers of prestigious universities and scientific societies the world over that conferred high praise on Walcott's academic accomplishments. He truly was a world-renown pioneer-paleontologist.

DID GOULD HAVE A HIDDEN AGENDA?

There is no doubt Walcott fully understood the importance of the Burgess Shale fossils. He instantly realized *each fossil destroyed* an important part of his own belief in something Darwinists still preach and something that Gould initially championed — *gradualism in evolution.* We have already mentioned Gould's view that Walcott's belief in God's gradual methods was the reason he *'shoehorned'* the fossils into already known categories. However, Gould's most harsh criticism was his claim Walcott's belief in God kept him from

[643] Article: *Charles Doolittle Walcott (1850-1927): A Biographical Memoir* by Ellis L. Yochelson © 1967 the National Academy of Sciences, Washington, D.C. http://www.nap.edu/html/biomens/cwalcott.pdf

realizing the significance of his find.[644] In his book, *The Science of God,* Dr. Schroeder quotes Gould's indictment and wrote: *"God has taken the rap for a host of human failures, but this charge takes the cake!"*[645] Furthermore, Schroeder also wrote: *"Let's be more realistic and more charitable to his* (Walcott's) *intelligence. Let's just ascribe his act to cognitive dissonance, humanity's inherent desire to ignore unpleasant facts."*[646]

Schroeder's suggestion that Walcott may have been influenced by cognitive dissonance was only a *speculation*. There may have been other reasons Walcott did not finish the study of his fossils that have nothing to do with his belief in God. Consider the following.

- From Yochelson's biography of Walcott, we learn a little bit about his responsibilities as director of the Smithsonian Institution, as well as the wide range of his service to other organizations and branches of government. So, one might ask the question: Was it really Walcott's cognitive dissonance, or was his reason the same reason Copernicus waited until the twilight of his life to make known his own work that disproved the Church-sponsored dogma of Geocentrism? Perhaps because of his other time-consuming commitments, Walcott was reluctant to take on the protracted fight he knew would come from the entrenched views of academics and other proponents of Darwinism — if he used his fossil evidence to challenge their dogma.

- And then, there were other things that may have been significant distractions during the last eight years of his life. For example, WWI started in 1914. Although the United States did not enter the war until 1917, Walcott had been actively involved (since 1898) as an advocate in the development of a troop-carrying airplane. He was a long-time member of the National Advisory Committee for Aeronautics. This committee wears another *"hat"* today — *The National Aeronautics and Space Administration* (or *NASA*) — as it is now more commonly called. In June of 1916 Walcott recognized the possibilities of the involvement of the United States in WWI and the importance of the use of the airplane in warfare — long before many of his predecessors. He was the one who organized and held the first general meeting of representatives of the American aircraft industry. The year was 1916. The United States entered the war in 1917.

- The government closed the Smithsonian Institution to the public on July 16, 1918. The Bureau of War Risk Insurance began using the museum as office space in October of that year and did not return it until April of 1919. How disrupting to Walcott's study of his fossils could that have been?

- Some of the things he was involved in during his time at the Smithsonian were: the *National Park Service* (getting it started); the *Mt. Wilson Observatory*; the *United States Geological Survey*; the *Carnegie Institution* of Washington, the establishment of the *National Gallery of Art, The American Association for the Advancement of Science* (serving as its president in 1923). The list goes on and on.

---

[644] Schroeder, *The Science of God,* Chapter 2, p. 38*a*
[645] Schroeder, *The Science of God,* Chapter 2, p. 38*a*
[646] Schroeder, *The Science of God,* Chapter 2, p. 38*b*

- Walcott was also given credit for being extremely active in the field of aviation after WWI. Upon his death, a special meeting of the *National Advisory Committee for Aeronautics* passed a resolution which read in part, *"We mourn his death as a loss to the entire scientific world and a distinct and irreparable loss to the science of aeronautics."*

So, in answer to Gould's criticism of Walcott's failure to fully understand the significance of his discovery and finish the study of his fossils — maybe Walcott had more pressing things on his mind. After all, there is a saying — *"Life is something that happens while you are busy planning something else."*

GOULD'S COGNITIVE DISSONANCE

All of Gould's criticisms centered on Walcott's belief in God. Since Gould's death in 2002, some scientists have argued — on some classifications, Walcott may have been closer to the truth than Gould thought when he accused him of misclassifying and misinterpreting the Burgess fossils because of his belief in God's gradual methods. For example, after Gould's book *Wonderful Life* was published, Gould's interpretation of some of these fossils has also been challenged by a number of paleontologists. It now seems the Burgess Shale animals weren't nearly as weird as Gould and some other researchers first thought. Gould's critics say many readily fit into a standard taxonomic tree, and their descendants are with us still! So, when Walcott supposedly "shoehorned" many Burgess Fossils into the classifications of modern-day animals, his doing so seemed to be a perfectly logical and in many cases, the correct thing to do!

Take for instance the case of a fossil so bizarre that it was named *"Hallucigenia."* Gould, following the prevailing interpretative thoughts of his day (and greatly influenced by Simon Conway Morris, who first described, classified, and named Hallucigenia in 1977), thought — *"those baffling squiggly things on its back were legs and those strange spiky things on its front were a puzzlement."*

In 1991, Lars Ramiskold of the Swedish Museum of Natural History and Hou Xianguang from the Nanjing Institute of Geology and Paleontology decided that the squiggly things that were legs were actually on the *front* of the animal and the strange spiky things on its other side were actually protective armor that was on the *back* of the animal.[647] They also decided *Hallucigenia* was an armored velvet worm, that belongs to the phylum *Onychophora*. They said Gould and others had *misclassified* Hallucigenia *because they were looking at the animal upside-down*. To his credit, Gould agreed with their interpretation and almost immediately replied in a clever and thoughtful article entitled: *"The Reversal of Hallucigenia: Natural History 101"* (Jan. 1992).[648]

GOULD WAS AN INFLUENTIAL ADVOCATE OF DARWIN'S THEORY OF EVOLUTION.

Dr. Stephen Jay Gould earned his Ph.D. degree in paleontology from Columbia University in New York in 1967. His academic accomplishments at Harvard University as a Professor of Geology and Zoology and his literary contributions to scientific journals and news media publications quickly established his reputation as an intellectual force. While at

---

[647] Article: **Hallucigenia Reconstruction Turned Upside Down**: by David J. Tyler 1991
http://www.biblicalcreation.org.uk/scientific_issues/bcs007.html
[648] Article: SJG Archive: *The Reversal of Hallucigenia, Natural History 101* (Jan. 1922):
http://www.stephenjaygould.org/library/gould_reversal-hallucigenia.html

Harvard, he was also named the Alexander Agassiz Professor of Zoology and Geology, became the Curator of Invertebrate Paleontology in the Harvard Museum of Comparative Zoology, and was appointed an adjunct member of the Department of the History of Science. Dr. Gould established a reputation as one of Harvard's most visible and engaging instructors, offering courses in paleontology, biology, geology, and the history of science. In 1996, he also became a Vincent Astor Visiting Research Professor of Biology at New York University and soon after began to divide his time between New York and Cambridge. Few academics have been as celebrated and honored as Stephen Jay Gould. He was an influential academic, and a complicated man. His specific area of expertise was paleontology. He was well known because he was such a prolific author who wrote many books on natural history. He was considered to be an expert on Darwin's core concepts of evolution. In his lifetime he was considered a formidable anti-creationist and an avid proponent of a modern-day synthesized version of Orthodox Darwinism, known as *Neo-Darwinism*. Neo-Darwinists added the new ideas of population genetics theory and some other evolutionary theories of the geologists and biologists of Gould's day — to Darwin's original ideas.

Although he was born into the priestly tribe of Levi, he was raised in a secular Jewish household.[649(*)] He could not decide *if* God existed, therefore he claimed to be *an Agnostic*. The evidence shows he also had a problem with Jesus Christ. How do we know Gould had a problem with Jesus Christ and God? Answer: He admitted it when he mused about his fascination with the Christian concept of *a Millennium*.

GOULD'S PROBLEM WITH JESUS CHRIST AND WITH GOD

For the next few pages, I am going to illustrate the complexity that is characteristic of Gould's writings. I will do this by discussing his fascination with what he called — *"the Christian idea of a Millennium."* I think this will be an important exercise because it will demonstrate *the confusing convolution of some of Gould's opinions and ideas*. I believe you will benefit from this discussion when you get to Chapter 21: *The Agenda of Darwinists* — because it will help you understand *why* Orthodox Darwinists and Neo-Darwinists are now criticizing Gould, and *why* they think Gould did great harm to their common cause.

THE IDEA OF "A MILLENNIUM" HAD FASCINATED GOULD.

Gould admitted he had always had a fascination with the idea of *"a Millennium"* — the Christian doctrine that Christ would come a second time as a conquering Messiah and establish a peaceful 1,000-year reign on earth. The Christian doctrine of *"a Millennium"* will be discussed later in this chapter.

When he was eight, Gould realized there was a good possibility he would live to experience whatever changes might happen to life on Earth in the year 2,000 when a new millennium would be ushered in. Since he had been born in 1941, he realized he would be 58 years old at the time of the millennial transition. However, in 1980 he was diagnosed with *peritoneal mesothelioma*, a rare and usually fatal malignancy. Fortunately, his treatment was successful, and he survived until the year 2002. So, Gould did live long enough to experience the beginning of the new *calendrical earthly* millennium in which we now live.

[649(*)] **Secular Jew:** a person of Jewish heritage who is not observant of Judaism.

I remember some of the hysteria of people who were predicting all sorts of unusual things were going to happen when the clock signaled the passing of 1999 and the birth of the new millennium. Some were saying that would be the moment Christ would come again to inaugurate his millennial rule of peace on Earth. Others were predicting the end of civilization and the fiery destruction of the Earth in the year 2,000. It was soon discovered however, that the biggest threat to our way of life turned out to be — computer programmers hadn't been far-sighted enough to program our computers to function after that date. As it turned out, that problem was solved *before* the year 2,000.

QUESTIONING THE CONCEPT OF A MILLENNIUM

Gould's book, *Questioning the Millennium,*[650] was published in 1997. In the Preface of the 1st edition of his book he explained why he felt the Christian concept of a millennium was a *myth,* and he told his readers he wanted to talk about "*calendars and numbers; fingers and toes; the perception of evenness; the sun and moon; the age of the Earth; and the birth of Jesus.*" Why? Because: "*These preciously definite, but wondrously broad calendrical questions all arise from a foible of human reasoning and also underlie all passionate arguments now swirling around the impending millennial transition.*"

As it turns out, the main subject of Gould's book *was not* what the title of the book, implied. The main thesis of his book was actually — "*the myth of Jesus Christ.*" Why do I think that? Let's take a look at what he wrote, how he wrote it, and what he concluded. At the end of this exercise, you can decide if you agree with me.

Gould told his readers (up front): "*He considered the* (Christian) *concept of a millennium a myth.*" In order to explain the myth of a millennium, he wanted to start by talking about:

- *¹Calendars and numbers—*
- *²Fingers and toes—*
- *³The perception of evenness—*
- *⁴The sun and the moon—*
- *⁵The age of the Earth—*
- *⁶And the birth of Jesus.*

Why did Gould want to talk about this seemingly diverse list of six subjects? Because he said: "*These were all broad calendrical questions that arise from a foible of human reasoning and underlie all passionate arguments now swirling around the impending millennial transition.*"

CALENDARS AND NUMBERS; FINGERS AND TOES; THE PERCEPTION OF EVENNESS; AND THE BIRTH OF JESUS.

In his Preface, Gould made some interesting observations about the decimal system of numbers based on the number 10. The decimal system came to us from Hindu and Arabic systems of mathematics. Why the base number 10? Because humans have 10 fingers and 10 toes. We call the numbers in the Hindu-Arabic numeric systems *digits* — the same name we assign to our fingers and toes. The number that represents a millennium of

---

[650] Gould, *Questioning the Millennium: A Rationalist's Guide to a Precisely Arbitrary Countdown.* Preface to the Original Edition—Our Precisely Arbitrary Millennium.

years is 1,000. Gould said the number 1,000 is *"a beautifully symmetric and even multiple of the base 10."*

So, where did Gould go with this musing about the decimal system (a numbering system that uses the base 10), and the specific *"even"* number of 1,000? We all know:
- Europe adopted the Hindu-Arabic numeric system.
- Then, Europe discovered the New World and conquered it.
- When Europe conquered the New World, it brought to the New World its missionaries and its Christian religion.
- Why did he mention the birth of Jesus? Since Jesus of Nazareth is the center of Christian belief, the Christian calendar divides history at the point of his birth. Time before Jesus in the Christian Calendar is designated as time *Before Christ* (BC) and time after his birth is designated as time *After Christ* (AD — for *Anno Domini,* which is Latin for *"The Year of our Lord"*).

Gould next speculated (or mused) there might not be the kind of wild things people were saying about the millennium before it came:
- *If* — the Mayans had domesticated a beast of burden.
- *If* — they had invented the wheel.
- *If* — they had invented gunpowder:
- *And If* — they had invented an efficient system of ocean navigation—
- *Then perhaps* — at that time when Europe was just a *'backwater,'*
- *If* — the Mayans had made an alliance with Imperial China and conquered the Old World,
- *Then possibly* — perhaps the concept of a millennium would never have developed.

Where did Gould's arguments go next? Gould further mused:
- *If* — the Mayans had conquered Europe:
- *Then* something that he called *'decimal Europe,'* *would not* have conquered the New World as it later did.
- A defeated and conquered *'decimal Europe'* (Gould continued to muse), which was under the influence of Christianity with its belief in the myth of a local god, Jesus Christ,
- And the myth of His millennial rule on Earth in the end times—
- Would have been relegated to the status of a curious myth of a primitive and conquered culture—
- Something that kids learn in their third-grade unit on global diversity.
- But, alas, *'decimal'* Europe did prevail.
- And *'decimal'* Europe did become Christian.
- Thus, Gould felt, ***"Christianity is responsible for the maintenance of an interesting historical <u>myth</u> about a millennium."***

His reasoning is a classical, complicated, and convoluted string of ***"Sitisams"*** (cf. with the definition of *Sitisams in Chapter 10*). Why did Gould pick the Mayan culture as an object of this speculation? Because the Mayans were an ancient, advanced South American culture that had a numeric system based on the number 20. Thus, the Mayans had what is known as a *vigesimal* system of numbers — from the Latin viginti meaning '*twenty.*' Gould speculated perhaps they counted both fingers and toes (clever and humorous).

GOULD'S LAST TWO POINTS: THE SUN & THE MOON, & THE AGE OF THE EARTH.
According to Gould, it was because of Christian belief that Western culture married this apocalyptic tale with a focus on intervals of 1,000 that any decimal system might be prone to favor.

"*So here we are engulfed in a millennial madness utterly unrelated to anything performed by the earth and moon in any of all their natural rotations and revolutions. People really are funny — and fascinating beyond all possible description*" — he said. [651]

By the way, he never actually said anything further about the sun.

In his musings, it seems '*decimal Europe*' gets a black eye, because he uses pejoratives such as '*backwater*', and '*primitive*' to describe it. It also seems Imperial China and the Mayans were civilizations (at the least) Gould had no problem with, and (at the most) he lauded because he didn't use any uncomplimentary or derogatory terms when he referred to them. We know Imperial China and the Mayans were not Christian, and '*decimal*' Europe was. However, current-day China is becoming more and more Christian minute by minute, but Gould certainly would not have known this because this statement is based on recent data. [652]

Why would Gould apply such words as '*backwater*' and '*primitive culture*' to 15th Century Europe? Was he just trying to be humorous, or was he intentionally being disdainful, derisive, and condescending? Was he seriously saying that 15th Century European culture was primitive? Did he think the 15th century Mayans were a more advanced culture? We don't know for certain. We'll go through Gould's list, but before we do, if he was seriously being contemptuous of Christianity, it may have been *his own cognitive dissonance* that caused Gould to consider the Mayans and the Chinese were superior cultures — because they were not influenced by Christianity. Gould believed: "*The Christian belief that Jesus Christ is God's Son*" — was a myth.

Let's take a brief look at each of the items Gould listed that could have reversed the course of history if the Mayans (instead of Europe) had had them. As you shall see, this discussion will include some interesting facts about the evolution of a fascinating animal. Now, let's look at Gould's list.

THE HORSE
This beast of burden and of war, that was such an important part of the Spanish conquest of Central and South America — originated as small dog-like animals in North America 60 million years ago during the Paleocene Epoch. They then spread to South America via the Isthmus of Panama. They also migrated overland to Alaska and from there to Asia by crossing prehistoric land-bridges between the continents that resulted from the lowering of sea levels during each of the Earth's many ice ages that occurred in the Pleistocene Epoch. The horse then vanished from the Americas during an extinction that

---

[651] Gould, *Questioning the Millennium: A Rationalist's Guide to a Precisely Arbitrary Countdown.* Preface to the Original Edition—Our Precisely Arbitrary Millennium.
[652] Micklethwait & Wooldridge, *GOD IS BACK,* Introduction, p. 1, 4-5, 6-9,18-19, & 224 (Book Published in 2009)

occurred in the Americas at the end of the Pleistocene Epoch about 15,000 years ago. They almost became extinct in the rest of the world as well. By about 7,000 years ago (in the Holocene epoch, which is Earth's current epoch of life), the worlds' only horses were confined to a small area in the still open grassland steppes of the Ukraine and central Asia. Thus, it was — the horse was first domesticated and used as a beast of burden by people in Eastern-Europe and Asia and was then later introduced into Western-Europe, before being brought again to the New World as a much larger animal by the Spaniards in their voyages of discovery and conquest in the 15th century AD.[653] There have been many changes in the horse since it first appeared 60 million years ago in North America as a small dog-like animal. The remarkable changes that occurred to produce the larger animals of today are a classic example of *Micro-evolution* — i.e., a gradual enlargement of the animal that involved changes in the traits of the animal that caused *no change* in its *basic-body-plan*. The Mayans did *not* have horses. This is only *one* of the reasons they were at a decided disadvantage when they warred with the Spanish. (We will wait until Chapter 18: *Evolution — Darwin vs. Modern Science & the Bible,* to explain the concept of *Micro-evolution.*)

GUNPOWDER

We know gunpowder was invented by the Chinese, and they were the first to use it in war.[654] The Mayans did *not* have gunpowder. But the Europeans did.

AN EFFICIENT SYSTEM OF OCEAN NAVIGATION

The compass was invented by the Chinese. The Chinese pioneered its use for transoceanic navigation.[655, 656] Did you know the Chinese were the first people to circumnavigate the globe? *Gavin Menzies,* an officer in the British Royal Navy, joined the Royal Navy in 1953 and served in submarines from 1959-1970. As a junior officer, he sailed the world in the wake of *Columbus, Dias, Cabral,* and *Vasco da Gama.* When he commanded the *HMS Rorqual* (1968-1970), he sailed the routes pioneered by *Magellan* and *Captain Cook.* Menzies was born in 1937 and lived in China for two years before WWII. After he left the Royal Navy, he returned to China and the Far East many times. He wrote a truly fascinating book: *1421: The Year China Discovered America.* His book was the result of years of research. He describes several incredible transoceanic voyages made by the Chinese between 1421 and 1423 AD. One of these (the voyage of *Zhou Man*), circumnavigated the globe! Three of the voyages actually visited the shores of the Americas (the voyages of *Zhou Man, Zhou Wen, and Hong Bao*)! Their compasses were rudimentary, but when combined with their celestial navigational skills, they were helpful. Indeed, the Chinese were skilled navigators whose transoceanic voyages preceded *Christopher Columbus'* voyage to *the 'New World'* by at least 70 years and Magellan's circumnavigation of the globe by 100 years![657] Since Magellan was killed in the Philippines in 1521, it was his men who completed that historic voyage.

[653] Article: *The horses origin - Where horses originated & evolved into what we know them as today; horses evolution* http://www.irishhorsesociety.com/horsedata/horsesorigin.html
[654] Article: query: *Invention of Gunpowder.* By Kallie Szczepanski
[655] Article: http://www.smith.edu/hsc/museum/ancient_inventions/compass2.html Compass, China, 220 BCE by Susan Silverman AC
[656] Article: *History of Chinese Invention - Invention of the Magnetic Compass.* http://www.computersmiths.com/chineseinvention/compass.html
[657] Menzies: *1421: The Year China Discovered America.* © 2002 by Gavin Menzies.

THE WHEEL

The wheel came from Ur, in Mesopotamia (the same place Abraham was born), where the oldest use of the wheel is shown in clay tablets that diagram its use as a potter's wheel. It is thought the use of the wheel in transportation came later.[658]

CHRISTIANITY

Christianity came to the world from a tiny area on the east coast of the Mediterranean Sea known to the ancients after Noah's time as *Canaan*[659](*) in the Middle East — where Jesus Christ was born. Christianity spread worldwide from there.

BACK TO GOULD'S MUSINGS ABOUT THE MAYANS

Although the Mayans had Llamas, there is no evidence they had any other large draft-animals, such as horses or oxen. Neither did they have gunpowder. Their oceanic navigational skills were not as sophisticated as those of the Chinese and the Europeans. Apparently, most of their maritime travel was in the dugout canoes they paddled through coastal waters close to the shorelines. So far as we know, they did not invent and did not have wheeled transportation. The Mayans had advanced architecture, agriculture, irrigation, and water conservation systems. They also had advanced mathematical, and astronomy skills. Their calendrical system was incredibly accurate. But their military technology and tactics were not as sophisticated or as lethal as those of the Spanish. It seems Gould thought their only advantage was — they were not encumbered by the '*myths of Christianity.*'

Since their numeric system was based on the number 20, Gould suggested maybe the number 1,000 would not have seemed so significant to them. I cannot see why he would think that. 1,000 is a multiple of both base numbers (10 and 20). While it is true that 100 times the base 10 is 1000, it is equally true that 50 times the base 20 is also 1,000.

Maybe the reasons Gould mused about a possible Mayan-Chinese alliance was because, compared to the military advantages of the Spaniards when they invaded Meso-America, the Mayans would have needed the Chinese to have any chance of victory over the Spaniards. The Chinese had gunpowder, the horse, the wheel, and trans-oceanic navigation skills that were equivalent to those of the Spaniards when they warred against the Mayans.

So, *if* in his musings Gould was really being serious, then the only conclusion one can reach is that he had a big problem with Jesus Christ, with Christianity, and thus also with '*decimal*' Europe because it was — Christian.

There is no doubt Gould had a fascinating mind. What *a labyrinth of thought* he put his readers through with these musings. Maybe *his maze of thoughts* in his writings were (in large measure), responsible for his success and notoriety. He makes you stop and think about **what it is you think he means!**

I must agree with Gould about one thing. People are funny and fascinating beyond all possible description. People were doing all sorts of crazy things just before the dawn of the year 2000, like hoarding water for instance, and stockpiling canned food. Although it is hurtful to Christians, I think Gould's opinion of Christianity is understandable. Although

---

[658] Article: The Origins of the Potter's Wheel by Victor Bryant http://www.ceramicstoday.com/articles/potters_wheel.html
[659] (*) **Canaan:** A pre-Abraham name for what became the Holy Land; the nation of Israel in modern times.

he was Jewish, he was raised in a secular Jewish household. For that reason, Jewish religious precepts (which Christians venerate) may not have been a part of his life or his belief. He may have read the Old Testament or parts of it, but did he study it? The fact remains — Gould said he was an Agnostic. And that is something I can "hang my hat on."

Some say Agnostics cannot decide *if* God exists. Others claim this view of Agnosticism is an over-simplification. They say Agnosticism is very close to the Christian belief that the ways of God are unfathomable, that human reason is fallible, and that man requires a different non-scientific path to the truth — such as faith. This depiction of Agnosticism views Agnostics as allies of the church. The notion that anything is unknowable (some say), undermines science and reinforces theology, thus inclining man to faith and inducing men to trust religious doctrines. The church does not anathematize Agnostics and even the Roman Catholic Church will accept Agnostics in its fold because an association with them may cause them to change their mind about Jesus and God.

Nevertheless, since Gould wrote that he considered Jesus Christ and the Christian belief in a millennial rule of Christ on Earth in the end times a *myth*, it would not be unreasonable to suspect Gould had anything other than a passing acquaintance with the teachings of the New Testament.

THE CHRISTIAN CONCEPT OF A MILLENNIUM

The word *"millennium"* is not found anywhere in the Bible. The concept of the peaceful millennial rule of Christ on Earth comes from the mention of the binding of Satan for a period of a thousand years in the Book of Revelation written by the apostle John.

Revelations 20:1-3 *"And I saw an angel coming down from heaven, having the key to the abyss and a great chain in his hand. And he laid hold of the dragon, the serpent of old, who is the devil and Satan. And bound him for a thousand years, and threw him into the abyss, and shut it and sealed it over him, so that he should not deceive the nations any longer, until the thousand years were completed. After these things he must be released for a short time."*

DR. RYRIE'S INTERPRETATION OF THE PHRASE: 'A THOUSAND YEARS'.

In the Ryrie Bible commentary on the phrase *'a thousand years,'* Dr. Ryrie wrote: *"Since the Latin equivalent for these words is 'millennium,' this period of time is called the millennium. It is the time when Christ shall reign in peace on this Earth* (see also Isa. 2:1-4, Dan. 7:13-14, & Zech. Chapter 14). *Satan will not be free to work, righteousness will flourish* (see Isa. 11:3-16), *peace will be universal* (see Isa. 2:4), *and the productivity of the Earth will be greatly increased* (see Isa. 35:1-2). *At the conclusion of the thousand years, Satan will be loosed to make one final attempt to overthrow Christ but will not succeed."* (This represents Dr. Ryrie's full commentary on the phrase: *"a thousand years"*—Rev. 20:2). [660]

You can see the concept of *the end-times* is also a Jewish concept by reading the Old Testament scriptures listed above. Christians believe Jesus Christ was and is the Messiah (so often mentioned in the Book of Isaiah), who first came as a servant and to be a sacrifice for our sins. Christians also believe when He comes again, He will return as The Universal Savior.

---

[660] The Ryrie Bible note on Rev. 20:2—*'a thousand years.'*

WHY DID GOULD REFER TO JOHN'S REVELATION AS AN APOCALYPTIC TALE?

The Greek word, *Acpokalypsis* (or, as in the English spelling, *Apocalypse*) means *'revealing, conveying a revelation, an uncovering, a disclosure — a prophetic disclosure.'* That is why the book of Revelation is sometimes called the *'Apocalypse of John.'* The New Testament ends with John's book — *The Revelation of John*. John was the apostle and prophet who conveyed his visions of what will happen in the end-times when Christ comes again and establishes His peaceful 1,000-year rule on Earth. The book ends with what happens at the end of Christ's peaceful rule.

WHY WAS THERE SO MUCH HYSTERIA NEAR THE ADVENT OF THE YEAR 2000?

Perhaps it was for the same reason so many Bibles collect dust while on the shelves of our homes—people don't read, much less study their Bibles. The truth is, if you read the 24th Chapter of Matthew, you will see Jesus told the disciples all sorts of things concerning the end-times. But he also told them no man would know when the end-times would come. Only the Father knew (Matt. 24:36). Nothing in the Bible gives anyone any reason to think the second coming of Christ will occur at the *start* of any *earthly* calendrical millennium. The Bible simply states when He returns, Satan will be bound for the thousand years of Christ's peaceful rule on Earth. After that, Satan will be released again for a short time and will deceive the nations once again. After his defeat in the battle of Gog and Magog, Satan will be thrown into the lake of fire and brimstone for eternity (Rev. 20:7-10).

So, you see, no believer in Christ should fear the coming of the end-times spoken of in the Bible. Christ told the disciples only the Father knew when Christ would come again (Matt. 24:36). Therefore, Christians should not be concerned with *when* the second coming of Christ will happen, or *when* the peaceful millennial rule of Christ will be. Instead, they should live their lives in such a way that they will be prepared for His second coming when it happens. Christ's second coming will be a time of great exaltation and rejoicing for all believers, alive and dead, for when He comes again, the living believers and the spirits of the dead believers will be raptured (Matt. 24:30-31; Matt. 24:40-41 and Rev. 4:1). This is bed-rock Christian belief.

There are different views of how the millennial rule of peace will occur in the end-times. I will not attempt to explain the different views because they are a matter of interpretation of the scriptures, and different Biblical scholars have different views and beliefs about that as well.

Perhaps it was easier for Gould, a Jew and secular Jew at that, to dismiss everything I have just discussed as myth. After all, if he had his questions about the possible existence of God, (I'll discuss that possibility in a minute), why would he seriously consider the Christian belief that God had a son named Jesus?

From his musings in the Preface of his book, *Questioning the Millennium*, you can see why I think Gould maintained *Christianity was an historical myth*. Because he wrote — Christians believe in *'the myth of a local god, Jesus Christ, and the myth of His millennial rule on Earth in the end times.'*

LEVITES, COHEN, & THE COHANIM

Dr. Stephen Jay Gould was a Levite — a descendent of Levi. What is the significance of that? I have a very dear friend who lives in Tel Aviv. She is a Radiologist (like me) whose primary professional interest (i.e., passion) is — Mammography. Mammography was also my passion. I met her in Falun, Sweden in 1999 when she and I were two of four Radiologists Dr. Laszlo Tabar accepted for a visiting-fellowship in Mammography. Dr. Tabar is an internationally recognized authority on Mammography and Breast Cancer. The other two Radiologist-visiting-fellows were from Scotland and Spain. Myra,[661] my Israeli friend and colleague, came with her husband Alphie (a retired Pediatrician), to meet us in Jerusalem when my wife and I toured the Holy Land in the spring of 2010. We spent a day together. During our visit, I discovered Alphie is a Levite. He told me he has a specific gene that identifies him as a descendant of Aaron and Moses. I asked: *'How do you know that?'* He told me *all* descendants of Aaron and Moses carry *a specific genetic marker.* According to Jewish tradition, only males from the direct line of Aaron could serve as priests in the holy temple of God. This tradition began when Moses brought his brother Aaron before God to be anointed as the first High Priest of the Israelites. Historical documentation confirms Aaron's lineage was stringently followed from the first temple of Solomon, through the Jewish exile in Babylon, and continued past the destruction of Herod's temple by Titus in 70 AD. These priests, called *The Cohanim* (also spelled *Kohanim*), persist today and are charged with performing all religious rituals for the Jewish people.[662]

Furthermore, it has now been demonstrated *the Cohanim* have a common genetic marker that is characteristic of only ~10% of the general Jewish population. This genetic marker is completely absent in Gentiles. While some scientists claim this is not a direct confirmation *the Cohanim* specifically descended from Aaron, it does demonstrate a separation and preservation of this priestly line that has persisted for over 3000 years. It is fascinating the Bible independently confirms *the Cohanim priestly pedigree* existed in the past and is expected to continue in the future, ready to fulfill any prophetic destiny Almighty God has for them.[663] That's really taking your genealogy seriously. I remember thinking: 'Alphie is from the same tribe as Moses! He is descended from Moses' brother, Aaron! Alphie is a Levite, and *he could have been a Cohen of Israel if he had so chosen!'* Yet there was no pretention on his part. What marvelous and wonderful people they are. My Israeli friends and I have stayed in touch ever since through the internet. They have also visited us on one of their trips to the USA. They visited us after I retired from Medicine, and moved to Savannah, GA. Our door will always be open to them.

THE ORIGIN OF THE LEVITES AND THE SIGNIFICANCE OF *THE COHANIM*

The nation of Israel started with Abraham and Sarah. Abraham is their patriarch. Abraham is also the patriarch of the Arabs because his first son was Ishmael (Ismaël), whose mother was Hagar, Sarah's Egyptian handmaiden. But, since we are concerned here with how the Levites got their name, we will turn our attention to the Jewish side of Abraham's descendants.

---

[661] My friend Myra was the head of the Breast Imaging Center and the Chairman of the Department of Diagnostic and Interventional Imaging at Meir Hospital in Tel Aviv, when I met her in 1999.
[662] Article: **The Lineage of Jewish Priesthood Confirmed** by Patrick Young, Ph.D.
http://www.creationists.org/patrickyoung/article10.html
[663] Article: **The Lineage of Jewish Priesthood Confirmed**—by Patrick Young, Ph.D.
http://www.creationists.org/patrickyoung/article10.html

Abraham later had a son with his first wife, Sarah. That son, named Isaac, was born 14 years after Ishmael. Isaac's sons were Esau and Jacob. The 12 tribes of Israel came from Jacob's twelve sons. Levi was the third of Jacob's twelve sons, the issue of Jacob and his first wife Leah. Moses, his brother Aaron, and his sister Miriam were Levites — i.e., of the tribe of Levi. They were born some 400 years or so after Levi's time. It was God who, during the Exodus and in the Sinai desert, appointed Aaron to be Israel's first High Priest (Exodus 28:1-2; and Leviticus Chapters 8 and 9). The story of the rebellion of Korah against the authority of Moses and Aaron is told in Numbers 16:1-50. God intervened and that didn't end well for Korah and his followers. The validation of the Aaronic Levitical priesthood with the budding of Aaron's rod in the tent of the testimony is told in Numbers 17:1-13. Finally, the duties and support of the Levites are codified in Numbers 18:1-32. Thus, the Levites were ordained by God to be the priestly tribe of Israel. They were appointed by God to serve in the tent-tabernacle and to be the tribe from which Israel's priests would come. That's it. **Appointed by God! That is the significance of being a Levite!** If you have been born into the tribe of Levi, and if you carry the gene that identifies you as a *Cohen* (meaning that you are a descendent of Aaron), you are genetically *qualified to become a Cohen* (i.e., a priest) of Israel should you so choose.

Since Gould was a member of the priestly tribe of Levi, he might have been a descendant of Aaron. *If* he carried the *Cohen* gene, and *if* he had wanted to be a priest of Israel, it could have been within his grasp.

Gould was a Levite. I don't know if he carried the Cohen gene, but being a Levite suggests it could have been possible. He was a gifted man who was born into one of the most holy tribes of Israel — a man who might possibly have been directly related to one of Israel's two most revered prophets — Moses. (The other was Elijah.) But Gould chose the path of *Agnosticism.* He was *not* a practicing Jew. He most certainly *did not believe* in God and *did not believe* in a God-directed scheme of evolution. When he blamed Walcott's belief in God as the reason Walcott did not realize the significance of his discovery, it was obvious Gould not only had a problem with Jesus Christ — he also had a problem with God. What evidence do we have for this?

IN PUBLISHED ARTICLES, GOULD MISQUOTED DARWIN.

Gould wrote two essays for *Natural History* magazine in which he quoted the closing statement Darwin wrote in his book *The Origin of Species.* Later, the way Gould quoted Darwin was republished in a Gould collection. Here is the quote Gould attributed to Darwin:

> *"There is grandeur in this view of life.* **[   ] Whilst** *this planet has gone cycling on according to the fixed law of gravity, from so simple a beginning endless forms most beautiful and most wonderful have been, and are being, evolved."*

The gap I marked with brackets in Gould's quote of Darwin — represents the words Darwin wrote that Gould *left out!* The following words that appear in the box below are *the part* of the quote Gould omitted.

> **["with its several powers, having been originally breathed by the Creator into a few forms or into one; and that"]**

In his book, *The Science of God,* Dr. Schroeder wrote:

"Gould placed a period after 'life' and capitalized the 'w' in 'whilst,' neatly leaving out any hint of God. It seems to me that Gould has a problem with Darwin as well as with God."

So, you see, Gould went to great lengths to leave out Darwin's words that showed Darwin believed in a Creator. In this way, Gould hid the fact that Darwin believed in a God, that Darwin called *'the Creator,'* who Darwin believed *"originally breathed life into a few forms or into one."* [664] Darwin's use of the phrase: *"life, with its several powers, having been originally breathed by the Creator,"* is extremely important because it comes close to being a direct quote of scripture. It comes from Genesis 2:7 and it indicates Darwin believed God was the source and cause of life. This is so important that I must show you what the King James Version of the Bible (undoubtedly the version of the Bible Darwin read) actually says in this verse.

"And the Lord God formed man of the dust of the ground and breathed into his nostrils the breath of life. And man became a living soul." (Genesis 2:7 King James Version)

Of this, Dr. Schroeder wrote that Darwin made this statement of faith in God — his closing statement in every edition of his book *The Origin of Species,* including the 6th Edition dated 1872, which was the last edition during Darwin's lifetime.[665] Dr. Schroeder also wrote Gould had said Charles Darwin was his hero and role-model, but:

"HE (i.e., GOULD) IS DESPERATE TO CHANGE DARWIN'S WORLDVIEW INTO GOULD'S."[666]

Why would Gould do this? The truth is, we don't know. But it leads to some speculation.

- Maybe Gould was anxious to get rid of the inconvenient truth that Darwin grew up believing in God and had been taught God was the source and cause of all life on our planet;[667] because everything Darwin had assumed in his book of opinions and assumptions about evolution fit into Gould's worldview — with the singular exception of Darwin's belief in God.
- Maybe it uncovers something much more serious — maybe Gould was not really an Agnostic as he had claimed. Could Gould have been an Atheist?
- Maybe Gould omitted God from Darwin's statement because *Gould's own Cognitive Dissonance* favored the 1st pillar of Classical Darwinism — *Random-chance reactions among atoms started the process from which life eventually arose.* You see, if life started by chance, and if the chance was random, then there would be no need for a God. The assumption that chaotic random helter-skelter reactions bumbling along with no plan had eventually led to life, certainly appealed to atheists. If that were the case, then it all could have happened without the need for a Creator. However, it is important to again mention here:

---

[664] Schroeder, *The Science of God,* Chapter 2, p. 38*c,d,&e*
[665] Schroeder, *The Science of God,* Chapter 2, p. 38*e*
[666] Schroeder, *The Science of God,* Chapter 2, p. 39*a*
[667] Article: About Darwin.com—Who was Darwin? www.aboutdarwin.com/darwin/whowas.html

- *"Since 1979, articles based on the premise that life arose through random chance reactions over billions of years are no longer accepted in reputable journals."*[668] That is a direct quote from Dr. Schroeder's book, *The Science of God.* May I suggest that you read Chapter 10 again to brush up your memory of the reasons why the 1st pillar of Classical Darwinism is dead.

Before we finish this chapter, let's take a look at the unedited statement Darwin made at the conclusion of his book. The quote that follows is the last paragraph in the original first edition of his book, and it has remained the last paragraph in all the succeeding published editions of Charles Darwin's *The Origin of Species.*

"There is grandeur in this view of life with its several powers, having been originally breathed by the Creator into a few forms or into one; and that whilst this planet has gone cycling on according to the fixed law of gravity, from so simple a beginning endless forms most beautiful and most wonderful have been, and are being, evolved."

We will never know exactly what caused Gould to attack Walcott's belief in God, or why he purposefully misquoted the last paragraph of Darwin's book. However, we can say that sometimes it is our sins of omission — the things we don't do, the things we fail to say, the words in a quote we omit — that resonate the loudest and give others a glimpse into the depths of our feelings, our thoughts, and our beliefs.

Summary Points:
- Much of the behavior of present-day Darwinists can be explained by the beliefs, the cognitive dissonance, and the influence of Dr. Stephen Jay Gould.
  - Gould criticized Dr. Charles Doolittle Walcott for: Erroneously *'shoehorning'* all the Burgess fossils by classifying them into the groups of known modern-day animals to maintain his belief in God's gradual methods.[669] This is ironic because Gould — like Darwin, and Walcott — also initially believed in gradualism in evolution, but Gould did not believe in God.
  - Next, Gould asserted Walcott *'misinterpreted the Burgess fossils in a comprehensive and thoroughly consistent manner'.*[670]
  - Finally, Gould claimed the reason Walcott made these mistakes is because *'His belief in God kept him from realizing the significance of his find.*[671]
- Walcott's defenders believe Walcott may have been closer to the truth than Gould thought.
- Gould unwittingly revealed his own bias against Christian belief in Jesus Christ and God the Father when he misquoted the last paragraph in Darwin's book: *The Origin of the Species.*
- Gould's misquote of Darwin hid the fact Darwin also believed in a God who Darwin called *'the Creator, who originally breathed life into a few forms or into one.'*

---

[668] Schroeder *The Science of God* Chapter 6 p 85c
[669] Schroeder *The Science of God* Chapter 2 p 38b
[670] Gould, *Wonderful Life: The Burgess Shale & the Nature of History.* Preface & Acknowledgements
[671] Schroeder, *The Science of God,* Chapter 2, p. 38a

❧

CHAPTER 16: CHARLES DARWIN—THE MAN

Although this chapter will be devoted to the life, work, and ideas of Charles Darwin, it must be mentioned Darwin had one thing in common with the 16th President of the United States — the date of his birth. As fate would have it, Charles Darwin and Abraham Lincoln were born on the same day, February 12, 1809. That date is significant because both men would have a significant impact on world history. Some people also believe both men struck a blow against 'slavery.' O.David

ABRAHAM LINCOLN

Abraham Lincoln was born in poverty but would rise to prominence through his own efforts and eventually become the 16th President of the United States of America. He was one of the founding fathers of the current Republican Party and was its first elected President. His election sparked the outbreak of the American Civil War. Lincoln rallied most of the northern Democrats to his cause of liberty for all. He would go on to manage and rally the Northern American States to victory over the pro-slavery Confederate states of the South thus preserving the union. The American Civil War ended in 1865. Robert E. Lee surrendered his Army of Northern Virginia to Grant on *Palm Sunday* April 9th, 1865. Perhaps due to another quirk of fate, Abraham Lincoln would pay *'the last full measure of devotion'* [672] to his country with his life when he was shot in the back of his head by John Wilkes Booth five days later, on the night of *Good Friday* April 14, 1865. He died early on the *Sabbath morning* of April 15th, 1865! Some of us see those dates as prophetic! Although Lincoln is credited with ending *slavery* in America, racism persists, and our nation is still struggling with the principles of freedom, equality, and justice for all that were supposedly ushered in by the victory of the North.

CHARLES DARWIN

Charles Darwin was not born in poverty. He was the son of a prominent Medical Doctor and was born into a distinguished English family. Arguably, his life and work had an equally momentous impact. He became the influential 19th century scientist who is credited with a revolutionary theory of evolution that has sparked much controversy, division, and debate. Generations of antireligious nonbelievers have claimed Darwin's idea of evolution *'freed'* them from the *'slavery'* of Judeo-Christian religious dogma because it provided *an alternative* to the Biblical explanation of our origins which attributes everything to an almighty deity called *'God.*

DARWIN WAS RAISED IN THE UNITARIAN CHURCH. [673, 674]

Although generations of atheists have touted Darwin their hero, the fact remains his mother believed in God. While still a boy, Charles was baptized in the Anglican Church of England. However, he regularly attended services in the Unitarian Church with his mother. Tragically, she died when he was eight. When the time came for him to choose a profession Charles began his study of Medicine at Edinburgh. This seemed the logical thing to do because he came from a family well represented in the profession of medicine. He soon discovered he was not *'cut out'* to be a Medical Doctor. So, in 1828 he dropped out of Medical School and transferred to Cambridge to train for the ministry. This also

---

[672] From Lincoln's Gettysburg Address

[673] Article: http://www.famousuus.com/bios/charles_darwin.htm Darwin attended the Unitarian Church with his mother.

[674] Article: *About Darwin.com—Who was Darwin?* http://www.aboutdarwin.com/darwin/whowas.html

seemed a logical choice because his family was equally well represented in the profession of the ministry. It was commonly known when he was a young man, he read and quoted the Bible regularly. However, while at Cambridge, he came under the influence of John Stevens Henslow and soon developed an interest in Zoology and Geography. So, he *'changed course'* again and became the *'naturalist'* who took ship on the *HMS Beagle* when it set sail in June of 1831 for a protracted voyage to South America and the Galapagos Islands.

Early in this voyage, there are accounts of times when Darwin quoted the Bible to some of the profane sailors and had discussions about the Bible with the ship's Captain. At this time his frequent quoting of the Bible caused people to think he was a Biblical literalist.

DARWIN'S CHRONIC ILL HEALTH AND PERIODS OF DEPRESSION

After his return to England, he suffered from various maladies and chronic ill health, which plagued him for the rest of his life. The evidence suggests his health problems started after that voyage. Some have surmised perhaps he was stung by some exotic insect while in the Galapagos Islands. Whatever the cause, Darwin's persistent state of ill health was complicated by episodes of vomiting and periods of profound melancholy. His melancholy intensified after the tragic death of his daughter, Annie Elizabeth, who died shortly after her 10th birthday.

Annie was Darwin's favorite daughter, *'the apple of his eye.'* She spent much time with her father and was his constant companion. She was an angelic, affectionate, intelligent, and inquisitive child. Annie was a gracious, gentle spirit. At all times she was considerate of the feelings of others. She took great interest in her father's work. He had many conversations with her in which he explained his ideas about evolution.

In 1849 Annie and her two sisters caught scarlet fever. After their recovery, Annie's health continued to decline. Some suspect she suffered from tuberculosis. When her protracted illness worsened, Darwin took her to the Worcestershire spa town Great Malvern in a futile pursuit of help from hydrotherapy — a treatment known as *'Gully's water cure.'* While there (in Montreal House on the Worchester Road, on April 23rd, 1851); she died in her father's arms. No specific cause of death was given. Some have speculated she died of pneumonia. She was buried in the Great Malvern Priory Church yard. Darwin was so distraught he could not attend her funeral. Both Charles and his wife Emma (who had remained at home because of pregnancy), were devastated for they *'had lost the joy of their household.'*

After his mother's death, Darwin had stopped his regular attendance at Church services. After Annie's death, Charles stopped going to church altogether. It was during this period he stopped professing his belief in God. In 1860, he wrote a famous letter to his American friend, the biologist *Asa Gray.* Darwin told him he couldn't understand how the sufferings produced by natural selection could be countenanced by *'a beneficent and omnipotent God.'*

Over the years, he had studied nature and observed and reflected on how fragile all life is. He saw the cruelty and certainty of death by predators in nature and decided almost all life is in the food chain of a higher and stronger order of species. As he evolved his ideas of *natural selection* and *the survival of the fittest* he began to lose his childhood instilled faith in the goodness of an all-loving and all-protective Creator-God. His faith in God seemed to have been completely broken by Annie's death.

DARWIN LOST SIGHT OF GOD'S ORIGINAL INTENT FOR MAN AND GOD'S PROVISION FOR MAN'S FUTURE.

He seems to have lost sight of the Bible's message. God's original intent was for man to dwell in a paradise God had created on Earth specifically for man. The Bible informs us: In the beginning, everything in the Garden of Eden was created *perfect for man by God*. Man's original home on Earth was a *Paradise* in which all things were *free — except for one prohibited thing —* The *Fruit* of the *Tree of Knowledge of Good and Evil*. In the 3rd Chapter of Genesis, the Bible relates the temptation of man and man's disobedience which led to God's judgments—

- of enmity between man and nature,
- enmity between man and the ground,
- enmity between man and other men,
- and man's separation from God.

Some have said the eviction of Adam and Eve from the garden after their disobedience was the act of a vindictive God. Others believe God's eviction of Adam and Eve was an act of love to prevent man from also eating of the fruit of *the Tree of Life* (the other tree in the center of the garden) — something that would have caused man to live eternally in an infinite state of separation from God (Genesis 3:22-24).

It is no accident. In the last chapter of the last book of the Bible (i.e., the *Book of the Revelation of John*); after Christ has returned in triumph; after the saints have been resurrected; after the Devil has been defeated; and after the final judgments — those whose names are written in *the Book of Life* (because they believe in Jesus who gave His life for our salvation) — find themselves in Heaven and in the presence of God and Christ where all things have been made new. There, in the middle of the New Jerusalem and on either side of the river of life, they find *the Tree of Life*, bearing twelve kinds of fruit, and giving its leaves for the healing of the nations. When all believers have been saved, and resurrected, and have entered Eternity Future where they will commune with God for eternity; they are free to partake of the fruit of *The Tree of Life*. Thus, the Bible comes full circle (Rev. Chapters 19-22).

These are the beliefs Darwin's wife Emma held onto. If only Darwin could have focused on the Bible's message of hope and God's alternate plan for the salvation of man whereby the death penalty of disobedience could be overcome — he might have found solace in faith, as Emma did. Perhaps he could have seen things differently and his state of melancholy could have been resolved. Nevertheless, two profound conundrums of faith are the questions:

- *"Why do good people suffer.*
- *And why do innocent children die?"*

There are no satisfactory answers for mortal man. Those mysteries will perplex all believers for as long as they are on this terrestrial ball. However, after Annie's death, Darwin feverishly worked through his grief by organizing and writing down his ideas about evolution. The result was his book: "*The Origin of Species.*"

DARWIN'S WIFE WAS A DEVOTED CHRISTIAN

Darwin's wife, Emma, was a Christian who had strong faith. She showed great concern and worry over her husband's gradual, but apparent systematic loss of faith. The evidence seems to show Darwin gradually fell away from a belief in God. After the tragic death of his eldest daughter, he stopped attending church. It was at this time he began describing himself as an *agnostic*. He also began to see religion as a strictly personal matter and regarded science as completely separate from religion. At that time, when *GOD* ceased to be *GOD* for him and became only *god*, he began to think the question of God's existence was outside the scope of scientific inquiry. Yet, the mystery remains he apparently did not think his theory of evolution contradicted the biblical concept of a God who created all things. He also did not think the natural laws of evolution (which he believed he had discovered) were created by God. So, Darwin *believed god 'created all things.'* but, he *did not* believe *god* created the *'natural laws of evolution?'* Apparently, Darwin did not see the contradiction.

AT VARIOUS TIMES IN HIS LIFE DARWIN MADE SEVERAL CONTRADICTORY STATEMENTS.

- He freely admitted: In his Cambridge days he believed in William Paley's *'Argument from Design'* as evidence for God's place in nature. But, by the time he completed *'The Origin of Species,'* he had changed his mind and wrote: *'The old argument of design in nature, as given by Paley, which formerly seemed to me as conclusive, fails, now that the law of natural selection has been discovered.'*

- In 1879 (three years before his death in 1882), he said he was never an atheist or denied the existence of *a god*, but rather he thought the term agnostic would be the more correct description of his state of mind.

- Regarding the questions — *'does God exist,'* and *'was there a beginning'* — near the end of his life Darwin wrote: *'I cannot pretend to throw the least light on such abstruse problems. The mystery of the beginning of all things is insoluble to us; and I for one must be content to remain an agnostic.'* (We have already talked about Gould's 'agnosticism.' (cf. Appendix V in Book III for more information).

- However, on other occasions — and more often — he referred to himself as a *'theist.'*

A theist *believes in one God who is the creator and ruler of the universe who is known by revelation.* By definition (i.e., *'ruler'*), theists believe — *God is in control.* This belief is called *Monotheism.* The belief that multiple *gods* control — is called *Polytheism.* The role that God assumes in the lives of people distinguishes *theists* from *deists.* A *deist* believes God exists and created the world but thereafter assumed *no control* over it or over the lives of people.

- Yet, we also know Darwin delayed writing down his ideas about evolution because he was worried about the religious consequences that might arise from his published work. If Darwin didn't believe in God (as some have claimed), or was uncertain if God actually existed, why would he do this? Was it simply because he may have been concerned how the publication of his ideas would affect his wife? Perhaps. Some say he gave the manuscript of his book to his wife and asked her to decide if it should or should not be submitted to a publisher.

DARWIN'S TORMENT

It seems Darwin was conflicted by a lifelong struggle with his conscience and lived a tormented life of existence between the *never lands* of belief versus unbelief. Darwin had always refused to discuss his own beliefs about a supreme being in public. But he once wrote to his friend Asa Gray:

"I feel most deeply that the whole subject is too profound for human intellect.
A dog might as well speculate on the mind of Newton."

And yet, he closed his *"The Origin of Species"* on a more inspirational note. It was this inspirational note—which appears as the final statement in every one of the editions of his book that were printed in his lifetime — that Stephen Jay Gould *misquoted,* and other Darwinists have *ignored.* Perhaps, in the final analysis, and in spite of his previous denials, this statement is the true window into his core belief — *Darwin really did believe in God!*

Not only did he believe in — **'The Creator who created,'** but he also believed in —

The Creator who — **'Originally breathed life into a few forms or into one.'**

In other words, the closing statement in his book makes one think Darwin believed God was the Author of all life on our planet. The last statement in his book also shows Darwin did not think his theory of evolution contradicted a belief in God. This revelation is so important that we should, once again, take a look at Darwin's closing statement in his book.

"There is grandeur in this view of life, with its several powers, having been originally breathed by the Creator into a few forms or into one; and that whilst this planet has gone cycling on according to the fixed law of gravity, from so simple a beginning endless forms most beautiful and most wonderful have been, and are being, evolved." [675]

Dr. Schroeder thinks Darwin's reference to the *'fixed law of gravity'* reflects his belief his theory of evolution would experience the same fate as Newton's Laws of Planetary Motion.

"At first it would be attacked as being sacrilegious. But eventually it would be seen to fall within a religious paradigm." [676]

When we discuss what Darwinists and Neo-Darwinists have done with their views of Darwin's ideas, you will see current-day society is sharply divided between those who believe in God and those who don't. It is now obvious — Darwin's views have never been viewed as — *a religious paradigm.* Unfortunately, they are now — *the center of the controversy that exists over that deep divide!*

---

[675] The Works of Charles Darwin: *The Origin of Species, 1876* Chapter XV *Recapitulation & Conclusion p.* 446-447
[676] Schroeder, *The Science of God,* Chapter 2, p. 38*d*

DARWIN MADE OTHER STATEMENTS ABOUT GOD & THE CREATOR IN HIS BOOK.

For those of you who (like Gould), would like to think Darwin did not believe in God, get ready for a revelation. Darwin made at least *five* other references to *"God"* and to *"the Creator"* in his book!

1. On pages 137-138 of his book, while discussing the simple variation of striped legs on several distinct species of the horse genus, he wrote: *"He who believes that each equine species was independently created will, I presume, assert that each species has been created with a tendency to vary, both under nature and under domestication, in this particular manner, so as often to become striped like the other species of the genus; and that each has been created with a strong tendency when crossed with species inhabiting distant quarters of the world, to produce hybrids resembling in their stripes, not their own parents, but other species of the genus. To admit this view* (i.e., that each species was independently created) *is, as it seems to me, to reject a real for an unreal, or at least for an unknown, cause. It makes the works of God a mere mockery and deception; I would almost as soon believe with the old and ignorant cosmogonists, that fossil shells had never lived / but had been created in stone so as to mock the shells living on the seashore."*

> In this 1ˢᵗ quote, when he wrote: *"It makes the works of God a mere mockery and deception;"* he seems to suggest he believes creation resulted from the works of God. And, if God *'created'* an inanimate something in stone that had never lived but *looked like* the shell of a previously living organism, then God would have been guilty of the sins of mockery and deception—something Darwin believed God would never do. So, I think Darwin would have agreed with me in the 1ˢᵗ volume of this book (i.e., The Introduction—Part V under "Some Christians feel Threatened by Science") when I said: *"There are some Christians who claim the fossil evidence of a very old earth, and the mountains of accumulating scientific data, which prove an even older universe, are deceptions of God because God purposefully planted fossils in geologic strata for the explicit purpose of deceiving man. These people have claimed the author of truth (God) has done something God would never do."*

2. On page 153 Darwin wrote: *'It is scarcely possible to avoid comparing the eye with a telescope. We know that this instrument has been perfected by the long-continued efforts of the highest human intellects; and we naturally infer that the eye has been formed by a somewhat analogous process. But may not this inference be presumptuous? Have we any right to assume that the Creator works by intellectual powers like those of man?'*

> In this 2ⁿᵈ quote, his statement: *'Have we any right to assume that the Creator works by intellectual powers like those of man,'* makes us think Darwin considered God's thoughts and ways are higher than man's. Darwin must have been familiar with and may, at one time, have believed Isaiah. 55: 8-9.
>
> *"For My thoughts are not your thoughts,*
> *Neither are your ways My ways, declares the LORD.*

> *For as the heavens are higher than the earth,*
> *So are My ways higher than your ways,*
> *And My thoughts than your thoughts."*

3. On page 154 (again comparing the eye to the telescope) he wrote: *"In living bodies, variation will cause the slight alterations, generation will multiply them almost infinitely, and natural selection will pick out with unerring skill each improvement. Let this process go on for millions of years; and during each year on millions of individuals of many kinds; and may we not believe that a living optical instrument might thus be formed as superior to one of glass, as the works of the Creator are to those of man?"*

> This 3rd quote: *"And may we not believe that a living optical instrument might thus be formed as superior to one of glass, as the works of the Creator are to those of man?"*—is evidence Darwin believed *creation* was the *work of God.* It also brings to mind these scriptures:
>
> *Ps. 86:8 "There is no one like Thee among the gods, O Lord. Nor are there any works like Thine."* And
> *Ps. 86:10 "For Thou art great and doest wondrous deeds. Thou alone art God."*

One can successfully argue these three quotes give us insight that deep down, Darwin still believed in an honest, truthful, righteous, and good God who created; and whose works, wisdom, and intellect were superior to and above all others.

4. In Chapter VI of his book (the chapter where he discusses *"Difficulties of the theory")*, and in response to the opinion of some naturalists that every detail of structure was produced for the good of its possessor — on page 167 he wrote: *"The foregoing remarks lead me to say a few words on the protest lately made by some naturalists, against the utilitarian doctrine that every detail of structure has been produced for the good of its possessor. They believe that many structures have been created for the sake of beauty, to delight man or the Creator (but this latter point is beyond the scope of scientific discussion), or for the / sake of mere variety, a view already discussed. Such doctrines, if true, would be absolutely fatal to my theory."*

> In this 4th quote, Darwin refers to 'the Creator,' however, it seems he is not making a statement of personal belief that the Creator would act in this way, but is talking about the beliefs of *others* which, if true, would be fatal to his theory.

5. On pages 445e-446a (near the close of his book), he wrote: *"Authors of the highest eminence seem to be fully satisfied with the view that each species has been independently created. To my mind it accords better with what we know of—the laws impressed on matter by the Creator—that the production and extinction of the past and present inhabitants of the world should have been due to secondary causes, like those determining the birth and death of the individual. When I view*

all beings not as special creations, but as the lineal descendants of some few beings which lived long before the first bed of the Cambrian system was deposited, they seem to me to become ennobled."

In this 5th quote, Darwin talks about: *"What we know of the laws impressed on matter by the Creator."* This suggests Darwin believed not only was there a Creator, but the Creator 'created' matter and the laws that govern matter.

Also, when he talked about *"Viewing all beings not as special creations, but as the lineal descendants of some few beings which lived long before the first bed of the Cambrian system was deposited"*—we are reminded Darwin was puzzled by the lack of any fossil evidence of *visible* animals (like those in the Cambrian Period), in the layers of deposits that were deeper and therefore older than the Cambrian layer. Scientists later referred to this puzzlement as *Darwin's Dilemma.*

The *microscope* had been experimented with in the mid 1590s by the Dutch spectacle makers *Hans and Zacharias Jensen*, and the first true microscope had been developed by *Anton van Leeuwenhoek* in the late 17th century. Therefore, Darwin was familiar with light microscopy. Darwin also knew about microbes because of the work of such men as—*Robert Heinrich Herman Koch* (1843-1910) who became the father of modern bacteriology; and the work of *Louis Pasteur* (1822-1895) who developed the pasteurization process that gave the world 'safe milk;' and the work of *Joseph Lister* (1827-1912) who was the English surgeon who spearheaded the medical use of antiseptic medicine. All of this had been published in his lifetime. However, Darwin didn't know:

- ***All life in the Pre-Cambrian Age* was *microscopic.*** He also did not know—
- **The *macroscopic* life-forms of the Cambrian Period were *the first visible* animals and plants to appear on Earth.**

Those discoveries were made 95 years after 1882 — the year Darwin died. It was not until 1977 that *Elso Barghoorn* published his article about his discovery of the evidence of the Earth's first life. He used an ***electron microscope*** to discover the microscopic fossils of the Earth's first life-forms (the Prokaryotes) in the 3.3-billion-year-old sedimentary deposits of ***the Pre-Cambrian Fig Tree Formation***. The age of those microfossils indicates they appeared in the Archean Eon early on the 3rd Day. (See the discussion of Barghoorn's discovery in Chapter 10 and the Summary of the Fossil Evidence of the Earliest Life-Forms on Earth in Chapter 12.)

Summary

- We have seen Charles Darwin was chronically ill when he returned from his voyage on the HMS Beagle. He suffered greatly from his undiagnosed illness for the rest of his life. The medical profession of his day was incapable of understanding and properly diagnosing his malady. No cure could be made, and the doctors of his day were powerless in their attempts to palliate his suffering. Nothing they did helped, and the only choice Darwin had was *'to do or to die.'* Darwin chose *'to do.'* I believe his determination to persevere through his pain and suffering was motivated by his love of his wife and family. We must remember — Darwin was an Englishman. *Perseverance until the goal is accomplished is an historical characteristic of the English. Perseverance is part of the moral fiber of England and is a virtue of the English people that is to be greatly admired.*

- He and his wife Emma experienced much tragedy in their lives. Although they were blessed with ten children, three died of childhood diseases. We thank the Lord for each of our children. A loving parent does all that is within his power to nurture and provide for his child. When our children scrape a knee or suffer from the measles, it is as if it is happening to us all over again. Thankfully, modern medicine does so much more for us today than the medical profession could do in Darwin's day. But, still, there are times the illness of a child cannot be reversed or rectified. When that happens, I have seen what it does to a grieving family. I also know from personal experience because it happened to my wife and me. It is a sad thing for a parent to see his child die. It is unexpected. It is unnatural. The helplessness of knowing nothing can be done to prevent it tests our faith in God to the extreme and out of the depths of our sorrow we all cry: ***"Why?"***

- In Darwin's case the loss of Annie Elizabeth was a crushing blow. It seems the tragic death of Annie caused Darwin to lose his faith in God. So often (both then and now), organized or formal religion can be more about judgment and retribution than about love and forgiveness. If judgment and retribution were what Darwin found in church, then perhaps we could understand why he ran from it. We don't know if that was the case, and I am not saying it was. However, in our attempts to understand the tragedies in our lives we often blame ourselves first, but when the pain becomes unbearable, we get angry — angry at God — and we start blaming God. We ask as Darwin did: *"How can an omnipotent, beneficent, and all loving and all forgiving God allow the death of an innocent child?"* We also ask: *"How can God allow good people to suffer?"* If we blame God and hold onto our anger, these experiences will eventually make us emotionally sick and cause us to turn away from God. I know — on both counts. Although I still went to church, it took me years to come back to God. God *is* all loving and all forgiving. But for us mortals, the questions: *"Why do innocent children die, and good people suffer,"* are unanswerable. **They betray our ignorance of God's Divine Omniscience! Like Job, when I realized that, I stopped blaming God (cf. "Darkens Council without knowledge," — in The Introduction: Part V).**

- The record tells us Darwin did turn away from God. For a long time, he considered that to speculate about the mind and purposes of God *"was too profound for human intellect — a dog might as well speculate on the mind of Newton."*

- As concerns the reasons for man's belief in God, late in his life Darwin wrote: *"I cannot pretend to throw the least light on such abstruse problems. The mystery of the beginning of all things is insoluble to us; and I for one must be content to remain an agnostic."*

- Nevertheless, the six places in *The Origin of Species* where Darwin mentioned the Creator, tell us that deep down, he did not give up his belief in God. There is no doubt he questioned what he had been taught as a child. But in Darwin's case, the final paragraph in his book tells us what he wrote there — and kept there in *all the editions of his book in his lifetime* — about *"The Creator, who originally breathed life into a few forms or into one;"* resonates the loudest and gives us a glimpse into the depths of Darwin's feelings, thoughts, and beliefs. I am convinced Darwin came back to God. I am also convinced Darwin did not believe his ideas about how life developed and evolved on Earth contradicted his belief in God. I think Darwin thought he had theorized how God created and evolved all life.

- Charles Darwin was a brilliant scientist. His chronic illnesses, his melancholy, the tragic deaths of three children, and a church that may have caused him to turn away from it — caused him to question his faith. His ideas about evolution satisfied a host of nonbelievers. His ideas have been championed by nonbelievers because they offer an alternative view of creation which nonbelievers think exclude God.

- In the final analysis, I am convinced his statements about the Creator in his book reveal — *Darwin did not entirely give up his belief in God.*

⚜
CHAPTER 17: HOW LIFE ORIGINATED—DARWIN VS. MODERN SCIENCE

We have just talked a bit about Darwin's life, his family, and the tragedy in his life. In this chapter, I will focus on the basics of his theory of how life originated and developed. O. David

We have learned, the first life on Earth was *microscopic*. Those life-forms *suddenly appeared* in the Pre-Cambrian Age on the dawn of the 3rd Day of Creation. The first *macroscopic* life-forms did not appear until the 5th Day of Creation. They appeared in the Cambrian Period, which was the 1st Period of the Phanerozoic Age (i.e., the Age of *macroscopic,* or *visible life*). The scientific evidence that told us when they appeared and how they evolved has also been presented. Modern science has recently informed us those first *visible* animals on Earth also *suddenly appeared*. This is something the Bible has claimed for the last 3,300 years. However, when it comes to the question of *how* life on Earth originated, we find there have been two very different competing views—

- The Bible's view, and
- What Charles Darwin *imagined and assumed* (i.e., Darwin's *'Sitisams'*).

'Sitisams' is an acronym I coined. I introduced the concept of *Sitisams* in Chapter 10 of this Book when I talked about "The *Wrong Science Theory on the Origins of Life"* in part III of Chapter 10. In this chapter we will now discuss the basic tenets of *Darwin's Abiogenic Theory of Life's Origins*. What Darwin thought may have happened will be compared with what Modern Science has discovered. However, before we discuss Darwin's ideas, let's review the meaning of the acronym *'Sitisams.'*

S-i t-i sams stands for *'Since-if…then-if… Serial Assumption Mistakes.'* I coined this acronym when I was studying how George Wald decided Stanley Miller had discovered how life originated on Earth. We have already discussed the *mistakes* George Wald made when he championed the idea that Miller's experiment *proved* Darwin's *wrong* idea that life came from *abiogenic random chemical-reactions in warm ponds*. Miller produced amino acids in a vacuum flask that contained the same volcanically produced gases that were in the early Earth's atmosphere 3.8 billion years ago. Miller subjected those gases to electrical charges. After two days, a slimy substance developed on the inner wall of the flask. That slimy substance proved to be *amino acids*. Amino acids were known to be *the building blocks of proteins.* When Wald examined the results of Miller's two-day experiment, he made three *speculative assumptions* that he projected onto *a flawed conjecture,* which led him to *a faulty conclusion.*

WALD'S SPECULATIVE ASSUMPTIONS, FAULTY CONJECTURE, AND FAULTY CONCLUSION:
1. ***Since-if*** amino acids are the building blocks of proteins—
2. ***Then-if*** random chemical reactions produced amino acids in only 2 days—
3. ***We Assume:*** given enough time—
4. ***We Conjecture:*** those amino acids— *would eventually evolve into proteins.*
5. ***Thus, We may Conclude****: those proteins would eventually bring forth life.*

#1—3 were Wald's Speculative Assumptions. #4 was Wald's (& Miller's) flawed conjecture. #5. was Wald's faulty conclusion.

Wall thought Miller's experiment had proved Darwin's Theory that 3.8 billion years ago, life on Earth came from *abiogenic random chemical-reactions* which *in time* produced amino acids which *ultimately* formed proteins that *eventually* turned into life. Wald believed this process played out over the 2 billion years he thought were available. I have already discussed the faulty reasoning in this *five-step 'Sitisams'* sequence (See Chapter 10). This was just a summary review.

HAROLD MOROWITZ & ELSO BARGHOORN

The statistical work of Yale's *Professor Harold Morowitz*, which demonstrated Wald's assumptions were statistically impossible, has already been presented. And the scientific discoveries of Harvard's Professor Elso Barghoorn have also been reviewed. Barghoorn proved beyond every shadow of a doubt:

- Wald's assumptions were wildly wrong.
- Life on Earth did not occur in the way Wald, Darwin, and the other proponents of the *Abiogenic Theory of how life originated on Earth — had supposed.*
- We also know the amino acids that were produced in Miller's experiment *did not produce any proteins and did not bring forth life.*

The scientific proof Harvard's *Professor Elso Barghoorn* discovered was so convincing that twenty-five years after it had published Wald's views, *Scientific American* retracted its support of Wald's assumptions in another article that reported Barghoorn's findings and stated Barghoorn's scientific discovery unequivocally proved Wald's assumptions were wrong. Today, no reputable scientific journal will accept any articles that tout *the random-chance chemical-reactions (over eons of time) theory* of the origin of life. (See Chapter 10.) Therefore, modern science has proved — *the Abiogenic Chemical-Reaction Random-Chance Theory of the Origin of Life is now dead.* Now we are ready for something new.

CIRCULAR LOGIC

Before delving into Darwin's ideas, we need to examine a fallacious form of reasoning known as *'Circular Logic.'* My Dad used to tease me with a clever saying called the *"Exception to Every Rule—Rule."* It goes like this:

"There is an exception to every rule. If this statement is true, then it must (in-and-of-itself) be a Rule. But if it is a rule, then there must be an exception to it. Now, if there is an exception to the rule that there is an exception to every rule, then there is a problem. The problem is: 'the-exception-to-the-exception.' Now if there is an exception to the rule that says, 'there is an exception to every rule,' then there can't be an exception to every rule! Therefore, the inescapable conclusion must be — For the Exception to Every Rule-Rule to be True — It Must Be — FALSE!"

This is an example of *"Circular Logic."* It really messes with your mind, doesn't it? Why? Because circular logic is *a formal logical fallacy* in which the proposition to be proved (*there is an exception to every rule*) is *assumed* to be *true.* This is a classic example of a formal *'Sitisam.'*

Obviously, the *'Exception to Every Rule-Rule' is* **false** because there are some rules to which there are no exceptions. If I were to say: ***"It is a rule of physics that an uninterrupted and uncushioned fall from an extremely great height will result in*** _death"_ — is unquestionably true. There are no exceptions to that rule. That's just pure physics.

However, there are other rules to which _there are commonly known exceptions._ For example, if I were to say: _"It is a rule that all great military leaders throughout world history have been tall men"_ — you would immediately think of the exception — Napoleon Bonaparte.

So, we cannot truthfully say there is an exception to every rule because _there are exceptions to some rules,_ but _there are no exceptions to others._

Wald's _'Sitisams' (**S**ince-if / **t**hen-if / **S**erial **A**ssumption **M**istakes)_ are a classic example of the fallacious reasoning of _Circular Logic._ Metaphorically speaking, _Circular Logic_ is like — a dog chasing his tail! It gets the dog — _nowhere!_

Now, let's dive into the _"nitty-gritty"_ of Darwin's Wrong Theory of Evolution.

DARWIN'S THEORY ON THE ORIGINS OF LIFE

Now that the acronym _Sitisams_ and the misleading form of reasoning known as _Circular Logic_ have been defined, we can proceed with an examination of Darwin's _"warm-pond abiogenic chemical-reaction idea for the origin of life"_ which has already been introduced in Chapter 10. Some of what follows will involve a review of what has been said. Then, we will delve into some new information that has proved Darwin wrong.

Like George Wald, but long before Wald's time, Darwin had _assumed_ life had to go through a sequence of events that led from the inanimate to the animate. Given enough time, he imagined these events would start with inanimate chemicals and eventually lead to the first biological cell. As a means of review, these events are again listed here. I call them — _the Five Pillars of Darwin's Origin of Life 'Sitisams.'_ Slow gradual development figures prominently in Darwin's ideas. His scheme _assumed_ life started with:

1. _Random-chance chemical-reactions among atoms (the 1st Pillar)—_
2. _Requiring eons of time (the 2nd Pillar)—_
3. _Gradually combining one chance-reaction with others (the 3rd Pillar)—until_
4. _Self-replication (the 4th Pillar)—then_
5. _Mutations eventually produced — the first living biological cell (the 5th Pillar)._[677]

We have just discussed — modern science has discovered the first three assumptions did not happen. Although we know life does reproduce (i.e., _self-replicate_), and mutations do occur in the reproductive process, modern science has found it is powerless to provide the answers to _how_ life happened. In chapter 10 this quote from Dr. Schroeder was presented.

"There is now overwhelmingly strong evidence, both statistical and paleontological, that life could not have been started on Earth by a series of random chance chemical reactions. Today's best mathematical estimates state that there simply was not enough time for random reactions to get life going as fast as the fossil record shows that it did. The reactions were either directed by some,

    (1) as of yet unknown physical force, or
    (2) a metaphysical guide; or
    (3) life arrived here from elsewhere.

---

[677] Schroeder, _The Hidden Face of God,_ Chapter 4 p 50_b_

But the 'elsewhere' answer merely pushes the start of life into an even more unlikely time constraint. For decades (since Darwin) many scientists have presented the misconception that there are rational explanations for the origins of the universe, life, and mankind. The shortcomings of the popular theories were merely swept under the rug to avoid confusing the issues. The knowledge that scientists do not have these explanations has now been coupled by the awareness of the fossil record's failure to confirm Darwin's or any other theory of the gradual evolution of life. The demonstration of these misconceptions has brought many scientists and laypersons to an uncomfortable realization: The problems of our origins, problems that most of us would have preferred to consider solved by experts who should know the answers, in fact have not been solved and are not about to be solved, at least by the purely scientific methods used to date." [678,679]

It is essential to understand science has not provided explanations for the two principal starting points in our lives:
(1) The start of the universe, and
(2) The start of life itself.

DARWIN'S IDEA ABOUT HOW LIFE PROGRESSED

Now let us turn our attention to the discussion of Darwin's idea of how life moved on from the formation of the first living biological cell. Since Darwin's 5 pillars of the origin of life just get us to the first living cell, he had to speculate how the first living cell could produce another living cell and then go on to produce a population of living cells that would eventually cause the diversity of life that we see around us.

- So, he *assumed* the first living cell would *self-replicate* to produce another cell. Then, the process would repeat itself until a population of living cells would exist.
- Eventually, he *assumed* these cells would *combine* to produce *the first simple organism.*
- Next, he *assumed* the first simple organism would *self-replicate and mutate* to produce *other simple organisms.*
- At some point, *combinations, self-replications, and mutations* would eventually *evolve a more complex organism from a simple one.*
- *Over time, mutations would produce other more complex and different living organisms which in turn would self-replicate and mutate and evolve* — the whole process repeating itself over and over until the complexity of life that is on Earth would eventually be.
- Darwin envisioned *an evolutionary tree of life* that *started* with the *simple* and then *evolved* into more *complex* forms; with each *branch* becoming *more complex* and at the same time *more diverse.*

Darwin's idea of how life began and then evolved from the simple to the complex is imaginative and ingenious. No wonder Darwin was welcomed by the scientists of his day. No wonder those who don't believe in God still champion his ideas of how life developed

678 Schroeder *Genesis and the Big Bang* Chapter 1 p 25 *b&c*
679 Schroeder *The Science of God* Chapter 1 p 10 *a*

and evolved. Darwin's scheme doesn't require a God. Absolutely brilliant — *but we now know it didn't happen that way!*

WHAT 20TH & 21ST CENTURY SCIENTIFIC DISCOVERIES HAVE TAUGHT US.

The scientific discoveries of the last 85 years have proved *the first life on Earth was microscopic* — the *Prokaryotes*, which were the first life-forms on Earth. They were simple, single-cell bacteria, single-cell algae, and the Archaea — that *suddenly appeared* at the juncture of the 2nd and 3rd Days of Creation, when *liquid water first appeared*. This is something *Darwin did not know* because the scientific discoveries that proved this were made 95 years after his death.

NATURE'S 1ST REPUDIATION OF DARWIN'S THEORY

The *sudden appearance* of the Prokaryotes is nature's *first refutation of Darwin's theory*. It disproves all 5 pillars of *Darwin's Origin of Life Assumptions*: i.e., that random-chance inorganic chemical-reactions — over eons of time — *gradually* combined with other random-chance inorganic chemical-reactions until — *after additional eons of time* — *self-replications and mutations* produced the first simple living biological cell. **No!** The microscopic fossils of the Prokaryotes show *they suddenly appeared* as *complete living simple single-cell life-forms! They did not evolve* in the way Darwin suggested. *They sprang forth fully developed!* They are the first example of *the sudden, abrupt, punctuated changes* the Bible proclaims *ten times over* in first chapter of the Genesis Creation Account!

PROKARYOTIC LIFE-FORMS APPEARED IN MASSIVE NUMBERS.

Although the Prokaryotes were single-celled organisms, when they arrived on the scene, they did *not* appear *as only one biological cell. They simultaneously and spontaneously appeared worldwide in massive numbers!* That is what the fossil record shows. This proves Darwin's assumption that eons of time were required to get from the first living simple cell to a worldwide population of living simple cells — *was wildly wrong!*

The 3.3 billion year-old *microfossils* of the Earth's first life-forms (the Prokaryotes), *are identical in every respect including size and scale to today's living Prokaryotes that are found in present-day aquatic environments!*[680] During their 2.5 billion year dominance as the only life-forms on Earth, *their one cell, no nucleus 'basic-body-plan' has remained unchanged!*[681] This refutes Darwin's idea that numbers of simple living cells would combine, mutate, recombine, and self-replicate the recombinations until the first simple living organism would eventually evolve. Even today (3.3 billion years later), the Prokaryotic single-cell bacteria and Archaea *have not evolved into more complex organisms. Neither have they undergone any recombinations nor mutations to produce any higher-order or more complex multicellular life-forms.*[682] They have indeed — *Long Endured!*

PLANTS MAYBE THE SPECIAL EXCEPTION.

However, scientists have discovered that single-cell algae have massive amounts of *unexpressed* DNA. For what reason? I will talk about that in another chapter. Nevertheless, science has now proved *there was no gradual steady progression from*

---

[680] Schroeder *Genesis and the Big Bang* Chapter 7 p 112*b*

[681] Schroeder *Genesis and the Big Bang* Chapter 9 p 145*b*

[682] Schroeder *Genesis and the Big Bang* Chapter 7 p 112*b*

one-celled life to complex multicellular animal organisms — no smooth transitions from the simple to the complex. The fossil record does not support this part of Darwin's assumptions. The Prokaryotic bacteria and Archaea were simple one-celled organisms when they first appeared, and the fact that they have not evolved into Eukaryotes or multi-celled or other more complex forms of life shouts out that these classes of the first life-forms on Earth have retained their simple structure during the entire 3.3 billion years of their existence![683] *When life's complex multicellular animal life-forms first appeared on the 5th Day, their appearance was also sudden, abrupt, punctuated, and worldwide.*

What actually happened was — *over 3 billion years* spanned the gap between the immediate appearance of one-celled *microscopic* life on the just-cooled Earth at the end of the 2nd Day, *and the explosion of multicellular macroscopic animal life* 570 million years ago in the Cambrian Period of the 5th Day. During all that time, *all* life on Earth remained confined to simple organisms.[684] So, for almost the entire duration of the 3rd Day (2 billion years), the only life on Earth was that of Prokaryotic life (cells with no nucleus) — the single-celled bacteria, single-celled algae, and the Archaea. (Note that the 2nd Eon of the Pre-Cambrian Age is the Archean Eon — which corresponds to the dawn of the 3rd Day). These first simple life-forms did not require oxygen. The consensus is: the first life that produced oxygen, the *cyanobacteria* (also prokaryotes) — began to appear late — near the end of the 3rd Day. (See the Chart on the last page of Chapter 12.)

During the 1-billion-year duration of the 4th Day, in the Mesoproterozoic Eon, *as oxygen levels increased*, and as Rodinia formed, *higher-order single-celled life-forms began to appear.* These life-forms, the *Eukaryotes* (higher-order single-celled life-forms with nuclei), needed *oxygen* to gain their energy. Some were oxygen producers, such as the simple photosynthesizing plant-forms that joined-in with the stromatolites to ramp up the production of volumes of oxygen *"big-time."* By the end of the 1-billion-year duration of the 4th Day, higher-order multicellular Eukaryotic life-forms had not only appeared, but dominated, and Earth's atmosphere had been completely transformed from its poisonous opaque atmosphere of the 2nd Day, through its anoxic translucent atmosphere of the 3rd Day, to its life-friendly oxygen-rich clear atmosphere on the 4th Day. For a review, see Chapter 11: *The 4th Day and the Luminaries.* Also, on the chart at the end of Chapter 12: *The Geologic Timetable Compared to the Six Days of Creation*; note that Eukaryotes dominated during the Neoproterozoic Eon of the Pre-Cambrian Age. The Neoproterozoic Eon was the last part of the 4th Day and the earliest part of the 5th Day.

Then, 650 million years ago, near the end of the Neoproterozoic Eon (the end of the 4th Day and very early part of the 5th Day, which was over 3 billion years after the 1st Prokaryotes appeared), *the Ediacaran forms* (simple soft-bodied globular life-forms of uncertain classification) *suddenly appeared.*[685,686] The fact of their *sudden appearance* is the 2nd example of nature's disagreement with the 1st, 2nd, and 3rd *Pillars* of *Darwin's Theory.* The Pre-Cambrian fossil-data show these globular simple unclassified life-forms

[683] Schroeder *Genesis and the Big Bang* Chapter 7 p 112*b*
[684] Schroeder *The Science of God* Chapter 6, p. 90*a*
[685] Schroeder *The Science of God* Chapter 2 p. 29*c*
[686] Schroeder *The Science of God* Chapter 6 p. 89*d*

lacked mouths and appendages. Although some have small portions of shells, they are mostly soft-bodied.[687] This is also the time when Rodinia broke apart.

Next, 570 million years ago on the 5th Day (in the Cambrian Period of the Paleozoic Era of the Phanerozoic Age), *and without any hint of any earlier fossils, the basic anatomies of all life extant today suddenly appeared simultaneously in the oceans.* This is known as the *'Cambrian Explosion of Life.'* This Cambrian Explosion of life is one of the greatest paleontological discoveries of all time.[688] This happened at the start of the Cambrian Period. The fossil-record now shows *the explosion phase of the Cambrian* was its earliest part and it only lasted about 5 million years. But the sediment deposits of this 5-million-year phase are 300 meters (327 yards) thick! Through the entire thickness of these deposits a multitude of varieties of animals appear with no change in the basic morphologies of the individual phyla of animals.[689] After that, for some unexplained reason, *no other new phyla (basic anatomies) ever appeared.*[690]

So, to summarize — in a leap, life had moved from the simple single-celled Prokaryotic life-forms that appeared at the juncture of the 2nd & 3rd Days of Creation; through both the single-celled Eukaryotes and multicellular Eukaryotic life-forms of the 4th Day; and then through the simple soft-bodied Ediacaran fauna that appeared at the juncture of the 4th and 5th Days. Next, after the stage had been set by the life-friendly transformations of the Earth's oceans, atmosphere, and continents that occurred on the 3rd and 4th Days, a literal explosion of complex animal and plant-life occurred in the early Cambrian Period of the 5th Day.[691] *These animals that suddenly appeared on the 5th Day* had heads, mouths, eyes, jointed legs, food-gathering appendages, intestines, and notochords — all of which had appeared *simultaneously, independently and fully developed!* Sponges, rotifers, annelids, arthropods, primitive fish, and all the other body plans represented in the 34 animal phyla that exist today appeared *'after their kind'* (as the Bible puts it) *as a single burst of life in the fossil record!* This is what the worldwide fossil record shows, **and no one disputes it!**[692,693]

> *According to the fossil record, gradual evolution has been found to be false at every major morphologic change.*[694] *All of the changes that have occurred have been sudden, abrupt, developments — just as the Bible states.*

Thus, this sequence of events has destroyed not only the 1st, 2nd, and 3rd, but also the 4th, and 5th Pillars of Darwin's assumptions as well. The idea of the self-replication of the combination of random-chance reactions that had combined with other random-chance events, and which required mutations to produce the first biological cell — simply did not happen. **No!** Complex, complete, fully developed, and different life forms suddenly sprang

---

[687] Schroeder *The Science of God* Chapter 6 p. 89*d*
[688] Schroeder *The Science of God* Chapter 2, p. *29c-30a*
[689] Schroeder *The Science of God* Chapter 6, p. 89*b*
[690] Schroeder *The Science of God* Chapter 2, p. 30*b*
[691] Schroeder *The Science of God* Chapter 6, p. 89b
[692] Schroeder *The Science of God* Chapter 6, p. 88*b*
[693] Schroeder *The Science of God* Chapter 6, p. 88-89*a*
[694] Schroeder *The Science of God* Chapter 2, p. 29*c*

into existence as individual creations that were completely independent of each other. ___It all happened the way the Bible says!___

Summary Points:

Science has failed to explain how life came to be. But the fossil evidence that scientific investigation has discovered:

- *Destroys Darwin's 1st pillar of random-chance reactions as the ignition point.*
- *Destroys the 2nd and 3rd pillars which posit that eons of time were required for these random chance reactions to gradually produce the first living biological cell.*
- *And also destroys the 4th and 5th pillars, which propose that self-replication and mutations not only produced the first simple organism, but also produced the diversity of complex life that exists today.*

If your teachers and professors are still teaching Darwin's ideas of how life originated, developed, and evolved — they are woefully behind the times. Darwin's 19th century scheme has now been refuted by the vast compendium of scientific discoveries that have been made in the 20th and 21st centuries. His theory is like the proverbial horse-drawn buggy — whose horse has died.

Ironically, there is a much older divinely inspired book (written 3300 years ago by Moses) that correctly names the Creator of all things, and gives us the precise, correct sequence of His Creations. Sadly, that book, which is the true guide to a blessed, happy, productive, moral-mortal-life, and Life Eternal — doesn't get the attention it deserves.

CHAPTER 18: EVOLUTION—DARWIN VS. MODERN SCIENCE & THE BIBLE

There are three basic tenets of Darwin's beliefs about how Earth's complex life-forms evolved. They are [1]*Gradualism,* [2]*Common Descent,* and [3]*Natural Selection.* Darwin's *concept* of *Gradualism* has been disproved. The idea of *Common Descent* has merit, but *his specific concept* of *Common Descent* has been refuted by the fossil record. We'll talk about this in Chapter 20 when the possibility of a *'tie that binds'* will be discussed. So, we will now briefly state Darwin's basic ideas about *Natural Selection,* and then direct our attention to a discussion of how Darwin derived his conclusions about evolution through Natural Selection. As we do this, we will compare Darwin's ideas with what modern science has discovered and what the Bible first stated 3,300 years ago. *O. David*

DARWIN'S "LAW" OF NATURAL SELECTION

Darwin claimed the *Law of Natural Selection* had been discovered in his lifetime. He said the discovery of that law was the reason he decided Paley's *'Argument from Design,'* as evidence of God's place in nature, was wrong.[695] So, we will now examine Darwin's Law of Natural Selection. Let's open this discussion by going to his book: "*The Origin of Species.*" In Chapter IV (pages 65-111 of his book), he explains his observations upon which he derived his *Law of Natural Selection.* He often referred to his Law of Natural Selection as *"The Law of the Survival of the Fittest."* Here is what he wrote in the first paragraph of his summary at the end of Chapter IV. I have underlined a few words for reasons I will explain.

"If under changing conditions of life organic beings present individual differences in almost every part of their structure, and this cannot be disputed; if there be, owing to their geometrical rate of increase a severe struggle for life at some age, season, or year, and this certainly cannot be disputed; then, considering the infinite complexity of the relations of all organic beings to each other and to their conditions of life, causing an infinite diversity in structure, constitution, and habits, to be advantageous to them, it would be a most extraordinary fact if no variations had ever occurred useful to each being's own welfare, in the same manner as so many variations have occurred useful to man. But if variations useful to any organic being ever do occur, assuredly individuals thus characterized will have the best chance of being preserved in the struggle for life; and from the strong principle of inheritance, these will tend to produce offspring similarly characterized. This principle of preservation, / or the Survival of the Fittest, I have called Natural Selection. It leads to the improvement of each creature in relation to its organic and inorganic conditions of life; and consequently, in most cases, to what must be regarded as an advance in organization. Nevertheless, low, and simple forms will long endure if well fitted for their simple conditions of life." Now look at the underlined words.

If—if there be—a severe struggle for life—then—it would be—if—But if ever do occur—assuredly—will have the best chance—will tend to produce offspring similarly characterized.

This is the characteristic language of the naturalists of Darwin's day. Their conclusions about the laws that govern nature were formulated by observing the conditions under which animals lived. They observed their character and behavior and noted the changes

---

[695] Article: *About Darwin.com—Who was Darwin?* http://www.aboutdarwin.com/darwin/whowas.html

they saw over time. They then imagined what they thought were the causes and the effects of the changes they observed. What this first paragraph of Darwin's summary demonstrates is — *a chain of assumptions and conjectures* that were *based on observations* which *were then projected on to a series of seemingly rational or logical conclusions, which he thought explained the things he saw.* This 19th century method of reasoning was *fraught* with *multiple possibilities for faulty conclusions.* In short, what we see here is just another example of the same old **'Sitisams'** method of reasoning that we have previously discussed. This type of reasoning *is vulnerable to the ills of Circular Logic.*

Conversely, Elso Barghoorn based his conclusions of when Earth's first life-forms appeared by using modern scientific methods of investigation, which produced the data that proved the validity of his discoveries. He used an electron microscope to study the 3.3-billion-year-old Pre-Cambrian chert rock of *the Fig Tree Formation* in the midst of the African Shield.[696] There, he found the microfossils of the Earth's first Prokaryotes. His conclusions did not rely on any assumptions that rested on reasoned conjectures, which were drawn from his observations. **No!** *He analyzed the scientific proof provided by his electron microscope.* Not only did he identify the Earth's first life-forms, but he also discovered — *their microfossils were identical in every respect with the same life-forms that are found today in Earth's aquatic environments, thus proving — in the entire 3.3 billion years of their existence, the Earth's first life-forms have not undergone any evolutionary changes.*[697] These organisms (the Prokaryotes) still exhibit the same basic-body-plan. They have not evolved into any higher or more complex forms of life. For 3.3 billion years the basic body plan of the earth's first life-forms has remained unchanged![698] Thus we see, the only idea Darwin expressed that science has confirmed, is in the last sentence of Darwin's statement (i.e., *"low and simple forms will long endure if well fitted for their simple conditions of life)."*

DISCUSSION

The concept of natural selection was originally developed in the absence of a valid theory of heredity. Although Deoxyribonucleic Acid (DNA) was discovered in the 1860s by the Swiss chemist Friedrich Miescher, it was not until the 1950s that the importance and significance of the role DNA plays in heredity was suggested. In 1953 Watson, Crick, and Wilkins reported what is now accepted as the first correct *double-helix chain-model of DNA structure.* Wilkins' contribution was not as readily recognized as that of Watson and Crick, but he was finally recognized when all three men were jointly awarded the Nobel Prize in Physiology and Medicine in 1962 for their work on DNA structure.[699] After the discovery of *the double helical-chain nature of the DNA molecule in 1953,* the idea that DNA is the driving force behind the Mendelian Theory of Genetics came about, and the science of modern genetics was born.[700] The 1865 Mendelian Theory of Genetics is attributed to the Augustinian friar — *Gregor Johann Mendel.*

---

[696] Schroeder *The Science of God* Chapter 6 p 86*b*.

[697] Schroeder *Genesis and the Big Bang* Chapter 7 p 112*b*

[698] Schroeder *Genesis and the Big Bang* Chapter 7 p 112*b*

[699] Article: Discovery of DNA Structure and Function: Watson and Crick by Leslie A. Pray, PhD © 2008 Nature Education. www.nature.com

[700] Article: Chromosomes, Mutation, and the Birth of Modern Genetics: by Thomas Hunt Morgan evolution.berkeley.edu /.../history_ 18

DARWIN'S DILEMMA—THERE ARE GAPS (JUMPS) IN THE FOSSIL RECORD.

The fossils of Darwin's time showed both complex and simple organisms but were limited to those forms of life that were visible to the naked eye. The fossil record of his day was discontinuous. There were massive gaps (or *'jumps'*) in the record. Darwin acknowledged that jumps in the development of the animals existed. He also admitted the fossils discovered in his time did not demonstrate the smooth gradual evolutionary flow from the primitive and simple to the complex that he theorized. He and his contemporaries were puzzled they were unable to discover any fossils in the layers of rock that were older than the Cambrian layer. This has been called *Darwin's Dilemma*. He did not know that the lack of any *macroscopic* fossils in the Pre-Cambrian strata *was because all* Pre-Cambrian life was *microscopic*! That discovery would not be made for almost a hundred years after Darwin died when Elso Barghoorn used an electron microscope to examine the Pre-Cambrian sedimentary rocks of *the Fig Tree Formation*. Darwin had hoped future fossil discoveries would find evidence of earlier life-forms in the Pre-Cambrian layers and fill in the jumps thus proving his theory of a slow smooth gradual evolution from the first simple organisms to the complex. For this reason, Darwin encouraged his followers *to continue to search for* the so-called *missing transitional forms* that he felt would prove the slow gradual smooth developmental changes he had imagined. Darwin was confident future fossil discoveries would find the missing links that would prove his idea of a smoothly trending life curve that led from bacteria to trees and mankind.[701] *Barghoorn solved Darwin's Dilemma, but his solution did not confirm Darwin's theory of Gradualism.*

DARWIN DID NOT BASE HIS THEORY OF EVOLUTION ON THE FOSSIL RECORD.

Because of the jumps in the fossil record of his day, and its lack of any transitional forms that would prove his theory of evolution via natural selection, Darwin ignored the fossil record and looked elsewhere for the *'proof'* he sought. Instead, he took note of the morphological changes that occurred in the *selective breeding* of various species of pigeons and other farm animals. He then assumed that if in tens of generations lean ancestral stock evolved into robust productive progeny — then gradually over tens of millions of generations vastly greater changes would have occurred. Thus, he imagined there could eventually be changes great enough to cause one phylum to morph into another phylum and that life could then rise ever higher on an evolutionary tree. Unfortunately for Darwin, there is no evidence of an evolutionary tree in the fossil record.[702] Notice the underlined words: *assumed—if—then gradually—vastly greater changes would have occurred—imagined there could eventually be—and life could then rise.* This language is a classic example of faulty *'Sitisams'* reasoning. It is the formal flawed language of *Circular Logic*. Although acceptable in Darwin's day, *this type of reasoning would not be called 'scientific investigation'* today!

It is incongruous Darwin chose *the more controlled* biological sequences of *selective breeding* to make the observations upon which the conclusions about *his imagined uncontrolled random processes of natural selection were reached.* This was ironic because his methods limited the expression of the 1st Pillar of his Theory of the Origin of Life—*Random Chance*—and minimized the possibility for *Mutations*—the 5th

[701] Schroeder *Genesis and the Big Bang* Chapter 9 p 134 *a&b*
[702] Schroeder *The Science of God* Chapter 1 p 9*b*

Pillar of his origin-of-life ideas, and an *imagined engine of change in his scheme of evolution*. By definition, and to a certain extent, *selective breeding* (as opposed to *inbreeding*) limits the possibly of *random-chance expressions, and mutations,* in the off-spring!

DARWIN ENCOURAGED HIS FOLLOWERS TO CONTINUE SEARCHING FOR TRANSITIONAL FOSSILS.

Because of the gaps in the fossil record of his day, and the lack of any transitional forms, Darwin urged his followers to continue to search for the missing transitional links he thought would prove his theory. His disciples did continue the search. That search has now been going on for the past 165[*] years.

165[*] — Darwin's Book: "The Origin of Species" was 1st published in 1859. 2024 – 1859 = 165 years.

However, the more extensive fossil record of today reveals:

- Transitional forms are totally absent at the basic levels of the phyla of life and are rare if present at all — in class.
- The fossil record shows: Only after the basic anatomies of the animals (i.e., the basic-body-plans) are well established are any fossil transitions observed.[703]
- However, the fossil remains of all the transitional changes that have occurred represent changes within the phylum that were all expressed at the level of the individual species.
- Stated another way, all the transitions that have been found in the vast abundance of fossil specimens discovered in the last 165 years — have occurred at the level of the species — five levels below the level of the phyla.
- The Bible actually tells us this!

THE BIBLE SAYS ALL LIFE WILL REPRODUCE ACCORDING TO THEIR SPECIES.

According to the Bible, all forms of life will self-replicate at the level of the species of life. Beginning with the first mention of life in the Bible (Genesis 1:11) on the 3rd Day and repeated for the life-forms that were made by God on the 5th Day (Genesis 1:21) and the 6th Day (Genesis 1:24), the Bible tells us the Earth's life-forms will reproduce *'after their kind'* (or *'according to their kind'*) — as English translations of the Bible put it. The Hebrew word that is translated as *'after their kind'* is *miyn. Miyn means Species.*[704, 705] Those fossil transitions that have been found within the various *species* of life are changes that occurred in the *traits* of the *species* (i.e., *Micro-evolution*). *No changes in the basic-body-plan of an animal or a plant have ever been found!* The extensive fossil record of today tells us that the *Macro-evolution* that Darwin imagined was fantasy — not fact.[706] *Micro-evolution* and *Macro-evolution* will be defined and further discussed after we have talked about how modern science classifies life.

---

[703] Schroeder *The Science of God* Chapter 1 p 10*a*
[704] The Interlinear Bible (Hebrew to English): *'after their kind'* in English is *'miyn'* in Hebrew. (See ref. 106)
[705] The Hebrew & Chaldee Dictionary in Strong's Exhaustive Concordance of the Bible: reference word #4327 — *'miyn'* means *'species.'*
[706] Schroeder The Science of God Chapter 2 p 36*e*-37*a*

To better understand what has just been stated, let's pause briefly to discuss how science classified the various forms of life in Darwin's day. An explanation of the *Linnaean Taxonomy,*[707] a well-known scientific classification of life-forms and the one most prevalent in Darwin's lifetime, will help us understand where *Micro-evolution* occurs in nature, and it will also help us understand where Darwin hoped the fossil evidence of his idea of evolution (what science calls *Macro-evolution*), would someday be found.

THE LINNAEAN TAXONOMY—A CLASSIFICATION OF LIFE.

The Linnaean Taxonomy is named for one of the most important scientists of the 18th century — a Swedish botanist and medical doctor named *Karl von Linné*. He wrote 180 books in which he described Earth's life-forms in extreme detail. Since his published writings were mostly in Latin, he is known to the scientific world as *"Carolus Linnaeus."* *The Linnaean classification* was widely accepted by the early 19th century and is still the basic framework of all taxonomy in the biological sciences today.[708] Linné divided the life-forms on Earth into two *Kingdoms — Animals & Plants*. To understand the divisions of the taxonomy of animals, let us look at how Karl von Linné classified the animals that we are — human beings, i.e., *Man*.

Man is the specific *species* of animal that is named *sapiens*. Man belongs to the *Genus* or *Family* of animals that are called *the Hominidae*; which are *an Order* of animals that are *primates*; that belong to *a Class* of animals called *the Mammals*. Mammals are *a Sub-phylum* or sub-division of animals that are *Vertebrates,* which in turn belong to a larger *Phylum* of animals that are known as the *Chordates*. In short, the classification of the animal we call *'man'* looks like this:

Phylum *(a group, race, or tribe)*: **Chordata**←(*The level where Darwin thought transitions would be found.*)
    Subphylum *(sub-division or clan)*: **Vertebrata**
      Class *(or Type)*: **Mammals**←(In Antiquity, transitions occurred at the level of *Class*)
        Order *(or sub-type)*: **Primates**
          Genus *(or Family)*: **Hominidae**
            Species *(or Sub-family)*: **sapiens**←**(Modern times,** *change @ species*)

So, man is classified as the Species (*sapiens*) of the Genus (*Homo*—for Hominidae) that science refers to as *Homo sapiens* — meaning *"Man Who is Wise."*

The Phylum is the major division of animal-life and exhibits the animal's basic anatomy—*its basic-body-plan.*[709,710] Darwin thought future fossil discoveries would yield the evidence that would validate his idea of *Macro-evolution* — the name that modern science now ascribes to Darwin's scheme. However, his ideas about evolution were *not derived* from any observations of changes at the level of the phylum.

Since Darwin got his ideas from observing the results of the selective breeding of pigeons and other farm animals, the changes he saw occurred at the level of the *species* of the animals.[711] What he observed are the *only* transitions that are observed in nature

[707] Article: Carl Linnaeus (1707-1778) http://www.ucmp.berkeley.edu/history/linnaeus.html
[708] Article: Classification of Living Things: Introduction—anthro.palomar.edu/animal/animal_1.html
[709] Schroeder *The Science of God* Chapter 2 p 30*a&b*
[710] Schroeder *The Science of God* Chapter 2 p 36*d&e*
[711] Article: Carl Linnaeus (1707-1778) http://www.ucmp.berkeley.edu/history/linnaeus.html

in modern times. They have *only* occurred at the level of the *species* of animals — *five levels below the level of the phylum.*

MICROEVOLUTION[712]

Changes that occur below the level of the phylum of an animal are classified as *intra-phylum* (i.e., *within* the phylum) changes. The transitional changes that have occurred within the phyla of animals, which the fossil record documents, are the only transitions that have occurred in modern times. They show changes in morphology or other features that happened at the level of the *species,* and which *only involve changes in certain traits* of animals without causing any changes in *the animal's basic-body-plan.* An animal trait, such as the heft of its bone structure, is something that distinguishes the animal but does not change its basic anatomy (i.e., its basic-body-plan). For example, Arabian horses differ from Clydesdale horses in the more streamlined features of their muscles and the lighter and less hefty character of their bone structure. The distinctive appearances of Arabian and Clydesdale horses are such a contrast that no one would mistake one for the other. However, Arabians and Clydesdales are still horses. Both belong to the Chordate *phylum.* They are *Vertebrates* of the *Mammal Class* in the *Order* of the *Perissodactyla* — of the Genus *Equus* — of the species *caballus.* Taxonomically, they are both classified as *Equus caballus* (common name—horse). The Arabians are a *breed* of horses that were *bred* for speed. The Clydesdales are another breed of horses that were bred for heavy work. Since they were *bred* for specific tasks, they are commonly referred to as *"breeds."* Changes expressed at the level of the species of animals, which result in changes in the traits of a species that do not affect the basic-body-plan of the animal, are changes science now calls *Micro-evolution.* Micro-evolution is observed regularly in farmyards and biology laboratories. Today, it is understood: *Micro-evolution is the type of selection that forms the basis for breeding and population genetics. It finds no dispute in the Bible.* [713]

MACROEVOLUTION

Darwin imagined a type of evolution of the Earth's animals that would have resulted in the change of one basic-body-plan into another — i.e., a *worm* evolving into an *insect*, then into a *mollusk*, and from there into a *fish*. Since worms belong to the phylum *Annelida*, and insects belong to the phylum *Arthropoda*, and mollusks belong to the phylum *Mollusca*, and fish belong to the phylum *Chordata* — for a simple worm to morph into a complex fish would mean the worm would have to go through two other phyla of more complex life and then into a third phylum of an even more complex form of life. This might have happened *if* fish came from worms — i.e., if worms were the common ancestors of insects, mollusks, and fish — that is *if* they were *all* related. This was the way Darwin imagined the first simple animals would have gradually become more complex over time as they climbed his imaginary evolutionary tree. In this scheme, gradualism is expressed. On the other hand, for a worm to suddenly transform into a fish would have created a tremendous gap or jump in development, which would have been the antithesis of slow gradual change. Darwin's scheme of the gradual evolution of the simple into the complex

---

[712] Schroeder *The Science of God* Chapter 1 p 16c Chapter 2 p 31 [**Micro-evolution]**
[713] Schroeder: The Science of God Chapter 1: p 16
[714] Schroeder *The Science of God* Chapter 1 p 16c Chapter 2 p 31 [**Micro-evolution]**

would necessarily be a change, which would have caused individuals of one phylum of animals to evolve into another new race of animals through mutations and interbreeding that would have involved a complete change of the animal's basic-body-plan. Scientists have decided to call Darwin's concept of evolution — "*Macro-Evolution.*" If evidence of this type of evolution were to ever be found, it would be a type of evolution that expressed itself on the grand scale — at the level of the phylum of an animal. Darwin imagined a type of evolution, which would have involved changes in animals that would have occurred five levels *above* the level of the species.[715]

Darwin's '*Sitisams*' had already caused him to buy into a false theory about how life originated. Now he again theorized another fallacious *Sitisams* scheme when he mused about how our planet's life-forms must have evolved.

BUT THE FACT REMAINS: NO CHANGES IN THE BASIC BODY PLANS OF THE PHYLA OF ANIMALS HAVE EVER BEEN DOCUMENTED!

The kind of theoretical change Darwin imagined (i.e., at the level of the phyla of animals) is what scientists call *inter-phylum* (i.e., *between* the phyla) — or *cross-phylum* change. As just discussed, the name scientists have applied to this kind of *theoretical* evolutionary change is — "*Macro-evolution.*" This is the kind of evolution Darwin encouraged his followers to find. However, after 165 years of searching, no one has found any fossils that demonstrate any animal, which belonged to a specific phylum of animals, subsequently morphed into a completely different animal of another phylum. Therefore, scientists have concluded Darwin's concept that *Macro-evolution* would have eventually caused *inter-phylum* changes — has been proved to be a fantasy.[716] There are no cross-phylum changes documented in the fossil record! There is no evidence that *Macro-evolution* has ever occurred in nature! The only place it has ever occurred was in Darwin's imagination.

Darwin mistakenly assumed the changes in the *traits* of the *species* of animals he observed, would later translate upward, and cause even greater changes at the level of the phylum to which the species belonged — if given enough time. He did not know the more extensive and complete fossil record of the future would show—

- The basic-body-plans of Earth's life-forms were established at the level of the phyla on the 5th Day![717]
- They have never been established at the level of the species!
- 165 years of scientific discovery has determined there are 34 distinct phyla of animals today.
- Within the thirty-four phyla that define the basic-body-plans of modern-day animals, there are approximately thirty million species.
- More than 34 phyla developed during the Cambrian Explosion on the 5th Day.
- But only 34 persisted.
- The rest became extinct.
- At their inception, the 34 phyla of animals that survived extinction looked very different from our modern-day animals.

---

[715] Schroeder *The Science of God* Chapter 1 p 16*c* Chapter 2 p 31 (**Macro-evolution)**
[716] Schroeder *The Science of God* Chapter 2 p 40*a*
[717] Schroeder *The Science of God* Chapter 2 p 30*a&b*

- The different appearances of our modern-day animals were the result of micro-evolutionary changes caused by **Major environmental changes:**
  - [1]Such as supercontinent formations and break-ups, reversals of the Earth's magnetic field, eruptions of super-volcanos, and mega-tsunamis—
  - [2]Population genetics, and—
  - [3]Extra-terrestrial macro-environmental events, (such as asteroid impacts, and T-Tauri solar winds).
- Nevertheless, the 34 phyla that survived extinction formed the basic-body-plans of all animals alive today.
- Since the Cambrian Explosion, no new phyla have ever appeared![718,719]
- Once again, Darwin's *Sitisams* and *Circular Logic* led him (and his disciples) — astray.

PUNCTUATED DEVELOPMENT—THE BIBLICAL SIGNS OF DIVINE INTERVENTION & INTELLIGENT DESIGN.

The Bible announces *sudden, abrupt, punctuated changes* on each and every one of the *Six Days of Creation.* In the First Chapter of Genesis, they are marked by *the tenfold repetition* of the phrase *"Then God said."*[720] These Biblically announced, punctuated developments, are the signs of the Creator's *Divine Intervention, and Intelligent Design. On each one of the Six Biblical-Days-of-Creation,* Elohim intervened by making something new.

The fossil record of today continues to document gaps or jumps in the development of the Earth's animals. These gaps defeat Darwin's principle of *Gradualism* in evolution because they document the *sudden, abrupt, punctuated developments* of complete and independent complex life-forms in strata, which are above the strata that contain the older simple life-forms that preceded them. Like the fossil record, the Bible's description of the unfolding of life is *sudden, abrupt,* and *punctuated — not* gradual — and certainly *not smooth.* However, between theologians and Darwinian paleontologists, there is a dramatic difference in *how* nature's punctuations are interpreted.

"THEN GOD SAID"

In Chapter One of Genesis, the Bible states the transition from the nonliving to the living and the appearance of plants and animals are all marked by this statement of God: *"Then God Said."* The theological understanding is — *All forms of life on Earth and all of the Earth's foundations and features were created by God!* They came forth by His pronouncements and direction. While science indicates environmental changes have at times played a role in determining which species flourished and which perished, science also tells us that there is within the material universe an *orthogenetic property — a developmental direction* that is determined *by internal genetic factors as well.* Nevertheless, the Bible holds that this *orthogenesis is God-directed and the result of a divine Plan!*[721]

---

718 Schroeder *The Science of God* Chapter 7 p 102-103
719 Schroeder *The Science of God* Chapter 2 30*b*
720 Schroeder *Genesis and the Big Bang* Chapter 10 p 158*b*
721 Schroeder *Genesis and the Big Bang* Chapter 9 p 136*d*

The above-described Biblical concept of *a Divinely Inspired Ultimate Cause of Life in Nature and a Purposeful Goal* is clearly *at odds with Darwin's theory of gradual random natural selection.* But, during the past few decades, some Neo-Darwinists have proposed modifications in Neo-Darwinian Theory. Their new proposals have brought their version of Darwin's *so-called natural selection theory* considerably closer to what the Bible says actually happened — perhaps without those Neo-Darwinists realizing it! The most dramatic shift in opinion has been the recent acceptance by some Neo-Darwinists that *gradual random mutations* are *probably **not** the sources of change within a species!*[722] One particularly prominent Neo-Darwinist has been recently criticized for his '*new*' idea of *"punctuated equilibrium"* — his explanation of the abrupt, sudden developments and gaps that are documented in the fossil record. We will talk a bit more about this in Chapter 21. I'll wager you will be surprised when you learn his identity.

DARWINISTS AND NEO-DARWINISTS ESCHEW THE MATHEMATICS OF STATISTICAL PROBABILITY.

Darwin thought it *highly probable that gradual random mutations were responsible* for the diversity of Earth's life-forms. However, statistical analyses of Darwin's theory have consistently shown *that belief is statistically highly improbable.* Dr. Schroeder thinks that is why Darwinists object to the tests of statistical analysis. Schroeder made this statement in his book: *The Hidden Face of God—*

"It is not surprising that so many of the texts on evolution eschew any semblance of a mathematical analysis of the theories that random reactions produced the ordered, information-rich complexity (of life—my edit). *When Lawrence Mettler and Thomas Gregg decided to add a few chapters on the mathematics of evolution in their book: 'Population Genetics and Evolution,' they brought Henry Schafer on board. The math Schaffer brings to this totally secular text states clearly that evolution via random mutations has a very weak chance of producing significant changes in morphology. Of course, this is exactly why you will search long and hard to find any spokespersons for random evolution. Their approach to evolution is atavistic, a throwback to the time of Darwin, when cellular biology was assumed to be a rather simple affair of slime within a membrane. As we've seen, molecular biology has revealed that it is a mountain more than that."*[723]

THE WORLD CONFERENCE ON MACRO-EVOLUTION IN 1980

The intense paleontological efforts of the past 100 years contain vastly greater evidence of the development of earlier life than in Darwin's day but have not produced the evidence Darwin hoped for. Today's fossil record is as discontinuous as it was in Darwin's time. This discontinuity has been brushed aside by supporters of his theory, but that is no longer possible. Dr. Niles Eldredge (of the American Museum of Natural History in New York) is on record for stating at the Chicago held World-Conference on Macro-evolution in 1980:

---

[722] Schroeder *Genesis and the Big Bang* Chapter 9 p 136*e*-137*a*
[723] Schroeder *The Hidden Face of God* Chapter 7 p 120

"The pattern that we were told to find for the last 120 years [since Darwin] *does not exist."*[724,725,726]

This means — in 1980, *Eldredge closed the door on Darwin's concept of Macro-evolution* (i.e., Macro-evolution never existed, never happened). As I write these words, 165 years have passed since Darwin made his claim, and no cross-phylum fossil transitions have been found.

Considering the scientific discoveries of the 20th century, the statistical probability that Darwin's assumptions were correct has become vanishingly small. After 165 years of searching, no fossil evidence has been discovered to support his views. His imaginary evolutionary tree has not been discovered.[727] In Chapter 2 (in Book I) it was stated Einstein's theory of Relativity is now a Law. What changed his theory into a law? The accumulating scientific data from many other independent disciplines of science and literally thousands of investigators the world over proved his theory to be correct. Science proved Einstein had discovered an overlooked law of nature. The proof came rather quickly. It all happened in his lifetime.

However, there are flaws in Darwin's ideas about evolution. Therefore, it cannot truthfully be said his theory has been proved. 165 years have come and gone since Darwin first published his book, and there is not one shred of scientific evidence that *any* of his ideas on the *origin of life* were correct.

YET, DARWIN WAS RIGHT ABOUT ONE THING — EVOLUTION HAPPENED!

Furthermore, the Bible supports it! Darwin deserves his place in history for putting forth his theory. The fact is — modern science agrees with some of his basic ideas about the evolution of life. For example:

- We know evolution occurred. Darwin was right about that.
- Accommodative adjustments to environmental changes result in specialization to adapt to new ecological niches — therefore populations do evolve. Darwin was right about that.
- Survivors do give rise to the next generation and new generations may differ in some way from their parents. Darwin was also right about that.

DARWIN WAS WRONG ABOUT HOW EVOLUTION OCCURRED.

Although these basic ideas were correct, *his schemes of development were wrong.* The more complete fossil record of the last 165 years refutes his ideas of how things changed. For example—

- Darwin's ideas about how evolution happened are very different from the type of evolution the Bible proclaimed and modern science has proved.
- His mechanisms for reproduction and the development of diversity are poles apart from what the Bible says, and modern science has validated.
- His idea of macroevolution through cross-phylum change did not happen.

---

[724] Schroeder *Genesis and the Big Bang* Chapter 9 p 134*c*
[725] Schroeder *The Science of God* Chapter 1 p 10*a*
[726] Schroeder *Genesis and the Big Bang* Chapter 1 p 25*b*
[727] Schroeder *The Science of God* Chapter 1 p. 9*b,c*

- The intra-phylum changes at the level of the species that the Genesis Code of the Bible said would happen are what actually happened. The Bible declared it. Modern science has proved the Bible correct.
- Science has refuted his ideas about how reproduction and specialization occur. Gradualism, random chance, and mutations were not the engines of change.
- In Darwin's mind, mutations led to beneficial changes. However, in real life, mutations are not always beneficial. More often than not, mutations create disadvantages, and many are lethal.
- Although mutations do occur, variations cannot be solely attributable to mutations. Some variations among survivors are attributable to genetic expressions of inheritance. However, variations have also occurred through adaptations triggered by the many environmental changes and extra-terrestrial events that have occurred throughout Earth's history. Science has discovered these macro-environmental events led to the activation and expression of inherited latent genetic information within the survivors which gave them the ability to adjust, survive, and thrive. The evidence for this will be presented later.
- The multiple major extinctions of life on Earth were not caused by the dominance of the more fit species over others but were the result of macro-environmental changes, extra-terrestrial impact events, and population genetics. This will be discussed later.
- The specialization that occurs among species has not resulted in any new phyla since the Cambrian Explosion that occurred 570 million years ago.[728,729]
- His concept that *all* animal organisms descended from a *single ancestor* fails. The particulars of this statement will be discussed in Chapter 20.

THE COUP DE GRACE

Darwin said: *"If it could be demonstrated that any complex organ existed, which could not possibly have been formed by numerous successive, slight modifications, my theory would absolutely breakdown."*[730] That is exactly what happened when the Burgess Pass fossils were discovered. The 1909 discovery of the fossils of the Burgess Shale Cambrian Explosion by Charles Doolittle Walcott dealt the *Coup de Grace* to Darwin's Theory of Random Gradual Evolution through Natural Selection. Why? Because—

1) The burgess Shale fossils show all 34 phyla of animals that exist today suddenly and simultaneously appeared in the brief span of the first five million years of the beginning of the Cambrian Period — on the dawn of the 5th Day of Creation.
2) They appeared as separate, independent, and fully developed complex animal life-forms that had fully developed complex organs such as eyes, brains, nervous systems, circulatory systems, lungs, and digestive tracts.
3) All of them literally exploded upon the scene — abruptly, simultaneously, and separately. They did not evolve in the way Darwin had imagined. (cf. Chapter 14.)
4) Thus, it was that the first animals that appeared on Earth were suddenly and independently **made** (asa) and **formed** (yasar) of the 5th Day of Creation (as the

[728] Schroeder *The Science of God* Chapter 7 p 103*b*
[729] Schroeder *The Science of God* Chapter 2 p 30*b*
[730] *The Origin of Species:* Chapter VI Difficulties of the Theory p. 154—Modes of transition.

Bible states). Since then, Earth's animals have evolved *"After Their Kind"* (i.e., their species) — as the Bible says — something that science now calls *Microevolution.*

5) In antiquity new *classes* of animals developed, but no change in the basic body plans of the phyla to which they belonged occurred. None survived. The Dinosaurs are an example.

6) Since then, all evolution in modern times has occurred at the level of the *Species* (the way the Bible proclaimed). We will talk more about the definition of *Antiquity* and *Modern Times* in the next chapter.

7) Darwin proclaimed gradual evolution is a fundamental tenet of his theory. He theorized the complexity and variety of present-day life came from the primordial and primitive through the slow, smooth, gradual evolution of the simple to the complex. He predicted the more complete fossil record of the future would validate his theory. He declared the fossil record would someday prove: *"Natura non facit saltum"* (i.e., *Nature does not make jumps*).

8) The fact is: the Cambrian Explosion and the vastly more complete fossil record that has been accumulated over the 165 years since Darwin's book was first published has proved: *"Natura solum facit saltum"* (*Nature only makes jumps*).[731]

9) If Darwin were alive today, he would admit the Cambrian Fossils (with their sudden appearance and their complex organs, and the more complete fossil record of today, which still demonstrates numerous examples of sudden, punctuated developments, gaps, and the continued absence of transitional forms); have delt the death blow to his theory of evolution! Darwin's idea of Macroevolution did not happen! What actually happened (in Antiquity) was the Microevolution which has been described. Microevolution also happened in Modern times and still happens today. The Bible has no dispute with Microevolution!

10) Absolutely nothing in Darwin's theory justifies the idea that God had nothing to do with Creation. Even Darwin thought God was the Creator. The last paragraph in his book proclaimed:

"The Creator originally breathed life into a few forms or into one."

11) The Genesis Code, which is imbedded in the Biblical Creation Account tells us — after Elohim created the Singularity, He then made and formed everything else during those *"Six Days of Old."* At the same time, He set in motion the "after their kind" reproductive processes by which life would continue to evolve.

12) In Chapters 23 and 27 (when I talk about the Nephilim and the Neshama), I will talk about what the Talmud scholars believed when they considered how Elohim may have evolved the first man.

13) The scientific discoveries since Darwin's time have confirmed for us — Our faith in the truth of the Bible's Account of Creation has not been misplaced.

---

[731] Schroeder: *The Science of God* Chapter 1 p 10a

Summary Points:

- Make no bones about it, science has proved Evolution occurred and still happens. There is no argument with Darwin about that.
- But science has disproved Darwin's ideas about how evolution occurred.
- There is no denying the scientific evidence that proved the Earth's first animal-life suddenly and abruptly appeared on the dawn of the 5th Day of Creation in the first 5 million years of the Cambrian Period.
- All of the Phyla of animals that exist today were established in that explosion of animal-life. They appeared *separately* and *independently* as fully developed complex animals. They did not evolve in the way Darwin imagined. The Cambrian Period Burgess Shale Fossils prove this.
- How do we explain it? Science can't.
- In his discussion of the origin of life, Dr. Schroeder said: *"For decades many scientists have presented the misconception that there are rational explanations for the origins of the universe, life, and mankind. The shortcomings of the popular theories were merely swept under the rug to avoid confusing the issues. The knowledge that scientists do not have the answers has now been coupled by the awareness of the fossil record's failure to confirm Darwin's or any other theory of the gradual evolution of life.*
- *The demonstration of these misconceptions has brought many scientists and laypersons to an uncomfortable realization: the problems of our origins, problems that most of us would have preferred to consider solved by experts who should know the answers, in fact have not been solved and are not about to be solved, at least by the purely scientific methods used to date.*
- *There is now overwhelmingly strong evidence, both statistical and paleontological, that life could not have been started on Earth by a series of random-chance chemical reactions.*
- *Today's best mathematical estimates[732] state that there simply was not enough time for random reactions to get life going as fast as the fossil record shows it did.*
- *The reactions were either directed by:*
  - *Some unknown physical force, or*
  - *A metaphysical guide, or*
  - *Life arrived here from elsewhere."*
- The same can be said about the question of the sudden appearance of the Earth's first animals. They were fully developed when they literally exploded upon the scene in the earliest phase of the Cambrian Period on the dawn of the 5th Day of Creation.
- Science tells us the Burgess Pass fossils established the 34 phyla that define all animal life today.
- They were the progenitors of all present-day animals.
- They were either created by:
  - Some unknown physical force, or

---

[732] Schroeder *Genesis and the Big Bang* Chapter 1 p 25

- o By a metaphysical guide, or
- o Life arrived here from elsewhere.
- For me, the answer lies in the realm of faith. Faith can go to those places science can never go. I have the Biblical Account of Creation, and I now know about the Cosmogony of the Ancient Jewish Sages, which they derived from their knowledge of the deeper meaning of the Hebrew words Moses wrote in the first two chapters of Genesis. For me, the answer is: *There was a metaphysical guide.* That metaphysical guide was the Hebrew God *Elohim* (in the first chapter of Genesis), who is also referred to as *Jehovah-Elohim* (in Genesis Two).
- Therefore, through faith, I think the animals that suddenly appeared on the 5th Day were *made* and *formed* by God from the primordial substance He *created* when He initiated His Creation on Day One.
- *The Genesis Code* that is embedded in the first chapter of Genesis tells us this.
- It also tells us: After the first animals were *made* and *formed*, they then *evolved* according to the laws of reproduction that Elohim formulated.
- The Bible tells us they would reproduce *"After Their Kind"* at the level of the individual species of animals.
- Since the Cambrian Explosion, the changes observed *in modern times* occur within the *species* and only result in changes in the *traits* of animals.
- Starting with the Cambrian Explosion and continuing to the present, today's fossil record (with its vastly greater number of specimens) *refutes* Darwin's conjectures.
- There is no example in the fossil record or in population genetics studies of any change which has ever resulted in a change in an animal's basic-body-plan. There is no example of any animal morphing from one species into an entirely different animal of a new phylum — no evidence that Darwin's macro-evolutionary concept of cross-phylum change has ever occurred.
- Science has not identified any examples of any species *'budding-off'* an entirely different type of animal. The differences observed between the progenitor and its offspring have been changes in the traits of the animals only — such as the larger size of modern-day horses as opposed to the small dog-like ancestor of the horse that suddenly appeared in North America 60 million years ago in the Paleocene Epoch in the middle of the 6th Day of Creation. The basic-body-plan of the horse has remained unchanged for the 60 million years of its existence.
- Science has no problem with Darwin's claim that the progeny which survive give rise to the next generation — or that the characteristics of the survivors in any generation may be different from the generation as a whole — so long as one recognizes the differences that result in succeeding generations involve changes in the *traits* of the animal and occur only at the level of the *species*.
- Science cannot attribute *all* changes that occur to genetic mutations. Many mutations are *lethal.* Others are detrimental and countless numbers of mutations do not convey any advantage.
- Furthermore, science has discovered: mutations do *not* play as important a role in *speciation* as Darwin supposed. *Genetic factors are the primary determinants* and often over-ride the mutation-effect.

- Modern science has no problem with that part of Darwin's idea of natural selection, which has to do with *specialization* to adapt to a new ecological niche. But there is a problem with his idea that such specialization will always lead to the emergence of new and improved species.
- Darwin thought *natural selection* would cause the development of entirely new and different animals with new basic-body-plans. That has never happened in nature!
- Science has disproved Darwin's scheme of *natural selection*.
- Darwin's concept of *Gradualism* has failed. The Burgess fossils absolutely disprove Darwin's idea of Gradualism.
- His idea of *common descent from a single ancestor* has also failed.
- I suspect — *if* there is a *chain* that binds us (pun intended because DNA's double helical-chain-structure is commonly called "a chain") — future genetic research will find it in our DNA.
- A common genetic link may eventually be discovered. If this happens, it will not prove the claim Neo-Darwinists will make that the discovery of a common genetic link proves the Bible wrong, that God had nothing to do with our orthogenesis, and that God doesn't exist. When they say that — I will say: *"Who do you think created DNA? Don't say — Random Chance — because modern science has also destroyed that faulty platform!"*
- Stephen Jay Gould said: *"Science simply cannot adjudicate the issue of God's superintendence of nature."* [733]
- I agree and think the discovery of a common genetic link may just put us one small step of faith further by strengthening our belief in God, and our belief that God created all things.
- Science will never be able to prove or disprove the existence of God.
- Belief will always be a matter of faith.
- *By faith alone in Christ, we are justified.* (Luke 23:39-43 — The thief on the cross who believed in Christ was saved. Also see Gal. 2:16 & 3:24.) Jesus promised him he would be in paradise with Him that very day!

---

[733] Schroeder *The Science of God* Chapter 1 p. 18*b*

✤
CHAPTER 19: MODERN TIMES vs. ANTIQUITY

This chart of the Taxonomy of man was presented in the previous chapter.

Phylum *(a group, race, or tribe)*: **Chordata**←(*The level where Darwin thought transitions would be found.*)
Subphylum *(sub-division or clan)*: **Vertebrata**
Class *(or Type)*: **Mammals**←(In Antiquity, transitions occurred at the level of *Class*)
Order *(or sub-type)*: **Primates**
Genus *(or Family)*: **Hominidae**
Species *(or Sub-family)*: **sapiens**←(**In Modern times**, *transitions occur in Species*)

So, man is classified as the Species (*sapiens*) of the Genus (*Homo* — for Hominidae) that science refers to as *Homo sapiens*: meaning *'man who is wise'*. O.David

This chart shows *Darwin thought* the diversity of modern-day life came through evolutionary transitional changes *that must have occurred over time* at the levels of the *Phyla*. Darwin thought *all* of complex modern-day life-forms must have originated from an ancient ancestor — a common progenitor. He hedged his bet by also considering the possibility that perhaps more than one ancient ancestor may have been involved.

WHAT ACTUALLY HAPPENED

Contrary to what Darwin thought, this Taxonomy of Man chart demonstrates — *in antiquity*, the fossil record shows transitions occurred at the level of the *Class* of the animals — two levels below the level of the *Phylum*. It also shows — *in Modern Times*, transitions *only occur* at the level of the *species*. So, what do we mean by *"Modern Times?"* And what does *'Antiquity'* mean?

THE DEFINITION OF 'MODERN TIMES'

So, take another look at the *Geologic Timetable Compared to the Six Days of Creation* chart at the end of Chapter 12. Notice: *Modern-day animals and plants appeared 5.3 million years ago* (late on the 6th Day of Creation), during the *Pliocene Epoch*. So, science defines *"Modern Times"* as that period, which began 5.3 million years ago, and extends to the present — i.e., *through* the entire Pliocene and Pleistocene Epochs *and into the Holocene Epoch — to the Present*. Stated another way, the beginning of the *Pliocene Epoch* marks the beginning of *"Modern Times."* According to the Geologic Time Scale, *The Holocene Epoch is part of "Modern Times."* The *Holocene* is the epoch in which Adam lived, Darwin lived, and we live. To say *"Modern Times"* began 5.3 million years ago seems wrong to those of us who believe the Bible's claim that Adam was the first man. Biblical scholars have made calculations based on the genealogies in the Book of Genesis that point to a period ~ 5700 years before the present as the time when God made Adam. However, we must be aware many scientists believe man came from the *'man-like'* Hominids that dominated the *Pleistocene* Epoch (1.6 million — to 12,000 years ago). And some scientists argue that *'man'* appeared much earlier and came from one or more of the earliest Hominids that appeared in the *Miocene Epoch* (23.7—5.3 million years ago). But bear with me for now. In coming chapters I will discuss how science and the Bible define *'man'* differently.

ANTIQUITY

What about those changes that occurred in *antiquity*? Since we are now talking about when the first animals appeared on Earth, we are talking about the ancient animals that suddenly appeared in the early phase of the 5th Day of Creation (570 million years ago). We are also talking about the rest of the 5th Day of Creation and that part of the 6th Day, from the *Triassic Period* up to and through the *Miocene* Epoch, which ended 5.3 million years ago, when their descendants lived. Thus, *antiquity* represents those blocks of Earth-time that started 570 million years before the present and extended up until 5.3 million years ago. Why 5.3 million years ago? Because, if you look at the Chart at the end of Chapter 12, you will see that is when *the Miocene Epoch ended* and *the Pliocene Epoch began*. The *Pliocene* was when *"Modern Animals and Plants"* appeared *"in a blink of the geologic eye!"*

WHAT KIND OF EVOLUTION OCCURRED IN ANTIQUITY? — MICROEVOLUTION.

In the last chapter we learned Darwin observed the results of the selective breeding of *modern-day domestic animals* and made conjectures about how life could have evolved from *antiquity* to *the present*. I pointed out — the more extensive fossil record of today has disproved his idea of *Macroevolution*. Since Darwin, we have learned: Beginning with the advent of *Modern Times* and for the last 5.3 million years, evolution has occurred *inside* the various phyla of animals at the level of the *species* and has only caused changes of the *traits* of the *species* — something that modern science has labeled *Microevolution*. Darwin's idea of cross-phylum change at the level of the phyla has never happened, *even in antiquity! But, in antiquity there are examples of some changes that occurred at a level that was different from the level of the species.*

AFTER THE CAMBRIAN EXPLOSION, MICROEVOLUTION OCCURRED AT THE LEVEL OF CLASS.

The facts are, in antiquity the fossil record *does* document that some *new animals* developed within each *phylum* at a level that is three classifications above the species — i.e., at the level of *Class*. Nevertheless, those classes of new animals did not display any changes in the basic-body-plan of the phylum to which they belonged. Neither did they show any cross-phylum (i.e., *Macroevolutionary*) changes.[734] Therefore, those evolutionary changes that occurred at the level of *Class* (in *antiquity*), were *micro-evolutionary* changes because they produced animals with new traits but did not create any new phyla of animals.

As in the Cambrian Explosion, those classes of new animals and plants suddenly appeared. The fossil record shows they were fully developed and specialized when they first appeared, they lasted their time, and then they suddenly disappeared, with no evidence that any new or better-adapted class of animals forced their disappearance or took their place.[735]

WINGS

The fossil record never gives any hint that a *change* in morphology was in the offing.[736] The origin of *wings* is a prime example. The fossil record gives us no clues of the coming of winged life prior to its development. Earth's first winged life-forms were the winged insects that suddenly appeared on the 5th Day of Creation in the Mississippian Period. The earliest fossils of winged insects show they were fully specialized and developed when they appeared — and as we have already discussed in Chapter 13, quite large. The

---

[734] Schroeder The Science of God Chapter 2, p. 30b
[735] Schroeder The Science of God Chapter 2, p. 30c
[736] Schroeder The Science of God Chapter 2, p. 30c

fossils of the closest relatives of the winged insects are the *wingless* insects which appeared 78 million years earlier in the Silurian Period — also on the 5th Day.[737] (See the chart at the end of Chapter 12.)

Nevertheless, these new classes of animals did not contain any transitional forms. That is, they did not represent any of the cross-phylum changes that Darwin had imagined. The morphologic changes demonstrated by these new classes of animals did not cause any changes in the basic-body-plan of the phyla to which they belonged.

DINOSAURS

The *Dinosaurs* are another example of a new class of animals (a new class of reptiles) that (in geologic terms), suddenly appeared 220 million years ago in the Triassic Period — early on the 6th Day. By the Jurassic Period they dominated. They lasted their time and then disappeared in the Cretaceous Period, having dominated, and lasted for about 150 million years. During the time they were the kings of the roost there were five extreme and three lesser mass extinctions of life on our planet. The Dinosaurs survived them all. But finally, 65 million years ago, something did them in.[738]

IRIDIUM

In many different geographic locations on our globe, the Nobel Prize winner, Luis Alvarez, and his son Walter, found an extremely rare metal in layers of sedimentary rock that all date to the time of the extinction of the Dinosaurs. That rare metal is *Iridium*. Iridium is associated with certain classes of meteorites. The concentrations of iridium in the 65-million-year-old strata of sedimentary rock that date to the time of the extinction of the Dinosaurs are 30 times greater than normally present in all other strata of sedimentary rock. They believe this implies a sudden extraneous increased input of iridium into Earth's global environment by an extra-terrestrial event that occurred 65 million years ago.[739]

AN EXTINCTION CAUSED BY A NUCLEAR WINTER

Scientists now believe that 65 million years ago, a large meteor ~ 10 kilometers in diameter collided with the Earth. That impact supplied the increased worldwide concentrations of iridium in the strata of the Earth that date to this period. Such an impact would have poisoned Earth's atmosphere. Quadrillions of tons of dust would have been blasted into Earth's stratosphere reducing the amount of sunlight reaching Earth's surface to an intensity less than that of a quarter-moon. This would have caused a nuclear winter. The result would have been a prolonged severe drop of global temperatures and a drastic lowering of photosynthetic rates with resultant decimation of plant-life worldwide. In this scenario of a drastically altered ecology of the Earth, only the most resourceful of species could have avoided the extinction suffered by the Dinosaurs. Apparently, it was the tiny mammals that managed to survive. For the 150 million years that the Dinosaurs dominated, the tiny mammals had scurried away from their feet. They only occupied a diminutive niche when the Dinosaurs ruled. But following the extinction of the Dinosaurs, mammals gained prominence. The greatest prominence extended to the primates who were able to extend their domain.[740]

---

[737] Schroeder The Science of God Chapter 2, p. 30d
[738] Schroeder Genesis and the Big Bang Chapter 9 p 139b
[739] Schroeder Genesis and the Big Bang Chapter 9 p 140b
[740] Schroeder Genesis and the Big Bang Chapter 9 p. 139-140

IN MODERN TIMES, MICROEVOLUTION HAS ONLY OCCURRED (AT THE LEVEL OF THE SPECIES).

In antiquity, classes of animals developed within each phylum of animals, but they always retained the basic-body-plan of their particular phylum.[741] More than 34 distinct phyla of animals were created during the Cambrian explosion, but only 34 persisted. The rest became extinct.[742] No other new phyla have appeared since the Cambrian Explosion of Life.[743] However, after the Earth-time-continuum moved onward into *modern times*, fossil transitions at the level of the *Classes* of animals <u>ceased to occur</u>. Beginning 5.3 million years ago, in the Pliocene Epoch and continuing to the present day, all evolutionary transitions have occurred just as the Bible says — <u>at the level of the *species*</u>.

Beginning with the Pliocene Epoch, 5.3 million years ago, the transitions that occur in nature are changes in the *traits* of the animals at the level of the *species* (i.e., five levels below the level of the *phylum*). Genetic inheritance is the driving force in the vast majority of cases. However, history has taught us that sometimes, evolutionary changes have also been directed by the environment. Nevertheless, whether or not the *evolution* of life is primarily directed by genetic factors or by necessary adaptations to massive environmental changes, the *Microevolution* that occurs in *modern times* expresses itself *only* at the level of the *species*. There is no fossil record of gradual change from the simple to the complex of any changes that cross phylum lines — i.e., no morphing of one animal into another as Darwin had theorized. So far, the fossil record of the past 165 years shows that *all* new plant and animal groups make their first fossil appearance highly specialized and fully developed. They suddenly appear. They last their time, and they disappear.[744] The fossil record indicates:

1. While it is true that *'fit'* animals usually survive long enough to produce progeny, Darwin's hypothesis of *'the survival of the fittest'* was an oversimplification. Rarely if ever are there any fossil indications that competition by a new and better adapted species of animals dominated and beat out an outdated ancestor in the race for food, shelter, and survival, thus driving the ancestor to extinction.[745] Perhaps with the singular exceptions of the *Woolly Mammoth*, and the *Mastodon*, there is no other evidence that the simple dominance of one species over another brought about the extinction of the less dominant species. Instead, macro-environmental changes resulting from Earth's many Ice Ages, the formation and breakup of supercontinents, and extraterrestrial impacts, have caused several mass extinctions of life on our planet. For example, not even the most *fit* of the dinosaurs survived the Asteroid impact that ended their existence.[746,747]

2. Concerning the major morphologic changes in *antiquity* that have occurred within the phyla of animals at the level of *Class*, the fossil record consistently fails to give any

[741] Schroeder The Science of God Chapter 2, p. 30b
[742] Schroeder The Science of God, Chapter 7, p. 102a
[743] Schroeder The Science of God, Chapter 7, p. 103b
[744] Schroeder The Science of God Chapter 2, p. 30c
[745] Schroeder The Science of God Chapter 2, p. 30c
[746] Schroeder Genesis and the Big Bang Chapter 9 p 138-141
[747] Schroeder Genesis and the Big Bang Chapter 9 p 145-146

hint at the basic anatomical levels that a change in morphology was in the offing. An example of this is *wings* which we have just discussed.

3. Another example of the sudden appearance and abrupt disappearance of an animal in the fossil record is that of the marine reptile that had a fish-like body — the *ichthyosaurus*. This animal first appeared in the Jurassic Period (on the 6th day) with fully developed fins, paddles, and a bill. A little over 100 million years later, when it disappeared from the fossil record (at its extinction), the fossil record shows that it had not changed in any way.[748]

4. Still another example of the lack of any fossil evidence of transitional change comes from the plant kingdom — the *angiosperms*.[749] (*) 140 million years ago (on the 6th day), they blossomed forth with no inkling in the older fossils of their relatives of their impending explosion. The angiosperms represent about 80% of all forms of plant-life on Earth today.[750]

5. Perhaps the most impressive display of what is alleged to be the scientific evidence for Darwin's concept of evolution is the one in the Natural History Museum in London. The exhibit shows how pink daisies can evolve into blue daises — how gray moths can evolve into black moths — how a wide variety of cichlid[751] (**) fish species evolved in Lake Victoria over a mere few thousand years. Does this exhibit really demonstrate Darwin's concept of Macroevolution?

Lets' see:

Daisies evolved into daisies — (of different colors).

Moths evolved into moths — (of different colors).

Cichlid fish evolved into cichlid fish — (of different varieties, but without any changes in their basic-body-plan).

What do these examples of so-called Macroevolution have in common? The basic-body-plans of each example remained the same. Daises remained daises. Moths remained moths. Cichlid fish remained cichlid fish. *Not one example of a change in the basic-body-plan of any life-form is shown in the exhibit.* There are no examples of the cross-phylum changes Darwin theorized — i.e., no examples of one animal of one phylum morphing into a new animal of a different phylum. Instead, the exhibit demonstrates many changes in the traits of the individual species of the various life-forms. Some of the changes in character traits are truly spectacular, but *there is not one example* of any change in any basic-body-plan. **What the exhibit actually demonstrates — is Microevolution.**[752]

---

[748] Schroeder The Science of God Chapter 2, p. 30d & 31a
[749] Schroeder The Science of God Chapter 2, p. 31a (*) Angiosperms: Those plants in which the sex organs are within their flowers & the seeds are in their fruit.
[750] Angiosperms—Nature Works: http://www.nhptv.org/natureworks/nwep14f.htm
[751] (**) Cichlid Fish: a tropical freshwater fish with spiny fins, popular as an aquarium fish. Phylum (family) Cichlidae.
[752] Schroeder The Science of God Chapter 2, p. 31d&e

Summary Points:

- Darwin imagined evolution occurred at the level of the *Phylum.*
- He was wrong.
- The Bible says evolution will occur at the level of the *"Miyn."*
- *Miyn* means *Species.*
- Science discovered (in *Antiquity*), evolution occurred at the level of *Class.*
- But in *Modern* Times evolution has only occurred at the level of the *species.*
- Science has proved the Bible right.
- *Antiquity* is defined as the time that began with the Cambrian Period (570 million years ago) on the 5th Day of Creation and ended at the beginning of the Pliocene Epoch (5.3 million years ago) on the 6th Day of Creation.
- The Pliocene Epoch was the time when modern animals and plants appeared on Earth. It marks the beginning of *"Modern Times."*
- In Modern Times, evolution is expressed by the changes in the *traits* of animals that occur *within the species* of each phylum of animals.
- In Modern Times, evolution has never caused any change in the basic-body-plans of the animals.
- We now know, the basic body plans of the progenitors of all Modern-Day animals were were established in the Cambrian Period at the level of the Phyla on the 5th Day.
- However, no new phyla of animals have been established since the Cambrian Period.
- Darwin's imagined scheme of *Macroevolution* has never happened.
- The only place *Macroevolution* has ever existed was in his imagination.

☘

CHAPTER 20: MODERN SCIENCE, THE GENESIS CODE, & THE TIE THAT BINDS

This chapter summarizes the history and tenets of the Big Bang Theory—summarizes the Cosmogony of the Ancient Jewish Sages, which they derived from their interpretation of the deeper meaning of Moses' words in Genesis One and Genesis Two & then ends with—"The Tie that Binds.".   O. David

As you read these summaries you will see the scientific discoveries of the last 85 years have brought about a convergence of agreement between modern science and the beliefs of the ancient Jewish Sages concerning the *fact there actually was a beginning.* Furthermore, it was also the Creator's *Will* that man would someday understand *what happened after the beginning.* As you read this chapter, you will experience a sense of *déjà vu* because these concepts were introduced in Chapters 1, 2, 4, 5, 6, and 7. Those chapters examined the particulars of the discoveries of science and compared them with the particulars of the beliefs of Nahmanides and other Ancient Jewish Sages. I am doing this here because you have just read about Darwin's scheme and how it differs from what modern science has recently discovered and what the Bible first stated 3300 years ago! So, this summary-review should provide an unambiguous and convincing contrast between the *fiction of Darwinism* and *the facts of science and the Bible.* The fact — that science now agrees with Moses should convince you — the Christian belief in the truth of the Bible has not been misplaced. The rest of this chapter will be devoted to — The possibility of a 'Tie that Binds.'

MODERN SCIENCE SAYS:

The following is a bullet-point summary of the conclusions the majority of current-day scientists have reached concerning the beginning.

- Modern science has discovered the Universe started as the result of a Big Bang.[753]
- The Big Bang Theory was the brainchild of Monsignor Georges Henri Joseph Édouard Lemaître (1894 – 1966), a Belgian priest, astronomer, and professor of physics at the Catholic University of Louvain.[754]
- In 1927 Lemaître theorized a colossal explosion created an infinitely tiny speck-of-space that comprised the Universe at its beginning.
- Lemaître called that point the 'Primeval Atom.' (See Chapter 2 in Book I.) Scientists now call that point – the Singularity.
- Scientists have concluded the Singularity was a mathematically untenable microscopic "Dot-of-Space" that inexplicably appeared. It was infinitely small, infinitely hot, infinitely chaotic, and infinitely unstable. It was the beginning of space and matter and time and all that exists.
- The Singularity contained the potential for all matter — i.e., quarks, free electrons, and the chaotic energy of a black fire.
- Very shortly after it formed, the Singularity was under the threat of self-annihilation because it was nature's first black hole.

---

[753] Schroeder: *Genesis and the Big Bang*, Chapter 3 p 65c

[754] Article: Where Did The Universe Come From? New Scientific Evidence of the Existence of God—by Dr. Hugh Ross, Ph.D., Astrophysicist—April 16, 1994. www.cosmicfingerprints.com/hugh-ross-origin-of-the-universe

- At a critical moment, the Singularity inexplicably underwent a sudden expansion which caused the separation that was needed to allow true matter to eventually form, thus saving the Singularity from self-annihilation.
- The sudden inflation-expansion of the Singularity allowed the formation of the first true matter.
- When the first true matter formed — Time began.
- The expansion of the Universe has continued ever since.
- Through several independent methods, Scientists have learned The Big Bang happened 15 ¾ billion years ago. (See Chapter 5 in Book I).
- Science has also discovered the proof of the beginning and what has happened since the beginning — but has admitted — what existed before the beginning and what caused the beginning can never be discovered by science.
- Science will never be able to prove the existence of a Beginner. But, more importantly, science will never be able to disprove Elohim's existence. Belief in The Creator will always remain in the realm of the spiritual. Belief will always be an act of faith.

THE BIBLE, THE GENESIS CODE, & HEBREW COSMOGONY
The ancient Jewish Sages believed God caused the Beginning and created all that exists.

The Hebrew Bible teaches the Author of life — was, is, and will forever be *the One True God*, whose name is *Elohim*. Elohim is — *'the Strong One, the Mighty Leader, the Supreme Leader.'* The Bible also teaches Elohim *is the Beginner* — the *One* who created everything there will ever be. The ancient Jewish sages and the framers of the Talmud believed *Elohim* has always existed. He is *'the Eternal One.'* He is outside of time. Prior to the beginning of time, all that existed was Elohim.

ELOHIM'S TZIMTZUM

Nahmanides believed creation was caused by a spiritual contraction of Elohim. According to Nahmanides, at a specific point in the eternity of Elohim, Elohim suddenly withdrew the tiniest part of *His Spiritual Being from His Infinite Unity,* and in so doing, caused the largest explosion in all history. This was the seminal cause of *the beginning of Creation* which allowed the physical complexity of the Universe with its laws of nature to emerge.[755] In Hebrew Cosmogony, this minute spiritual contraction of God — that caused the beginning of all things — is called *"Elohim's Tzimtzum."* From his knowledge of the Hebrew language, Nahmanides deduced the deeper meaning of the Biblical Creation Account. *The Genesis Code* tells us — at the moment of the beginning, Elohim created all there will ever be. That is, He *created* the substrate He would later use to *make* and *form* everything that exists today.

THE "BLACK-FIRE" OF A "GRAIN-OF-MUSTARD-SIZED SPECK-OF-SPACE"

In 1250 A.D. Nahmanides hypothesized, at the briefest instant following the beginning, all the matter of the universe was concentrated in a very small space no larger than *a grain of mustard.* He thought that tiny speck-of-space was the beginning of the Universe. He theorized the matter within that speck-of-space at the moment of the beginning was so thin, so intangible, it did not have real substance. It was not tangible matter. However, it did have the potential to gain substance and form. That is, it had the potential to become

---

[755] Schroeder: *The Science of God*, Chapter 1 p 16-17

tangible matter. According to Nahmanides, the initial concentration of this intangible primordial pseudomatter (in its minute location) was infinitely dense, infinitely hot, and infinitely chaotic — so chaotic, that he thought it was *"a black-fire."*

From the shape of the first letter in the first word of the Bible (*the Bet /or Beth*), Nahmanides also deduced man would never be able to determine what existed before the moment of the beginning, but man would be able to discover what happened after that moment.

CREATION EX NIHILO

So, Elohim's Tzimtzum (His *'barah'* that caused the largest explosion in history), created a tiny speck-of- space that was no larger than a grain-of-mustard. The Hebrew word *"barah"* means: *"to create something from nothing — something only Elohim could do."* *"Creation of something out of nothing"* is a central principle of Hebrew Cosmogony and according to Maimonides is at the root of biblical faith.[756] This principle of *creation from nothing* is called — *"Creation Ex Nihilo."* This was discussed in Chapter 4 in Book I. What Elohim *created* at the moment of the beginning *was the substrate* He would use to make (*asa*) and form (*yasar*) all that has come to be.

THE RUACH ELOHIM

From the Ancient Hebrew Script of Genesis One, Nahmanides also envisioned: shortly after its creation, the grain of mustard-sized speck-of-space was so unstable it was under the constant threat of self-annihilation. But, at a critical moment, Elohim intervened with his *'Wind of God'* in Genesis 1:2c (i.e., His *"Ruach Elohim"* — in Hebrew and/or *The Holy Spirit or Holy Ghost* — in English). The *'Wind of God'* suddenly expanded the tiny speck-of-space to the size of *"a grapefruit"* (i.e., Nahmanides' description). This separated the wildly colliding primordial particles of pseudomatter and eventually brought about cooling to the point where true matter could form and visible light could emerge from *the black-fire-darkness of the beginning* (cf. Chapter 7).

THERE WAS A BEGINNING

The opening sentence of the Hebrew Bible declares: *"In the beginning."* Centuries later, and perhaps beginning with Aristotle, scientists thought there was *no* beginning. They thought the universe was *eternal.* We now know Aristotle was wrong. The Universe is *not* eternal — *it has not always existed!* However, after Moses wrote the Book of Genesis, 33 centuries passed before science proved what the Hebrew Bible had claimed all along — *There was a beginning!* (See Chapters 2 and 6 in Book I.)

INTELLIGENT DESIGN

Hebrew Cosmogony claims: every plant, every animal, every planet, and every star — in fact all of Elohim's creation — shows the undeniable evidence of *Intelligent Design*. All of Elohim's *creations* sprang forth *suddenly* and *abruptly* when He *commanded* their *appearance* by *the pronouncements of His Word.*

ABRUPT SUDDEN CHANGES

The Creation Account of Moses tells us: on each of the *Six Days of His Creation*, Elohim introduced something new with His pronouncements of *abrupt and sudden change*. When Elohim *created, made, and formed* the life-forms on our planet, He caused the Earth to bring forth life, and He made and formed whole races, clans, types, sub-types, families,

---

[756] Schroeder Genesis and the Big Bang Chapter 3 p 62d

and sub-families of different creatures and plants. In His acts of *creating, making, and forming,* Elohim gave the Earth's plants and animals the ability to reproduce their progeny *"after their kind,"* meaning, *"according to their species."* He also gave them the ability to adjust to environmental changes through the process that science now calls — *Microevolution.* Then, when one or more of the species (or sub-families) of animals required basic similar body parts or organs, He *made* and *formed* them in the species of animals that needed them. (We will talk about that next.) The differences in these *basic-organ-plans* that different species of animals have in common, Elohim *evolved* through the mechanism that we have come to understand is *Microevolution. Microevolution is the way Elohim actually evolved and is still evolving things.*

Perhaps, you can now understand the points of similarity that the current-day view of modern science and the ancient Hebrew cosmogony have in common. Perhaps you will now agree that modern science has confirmed the Biblical Account of Creation.

THE POSSIBILITY OF A TIE THAT BINDS—OUR DNA IS THE CHAIN THAT BINDS US TOGETHER.

The Biblical phrase *"after their kind"* (or *"according to their kind"*) is the way our English Bibles translate the Hebrew word — *"miyn." Miyn* means *"Species." "After their kind"* refers to the ability of Earth's different life-forms to reproduce progeny at the level of their *species —* i.e., at the level of their *sub-family* which is five levels *below* their group, race, or tribe. The scientific name *for a group, race, or tribe is —* *"Phylum."* The plural of phylum is — *"Phyla."* The Creator not only gave the various *species* of animals (and plants) the ability to reproduce, but He also gave them *the ability to adapt to environmental changes.* Modern science has *now verified the Biblically proclaimed reproductive capability and adaptation of the various species of life* and calls it — *Microevolution.*

SOMETHING NEW

Through the science of *Comparative Anatomy,* we have discovered there are different *classes* and even different *phyla* of life that have certain abilities and even some organs, in common.

ANIMALS THAT CAN SEE

With the eye for example, once Elohim had fashioned an optical organ, He didn't *'reinvent the wheel,'* so to speak. There are five distinctly different phyla of animals that have sight — *Flatworms, Ribbon-Worms, Mollusks, Insects, and Chordates.* Even though the animals with sight are extremely diverse in their *basic-body-plans,* and even though they live in radically different environments — all animals with sight have the same gene for vision![757]

THE PAX-6 GENE GROUP AND IT'S ANALOGS

The *Pax-6 gene group* is a key regulator in the development of the visual systems in all *Vertebrates. Vertebrates* belong to the *phylum* of animals that have been classified as the *Chordates.* The *Vertebrates* are a sub-phylum or clan of the *Chordates* to which the species of man (i.e., *sapiens*) belongs. (See the *Taxonomy of Man* chart at the beginning of Chapter 19.) The *analogs* of the *Pax-6 gene group* (not the identical gene but other very similar genes), have been found to control the development of the visual systems of the *four* other different phyla of animals with sight that science has classified as belonging

[757] Schroeder *The Science of God* Chapter 7 p 105f

to the separate and distinctly different phyla of *Mollusks, Insects, Flatworms, and Ribbon-worms*. The molecular similarity among these analogs is nothing less than astounding.[758]

THE MASTER PLAN FOR VISION

The basic parts of the visual organs in all of the animals that have sight (irrespective of their different phyla) — *show Elohim's Master Plan*. Their organs of sight have the same basic components.

- There is the *receptor* — the eye itself.
- There are the *conductors of sight* — the retina that receives the images and the nerves that transmit those signals.
- And there is the *processor* — the visual cortex of each animal's brain that processes the information received.

DIFFERENCES

There are differences in each of these basic parts that vary from animal to animal and from phylum to phylum. Some of these differences are in *structure*. Some are in what *type* of *embryonic cells* the Creator used to fashion the *receptors* of sight. There are differences in the way the basic parts *function*. Many differences in structure have to do with *what kind of environment* the visual organs must function in — for example, in fresh water, in salt water, in air, in the daytime, in the night, or in the ground.

SIMILARITIES AND BASIC RESULTS

These differences in the sight receptors and processors of each phylum of the sighted animals are many. But the *basic components* of sight and the *basic results* — are the *same!* The differences in the evolution and function of the various sight-organs of each animal serve the special needs of that animal and are primarily determined by their genetic code, which has been pre-programmed by the Creator to allow the species within each genus to adapt to present and future environments.[759,760] These differences are the result of what scientists now understand to be *Microevolution*. However, *no chordate, no mollusk, no insect, no flatworm, or ribbon-worm* — will reproduce any progeny that will have a sight-organ that is different from the sight-organ of its individual parent.

LATENT GENETIC INFORMATION

The information to produce the *basic-body-plans* has been put by our Creator into the DNA of all creatures and all plants. Scientists have discovered that genetic information (*often latent for generations*) is there *in excess* of what is actually needed so that future generations which might have additional needs to adapt to changing environmental conditions — might do so.[761]

For example, the first life the Bible mentions is vegetation (in Genesis 1:9-13), where the Bible says the Earth brought forth grass, herbs, and fruit trees on the 3rd Day (2.5 billion years ago). Note that grass, herbs, and fruit trees are plant-forms that vary from the simple to the complex.

---

[758] Schroeder *The Science of God* Chapter 6 p 91*d*

[759] Schroeder: *The Science of God* Chapter 6 p 92*f*—94*a*

[760] Schroeder: *The Science of God* Chapter 7 p 104-114

[761] Schroeder: *The Science of God* Chapter 6 p 90-92

On the other hand, science says the first plant-life was much less complex and consisted of single-celled algae. According to science, the more advanced land-plants appeared in the fossil record only 400 million years ago (in the Silurian Period on the 5th Day), and the even more advanced flowering plants and trees first appeared 120 million years ago (on the 6th Day, in the Cretaceous Period).[762] Therefore, according to the Bible, plant-life appeared on the 3rd Day of Creation — but according to science, plants appeared much later. *At first glance*, it would seem science *disagrees* with the Bible.

PLANTS ARE A SPECIAL CASE.

Science has discovered the first life on Earth were the single-cell Prokaryotes. Some of those simple Prokaryotes were microscopic single-cell algae. Molecular biology has discovered microscopic single-cell algae have as much as one hundred times the amount of DNA per cell as mammals do! Why would nature put such a large amount of genetic information into such a simple, primitive organism? Scientists have theorized *a genetic library that large* could contain the basic information for all of the forms of advanced plant-life that appeared much later.[763] Scientists now think the Earth's first simple single-cell algae had an excess of genetic information that would enable the development of higher more complex plant-life. That *latent genetic information* remained *dormant* until such time as the environmental conditions on Earth existed to foster its expression. Thus, scientists believe — *The Earth's first simple plant forms would later enable the development of higher plant-life. The necessary genetic information for this to happen was in the DNA structure of the simple plants that appeared on the 3rd Day!*

CAN PALEONTOLOGY BE RECONCILED WITH THE BIBLICAL DATES?

Nahmanides provided us with the answer. According to Nahmanides' 700-year-old commentary on Gen. 1:12: *"There was no special day assigned for the command for the appearance of the various forms of vegetation alone, since it is not a unique work."*[764] We have previously discussed this principle in Chapter 10 in this book.

THE ATHEIST RICHARD DAWKINS MADE THIS STATEMENT:

"The great achievement of Darwin's Theory of Evolution and Natural Selection is that it shows how creatures that appear to be designed have in fact evolved according to the pressures of chance and survival. Atheists now have an alternative explanation for why fish have gills, why birds have wings, and why human beings have brains and arms and lungs."

Indeed, in the atheist view, Darwin's Theory of Evolution refutes the Biblical Account of human creation and exposes it as a crude and primitive myth.[765]

THE REBUTTAL OF DAWKINS' STATEMENT

We now know the *real myth* is *Darwin's view of evolution that Dawkins championed.* Modern science has now *refuted* Darwin's Theory of the Origin of Life and has *disproved* his concepts of how life reproduced, specialized, and evolved. Darwin's imagined scheme of random chance, mutations, and natural selection were *not* the engines of change. His concept of *gradualism* has been disproved, and his *'law of natural selection'* (i.e., what he frequently referred to as *'the survival of the fittest'*) has been found to be a vastly over

---

[762] Schroeder: *The Science of God* Appendix E p 204*a*

[763] Schroeder: *The Science of God* Appendix E: p 204*b*

[764] Schroeder: *The Science of God* Appendix E p 204*b*

[765] D'Souza: *What's So Great About Christianity* Chapter 3 p. 26-27

simplified explanation for the cause of the extinction of whole classes of animal-life. The multiple major extinctions of life on Earth were not caused by the dominance of the more fit species over others but were the result of macro-environmental changes and extra-terrestrial impact events. Modern science has also discovered the real reasons why fish have gills, why birds have wings, and why human beings have brains, arms, and lungs. *The Creator programmed it all into our DNA!*

MAPPING THE HUMAN GENOME

Scientists have started the colossal task of mapping the human genome. As of this writing, their work is not complete. I suspect when that monumental work has been completed and when the research of animal and plant DNA is more complete; we will discover that if there is a 'chain' that binds us (pun intended), we will find it is in our DNA. I say: "Pun intended," because the molecular structure of our DNA has been described as "a chain." I am also saying — I believe DNA is "The Chain that connects all life." I believe Our DNA is — "The Tie that binds."

COMPARATIVE ANATOMY & VARIATIONS ON A THEME

From Comparative Anatomy, we know some *nonhuman vertebrates* have certain organs and anatomical features in common with humans, but within their commonality, they express *variations-on-a-theme* which are significantly different. Nevertheless, within the embryos of the various vertebrates (humans included), *the potential for multiple themes of animal development exists*. We know there is something in our genetic material that causes some of these themes to dominate while others regress and disappear. *If* some of these animal-themes persist in the development of the human embryo, problems may be presented at birth that can range from an *inconsequential unsightly cosmetic aberration* on the one hand, to *a major organic malformation or anomaly* that poses a threat to the survival of a newborn.

FISH-LIKE GILL SLITS

An example of an *inconsequential unsightly cosmetic aberration* in some human embryos is the persistence of a few embryonic *fish-like cells* that try but *fail* to develop *fish-like gill-slits in some newborns*. A tiny number of human infants are born each year with *incomplete expressions of fish-like gill slits!* How can this happen? Was Dawkins right? Could this aberration be the result of Darwin's idea of *"natural selection and random chance?"* No! Through genetic research, we have learned the human embryo has programmed within its DNA the *pluripotential* for the formation of fish-like gill slits! That is why some babies are born with unsightly *branchial-cleft-cysts* (i.e., *incomplete expressions of fish-like gill slits*) that require surgical removal.

In fish, the gill-slit potential of the fish-embryo goes on to develop fully functioning gill-slits that give fish the ability to extract oxygen from their watery environment.

In human embryos, the most proximal (i.e., those in the upper neck near the jaw) of the fish-like gill-slits normally take another pathway of development and contribute to the development of the human middle ear. In human embryos, our DNA directs a uniquely different human pathway of development, and the embryonic cells that go on to develop gill-slits in fish, contribute instead to the development of the human malleus, incus, stapes, and the Eustachian tube.[766] The human malleus, incus, and stapes are the three tiny bones in our middle-ear, which articulate with eachother.[767] They transmit the sound-wave vibrations that impact our eardrums. They transmit those vibrations into our inner ear. In our inner ear, those transmitted vibrations are transformed into electro-chemical impulses that travel our neural pathways to those parts of our brain that interpret sounds and also help us maintain our equilibrium in our three-dimensional world. As it turns out, those persistent fish-like gill-slit embryonic cells that cause the development of brachial-cleft cysts in some newborns are *superfluous*. That is to say, they do *not* interfere with the development of our hearing, and they don't develop into actual gill-slits. Simple surgical removal is all that is required to make those infants look normal.

Scientists now believe (for some unknown reason), *the genetic switch* that is supposed *to prevent the developmental expression of fish-like gill-slits in human embryos* fails in some human embryos. This mystery is believed to reside in our DNA. Someday when the mapping of the human genome is complete, I suspect we will learn more about the cause of this cosmetically unsightly and functionally inconsequential aberration.[768]

DOES IT SURPRISE YOU THAT WE AND FISH ARE GENETICALLY CONNECTED?

We are *remotely* genetically connected. I say "remotely connected" because *'Fish'* are much more primitive. Their ancestors first appeared on the 5th Day of Creation (505—438 million years ago) in *the Ordovician Period*. Debatably, the case can be made that the Bible says the first of our species (*Adam*) first appeared ~ 5700 years ago in *the Holocene Epoch at the end of the 6th Day of Creation* (cf. the Chart at the end of Chapter 12) — I will talk *'a whole lot more'* about that — much later.

We and *'Fish'* are *Chordates* that have *Vertebrae* (i.e., *Chordate-Vertebrates*). So, *'fish'* belong to the same *phylum* (Chordata) and the same *Sub-phylum* (Vertebrata) of animals that we do. However, that is where our similarities end. It is also the point in the Taxonomic Tree where our development completely diverges! We are of an entirely different *Class, Order, Family, and Sub-family* of animals. All of which are very different from the *Classes, Orders, Families and Sub-families of 'the fishes!'* Our genetic connection dates to 505 million years ago. Some scientists argue our Class, Order, Family, And Sub-family *'branched-off'* from the taxonomic *'tree'* of the fishes some 1.6 million years ago in the *Pleistocene Epoch*. Other scientists say we branched off 5.3 million years ago in the *Pliocene Epoch*. And then there are some who say we branched off 23.7 million years ago in the *Miocene Epoch*.

The Bible says the first man (Adam) was "created" when God breathed the breath of life into his nostrils near the close of the 6th Day of Creation. I'll talk about those *'opinions'* in Chapter 22 (in this book), and also in Chapters 23, and 27 (in Book III). That's because science and the Bible classify *'man'* differently, and a whole lot of scientists argue over exactly *what* animal can be properly called *'the 1st man.'*

[766] Article: **UNSW Embryology Development of the Organs of Audition and Equilibrium Middle Ear © Dr. Mark Hill (2010)** http://embryology.med.unsw.edu.au/Notes/ear7.html
[767] In Anatomy the word "*articulate*" defines the point of connection between two bones or elements of a skeleton that allows motion.

[768] Schroeder The Science of God Chapter 6 p 90-91

AN EXAMPLE OF A MAJOR ORGANIC MALFORMATION—THE AORTIC ARCH & VARIATIONS ON A THEME.

For an example of a major life-threatening aberration of embryonic development, we only need to look at the embryonic formation of the aortic arch (the large artery that receives the arterial blood from the heart and distributes it to the rest of the body). We now know — in the human embryo and in certain other species of mammals — six pairs of aortic arches develop but are not all present at the same time. In the majority of human embryos these six pairs of aortic arches appear in the 5th week of embryonic development and their transformation occurs during the 6th and 7th weeks of fetal development. Normally, the 1st and 2nd arches disappear early. The 5th arches are also transitory and disappear later. In the vast majority of human embryos, *the final configuration of the aortic arch* presents in a *normal and usual pattern*. But in some, *variations and anomalies may persist that can cause maladies* that present threats to the health and survival of the newborn. In infants who have life-threatening anomalies of the aortic arch, surgical intervention is required to make their survival possible. Fortunately, the animal-theme embryonic variations that threaten human life are rare. I mention this only to inform you they can occur in the development of the human embryo. Entire books have been written on this subject. But I leave this subject now because it is beyond the commitment and focus of this book.

VARIATIONS OF THE AORTIC ARCH THAT ARE COMPATIBLE WITH A NORMAL LIFE:

When I was practicing Radiology, I was frequently asked to perform *contrast enhanced x-ray pictures* of the arteries of the brain (i.e., *cerebral arteriograms*) for patients who were suffering from brain tumors, aneurysms, strokes, vascular malformations, and various other maladies that had developed in their brains. *"Contrast enhanced"* means I injected contrast into the arteries that supply the brain so that they could be seen on x-rays. These special x-ray procedures must be performed in a sterile environment using the same precautions and techniques a surgeon uses when he performs a surgical operation. However, no knives or cutting is involved. An artery (in the groin or the arm) is entered with a needle. A tiny flexible metallic guide is inserted through the hollow of the needle. The needle is then withdrawn, and a small flexible catheter is inserted and threaded over the guide. Under fluoroscopic observation, the Radiologist manipulates the guide-catheter combination from the point of entry into the aortic arch. The cerebral arteries (i.e., the right and left carotid arteries, and the right and left vertebral arteries) that supply the brain, originate from arteries that arise from the aortic arch. Once the aortic arch has been entered, tiny amounts of contrast material are injected. This is necessary because our arteries are invisible to x-rays. The contrast material shows up on the fluoroscope (and contrast enhanced x-ray films) and allows the Radiologist to manipulate his catheter into the arteries that supply the brain. Once the catheter is successfully manipulated into the selected artery, a larger volume of *contrast material* is injected, and a rapid sequence of x-ray films are exposed during the injection. Eight separate injections and film-sequences are made — two (frontal and lateral projections) for each of the four arteries that supply the brain. These arteriograms of the arteries in the brain are necessary to determine if surgery can offer a chance for cure.[769,770] They are also the "maps" of the arteries of the brain that guide the neurosurgeon when he operates.

In the majority of people, the origins of the arteries to the brain conform to a certain pattern that is considered a *normal configuration of the aortic arch*. Usually, the normal pattern does not present any difficulty to a Radiologist who is skilled and experienced in performing these special procedures. *However, in a small number of people, an embryonic variation or what is called an anomalous pattern of the aortic arch, can be present. The possibility a patient may have a non-lethal embryonic variation of the aortic arch is the reason why Radiologists have to be familiar with the embryonic developmental variations in the configuration of the aortic arch. Knowledge of the pattern of these variations is essential in knowing the various places to search for the origins of the arteries that supply the brain.* (The research for the reference article on the embryonic development of the aortic arch was performed on the embryos of mice. The developmental changes in the aortic arch that occur in the embryos of mice are the same as those that occur in the embryos of humans.)

THE QUESTION OF COMMON ANCESTRY

One might claim the examples just given are evidence of the correctness of Darwin's assumption we *all* developed from one primordial common prototype ancestor or a few. While there is **no** possibility that *all* animal-life descended from a single common ancestor, it is possible that *each separate phylum* of animals may have a common ancestry. Many scientists now think animals that belong to *the same phylum did indeed develop from a common prototype ancestor.*

Both Fish and Humans are *Chordates with Vertebrae*. The examples just given concerning the development of fish-like gill slits are examples that involve *fish and certain other vertebrates*. The example of variations of the aortic arch involves some *Mammals*. Fish are not *Mammals*. *Mammals* are only one of the *classes* of animals that belong to the *phylum* of animals that is classified as the *Chordates*. The *subphylum* to which mammals and fish belong is that of the *Vertebrates*. Vertebrates are animals that have an inner skeleton with a backbone and spinal cord. *Mammals are Vertebrates* because they have an inner skeleton with a backbone and spinal cord — but (unlike fish, who extract oxygen from their watery environment through their gill-slits), with the exception of whales and dolphins,[771] most mammals also live in the open atmosphere of the Earth. Fish lay eggs. Mammals breathe *'open' air* and give live birth. Most mammals feed milk to their young — (i.e., they have mammary glands that produce milk for their young, hence the name — *'Mammals'*). Human beings are members of the Mammal *Class*. So are *dogs, cats, deer, mice, squirrels, raccoons, bats, opossums, apes, whales, and dolphins.*[772,773] These animals have appendages for locomotion. For *dexterity*, some non-human mammals also have feet with toes, and hands with fingers and thumbs (i.e., apes, and

---

[769] Article: *The Embryonic Development of the Aortic Arch:* [PDF] Aortic Arch Development by Dr. Effmann et al: radiographics.rsna.org/content/6/6/1065.full.pdf (**rsna means: Radiological Society of North America**)

[770] *The Essentials of Roentgen Interpretation* by Lester W. Paul, M.D. & John H. Juhl, M.D.: 3rd Edition, Published by Harper & Row, New York, N.Y. © 1972 (Anomalies of the Aortic Arch and its Large Branches. p. 1010-1012)

[771] Whales and Dolphins also breathe air from the atmosphere but must surface from their watery environment to do so.

[772] Article: *Glossary mz:* http//www.fcps.edu/islandcreekes/ecology/glossary_hp.html

[773] http://www.mcwdn.org/Animals/Chordate.html

monkeys). *The Taxonomy of Man Chart* in Chapters 18 and 19 will help you understand this explanation.

There are other Chordate/Vertebrates with spinal cords aside from mammals. The broader category of the *Chordate Phylum* includes other subdivisions and classes of animals that also have an inner skeleton with a backbone and a spinal cord (like fish); but instead of legs and arms, they have wings (*birds*), or fins/flippers and fin-like tails (i.e., *fish* and *some mammals such as dolphins and whales*). The chordates also have the most developed brains and complex nervous systems of all the phyla of animals. These are just a few distinguishing characteristics of the *Phylum Chordata*, but a complete listing of all the animals in the various subdivisions and classes of animals belonging to the Chordate Phylum, and a description of the other 33 phyla of life is beyond the scope of this book and is unnecessary for our purposes.

THE CAMBRIAN EXPLOSION & COMMON GENETIC BACKGROUNDS

Suffice it to say the genomes of the *Chordate phylum* (which includes the *Classes* of Mammals, Birds, Fish, Reptiles, etc.); *share a common genetic background that started 570 million years ago in the Cambrian Period on the 5ᵗʰ day of Creation.* When we say '*genome*,' we are referring to the genetic information that is held on the DNA of the chromosomes of these animals.

Bats, birds, whales, and dolphins are all species that find their way by sonar. All of these are vertebrates as we are. These animals send out sounds and listen for the echo. Based on such parameters as the delay of the returning sound, and changes that have occurred in the frequency of the returning echo, a bat can fly its way through a maze of closely spaced trees in a forest, and a dolphin can track and catch its dinner in muddy channel waters. The development of similar sonar capabilities among these diverse animals is not surprising. *These animals have many similarities. All resemble a more ancient form of land-dwelling quadruped. Why?* All fall into the same phylum (or race) of animals known as the *Chordata* (animals that have vertebrae). *All have genes that share a common background that started 570 million years ago!* Because of their long common ancestral history, we should not be surprised their genomes contain many similar inherited genes with which to construct similar organs.[774]

Since humans are mammals and belong to the *Chordate Phylum*, and since fish belong to a different *Class* but still belong to the *Chordate Phylum*, it is not surprising the human embryo has programmed within its DNA the *pluripotential* for the formation of fish-like gill slits. Fish and humans have *a common genetic historical beginning* because they belong to the same phylum of animals. *Therefore, since the Chordate Phylum of animals have a common genetic history, the animals of that phylum may have had a common ancestral history as well — i.e., may have originated from a specific progenitor.*

Nevertheless, the *Chordate Phylum* of animals developed separately and independently from the other phyla of animals that also developed separately and independently and suddenly appeared on the 5ᵗʰ Day. Therefore, there is *no possibility* for there to have been one or even a few progenitors that gave rise to *all of* the distinctly separate 34 phyla of animal life. Since there are 34 phyla of animals that exist today, some scientists now believe each phylum developed from an ancestor that was *the*

[774] Schroeder: *The Science of God* Chapter 7 p 104b

progenitor of the basic-body-plan that defines each phylum. Therefore, it may have been that each phylum of animals today could have originated from one of 34 distinctly different progenitors that suddenly and independently appeared 570 million years ago in the ocean shallows during the Cambrian Explosion of visible animal-life that occurred at the dawn of the 5th Day of Creation when God said: *"Let the waters teem with swarms of living creatures... (Gen. 1:20)"*

THE FIVE PHYLA WITH SIGHT DO NOT SHARE A COMMON ANCESTRAL HISTORY.

Although the animals of the *same* phylum may share a common ancestral history, the animals of *different* phyla *do not* share a common ancestral history. 570 million years ago, in the Cambrian Period, the basic anatomies of all the different phyla of currently existing animals, from sponges to vertebrates, suddenly, simultaneously, and independently appeared. They literally *exploded* onto the scene. Because *all* of the phyla, including the Chordates, appeared *separate and independent* of each other, the *different* phyla of other life-forms do not share a common genetic history above the level of the *protozoans*.[775] They separated in a *'bush'* of life (not a tree) at their inception in the early Cambrian Period at the beginning of the 5th Day of Creation. Therefore, *there is no common 'stem or trunk' to 'connect' them.* That is why the term *'bush'* (as opposed to *'tree'*), is now used to describe their origins. A true bush has several independent and separate stems that arise from the Earth. The fossil evidence from the Cambrian Period tells us the 34 *separate and different phyla* of animals that comprise all animal life today came forth from the Earth in the same way a bush arises from the Earth — as *'stems'* that are *separate and independent of each other.* This complete separation allows us to calculate the statistical likelihood that analogous organs in different phyla (such as the example previously given of the five different phyla that have sight) *evolved independently* — i.e., via a process that science calls *convergent evolution.*[776]

It has been statistically proved — the convergent evolution that is documented in the fossil record and is observed in today's life-forms — *did not happen by independent random reactions.* Since it could not have happened by random chance, scientists currently think it must have been preprogrammed.[777]

The following is a direct quote from Dr. Schroeder.

"Science has shown that in the five-million-year transition from Pre-Cambrian to Cambrian life, the basic anatomy of every animal alive today developed. Massive morphological changes were required in every part of the ancestral genome. Even more confounding to the traditional logic of evolution; there is no evidence of evolution within the five-million-year span of the Cambrian explosion. Each of the animals in this era makes its first appearance fully developed. It was the sudden nature of this 'evolutionary' development that led to Walcott's reinterrment of the Burgess Shale fossils. The idea of a hopeful monster, a massive and multifaceted evolutionary change, occurring in a single generation — or even in a few generations — simply does not stand up to the scrutiny of statistics. This was established in 1967 at the Wistar Institute symposium, which brought

---

[775] Protozoans: Ancient, Pre-Cambrian, microscopic single-cell eukaryotic organisms such as amoeba that made their appearance in the Paleoproterozoic Eon on the 3rd Day of Creation. They feed on organic matter, and debris.

[776] Schroeder: *The Science of God* Chapter 7 p 104*c*

[777] Schroeder *The Science of God* Chapter 7 p 112*c*

together leading biologists and mathematicians in what turned out to be a futile attempt to find a mathematically reasonable basis for the assumption that random mutations are the driving force behind evolution. Unfortunately, each time the mathematics showed the statistical improbability of a given assumption, the response of the biologists was that the mathematics must be somehow flawed since evolution has occurred and occurred through random mutations." [778]

DR. SCHROEDER CONTINUED—

"The fossil record implies an exotic developmental occurrence at the Cambrian. These data are reported in the leading scientific journals. But how to explain the data is a mystery that becomes more mysterious with each new fossil. When Darwin wrote 'natura non facit saltum' (nature does not make jumps) he was so very wrong — 'gloriously and utterly wrong' (to quote Richard Dawkins, though admittedly out of context). It seems that nature only makes jumps (natura sola facit saltum). Sudden appearances are the trademark of the Fossil record.[779] Fossils reveal the events. Unfortunately, they do not disclose the processes by which those events occurred. It is true that Hox genes have been discovered to control the location and development of entire organs. But the genes that actually form these organs must already be present in the genome. We are forced to revert to the idea of latent genes waiting patiently to be queued by the environment for expression."[780]

THE SCIENCE OF GENETICS SUGGESTS THAT ONLY ANIMALS IN THE SAME PHYLUM HAVE A COMMON GENETIC HISTORY.

More than 34 phyla of animals appeared on the 5th Day, but only 34 phyla survived extinction. At their inception those 34 phyla of animals that survived looked very different from our modern-day animals. But the different appearances of our modern-day animals are the result of the changes caused by *microevolution resulting from major environmental changes, population genetics, and extra-terrestrial macro-environmental events.*

Some *classes* of animals within some of the 34 phyla that survived the 5th Day became extinct during the 6th Day. An example of this is the *Dinosaurs*. They were of the *Phylum*: **Chordata** — of the *Sub-phylum*: **Vertebrata** — that belonged to the *Class*: **Reptilia**. As we have discussed, they developed on the 5th Day and through microevolution they evolved into the giants we call Dinosaurs during the Jurassic Period on the 6th Day. But they suddenly died out during the Cretaceous Period on the 6th Day. We think their extinction was the result of an asteroid impact with the Earth — *an extra-terrestrial macro-environmental event.*

Darwin attributed the extinctions of classes of animals to the dominance of other classes of animals that caused their extinction because they were '*more fit.'* This is how Darwin derived his evolutionary idea of *"natural selection,"* which he said was *"The Law of the Survival of the Fittest."* Darwin's hypothesis of the survival of the fittest was a vast *"oversimplification."*

---

[778] Schroeder *The Science of God* Chapter 7 p 113a (quoting Schroeder)
[779] Schroeder *The Science of God* Chapter 7 p 113a (quoting Schroeder)
[780] Schroeder *The Science of God* Chapter 7 p 113b,c (quoting Schroeder)

DR. SCHROEDER ALSO SAID:

"Rarely if ever are there any fossil indications that competition by a new and better adapted class of animals dominated and beat out an outdated ancestor in the race for food, shelter, and survival, thus driving the ancestor to extinction. There simply is no evidence the simple dominance of one class of animals over another brought about the extinction of the less dominant class, through what Darwin called 'natural selection.' On the other hand, science attributes Earth's several episodes of mass-extinctions of life to macro-environmental changes that were brought about by the several separate ice ages, global floods, and supercontinents that have occurred in Earth's history. Extra-terrestrial macro-events such as major asteroid impacts have also caused macro-environmental changes which classes of life could not survive.[781]*"*

In general terms, the new science of genetics does not argue with Darwin's idea of common ancestry.[782] However, there is an argument.

THE ARGUMENT LIES IN THE SPECIFICS:

- Darwin thought all life had one common progenitor. Then he hedged his bet when he also said maybe instead of one, there were *'a few.'*
- Darwin thought the different varieties of life came through changes, which were the result of gradual random chance that happened at the level of the phylum — *over* eons of time.
- Since the fossil record of his day did not support his ideas, he wanted his disciples to continue to search for the transitional forms he believed would prove his theory.

THE MODERN SCIENCE OF GENETICS SAYS:

- *Each phylum* of animals shares a common genetic history.
- Therefore, *each phylum may have started with a specific patriarch or progenitor.*
- However, the 34 phyla of animals alive today *do not* share a common genetic history above the level of the protozoans.
- This is because *each* of the 34 phyla of animals alive today *originated separately and independently of the other phyla during the Cambrian Explosion of life.*
- *Each phylum appeared suddenly — mature, complete, and fully developed.*
- Therefore, there was no slow, gradual, or random chance development.
- Reproduction and development happen at the level of the *species* — not at the level of the *Phylum* as Darwin had supposed.
- *No cross-Phylum changes or developments have ever occurred!*
- *No new Phyla have developed since the Cambrian Explosion!*

CONCLUSIONS

So, when people talk about evolution, it would be helpful to know exactly what they mean when they say *'evolution.'* And, when people ask the question: "Did Darwin get it *all* right?" The answer is: *"No. Darwin did not get it all right."* (These quotes also come from Dr. Schroeder who attributes them to an article in the journal *Science*.) Most of Darwin's conjectures have been refuted by the scientific discoveries that were made after his death. Unlike Einstein, whose Theory of Relativity has been scientifically proved to be —

---

[781] Schroeder: *Genesis and the Big Bang* Chapter 9 p 138*d*-141*b* (A direct quote of Schroeder)
[782] Schroeder *The Science of God* Chapter 2, p. 30*c*

The Law of Relativity: Darwin's theory has *not* been confirmed by science even after 165 years of scientific investigation. The same must be said for Neo-Darwinian theory.[783]

When one reads Darwin's book, *The Origin of Species,* one finds such phrases as:

"Thus we can hardly believe...we cannot believe...we may safely attribute...we may further venture...we may safely believe...probably through the...It is scarcely possible to decide...we may conclude" (reference p. 168)...

"As far as ignorance permits us to judge...If it profit a plant...I can see no greater difficulty...modifications in the adult may affect the structure of the larva; but in all cases Natural Selection will ensure that they shall not be injurious; for if they were so, the species would become extinct" (reference page 70)...

"I suppose that the inhabitants of each region underwent a considerable amount of modification and extinction...and that there was much migration from other parts of the world...we are very far from concluding...I suspect that cases of this nature occur in Europe...If the several formations in these regions have not been deposited during the same exact periods...and if in both regions the species have gone on slowly changing during the accumulation of the several formations...in this case the several formations in the two regions could be arranged...and the order would falsely appear to be strictly parallel" (reference page 314)...

"It is probable that more than one species would vary...If in the diagram I have assumed...after fourteen thousand generations, six new species, marked by the letters n^{14} to z^{14} are supposed to have been produced...for these will have the best chance...may for long but unequal periods continue to transmit unaltered descendants...but in the process of modification...extinction, will have played an important part...there will be a constant tendency in the improved descendants...to supplant and exterminate in each stage of descent their predecessors and their original progenitor...will generally tend to become extinct." (Reference page 99).

I selected these pages — *BY RANDOM CHANCE.* These phrases are examples of Darwin's reasoning and thought processes. This type of language appears on every page of his book. Although this type of writing may have been considered *scientific inquiry* in Darwin's day, *it would not be considered the language of scientific inquiry today.* If a scientist were to use this kind of language today, his contemporaries would think it to be the language of — *assumption, belief, conjecture, deduction, guessing, hypothesis, imagination, possibility, presumption, supposition, and speculation.*

In the 447 pages of his book, Darwin freely exercised his imagination. But Darwin never once offered what the scientists of today would consider — *any valid scientific proof to substantiate his assumptions.* His own words tell us Darwin's conclusions were founded on a type of reasoning that was based on a series of — *'Since—If—Then—If—Serial Assumption Mistakes'* (or *'Sitisams'*). His so-called *'Theory of Evolution'* is full of this kind of *Circular Logic.* It is like a dog chasing its tail. (cf. Chapter 17.)

---

[783] Schroeder: *The Science of God* Chapter 7 p 114*b*

We have mentioned the University of Cambridge honored Charles Doolittle Walcott with an honorary D.Sc. degree during the Semicentennial celebration of the publication of Darwin's book: *The Origin of Species.* Has no one noticed — more than three times that interval of time has passed since Darwin's book was first published, and yet after 165 years of scientific investigation, his ideas are still unproved. Why is his *'theory'* now treated as if it were *'Law?'* When will people wake up? *All of his major assumptions have been refuted by modern science!*

Nevertheless, Darwin's ideas have been fraudulently elevated to the status of proven scientific principles and they are taught as if they are factual truths. Why? Because they satisfy the social and political agendas of a whole class of people who are enemies of God. These people are using their teachings to change public opinion so that they can engineer their beliefs and philosophy into secular law.

The fact that secular law now promotes Darwin's views, while preventing prayer, any mention of the Biblical Creation Account, and any mention of God in our schools — is ample evidence of the truth of this statement. I will document my reasons for this opinion in the next chapter — **Chapter 21: The Agenda of Darwinists.**

Darwinists and other non-believers say religious people believe in *"the myth of God,"* and they claim the Biblical Creation Account is *a myth* as well. In answer to this, believers can truthfully say *the Biblical account* of the development of life on our planet *is right* and *the way Darwin imagined and assumed life developed was wrong.* Science has now proved it. Believers should also remind non-believers — science will *never* be able to *disprove* the existence of God.

Although the Biblical Creation Account has been relegated to the status of a myth and Darwin's ideas are taught as the only explanation of our origins, modern science has now proved: the real myths are Darwin's ideas. His assumptions amount to nothing more than a belief system that has been used to discredit the Bible and promote the anti-God social and political agendas of its advocates.

So, does it all boil down to belief? No! Something major has happened. The Biblical Account has now been validated by modern science, and a major paradigm shift has been brought about by the scientific discoveries of the last 85 years.

MODERN SCIENCE NOW AGREES WITH MOSES!

- Although most people do not yet realize it, science now agrees with the Biblically defined type of Evolution that is revealed to us by the deeper meaning of the original Hebrew text of Genesis 1 and Genesis 2 — something that I call — *'The Genesis Code.'*

- Modern science now agrees with the sequence of creation that is stated in the Bible. The development of the visible life-forms on Earth (forms that we can see with unaided vision), occurred in the order of development that is described in the Bible.

- The fossil record supports the Bible's declaration of *sudden, abrupt, punctuated change,* and modern science is just now beginning to fill in the particulars.

- Scientists are now marveling at the abundance of evidence that is found everywhere they look. Everything shows the imprint of an all-pervading *Intelligent Design.* And science has proved the *Intelligent Design* that is so evident was *not* the result of random chance.

- The rapprochement between science and the Bible (which started in high energy physics and has slowly spread to astronomy, geology, paleontology, and biology); gives believers the encouragement and hope that more and more people will come to the realization — *God is real! God matters! God is the source of all life and all that exists!* That is what the Bible teaches, and I have the conviction of the truth of that belief.

- When The Genesis Code becomes generally known, people will realize God told Moses how He *created*, *made*, *formed*, and *evolved all things*. The Account is recorded in Genesis, Chapters One and Two.

- There now is a definitive answer to the question: *Is there such a thing as Evolution?* The answer is: *Yes, there is such a thing as Evolution. But it is not the type of evolution Darwin imagined*. Darwin's 19th century ideas of random chance gradualism in the development of life, macroevolution, and survival of the fittest (his supposition of natural selection) — have all been disproved by a compendium of 20th and 21st century scientific investigations. Darwin's faulty platforms of 19th century thought have been erroneously elevated to the status of law and have been used to promote an anti-God political and social agenda.

THE EMPEROR'S NEW CLOTHES

In 1837, Hans Christian Andersen wrote a Fairy Tale entitled *'The Emperor's New Clothes.'* This famous story is about an Emperor who cares for nothing but his appearance and his attire. He hires two tailors who promise him the finest suit of clothes from a fabric that *will be invisible* to anyone who is *hopelessly stupid* and *unfit* for his position. The deceitful tailors hold out their empty hands to the Emperor and proclaim they are holding a bolt of the magic fabric, which the stupid and unfit will not be able to see. Does he approve? The Emperor *cannot see* the cloth, but for fear he will appear stupid and unfit, he pretends he *can see* the fabric from which his suit will be fashioned. His ministers do the same. When the swindlers report the suit is finished, they mime dressing him and the naked Emperor then marches through his castle in procession before his ministers and royal court.

The procession (led by the Emperor) proceeds with much pomp and ceremony through the streets of the Emperor's city. Everyone clearly sees the Emperor is naked! But, word of the magic fabric has spread, and fearing the pretense might indeed be true, the crowd also plays along. All along the way the Emperor hears loud proclamations concerning the magnificence of his new attire.

Suddenly, an innocent and guileless child in the crowd (too young to understand the desirability of keeping up the pretense), blurts out: ***"Look Mama! The Emperor is naked!"*** When the obvious has been loudly proclaimed by a child, the cry is finally taken up by all in the crowd. The Emperor cringes, suspecting the assertion is true; but he holds himself up proudly, and arrogantly continues the procession.

For 165 years, Atheists and secularists have been parading Darwinism through the institutions and streets of society proclaiming it is their hero and using its ideas to discredit the Biblical Account of Creation. All, it seems, have proclaimed *Darwinism their Emperor*. It is doubtful many have ever read Darwin's book. But most accept the myth that Darwinism has been scientifically proved. Respected teachers in prestigious universities, seminaries, & institutions; public officials, leaders in government, journalists, and all media — claim the tenets of Darwinism are Law. They believe Darwin's scheme of Evolution is the way Evolution actually happened. They also believe the claim of nonbelievers that the Biblical Account of Creation is a childish myth. Although Darwin's body of work was impressive in his day, it is riddled with *'Sitisams'* and *Circular Logic*. It does not rise to the standards of what would be considered true scientific inquiry today.

In reality, modern science has now proved "Darwinism" and "Neo-Darwinian Theory" are nothing more than a façade! We now know the last 85 years of true scientific inquiry overwhelmingly confirms the Biblical Account of Creation. This convergence of opinion is not yet widely known.

However, someday, some brave, guileless, esteemed scientist or prestigious, respectable, and laudable college faculty, or scientific group, will stop looking at the individual leaves in the 'Forest of Discovery' and will focus on the 'Big Picture' — (i.e., 'the Forest itself')! When that happens, they will discover — modern science not only now agrees with the Bible but has also proved Darwinism wrong! Like the guileless child in the crowd, they will then shout out the truth for all to hear— "Look! Darwinism is naked!"

AFTER THE NAKED TRUTH HAS BEEN DECLARED—

- *What* will people do?

- Will they *acknowledge* the *truth* of the *Bible*?

- Will they *repeal* the secular laws that have driven God out of our public schools?

- Will they *add* the deeper meaning of the Biblical Account of Creation to the curriculum?

- Will they *allow* public prayer and devotions to God in our schools again?

- Or, like the prideful, supercilious, and ignorant Emperor, will they *ignore the truth* and continue to pay homage to the breeder-pigeon spawned, 'Since-If-Then-If' faulty Circular Logic & flawed assumptions of Darwinian & Neo-Darwinian Theory?

CHAPTER 21: THE AGENDA OF DARWINISTS

In this chapter, we will discuss the damage Darwinism is doing to those who believe in God and how the type of evolution Darwin imagined has enabled anti-God people to exclude God from public life and claim God doesn't exist!
                                                                                    O. David

Stephen Jay Gould was one of the most famous Darwinists of modern times. Until his death in 2002, he was widely considered the unofficial chair of evolutionary biology in the pages of the *New York Review of Books*. Like Darwin, Gould said he was an Agnostic. Unlike Darwin, Gould never professed any belief in God. In Chapter 15, I talked about Gould's misquote of Darwin, gave an illustration of his convoluted style of writing, and discussed his criticisms of Charles Doolittle Walcott. Although Gould was a formidable anti-creationist, *It is not generally known Gould became the chief critic of contemporary Neo-Darwinism in his day!*

Gould realized the more complete fossil record of today overwhelmingly refutes two major tenets of Darwinian Theory:

(1) *Gradualism* in evolution, and
(2) *The smooth natural flow of the transitions that must have occurred.*

Contrary to what Darwin claimed, the accumulating "pile" of the fossil record over the past 165 years since Darwin's time — shows *big jumps* in the development of animal life and documents *rapid changes* in the development of inherited character traits!

Therefore, the *staccato nature of the rapid development that the fossil record demonstrates* so much bothered some paleontologists who had hitched their wagon to Darwin's ideas that they felt they had to come up with a way to explain both the lack of gradualism and the lack of any fossil evidence of slow gradual transitions from some original ancestor into later generations of improved and more highly advanced progeny.

- Since the past 165 years of fossil data has failed to find any evidence of the continuity of development and gradualism in evolution that Darwin thought would be found, Gould and some of his Neo-Darwinist-friends decided — *'rapidity in development' must be the answer!* Therefore, they postulated *rapid changes* will not likely leave any fossils to record the morphological flow from the old to the new type of animal. So, they proposed *that* must be a *major* reason there is no evidence of slow gradual evolution in the fossil record.

- Furthermore, they claimed *the other reason* for a lack of gradualism is because new and more fit species must have competed for natural resources more effectively and in a short time destroyed the older less fit species. So, their new reasoning goes.

- However, they have not given up hope that new future fossil discoveries will vindicate their new view.

- Millennia later, so their new modification of the old assumptions goes, someone will find a fossil record of the new morph directly above the old morph with no transitional link which might embody an animal that was part of the older and part of the newer species.[784]

Without realizing it, their new idea of rapid development agrees with the Biblical proclamations of rapid development that were announced on each of the Six Days of Creation by this statement of God — *"Then God said."* The ten-fold repetition of this statement of God heralds the Biblical tenets of (1) *Divine Direction* — (2) *Divine Intervention* — (3) *Divine Punctuated Development* — and (4) *Divine Intelligent Design in Creation! The Genesis Code* meaning of these statements of God *is the Biblical evidence of* — the *God-Directed Orthogenesis in Creation that actually occurred* on each Day of Creation when following the phrase *"Then God said:"* The Creator spoke — *"Let there be"* ... (See Chapter 8 in Book I).

IF THE "PACK" THINKS YOU HAVE TURNED ON THEM, THE "PACK" WILL TURN ON YOU!

PUNCTUATED EQUILIBRIUM: AN UNWELCOME, "NEW REVOLUTIONARY IDEA."
In 1972, Stephen Jay Gould and Niles Eldredge proposed their idea of *"PUNCTUATED EQUILIBRIUM."* Only two months before Gould's death in 2002, their 1433-page Book: "*The Structure of Evolutionary Theory*" was published.[785] Their book put forth their new idea of *PUNCTUATED EQUILIBRIUM* as an alternative to Darwin's *Random Chance Natural Selection Theory.* The three main arguments for punctuated equilibrium are what they called: (1) *LAMARCKIAN INHERITANCE,* (2) *ORTHOGENESIS,* and (3) *SALTATIONISM.* They thought these new ideas would be accepted as critical improvements to Neo-Darwinian Theory. Sounds really sophisticated — doesn't it? As you shall see, the Neo-Darwinists *"across the pond"* had a low opinion of it. They were especially critical of Stephen Jay Gould.

- (1)Gould's and Eldredge's concept of the *LAMARCKIAN INHERITANCE* of acquired characteristics was their denial of the Darwinian and Neo-Darwinian idea of variation through *random chance* and *natural selection.* Gould's and Eldredge's adaptation of *Jean Baptiste Lamarck's* idea that animals will lose the inherited characteristics they don't use and develop the ones they do use (called "*LAMARCKIAN INHERITANCE*") — has now fallen out of favor.
- (2)Their claim of *ORTHOGENESIS* argues that *evolution is directed!* (The *Bible* proclaims evolution *is directed* and attributes the directing force of evolution *to God.*) Nevertheless, Gould's and Eldredge's claim of an orthogenesis in evolution contradicted Darwin's view that *variation in the inherited characteristics of offspring is undirected.*
- (3)With their resurrection of the old idea of *SALTATIONISM* (i.e., a refutation of Darwin's *"natura non facit saltum" i.e., nature does not make jumps*), they claimed the changes that occurred in evolution are *big* jumps — a denial of Darwin's claim that variation requires *many small gradual steps.*

They gave their so-called *"new ideas"* of Lamarckian Inheritance, Orthogenesis, and Saltationism a name. They called it: *"PUNCTUATED EQUILIBRIUM"* — their term for the whole process they felt explained the persistent lack of gradualism in the fossil record.

[784] Schroeder *The Science of God* Chapter 6 p 94e-95a
[785] Stephen Jay Gould *Punctuated Equilibrium* Harvard University Press www.hup.hardard.edu>edu>catalog....

"Punctuated Equilibrium" seems dangerously close to the *Biblical concept of Punctuated Development!* Doesn't it?

Gould thought he had offered a valid explanation for the *punctuated development* that the past 165 years of scientific investigation *has proved.* He believed his scheme explained *the big jumps* and the *persistent lack of gradualism* in the fossil record. His idea that evolutionary development *is directed* factually agrees with the Bible. However, he offered no explanation for the *source* of orthogenesis. Without realizing it, his arguments for *big jumps, and sudden directed developments* — actually agree with the type of evolution the Bible has proclaimed for the past 3300 years.

GOULD OFFERED HIS ARGUMENTS TO IMPROVE NEO-DARWINIAN THEORY.

Instead, the Darwinists of his day had a low opinion of his new ideas. He should have been prepared for their reaction. Instead of the acclamations he expected, he became a target of Neo-Darwinian criticism because he had proposed putative corrections and alternatives to mainstream Darwinian Theory.[786]

The Neo-Darwinist criticisms of Gould were over his disagreement with Darwin's idea that *adaptation through random chance natural selection* is the main engine of evolutionary change. The Orthodox Darwinists and contemporary traditional Neo-Darwinists of his day claimed Gould had offered: *"No truly original and genuinely significant contributions to evolutionary theory!"* Instead, they claimed Gould created *"a vast rhetorical tissue of sophistical equivocations."* My Oh My! **They called his 1433-page book a "*tissue!*"** Not just a *'tissue,'* but a *rhetorical tissue of sophistical equivocations!"* Synonyms of *rhetorical* include pejoratives such as *"pretentious, bombastic,* and *pompous!"* They really were unkind!

Maynard Smith (a famous Neo-Darwinist) asked this question: *"If Gould had formulated no significant revisions of Darwinian theory, then why was it necessary to take account of his views?"* He answered his question with this statement:

"Gould occupies a rather curious position, particularly on his side of the Atlantic. Because of the excellence of his essays, he has come to be seen by non-biologists as the preeminent evolutionary theorist. In contrast, the evolutionary biologists with whom I have discussed his work tend to see him as a man whose ideas are so confused as to be hardly worth bothering with, but as one who should not be publicly criticized because he is at least on our side against the creationists. All this would not matter, were it not that he is giving non-biologists a largely false picture of the state of evolutionary theory."

Another prominent Neo-Darwinist, *John Alcock*, declared:

"Gould's situation is something like that in the story of the man, hungry for fame, who made a particularly ingenious bargain with the devil—ingenious, that is, on the devil's side. In return for his soul, the man would be famous in his own day, but only on the condition that after his death all trace of his works would be eradicated from the memory of men."

---

[786] University of Missouri–St. Louis
Modern Darwinism and the Pseudo-Revolutions of Stephen ...
This is an excellent informative Article on Darwinist Criticism of Gould's "Punctuated Equilibrium." It also reveals why Marxism is so actively promoted by many university professors who oppose Christianity & the ideas of the Founding Fathers of the American Revolution.

Other prominent Darwinists who were critical of Gould were *Daniel Dennett, Richard Dawkins, Simon Conway Morris, and E. O. Wilson.*[787] So it is that Darwinists are not only against *"Creationists,"* but there are also serious disagreements between those Darwinists who think Darwin's ideas are sacrosanct and those who do not. Yet, many of them feel it unwise to criticize each other publically because it might weaken their cause. They wish to maintain their carefully constructed façade that they are all united behind Darwin's original thoughts and 'theory.' So, what is their common cause? Most of them deny the existence of God. Some (who won't go that far) say — if God exists, he is irrelevant.

THE FACT IS: DARWIN WAS WRONG!

I have already presented the basic ideas of Darwin's original theory and have explained that Darwin's idea of *macroevolution* has not been verified by modern science. I have also explained that modern science has proved — *Evolution happened via microevolution*. The microevolution that the Genesis Code of the Bible describes is very different from what Darwin thought. The fact has also been mentioned: modern science has now verified the type of evolution presented in the Bible — i.e., *"Modern science now agrees with Moses."* And, I have said this convergence of agreement between modern science and the Bible is something *academia, secularists,* and *the media* either have not understood, or have ignored.

Nevertheless, Darwinists and other anti-God groups have labeled the Biblical Account of Creation — *"Creationism."* And *Creationism* is something they disdain. Darwinists have been so successful in convincing the public their ideas have been founded on science and proved by scientific investigation that the Biblical Creation Account is now treated by most American secularists as *a myth*. There is a great divide of opinion that exists today between believers and nonbelievers. Darwinism has been placed in the middle of that great divide.

AN EXAMPLE OF MEDIA BIAS AND DISDAIN FOR 'CREATIONISM'

The disdain of the media for the *Biblical Account of Creation* was highlighted in a national television broadcast on the Fox TV News Channel on Thursday night, May 5th, 2011. On that night, in South Carolina, the first Republican Presidential Campaign Debate for the Presidential election in 2012 was held. The respected TV Journalist, Juan Williams, asked the former Republican Governor of Minnesota a question concerning his position on teaching 'Creationism' in the public schools. Mr. Williams, as always, was respectful, but the tone and inflections of his voice and his body language conveyed to the audience his disdain for what he thinks was an action that was taken in Minnesota, which equated 'Creationism' with science.

Juan Williams: *Governor Pawlenty, when you served as governor of Minnesota you named an education commissioner who equated the teaching of creationism with the teaching of evolution. Do you equate the teaching of creationism with the teaching of evolution, as the basis for what should be taught in our nation's schools? And I ask that in this sense, do you personally equate a faith-based theory with scientific inquiry?*

---

[787] ibid

Tim Pawlenty: *Well, Juan, the approach we took in Minnesota is to say that there should be room in the curriculum for study of Intelligent Design. Didn't necessarily need to be in a science class, it could be in a comparative theory class. But we didn't decide that at the state level. We left that up to the local school districts, and the communities, and parents in that area. I think that's a reasonable and appropriate approach. . .*

I have omitted that part of Pawlenty's answer that segued into his position on unions and the heavy hand of the federal government in the jobs market. Mr. Williams brought the discussion back to creationism with his follow-up question.

Williams: *I understand, Governor, but you didn't answer my question about what you believe about teaching creationism in the schools. What do you believe, Governor?*

Pawlenty: *I believe that should be left up to parents and local school districts and not to states or the federal government.*[788]

SECULAR SUPPRESSION OF CHRISTIANITY

Beginning in the 20th Century, and continuing to today, modern-day secularists and atheists have turned a blind eye to the most recent discoveries of science that have proved Darwin's assumptions on evolution wrong. They continue to revile what they call "Creationism," and they continue to label the Biblical Account of Creation "false and politically incorrect." Current law, under the guise of separation of church and state, prevents any mention of the Biblical Account of Creation in America's classrooms. They have been so successful in promoting their views that the term "Creationism" is now considered a *bad* word. Modern-day secularists have turned the intentions of our founding fathers *upside down.* They have sold the public on the idea the founding fathers' principle of "freedom *of* religion" should be interpreted to mean "freedom *from* religion."

THE SCOPES 'MONKEY' TRIAL

In Darwin's day, and in the day of the famous *Scopes Trial in Tennessee*, when Clarence Darrow and William Jennings Bryan represented opposing views, the *Genesis Code* was unknown to all but only a small number of Jewish rabbis who were familiar with the writings of Moses Maimonides and Moses Nahmanides. So, the trial debated the merits of Darwin's assumptions as measured against what was then believed to be "*the truth of the Bible.*" Sadly, because the Genesis Code was generally unknown, the prevalent interpretation of the "truth of the Bible" was based on *misinterpretations* of the ancient text. Those misinterpretations were from a lack of knowledge of the deeper meaning of the Hebrew Creation Account. I wonder — if William Jennings Bryan had known about the *Genesis Code* — would the Scopes Trial have turned out differently? If he had known the ancient Hebrew text factually tells us how Elohim *"evolved"* the life-forms on our planet, he could have made the trial an argument over the true Biblical concept of evolution versus how Darwin envisioned it. Now, that would have been something.

(I talked about this in the Introduction—Part II as part of the Preface to Book I.)

---

[788] Article Query: "Juan Williams Channels Chris Matthews, Grills Pawlenty on Evolution in Debate By Kyle Drennen" [Note]: The transcript from this source accurately quotes this particular exchange between Williams and Pawlenty. Mr. Williams' *disdain* for what he called 'creationism' was also noted by several of my friends.

YES, THERE IS SUCH A THING AS EVOLUTION.

So, in answer to the question: *'Is there such a thing as Evolution?'* The answer is: *'Yes!'* However, the type of Evolution the Genesis Code discloses in the Genesis Creation Account is very different from the type of Evolution Darwin postulated.

DARWINISTS HAVE ALWAYS HAD AN ANTI-GOD AGENDA.

The ideology of Darwinists has always been driven by atheism. At first, some of the proponents of Darwin's ideas did not openly declare their anti-God agenda. But, today, they have proudly declared it. We will examine the evidence for this statement in more detail in the last part of this chapter. But, for now, let's look at the following direct quote from the Introduction to Dr. Grant R. Jeffrey's book: *Creation: Remarkable Evidence of God's Design.*

"The real agenda of many of those scientists and educators who embrace evolution (*i.e., 'Darwinism'*) is to use it to destroy man's faith in the Word of God, divine creation, and the Christian faith. This fact is demonstrated by the very words of leading atheists and supporters of evolution. For example, *Professor J. Dunphy* wrote in his revealing article entitled *'A Religion for a New Age'* in *Humanist* magazine (an atheist publication) about their plan to replace orthodox Christianity with their new atheistic 'religion' called "Humanism."

Dunphy — "*I am convinced that the battle for humankind's future must be waged and won in the public-school classroom by teachers who correctly perceive their role as the proselytizers of a new faith: a religion of humanity that recognizes and respects the spark of what theologians call divinity in every human being. These teachers must embody the same selfless dedication as the most rabid fundamentalist preachers, for they will be ministers of another sort, utilizing a classroom instead of a pulpit to convey humanist values in whatever subject they teach, regardless of the educational level — preschool, day care, or large state university. The classroom must and will become an arena of conflict between the old and the new — **the rotting corpse of Christianity** — together with all its adjacent evils and misery, and the new faith of humanism...It will undoubtedly be a long, arduous, painful struggle replete with much sorrow and many tears, but humanism will emerge triumphant. It must if the family of humankind is to survive.*" [789],[790]
[The *i.e., 'Darwinism,'* bolding, and underlining are mine.]

UNLIKE DARWIN, DARWINISTS LEAVE GOD OUT OF THE EQUATION.

There are some people who promote a body of assumptions about evolution they say originated from the work and mind of Charles Darwin; however, like Gould, they make no mention of Darwin's belief in God. There are people who call themselves *'Darwinists'* who are, at the worst, Atheists and/or Gnostics, or at the best — Agnostics. Many of them have the same agenda as Professor J. Dunphy. You see, if life originated on Earth from random chance reactions over periods and epochs of time, until finally one-celled living organisms emerged by chance; and, if over additional epochs of time, those one-celled living organisms just happened to evolve into more complex life-forms, which through the

[789] *CREATION: Remarkable Evidence of God's Design* Introduction p. 15 & 16
[790] J. Dunphy, *"A Religion for a New Age," The Humanist,* Jan.-Feb. 1983, 23, 26 (emphases added), cited by Wendell R. Bird, *Origin of the Species—Revisited,* vol. 2, p. 257

mechanisms of self-replication and random chance mutations caused the plethora of life on our planet that eventually came to be; then it all could have happened spontaneously, and there would be no need for a God. These people ignore the fact — the Cambrian explosion of life has disproved Darwin's Theory.

When the Big Bang Theory gained credibility, these anti-God people argued it was not inconsistent with their view of a type of evolution that does not require the existence of a God. They thought you could have *a Big Bang* without any need for there to be *a Big Banger.* These people have fought an appalling fight. They have managed to kick God out of our schools. And they are trying to kick God out of our history, our historical traditions of government, and our laws, which have a solid foundation on the Ten Commandments, the Commandment of Christ (John 13:34), Roman Law (tempered by Judeo-Christian Law), and English Common Law. They have managed to promote the idea that people who believe in God and the Biblical Account of Creation are not only *nuts,* but they are *stupid* as well. They claim those who believe in a Creator and a Savior are trapped in a mindless mythology that enslaves them and serves as a soporific for their minds (*what Marx believed).* They have been successful in their fight to prevent any mention of the Biblical Account of Creation in our schools as an alternative view that opposes Darwinism.

DARWIN DID NOT THINK HIS IDEAS CONTRADICTED THE BIBLE OR EXCLUDED GOD.

At the time of this writing, it has been 165 years since Darwin's book was first published. During all of this time Christians have attacked his concepts of evolution because the proponents of his theory have been so successful in hiding the inconvenient truth that Darwin saw nothing in his theory that any reasonable person would think contradicted the Biblically founded belief in the existence of a God who created all that exists. But Darwinists have been so successful in using their views of his ideas to promote their anti-God agenda that his theory is still considered sacrilegious by most people who believe in God.

It is a sad thing that many if not most people who believe in the One True God (i.e., Unitarians as Darwin was, and Jews, Christians, and Muslims) do not know that something in Darwin compelled him to reveal he had a belief in God as well. It is doubtful Darwin's hope will ever be realized that his theory would someday fall within what he would have considered a religious paradigm. While it is true his proponents pursue their agenda with a religious zeal, their goals are secular, and their zeal is used to discredit God's word. I suspect if Darwin could see how his ideas have been misrepresented and misused, he would be greatly saddened.

As you shall see in the following discussion of the militancy and aggression of modern-day atheists — they have used Darwin's ideas to declare God is dead. They claim Darwin's ideas are the nails in God's coffin. So far as Gould's misquote of Darwin is concerned, sometimes it is our sins of omission; the things we don't do, the things we fail to say, the words in a quote that we omit; that resonate the loudest and give others a glimpse into the depths of our feelings, our thoughts, and our beliefs.

THE MILITANCY AND AGGRESSION OF MODERN-DAY ATHEISTS

Modern atheism has become extremely aggressive in its so-called intellectual militancy and moral self-confidence. In recent years, there have been several books published that have been widely read: books like Richard Dawkins's *The God Delusion* — *The End of Faith* by Sam Harris — Victor Stenger's *God; The Failed Hypotheses* — Christopher Hitchens's *God Is Not Great* — and Michel Onfray's *Atheist Manifesto,* which posits a 'final battle' against the forces of Christianity.[791] On this, both Onfray and the Bible agree. (See Revelations, Chapters 19 and 20.)

Dawkins said: *"The great unmentionable evil at the center of our culture is monotheism. From a barbaric Bronze Age text known as the Old Testament, three anti-human religions have evolved: Judaism, Christianity, and Islam."*[792]

The Nobel laureate Steven Weinberg wrote: *"Anything that we scientists can do to weaken the hold of religion should be done and may in the end be our greatest contribution to civilization."*[793]

DINESH D'SOUZA

What has given these atheists the confidence to openly criticize religion is the so-called modern *'science'* of Darwinism. In making their case, the atheists of today point to what they refer to as the revolutionary influence of Charles Darwin. Dawkins, in his book "*The Blind Watchmaker*" wrote*: "Darwin made it possible to be an intellectually fulfilled atheist."*[794] In his explanation of the new atheist militancy, Dinesh D'Souza states the atheists' case so eloquently in his book: "*What's So Great about Christianity,"* that the following is a direct quote from his book.

"He (Dawkins) *points out that the universe and its creatures show irrefutable evidence of design. Before Darwin, there was no plausible explanation for that design other than to posit a designer. So, atheists had no way to account for life's diversity and complexity. Many—including skeptic David Hume—were forced to concede that each creature was fitted with the equipment needed for its survival by some sort of higher being. The great achievement of Darwin's theory of evolution and natural selection, Dawkins and others say, is that it shows how creatures that appear to be designed have in fact evolved according to the pressures of chance and survival. Atheists now have an alternative explanation for why fish have gills, why birds have wings, and why human beings have brains and arms and lungs. Indeed, in the atheist view,* (Darwin's view of) *evolution refutes the biblical account of human creation, exposing it as a crude and primitive myth."*[795]

Dawkins sounds like Gould, doesn't he? In the last chapter I discussed the real reasons why fish have gills, birds have wings, and why human beings have brains and arms and lungs. *The Creator programed all of it into the "TIE THAT BINDS US" — OUR DNA!*

D'Souza goes on with his detail of the statements and publications of modern-day atheists. And I encourage you to read his book. But I think I have stated enough of the evidence, which shows their boldness has come directly from their views of Darwin's assumptions — that we can move on to a discussion of what modern-day atheists are now doing with their newfound militancy.

[791] D'Souza: *What's So Great About Christianity* Chapter 3 p. 24
[792] D'Souza: *What's So Great About Christianity* Chapter 3 p. 25
[793] D'Souza: *What's So Great About Christianity* Chapter 3 p. 25
[794] D'Souza: *What's So Great About Christianity* Chapter 3 p. 26
[795] D'Souza: *What's So Great About Christianity* Chapter 3 p. 26-27

THE MISSION OF MODERN-DAY ATHEISTS

Dinesh D'Souza gives us the evidence that the mission of atheists today is to correct the *"miseducating* (of) *the young: (*thus) *saving children from their parents"* — the title of Chapter 4 of D'Souza's book. Their manifesto is to take the children religious people breed and educate them to despise their parents' beliefs. In recent years some parents and school boards have asked public schools to teach alternatives to Darwinian evolution. Does this cause any sense of déjà vu? It should, because I have already discussed the exchange between Juan Williams and Governor Pawlenty in the first Republican debate of the 2012 Presidential campaign. In response to such requests, there has been a powerful outcry from non-believing scientists and non-believing people in our society. They equate such requests to the equivalent of retarding the acquisition of scientific knowledge in the name of religion. The magazine, *The Economist*, published an editorial that stated: *"Darwinism has enemies mostly because it is not compatible with a literal interpretation of the book of Genesis."* [796]

The great divide in our society has now become the gap that has developed over deep-seeded personal beliefs. It is the gap that has developed between the people of faith and those who are non-believers. And strangely enough, both sides pursue their goals with a religious zeal. While non-believers have been active in pursuing their agenda for years, it seems the people of faith are just beginning to awaken from their apathy and take note of the tremendous changes non-believers have now made in our society.

JESUS SAID:
'RENDER UNTO CAESAR THE THINGS THAT ARE CAESAR'S.
AND RENDER UNTO GOD THE THINGS THAT ARE GOD'S.'" (MATTHEW 22:21)

It seems the new mantra of atheists the world over is now a perverted version of Christ's words:

RENDER ALL THINGS UNTO CAESAR, FOR THERE IS NO GOD!

Today, we have people who proudly declare themselves to be *Darwinists.* Darwinism has become an ideology. You don't hear anyone declaring themselves to be an *Einsteinian,* or a *Newtonian,* or an advocate of *Keplerism.* And yet, unlike Darwin, the theories of Einstein, Newton, and Kepler have been proven to be true. Their theories are now clearly labeled *Laws* that science has proved beyond every shadow of a doubt.

But today's Darwinists openly state their agenda is to get society to reject—

"Irrational and supernatural explanations of the world, the demons that exist only in their imaginations, and to accept a social and intellectual apparatus — science — as the only begetter of truth."

That is a quote of from biologist Richard Lewontin.[797]

THE STRATEGY OF ATHEISTS

And just how do they propose to accomplish this? They will do their work through the secular professors and teachers in our universities and public schools.

---

[796] D'Souza: *What's So Great About Christianity* Chapter 4 p. 33
[797] D'Souza: *What's So Great About Christianity* Chapter 4 p. 35

According to Philosopher Richard Rorty, the secular professors in the universities should: *"Arrange things so that students who enter as bigoted, homophobic religious fundamentalists will leave college with views more like our own."*

Rorty added that his students are fortunate to find themselves: *"Under the benevolent Herrschaft* [*] *of people like me, and to have escaped the grip of their frightening, vicious, dangerous parents."*

Rorty continued: *"We are going to go right on trying to discredit you in the eyes of your children, trying to strip your fundamentalist religious community of dignity, trying to make your views seem silly rather than discussable."*[798]

ACCORDING TO D'SOUZA, THE STRATEGY OF TODAY'S DARWINISTS AND ATHEISTS IS:

"...not to argue with religious views or to prove them wrong. Instead, it is to subject them to such scorn that they are pushed outside the bounds of acceptable debate. This strategy is effective because young people who go to good colleges are extremely eager to learn what it means to be an educated Harvard man or Stanford woman. Consequently, their teachers can very easily steer them to think a certain way merely by making their point of view seem fashionable and enlightened. Similarly, teachers can pressure students to abandon what their parents taught them simply by labeling those positions simplistic and unsophisticated. A second strategy commonly used to promote atheism on campus utilizes the vehicle of adolescent sexuality. 'Against the power of religion,' one champion of agnosticism told me, (D'Souza wrote) 'we employ an equal if not greater power—the power of the hormones.' Atheism is promoted as a means for young people to liberate themselves from moral constraint and indulge their appetites. Religion, in this framework, is portrayed as a form of sexual repression."[799] (**)

D'Souza ends the 4th Chapter of his book with these words:
"Children spend the majority of their waking hours in school. Parents invest a good portion of their life savings in (a) college education to entrust their offspring to people who are supposed to educate them. Isn't it wonderful that educators have figured out a way to make parents the instruments of their own undoing? Isn't it brilliant that they have persuaded Christian moms and dads to finance the destruction of their own beliefs and values? Who said atheists weren't clever?"[800]

Professor J. Dunphy was also clear about what he thought. When he wrote:
"The rotting corpse of Christianity, together with all its adjacent evils and misery... (versus) the new faith of humanism" ... There was no mistaking what he meant.

What is happening in our schools is a perversion and a travesty. For many years the true agenda of secular Darwinists was kept secret. But they are now being more open, more forthright, and more militant. We now know for certain there are people like Dunphy who want to influence our children and young adults to their views of what they call *'humanism.'* And, at least we are forewarned there are other people who variously label themselves as *secularists, nonbelievers, non-theists, anti-theists, apatheists, agnostics, skeptics, free tinkers, and humanists,* who want to turn our nation away from a belief in

---

(*) **Herrschaft:** an institutionalized authority inducing obedience.
[798] D'Souza: *What's So Great About Christianity* Chapter 4 p. 38
[799] D'Souza: *What's So Great About Christianity* Chapter 4 p. 38 (**) Paragraph a direct quote from D'Souza's book.
[800] D'Souza: *What's So Great About Christianity* Chapter 4 p. 39

God. Dunphy has told us humanists wish to direct society toward a *'new religion of humanism.'*

While agnostics say they don't know if God exists, apatheists say they don't care. Even though some of these groups would argue if you labeled them 'atheists,' they are in effect, *defacto atheists,* because their ignorance and indifference amount to a practical rejection of God. In his book, *"What's So Great about Christianity,"* Dinesh D'Souza, talks about these groups and declares there is a war over religion that has been declared by leading Western atheists who have commenced hostilities.[801]

THE WAR FOR THE CONTROL OF THE MINDS OF OUR CHILDREN.

D'Souza has given us the evidence there are powerful people in the kindergartens, elementary schools, high schools, universities, and institutions of higher learning that want to turn our children and young adults away from God. They want to send them out into our society believing either there is no God, or that God (if he exists) is irrelevant. There are still others who want to *convert people to a new religion of humanism* and send them out into our society imbued with the idea that converting others to a new religion of humanism should also be their mission in life. A surprising number of these people are in positions of power and influence in our educational institutions. Tuitions now range from $7,600—$50,000 or more per year![802] At prestigious private colleges, the total 4-year cost of an undergraduate degree can be as high as $200,000—$235,000! That is a high price to pay for teachings (many of which) are actually *pseudoscience,* and it is also a high price to pay *for spreading a sinister anti-religious agenda!* However, I think the monetary cost becomes infinitely small when compared to the spiritual cost — for no one can place a cost figure on the value of a person's soul. Here is what Jesus Christ said about that.

> *"For what does it profit a man to gain the whole world, and forfeit his soul? For what shall a man give in exchange for his soul? For whoever is ashamed of Me and My words, in this adulterous and sinful generation, the Son of Man will also be ashamed of him when He comes in the glory of His Father with the Holy angels." (Mark 8:36-38)*

Christians must wake up to the fact that anti-god people in the world have used Darwinism to engineer society away from a belief in God. The Bible is right. The Genesis Code tells us how God created and evolved all things. The Genesis Account of Creation is science. And we now know the scientific discoveries of the last 85 years agree with The Genesis Creation Account. In it, God told Moses how He created, made, and formed all things.

Charles Darwin was a brilliant man. I admire his intellect, his efforts, and his work. His Theory of Evolution was truly extraordinary for his time. I also have a great deal of empathy for him because of his struggle with his faith, which seems to have been caused by the sorrow and tragedy in his life. But how do I feel about 'Darwinism' and 'Neo-Darwinian Theory?' They are something else altogether because of their anti-God agenda. I think Darwin would be greatly dismayed if he knew what those who ascribe to his ideas have accomplished.

---

[801] D'Souza: *What's So Great About Christianity* Chapter 3, p. 23,24
[802] Article: *Live and Learn: Why We Have College*—The New Yorker Magazine: p.74-79 by Louis Menand. June 6, 2011 Issue

Summary Points for Chapters 14—21:

- The way Darwin assumed life evolved (an idea that science has labeled Macro-evolution) has now been disproved.

- Darwin did not base any of his ideas of evolution on the fossil record. Instead, he looked at the results of the crossbreeding of the various species of pigeons and the species of other domesticated animals and assumed the changes he observed (that occurred at the level of the *species* of animals), if multiplied by tens of millions of generations, could eventually cause even greater changes to eventually be expressed at the *phylum* level.[803] Science has proved life did not happen the way Darwin imagined. No evidence of his imagined "Evolutionary Tree of Life" has ever been discovered.[804]

- Darwin thought the development of the Earth's animals occurred at the level of the various phyla of animals, and then, through cross-phylum changes, the evolution of other animals took off from there. Science has proved evolution did not happen that way. Darwin's idea finds no support in the fossil record, in the lab, or in the Bible. [805]

- His imaginings that life had evolved from the simple to the complex, that invertebrates had evolved into vertebrates over one hundred to two hundred million years, and that the other simple phyla that also appeared on the "morning" of the 5th Day had evolved into more complex and different phyla — was fantasy, not fact.[806]

- Darwin's opinions, Miller's experiment, and Wald's claim that life had originated from random-chance-reactions among inanimate chemicals in warm ponds over eons of time and then progressed through an elaborate scheme of self-replications, combinations, mutations, and recombinations—has been proved false by the accumulated fossil data of the past 165 years.

- In his book, Darwin wrote: *"If it could be demonstrated that any complex organ existed, which could not possibly have been formed by numerous successive, slight modifications, my theory would absolutely break down."* [807]

- **Although the world still does not know it — that is exactly what has happened! His theory broke down when Charles Doolittle Walcott discovered the Burgess Pass Fossils of the Cambrian Explosion of Life in 1909. The Cambrian fossils were the first discovery — the first conclusive scientific evidence — that *absolutely destroyed* Darwin's theory. However, the world would not know that until the mid-1980s—when the complete analysis of all 60,000 of Walcott's fossils was completed!**

- If the famous historian Lecky (1838-1903), had lived to witness the impact of the full report of Walcott's 1909 discovery of the Burgess Pass fossils — he would have said: *They were the 'hard evidence'*[808] *that destroyed Darwin's Theory of Evolution.*

---

[803] Schroeder *The Science of God* Chapter 1 p. 9*b*

[804] Schroeder *The Science of God* Chapter 1 p. 9*c*

[805] Schroeder *The Science of God* Chapter 1 p 16*c* and Chapter 2 p 31 [**Macro-evolution]**

[806] Schroeder *The Science of God* Chapter 2 p. 37*a*

[807] Schroeder *The Hidden Face of God* Chapter 4 p. 51*c*, 50*b*, 50*d*,

[808] In the Introduction—Part VI, William Edward Hartpole Lecky objected to Wellhausen's Documentary Hypotheses. He said Wellhausen's conjectures — "totally lacked '*hard evidence.*'"

- Not only did the Burgess Pass fossils destroy Darwin's Theory, but the vastly more complete fossil-record of today (with its millions of specimens), absolutely refutes Darwin's Theory *and* confirms the Biblical Creation Account and the Biblical concepts of sudden, abrupt, punctuated development at the level of the individual species of life.

- Earth's first life-forms were the *microscopic* life-forms (*i.e., not visible to the naked eye*) that suddenly appeared on *the 3rd Day* after the appearance of liquid water.

- Earth's first *visible* life-forms exploded upon the scene at the dawn of *the 5th Day*. That's why the appearance of the complex, fully developed animal-life that suddenly and abruptly appeared on *the 5th Day* is called *the Cambrian Explosion of life*. It all happened suddenly, in the first 5 million years of the early Cambrian Period. It did not require the 100-200 million years of time that Darwin had imagined. Although some of those animals did not survive, the ones that did — represent the progenitors of all animal-life on Earth today. [809, 810]

- The Burgess fossils that Walcott discovered do not question the development of *classes* of life. It is no secret that each individual phylum first appeared as simple aquatic forms and, through the mechanism of *Micro-Evolution* (occurring at the level of the *species*) — became more complex with the passage of time. The Book of Genesis proclaimed this fact 3300 years ago. First came aquatic animals, then winged-creatures and land-animals, then mammals. That's Genesis One. The Bible knows about development. The Bible says Humans were the last species to develop.

- It is Darwin's idea of *cross-phylum* development that has been proven to be a fantasy.[811(*)] His wrong idea is what modern science refers to as *Macro-Evolution*.

- Modern science has now proved *Micro-Evolution* is the way Elohim factually evolved the current morphologies of today's life-forms from the old ones He had previously created and made. Micro-Evolution is the process by which genetic changes occur in the traits of the species of animals that only slightly alter the morphology of those traits without causing any changes in the *basic-body-plans* of the species.[812] Micro-Evolution *only occurs* at the level of the *species* of the various animals. This is what the Genesis Code of the Bible says.

- When Dawkins wrote: *"Darwin made it possible to be an intellectually fulfilled atheist,"[813]* he had bought into a belief system that was based on the false assumptions of a form of mid-nineteenth century pseudoscience.

- What Mr. Juan Williams called *'scientific inquiry'* when he questioned former Governor Pawlenty and inferred that Darwinian theory represented scientific inquiry; is in fact a compendium of Darwin's wrong ideas, imaginings, and assumptions about how life originated and evolved.

- 165 years of true scientific inquiry has now proved Darwin's ideas and assumptions were wrong beyond every shadow of a doubt.

---

[809] Schroeder *The Hidden Face of God* Chapter 4 p.51*b&c* and Chapter 7 p 121
[810] *The Origin of Species:* Chapter VI: Difficulties of the Theory—p. 154
[811] Schroeder The Science of God Chapter 2 p. 39*e*-40*a* *(*) A direct quote from Schroeder's book.*
[812] Schroeder *The Science of God* Chapter 1 p 16*c* Chapter 2 p 31 [**Micro-evolution**]
[813] D'Souza: *What's So Great About Christianity* Chapter 3 p. 26

- The same scientific body of evidence that has proved Darwin wrong has confirmed the authenticity of the Biblical Creation Account. The Bible's account of creation is what Mr. Williams referred to with disdain as *"Creationism."* The implication that Williams communicated to his audience was that *"Creationism"* has nothing to do with science and Darwin's ideas do.

- Someday a critical mass of scientists will realize Darwin was wrong and shout out to the world that science has proved him wrong.

- When Gould put forth his idea of *"Punctuated Equilibrium,"* he *repudiated* Darwin's ideas of *undirected random chance development, slow smooth gradual evolutionary change, and adaptation through natural selection.* His proposition of *Punctuated Equilibrium* accommodates the **sudden**, punctuated, simultaneous, independent, and separate development of all existing life today that the fossils of the Cambrian Explosion of life demonstrate.

- The discovery of the Cambrian fossils *reaffirmed* the Genesis Code revealed Biblical concepts of *Intelligent Design, Divine Intervention, and God's institution of abrupt, sudden punctuated development* in all things that we have emphasized so much in the preceding chapters. No wonder the *"hornets came out of their Neo-Darwinian hive"* to attack Gould's adjustments to Neo-Darwinian theory.

- Although it is not generally known, the political agenda of atheists and other nonbelievers is a house of cards that is built on a foundation of 19th Century pseudo-science. Darwin's imaginings are an unstable foundation of *"shifting sand."* Darwinism has nothing to do with the truth of what factually happened.

- Modern science has confirmed the abrupt, sudden, punctuated development of the visible forms of life that appeared on the 5th and 6th Days of Creation. What the Bible said — is exactly the way life happened.

- Modern Science has also confirmed the Biblical sequence of the development of all things![814]

- The Genesis Code has revealed to us the true account of the origins of the universe and our origins. It all happened the way the Bible says. The Bible begins with the Biblical Creation Account. The first two chapters of the first book of the Bible (Genesis) tell us how creation happened. God dictated that account to Moses.

Now, we can resume our study of the Biblical Creation Account. The subject of the next chapter will be about the modern-land animals, the mammals, and the man-like hominids that God made and created on the 6th Day.

---

[814] Schroeder *The Science of God* Chapter 4 p. 66c

✤

CHAPTER 22: GENESIS 1:24-25: THAT PART OF THE 6TH DAY, WHEN GOD MADE LAND ANIMALS, MAMMALS, & MAN-LIKE HOMINIDS[815]

THE 6TH DAY OF CREATION LASTED APPROXIMATELY ¼ BILLION (250 MILLION) EARTH-YEARS.[816]

The 6th day: 24 hrs of God' Time	Started ¼ billion years ago	Ended 5,700 years ago
God's Time Perspective	Earth-years before Adam	Ended with Adam

INTRODUCTION

From science we have learned the 6th Day started ~ 250,000,000 years ago.[817] From the genealogies in the Book of Genesis, we learned a literal interpretation of the Bible tells us the first man, Adam, was created ~ 5,700 years ago (before the present or BP).[818,819] The Bible also informs us the 6th Day of Creation ended with the making of Adam.[820] Since a lot of scientists view the *man-like hominids* that appeared in the *Pleistocene* Epoch as the first humans on Earth, they strongly disagree with the Biblical date of ~ 5,700 years ago for the appearance of Earth's first man. However, they still argue over which *one* of the two man-like hominids was the first "*human.*" Moreover, there are some who claim "*the first man*" appeared even earlier, in the form of one or more of the controversial hominid species that belong to the *Pliocene* Epoch. This controversy among scientists will be briefly discussed in this chapter. *Near the end of this chapter, when we discuss "the beasts of the Earth," you will see the Bible and Science define "man" differently.*

This chapter will be about that part of the 6th Day that is told from God's Perspective and in a God-based Time-flow. Verses 24 through 31 of the 1st Chapter of Genesis are devoted to the major events of Creation that happened on the 6th Day. In the Introduction—Part IX, in the section entitled: 'TIME-FLOW REITERATED,' I said that *Time-Flow* in the first 25 verses of the 1st Chapter of Genesis is *God-based,* and that the *God-related time-flow* in the 1st Chapter of Genesis covers the first 5 Days of Creation and the majority of the 6th Day.

Of the eight verses in the 1st Chapter of Genesis that talk about the 6th Day, only two — Gen. 1:24 and 1:25 — mention the events that *preceded* the making of man. The actual amount of Earth-time those two verses cover is, by far, the majority of the 6th Day! The other six verses about the 6th Day are devoted *to the making and the creating of man.* However, the *creating* of man was the *next to the last act* of Elohim on the 6th Day — that is to say: *When God created Adam (and Eve), He was finished with His Creation of the Earth. Eve was His finishing "touch."* Therefore, the reader must understand the events I am going to discuss in this chapter (Gen. 1:24 and 1:25), actually occurred over the vast majority of the 250-million-year duration of the 6th Day. Apparently, it did not take God much time to *create* Adam and Eve. The ancient Jewish Sages had an interesting take

---

815 Schroeder *The Science of God* Chapter 4 (Table) p 67
816 Schroeder *The Science of God* Chapter 4 (Table) p 67
817 Schroeder *The Science of God* Chapter 4 (Table) p 67
818 Schroeder *Genesis and the Big Bang* Chapter 1 p. 11a
819 Schroeder *The Science of God* Chapter 4 (Table) p 67
820 Genesis 1:26-31

on this. We will talk about that in the next chapter (in Book III). However, the Bible is so eager to get to the *making* of man that no details of *the making of the other animals* on the 6th Day are given— other than to mention (in the most cursory way) the broad categories of animal-life to which they belonged.

MAN-RELATED TIME-FLOW

When God *creates* man, the 6th Day is over. That is to say, the *2nd Telling* of the Creation Account ends with the making of God's next to last creation — the first man. But as you shall see (in the next chapter in Book III), when God *made* man, he also *made* woman. This actually happened in Gen. 1:27, but the *'how'* of *how God did it* — is not explained until Gen. 2:7. The *enigmatic details* of how God *made* woman are not mentioned until the Bible is well into the *3rd Telling*. (See Chapter 29 in Book III.) Although the name of the first man is not mentioned in the Bible until the 5th Chapter of Genesis, the creature that God named *'Man'* (i.e., the *'Adam'* in Gen. 5:2) is the *penultimate creation* of God (i.e., the next to last in a sequence). Woman was God's *ultimate* or *final 'creation.'* The minute that man appears on the Earth, and for all the time in the Bible thereafter, Time-Flow in the Bible switches from a God-related time-flow to a time-flow that is related to man. (See Introduction—Part IX.)

THE PART OF THE 6TH DAY THAT INVOLVES A GOD-BASED TIME-FLOW PERSPECTIVE.

In this Chapter we will examine that part of the 6th day of Creation (verses 1:24 and 1:25) which is told from a *God-based Time-Flow perspective*. When we have finished our discussion, we will have finished *'The 2nd Telling'* of the Creation Narrative. These two short verses actually cover the majority of the time God allocated to the 6th day.

If you will refer to the *Geologic Timetable of the 6th Day* in this chapter, you will see the 6th Day is depicted in *blue*. Scientists tell us the *Holocene Epoch* started ~ 10,000 years BP (Before the Present). From the genealogies in the Book of Genesis, calculations have been made that point to 5,700 BP as the time when God made *Adam*.[821] That is why the chart at the beginning of this chapter places the end of the 6th Day of Creation at ~ 5700 years ago. It acknowledges that approximate date as the point in time when God *created Adam*. In Chapter 23 in Book III, we'll discuss how the Jewish sages concluded God *'made' man before He 'created'* him.

Judaism, Christianity, and Islam agree *Adam was the 1st 'Man.'* Since the Biblical 6th Day ended with the creation of the 1st *Man (Adam)*, and since three major religious traditions hold that the 6th Day ended with the creation of Adam (~ 5700 years BP, or ~ 3700 BC), then this book considers that the 6th Day ended ~ 4,300 years after the Holocene Epoch had begun. (10,000 BP minus 5,700 = 4,300 BP). That is why I assigned *two* colors to the Holocene Epoch. The *early Holocene* belongs to the 6th Day of Creation. I have therefore included it in the 6th Day and have depicted *all* of the Geologic Periods and Epochs which I *believe* belong to the 6th Day in *blue*. However, once Adam was created, the time-reference-frame shifted to the same 24-hour day that we experience (*see Chapter 25 in Book III*). So, that part of the Holocene Epoch from *Adam* to the present — has been depicted in *green*. The green part of the Holocene Epoch is the part in which Adam lived and we presently live.

---

[821] Schroeder *Genesis and the Big Bang* Chapter 1 p. 11a

In the next chapter we will begin our discussion of *'The 3rd Telling'* of the Creation Narrative (i.e., Book III of this series) — a narrative that begins with Genesis 1:26 and concludes with the final verse of the 2nd Chapter of Genesis. *'The 3rd Telling'* is a tale that is told from man's perspective and represents the establishment of the same Earth-based time-reference-frame of the same 24-hour day-night cycle we experience today. Now, let's look at what the Bible says about Genesis 1:24 in the New American Standard Bible (NASB) and The Interlinear Bible (TIB).

Gen. 1:24 Then God said: "Let the Earth bring forth living creatures after their kind: cattle and creeping things and **'Beasts of the Earth'** *after their kind; and it was so."* (NASB)
Gen. 1:24 And God said, "Let the Earth bring forth **the soul of animal life** *according to its kind: cattle, and creepers, and its* **'beasts of the Earth'**, *according to its kind. And it was so." (TIB)*

Applying the Genesis Code to the Interlinear Bible translation of Genesis 1:24

Gen. 1:24: Then Elohim commanded ('amar): Let the ground ('erets) form (yatsa/or yasar) living, breathing creatures with a <u>soul of animal life</u> *(nefesh), each according to its species (miyn); the large dumb domesticated four footed animals, such as cattle and other domesticated animals (behemah), and reptiles (remes) and other rapidly moving animals that creepeth (remes), and other multitudes of quick, running, springing living things (chay), and* <u>'beasts of the ground,'</u> *according to their species (miyn). And it came to pass (haiyah).*

DISCUSSION OF GENESIS 1:24 "THE SOUL OF ANIMAL LIFE"

Like all of the preceding days of creation, the 6th Day starts with the same command of Elohim: *'Then Elohim said.'* The various English translations tell us Elohim said: *'Let the Earth bring forth living creatures after their kind.'* However, the *Interlinear Bible* (which translates the Old Testament Hebrew into English), states Elohim said: *'Let the Earth bring forth the <u>soul</u> of <u>animal</u> <u>life</u>, each according to its kind...'* The Interlinear Bible translates the Hebrew word, *nefesh and/or nephesh,* as *'the soul of animal life.'* This Hebrew word for *the soul of animal life,* is the same word that is found in the Interlinear Bible translation of Genesis 1:24 and Genesis 1:20. We discussed this in Chapter 13. Remember, Hebrew has two words for *soul — nefesh* and *neshama. The nefesh is the soul of animal life.* The Bible, the Talmud, and Jewish tradition teach *all* animals have *the soul of animal life — the nefesh.* Biblically, an animal is defined as a *living nefesh* (a *nefesh haiyah*). The ancient Hebrews believed this *'soul of animal life'* provides *all* animals (*man included*) with the freedom to process and evaluate the information of their sensory input. Animals quickly learn which experiences cause pain and those that cause pleasure and satisfy their needs. The nefesh guides their behavior to exploit pleasure, maximize their chances for survival, and minimize their chances for pain and injury. The nefesh fuels the behaviors that seek food, reproduce, protect, and nurture the young, seek pleasure, and avoid pain.[822] Some think the basic animal drive to reproduce is mostly *eros.*

---

822 Schroeder, *The Science of God,* Chapter 11, p. 171-172

GEN. 1:24. THE ANIMALS OF THE EARTH THAT APPEARED ON THE 6TH DAY:
(i.e., The remes, the chay, and the b^ehemah — according to their 'miyn.')

Look at the Geologic Timetable of the 6th Day in *this* Chapter. This *new* chart focuses on the life-forms science says lived on the 6th Day. It is slightly more detailed than my first chart — *"The Geologic Timetable Compared to the Six Days of Creation"* at the end of Chapter 12. Both charts include the *broad* categories of animals modern science has listed for each Period of the 6th Day. Just as in Chapter 12, I have greatly simplified what science has discovered about the animal-life that appeared on the 6th Day. By doing this, I have attempted to summarize the astounding changes that occurred by mentioning only the broadest categories of animals that *'came forth from the Earth'* (as the Bible puts it) on the 6th Day. Otherwise, we would become lost in the details science has discovered, and that would defeat the purpose of this book. So, to those of you who have devoted your professional lives to the discovery of the details of what occurred in the development of life on our planet during the most recent 250 million years before the present, please accept my apologies. Perhaps I may be forgiven the following cursory explanation because I have attempted to focus on *the Big Picture*, so that readers can see — what modern science has discovered now shows an *ever-converging agreement* with what the ancient Hebrew Biblical text said about the 6th Day 3,300 years ago.

THE 6TH DAY FROM THE PERSPECTIVE OF SCIENCE

- Between 245-208 million years before the present (look at the chart at the end of Chapter 12) during the Triassic Period of the Mesozoic Era (i.e., the 1st Period of the 6th Day), reptiles dominated. The *'remes,'* refers to two categories of reptiles. The reptiles were —

  1) Those *without legs*, like the Miocene Epoch snakes (23.7 million years ago), and more modern-day Pliocene Epoch snakes (5.3 million years ago) that glided swiftly along the ground. However, the fossil record also shows evidence of *'slithering'* snakes as early as 128 million years ago, during the *Cretaceous Period* on the 6th Day.

  2) There were also other rapidly moving reptiles, which were those with legs, like the *Archosaurs*[823] (who, although markedly different from snakes), were ancestors of a great variety of reptiles that crept and crawled in various periods of the Earth's history that occurred on 5th Day of Creation. In Chapter 13, I mentioned some scientists think the *Archosaurs* originated ~ 397 million years ago in the *Devonian Period* on the 5th Day.

  3) The Bible also mentions the non-reptilian *'chay.'* The chay were the *'quickly running, springing, living multitude of wild creatures, beasts, and things'* that also appeared on the 6th Day of Creation.

- Between 208-144 million years ago, *the giant reptiles* (i.e., the *Dinosaurs* or the *'Terrible Giant Lizards'* of the reptile family) dominated. This was in the Jurassic Period of the Mesozoic Era (i.e., the 2nd Period of the 6th Day, ~ 208 million years ago). They died out ~ 65 million years ago. (*cf. the Chart at the end of Chapter 12.*)

---

[823] Article: *Before the Dinosaurs*—Pelycosaurs, Archosaurs, & Therapids: The Story of the Reptiles that preceded the Dinosaurs by Bob Strauss, About.com Guide http://dinosaurs.about.com/od/otherprehistoriclife/a/beforedinos.html

ARCHAEOPTERYX—THE EXCEPTION THAT PROVES THE RULE?

Some scientists believe the first birds had teeth and appeared in the *Jurassic Period*. They point to the *Archaeopteryx* and say the fossils of this peculiar animal prove evolution produced *cross-phylum changes* in animals. The Archaeopteryx appeared *150 million years ago*, in the *late Jurassic Period*. It was in the Jurassic Period that the most fearsome reptiles the Earth will ever see dominated. We call them the *Dinosaurs*. Yet, the Archaeopteryx was a tiny animal. At the time, Central Europe, including Germany (where all seven of the fossils of this creature have been found) had a tropical climate. *Only* seven fossils of this small animal have been found. All seven fossils of the Archaeopteryx (meaning *"ancient wing"*) were found in the Solnhofen limestone pits of southern Germany within strata that date to the late Jurassic Period. This animal had a full set of teeth, a flat breastbone, a long bony tail, gastralia (or 'belly ribs'), long legs with short thighs, and claws at the end of its legs with three toes facing forward and one facing backwards. This animal also had three claws on each wing. One of the seven fossils of this creature had such poorly preserved feathers that it was originally described as the skeleton of a *small bipedal dinosaur*.[824,825] The presence of feathers (the imprints of which were well preserved on the other six fossils of this animal) suggests this creature belongs in the bird family. However, some claim the animal represents a *transitional* form that was *half-bird, and half-dinosaur.*

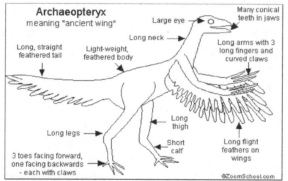

Image Courtesy of ZoomSchool.com [826]

The third book of the Bible gives us a list of ritually pure and impure animals. The impure (unclean) are "forbidden food." Three unclean birds are listed in Leviticus 11:18. According to Dr. Schroeder, one of these is a bird called the *"tinshemet"* (Hebrew). Only a few verses later (Leviticus 11:30), *reptiles* are listed. Once again, the *tinshemet* appears. So, the Third Book of Moses (Leviticus)*, records the same name,* spelled identically, for an animal *that the Bible classifies as both a bird and as a reptile, which is unclean for eating.* Dr. Schroeder thinks the same name is given for a bird and for a reptile because — at one level of Biblical meaning — the animal fell into both categories. Also, according to Dr. Schroeder, *in the entire Bible* there is *only one reference* to an animal that falls into two distinctly different categories of animals — the *tinshemet*. Schroeder also says: in the entire fossil record to date, there are only *seven fossils* of one animal that some scientists believe fall midway between two *phyla* of animals. They point to the

---

[824] Schroeder, *The Science of God,* Chapter 6, p. 95-96

[825] Article: ***Archaeopteryx: an Early Bird***: http://www.ucmp.berkeley.edu/diapsids/birds/archaeopteryx.html

[826] ***Archaeopteryx: The Image is at—*** www.enchantedlearning.com/subjects/dinosaurs/dinos/Archaeopter...

Archaeopteryx and say it *may have been* an animal that was *part-bird and part-reptile.* Therefore, it may be *the 'link' that was never missing.*[827] Could the Archaeopteryx be — *'the exception to the rule?"*

Some scientists are now questioning the classification of the Archaeopteryx. These scientists believe it was *not* a bird at all — but *was really a flying dinosaur.*[828] If this new way of looking at the Archaeopteryx becomes the prevailing view, then some day we may say the Archaeopteryx *does not* represent an animal that was part-dinosaur and part-bird. *If* the new proposed classification of the Archaeopteryx as *a flying dinosaur* becomes the accepted view, then there would be *no* examples in the fossil record of any transitional forms — i.e., no examples of the type of *cross-phylum* (*or inter-phylum*) change that Darwinists claim these fossils represent.

Nevertheless, there are some who say a decision that labels the *Archaeopteryx* half-bird and half-dinosaur would *"fly"* in the face of the 165 years of fossil data (accumulated since Darwin), in which *no* transitional forms have been found. They believe the seven known fossils of the *Archaeopteryx* "crashed against the rocks of history" somewhere around *144 million years ago* (in the Cretaceous Period on the 6th Day of Creation when it became extinct (cf. my chart of the 6th Day that is in this chapter). That was at least 144 million years before God created Adam. The argument can be made that *a single exception to the rule cannot be the basis of any sound theory.*

Furthermore, I doubt the *tinshemet* and the *Archaeopteryx* were the same animal. The *Archaeopteryx* lived for a moment *in antiquity and then disappeared 144 million years ago!* It was *"long gone"* before Adam was created! So, it could not have been *"a forbidden food"* for Adam! Since the *tinshemet* is listed in Leviticus, it must have lived only a few thousand years ago during the period of the oral tradition of the *Torah* that was started by Adam ~ 3,700 BC, because it was listed twice in the book of Leviticus as *"an unclean animal and a forbidden food."* It apparently also lived in the time when Moses wrote the *Torah* (~ 2,250 years after Adam, or ~ 1,450 BC. And then there are those who think Moses wrote the Torah about 3,300 years ago. If that is true, then the *tinshemet* would have still been around in 1,300 BC. So, I don't think the fossils of the *Archaeopteryx* can settle the argument, because the *Archaeopteryx* became extinct ~ 144,000,000 years BC! Dr. Schroeder says the Bible classifies the *tinshemet* as *both a bird and a reptile.* Maybe it was indeed a transitional animal. However, we have no idea *exactly what the tinshemet actually was.* I think — for the present — *the tinshemet* must remain one of the Bible's many "*mysteries.*"

NOW, LET'S CONTINUE THE DISCUSSION OF THE 6TH DAY FROM THE PERSPECTIVE OF SCIENCE.

(Frequent Reference to the Chart of the 6th Day in this chapter will be helpful.)

• In the 3rd part of the 6th Day, between 144-66.4 million years ago, during the Cretaceous Period of the Mesozoic Era, the Dinosaurs and the so-called '*toothed birds*' (the Genus to which the Archaeopteryx is believed to have belonged) died out. Although mammals may have existed in the late Jurassic when the Dinosaurs dominated, the first mammals on Earth were tiny animals when they first appeared.

---

[827] Schroeder, *The Science of God*, Chapter 6, p. 96c
[828] Famed fossil isn't a bird after all, analysis says - Phys.org
p. 2A

- The Cenozoic Era (*cf. the chart at the end of Chapter 12*) began 66.4 million years ago and extends to the present. Cenozoic means *new or recent animal life*. The Cenozoic Era is characterized by the development and dominance of mammals. The first mammals began to appear during the Cretaceous Period of the Mesozoic Era. Then, as mammals evolved through the process of microevolution, they became dominant in the Eocene Epoch of the Cenozoic Era. The Hebrew word *'chay'* could be considered the broad category of the wild animals of the Earth; a category that includes the animals that became dominant — i.e., the Class of animals that we categorize as mammals today. *Later, you will see that the 'beasts of the ground' may be something else entirely. The Talmud considers them a special sort of mammal that appeared in the Pleistocene Epoch. Talmudic scholars have theorized — one or more of the females of the 'beasts of the ground' may have cohabited with Adam after the death of Able. Therefore, the 'beasts of the ground' may refer to one of the species of the man-like hominids that appeared late on the 6th Day.*

- Earth's first giant mammals appeared in the Paleocene Epoch of the Tertiary Period of the Cenozoic Era, between 66.4-57.8 million years ago (the 4th part of the 6th Day).

- The Giant mammals dominated all other species during the Eocene Epoch, between 57.8-36.6 million years ago (the 5th part of the 6th Day). They lasted their time and then disappeared.

- Higher-order mammals which were much smaller than the giant mammals of the Paleocene and Eocene appeared in the Oligocene Epoch, between 36.6-23.7 million years ago (the 6th part of the 6th Day). They lasted their time and disappeared.

- According to scientific discoveries, Earth saw its first Hominids in the late Miocene Epoch (the 7th part of the 6th Day). However, they disappeared before the advent of the 8th part of the 6th Day — i.e., during the Pliocene Epoch. Some scientists believe the earliest Hominids were the first primates to walk the Earth. Primates are the most highly developed order of animals. They are mammals with a large brain and complex hands and feet. They make up the group of animals that are classified as the Genus *Hominidae*. According to science, the earth's first Hominids are thought to have been the ancestors of the great apes. Science also classifies *'man'* as belonging to the Genus or family of the *Hominidae*.

- Even though the giant mammals of the Paleocene and Eocene Epochs had passed into extinction, with the advent of the Pliocene Epoch — the saga of the giant mammals of the Earth was not completely over. Several new species of giant mammals again appeared in the Pliocene and Pleistocene Epochs of the Cenozoic Era. These *'latter day'* Giant Mammals included what we would consider many unusual species (all extinct today), such as the Giant Beaver, the Giant Sloth, the Giant Wombat, the Giant Cave Bear, the Giant Short-Faced Kangaroo, the Giant Woolly Mammoth, the Giant Mastodon, and the Giant Saber-Toothed Tiger — just to name a few.

- 5.3-1.6 million years ago, the Pliocene Epoch saw the introduction of modern-day animals, birds, and plants. Through the continuing process of microevolution, the earliest ancestors of today's modern-day animals (the *remes* and the *chay* that the Bible again mentions in Genesis 1:25 — began to make their appearance about 5.3 million years ago. These are all of the wild animal species that are extant today.

- Today's modern animals include another broad category of animals known to the ancient Hebrew as the *b*ehemah*. Because the Hebrew Bible mentions the cattle by their name, could it be that the '*b*ehemah*' may refer to all of the other different types of animals that '*man*' domesticated on the 6th Day? Some believe '*the b*ehemah*' refer to the large four-footed dumb animals, such as the cattle, that are so helpful to man.

- Although the first Hominids had appeared in the Miocene Epoch; a new species of animals—the **'Man-like' Hominids** began to make their appearance in the Pleistocene Epoch (1.6 million years to ~ 10,000 years BP). Modern science considers these 'Man-like' Hominids the Earth's first humans. *However, the Bible defines "man" differently — and the Bible gives a different "Timeline" for the appearance of the Earth's "first man." That "Timeline" is believed by some to be ~ 5,700 years ago before the Present.*

- The European and Asian Giant Mastodons and Woolly Mammoths died out millions of years ago, during the late Pleistocene Epoch, before the end of the last Ice Age of the Pleistocene. But the Giant Mastodons and Woolly Mammoths in North and Central America persisted a bit longer, almost to the end of the last Ice Age, becoming extinct around 13,000 years ago,[829] or about 3,000 years before the end of the Pleistocene Epoch.

- Scientists have reason to believe the Giant Mastodons and Woolly Mammoths of the Americas may have been hunted to extinction by what modern science considers early human settlers (*the 'Man-like Hominids', i.e., the Cro-Magnons that will be discussed later in this chapter*). These early '*humans*' (as science now classifies them) coveted their meat, fur, and their massive tusks.[830]

- Notice that the original Hebrew language of Genesis One that pertains to the events of the 6th Day says that all of the animals of the 6th Day came forth from the ground of the Earth according to their *miyn*. The proper English translation of *miyn is species*.

IN MODERN TIMES, EVOLUTION TAKES PLACE AT THE LEVEL OF THE SPECIES

Remember, in antiquity (that is, prior to the Pliocene Epoch in the 6th Day, when modern animals and plants appeared), new *Classes* of animals came forth. These new classes of animals and plants suddenly appeared and were fully developed and specialized when they first appeared. They lasted their time and then suddenly disappeared with no evidence that any new or better-adapted class of animals or plants forced their disappearance or took their place.[831] The Dinosaurs are just one example. This was discussed in Chapter 19. As stated, these changes in antiquity took place at the level of *Class*, two levels below the level of the *Phylum* (which was the level that Darwin imagined evolution occurred). These changes at the level of Class do not represent the inter-Phylum (same as *cross-Phylum*) changes that Darwin had imagined because the new classes of animals did not cause any changes in the *basic-body-plans* of the Phyla to which the new classes of animals belonged.

---

[829] Article: **Mastodons:** http://www.robinsonlibrary.com/science/geology/paleontology/mastodons.htm
[830] Article: **Prehistoric Megafauna—The Giant Mammals of the Cenozoic Era**: by Bob Strauss; http://dinosaurs.about.com/od/mesozoicmammals/p/.html
[831] Schroeder, *The Science of God,* Chapter 2, p. 30c

After the extinction of the Dinosaurs, as one examines the appearance, development, and disappearance of the various animals that once roamed the Earth during the 6th Day (and as one gets closer to the time reference-frame of the present); one finds that changes no longer occur at the level of *Class*. This is especially true when the Pliocene Epoch is reached (i.e., the Epoch in which our modern-day animals developed). Beginning with the Pliocene Epoch and continuing through to today, the evolutionary changes that occur in nature occur only at the level of the individual species. The Bible says this by its use of the Hebrew word, *miyn* — which means *'species.'*

MICROEVOLUTION: THE KIND OF EVOLUTION DESCRIBED IN THE BIBLE.

Science has labeled the kind of evolution that is found in nature — *microevolution*. Microevolution only takes place at the level of *species*. It involves genetic changes in the *traits* of a *species* with no alteration of the animal's *basic-body-plan*. As we can see from the meaning of *miyn* (i.e., the deeper meaning of the Genesis Code), the Bible has no problem with microevolution. *It confirms it.*

MACROEVOLUTION: DARWIN'S FOLLY

In truth, it was from the changes in the traits of several different *species* of breeder pigeons that Darwin saw occur over only a few generations (what science now calls *microevolution*), that he imagined even greater changes could occur if given eons of time. He then imagined even more astonishing changes would eventually begin to occur at the level of the Phylum that would result in a change of the *basic-body-plan* of the animal and necessitate its re-classification under an entirely new Phylum of animals. In this way he thought an animal could morph into an entirely new race, tribe, or group of animals. Science has labeled this type of imaginary evolution — *Macroevolution. Macroevolution finds no support in the fossil record, in the lab, or in the Bible.*[832]

WHAT ACTUALLY HAPPENED

The 34 Phyla of animals that exist today were established in the first five million years of the Cambrian period. They appeared as *a single burst of life in the fossil record* on the 5th Day. Ever since the Pliocene Epoch of the 6th Day, when modern-day animals and plants appeared, all of the basic-body-plans that are represented in the 34 animal Phyla that exist today, reproduce *'according to their kind'*, as the various English Translations of the Bible translate the Hebrew word *'miyn.'*

This is what the worldwide fossil record shows, and no one disputes it. [833,834]

The Genesis Code informs us the kind of evolutionary changes that have occurred since the Pliocene Epoch are the *microevolutionary* changes that we observe at the level of the *miyn*, as the Hebrew Bible puts it (i.e., at the level of the individual *species*). Thus, you can see the discoveries of Modern Science now show an agreement with the Bible. This has already been discussed.

The next chart summarizes the timeline of the 6th Day that was just discussed. *Time is expressed in Millions of Earth-years. Start at the bottom of the chart and read to the top.* Keep in mind — the most recent Epoch of Earth's history is the Holocene Epoch

---

[832] Schroeder, *The Science of God*, Chapter 1, p. 16c
[833] Schroeder, *The Science of God*, Chapter 6, p. 88b
[834] Schroeder, *The Science of God*, Chapter 6, p. 88-89a

— the epoch in which Adam lived and we live. The earliest part of the Holocene belongs to the 6th Day because God *'made'* Adam at the end of the 6th Day. The 6th Day is color-coded in blue. The rest of the Holocene (from the advent of the *'creation'* of Adam to the present) is depicted in green. *This chart correlates Biblical Time with the Geologic Timetable.*

THE GEOLOGIC TIMETABLE AND THE 6TH DAY OF CREATION (MY CHART)

Period/Epoch /Main Events	Earth-Time	Biblical Time in Earth-Years
Holocene Epoch: Humans populate, dominate & persist. Adam & Eve were created ~ 5700 earth-years ago.	0.0057	**The Beginning of the Present Started with Adam's Creation**
That Part of the 6th Day that belongs to the Early Holocene Epoch	0.01	**6th Day ended when God made Adam**
Pleistocene Epoch: Two man-like hominids appear. One vanishes. Other Giant Mammals appear then vanish.	1.6	
Pliocene Epoch: Modern animals, birds, plants, appear & persist. New Giant Mammals appear then vanish.	5.3	
Miocene Epoch: Earth's 1st Hominids appear then vanish.	23.7	**The**
Oligocene Epoch: Higher Mammals appear then vanish.	36.6	**6th**
Eocene Epoch: Smaller Mammals appear then vanish.	57.8	**Day**
Paleocene Epoch: Earth's 1st Giant Mammals appear then vanish.	66.4	
Cretaceous Period: Earth's 1st Mammals & 1st Trees appear. Dinosaurs & Archeopteryx (i.e., Toothed 'Birds') die out.	144	
Jurassic Period: Dinosaurs Dominate. Archaeopteryx appears. Pangaea ends near the beginning of the Jurassic Period	208	
Triassic Period: Reptiles Dominate. Pangaea fractures.	250	**The 6th Day Begins**

Massive extinctions destroy over 90% of life multiple times on the 5th and 6th Days. In the Pliocene & Pleistocene epochs of the 6th Day, Earth was repopulated: hominids and then humans. (In the date of ~ 5700 BP for the 1st Biblical Man, BP stands for "years ago — Before the Present.") Earth-time in millions of years.

More than 34 phyla of animals appeared on the 5th day, but only 34 survived extinction. Through Microevolution, those that survived look very different today. The multiple mass extinctions of life that have occurred in the past were the result of cataclysmic events involving macro-environmental changes brought on by such things as extraterrestrial asteroid impacts, multiple ice ages, and the formation and break-up of supercontinents.

The Pliocene Epoch was when all of the Earth's modern animals and plants appeared and persisted. Prior to the Pliocene, some changes occurred at the level of "*Class.*" Since the Pliocene, all life has reproduced as the Bible says—"after its *miyn*"—i.e., "after it *species*."

HOMINIDS

We should take a closer look at the terms '*Hominid*' (singular) and '*Hominidae*' (plural). Over the past few decades, the meaning of 'Hominid,' has been revised several times. At first, scientists used the word to refer to humans and to the animals they considered the closest relatives of humans (excluding the great apes). But the classification of the great apes has been revised several times since, and in the last few decades more recent categorizations have included the great apes. Today, the term: '*Hominid*' is generally accepted to refer to the four Genera which are considered to be members of the biological family *Hominidae,* which includes humans and the great apes — i.e., *chimpanzees, gorillas,* and *orangutans.*[835] Unfortunately, much confusion still reigns, and various classifications persist. No consensus seems to have yet been reached among scientists. However, as DNA research progresses, consensus and agreement among the various scientific specialties that are studying the origin of man will someday be reached. Among the four genera that now seem to be accepted as belonging to the *Genus Hominidae,* we will concentrate on the one species that science calls '*humans,*' (i.e., the species sapiens that is of the Genus Homo: or *Homo sapiens.*)

A REVIEW OF THE LINNAEAN TAXONOMY OF MAN (FROM CHAPTER 19)

Man is the specific species (*miyn* — Hebrew) of animal that is named *sapiens*. Man belongs to the *Genus* or family of animals called the *Hominidae*; which are an *Order* of animals that are *Primates*; that belong to a *Class* of animals called the *Mammals.* *Mammals* are a *Subphylum* or subdivision of animals that are *Vertebrates* which, in turn belong to a larger *Phylum* of animals that are known as the *Chordates*. In short, the Linnaean classification of the animal, man, looks like this.

> **Phylum** *(a group, race, or tribe)*: **Chordata.**←(*The level Darwin thought evolutionary transitions would be found.*)
> > **Subphylum** *(sub-division or clan)*: **Vertebrata**
> > > **Class** *(or Type)*: **Mammals**←(*Prior to the Pliocene Epoch, transitions occurred @ the level of Class*)
> > > > **Order** *(or sub-type)*: **Primates**
> > > > > **Genus** *(or family)*: **Homo** (for **Hominidae**)
> > > > > (*Since the Pliocene Epoch, transitions occur only @ the level of* **species:**→ (*or sub-family* — **sapiens**)

So, man is classified as the species (*sapiens*) of the Genus (*Homo* — for Hominidae) that science refers to as *Homo sapiens*: meaning '*man who is wise*'.

SO, WHAT DOES MODERN SCIENCE THINK WAS THE ORIGIN OF 'MAN'?

Much of what follows is controversial and difficult to 'piece' together. The various issues of exactly how the human race 'evolved' are still being hotly debated by scientists. It is fair to say there is no firm consensus concerning which species represented the first or

835 Article: **Hominidae-Science Daily**: http://www.sciencedaily.com/articles/h/hominidae.html

earliest 'human' on Earth; or exactly how, when, and where the modern human 'evolved.' In no way can my discussion of the so-called proto-human ancestors be considered complete. But I think the same can be said of any currently existing papers on the subject. As you shall see, there was often a great deal of timespan overlap in the existence of some of these creatures. Many species co-existed on Earth in close proximity and in various places in the same or near-same time periods. In some instances, there is evidence they interbred. In a surprising number of the fossil remains that have been touted as representing new and different species of proto-typical human ancestors, charges of fraud have been made. Some of these charges have been proved. The fossils had been tampered with to make them appear authentic. Other discoveries have been verified because they have stood the test of further scientific investigation. So, with this in mind — 'here goes.'

HOMO HABILIS[836] may be the earliest hominid assigned to the genus Homo. Its brain-shape, though much smaller than what some scientists consider to be other 'man-like' creatures that appeared later, is somewhat human-like because its fossils show it had a rather large area in its brain that may have made it possible for this creature to vocalize. Thus, this animal may have been capable of rudimentary speech. The fossils of this animal date to between 2.3 and 1.6 million years ago in the late Pliocene Epoch. This is also the time when other modern animals of the 34 phyla of animals extant today, and when modern-day plants began to appear. (See the Geologic Timetable and the 6th Day of Creation Chart—in this chapter.)

Homo habilis has been a controversial species since it was first described in the mid-1960s. But H. habilis is now widely accepted as a species. It was a fairly small creature; maybe 4 feet 6 inches or so, with long arms, and a more ape-like appearance than the other hominids. Recent claims make Homo habilis another 'aunt/uncle' species to humans (i.e., not in the direct human line). Some scientists still insist many of the earliest fossils assigned to H. habilis are too fragmented and separated in time for conclusions about their relationships or species compositions to be possible. This is the primary reason Homo habilis is so controversial. Nevertheless, Homo habilis (meaning 'handy man') is so called because some crude tools have been found with some of its fossils. Whether or not the tools of this creature were fashioned by H. habilis or by nature has not been settled, and probably never will be.

HOMO ERECTUS [837,838] made its first appearance somewhere around 2 million years ago, in the late Pliocene Epoch. Because of his antiquity, only a few nearly complete Homo erectus skeletons have been found. One such specimen, named **Lake Turkana Boy,** was found in an arid region of Kenya. Lake Turkana Boy lived 1.6 million years ago.

Another famous fossil of Homo erectus, named **Peking man,** was found near Cho-k'ou-tien, China, in a limestone cave. Peking man lived 300,000 years ago, in the Pleistocene Epoch. So, it is that we know Homo erectus walked this earth for a period of

---

[836] Article: **Homo habilis and Homo erectus**: **The Origin and Evolution of Human Language**—by Professor Suzanne Kemmer: Rice University: http://www.ruf.rice.edu/~kemmer/Evol/habiliserectus.html
[837] Article: **Homo habilis and Homo erectus**: **The Origin and Evolution of Human Language**—by Professor Suzanne Kemmer: Rice University: http://www.ruf.rice.edu/~kemmer/Evol/habiliserectus.html
[838] Schroeder, Genesis and the Big Bang, Chapter 1 p. 13a,b

about 1.7 million years. He appears to be a creature that crossed the timeline of two Epochs in Earth's history.

Homo erectus has many skeletal features similar to modern humans. Scientists believe this animal walked erect with a smooth bipedal stride as early as 2 million years ago, with hands free for grasping and using objects. Yet, during almost this entire period, the manufacture of tools evolved only slightly, being confined to the making of stone cores and flint blades. Yet it is believed Homo erectus discovered how to make fire. However, given the attention many city-dwellers pay to the people around them when they are rushing around in their harried daily routines — Homo erectus might be unnoticed if he were alive today and walking among them. Nonetheless, at least some people might notice his markedly shortened forehead. That is to say, if they noticed him, some people might think: *'Goodness, that really is a weird looking guy!'*

There are *many* specimens (discovered at various places on our globe) that have been touted as different species of proto humans. Some of these are:

- *Australopithecus afarensis* (discovered in Africa and discussed later).
- *Homo ergaster*[839] (also found in Africa; this creature is one of the more problematic of the somewhat accepted species tossed around in anthropological literature. Supposedly *H. ergaster* had a higher cranial vault and lighter frame and facial structure than *H. erectus*).
- *Homo antecessor* [840, 841] (controversial — may have been a link between *H. ergaster* and *H. heidelbergensis* — best preserved fossil is the mandible of a 10-year-old found in Spain— supposedly lived between 1.2 million and 800,000 years ago in the Pleistocene Epoch).
- *Homo cepranensis*[842] is known from *one skull cap* discovered near Rome, Italy in 1994 that is estimated to be between 350,000 and 500,000 years old. There is not enough material to make a complete analysis of the individual, *and no other fossils of H. cepranensis have been found.*
- *Homo heidelbergensis*[843] (found near Heidelberg, Germany — specimens date between 700,000 and 200,000 years ago — used tools very similar to those of *Homo erectus* — maybe the direct ancestor of both *H. neanderthalensis* in Europe and *H. sapiens*).
- *Homo rodensiensis*[844] ('*Rhodesian Man*' — specimens found in Africa date between 300,000 and 125,000 years ago — controversial and not well accepted as a human prototype).
- There are others, believe me, but I will not discuss them. I think I have given enough that you get the idea — many fossils have been claimed to be *protohuman*, and much controversy prevails.

[839] Article: **Homo ergaster:** http://archaeologyinfo.com/homo-ergaster/
[840] Article: **Homo antecessor** http://australianmuseum.net.au/Homo-antecessor
[841] Article: **A New Species?** (referring to Homo antecessor) by Mark Rose http://www.archaeology.org/online/news/gran.dolina.html
[842] Article: **Homo cepranensis** http://www.macroevolution.net/homo-cepranensis.html
[843] Article: **Homo heidelbergensis** (Smithsonian National Museum of Natural History) http://humanorigins.si.edu/evidence/human-fossils/species/homo-heidelbergensis
[844] Article: **Homo rodensiensis—a cave man of uncertain age & status:** http://www.macroevolution.net/homo-rhodesiensis.html

- Two man-like hominids appeared in *the Pleistocene Epoch. We will pay a lot of attention to them.*

  ✓ ***Neanderthal man, and***
  ✓ ***Cro-Magnon Man.***

Neanderthal Man appeared first, lasted his time and then disappeared. Cro-Magnon Man appeared later, coexisted with Neanderthal Man for a while, and lived on into the Holocene Epoch. According to science, Cro-Magnon Man was anatomically identical to modern man when he appeared, **and he behaviorally became modern man in the early Holocene Epoch.**

As we shall see in the next chapter, Genesis 1:26 tells us Elohim said, *'Let Us make man.'* Genesis 1:27 says, *'And Elohim created man.'* The Ancient Jewish sages thought the mention of the *making* of man in Gen. 1:26 and later, the *creating* of man in Gen. 1:27 suggested some time passed between the 'making' and the 'creating' of the first man.[845] When we talk about this in the next chapter, this interesting subtlety, and the conclusions the sages drew from it may help us see why scientists and the ancient Jewish sages define man differently.

HOMO SAPIENS NEANDERTHALENSIS[846]

In the land of Israel, just inland from the coast of the eastern most shoreline of the Mediterranean Sea, and just north of the ancient city of Caesarea by the Sea; halfway up the westward facing steep slope of Mt. Carmel — the mountain on which, in ~ 860 BC Elijah challenged Ahab's priests of Baal (cf. I Kings Chapter 18) — there are the large black openings to several huge caves. Today, these cave openings are clearly visible from any offshore vessel plying those pristine waters. Stand in the openings of these caves and you can gaze westward toward the open expanse of the Mediterranean Sea. Within these huge caves lie the fossils and artifacts of a prehistoric animal that lived in and on Mt. Carmel many tens of thousands of years before Elijah. Science has named this animal *Homo neanderthalensis* or Neanderthal *Man*. Others maintain this animal was a protohuman ancestor and claim he should be named *Homo sapiens neanderthalensis*.

The bones of *all animals (including man)* contain carbon. Carbon is a principle structural element of bone. However, the bones of Neanderthals are too old to date using Carbon[14] (i.e., radioactive Carbon dating) techniques. Carbon[14] decays 50% of its radioactivity every 5,600 years. Therefore, C^{14} dating of ancient fossils is unreliable. So, the approximate age of the fossils in the caves on Mt. Carmel has been determined by the age of the geologically known rock strata in which the fossils have been found. Thus,

---

[845] Schroeder, *Genesis and the Big Bang*, Chapter 9 p. 138*d*
[846] Schroeder, *Genesis and the Big Bang*, Chapter 1 p. 11-12

the Mt. Carmel Neanderthal fossils have been determined to be about 60,000 years old.[847] These particular fossils of Neanderthal Man are relatively young compared to other Neanderthal fossils from North Africa, Europe, and Asia that have been dated as early as 150,000 years before the present. Some scientific articles claim Neanderthals appeared as early as 250,000-200,000 years ago and that they descended from an earlier human species, i.e., *Homo erectus*, between 500,000 to 300,000 years ago).[848] Neanderthals became extinct somewhere around 30,000 years ago.[849] So, science considers Neanderthals to be 'man-like' hominids that lived during the Ice Ages in the late Pleistocene Epoch — specifically, in the Middle Paleolithic Period (discussed and defined later in this chapter).

The first fossils of Neanderthals were discovered in the Neander Valley near Dusseldorf, Germany in 1856.[850] *Neanderthal* (a German word) means *'Neander Valley.'* The valley was named in the early 19th century AD to honor a prominent clergyman, *Joachim Neander*. In 1901, the spelling of the German word for '*valley'* was changed from '*Thal'* to '*Tal.'* So, if you read any German papers written after 1901 that concern this creature, his name will likely be spelled — *'Neandertal Man.'* Some have claimed *Homo neanderthalensis* should be properly named *Homo sapiens neanderthalensis*. They also claim he is related to H. habilis, H. erectus, Australopithecus, H. ergaster, H. rodensiensis, and H. heidelbergensis. Who really knows?

Others say some day, when DNA research is complete, we will know. To that claim one might ask the question: Do we really have enough DNA evidence to make a conclusive determination? After all, no complete skeletal fossil of a Neanderthal has yet been found![851] Most of the DNA samples we have from Neanderthals is not only insufficient for accurate and conclusive analysis, but in some of the DNA samples that have been analyzed so far, the chains of DNA are incomplete or have been tainted by microbial or fungal digestion.[852,853]

Nevertheless, we know Neanderthals had a very distinctive appearance. The Neanderthal's skull had prominent protuberant frontal orbital ridges. His frontal bones sloped backwards rather quickly and did not present the higher vaulted appearance of the modern-day human forehead. The size of his brain was equivalent to ours. Some say it was a bit bigger. He was also more muscular than modern-day humans. His bones were more massive, and his pelvis was bigger and wider. Neanderthals were generally shorter than modern-day humans. The average male stood 5 feet 6 inches tall. The average female was 5 feet tall. Neanderthal man used crude tools that he fashioned from stone.

---

[847] Schroeder, *Genesis and the Big Bang*, Chapter 1 p. 12*d*

[848] Article: **Rethinking Neanderthals:** By Joe Alper: *Smithsonian* Magazine June 2003 p 2
http://www.smithsonianmag.com/science-nature/neanderthals.html?c=y&page=2

[849] Article: **Ancient DNA reveals secrets of human history. Modern humans may have picked up key genes from extinct relatives.** By Ewen Callaway http://www.nature.com/news/2011/110809/full/476136a.html

[850] Article: **Evolution of Modern Humans: Neandertals.** http://anthro.palomar.edu/homo2/mod_homo_2.htm

[851] Article: **Neanderthal—BBC** (Science and Nature TV & Radio follow-up)
http://www.bbc.co.uk/sn/tvradio/programmes/horizon/neanderthal_prog_summary.shtml

[852] Article: **What will the Neanderthal Genome Teach Us about the Human Brain?**
http://neurophilosophy.wordpress.com/2006/08/07/499/

[853] Article: **Biochemical & Physical Correlates of Contamination in Archaeological Human Bones & Teeth Excavated at Matera, Italy: by M. Thomas Gilbert, et al. From the Journal of Archaeological Science 32 (2005) 785-793** http://www.eva.mpg.de/evolution/staff/c_smith/pdf/Gilbert_et_al_MateraJAS05.pdf

He lived mostly in caves and wore the skins of the animals he killed for food. His diet was almost completely the meat of the animals he killed. His weapons were mostly crude clubs or sharp stones that he used as knives for chopping, scraping, and cutting. There are indications he was acquainted with a heavy spear that he used for thrusting. But there is *no* evidence he was acquainted with any projectile weapons[854] other than the throwing of rocks. This animal was the dominant mammal during the middle part of the Old Stone Age (i.e., the Middle Paleolithic Period). Although Neanderthals became extinct about 30,000 years ago BP, there is evidence they coexisted for a few thousand years with another younger man-like animal that many scientists believe was our direct ancestor — Cro-Magnon Man (now called *Homo sapiens sapiens*).

It is believed Cro-Magnons and Neanderthals were competing enemies. However, since Neanderthals became extinct somewhere around 30,000 years ago and Cro-Magnons appeared on Earth somewhere around 50,000 years ago BP, there are a growing number of scientists who claim Neanderthals and Cro-Magnons co-existed on Earth for at least 20,000 years. They also claim DNA evidence indicates some Neanderthals interbred with Cro-Magnons. Supposedly interbreeding happened in the Middle East prior to the migration of Neanderthals to Europe and Asia. Thus, it is claimed interbreeding between the two species is the reason that 1-4% of people from Eurasia have DNA in their genome that has been contributed by Neanderthals.[855,856]

CRO-MAGNON MAN—NOW CALLED HOMO SAPIENS SAPIENS[857]

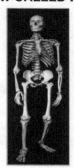

Cro-Magnon Man was so named because the fossils of this animal were first discovered in the Cro-Magnon cave at Dordogne, France near the village of Les Eyzies in March of 1868. From the abundance of fossil evidence discovered since, it has been determined Cro-Magnon Man appeared about 50,000 years ago BP in the very late Pleistocene Epoch. Scientists now believe this animal (that science claims is our direct ancestor), originated in the Middle East and Asia. Supposedly, Cro-Magnons then migrated to Europe, the Ukraine, China, Siberia, and finally into the Americas before a land-bridge

---

[854] Article: ***Neanderthal Weaponry Lacked Projectile Advantage:*** by Jennifer Viegas; Discovery News Jan. 14, 2009 (article quotes Assoc. Prof. Steven Churchill & colleague Jill Rhodes of Duke University)
http://dsc.discovery.com/news/2009/01/14/neanderthals-weapon.html

[855] Article: ***Neanderthal—Cro-Magnon—Hybrid?*** By Spencer P.M. Harrington
http://www.archaeology.org/online/news/neanderkid.html

[856] Article: *N.Y. Times* April 25, 1999, By JOHN NOBLE WILFORD: ***Discovery Suggests Humans Are a Bit Neanderthal***
http://cogweb.ucla.edu/ep/Neanderthal.html

[857] Article: ***Evolution of Modern Humans: Early Modern Homo sapiens.***
http://anthro.palomar.edu/homo2/mod_homo_4.html

connecting North America and Asia was closed by rising ocean levels that occurred from the global warming which ended the last glacial period of the Pleistocene Epoch. The migration of Cro-Magnons to North America supposedly happened around 10,000 years ago BP. There is archeological evidence that a land-bridge between Siberia and Alaska (called 'Beringia') was exposed several times over the last 60,000 years by the waxing and waning of sea levels caused by the many glacial and interglacial global warming periods of the Pleistocene Epoch. [858]

Most archaeologists claim the Cro-Magnons were tall.[859] Some say the average male was between 6 feet 4 inches and 6 feet 7 inches tall. The average female was between 6 feet and 6 feet 1 inch tall. If these were the average heights of the typical Cro-Magnon male and female, then about 68% of Cro-Magnons would have conformed to these average heights, representing a population that was within one standard deviation of the mean in either direction, and a people who were very tall — certainly tall when compared to the average height of the Neanderthals. This means that a small percent of Cro-Magnon men were taller than 6 feet 7 inches and a small percent were shorter than 6 feet 4 inches. That is not guessing. That is just the statistical distribution of the Cro-Magnon population by height as determined by a normal Gaussian Distribution (or Bell Curve).

I remember visiting the Museum of Liberation in Cherbourg, France, in 1968. There, I saw a mannequin dressed as a U.S. Infantry soldier with a caption that stated the average U.S. Infantryman in WWII was 5 feet 6 inches tall, wore size 6 boots, and weighed 140 pounds. That certainly would not represent the average height and weight of a typical young adult North American male today. The average U.S. Infantryman of WWII was short by comparison. Today, many young adult North American males are over 6 feet tall, and a considerable number are 6 feet 5 inches or taller. So, it seems to me the average height of our modern-day young adults is just now approaching the average height of the ancient Cro-Magnons.

THE SKELETONS OF CRO-MAGNONS ARE IDENTICAL TO THE SKELETONS OF MODERN HUMANS. Scientists tell us the Cro-Magnon skull is identical to the skull of modern-day humans, with an average brain size about the same as that of humans today. Their oral anatomy is identical to modern humans, and they probably could speak. Their other skeletal features are also identical to ours and because their legs were longer than those of the Neanderthals, and their pelvis was narrower and more streamlined — they were fast runners. Because Cro-Magnon skeletal anatomy is identical to the anatomy of modern Homo sapiens; scientists point out this fact and call them 'AMHs' (for 'Anatomically Modern Humans'). [860]

They were less muscular than the Neanderthals, and thus employed other skills to bring down their prey (as opposed to the brute force that was characteristic of the Neanderthals). Cro-Magnons hunted in packs that were highly organized. Early on, one

[858] Article: **Prehistoric Beringia: a Beginner's Guide.** http://weber.ucsd.edu/~dkjordan/arch/beringia.html
[859] Article: **Cro-Magnons: Why don't we call them Cro-Magnons anymore?** (states av. Height 6`7``) http://archaeology.about.com/od/earlymansites/a/cro_magnon.html
[860] Article: **Cro-Magnons: Why don't we call them Cro-Magnons anymore?** (states av. Height 6`7``) http://archaeology.about.com/od/earlymansites/a/cro_magnon.htm

of their favorite weapons was a lightweight throwing spear (called the "Atlatl" — described later in this chapter). It is believed the bow and arrow were developed much later. Archaeological evidence suggests a group of Cro-Magnon hunters would divide their responsibilities when hunting the large mammals. One group would distract the animal while another group would throw their Atlatl darts (i.e., "*spears*") from a safe distance.

By contrast, Neanderthals may have hunted in smaller groups. But the weapons of the Neanderthals were crude. Their spears were heavy and more suitable for thrusting than throwing. Therefore, it is thought the Neanderthals, who primarily hunted in forests, waited in ambush for their prey to approach. Then, Neanderthals would spring forth from their concealment and one or more Neanderthals would distract and thrust their spears at the animal while another Neanderthal would attack from behind by jumping onto the back of the animal to do mortal hand-to-hand combat.[861,862] Neanderthal tactics often resulted in severe injuries to the hunters, as evidenced by a number of Neanderthal fossils that show evidence of severe healed fractures of their long bones and ribs.[863] Such grievous evidence of severe bony injuries are not as common in Cro-Magnon fossils.

Cro-Magnons made tools from flint-stone for use in preparing animal skins. They used pierced shells and tooth and bone pendants for body ornamentation. Their art extended to *Venus figures* (small statuettes of bone), and they made simple drawings on the walls of their caves of woolly mammoths, cave bears, and the other animals they hunted. To make their cave drawings, they used colors like red, black, and brown, from the different types of berries they ate and other materials they possessed — like the charcoal that came from their fires. Both Neanderthals and Cro-Magnons ate meat, but tooth-analysis indicates Cro-Magnons were not such extreme carnivores as the Neanderthals were. Their diet also included plants and berries.[864,865]

THE ORIGINS AND DEVELOPMENT OF EARLY HUMAN CULTURE [866]

Archaeology is the branch of science that involves the study of ancient cultures through the examination of their material remains. *Anthropology* is the study of humankind in all of its aspects, especially in relation to human culture and development. Anthropology differs from *Sociology* in that it takes a more historical and comparative approach. In the past century much has been discovered about the earliest human cultures. Scientists now believe sometime in the Pleistocene Epoch an animal (a mammal — a 'man-like' hominid), began to make and use tools. That seminal event, scientists believe, marked the beginning of the earliest 'human' culture on our planet. This conclusion has come from the study of the fossils of these animals that have been discovered in the cave

---

[861] Article: **Neanderthal—BBC** (Science and Nature TV & Radio follow-up)
http://www.bbc.co.uk/sn/tvradio/programmes/horizon/neanderthal_prog_summary.shtml
[862] Article: **Neanderthal's Strong-arm Tactics Revealed.** By Kurt Kleiner: *Journal of Archaeological Science* (vol. 30, p 103) http://www.bbc.co.uk/sn/tvradio/programmes/horizon/neanderthal_prog_summary.shtml
[863] Article: **Rethinking Neanderthals:** By Joe Alper: *Smithsonian* Magazine June 2003 p 2
http://www.smithsonianmag.com/science-nature/neanderthals.html?c=y&page=2
[864] Article: **Cro-Magnon 1/ The Smithsonian Institutions' Human Origins:**
http://humanorigins.si.edu/evidence/human-fossils/fossils/cro-magnon-1
[865] Article: **Cro-Magnon Man (Anatomically Modern or Early Modern Humans.**
http://www.elephant.se/cro-magnon.php?open=Man%20and%20elephants
[866] Article: **The Stone Age: Prehistoric Cultural Stage, or Level of Human Development, Characterized by the Creation and Use of Stone Tools**—by Robert A. Guisepe—http://history-world.org/stone_age.html

dwellings and graves in which the fossils and artifacts of these animals have been found. Thanks to the efforts of generations of Archaeologists and Anthropologists we now know a great deal of the life and times of the Earth's earliest man-like hominids. Based upon the degree of sophistication in the fashioning and use of the tools and the materials used to make the tools and artifacts that have been discovered, the segment of Earth-time in which the beginning of early 'human' culture happened has been named '*The Stone Age.*' This is because the earliest tools were made of stone.

THE PLEISTOCENE EPOCH/ICE AGES[867]/ STONE AGE TOOLS/ THE STONE AGE [868]
FREQUENT REFERENCE TO THE CHART AT THE END OF CHAPTER 12 WILL BE HELPFUL WHILE READING THIS SECTION.

The Stone Age was approximately *coextensive* with *the Pleistocene Epoch*. The Stone Age 'saw' a number of dramatic climate changes that profoundly affected the Earth and its life-forms. In the Pleistocene Epoch (1.6 million years ago until 12,000 years BP—i.e., 10,000 BC), the northern latitudes and mountainous areas of our planet were subjected to numerous cycles of *Glaciation* and *Global Warming*. However, even before the Pleistocene Epoch, it appears our planet was 'well acquainted' with these *cycles*. They have been a principal force in determining earth's history. **Our current Global Warming Epoch started in 10,000 BC!** It ended the last Ice Age in the Pleistocene Epoch that started 70,000 years ago and ended in 10,000 BC (~ 12,000 years Before the Present). That Ice Age (the Wisconsinan Ice Age) lasted 60,000 years! Its end marked the beginning of our current age of Global Warming and ushered in the Holocene Epoch, which so far, has been an epoch of Global Warming. **Our current Epoch of Global Warming has fostered the birth of Earth's current-day human civilizations! No one knows what causes these cycles!** Many theories exist, but no one theory satisfactorily explains *all* drastic global climate changes.

- Are there variances in the earth's orbit that cause earth to 'wobble' a degree or two toward or away from the sun? Yes! Variances occur!
- Does the tilt of the earth's axis ever change? Yes! Tilts frequently occur.
- Does the sun generate a varying amount of heat from time to time? Yes! We call them "solar flares!"
- What part does continental drift play when it redirects the ocean currents? Major changes have occurred!
- Do reversals of the Earth's Magnetic Field play any role? Yes! Extinctions of life have resulted!
- What about the world-wide volcanic eruptions that spew ash, CO_2, and other nocuous volcanic gases by the billions of tons into the Earth's atmosphere every day? Scientists are re-examining this subject.

VOLCANISM
Current-day environmental activists say fossil fuel emissions that began with the Industrial Revolution in the mid 18th Century — along with human and animal CO_2 production are the root causes of our current-day epoch of Global Warming. Some have said forest fires and volcanic eruptions are *not* major contributors. No! CO_2 is the main culprit, and man

[867] Article: *Ice Ages:* http://essayweb.net/geology/quicknotes/iceage.shtml
[868] Article: *Ice Age—Discussion and Encyclopedia Article*—www.knowledgerush.com/kr/encyclopedia/Ice_age/

(alone) is responsible. The people who preach this idea say man can solve "the problem" through "smart legislation." All we have to do is stop using fossil fuels — kill coal mining and coal-fueled plants that generate electricity — stop oil and natural gas production — switch to electric cars, trucks, buses, and trains — switch to solar panels and wind-driven turbine farms — stop raising cows — become vegetarians — and start using "clean energy." They point to the "scientific studies" that support this ideology. But no one has noticed these "scientific studies" are funded by government grants! *Uhmm ???!!!*

Furthermore, the rich and famous who wholeheartedly support this idea — fly their private jet airplanes all around the world to conferences which are attended by like-minded wealthy people — so they can hobnob and demonstrate their support for the politically motivated anti-global warming movement. Some make an even bigger *"Carbon-footprint"* entry when they sail to these resorts on their luxury mega-yachts. Not too long ago, one member of a Royal Family (who recently turned his back on his family) gave a speech at a private Google-sponsored environmental event held at the exclusive Verdura Resort in Sicily — *sans shoes.* Yes, he went *barefoot* to that *"well-dressed Google sponsored meeting"* where he gave a speech that showed his support for *the Anti-Global Warming Efforts to Save the Planet.* That event was attended by a crowd of A-list celebrities who flew there in their 114 fuel-guzzling jets. I suppose he was barefooted because he wanted everyone to notice — *no animal had to die for him to be clothed!* [869]

Just recently, *"a Big Blue Norther"* (as we said when I lived in Texas) hit Texas and caused an extended period of below freezing temperatures that brought the state to its knees. [870] The wind turbines froze. The solar panels (beneath the cloud cover) iced over and stopped producing electricity. The commercial trucks shut down due to icy roads. The aging coal-fired plants and natural gas electricity generating plants were overwhelmed by the demand, and for several days, Texans suffered. Furthermore the severe cold caused a 40% decrease in the range of most EVs! Severe extremes of cold and heat severely affect the efficiency of EVs. For this reason, EVs are not popular in Alaska. Texas is now re-evaluating its electric-grid requirements and capacity. Points further north didn't suffer the same consequences because their fossil-fuel electric plants were able to meet the demand. If everyone were to start driving electric powered vehicles, the increased demand for electric power could not be met with our current day *"clean energy"* generating capabilities. Approximately 63% of our electricity is supplied by fossil-fuel generating plants; ~ 19% comes from nuclear powered plants; ~ 12% comes from wind farms and solar panels; and only ~ 6% comes from hydropower. I suspect most people who drive electric cars don't know they are recharging their cars every night with electric power that has been generated by a fossil-fuel generating plant!

Nevertheless, the fact remains — no one has calculated the volumes and environmental impact of the *continuing* emissions of CO_2 and other noxious volcanic gasses that active volcanos spew into our atmosphere on a daily basis. And no one seems

[869]'Barefoot' Prince Harry criticized as stars arrive for global ...

[870] Why the Deep Freeze Caused Texas to Lose Power

to know our current epoch of Global Warming started in 10,000 BC! That was 12,000 years before the advent of The Industrial Revolution, which climate activists say caused our current-day epoch of global warming! Our current-day epoch of global warming allowed the Cro-Magnons to come out of their caves! It was the seminal cause of the beginning of our current-day civilizations!

Mount St. Helens erupted on the 18th of May in 1980. That mountain is 50 miles west of Yakima, Washington (as the crow flies). There are several mountain ridges and mountain-passes that separate Yakima from Mt. Saint Helens. That is a day I will never forget! I had just finished playing my trumpet in the worship service at Wesley Methodist Church of Yakima and was driving west to attend the morning worship service of Westminster Presbyterian Church (my church). As I parked in my church parking lot, I saw this ominous black cloud of ash approaching Yakima from the west and towering overhead! At the time I didn't know the jet stream was moving that ash-cloud at 90 mph from west to east! There were horrendous flashes of lightening in the cloud. The mountain was booming — thundering out its major volcanic eruption. The booming of the mountain was many magnitudes louder than the thundering sounds of the barrages of 155 mm cannon-fire my army artillery battalion produced when firing all its howitzers simultaneously. I could literally *feel* the concussions of the eruption even though that darned mountain was 50 miles away ("as the crow flies")! Volcanic ash and mud balls were falling around me, and I could smell the hydrogen sulfide gas. When I saw the lightning flashes, I thought rain would soon be falling. I feared it would soon be raining down *sulfuric acid!* However, there was no water in that gigantic cloud. The lightning was caused by the electrically charged ash in the cloud. My town (Yakima, Washington) was covered by hundreds of thousands of tons of volcanic ash on that day and for the three days that followed. "Midnight" fell at 10 AM that Sunday morning and lasted 3 days! Yakima made the cover of *National Geographic* that month. The magazine showed the world what downtown Yakima looked like that Sunday at noon. We did not see the sun for a week after the eruption. Even then, the atmosphere was partially opaque from the still unsettled ash in the air. Our first "clear" day came about a month later.

When I visited the volcano 10 years later, the devastation of that eruption was still evident. The 17 pyroclastic flows, which followed on the heels of the lateral blast of the volcano, had flattened and burned all of the trees for miles around. The pyroclastic flows that swept up, over, and down the 5,000-foot mountain ridges (surrounding the north face of the volcano where the lateral blast occurred), killed 57 people who had been in the blast zone! It caught Dr. David Alexander Johnston (an experienced volcanologist) by surprise. He thought his observation post (on a peak six miles distant) was safe. He uttered his last words when he transmitted: *"VANCOUVER, VANCOUVER, THIS IS IT!"* — just moments before the lateral blast pyroclastic flow engulfed him going at a speed of 450 mph and incinerated his body with its 1830 F ° temperature! His body has never been found![871]

As I observed the devastation 10 years later, it seemed as if some giant had spilled a big box of colossal toothpicks across the forest floor. Small flora was returning to an

---

[871] **David A. Johnston - Wikipedia**

otherwise "moon-like" landscape. But no living or upright trees could be seen. The bears, mountain goats, cougars, deer, and the elk were still avoiding the area. There was a continuous column of steam and other volcanic gasses rising into the atmosphere from the ongoing volcanic emissions, which were still visible 10 years later! Even from a great distance I could smell the hydrogen sulfide gas (H_2S) which smells like rotten eggs! The Mount St. Helens 'SNIF' project has proved that volcano is still daily emitting sulfur dioxide, hydrogen sulfide, carbon dioxide gases, and steam![872] We know major volcanic eruptions throw hundreds of millions of tons of volcanic debris and volcanic gases into the atmosphere and stratosphere that encircle the earth. **But no one has done a global study of the accumulative daily volcanic pollution of our atmosphere that comes from the hundreds of the earth's active volcanos on a daily basis!**

Scientists say the Mt. Saint Helens eruption disgorged 540 million tons of ash! Ash settled as far as 2,000 miles away, in Oklahoma! After the eruption, it took several weeks to remove the ash from Yakima's streets. 600,000 tons of ash (enough to fill 31,189 dump trucks) were dumped on the banks of the Naches River at its juncture with the Yakima River near the downtown area. The ash was used to construct 7 soccer fields — now called Chesterley Park. Yakima now hosts an annual state-wide soccer tournament. [873]

- Does man-made atmospheric pollution really exceed our planet's continuous and ongoing volcanic pollution?
  - ✓ We know there are about 600 active volcanos on earth.
  - ✓ Between 50 and 60 volcanoes erupt each year somewhere on earth (about 1 major eruption every week of every year)!
  - ✓ Overall, there are 45 volcanoes (like Mount St. Helens) which are continually emitting CO_2 and other noxious volcanic gases into earth's atmosphere on a daily basis!
  - ✓ The daily continuing CO_2 emissions from Mt. St. Helens alone is 500 — 1,000 tons per day!
  - ✓ In the summer of 1959, I worked as a tour guide on Yellowstone Lake. On August 17th, after I went to bed, I was awakened by a 7.3 magnitude earthquake that triggered a landslide in Madison Canyon at Hebgen Lake, Montana. That landslide killed 28 people who were camping. After shocks continued for several days. I wanted to be in my boat on the lake during those aftershocks because they could not be felt. However, In 1959, we did not know Yellowstone is one of the earth's largest Supervolcanos! A major portion of the Yellowstone lakebed is a part of the giant Yellowstone caldera that was formed by a major volcanic eruption 640,000 years ago! This was discovered by a United States Geological Survey that was conducted in the 1970s.
  - ✓ The Yellowstone supervolcano has erupted three times over the past 2.1 million years, most recently 640,000 years ago. A major Yellowstone eruption today would

---

[872] **Volcanic Gas Monitoring at Mount St. Helens - USGS.gov**

[873] **It Happened Here: Mount St. Helens turns Yakima into an ...**

be unlike anything humankind has ever experienced! Scientists predict a nuclear winter, and a major extinction of life would follow!

* We now know our planet was born in fire. The fires that formed our earth still rage in the molten mantel layer of the earth. We also know volcanism formed our atmosphere and oceans. Furthermore, volcanism is still a major force that continues to change the landscape, the atmosphere, and the environment of our earth.

* If man-made fossil fuel emissions are to blame for our current epoch of global warming, how does one explain the many epochs of global warming that have occurred in our planet's history — before man arrived on the scene? We overlook one important fact. **Geologic history tells us each period of global warming was followed by an Ice Age!**

* Now, I want to give a summary of the history of the Earth's many Ice Ages and its longer periods of interglacial Global Warming.

THE HURONIAN ICE AGE

We have already talked about how the Earth was 'born' in space as a 'Fiery Ball' on the 2nd Day of Creation; then morphed into a Toxic Water-World with a Toxic Atmosphere by the end of the 2nd Day. Late on the 2nd Day, in the Archean Eon, the longest ice age (the Huronian Ice Age) occurred. It started about 2.7 billion years ago and lasted into the Paleoproterozoic Eon, ending about 2.3 billion years ago, on the 'morning' of the 3rd Day. On the 3rd Day the Earth also changed again into a 'Granite Planet' as the first continents rose to separate the 'waters below.'

THE CRYOGENIAN ICE AGE ('SNOWBALL EARTH')

On the 4th Day of Creation, Earth got its clear-blue life-friendly oxygen-rich atmosphere and life-friendly oceans. But when the first supercontinent (Rodinia) formed about a billion years ago, the Earth became a 'Snowball Earth' as Rodinia blocked the circulation of warm ocean currents and brought about the 2nd longest, but the most severe Ice Age our planet has ever seen! This is known as the Cryogenian Ice Age. It happened about a billion years ago on the 4th Day of Creation in the Mesoproterozoic Eon. The whole earth was covered in a great depth of snow and ice. The global warming that followed the breakup of Rodinia near the end of the Neoproterozoic Eon (late on the 4th Day), fostered the 'Cambrian Explosion of life' that occurred on the 'morning' of the 5th Day. But our planet was yet to see other periodic Ice Ages in its future.[874]

THE ANDEAN-SAHARAN ICE AGE

An Ice Age known as the Andean-Saharan Ice Age developed during the Ordovician Period of the 5th Day of Creation about 460 million years ago and lasted into the Silurian Period, ending about 430 million years ago.[875] During this severe Ice Age, glaciers covered much of our globe and extended as far south as North Africa into what is today the Saharan desert!

THE KAROO ICE AGE

Another Ice Age known as the Karoo Ice Age occurred in the 'afternoon' of the 5th Day of Creation in the Mississippian Period (350 million years ago) and persisted through the

---

[874] Article: *Ice Age—Discussion and Encyclopedia Article*—www.knowledgerush.com/kr/encyclopedia/Ice_age/
[875] Article: *Ordovician Period:* http://science.nationalgeographic.com/science/prehistoric-world/ordovician/

'*evening*' of the 5th Day. The Karoo Ice Age ended in the Triassic Period with the beginning of the 6th Day of Creation (250 million years ago) — when Pangaea broke apart.

THE ICE AGES OF THE PLEISTOCENE EPOCH[876,877,878]

There were so many cycles of Glaciation and subsequent Interglacial Global Warming in the Pleistocene Epoch that the whole span of the Pleistocene has been considered by some an extended Ice Age. The glacial phases of the Pleistocene are listed below, from most recent to most distant. As follows, the names before the *(/)* are North American names, and those after it are the Northern European names of the various Ice Ages. **The dates are listed in thousands of years before the present (i.e., BP).** Notice, in Eastern Europe and in the Alps other names are used. The Pleistocene '*saw*' six Ice Ages, and five periods of Interglacial Global Warming.

- The Wisconsinan/Weichsel or Vistula (*Glacial Age*, 70-10) — *This Ice Age* lasted *60,000* years.
- The Sangamon/Eem (Interglacial Age, 130-70) — This Age of Global warming lasted 60,000 years.
- The Illinoisan/Saale (*Glacial Age*, 180-130) — *This Ice Age* lasted *50,000* years.
- The Yarmouth/Holstein (Interglacial Age, 230-180) — This Age of Global warming lasted 50,000 years.
- The Kansan/Elster (*Glacial Age*, 300-230) — *This Ice Age* lasted *70,000* years.
- The Aftonian/Cromer (Interglacial, 330-300) — This Age of Global warming lasted 30,000 years.
- The Nebraskan/Gunz (*Glacial Age*, 470-330) — *This Ice Age* lasted *140,000* years.
- The —/Waalian (Interglacial Age, 540-470) — This Age of Global warming lasted 70,000 years.
- The —/Donau II (*Glacial Age*, 550-540) — *This Ice Age* lasted *10,000* years.
- The —/Tiglian (Interglacial Age, 585-550) — This Age of Global warming lasted 35,000 years.
- The —/Donau I (*Glacial Age*, 600-585) — *This Ice Age* lasted *15,000* years.

ICE AGE SUMMARY

The *Huronian* Ice Age lasted 400 million years — the *Cryogenian Ice Age* lasted 215 million years — the *Andean-Saharan Ice Age* lasted 30 million years — and the *Karoo Ice Age* lasted 100 million years. *The Ice Ages of the Pleistocene Epoch* total 345,000 years. **Folks, when you add this data, you will find that Ice ruled the earth for 745 million 345 thousand years (i.e., 745,345,000 years) of its history!** Are you surprised? As the guy says in the TV commercials — ***"BUT WAIT! THERE'S MORE!"***

The Interglacial periods of Global Warming in the Pleistocene Epoch total 245,000 years. *There is no possibility that man could have caused them.* According to some scientists, AMHs didn't make their appearance until the glacial Wisconsinan/Weichsel part of the Pleistocene Epoch (somewhere around 50,000 years ago) — i.e., in *the Upper Paleolithic Epoch*. The *Wisconsinan* was an Ice Age! By the time the Cro-Magnons

[876] Article: **Pleistocene:** http://en.wikipedia.org/wiki/Pleistocene
[877] Article: The Pleistocene Epoch: Annenberg Media
http://www.learner.org/courses/envsci/unit/text.php?unit=12&secNum=5
[878] Article: Ice Age—Discussion and Encyclopedia Article—www.knowledgerush.com/kr/encyclopedia/Ice_age/

appeared on our planet (in their Wisconsinan ice age 50,000 years ago), the 1.6 million-year long geologic *epoch* (at the end of which they appeared—the *Pleistocene*) had already experienced a cumulative total of 245,000 years of Global Warming! (Granted, all interrupted by the six intervening Ice Ages of the Pleistocene.)

NEVERTHELESS, GLOBAL WARMING HAS DOMINATED THE HISTORY OF OUR EARTH!

If you subtract the earth's Ice Ages from the 4.5-billion-year age of the earth, you will find earth's warm periods total ~ 3.755 billion **(or 3,755,000,000) years)!** Many of those who write about Ice Ages and Global Warming admit they don't know the cause. Yet, current-day environmentalists blame the most recent period of global warming on man.

THE LITTLE ICE AGE[879]

The most recent of the Ice Ages of the Pleistocene Epoch ended ~ 12,000 years ago (BP), about 2000 years before the close of the Pleistocene.

The global warming that followed has continued into our day and has allowed and fostered the growth and development of our present modern-day societies and civilizations! Nevertheless, our current age of Global Warming has already been interrupted by a "Little Ice Age!"

There is a reason Greenland was named *Greenland.* As the Ice Caps of the last Pleistocene Ice Age melted, Greenland's glaciers receded and withdrew from the coastal margins. When Eric the Red discovered Greenland in 982 AD, the small area he settled had green meadows. So, he gave the 'new' land an inviting name and called it *Greenland,* to induce other Vikings to settle there.[880] However, even our current Epoch of global warming (*the Holocene Epoch*), has been interrupted by an Ice Age. *The Little Ice Age* happened between 1,300 AD and 1,870 AD. It had two phases. The first phase began around 1,300 AD and lasted until the late 1,400s. There were generally warmer global temperatures in the 1500s, but then the cold returned with a vengeance. The second phase started around 1600 AD and lasted until 1870. The second phase marked the height of the Little Ice Age. The Vikings flourished in Greenland until the advent of the first phase of the Little Ice Age. The adverse effect of the severe sustained cold, the heavy snow falls resulting in the buildup of ice, and the failure of the Vikings to adapt to the drastically changing conditions; were the major factors that drove the Vikings out of Greenland.

THE LITTLE ICE AGE AND THE AMERICAN REVOLUTION

When George Washington crossed the Delaware River on the night of December 25th, 1776, and defeated the Hessians at Trenton, N.J., huge chunks of ice partially blocked his way. When his army went into winter quarters at Valley Forge, Pennsylvania in 1777 his troops suffered mightily from the severe winter cold. The major reason Washington and his soldiers were exposed to such severe cold is because those events occurred during *the last phase of the Little Ice Age.* We also know his troops were not adequately

---

[879] Article: ***Environmental History Timeline: The Little a, Ca. 1300-1870 A.D.***
http://www.eh-resources.org/timeline/timeline_lia.html
[880] Article: ***Discovery of Greenland by Eric the Red:*** by George Upton
http://search.aol.com/aol/search?q=Greenland%2C+Eric+the+Red%2C+discovery%2C+green&s_it=tb50-ie-aolmail-chromesbox-en-us

provisioned by the Continental Congress and that was also a major contributing factor in their suffering. Today, it is indeed a rare thing for the Delaware River to freeze over. And, current-day winters at Valley Forge are much more temperate.[881,882]

ICE AGES IN OUR FUTURE?

If past history is any harbinger of the future, there will be more Ice Ages ahead of us in spite of the hysteria that exists over our current epoch of global warming which began ~ 12,000 years ago in 10,000 BC.

Environmentalists claim man-made pollution is responsible and they point to man's use of fossil fuels (our so-called 'carbon footprint') as the cause. The arrogance of their ignorance is astounding! Our current epoch of global warming is only one of many epochs of global warming the earth has experienced in its 4.5-billion-year history. It started ~ 12,000 years before the advent of the Industrial Revolution and the invention of the internal combustion engine! So, it cannot be truthfully said 'man' caused it. Don't get me wrong! I'm not saying we should not be good stewards of our Earth. Of course, we must be responsible for what sort of footprint we leave behind. But I am saying I think we are showing our ignorance of the miraculous homeostatic mechanisms the Creator put in place to ensure the continued life-friendly environment of our planet. And I'm also saying "progressives" demonstrate their ignorant arrogance when they say they can stop Global Warming and reverse it with government legislation. In view of what we have learned since 1980 about the long-term effects of volcanic eruptions, some haughty, self-serving, barefooted politician may someday give a speech saying: "GOVERNMENT MUST OUTLAW VOLCANOS!" However, I do not wish to be "legislated" back into the Stone Age, especially when the real polluters of our planet like China and India are allowed to continue on their current course in order to allow their economies to "catch up!"

LET'S NOW TAKE A LOOK AT THE STONE AGE. LET'S START WITH STONE AGE TOOLS.[883]

In the Stone Age, early 'man' was a food gatherer. For his sustenance, he depended on fishing, hunting, and the collecting of wild fruits, nuts, and berries. The imperishable artifacts of his culture were those made of stone, bone, antlers, and horns. These artifacts, the cave wall-drawings that survive, and the skeletal fossils of these creatures are all we have from which to draw conclusions about early man's existence and culture. The tools these creatures fashioned range from the earliest tools, which were simple — to later tools which showed increasing degrees of complexity. In the making of stone tools, four fundamental traditions were developed by Stone Age Hominids:

- *Pebble-tool traditions,*
- *Flake-tool traditions,*
- *Hand-ax traditions, and*
- *Blade-tool traditions.*

---

[881] Article: ***Vikings in Greenland-an Overview: Collapse of the Greenland Viking Settlements***. http://search.aol.com/aol/search?q=Vikings%2C+Greenland%2C+little+ice+age&s_it=tb50-ie-aolmail-chromesbox-en-us

[882] Article: ***Northern Lights—Little Ice Age***: by Barbara Fifer http://lewis-clark.org/content/content-article.asp?ArticleID=375

[883] Article: ***The Stone Age: Prehistoric Cultural Stage, or Level of Human Development, Characterized by the Creation and Use of Stone Tools***—by Robert A. Guisepe—http://history-world.org/stone_age.html

PEBBLE AND FLAKE TOOL TRADITIONS

The first stone tools were primitive and rudimentary. They were most likely naturally broken, sharp-edged rocks that were picked up by early hominids and used as hand-held tools. There is archaeological evidence later hominids began selecting stones and fashioning them to make their own sharp-edged stone tools. The earliest examples of this activity have been called *the Pebble-Tool and Flake-Tool Traditions*, because pebbles and small cobbles of stone were selected and formed into specific shapes for certain purposes.

The first stone tools may have been made and used by Australopithecus in East Africa about 2.5 million years ago BP in the Pliocene Epoch. The question is: 'Did the animal we call Australopithecus afarensis make these early tools, or were they naturally broken sharp-edged rocks he found, picked up, and used?'

Tools of the Pebble and Flake traditions were also discovered with the fossils of *Homo habilis* at Olduvai Gorge in Tanzania. Tools of this type have been called *Oldowan tools* ever since, after that location. Homo habilis lived between 2.3 and 1.6 million years ago BP, in the Pliocene Epoch. Again, the question is: *'Did H. habilis make his tools or find them?'* We think these early tool users were selective in choosing the stones for their tools. They probably chose water-worn creek cobbles formed out of volcanic rock. The tools of the Pebble and Flake traditions consisted mainly of two basic types:

- Core tools, and
- Flake tools.

Core tools were stone cobbles with several flakes knocked off at one end producing a jagged, chopping or cleaver-like implement for hand use. *Flake tools* were sharp-edged, naturally occurring *stone flakes* that were used *'as is,'* without any improvement, for knives and scrapers. Thus, these basic *Oldowan tool-types* were examples of the *Pebble-Tool and Flake-Tool Traditions*. *Homo habilis* used Oldowan tools for nearly a million years. *Homo erectus* also used tools that could be described as *'evolved'* Oldowan tools.

HAND-AX TRADITIONS

Homo erectus appeared between 2 million and 1.5 million years ago — at the juncture of the *Pliocene* and *Pleistocene* Epochs. He lived onward into the Pleistocene Epoch, as the 300,000-year-old H. erectus fossil of *Peking Man* tells us. The more advanced tools of H. erectus included stone tools that were fashioned to be choppers, cleavers, hammers, and flakes. These were all hand-held. They have been found mostly in Africa, the Middle East, India, Spain, Italy, Greece, and Turkey. These tools are now called *Acheulian tools*, named for the *Saint Acheul site in France* where these types of tools were first found. However, it is believed this tradition of tool making actually started in East Africa. *The Hand Ax is the prototypical Acheulian tool.* Hand-axes were made from large rock cores or very large flakes that were persistently worked into an elongated oval shape that fits nicely in the palm of the hand. They have one pointed end and sharp edges on both sides and faces. Therefore, they are called *bifacial* tools. Hand-axes were used for chopping of wood, digging up roots and bulbs, butchering animals, and cracking nuts and small bones. They were portable tools that could be carried from place to place. *Acheulian* tools began in Africa about 1.5 million years ago and reached Europe at least

500,000 years ago. But not all Homo erectus animals possessed Acheulian tools. Some only had the simpler tools of the older Oldowan tradition.

THE BLADE TOOL TRADITION

Blade tools appeared in the Upper Paleolithic Period. They were typically a thin tool that is at least twice as long as it is wide. The sides were roughly parallel. They were fashioned by removing the longest possible flake from a stone or flint-rock core, and then carefully retouching the edges to achieve exactly the shape and cutting edge that was desired. Suffice it to say blade tools required considerable skill to fashion without breaking them because they were thin enough to be fragile. Blade tools were typically hafted (i.e., attached to a wooden or antler handle to make a knife, ax, spear, or other weapon or tool). These tools were excellent weapons and hunting tools. They were used to make deep holes, including deep wounds in prey animals. They were also useful in many other ways. They represented a marked improvement in the amount of cutting edge that could be gleaned from a single piece of stone.

THE CHRONOLOGY OF THE STONE AGE

Since we have been talking about '*Paleolithic*' periods, now is a good time to examine the meaning of the word. *Paleo* means '*old.*' *Lithic* means '*stone.*' So, Paleolithic literally means '*old stone.*' The Stone Age has been subdivided into three basic Periods of time based upon the degree of complexity and sophistication of the tools that the Earth's earliest tool-using hominids fashioned and used during these Periods. The first Period of the Stone Age was the longest and is divided into three Subdivisions. Since environmental and climatic factors were the major influencing factors in the development of hominid culture and society, the time parameters that are given below for each Period and Subdivision are approximate, and for that reason are indicated by the symbol ' ~ '. The Periods and Subdivisions of The Stone Age are listed as follows:

THE PERIODS OF THE STONE AGE

I. *THE PALEOLITHIC PERIOD (MEANING 'OLD STONE AGE')*
    From ~ 2.5 million yrs. ago to 12,000 BP (or ~10,000 yrs. BC)
    The Subdivisions of the Paleolithic Period
    o *The Lower Paleolithic Epoch* (or The 'Lower Old Stone-Age').
       From ~ 2.5 million yrs. ago to ~ 300,000 yrs. BP.
    o *The Middle Paleolithic Epoch* (or The 'Middle Old Stone-Age')
       From ~ 300,000 yrs. ago to ~ 30,000 yrs. BP (Neanderthal's Primacy)
    o *The Upper Paleolithic Epoch* (or The 'Upper Old-Stone Age')
       From ~30,000 yrs. ago to ~ 12,000 yrs. BP (Cro-Magnon's Primacy)

II. *THE MESOLITHIC PERIOD (FOR 'MIDDLE STONE' AGE)* ~12,000 BP to ~ 3,000 BP *in Europe;* and ~10,000 to ~ 9,000 years BP *in the Mid-East.* Advancement occurred more rapidly in the Mid-East than elsewhere probably due to the warmer climate and longer growing season.

III. *THE NEOLITHIC PERIOD (FOR 'NEW STONE' AGE).* ~ 9,000 to ~ 6,000 yrs. BP *in the Mid-East*, ending with the beginning of the *Bronze Age* (~ 5500 BP/ ~3500 BC).

A MORE DETAILED 'LOOK' AT THE STONE AGE

I. THE PALEOLITHIC PERIOD (OR 'OLD STONE AGE'): ~ 2.5 million yrs. BP to 12,000 BP Modern Science claims The Paleolithic Period (or The Old Stone Age) is the earliest and longest phase of mankind's history. The 'Old Stone Age' was 'approximately coextensive' with the Pleistocene Epoch and a portion of the earlier Pliocene Epoch; beginning about 2.5 million years ago and ending approximately 12,000 years BP (10,000 BC) when it was succeeded by The Mesolithic Period. ***Science has concluded the main event of the Paleolithic Period was the 'evolution' of the human species from an apelike creature, or near-human creature, to true Homo sapiens.*** Science claims such development was *exceedingly slow and continuous throughout the entire extent of the Old Stone Age.* In the chart of *'The Geologic Timetable & the 6th Day of Creation'* in this chapter, notice that the Pleistocene Epoch ended ~10,000 years BC (i.e., 12,000 years ago), and was succeeded by the Holocene Epoch. The Holocene Epoch is the Epoch in which we live.

o   *Lower Paleolithic Epoch Tools and their Makers (From ~ 2.5 million yrs. ago to ~ 300,000 years BP).*

In the first or earliest phase of the Old Stone Age (i.e., the *Lower* Old Stone Age) the first tools made were simple stone choppers such as were discovered in East Africa at Olduvai Gorge in Tanzania. It is arguably thought these simple tools were made about 2.5—2 million years ago by a creature that walked upright with a bipedal stride but had a brain that was much smaller than Neanderthals and Cro-Magnons. Nevertheless, the shape of its skull suggests its cerebral hemispheres *were more developed* than those of *gorillas, apes, and chimpanzees.* That creature has been named *Australopithecus afarensis.* Perhaps the best-known specimen of A. afarensis is *'Lucy,'* a partial skeleton that was found in 1974 AD at Hadar, Ethiopia. The two features used to distinguish other primates from humans are an *erect bipedal gate*, and a *large brain size.* While *A. afarensis* is believed to have had an upright bipedal gait and cerebral hemispheres that were larger than the great apes, there is still controversy as to whether or not *'it'* can be properly considered an early human. Nevertheless, it seems some scientists think *'he'* more properly should be considered an early ancestor of modern man. The tools of *Australopithecus afarensis* were those of *the Pebble and Flake Tool Tradition*s. The question is: *'Did he fashion his tools, or did nature fashion them?'*

Two other species that made stone tools during the *Lower* Old Stone Age were also creatures we have already mentioned — *Homo habilis* and *Homo erectus.* H. habilis began using the Oldowan tools (of the Pebble and Flake Tool traditions) about 1 million years ago. The fossils of *H. erectus* and the tools he made have been found in China, Asia, Africa, and Europe. They date from 1.5 million to 300,000 years BP. The stone tools of *'his'* early period were also of *the Oldowan type.* They were *core tools*, made by chipping a stone cobble to form a cutting edge, *and flake tools*, made by striking fragments off of a *'flake'* of stone. But, by the time H. erectus migrated to Europe about 500,000 years BP, many of them were fashioning the more advanced *Acheulian tools and were using Hand axes.*

   o *The Middle Paleolithic Epoch (The Middle* Old Stone Age*)* ~ 300,000 to ~ 30,000 yrs. BP.

(NEANDERTHAL'S PRIMACY.)

The *Middle* Old Stone Age in Europe began around 300,000 BP and lasted to about 30,000 BP. It was succeeded by the *New* Old Stone Age, or Neolithic Period. In the Middle East, cultures advanced more rapidly than in Europe and Neolithic communities developed in the Middle East as early as 9,000 years BP. The *Middle* Old Stone Age is associated with *Neanderthal Man*, a higher order primate that we have already mentioned, which appeared around 150,000 years BP and became dominant around 100,000 years ago. *Neanderthal Man* became extinct about 30,000 years BP. The Neanderthals were typically cave dwellers. Archaeological findings show he was well acquainted with the use of fire. His cultural remains, though predominately found in Europe, have also been found in North Africa, Israel, and Siberia. The Neanderthal tools are mostly of the *flake tool tradition* but were much more sophisticated than the tools discovered with the fossils of H. habilis and H. erectus. The presence of bone needles indicates Neanderthals fashioned crudely sewn clothing from furs and animals' skins. They also painted their dead before burial, suggesting that a primitive religion may have been practiced. At least, this practice indicates they honored their dead.

   o *The Upper Paleolithic Epoch* (The *Upper* Old Stone Age) ~30,000 yrs. BP to ~ 12,000 yrs. BP

(CRO-MAGNON PRIMACY)

In the last phase of the Old Stone Age, (i.e., the *Upper* Old Stone Age or Upper Paleolithic Epoch), Neanderthals disappeared and were replaced by *Cro-Magnon Man*. There is no evidence to suggest *Cro-Magnon Man* was descended from or related to *Neanderthal Man*. Both species of these two 'Man-like' Hominids are believed to have appeared *as separate and independent creations*, but some scientists argue this point.

     The *Upper* Old Stone Age includes the period of time during which the *Cro-Magnons* were the only surviving man-like hominids on Earth. *Cro-Magnons* appeared ~ 50,000 years ago BP just before the end of the *Middle* Old Stone Age during the time of the *Neanderthal's Primacy*. Science refers to them as the *"AMHs,"* for *"Anatomically Modern Humans."* Scientists believe the Cro-Magnons, who were anatomically identical to modern-day man, *behaviorally* became modern humans. Thus, many scientists believe the advent of modern-day man on Earth occurred about 50,000 years BP, when the *Cro-Magnons* first appeared. That is how most scientists interpret the fossil record.

     The *Upper* Old Stone Age (or Upper Paleolithic Epoch) saw an astonishing number of Cro-Magnon cultures. The beginnings of communal hunting and extensive fishing became prominent practices world-wide. Cro-Magnons also developed belief systems (early religions as it were) based mostly on magic and the supernatural. *'Venus figurines,'* the name given to a nearly universal type of art found in association with Cro-Magnon fossils and artifacts, appeared first in the *Upper* Old Stone Age about 30,000 years ago. These small statuettes are thought to be the *'hard'* evidence that Cro-Magnons may have been the first culture on Earth to have developed some form of primitive religion.

Some Cro-Magnons left their caves and started building their own homes. The so-called *'Pit houses'* are an early example of this practice. Although better than their cave dwellings, the living conditions in Pit Houses was very bleak — or so I thought when I visited a Pit house community on the shore of the North Sea in Scotland in 2002. Nevertheless, Archeologists tell us Cro-Magnons wore sewn clothing and *originated sculpture* and *painting*. Over time, Cro-Magnon tools became even more advanced and of a greater variety, including flint and obsidian tools and projectile points of *the Blade Tool Tradition*. They also made necklaces and other personal ornaments of bone, ivory, and horn. As mentioned before, their art included outline drawings using various colors.

THE MAGDALENIAN CULTURE

One of the most impressive cultures of the entire Stone Age was a Cro-Magnon culture that developed in the last phase of the Upper Paleolithic Epoch. This Cro-Magnon culture is known as the *Magdalenian Culture.* Named for a rock shelter in the Vézère valley in France, the Magdalenian culture developed about 17,000 years BP and extended to about 9,000 BP towards the end of the last major Ice Age. The Magdalenian culture was actually widespread and initially extended from Portugal, in the West, to Poland in the East! The artifacts of this culture reflect a society of communities of *fishermen* and *reindeer hunters*. Their tools ranged from tiny microliths to implements of great length and fineness that were indicative of advanced technological skill. For a Stone Age People, their weapons were highly advanced, refined and varied. Along the southern edge of the great ice sheets, these people fashioned boats and developed harpoons with which they attacked the great sea mammals. Eventually the weapons technology of this culture spanned the entire world. Perhaps the *atlatl* represents the most advanced weapon of their culture and became the preferred long-range weapon of the world until it was replaced by the bow and arrow. Because the *atlatl* is so innovative, and because an understanding of the uniqueness of this weapon will impress you and give you some insight into the intelligence of these early people, I want to take a bit of ink and paper to describe it and its history.

AN ATLATL IN POSITION FOR THROWING A FLEXIBLE DART.[884]

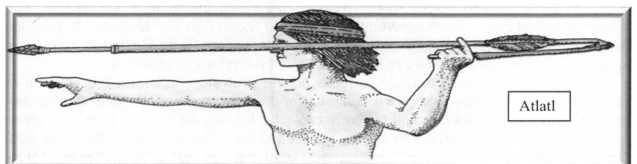

Atlatl

Image Courtesy: aol.com. query 'atlatl' and select: 'Search for images of atlatl.'

---

[884] Article: ***Atlatl:*** by Kathy Goldner Query: *atlatl*
   http://associations.missouristate.edu/mas/macquest/desk/atlatlindex.html

THE SAGA OF EARTH'S 1ST SOPHISTICATED COMPOUND WEAPON—THE ATLATL & DART SYSTEM. Although the sling may be older, the atlatl is a more sophisticated compound weapon. It is a short stick (about 2 feet long — about the length of one's forearm). It has a tiny hook on its end. The weapon is gripped by placing the throwing hand on the end opposite the hook. The atlatl is placed parallel to the shaft of a flexible lightweight 5-6-foot-long dart with its hook fitted into a tiny hole bored into the butt end of the dart. It is held by firmly gripping the throwing handle on the most forward part of the atlatl after it is placed parallel to the shaft of the dart. The thumb and index finger of the throwing hand keep the lightweight dart parallel to the shaft of the atlatl. As the dart is thrown, the thumb and index finger are released. The atlatl then becomes a lever for catapulting the dart down range. During the throwing motion the only part of the atlatl that maintains the longest period of contact with the dart shaft is the tiny hook which contacts the butt end of the dart. With training, the thrower can effectively use the atlatl to increase his leverage power in throwing the dart. Unlike a heavy rigid spear, which was Neanderthal's most advanced weapon, the dart used with *the Cro-Magnon's atlatl* is lightweight, extremely flexible, and shorter than a spear. However, it is longer than an arrow. When thrown, the force of the throw sets up a force of *'spring-like' kinetic energy* in the dart that causes the shaft of the thrown dart to *oscillate* while it is in flight. *This pent-up kinetic energy* that is imparted to the dart at release, *increases* both the *range* and *the striking power of the dart.* With the leveraged power provided by the atlatl, darts were easily thrown 100 yards or more! This is what is meant by the term *'compound weapon.'* It is a matter of physics.

A compound weapon is one that enhances human power. Because the atlatl is essentially a lever that doubles the length of the thrower's forearm, a dart thrown with an atlatl can easily deliver 200 times as much power and 6 times the range of *a traditionally thrown spear.* With the leverage the atlatl provides, a 5-ounce 6-foot dart can be thrown at 100 mph and have as much impact as an arrow fired from a 60-pound compound bow! The atlatl is certainly a very powerful and impressive example of a highly advanced weapons technology. The fact that it *"sprang forth"* (pun intended) from the minds of prehistoric ancient man-like hominids is even more impressive.

In some remote places in our modern-day world the atlatl is still in use. The effectiveness of this weapon allowed the *Upper* Old Stone Age Cro-Magnons to hunt Ice Age mega-fauna such as the *Giant Woolly Mammoth and the Giant Mastodon.* They were so successful it is believed they hunted these giant mammals to extinction.

Eventually the bow and arrow replaced the prehistoric atlatl as the weapon of choice because the bow was more compact, and easier to carry. Arrows were lighter, shorter, and more of them could be carried by the hunter. Also, more than one arrow could be made from the length of wood required to make one atlatl throwing dart. Nevertheless, we must remember that the atlatl was an extremely effective force-multiplier weapon, which may have preceded the bow and arrow by as much as 9,000 years!

Largely replaced by the bow and arrow in the *Middle* Stone Age, the atlatl was still the major long-range weapon being used by some Native Americans 520 years ago, when Columbus encountered natives armed with atlatls during his voyages to the New World in 1492 AD. Although the atlatl had been invented by pre-historic Cro-Magnons in

Europe, the Spaniards (who had never known the weapon) soon discovered their vulnerability to it when they waged their wars of conquest in the New World. In the 16ᵗʰ Century AD, when the Spanish Conquistadors invaded Central America, the Aztecs re-adopted the atlatl because of its incredible power. They weren't able to triumph over the massed firepower of the Spanish firearms, but many a Conquistador was killed when an armor-piercing dart (that was thrown from a considerable distance) completely passed through his steel breastplates — both front and back. The Aztecs are all gone now, but at one time or another, people everywhere have used the atlatl as their main weapon for hunting and for war. The atlatl is still used today by natives of Alaska, Australia, and Papua New Guinea. Some tribes in South America and Northwest Mexico still use the atlatl. The aborigines of Australia call it the *Woomera*. Native Alaskans of the lower Yukon call it the *Nuqaq*.

Archeologists tell us that in the last Ice Age of the Pleistocene Epoch, hunters tracking herds across the frozen tundra crossed *Beringia* (the land bridge between Siberia and North America). Somewhere around 20,000 years ago, across the frozen tundra of what is now the state of Alaska these hunters became the first immigrants to enter the North American continent. These hunter-gatherers brought with them the atlatl, a weapon that reigned supreme among them and their descendants for thousands of years to come. It was the first true weapons-system developed by *anatomically modern humans (AMHs)*.

The atlatl originated in Europe somewhere around 20,000 years ago and spread to every corner of the globe. In fact, the *Atlatl* and *Dart* were used and improved upon for so long by *early man-like hominids and modern man* that (by comparison), *the Bow and Arrow* can be considered *a recent development in projectile technology!* So powerful and effective was the atlatl that scientists and scholars speculate (along with the overkill tactics so common to the human race), the atlatl may have been responsible for the *extinction* of *the Giant Mastodons and the Giant Woolly Mammoths* in North America before the end of the last Ice Age of the Pleistocene Epoch. Thus, we see that with the appearance of this weapon on the scene of world history, we have the most dangerous species in the world — 'man' — possibly causing the only examples of one species of life driving two other species of life into extinction in early "*modern times.*" However, it was in what is now Alaska, that the weapon was developed to its fullest potential. Typically for our species, Native Americans tinkered and toyed with this weapon system, developing, and improving the technology to such a high level of sophistication that it is impressive even by today's standards.

Today, you can see demonstrations of the Atlatl in many places. I was exceptionally impressed by one at Meadowcroft (an Upper Paleolithic rock-shelter, i.e., an Upper Old Stone-Age rock-shelter-community) museum near Pittsburgh, PA. that dates to ~19,000 years ago BP, and also another at the Revolutionary War Museum in Camden, SC. At both places they let me try my "hand" at throwing an atlatl dart.

II. **MESOLITHIC PERIOD CULTURES (THE MIDDLE STONE AGE)** ~ *12,000 — ~ 9000 BP Mid East or ~ 3,000 BP in Europe:* A wide variety of hunting, fishing, and food gathering techniques developed during this period of man's history. Changing ecological conditions associated with global warming caused the end of the Ice Ages of the Pleistocene Epoch. The resultant world-wide retreat of glaciers caused the growth of forests in the temperate zones and the appearance of deserts in North Africa. Gone were the giant mammals of the last vestiges of the Pleistocene. For the first time, one animal ('*man*'), had contributed greatly to the extinction of at least two other animals. In the Mesolithic Period:

- Small Settled communities developed — i.e., hunting and fishing settlements grew up along rivers and lake shores where fish and mollusks were plentiful.
- Microliths (which were typical stone implements of the Middle *Old-Stone* Age) became much smaller and even more delicate than those in the Upper *Old-Stone* Age.
- Crude Pottery appeared.
- *The bow and arrow replaced the atlatl.*
- Hafted axes (axes with handles attached — an improvement over the Old-Stone Age hand-ax), and tools made of bone appeared.

IV. **NEOLITHIC PERIOD CULTURES (I.E., NEW STONE AGE)** ~ *9,000 to* ~ *6,000 years BP in mid-east—ended with the advent of the Bronze Age—which began much later in the less advanced areas of the world.)*

Transitions from the *Middle Stone Age to the New Stone Age* took place at various times in different places. The more temperate zones favored more rapid advancement, so the New Stone Age occurred earlier in the Middle East than in Europe. **So, in the Middle East, the New Stone Age saw the advent of *Adam* (the Biblical first man), who the Bible says was created ~ 5,700 years ago BP.** The New Stone Age ended ~ 6,000-5,000 years ago BP in the Middle East with the advent of ***the Bronze Age*** somewhere around ~ 5500 BP (i.e., ~ 3500 BC in the Mid-East).

Archaeology and anthropology use the term '*Neolithic*' to designate a stage of cultural evolution and technological development characterized by:

- The lack of the discovery of any materials superior to stone for the construction of tools.
- The existence of settled villages (larger than Mesolithic communities). And—
- Societies that became dependent on:
    - Domesticated animals,
    - Domesticated plants —
    - And crafts such as pottery and weaving (baskets from reeds).

That is to say, *Neolithic People* still used tools made of stone and bone, but their stone tools were much more advanced than the tools fashioned in the Paleolithic and Mesolithic Periods. They also domesticated plants. This means they planted and harvested crops. Thus, the Neolithic Period saw the invention of ***agriculture.***

> *The Bible says Cain, (Adam and Eve's first son), was a tiller of the ground (Genesis 4:2). He brought an offering to the Lord of the fruit of the ground (Genesis 4:3).*
> *So, Cain was a farmer (in the New Stone Age—or Neolithic Period).*

Neolithic People also domesticated animals such as cattle, sheep, goats, horses, donkeys, camels, and pigs — i.e., the '*behemah*' as the Bible puts it.

Genesis 4:2 tells us Adam and Eve's second son, Able, was a keeper of flocks. And Genesis 4:4 says Able brought of the firstlings of his flock and of their fat portions to sacrifice to the Lord God. *So, Able was a herder. He tended flocks of animals* (in the New Stone Age—or Neolithic Period).

THE NEOLITHIC PERIOD CROSSED THE TIME-LINE OF ADAM (~ 5,700 YEARS AGO BP).
The *domestication* of *plants* and *animals* is what distinguishes Neolithic culture from the earlier Paleolithic or Mesolithic hunting, fishing, and food-gathering cultures. The people of the Neolithic Period used their animals to help them in their work; provide them with a more efficient form of transportation; provide them with meat, milk, and cheese for food; and serve as valuable commodities for barter and trade. *Neolithic people* were definitely intelligent and resourceful. They were able to change their society from one that primarily *collected* food to one that *produced* food. The people of the Neolithic Period not only developed more abundant and reliable food sources, but they made and used *pottery* and they began to *weave malleable materials*, such as flexible reeds, into practical conveniences, such as *baskets.*

THE LEVANT

One of the most impressive Neolithic cultures was begun by the *Natufian*[885] *people* in the late Neolithic Period in the *Levant*. The Levant is defined as those countries bordering on the eastern Mediterranean Sea, from the Isthmus of Suez to the Taurus Mountains in southern Turkey. The Levant includes present-day Israel, Lebanon, Western Jordan, the Sinai in Egypt, and that part of Syria defined by the Orontes Valley and the region of Aleppo (perhaps the oldest city in Syria). One of the Sultanian entities in the Levant (*Jericho* — in present day Israel), was a key site. Jericho may be the *oldest city* in the world — dating back to the beginning of the Holocene Epoch. On my first tour of Israel, when I entered Jericho, I remember being puzzled by a sign. Their sign said Jericho was founded in 10,000 BC! Now, I understand. Jericho really is that old! The late period Natufian-settled villages played a major role in the emergence of early Neolithic farming communities and brought about an agricultural revolution based upon the cultivation of cereals, such as wheat, barley, and millet. They also domesticated cattle, camels, sheep, goats, and pigs.[886] *Jericho may have been the first city founded by the Natufian people in the Levant.*

Between 8000-4000 BP (6000-2000 BC) Neolithic culture spread through Europe, the Nile River valley (in Egypt), the Indus valley (in India), and the Huang He valley (in Northern China). In the Tigris and Euphrates River valleys of Mesopotamia the Neolithic culture of the Middle East developed into the urban civilizations (i.e., cities) of the Bronze Age by 5500 BP/3500 BC.[887] Before 4000 BP (i.e., before 2000 BC), a distinctive Neolithic culture based on rice cultivation developed in SE Asia.

In the New World, some believe the domestication of plants and animals occurred independently of Old-World developments. In Mexico and South America, the cultivation

[885] Article: *The Natufian Culture in the Levant, Threshold to the Origins of Agriculture:* by Ofer Bar-Yosef—Evolutionary Anthropology p. 159-177 http://www.columbia.edu/itc/anthropology/v1007/baryo.pdf
[886] Article: *The Stone Age: Prehistoric Cultural Stage, or Level of Human Development, Characterized by the Creation and Use of Stone Tools*—by Robert A. Guisepi—http://history-world.org/stone_age.html
[887] Article: *The Stone Age: Prehistoric Cultural Stage, or Level of Human Development, Characterized by the Creation and Use of Stone Tools*—by Robert A. Guisepi—http://history-world.org/stone_age.html

of corn, beans, and squash led to the rise of the Inca and Aztec civilizations ~ 3500 BP (i.e., ~ 1500 BC). Thus, the transition from Mesolithic to Neolithic culture (i.e., from a food-collecting culture to a food-producing culture) gradually took place at different times in different areas. In general terms, advancement occurred sooner in warmer climates and more temperate zones. The Neolithic Period ended when metal tools, writing, and the development of urban centers occurred.[888]

CITIES

It is noteworthy the Bible gives us quite a bit of information about the Neolithic culture of the Mid East, and its transition to the building of cities. For example, when God punished Cain for the murder of his brother, Able, God told him he would become a vagrant and a wanderer on the Earth because the ground would no longer yield crops to him (Genesis 4:12). Then in Genesis 4:17, we are told Cain had relations with his wife and she conceived and gave birth to his first son — Enoch. Next, Cain built a city and named the city *Enoch*, after his son. The transition from small villages to urban centers (cities) was a major transition and would not have been possible if men had not managed to become efficient producers of food. With the creation of cities came the development of a multitude of trades other than farming and animal husbandry. With the growth of urban centers, as the trade for goods and services grew, *writing* became necessary first to record business transactions, and later for other purposes. When men began to write, they began to record their history. The word "***prehistoric***" means *"before recorded history."* Read that: "***Before Writing!***"

CRO-MAGNON PRIMACY, FARMING, WEAVING, POTTERY, BRONZE AGE, AND WRITING[889]

About 30,000 years ago Neanderthal man disappeared and was replaced by Cro-Magnon man. The timeline on Earth of these two species over-lapped for about 20,000 thousand years, but Neanderthals and Cro-Magnons were very different species — arguably unrelated to each other. Cro-Magnon morphology was the same as we humans today. For that reason, modern science treats the Cro-Magnons as the ancestors of modern humans. With the appearance of Cro-Magnons, we see evidence of a geometric degree of advancement of motor skills over and above the motor skills possessed by the Neanderthals. Finely shaped bone tools and trinkets were buried alongside the skeletons of deceased Cro-Magnons. Even before 10,000 years ago (BP), at the close of the Pleistocene Epoch, Cro-Magnon settlements spread from Europe to the Ukraine and Siberia, and then across northern Canada. Stone lamps with niches carved for the placement of lamp wicks appear among their artifacts and are evidence they used fat or oil as fuel for their lamps. Finely fashioned bone needles indicate they possessed the skills for sewing garments of a higher order of refinement than those worn by Neanderthals.

FARMING, WEAVING, & POTTERY

Somewhere around 10,000-8,000 years ago the beginning of farming occurred in what is present-day central Israel and northern Syria. By 9,000 years ago, reeds were

---

[888] Article: ***The Stone Age: Prehistoric Cultural Stage, or Level of Human Development, Characterized by the Creation and Use of Stone Tools***—by Robert A. Guisepi—http://history-world.org/stone_age.html
[889] Schroeder *The Science of God* Chapter 9 p 130

being woven into baskets, and by 8,000 years ago pottery had been developed. All this — and yet, according to the Bible — no Adam!

In the 11th Chapter of Leviticus, when the Bible talks about the commandments to avoid a list of unclean animals and the carcasses of any unclean animal, this statement is made:

> 'As for an earthenware vessel into which one of them
> May fall, whatever is in it becomes unclean and you
> Shall break the vessel.'   Leviticus 11:33

Thus, the Bible talks about *pottery*, its purity and contamination, but makes no mention of when and where it was invented or who invented it. Perhaps no mention of the inventor is made because the invention of pottery (8,000 years ago), *preceded Adam!*[890]

BRONZE AGE

However, as concerns *metalwork*, Genesis attributes *the beginning of the forging of copper and brass* to a particular individual— a son of Lemech who was a descendant of *the* Cain that *murdered* Able.[891]

> 'As for Zillah (the 2nd wife of Lemech) she also
> Gave birth to **Tubal-Cain**, the forger of all **Bronze...**' Genesis 4:22

This seminal event, the Forging of Bronze, marked the end of the Neolithic Period and the beginning of the Bronze Age. The advent of the Bronze Age occurred at different times in different places. When the Bronze Age started in a particular region of the world depended upon the cultural advancement of the people in the various regions. Scientists tell us this happened around 5000 years ago (i.e., ~ 3000 years BC), in the Middle East. According to the Bible, the Bronze Age began *after* the advent of Adam and was started by the discovery of *Tubal-Cain*, a descendant of Adam's first son (Cain) approximately 700 years after Adam. Biblical scholars think Tubal-Cain forged his first batch of Bronze somewhere around 5000 years BP (i.e., ~ 3000 BC).[892]*

ADAM, WRITING, & HISTORY

The Bible tells us Adam was created by God ~ 5700 years ago BP. We get that date from the Genealogies of the descendants of Adam listed in the Book of Genesis. Also, according to the Bible, *the Genealogy of Adam* (one that goes from Adam to Noah) which is in the 5th Chapter of Genesis — had been recorded in a Book — *The Book of the Generations of Adam* (Genesis 5:1). The implication of this phrase is that *books existed at the time* and *the Genealogy of the Generations of Adam to Noah was recorded in a book*. Thus, if books existed at that time, then the ability to write had existed *prior* to *the Book of the Generations of Adam*.

There is an Arab legend that credits *another Enoch* with inventing writing. *This Enoch was a descendant of Adam through Seth — not* the descendant of the same name through Cain's line. This *Enoch* was the father of Methuselah and pleased God so much that God took him straight to heaven (Gen. 5:18-24). He, Elijah, and possibly Melchizedek

---

[890] Schroeder *The Science of God* Chapter 9 p 130*c*
[891] Schroeder *The Science of God* Chapter 9 p 130*c*
[892] Schroeder *The Science of God* Chapter 9 p 130*c* ***(Some scientists say it occurred ~ 3300 BC/about 400 years after Adam.)**

are the only persons in the Bible who were spared mortal death (Gen. 5:21-24; II Kings 2:1-11 [cf. Mal. 4:1-6 and Heb 7:1-10]). If I could have only two mysteries in the Bible explained to me, I would ask God to tell me more about Melchizedek and this particular *Enoch*.

Archeologists have made discoveries that *predate the invention of writing to ~ 5000—6000* years ago.[893] Archeological discoveries that *predate* the invention of writing are referred to by scientists as being *'prehistoric' (i.e., before written history).* Cuneiform (the first form of writing), dates to the Biblical time of Adam and Eve.[894] Theologists refer to *the time of Adam as the beginning of humankind (i.e., humanity), and Civilization.* Archaeology holds that *the invention of writing marked the beginning of history.* By this, they mean *'written history.'* Perhaps these two perspectives have something in common. *The Chinese word for civilization means: 'the uplifting force of writing.'*[895]

I have found the following charts from Dr. Schroeder's book, *The Science of God*, to be most enlightening.

A TIMELINE FROM CREATION TO ABRAHAM[1]

Big Bang 15.75 Billion	Sun 4.6 BP	Earth 4.5 BP	Neandertal Man 150,000 BP	Cro-Magnon Man 50,000 BP	Agri-Culture 10,000 BP	Pottery 8,000 BP	Adam Writing Neshama 5,700 BP	Bronze Age 5,000 BP	Noah's Flood 4,000 BP	Abraham ~3,800 BP ~2,000 BC

According to the Jewish Calendar, Abraham was born in 1948 years after Adam and Eve. The modern state of Israel was established in 1948 AD. The coincidence is intriguing.[2]

A TIMELINE FROM CREATION TO THE PRESENT

I← Six Days of Creation (billions of *years ago before Adam*).	→IAdam ← ~5700 Years BP to Present)

I Start of the 6ᵗʰ Day IAdam created @ the end of the 6ᵗʰ Day.
I (250 million years before Adam)

Day One	Day Two	→through Day Five	→ Day Six	→ I ←Adam	0	1948 AD
15.75 Billion BP	7.75 Billion BP		250 million			
BEGINNING			yrs. BP	Adam~3700 BC	Christ	Modern Israel

This concludes our discussion of what the Bible says in Genesis 1:24 and how the broad categories of animals mentioned in this verse are interpreted by the Genesis Code. This also concludes my cursory summary of what modern science has to say about the animals of the 6ᵗʰ Day of Creation that this verse covers. I hope this discussion has been succinct enough for you to see there is an incredible continuity of the convergence of agreement between the Bible and Modern-Day Science concerning the 6ᵗʰ Day.

⚜

A DISCUSSION OF GENESIS 1:25

Now, look at the next verse, Genesis 1:25. Then, we will talk a bit about what the ancient Jewish sages had to say about this verse.

Gen.1:25 *And God made* **the beasts of the Earth** *after their kind, and the cattle after their kind, and everything that creeps on the ground after its kind; and God saw that it was good. (NASB)*

---

[893] Schroeder *The Science of God* Chapter 9 p 130*d*
[894] Schroeder *The Science of God* Chapter 9 p 130*d*
[895] Schroeder *The Science of God* Chapter 9 p 130*e*

THIS IS HOW THE KING JAMES BIBLE PUTS IT.

Gen. 1:25 *And God made **the beasts of the earth** after his kind, and cattle after their kind, and everything that creepeth upon the earth after his kind: and God saw that it was good. (The King James Version)*

APPLYING THE GENESIS CODE TO GENESIS 1:25

Gen. *1:25 And Elohim made ('asah'— to make from some already created substance) the creatures and things (chay), and '**The beasts of the ground**' of the Earth according to their species (miyn), and the large four-footed dumb animals such as the domesticated cattle (bᵉhemah) according to their species (miyn), and every reptile (remes) and creeping thing (remes) of the ground ('adamah) according to their species (miyn). And Elohim saw (ra'ah) that it was good — a good thing (towb).* (The Genesis Code)

Since we have already talked about the chay, the remes, the bᵉhemah, and the Hebrew word for species (miyn) in our discussion of Genesis 1:24, we now need to turn our attention to the phrase: '**The beasts of the ground**' (the Interlinear Bible), or '**the beasts of the Earth.**' (as the New American Standard Bible and The King James Version put it).

BEASTS OF THE EARTH/BEASTS OF THE FIELD/RULERS OF THE FIELD [896]

Let's now examine the phrase '**the beasts of the Earth.**' This phrase (in Genesis 1:24 and 1:25) is found not only in the New American Standard Bible, but also in the Revised Standard Translation, the King James Version of the Bible, and the Interlinear Bible — a Hebrew to English translation. Most of us pass over this phrase as if we know its meaning. Most people *assume* it is simply a reference to the wild animals that roam the Earth. But the ancient Hebrew sages attached a different meaning to the phrase. Their different interpretation came from the deeper meaning of the original Hebrew text. Simply put, they considered '**the beasts of the Earth**' to be **nonhuman creatures (animals) that had a human morphology.** According to Dr. Schroeder, there are many ancient references to 'beasts' (in the wording of the Talmud), *that lacked only the neshama to make them human!* In one reference in *the Talmud Keliim* (8:5), this type of beast (*rulers of the field* is their formal name), *is described as being so human-like in bodily appearance that the ancients gave the same respect to its corpse as they did a human corpse!*[897] The scholars of the Talmud understood that with death, *the neshama leaves the body.* Therefore, *with the neshama gone,* there would be no way to distinguish a human corpse from the corpse of one of *the beasts of the Earth* that the Bible mentions.[898] We will touch on this subject again when we reach Genesis 2:7 (in Book III); but for now, let's next consider what Maimonides believed.

MAIMONIDES: ON THE BEASTS OF THE EARTH [899]

[896] Schroeder *The Science of God* Chapter 9 p. 140c
[897] Schroeder *The Science of God* Chapter 9 p. 140c
[898] Schroeder *The Science of God* Chapter 9 p. 140c
[899] Schroeder *The Science of God* Chapter 9 p. 141a

In 1190 AD, Maimonides wrote about a passage in the Talmud that discusses the possibility of the existence of nonhuman creatures on the Earth in Adam's time that had a human morphology but were not truly human *because they lacked the neshama* (i.e., the God-breathed soul of human life). This passage in the Talmud deals with what *may have happened* between Adam and Eve after their first son, Cain, murdered their second son, Able.

GENESIS 4:25 TELLS US:
"And Adam knew again his wife and she bore a son
And called his name Seth." (The Interlinear Bible: Hebrew to English)

ONLY FOUR VERSES LATER, GENESIS 5:3 TELLS US:
"And Adam lived 130 years, and fathered a son
In his own likeness, according to his image
And called his name Seth." (TIB: Hebrew to English)

Maimonides said the Talmud held that a subtle fact *was implied* by the Biblical description of the same event from two slightly different perspectives.[900] The Talmud *deduces* from these two verses that following the trauma of Cain murdering Abel, Adam and Eve separated. It was not until 130 years after Cain murdered Abel that *"Adam knew again his wife Eve"*[901] From the Talmud's perspective, the — 'again knew his wife Eve' — is superfluous and therefore it teaches something. The scholars who wrote the Talmud thus agreed *that the something which was being taught was that during those 130 years of separation, Adam had sexual relations with other beings.* The nature of those beings is not clear. However, according to the Talmud, from these unions with other beings came children that were *not human* in the true sense of the word. *They did not have the spirit of God (i.e., the neshama, which is the God-breathed spirit of life).*

According to Jewish tradition it has been acknowledged from ancient times that a being, which does not possess the spirit of God (*the neshama*) is not human. Such a creature was merely an animal — an animal that had human shape and form, but an animal that lacked *the neshama* and was thus not truly human.[902] Thus, it is there are ancient, accepted sources that describe animals with human shape, form, intelligence, and judgment that looked exactly like human beings, but were nevertheless not truly human! Suddenly cave paintings that predate Adam by 20,000 years and the archeological evidence that proves the pre-Adam 10,000-year-old inception of agriculture and the pre-Adam 8,000-year-old inception of pottery become understandable. *These less-than-human creatures had human-like skills.* According to the Talmud and ancient Jewish tradition — *what they lacked was human spirituality.*[903]

So, Dr. Schroeder asks the question: *With whom did Adam have relations? Eve was the only other human woman there.* The answers given in the ancient commentaries imply there were other mates available to Adam that were not human. Could they have been Cro-Magnon creatures?[904] The ancient sages knew nothing about the fossil

[900] Schroeder *The Science of God* Chapter 9 p. 141*b*
[901] Schroeder *The Science of God* Chapter 9 p. 141*c*
[902] Schroeder *The Science of God* Chapter 9 p. 141*d*
[903] Schroeder *The Science of God* Chapter 9 p. 141*e*
[904] Schroeder *The Science of God* Chapter 9 p. 141*f*

evidence of the existence of Cro-Magnon creatures when these ancient commentaries were written, but the paleontological discoveries of modern science certainly prove that Cro-Magnon creatures existed on Earth in Adam's day. In Chapter 23 and in Chapter 28 (both in Book III), we will expand the discussion of this possibility.

THUS ENDS THE 2ND TELLING OF THE CREATION ACCOUNT.

The 2nd Telling has been the most difficult part of this book to write because so much science and history is involved. I also think the 2nd Telling is the most difficult part of the book to read — for the same reason. This is the part of the book where I expected to find conflicts between the Biblical Account of Creation and Modern Science that could not be resolved. For several years I struggled against the Holy Spirit and resisted the idea of writing of this book. I often prayed and asked: *Who am I to write such a book — why me — of all people — and to what purpose?* I knew the undertaking would require several years of Biblical and Scientific research, study, and writing. I also knew the writing of this book would consume me. Furthermore, I sensed that *if* the book were ever written and read, it could cause controversy and criticism. For five years I felt His urging — but still resisted. Nevertheless, the Holy Spirit was persistent. So, I finally gave in with the proviso that if I ever encountered an impasse that could not be explained and resolved (either by bad science or a misinterpretation of the scriptures)—The Holy Spirit would allow me to quit, walk away, and this book would never *see the light of day.* To my surprise, that did not happen. There were times I thought an impasse had been reached — only to be given the answer in a dream. If you have read this far, you have also been persistent and must have found something of value. Take heart. Book III has been much easier to write. I also suspect it will be easier to read.

THE 6TH DAY OF GENESIS[905] LASTED 250 MILLION EARTH YEARS

Day #	Start of Day 6	End of Day 6	Bible's Description	Scientific Description
Six	250 Million yrs. Before Adam	~5,700 yrs. Before the Present when Adam Was Created	God willed the Earth to bring forth a large variety of living creatures and "the beasts of the earth" after their kind. At the end of the 6th Day, God declared them good. (Gen.1:24-25)	A series of cataclysmic changes occurred in which the multiple varieties of life created went through multiple extinctions. Giants came and went. In the evening of the 6th Day, Hominids and two Man-like Hominids appeared. At the end of the 6th Day God created Adam, and the primacy of "man" was established.

Summary Points:
- The Bible and Science define *'man'* differently.
- According to the Bible, the final creation was the *making* and the *creating* of *man* at the close of the 6th Day.

---

[905] Schroeder The Science of God Chapter 4 (Table) p 67

- After that, God rested, on the 7th Day.
- The Bible is so eager to get to the making of man at the end of the 6th Day — that no details of the other animals that were made on the 6th Day are given.
- Time-flow in the first Chapter of Genesis for verses 1 through 25 is God-based. Time-flow in the rest of the first Chapter of Genesis (verses 26—31), and for all of Genesis Two and the rest of the Bible, is man-based.
- The man-based time-flow in the Creation Account is referred to in this study as 'The 3rd Telling.' It is the same 24-hour day-night cycle that we experience today.
- The Genesis Code informs us the animals Elohim made and formed on the 6th Day (including the first man — Adam), had the God-given soul of animal life (i.e., the *nefesh* or *nephesh,* in Hebrew).
- The *nefesh* directs animal behavior, and according to Hebrew Theology, it influences the behaviors that induce animals to seek food, reproduce, protect, and nurture their young, seek pleasure, and avoid pain and injury. The *nefesh* maximizes an animal's chances for survival
- One might say the *nefesh* could in some ways be considered the driving engine of our eros, or what the New Testament refers to as our *'lower nature.'* Some Psychiatrists might even consider it synonymous with the Freudian concept of the *'id.'*
- The Bible says the animals that Elohim made on the 6th Day came forth from the Earth *'according to their kind.'*
- The Genesis Code informs us they came forth from the Earth according to their species (*miyn* — in Hebrew).
- Today, the evolutionary changes that are observed in nature occur only at the level of the species and involve genetic changes in the *traits* of an animal that do not involve any change in the animal's *basic-body-plan.* This type of evolution is now called — *'microevolution.'* On this point, science now agrees with what the Bible has stated all along.
- Darwin's concept of evolution is what modern science now calls — *'macroevolution.'* It finds no support in the Bible, in the fossil record, or in the lab.
- There is no firm consensus among scientists concerning *which* hominid species represented the first or earliest human on Earth; or exactly how, when, or where the first modern human *'evolved.*
- On the other hand, the Bible is very specific about who the first human was and when he appeared. That individual will be the main topic of the next chapter.
- Scientists agree, the orbit of the Earth, which dictates the changes of the distance between Earth and the Sun, is the root cause of the micro-seasonal changes we experience (i.e., winter, fall, spring, and summer).
- **But the notion that man's use of fire, fossil fuels, and fondness for meat (and therefore his raising of cattle and poultry) are responsible for Global Warming — is sheer lunacy!**
- **The fires within the Earth's interior that are evident in the volcanic eruptions that have occurred for billions of years — not only formed the Earth's atmosphere and oceans and dictated the many geographic changes the**

Earth has undergone; but (according to OCCAM'S RAZOR, cf. Chapter 27 Book III), the geologic history of the Earth tells us the "waxing and waning" of Volcanism is the root cause of the cyclical macro-environmental EPOCHS OF GLOBAL WARMING and ICE AGES the Earth has experienced during its 4.5-billion-year history!

- Our most recent epoch of Global Warming (i.e., the Holocene Epoch) fostered the development of our current-day civilizations. When it began at the end of the Pleistocene Epoch (some 12,000 years ago), the man-like hominids — came out of their caves!

- The idea man can legislate an end to Global Warming is not only ignorance. It is arrogant ignorance and pure insanity!

- Imagine what will happen when we enter another ICE AGE! We could go back to the time when the earth was a SNOWBALL, AND ALL LIFE BECAME EXTINCT.

- However, St. Peter prophesied the old Earth and old Heavens will be destroyed by fire. The fire is already here and has been here for the last 4.5 billion years! <u>It is about 30 miles beneath your feet (</u>cf. Chp. 12 Book II)!

- If you are a Christian, don't worry about the future destruction of the Earth by fire — because you won't be here when it happens (cf. "THE DAY OF THE LORD" prophecy by the Apostle Peter: in Chapter 7 of Book I near the end of the discussion of "BLACK HOLES TODAY."

Thus ends Book II.

THE COSMOGONY OF THE ANCIENT OF DAYS:
MODERN SCIENCE AGREES WITH MOSES & NAHMANIDES
Book III—Act III: The 3rd Telling

FROM THE END OF THE 6TH DAY TO THE END OF THE 7TH DAY (24 HOURS) FROM MAN'S PERSPECTIVE, WITH THE MAKING & CREATING OF EARTH'S FIRST MAN, ADAM—IN MAN'S TIME-FLOW

ON THE 7TH DAY ELOHIM RESTED, REPOSED, AND RESET THE EARTH'S CLOCK TO THE SAME 24-HOUR PER DAY RATE OF TIME-FLOW THAT ADAM WOULD EXPERIENCE AND THE EARTH EXPERIENCES TODAY.

HE CALLED THE 7TH DAY 'THE SABBATH' & DECLARED IT HOLY. ELOHIM ALSO MADE A HELPER FOR ADAM

AND CREATED THE GARDEN OF EDEN IN WHICH ALL THINGS

WERE FREE EXCEPT FOR ONE FORBIDDEN THING.

BY: Dr. David E. Marley, Jr. M.D. (O. David)

BOOK III IS FROM ADAM'S PERSPECTIVE
CONTENTS OF BOOK III:

BOOK III ILLUSTRATIONS:

CHAPTER 23: THE 6TH DAY—MAN: 'MADE' in 'HIS IMAGE': Gen. 1:26-27

The following verses are quoted from the New American Standard Bible (NASB). Some of the original Hebrew words are included. The Hebrew words (in parentheses) are the words the underlined words in the English translation represent. They can be found in the Hebrew to English translation of Genesis 1:26 and 1:27 in The Interlinear Bible (TIB): a Hebrew-English translation.   O.David

Genesis 1:26 Then <u>God</u> (Elohim) said, "Let Us '<u>make</u>' ('asah) <u>man</u> (adam) in Our <u>image</u> (tslm), according to Our <u>likeness</u> (demusth); and let them <u>rule</u> (radah — i.e., <u>have dominion</u>) over the fish of the sea and over the birds of the sky and over the cattle and over all the Earth, and over every creeping thing that creeps on the Earth." (NASB/TIB)

Genesis 1:27 And <u>God</u> (Elohim) '<u>created</u>' (barah) <u>man</u> (adam) in His own <u>image</u> (tslm); in the <u>image</u> (tslm) of <u>God</u> (Elohim) He '<u>created</u>' (barah) him; <u>male</u> (zakar) and <u>female</u> (neqebah) He '<u>created</u>' (barah) them. (NASB/TIB)

The 3rd Telling of the Creation Account begins with Genesis 1:26. It is an account of creation events told from man's perspective. It differs from the 1st and 2nd Tellings in that respect. Notice the Hebrew word for 'man' in these verses is 'adam.' Also notice that adam is spelled using the lower case. In our discussions of the First Chapter of Genesis, we have already noted Elohim named some of the things He formed. In Genesis 1:5 He called the light — 'Day' — and the darkness He called — 'Night.' In Genesis 1:8, He called the expanse that separated the waters above from those below — 'Heaven.' When He caused the dry land to appear, He called it — 'Earth.' And the gathering of the waters below, He called — 'seas.' But, in the five English translations of the Bible I have read, the First Chapter of Genesis does not specifically tell us what name Elohim gave to the first 'man.' They do not say God named the first man 'Adam.' The First Chapter of the Creation Account doesn't mention any specific name for the first man other than the generic name, 'man.' In fact, in the New American Standard Bible, we have to wait for Genesis 2:20 to see the name 'Adam' appear. Even then, we are not specifically told Elohim named the first man — 'Adam.'

In various English translations of the Creation Account, the words 'man' and 'Man;' and the words 'adam' and 'Adam' appear at different times and in different verses. For example, in the King James (KJ) and Modern Language (ML) translations I have in my library, the first time the Hebrew word 'Adam' appears in the upper case (as befits a proper name), is in Genesis 2:19, where God brought all of the animals to Adam to see what he would name them. But we are not specifically told God named the first man — Adam.

The first time the first man's name appears in the Revised Standard Version (RSV) as 'Adam' is in Gen. 3:17; where God reprimands 'Adam' for listening to his wife and eating of the fruit of the forbidden tree. The name Adam (in the upper case) appears, but we are not actually told God named him — 'Adam.'

The first time The Interlinear Bible (TIB) changes the name of the first man to the upper case, 'Adam', is in Gen. 4:25; where after the trauma of Cain's murder of Abel, the Interlinear Bible says 'Adam' had relations with his wife again, and their third son, Seth, was born. Again, there is no formal naming.

It is not until *the Fifth Chapter of Genesis* that we are told Elohim named the first humans. This happens after we assume the Creation Account has been completed. Although the Second Chapter describes the idyllic home God planted for the man that He formed — *The Garden of Eden:* and describes the helper and companion He fashioned for *"the man,"* *the man* and *his helper/companion/wife* are not named. The Second Chapter ends with these words:

> *"And the man and his wife were both naked and were not ashamed."*

The Third Chapter of Genesis has nothing to do with Creation. Instead, it describes the temptation of *the woman*, the downfall of *man*, and the *banishment* of the man and his wife from the Garden. Again, in this Chapter, no names are given to *the man and his wife.*

In the Fourth Chapter, darkness envelops man when Cain murders his brother Abel, and Cain is banished and sentenced to become a vagabond and a wanderer. The rest of the Fourth Chapter deals with the genealogy of Cain and the saga of the Bible seemingly moves even further from the Creation Account.

But then, late in the Fourth Chapter, hope is reintroduced when we are told Adam and his wife came together again and produced a third son, Seth — the son from whom we are all descended. Even in the Fourth Chapter there is no formal naming of the first man.

Then, in Genesis 5:1 by mentioning a Book — *the Book of the Generations of Adam*, we are told Elohim named the first humans. We are also told — when God created *'Man'* (Gen. 5:1), He created *"them"* — *"male and female"* — and He blessed them and named them — *"Man"* (Gen. 5:2). Here, *"Man"* is capitalized indicating that *"Man"* is a new species. Here is what the New American Standard Bible (the NASB) says in Gen. 5:1-2.

> *"This is the Book of the Generations of Adam.*
> *In the day when God created man, He made*
> *him in the likeness of God.* (Gen. 5:1)
>
> *He created them male and female, and He*
> *blessed them and named them Man in the day*
> *when they were created."* (Gen. 5:2)

In Genesis 5:2, some English Bibles say: *"and named them Adam."* The Hebrew word 'adam,' which means 'the man', comes from another Hebrew word, 'adamah,' which means 'the earth', or 'the soil' or 'the dust of the ground'.[906] So it is that we see there is a morphing of the Hebrew word for man into the Hebrew name of the first man that occurs at different times in different English translations of the Bible. The name of the first man, 'Adam', morphs from the lower case 'adam' which means 'the man' to the upper case 'Adam' which is the name of the first man.

Notice in Gen. 1:26, after Elohim decides to 'make' man, the same verse says: *"And let them rule over* (i.e., have dominion over) *the fish of the sea and over the birds of the sky and over the cattle and over all the Earth, and over every creeping thing that creeps on the Earth."*

---

906 Schroeder: *The Science of God* Chapter 9 p. 139*b*

Also notice Gen. 1:27 says: *"He 'created' (barah) him; male (zakar) and female (neqebah) He 'created' (barah) them.'*

Although we will have to wait for the second Chapter of Genesis to learn how God made and created the woman (Adam's wife), Gen. 1:26 gives us the hint that when God decided to make and create *the man*, He also decided to make and create his companion. How do we know this? Genesis 1:26 says: *"let them rule,"* and Genesis 1:27 says: *"He created him; male and female He created them."*

There is so much to talk about in Genesis 1:26 and Genesis 1:27. We will begin our discussion by concentrating on the words: *man, made and created*. Later, we will take a look at *image, likeness, and image of God*. And finally, we will talk about: *"Us" and "Our."*

I.   MAN: FIRST 'MADE' AND THEN LATER 'CREATED'

In Gen. 1:26 the Bible tells us God decided first to *'asah'* (to make) man. Then, in verse 1:27, after He had *'made'* man, we see God then *barah* ('created') *man in his own image.* Thus, it is that man was *first 'made' and then later, 'created.'* Previously, when we discussed the deeper meaning of the Hebrew verb *barah* in Genesis 1:1, we learned *barah* is the only word in the Hebrew language that means: *'to create something from nothing.'* Thus, it is that the Bible says that when Elohim began creation, *the universe was first 'created'* (Gen. 1:1) *and then later, 'made'* (over the ensuing 6 days of creation).

Exodus 31:17 adds emphasis to this salient point that God made everything from the substance that He created at the moment of the beginning. This is so important that we must take a moment to look at how Moses recorded that part of a conversation he had with God on Mount Sinai when God gave him the Ten Commandments that God wrote on two tablets of stone with His finger. When speaking to Moses about the Sabbath this is what the LORD said to him.

> *"It (i.e., the Sabbath) is a sign between Me and the sons of Israel forever:*
> *for in six days the LORD made heaven and earth, but on*
> *the seventh day He ceased from labor and was refreshed." (Ex. 31:17)*

When reading this verse, it is important to know the word 'Sabbath' comes from the Hebrew word 'shabat,' meaning 'to rest — to cease from work.' So, the essence of the Sabbath is rest — that on the 7th Day, God rested from all of His labors on *the Six Days of Old*. [907]

Resting on the Sabbath honors God by demonstrating to all who witness our obedience to God's command — we are proclaiming:
- He alone is God!
- Without any help, He single-handedly created all that exists!

The Creator labored on each of the six days of creation to make and form all that now exists — the universe, our Earth, and all life — ourselves included.

So, in the beginning God first created the substrate from which He would later make everything else. Why? Because before Elohim began creation, there was nothing

---

[907] Schroeder The Hidden Face of God Chapter 11 p 181c

with which to make anything! [908] However, in the case of the first human being, the Bible tells us the animal God would later name 'Man' (in Gen. 5:2) was first 'made' (in Gen. 1:26) and then only later 'created' (in Gen. 1:27 and Gen. 2:7). Thus, we see the order of first creating and from then on making, which was applied to everything else in the Creation Account, was reversed when it came to 'the making' of the first human being. The 'Man' who was later named 'Adam' is the only thing in the Creation Account that God first made and then later created.

HOW THE JEWISH SAGES INTERPRETED THIS ORDERING OF EVENTS

The ancient Jewish sages attached a special meaning or interpretation to this ordering of things when it came to the Bible's description of how the first human being came to be. This change of ordering, they claimed, informs us unequivocally that some amount of time passed between the making of the animal man in the lower case — that had only the nefesh (i.e., the animal spirit of life in Gen. 1:26) — and the creating of that particular man (in Gen.1:27 and Gen. 2:7), that God would later (in Gen. 5:2) name 'Man'/or 'Adam' in the upper case.[909]

According to Dr. Schroeder, the amount of time between the making and the creating is not certain from the Biblical text.[910] In their interpretation of these verses the ancient Jewish sages felt what was certain was that the making of Adam's body was not instantaneous. They also were convinced the making of man's body preceded the introduction of the neshama. *Making takes time*, they concluded. Thus, it is — the ancient sages reasoned: ~ 5,700 years ago, the *neshama* (the breath of God/ i.e., the soul of humankind), was implanted into one of the many man-like animals God had already made on the evening of the 6th day. This happened when the Creator breathed *the breath of life* into 'the adam' in Genesis 2:7 and later named the first human being, 'Man'/or 'Adam,' in Genesis 5:2. 'The adam' became 'Adam' only after the making of that first distinctly unique *human* was complete — i.e., had been molded by Elohim into its final form and became *'the specific man, Adam,'* when Elohim breathed the breath of life (the neshama) into his nostrils. Thus, 'Adam' was the first being to possess *both* the nefesh and the neshama. The Sages felt the possession of both the nefesh and the neshama is what distinguished Adam from the anatomically modern humans they called the Nephilim (cf. Genesis 6:4). We call them Cro-Magnons.

We will mention this again when, in the development of our discussion of The 3rd Telling of the Creation Account, we specifically look at the Biblical text in Genesis 2:7.[911]

II.   IMAGE (TSLM), LIKENESS (DEMUSTH), AND IMAGE OF GOD.

Before we talk about the Genesis Code meaning of the Hebrew word most English Bibles have translated as 'image,' I want to talk about my brother-in-law, his tiny pet dog, and the name he gave her.

JOE

My sister was married to the most wonderful man you can imagine. My brother-in-law, Joe, was in his mid-80s when he passed away. He married my sister in 1954. Joe

---

[908] Schroeder The Science of God Chapter 9 p. 138d
[909] Schroeder The Science of God Chapter 9 p. 138e
[910] Schroeder The Science of God Chapter 9 p. 138e
[911] Schroeder The Science of God Chapter 9 p. 139a

belonged to the generation of Americans Tom Brokaw called *'The Greatest Generation.'* After the surprise attack on Pearl Harbor on December 7th, 1941, Joe enlisted in the U.S. Navy. He was underage but was granted permission to enlist by his parents. He served as a radar operator aboard a destroyer (*the USS Mayo*) during the entire U.S. involvement in the European Theater of WWII until the Germans surrendered. He was then transferred to the Pacific fleet and served as a radar operator on another destroyer (*the USS Waller*) until the Japanese surrendered. So, Joe was a veteran of both the German and Japanese theaters of War in WWII. He remembered the historic Japanese surrender to the Allied Forces that took place in Tokyo Bay on September 2nd, 1945, as if it were only yesterday. He was one of the many sailors, soldiers, and airmen who witnessed it.

After WWII, my brother-in-law worked his way through college. He enrolled at the University of Alabama, in Tuscaloosa, and studied Industrial Engineering. However, before he could graduate, Korea happened, and he was reactivated for service in that war. Once again, he served on a USS destroyer as a radar operator. I believe it was *the USS Waller* again. After July 27th, 1953, when the Korean War ended, he returned to Tuscaloosa and finished his degree. In 1954 he graduated from college with a degree in Industrial Engineering. That was also the year he met and married my sister.

Like so many of those who have experienced combat, Joe would not talk about his war experiences. I remember going to his 75th birthday party in Troy, Alabama. A large number of friends and family, and members of Joe's extended family, who I had not seen since the wedding in 1954, were also there. (Joe grew up in Congers, New York, which is about 35 miles north of New York City, near West Point, on the western shore of the Hudson River. Most members of his family live in New York State.)

On the day of his birthday party, my sister placed something new on their living room wall. A few weeks before his birthday party, while rummaging in some old trunks in the attic, my sister discovered a box. In the box, she found eleven Battle Campaign Metals and Citations that he and his ship's company had been awarded for their service in WWII and Korea. Sister had them framed, and after the party in Troy, in the presence of friends and family, she brought them out and proudly hung them on their living room wall. Even then, with everyone questioning him, he would not talk about his war experiences. All he would say was: *"I just served."* Dear reader, please pause a moment. Think about those three words. Joe served in two theaters in WWII, and he fought in the Korean War. His life was on the line every day. Joe served with honor and distinction.

Yes, Joe proudly wore his *"Tin-Can Sailor WWII / Korean War baseball style hat,"* and he was one of the 957 Honor-Flight Vets Baldwin County, Alabama flew to Washington, DC to visit the WWII and Korean War Memorials that honor their service and sacrifice for freedom — but he never talked about his war experiences. Joe was a man of few words, but he was *"a true patriot, and 'gooder' than gold!"* My brother-in-law lived his life — in God's Image!

SHADOW

Several years ago, Sis and Joe moved from Brundidge, Alabama to Daphne, Alabama. Daphne is a small town near the east shore of Mobile Bay. A few months before the move, Joe bought a pet — a Miniature Pinscher, or 'Min Pin.' Although the *Min Pin* looks like a tiny Doberman, it is *not* a Miniature Doberman. Both breeds exist today. However, the

Min Pin predates the Doberman by about 200 years. This dog was one of the cutest dogs imaginable. Joe's tiny dog was exceptionally affable and loveable. She truly loved Joe. My brother-in-law couldn't go anywhere without his dog scrambling to be as near him as possible. As soon as Joe sat in his favorite chair, that little dog would immediately jump in his lap and curl up for a nap. So great was the love of his dog for him that she *shadowed* his every move. That is why he named her — *'Shadow.'*

Some animals are more perceptive than others. If they are loved and treated well, dogs are among the most loyal and loving of all pets. Treat a dog well — care for him — and you will have a friend for life. There are many stories of faithful dogs that have given their lives for their owners. Perhaps that is the ultimate sign of unconditional love. There are some animals that are able to sense the goodness and integrity of a person. They can also sense when a person is a threat. Shadow was one of those dogs. Is it any wonder that man has chosen to name this friend of man — *'dog?'* Perhaps it has not escaped your notice that *'dog'* is *'god'* spelled backwards. Every time I saw Shadow in Joe's lap, I saw an example of unconditional love, and thought of God's unconditional love for us.

"For God so loved the world,
That He gave His only begotten Son,
That whosoever believeth in Him should not perish,
But have everlasting life (John 3:16)."

THE GENESIS CODE MEANING OF 'IMAGE' AND 'LIKENESS.'[912]

Then Elohim said, 'Let Us make man in Our image (tslm), according to Our likeness (demusth). . . Genesis 1:26

The ancient Hebrew word that has been translated in our English versions of Gen.1:26 as *'image,'* is *'tslm.'* For generations English-speaking peoples have believed this phrase means — *'we look like God'* — i.e., there is a corporeal or physical similarity between man and God. In Colossians 1:15, Paul said: *"He (Jesus) is the 'eikon,'* (in Greek / *'icon'* in English) *of the invisible God, the first-born over-all creation." Dr. David Jeremiah said: "This means Jesus is the "exact 'likeness' of God the Father!"* So, on one level of meaning, *"Let Us make man in Our image"* (in Gen. 1:26) means: *When Jesus was born of the Holy Spirit and the virgin Mary, Jesus took on the form of a man and became a human without ceasing to be God. But Jesus gave up His divinity, humbled Himself, and took the form of a bondservant (Phil 2:5-8).* So, Jesus Christ looks like us, and Jesus looks like God. However, Dr. Gerald L. Schroeder says: the deeper meaning of the root of the Hebrew word *"tslm"* and the root-meaning of its Hebrew modifier *"demusth"* is — *"shadow."* So, on another level of meaning, Man was not only intended to present a *"likeness"* of God, but God also intended us to be a *"projection;"* or a *"silhouette,"* or a *"shadow"* of God's acts as we appear in this world. God intended us *"to act like His shadow."* His intent was for us to emulate Him as we perceive His interactions projected in our world. God meant for us — *"to walk in His shadow."*

When I contemplate the deeper meaning of *tslm*, I recall what Nahmanides said:

---

[912] Schroeder, Genesis and the Big Bang, Chapter 9 p. 152a

'God knows all life, but the degree of Divine direction to an individual person depends on that person's individual choice of how close to God he or she wishes to be.'

In his Guide of the Perplexed, Maimonides made the same observation. Dr. Schroeder puts it this way: *'Only the totally righteous have one-on-one Divine direction, and even that guidance may not ensure a life free of pain and suffering. For the rest of us, chance and accidents do occur. It's our choice as to where we, as individuals, fall within that spectrum of behavior that stretches from intimate Divine direction to total random chance.'*[913]

When I think about the foremost commandment:
'Thou shalt love the Lord thy God with all of thy heart, with all of thy soul and, with all of thy might'— Moses (Deut. 6:5) — and Jesus Christ (Matt. 22:37), who essentially said the same thing — I get this mental picture of my brother-in-law's pet dog, *Shadow* — who, with the confidence that came from being as close to Joe as she could possibly be, rested securely and contentedly in the lap of her master.

Somewhere around 1,200 to 1,400 years after Moses wrote the Book of Deuteronomy, a Pharisee who was a lawyer asked Jesus a question testing Him (Matt. 22:35) —
"Teacher which is the greatest commandment in the Law (Matt. 22:36)?"

This question was part of an attempt to trap Him in what He said. Jesus replied:

"You shall love the Lord your God with all your heart, and with all your soul, and with all your mind. This is the great and foremost commandment. And a second is like it: You shall love your neighbor as yourself. On these two commandments depend the whole law and the Prophets." (Matthew 22:36-40)

(Note that Moses said 'heart, soul, and *might*,' and Christ said, 'heart, soul, and *mind*.')

Earlier, Jesus also said: *"Therefore, however you want people to treat you, so treat them, for this is the Law and the Prophets."* Matthew 7:12 (Christ's Golden Rule)

The Gospel of Luke quotes Jesus this way: *"And just as you want people to treat you, treat them in the same way."* (Luke 6:31)

Can you imagine how this world would be *if* each of us loved the LORD GOD so much that we tried to emulate Him as we perceive His interactions projected in our world? What would happen *if* we constantly, in each of our actions and interactions with others, tried to act as if we were walking in God's shadow? Can you visualize how the world would be *if* we treated each other in the way we would wish to be treated? Wouldn't *that* be the same as *'loving your neighbor as you love yourself?'* In the Fifteenth Chapter of John, Jesus gave us His Commandment.

"This is My commandment—That ye love one another, as I have loved you .Greater love hath no man than this: 'that a man lay down his life for his friends.' Ye are my friends, if ye do whatsoever I command you (John 15:12-14)."

[913] Schroeder, The Hidden Face of God, Chapter 11 p. 177a

We have just talked about loving others as we love ourselves. Now, Christ says we must love one another as He loved us. Then, He gives us a definition of 'greatest love' — the example of *"laying down one's life for his friends."*

Chances are, if you ask someone to explain what Christ meant when He said this, they will give the example of someone, whose very act of saving another from death, costs him his life (i.e., the man who rushes forward just in time to push a child out of the path of an oncoming truck or train and, in doing so, is crushed to death in the place of the child). There are other examples such as the combat soldier who performs an act of heroism that costs him his life but saves the lives of his brothers. Or the fireman who loses his life while carrying others to safety. Christ died an unimaginably cruel death for us! These certainly are examples of — greatest love.

However, I submit to you there are other ways to love others as Christ commanded without dying in the process. What if you were to '*live*' your life in the service of others — always seeking to serve their best interests? Would not that be — loving others as you love yourself? Would not that be — loving others in the same way Christ loved us? If one approached life in this way, one would literally be — *living for others.*

IF YOU LIVE TO SERVE OTHERS, YOU WILL BE LAYING DOWN YOUR LIFE FOR YOUR FRIENDS.

I suggest to you this is another way of expressing 'greatest' love. Living our lives in the service of others is a way of living that can be repeated every day of our lives. We can and should do this in the conduct of our professional, personal, and business lives. We should do this in our everyday interactions with others. How would this affect our standing with God? Christ said:

'Many that are first shall be last; and the last shall be first.'
(Matt. 19:30, 20:16, and 20:20-28; also Mark 9:35 and Mark 10:31)

When we live to serve others: are we not putting ourselves last and putting others first? This kind of behavior is what God intended for us when He decided to 'make' and 'create' us.

Jesus Christ meant for us to be His shadow in the world. He meant for us to emulate His actions in our world by loving others as we love ourselves and by living our lives in the service of others. How do we know this? That is exactly what the Genesis Code meaning of "image' and 'likeness" in Genesis 1:26 tells us.

III.   "US" AND "OUR"

Then Elohim said, Let Us make man in Our image, according to Our likeness (Gen. 1:26).

There are several interpretations of the meaning of this verse. Some have said the 'us' and 'our' refer to '*the royal we.*' They say God is having a conversation with Himself, or with the angels, or His heavenly court. Still others have claimed when God made man, He took the best qualities of the various animals to make the first human and the conversation He is having is with the animals He created. Others have claimed the conversation is between the Creator and the human race in general. There are other opinions about who the 'us' and the 'our' represent. But no matter how convinced one might be of the correctness of his individual interpretation; most scholars would agree there is much mystery in these words.

The traditional Jewish explanation of 'us' and 'our' is: *The Creator* formed a partnership with the Earth. They think this verse is a conversation between the Creator and the Earth, which acknowledges the joint contributions of God and the Earth in the making of the first man.

The sages believed God placed in the Earth all of the ingredients necessary *to form* the first man. With God's single act of *Tzimtzum, The Creator* had *created the stuff from which He would make and form all things* in the beginning. Then about 5,700 years ago, something happened. That something was the reason for the biblically stated partnership between God and the Earth in creating the first man. So intimate is mankind's connection with the Earth that the name chosen for the first of our species was Adam, which comes from the Hebrew word, 'adamah' — meaning 'soil.' That 'something' was the *neshama* — the God given '*Breath of Life*' — the additional spirit or soul of human life that God breathed into *the adam's* nostrils (mentioned in Genesis 2:7), thus creating '*the Adam*' (i.e., the first man) from the already formed 'adam' which had been previously made through the joint partnership of the Earth and God.[914]

THE TRINITY

Most of the English translations of this verse capitalize the words '*Us*, and *Our.*' That's because many Christian Scholars believe this particular verse of scripture is the first overt reference to *The Trinity of God* in the Bible. This is the explanation I believe. This is why I believe this.

- We have already pointed out that Elohim, is plural —greater than two— indicating plentitude of power and majesty, thus allowing for the New Testament revelation of the *Doctrine of the Trinity* (cf. Chapter 4 in Book I — in the discussion of "Elohim").
- Therefore, the '*Us*' and the '*Our*' in the same verse refer *to a plurality of the persons in the Godhead* that is also — *greater than two*.
- In this verse of scripture, I believe God the Father, is talking to the Pre-incarnate Jesus Christ, *and* the Holy Spirit.
- I have already discussed why I believe *the First Wisdom of God* mentioned in the Onkelos translation of Genesis 1:1 was *The Pre-incarnate Jesus Christ,* and that the Spirit of God, which was hovering over the surface of the waters in Genesis 1:2c was the Holy Spirit (cf. Chapters 3, 7, and 8).
- Those who criticize the *Doctrine of the Trinity* by saying God is '*One,*' seem to interpret the principle of the '*Oneness*' of God (i.e., the '*Unity*' of God), which is proclaimed in Deut. 6:4 — *is a simple 'oneness' or a simple 'unity.'*

*"Hear, O Israel! The LORD is our God, the LORD is ONE! (*Deut. 6:4).*"*

This familiar verse of scripture begins the celebrated *Shema* (from the first word '*Hear*'), which became Judaism's basic confession of faith. According to rabbinic law, the Shema was to be recited morning and night. This verse has been subject to various translations, one of which is — '*The LORD is our God, the LORD alone.*' That is, the Lord's uniqueness precludes the worship of any other, and demands a total love commitment.[915] However, the Unity of God is not simple. It is incredibly complex. So, let us now take a brief look at

[914] Schroeder Genesis and the Big Bang Chapter 9 p 150-151
[915] The Ryrie Bible Commentary on Deuteronomy 6:4

the *Doctrine of the Trinity* and in so doing, see if we can offer at least some insight into this controversial Christian Doctrine.

A BRIEF DISCUSSION OF THE DOCTRINE OF THE TRINITY

The New Testament's *Doctrine of the Trinity* is much more fully developed than that of the Old Testament because God's revelation of Himself is progressive. Like Judaism and Islam, Christianity claims to be monotheistic and rejects polytheism. At the same time, Christian Doctrine acknowledges there are three persons in the Godhead of the One True God, which is still *One Essence.* This sentence necessarily defies syntax. God is indeed One, but that *Oneness* is not simple. It is complex. This is something both Judaism and Islam reject. Perhaps that is because Judaism and Islam consider the Oneness of God to be a simple Oneness.

In the last Chapter of the Gospel of Matthew, Jesus Christ charges His disciples with *'The Great Commission.'*

"Go and make disciples of all the nations, Baptizing them in the name of the Father, and of the Son, and of the Holy Spirit (Matthew 28:19)"

The case of the noun, *'name'*, in this verse is singular. This is the appropriate case for the One True God. But these words the Son of God spoke tell us the One True God exists in three persons. The Ryrie Bible Commentary on this verse informs us: *"Here is evidence of the Trinity of God — One God who subsists in three persons — The Father, The Son, and The Holy Spirit."*

Each of the three persons is distinguished from the others. Each possesses all the divine attributes—yet *'the three'* are *'One.'* This is a mystery, which no analogy man can think of can satisfactorily illustrate or explain, because the time-space-continuum that defines the laws of our existence does not allow for the possibility of *'a three-in-one'* existence of anyone or anything.

However, we must be cognizant of the fact we are discussing the *One* entity that exists *outside* of the time-space-continuum, which defines our existence. Here, we are talking about God, who is outside of the 'bubble' that we call the universe, and who is not constrained by anything. He, who created the universe, our Earth, and all that exists is eternal and is outside of time and space. The Bible tells us, for the briefest of moments in His eternity (in the beginning), He did enter the time-space-continuum of the universe when He created, made, and formed it. He also interacted with men in ancient times and sent His Son to us. After Christ ascended into heaven, Christ sent His Holy Spirit to each believer. The Holy Spirit continues to do His work within us. Nevertheless, the Triune God, has always existed. He has no beginning and no end. He will still exist even after all that we know has passed away. In the sense that He is *'Three-in-One,'* His Holy Spirit is with us still, and someday, each believer will join *Our Abba, His Son, and the Holy Spirit in Heaven* in order to spend *Eternity Future* in *His Company.*

MODALISM

There was a Christian heresy in the early Christian church that taught God appeared at different times in three different modes or forms — as Father, then as Son, and finally as the Holy Spirit. That heresy has been named *'Modalism,'* and was offered as a simplistic explanation of the *Doctrine of the Trinity.* The analogy of the three different forms of water has served as an analogy for the Modalists' concept of the Trinity of God. For example, under different temperature conditions, water can appear as a liquid, as a solid (ice), or as a vapor (a gas). Yet, all three forms of water are still the same substance — H_2O.

Do not let it escape your notice — the Modalists' concept of the Trinity visualizes the existence of God in three different forms — *at three different times!* What is wrong with this analogy? The Bible teaches God exists as three different persons — *at the same time! That* is something only God can do. To those who say this is not possible, I say — *nothing is impossible for God!*

- God is unchangeable. God is not $1 + 1 + 1 = 3$. No. The Unity of God is complete. We cannot add to God.

- God is unchangeable. God is not $1 - 1 - 1 = -1$. No. The Unity of God is complete. God is not a negative force. We cannot subtract from God.

- God is unchangeable. Like the integer one, if we try to divide God by Himself, we find God is: $1 \div 1 \div 1 = 1$. The Unity of God is complete. God cannot be divided.

- God is unchangeable. If we try to multiply God by Himself, we discover God is — $1 \times 1 \times 1 = 1$. The Unity of God is complete. God cannot be multiplied.

In this analogy of the integer one, notice: the unity of the integer one is *not simple.* While it can be added to itself and subtracted from itself, it remains the same when we attempt to multiply it or divide it by itself. Therefore, if the unity of the integer one is not simple: *How can we expect the Unity of God to be a simple oneness?*

For those who deny the Doctrine of the Trinity of God, it must be emphasized the greatness of the LORD GOD cannot be described or fully understood by man. His wisdom and ways are beyond our understanding. For those who deny The Biblical Concept of the Trinity of God and defend a simple explanation of the Unity of God, I would remind them: Beginning with the 38th Chapter of Job, and continuing through the 41st Chapter of Job, the following are some of the questions God asks Job — a man who questioned God's ways, His fairness, His justice, His purposes, and His motives.

"Who is this that darkens counsel by words without knowledge? Now gird up your loins like a man and you instruct Me! Where were you when I laid the foundation of the earth! Tell Me if you have understanding. Who set its measurements since you know? Or who stretched the line on it? Or who laid its cornerstone? Or who enclosed the sea with doors, when bursting forth, it went out from the womb. When I made a cloud its garment, and thick darkness its swaddling band, and I placed boundaries on it, and I set a bolt and doors, and I said,' Thus far you shall come, but no farther. And here shall your proud waves stop! Have you ever in your life commanded the morning, and caused the dawn to know its place? Have you entered into the springs of the sea? Or have you walked in the recesses of the deep? Have the gates of death been revealed to you? Or have you seen the gates of deep darkness? Have you understood the expanse of the earth? Tell Me if you know this! Where is the way to the dwelling of light? And darkness, where is its place, that you may take it to its territory. And that you may discern the paths to its home? You know, for you were born then, and the number of your days is great? Have you entered the storehouses of the snow, or have you seen the Storehouses of the hail, which I have

reserved for the time of distress, For the day of war and battle? Where is the way that the light is divided, or the east wind scattered on the earth? Who has cleft a channel for the flood, or a way for the thunderbolt? To bring rain on a land without people, on a desert without a man in it. To satisfy the waste and desolate land, and to make the seeds of grass to sprout? Has the rain a father? Or who has begotten the drops of dew? From whose womb has come the ice? And the frost of heaven, who has given it birth? Can you bind the chains of the Pleiades, or loose the cords of Orion? Can you lead forth a constellation in its season, and guide the Bear with her satellites? Do you know the ordinances of the heavens, or fix their rule over the earth? Who has put wisdom in the innermost being, or has given understanding to the mind? Who can count the clouds by wisdom, or trim the water jars of the heavens?"

Job's complaining and questioning made God angry. For God answered him out of a ferocious whirlwind — a *'tornado.'* The Hebrew word for the storm that is translated as *'the whirlwind'* in The New American Standard Bible of Job 38:1 is *'cᵉ`arah,'* which can mean: *"a storm, tempest, whirlwind, hurricane, or tornado."* Consider this. Which of these five best matches the majesty of God's words? A hurricane is a mega-event that has a quiet center, and a mere whirlwind can be a harmless *'dirt devil'* such as I used to chase when I was a child. I suggest a storm, or tempest, would provide an appropriate background for this majestic encounter between God and Job. If God pulled up right next to Job, and spoke to Job from a *tornado*, He most certainly would have commanded Job's attention! In Job 40:1 these words are found:

"Then the LORD said to Job, 'Will the faultfinder contend with the Almighty? Let him who reproves God answer it.'"

The crux of the whole discourse is:

"Who is this that darkens counsel by words without knowledge? Tell Me if you have understanding! Who is it that would reprove God! Let Him answer it!"

Greatly humbled by God's words, which God thundered out from the tempest of a tornado (in Chapters 38—41), in Chapter 42, Job replied:

"...I have declared that which I did not understand, Things too wonderful for me, which I did not know. Hear, now, and I will speak. I will ask Thee, and do Thou instruct me. I have heard of Thee by the hearing of the ear; But now my eye sees Thee; Therefore, I retract, And I repent in dust and ashes (Job 42: 3-6)."

The narrative continues in the 42nd Chapter of Job to inform us God instructed Job's friends of the error of their advice, because they had not spoken of God what is right as His servant Job had. God told them to go to Job and offer sacrifices. After they did so, and Job prayed for them, God restored Job's health, and multiplied his fortune. God gave Job seven more sons and three more daughters. Job lived another 140 years and saw his sons and his grandsons, four generations, and Job died an old man full of days.

So, to the critics of the *Doctrine of the Trinity* that the Son of God proclaims in numerous places in the New Testament, I say: Who are you to question God's ways and God's Word? But then, to Jews and Muslims I must acknowledge you do not believe Jesus Christ is the Son of God. And you do not accept the New Testament in the Christian Bible as the revealed word of God. Yet, I do not apologize for my beliefs — nor do I expect you to apologize for your beliefs. Would that we all would simply treat all others, regardless of our beliefs, our religion, our race, and any other differences the mind of man can conceive — that we would treat all others as we ourselves would wish to be treated. Would that we all would live our lives in the service of others. If all of us would do these two things, there would be peace among men and nations and there would be peace on earth!

Summary Points:
- The Hebrew word 'adam,' which means 'the man,' comes from another Hebrew word, 'adamah,' which means 'the earth,' or 'the soil' or 'the dust of the ground.'
- In the Creation Account, the Bible does not say God named the first man — Adam.
- We have to wait until Genesis 5:2 to learn God named the first man — '*Man.*'
- The name of the first man comes from the Hebrew word for 'the earth,' (i.e., the *adamah*).
- In various English translations of the Bible, the name of the first man morphs from the generic lower case 'adam' (meaning '*the man*'), to the upper case 'Adam' (that is befitting for the name of the first Man) — at different places in the different English translations of the Bible.
- When God named the first Man, He made both male and female and named them, '*Man.*'
- When God created the first man, He created both male and female and called them, '*Man.*'
- Man is the only creature God first made and then created.
- This reversal of the order of creating and then making which was originally described in Genesis 1:1, carried great weight with the ancient Jewish sages.
- They concluded: when it came to the Bible's description of how the first human being came to be, the ordering of things informed us that some amount of time passed between the making of the animal man (in the lower case — that only had the *nefesh*), and the creating of the first Man (Adam — in the upper case), that already had the *nefesh* when God made him — but then acquired the *Neshama* when God later breathed the *Neshama* (i.e., God's breath) into his nostrils.
- When we rest on the Sabbath, we are acknowledging the Supremacy of the Father, and we are proclaiming:
  - He alone is God!
  - Without any help, He single-handedly created all that exists!
- Moses said to love God with all of your heart, soul, and *might*.
- Jesus said to love God with all of your heart, soul, and *mind*.
- This essential change in the interpretation of the first of the Ten Commandments (which says: '*Thou shalt have no other gods before me*'—Ex. 20:3), is a perfect example of God's progressive enlightenment of His people through scripture.
- The New Testament is God's New Covenant with His people. This substitution of the word '*mind*' for '*might*' tells us God wants us to not only seek to know Him in our hearts and souls, but He also wants us to seek to know Him with our *minds* — our intellect.

- God does not want any mindless automatons in His Company. He wants us to make a conscious decision to cross the line and voluntarily (by exercising our own initiative, and free will), join Him as a believer who is completely committed to Him in our hearts — in our souls — and in our minds.
- Our decision to choose God honors Him.
- When God made us in *His image, according to His likeness*, His intent was *for us to be His shadow* — a representation of *His silhouette* in this world.
- This means our duty to Him is to emulate Him by our conduct and actions toward others as we perceive His will, His laws, and His interactions projected in our world.
- The best way for us to be God's shadow in our world is for each one of us to always treat others in the same way that we would want to be treated — each and every day of our lives — in all that we do.
- We should also live our lives in the service of others. If we would do this, then our actions would be an outward reflection of loving God with all of our heart, soul, and mind; and a demonstration that we love our neighbor in the same way that we love ourselves and that we love others in the same way that Jesus loves us.
- If all of us would do this, there truly would be peace on earth.

THUS ENDS MY DISCUSSION OF 1ST CHAPTER OF GENESIS.

❧

CHAPTER 24: THE END OF THE 6TH DAY—Gen. 1:28-31
God Blessed Man and gave him Dominion and Food.

Somewhere around 3000 years ago (~ 1000 BC[916]), or about 2700 years after Adam and Eve (who date to ~ 5700 years BP or ~ 3700 BC[917]), and about 400-500 years after Moses (circa ~ 1450 BC[918]) — in an obvious reference to the Genesis One Creation Account — King David wrote:

"O LORD our Lord, how excellent is thy name in all the earth! Who hast set thy glory above the heavens. Out of the mouth of babes and sucklings hast thou ordained strength because of thine enemies, that thou mightest still the enemy and the avenger. When I consider thy heavens, the work of thy fingers, the moon and the stars, which thou hast ordained. What is man, that thou art mindful of him? And the son of man, that thou visitest him? For thou hast made him a little lower than the angels, and hast crowned him with glory and honour. Thou madest him to have dominion over the works of thy hands. Thou hast put all things under his feet: All sheep and oxen, yea, and the beasts of the field. The fowl of the air, and the fish of the sea, and whatsoever passeth through the paths of the seas. O LORD our Lord, how excellent is thy name in all the earth!" (Psalm 8: a Psalm of David: The King James Version)

IN ANOTHER PSALM, DAVID WROTE:

"O LORD, what is man that thou dost regard him, or the son of man that thou dost think of him?" (Psalm 144:3 a Psalm of David)

[Quoted from my red letter 1946 Edition of The King James Version of the Bible, given to me by my parents on December 25th, 1949, when I was nine years old—the only thing I asked for on that Christmas—four years after the end of WWII.]

In this verse and in Psalm 8, note: *'the son of man'* is not capitalized and therefore is not a reference to Jesus Christ (who often referred to himself as *'the Son of Man'*). Jesus was not a contemporary of David and would not appear on the world scene until about 1,000 years after David. To the contrary, David is most likely referring to the offspring of man, i.e., the descendants of Adam and Eve through Seth—those who survived Noah's flood. In all probability, David is marveling God would *'have regard for and visit with and think about'* people like him. Since the Bible is a book for all times, when we read these words, we can also wonder why and marvel at the thought that God would have regard for, visit with, and think about us.

Job, who may have lived during or shortly after Abraham's lifetime,[919] and who himself probably preceded David by ~ 1,000 years; asked a similar question and wondered why God would have regard for man when he wrote:

"What is man that thou shouldest magnify him, and that thou shouldest set thine heart upon him (Job 7:17 The King James Version)?"

Since Job worshipped God and was the priest of his family,[920] in all probability Job's question was influenced by the oral tradition of the Genesis Creation Account handed down by succeeding generations of his ancestors since Adam. Nevertheless, when one reads the rest of Job's soliloquy (verses 18-21), unlike David, Job's questioning was not

---

[916] The Ryrie Study Bible: Genesis Timeline.
[917] Schroeder: Genesis and the Big Bang Chapter 1 p. 11 (calculations based on the Genealogies listed in the Bible.)
[918] The Ryrie Study Bible: Introduction to the Book of Genesis.
[919] The Ryrie Study Bible: Commentary and Introduction to the Book of Job.
[920] The Ryrie Study Bible: Introduction to the Book of Job. Also, Job 1:5.

motivated by wonder or thankfulness. Job's question came out of the misery of his own suffering. He wondered why God would allow his suffering. But the verses that inspired David when he wrote Psalm 8 are the following verses at the end of the first chapter of Genesis that recount what God did at the end of the 6th Day.

Gen. 1:28 *"And God blessed them, and God said to them: 'Be fruitful and multiply, and fill the Earth, and subdue it; and rule over the fish of the sea and over the birds of the heavens, and over all living things creeping on the Earth.*

Gen. 1:29 *And God said: 'Behold, I have given you every plant seeding seed which is on the face of all the Earth, and every tree in which is the fruit of a tree seeding seed—it shall be food for you.*

Gen. 1:30 *And to every living thing of the Earth, and to every bird of the heavens, and to every creeper on the Earth, in which is a living soul (a nephesh), every green plant is for food.' And it was so.*

Gen. 1:31 *And God saw everything that He had made; and behold, it was very good. And there was evening and there was morning, the sixth day."*   The Interlinear Bible

In Genesis 1:28-31, God does four things:
1. God blessed the Man and Woman that He made and then created.
2. God charged the Earth's first Man and Woman with their responsibilities.
3. God gave food to the Man, and the Woman, and to the animals He made.
4. And God saw everything He had made was very good.

The 6th Day concludes with this familiar Genesis One statement:

"And there was evening and there was morning, the 6th Day."

I.   GOD'S BLESSING AND CHARGE

When the Almighty Creator blessed the Earth's first Man and Woman, His blessing was much more than a simple go forth, reproduce, and populate the world, be happy, and hope all goes well wish. No. Every time in scripture that the Lord God bestows His blessings upon someone, He genuinely desires that person will take their mission seriously and diligently pursue the goals He has in mind for that person. He also pledges His divine support. The same expectations exist today. The message of scripture is — God does not simply send us out into the world with a mission to accomplish without giving us all that we need to be successful. Neither do we have *carte blanche* to do all that strikes our fancy. We must be cognizant of the fact that when we are given God's blessing and God's work to do, that mission is an imperative. The charge to perform that mission is also sacrosanct, and those works carry with them an obligation. In doing God's work, we have the obligation and responsibility to be prudent stewards of our charge. We learn this from similar charges God gave other people that are chronicled elsewhere in scripture. A prime example of this is the Covenant God made with Abraham.

In the 12th Chapter of Genesis, God blessed Abraham to be a blessing to others, so that *all* the families of the Earth shall be blessed. When we 1st 'meet' Abraham, his name is Abram. (cf. the footnote on the next page.) The New American Standard Bible records that story this way:

NOW THE LORD SAID TO ABRAM,
"Go forth from your country, and from your relatives,
And from your father's house to the land which I will show you.

And I will make you a great nation,
And I will bless you,
And make your name great.
And so you shall be a blessing.
And I will bless those who bless you,
And the one who curses you I will curse.

And in you all the families of the earth shall be blessed.

So Abram went forth as the LORD had spoken to him, and Lot went with him.
Now Abram was seventy-five years old when he departed from Haran." (Gen 12:1-40)

These verses are God's 1ˢᵗ Covenant with Abraham.[921]

In commercial law, a Covenant is a solemn agreement that is binding on all parties. It is a legally binding agreement that requires an owner and a steward to do some things and refrain from doing other things. In the Old Testament, God's Covenants are also binding agreements in which God issues a command, or charges a person with certain responsibilities, but also promises certain things that He will do as a reward for obedience to His command. In regard to the party to whom the Covenant is directed, God requires faithful obedience to His command.

In this Covenant (God's 1ˢᵗ Covenant with Abram), God commands Abram to separate himself from the idolatrous society in which he was born (Ur of Mesopotamia), and journey to a particular land God had chosen (the land of Canaan) — i.e., current-day Israel.

The promise to bless all of the families of the Earth through Abraham was fulfilled later through the life and the sacrifice of Jesus Christ. Jesus is in the lineage of Abraham.

Here, in Genesis 1:28-31 we read about the First Covenant in the Bible. It is the Covenant between God and the first Man and Woman He made and created — Adam and Eve. The first part of God's First Covenant details those things God commanded Adam and Eve to do:

- Be fruitful and multiply.
- Fill the Earth and subdue it.
- And Rule:
  - over the fish of the sea—
  - the birds of the heavens—
  - and all living things that creep on the Earth.

In short, have dominion and control over the Earth and all living things on the Earth. This is the reason David later wrote in Psalm 8 that God had crowned man with glory and

---

[921] Abram vs. Abraham: God changed Abram's name to Abraham in Gen. 17:5, when he was 99 years old. Abram means 'Exalted Father.' Abraham means 'Father of a great number.' In Gen. 17:5, God renewed His promise to make Abraham 'exceedingly fruitful' and promised to extend His original Covenant with him (made when he was 75 years old), to include the nation of Israel, which God promised would come forth from him.

honor; had given man dominion over the works of God's hands (God's creation); had put all things under man's feet; and thus, had made man a little lower than the angels.

II.   GOD'S GIFT OF FOOD

This first part of God's Covenant also details the reward for obedience to His command. God promised food. The first food God gave man and woman was:

- Every plant seeding seed—
- And every fruit of a tree seeding seed.
- God also promised to give every green plant for food to every living thing on the Earth, which has the living animal soul.

Perhaps it has not escaped your notice the first food God gave all living things was a vegan diet. Meat was not specifically given to man to eat until after Noah's flood (Genesis Chapter 9). This happened several hundred years after *the Fall of Man* (which occurred in the Third Chapter of Genesis). Adam and Eve fell from grace when they disobeyed another command God gave them in Genesis 2:17.

Some of you may object to this explanation of man's first diet and criticize it as being a 'too literal' interpretation of scripture. For example, some claim the reason Able's sacrifice in Chapter 4 of Genesis, was more pleasing to God than Cain's offering (for which God had no regard); was because God favored Able's offerings of meat and its fat portions more than Cain's offerings of grain. They further claim this implies meat had been offered as food for man long before the time in which the Bible makes mention that meat was declared by God to be an acceptable food source for man. That happened after Noah's flood.

However, there is perhaps a more plausible explanation for why God had no regard for Cain's offering. It may have been Cain's heart was not right with God at the time he made his offering. According to Levitical Law, a *flawless* offering of the first fruit of the ground was just as acceptable to God as a *flawless* offering of the first born of the flock of an acceptable animal.[922] It is therefore just as likely or perhaps more likely that Cain's attitude toward his obligation to make a sacrifice of the first fruits of his harvest was what displeased God and rendered his sacrifice unacceptable. *An offering to God that is not flawless and is not freely given in a spirit of love and gratitude — does not honor God!* Instead, an offering that is not made out of gratitude and with a thankful and respectful heart — offends Him. Only those flawless offerings that are made by those with contrite and righteous hearts are acceptable to God — (cf. Malachi 1:6-14 and 3:3-4). Hebrews 11:4 seems to verify this interpretation because this verse of Hebrews says that it was — *"by faith that Able offered a better sacrifice than Cain"* — meaning that the difference in the two offerings was in the heart and attitude of the person making the offering. While Cain was resentful, Able's love of God and his faithfulness to God shaped his thankful attitude.

The second part of God's first Covenant with Adam and Eve involved a specific command of God which they later disobeyed. We will talk about that when we discuss the 2nd Chapter of Genesis.

---

[922] A Ryrie Study Bible note concerning Genesis 4:3.

III.   **GOD'S PRONOUNCEMENT OF — "IT WAS VERY GOOD."**

Gen. 1:31 *"And God saw everything that He had made; and behold, it was very good. And there was evening and there was morning, the 6th Day."* NASB

With this verse, Chapter One of Genesis closes. With this pronouncement of God, the 6th Day of Creation ends. At this point in the Biblical text, *'The Ancient of Days'* (Elohim) considers His rudimentary work of creation that He did during *'the Six Days of Old'* (i.e., the six days of creation) — completed. Most of our English translations of the Hebrew text of the Torah and the Greek text of the Pentateuch, tell us when Elohim surveyed His work, He said: *'it was very good.'* This phrase differs from Elohim's other pronouncements of *'it was good'* that appears at the end of each of the other five days of creation. The 1900-year-old Onkelos translation of Genesis into Aramaic translates the phrase, *'it was very good,'* this way:

"It was a unified order."

Thus, according to Onkelos, all of God's labor during the six days of creation forged a state of *'unity and order'* out of the extreme chaos of the beginning. This state of *unity and order* are the hallmark, the trademark, the stamp of completion, and/or the end result of God's creative activity, as recounted in the first chapter of Genesis.[923]

The end result of unity and order out of the chaos of the beginning would not have happened if the universe had developed through the devices of *random chance* as the disciples of Darwin have claimed. If that had been the way the universe came into being, nothing would have changed from the chaos of the beginning and no development of the universe would have occurred. The chaos would have continued and would have prevailed. All would have ended in the overwhelmingly fatal gravitational vortex of a super black hole. We have already discussed this in Chapter 7 when we said the Singularity was the first black hole. However, God intervened, and order and unity were the end result. Six times over, the Bible tells us of the unifying passage to ever more complex and orderly arrangements of the chaotic matter of the beginning that resulted from God's labor on each and every one of the six days of creation by this simple statement that appears at the end of each of the six days:

'And there was evening (erev) *and there was morning* (boker)*'...Day One...the 2nd Day...the 3rd Day...Etc.*

As we discussed in Chapter 8, the Genesis Code meaning of *'erev'* is chaos; and the deeper meaning of *'boker'* is order. Nahmanides concluded the deeper meaning of the text tells us something crucial about the God-directed flow-of-matter in the universe. God caused a systematic flow-of-order to emerge out of *the chaos of the beginning* on each and every day of creation. That is, there was a systematic flow from disorder (the chaos of evening) to order (the unifying cosmos of morning) that resulted from each day of His labor. This is the opposite of what would have happened if the chaos of the universe had been left to the governing forces of — *random chance.*

The entire saga of God's creation ends with the appearance of human life. Approximately eight hundred years ago, Nahmanides (circa 1194-1270 AD) agreed with

---

[923] Schroeder: *The Hidden Face of God,* Chapter 3, p 33c

Onkelos. In his commentary he interpreted the deeper meaning of the original Hebrew text of Genesis 1:31 to mean:

'And God saw everything that was made and behold it was a unified order.'

Dr. Schroeder, commenting on the general consensus of other ancient Jewish sages, many of whom preceded Nahmanides by several hundreds of years, puts it this way: *'Two thousand years ago, the commentators on the Hebrew text of Genesis 1:31 saw within the words a wondrous transition from chaos to cosmos; from a jumble of energy and atoms to the dazzlingly complex and unified order of life.'*— a direct quote.[924]

Summary Points:
- At the end of the 6th Day of Creation, God blessed the Man and the Woman that He had made and created.
- God charged them to be fruitful, multiply, and fill the Earth.
- God also commanded them to have dominion over the Earth and every living thing that He had made.
- In return for their obedience to His command, He gave them the gift of the food of every green plant and the food of every plant that produced fruit.
- He also gave the food of every green plant to the animals He had made.
- At the end of the 6th Day, God surveyed His creation and was satisfied that everything He had created and made had resulted in a unified order.
- The verses of Genesis 1:28-31 chronicle the first part of the First Covenant that God made with Man.
- In Psalm 8, David wondered: *"What is man that You are mindful of him and the son of man, that thou visitest him?'*
- Saint Augustine said: *"You stir man to take pleasure in praising You, because You have made us for Yourself, and our heart is restless until it rests in You."*[925]
- The simple truth is — God made and created us for Himself. That is why our soul:
  - 'Thirsts for the living God'— Psalm 42:2; and 63:1.
  - And our souls: 'thirsteth after God as a thirsty land.' Psalm 143:6.
  - That is also is the reason Jesus said to the woman at the well:

"Whosoever drinketh of the water that I shall give him shall never thirst.
But the water that I shall give him shall be in him a well of water,
Springing up into everlasting life." John 4:14

---

924 Schroeder *The Hidden Face of God* Chapter 4, p 59
925 Charles Martin: *When Crickets Cry* Chapter 10, p 59

✦
CHAPTER 25: THE 7ᵀᴴ DAY—THE 1ˢᵀ SABBATH: REST & REPOSE

Gen.2:1 *"And the heavens and the Earth were finished, and all their host.*

Gen.2:2 *And on the seventh day God* (Elohim) *completed His work which He had made. And He rested* (shabath) *on the seventh day from all His work which He had made.*

Gen.2:3 *And Elohim blessed the seventh day and sanctified* (qadash, qodesh, or kodesh) *it, because He* (shabath) *rested from all His work on it, which God* (Elohim) *had created to make."*   TIB

Since Adam had been *made,* and near the end of the 6ᵗʰ Day *created* by God, the first day *after* the end of the 6ᵗʰ Day of Creation was *Adam's first full day.* It was the beginning of the time-flow Adam would experience and all humanity since Adam (including us) have experienced and will experience. Stated another way, Adam's first day began that portion of the Biblical Calendar that satisfies our perception of reality. Adam's first day was the first Sabbath. The first full day Adam lived gets its name from the Hebrew word God used that our English translations interpret as *"rest"* (*"shabath or shabat"*). That first Sabbath marks the start of Adam's time, and the Post-Adam Period — which is our Post-Adam Calendar in which the time-flow we experience was established. On that day, all of our English translations of the Bible, including the Interlinear Bible, tell us God *rested* from all of His labors He had done during the *"Six Days of Old."* So, it is our English translations of Genesis 2:1-3 that tell us — on the 7ᵗʰ Day, after the heavens and the Earth *were finished* along with *all* of their hosts, *The Ancient of Days* did three things:

- He *blessed* the 7ᵗʰ Day, by *separating* it and *setting it apart* as a special day.
- He *sanctified* the 7ᵗʰ Day, meaning He *commanded it to be kept free from sin.*
- And He *rested* from *all of His work that He had done* on the *Six Days of Old.*

When God blessed the 7ᵗʰ Day, He set it apart for praise and holiness. One meaning of the Hebrew word for 'holy' ('kodesh') is *'separate and set apart.* [926] The Sabbath is the first thing in the Bible God made 'holy' in the Biblical sense of being kept separate from the remainder of existence. [927]

When English Bibles say God *"sanctified"* the 7ᵗʰ Day, they translate the Hebrew word qadash (or from the same word when speaking of an object or thing, qodesh), as meaning — He made the 7ᵗʰ Day *'holy'* in another way. He made it holy in the sense *of making it sacred by commanding it be kept free from sin.* The Hebrew words qadash and qodesh can also be spelled with a 'k' — i.e., kadash and kodesh; and can also be interpreted to mean: *to purify, dedicate, hallow, and sanctify.* The English word *"sanctify"* comes from the Latin *Sanctus* (holy) + *facere* (to make); meaning *'to make holy, to make sacred, to purify, to make free from sin.'* The rest of this chapter concerns the deeper meaning (i.e., the Genesis Code meaning) of the phrase — *'He rested.'*

ON THE 7ᵀᴴ DAY ELOHIM "RESTED."

The Creator's *rest* on the day after He created Adam is also mentioned in the Book of Exodus. God's command to observe the Sabbath is the 4ᵗʰ of the 10 Commandments God gave Moses on Mt. Sinai (Exodus 20:8-10). The 10 Commandments were first given verbally (Ex. 20:1-17) and were later written by God on two stone tablets. In the 31ˢᵗ Chapter of Exodus, Moses wrote about a conversation he had with Jehovah when he was

---

[926] Schroeder *The Science of God* Chapter 5 p 77*a*
[927] Schroeder *The Hidden Face of God* Chapter 11 p 181*a*

on Mt. Sinai. Just before Jehovah handed Moses the two stone tablets on which He had written the *Ten Commandments*, He talked with him about the *"Sign of the Sabbath."* Jehovah instructed Moses to:

"Speak to the sons of Israel, saying, You shall surely keep My Sabbaths. For it is a sign between Me and you for your generations to know that I am Jehovah your sanctifier. And you shall keep the Sabbath, for it is holy for you. The profaners of it shall surely be put to death. For everyone doing work in it, that <u>soul</u> shall be cut off from the midst of his people. Work may be done six days, and on the 7th Day is a Sabbath of rest, Holy to Jehovah. Everyone doing work on the Sabbath day surely shall be put to death. And the sons of Israel shall observe the Sabbath, To do the Sabbath for their generations. It is a never-ending covenant. It is a sign forever between Me and the sons of Israel. For in six days Jehovah made the heavens and the earth. And on the 7th Day He rested (shabath) *and was refreshed. And when He* (Jehovah) *finished speaking with him* (Moses)*On Mt. Sinai, He gave Moses the two tablets of the Testimony, tablets of stone, written by the finger of God"* Ex. 31:12-18 *TIB.*

This day that has been named *"the Sabbath,"* is a perfect example of the claim — *God's revelation of Himself to man in scripture is progressive.* In Genesis 2:1-3, when God established the very first day He set aside for rest, He blessed it, sanctified it, and ended His daily interventions of creative activity He had done on each and every one of the preceding six days of creation. This happened immediately following the moment at the end of the 6th Day when He created the first man and woman who would become the progenitors of the whole human race. Nevertheless, there is *no* mention in the Genesis Creation Account of God's requiring Adam and Eve *to observe the Sabbath*. However, in the Book of Exodus, after the family of God's chosen people had been firmly established through the lineage of Adam—Noah—Abraham—Isaac—and Jacob: God raised up Moses to lead an abused and confused multitude of slaves out of the four-hundred-year-old bondage of Egypt, and to begin the slow and arduous process of teaching them about their God whom they had stopped worshipping. Moses' task was not only to teach them, but also to lead them through the wilderness to a promised land of plenty where God would eventually forge them into the nation of Israel.

So, Exodus 31:12-18 is a recounting of the 4th of the Ten Commandments (the commandment to observe the Sabbath) that was part of the 10 Commandments God first spoke to Moses in the 20th Chapter of Exodus. The Bible often emphasizes the importance of a passage of scripture by revisiting or repeating the essence of the original statement of an event or subject at another place in scripture. When this happens, the recounting not only emphasizes its importance, but also adds additional information and detail. *The School of the Higher Biblical Criticism* sees such recounting as evidence that supports their theory of the multiple unknown authorship of the Torah. However, the repetition and revisitation of the 4th Commandment that is chronicled in Exodus 31:12-18 can also be seen as a literary device, an author's poetic license (as it were) that Moses used to emphasize and add additional detail concerning the importance of the 4th Commandment. These seven verses of Exodus detail the last part of a lengthy conversation God had with Moses on Mt. Sinai, which occurred early in the wilderness experience of the Exodus — after the pursuing Egyptian Army had been destroyed by

God in the Red Sea, and after the Israelites defeated the attack by Amalek and his tribe at Rephidim. Here, God reiterates to Moses the 4th Commandment which shall, from that moment onward, be required of all of God's faithful. They, under the penalty of death and being cut off from the midst of their people for failing to obey, shall:

- Faithfully observe each and every 7th day.
- They shall call that day of observance, *'the Sabbath.'*
- On each Sabbath they shall cease from work, and they must rest.

They must also understand the observance of the Sabbath was established by God as a sign between God and His people which acknowledges —

- o During the *'Six Days of Old,'* God made the heavens and the Earth.
- o On the 7th Day of Creation, He rested (shabat**)** and was refreshed**.**

When reading these verses, it is important to know the word *'Sabbath'* comes from the Hebrew word *'shabat'*, meaning *'to rest — to cease from work.'* So, *at one level of meaning, the level of meaning that specifically applies to us,* the essence of the Sabbath is *rest. When we rest on the Sabbath, we honor God by demonstrating to all who witness our "Sabbath Rest" — we are proclaiming —*

- He alone is God!
- Without any help, He single-handedly created all that exists! [928]

Exactly what does the "penalty of death" and "being cut off from the people for failure to obey," mean? This penalty is stated twice in God's warning. The repetition of the warning emphasizes its importance. God made it abundantly clear — anyone doing work on the Sabbath shall be put to death and separated from the people. Does it mean instant death? Or could it mean: *Under the Old Testament Dispensation of the Law,* the failure to obey this command would affect *one's eternal life and one's relationship to God and the faithful in the hereafter?* That may be the case, because not only will the profaners of the Sabbath die, but their *soul* shall be cut off from the midst of the people.

Thanks be to God. We no longer live under *the Old Testament Dispensation of the Law.* We now live under *the New Testament Dispensation of the Grace of Jesus Christ!* (See: THE APOSTLES STARTED AND CONTINUED THE TRADITION OF CHRISTIAN WORSHIP ON SUNDAY — at the end of this chapter.)

IS THERE ANOTHER LEVEL OF MEANING TO SHABAT/SHABATH?

Our experience with the Genesis Code certainly suggests the answer to this question is: *Yes.* To understand the Genesis Code's deeper meaning, we first need to briefly review what we have learned about the relativity of time and then we need to take another look at Exodus 31:17 and examine how Maimonides intuited the deeper meaning of — *Shabat.*

THE RELATIVITY OF TIME.

We now know during the *first Six Days of Old,* (i.e., *the Six Days of Creation*), when God created and made all that now exists, the eternal clock literally saw 144 hours pass. But, because of Einstein's discovery of the Laws of Relativity, and also because of many of the other discoveries of modern science over the past 85 years, we now know the 144 hours of those *'Six days of Old'* need not bear any similarity to the time lapse measured at another part of the universe. In Chapter 5 we learned our sense of the passage of time is determined for us by our particular local time-reference-frame within the universe at

---

[928] Schroeder *The Hidden Face of God* Chapter 11 p 181*c*

large, which in turn is determined for us by our spaceship—Earth. The various 'clocks' on our Earth — such as radioactive dating, the placements of the various geologic rock strata, and our measurements from the Earth of rates and distances in the ever-expanding universe, are our tools by which we estimate the passage of time.[929]

The Creation narrative in the first chapter of Genesis that describes what happened on each day after the beginning in terms of *days*, truly considers those *days* as *six 24-hour days*. But we are just now beginning to understand the time-reference-frame of those days truly encompassed the entire universe, and also contained all of the mysteries of the Ages.[930]

The ancient Jewish sages warned us our perception of the events of *the six days of Genesis One* would be inconsistent with our understanding of nature for the time following Adam. Why did they warn us, and how did they perceive this conundrum? Their warning comes from, and was inspired by, their understanding of the declaration of *'Sabbath rest'* in Genesis 2:2-3, and the descriptions of *'Sabbath rest'* in two additional passages in the Bible that concern the *Ten Commandments,* as well as two other verses of scripture which contain a Hebrew word our English translations of the Bible have interpreted as *'rest.'*

So, in addition to Genesis 2:2-3, the Jewish sages also took special note of Exodus 31:17 — Exodus 20:11— Zechariah 5:11 — and II Samuel 21:10.[931]

THE DEEPER MEANING OF SHABAT—"REST AND REPOSE"

When speaking to Moses about the *Sabbath,* this is what the LORD said to him in Genesis 2:2 and 2:3. *"And He rested* (shabath) *on the 7th Day from all His work which He had made. And Elohim blessed the 7th Day and sanctified it, because He* (shabath) *rested from all His work on it, which Elohim had created to make." TIB*

When speaking to Moses about the Sabbath, this is what the LORD said to him in Ex. 31:17. *"It is a sign forever between Me and the sons of Israel. For in six days Jehovah made the heavens and the earth; And on the 7th Day He rested* (shabath/or shabat) *and was refreshed" TIB.*

In these verses, English translations of the Bible interpret the Hebrew word, *shabath* and/or *shabat,* as *'rested.'* The Hebrew and Chaldee Dictionary interprets shabat and/or shabath to mean *'to repose, or to rest, or be still.'* So, on at least one level of meaning, there is an agreement of interpretations. However, the Hebrew and Chaldee Dictionary also mentions — shabat and/or shabath *can mean 'to take away,'* or *'to be rid of.'* So, on another level of meaning, something more than simple 'resting,' or 'reposing,' may have been involved. Therefore, we see — in these verses about the Sabbath, the word *'shabath and/or shabat,'* has *two very different meanings.* Earlier, in the Book of Exodus, *in another statement about resting on the Sabbath*, the Bible uses *a different Hebrew word for 'rest.'* In Exodus 20:11, this is what the Bible says: *"For in six days Jehovah made the heavens and the Earth, the sea, and all which is in them, and He rested* (nuwach) *on the 7th Day. On account of this Jehovah blessed the Sabbath day and sanctified it TIB.'*

---

[929] Schroeder *Genesis and the Big Bang* Chapter 2 p 53*b*
[930] Schroeder *Genesis and the Big Bang* Chapter 2 p 53*c*
[931] Schroeder *Genesis and the Big Bang* Chapter 2 p 53*d*

In this verse, English versions of the Bible interpret another Hebrew word, 'nuwach,' to mean 'rested.' The Hebrew and Chaldee Dictionary agrees and says nuwach means — *'to dwell, be quiet, make to rest, cease.'* So, we see another Hebrew word for 'rest' is used, but this word has only *one meaning. Therefore, only one level of meaning can be applied.*

Thus, in the three verses of scripture just mentioned (that specifically apply to the Sabbath), two different words for 'rest' have been used — shabat and nuwach. In the first two examples, shabat has more than one meaning and can be interpreted two ways — i.e., *to rest/ or to take away/ or be rid of.* In the third verse, the word nuwach, means only one thing — *rested.*

THERE ARE TWO OTHER SCRIPTURES THAT SPEAK OF 'RESTING,' BUT HAVE NOTHING TO DO WITH THE SABBATH. In the Book of Zechariah, when the LORD commanded Zechariah to build a house in the land of Shinar, still another Hebrew word for 'rest' was used. But that word, which is very different from shabath and shabat, also has more than one meaning. *But both meanings have something to do with 'resting.'*

(Zechariah 5:11 TIB) "And He said to me, to build a house for it in the land of Shinar; and it shall be fixed and be set on its own place (i.e., yanach*)."*

In this verse, the Hebrew word, 'yanach' (reference word # 3240 in the Interlinear Bible), is interpreted to mean 'to be fixed and be set.' However, an additional note in the definition of reference word # 3240 in the Hebrew & Chaldee Dictionary says: *"In accordance with the older grammarians, the meaning of this verse should rather be referred to reference word # 5117 — 'nuwach,' — which means 'to dwell, be quiet, make to rest, set down, cease.'* So, we see — 'yanach' and 'nuwach' have essentially the same meaning — i.e., they *are synonyms.*

In another passage of scripture *which also has nothing to do with the Sabbath*, the word 'nuwach' (which has only one meaning — *'rest'*), was used.

*"And Rizpah the daughter of Aiah took sackcloth and stretched it out for herself on the rock, from the beginning of harvest until water dropped on them out of the heavens. And she did not allow a bird of the heavens to rest (*nuwach*) on them by day, nor the beast of the field by night."*   II Samuel 21:10 TIB

In this verse, the Hebrew word, *nuwach*, is interpreted in English translations to mean, *'rest.'* *The Hebrew and Chaldee Dictionary* agrees and indicates that *nuwach* has only one meaning — *'to rest, set down, cease, etc.'*

HOW MAIMONIDES INTERPRETED THE GENESIS CODE.

As we have just seen, in Genesis 2:2-3 and Exodus 31:17, Moses could have used the Hebrew words *nuwach* or *yanach* instead of *shabat* when he talked about resting on the Sabbath. If he had, only one level of meaning (*resting*) could have been applied. In fact, he did use the word *nuwach* in Ex. 20:11 when he mentioned God sanctified and blessed the Sabbath. But, in Genesis 2:2-3 and Exodus 31:17, the word he used for resting was *shabat* — a word that has *two contradictory meanings.* Maimonides decided the answer to this riddle was: *On the level of meaning that applies specifically to us, it was God's intent that we rest on the Sabbath.*

Since Shabath (or Shabat) means *'to repose, or to rest;'* the next question for consideration is this. *Are reposing and resting the same thing? That is to say — is it possible to repose without resting, or rest without reposing?* Both words have multiple meanings and, many of those meanings are synonymous. However, when one looks at the root meaning of *repose*, one finds: *('re'* in Latin = *'back + ponere* (or *positus*) = *to place'*), meaning — *"to place back."*

Furthermore, so far as God Almighty is concerned, why would *the Eternal One* ever need to rest? Therefore, Maimonides decided the deeper meaning of shabat — i.e., the *'get rid of'* and *'take away'* level of meaning — must apply to what the Creator *actually did* on that First Sabbath. He decided — *something more than simple resting must have been involved.* Maimonides concluded the deeper meaning of the original Hebrew text was informing us:

The intent is not that God 'rested' on the First Sabbath. Instead, the Creator caused a repose to encompass the entire universe that He had made during the first six days. Our perception of this repose, according to Maimonides is — on the first Sabbath and for all days thereafter, the laws of nature, including the flow-of-time, would function in a 'normal manner.[932]

What effect would this have on the Earth? Maimonides decided during *'God's repose'* on the 7th Day, *"God placed something back/ or got rid of something."* He decided God changed the *flow-of-time-on-Earth* so that the time-flow Adam would experience would be different from the time-flow that had occurred during the *Six Days of Creation.* It would also be the same rate of time-flow the generations following Adam would experience.

That is to say, during God's repose on the 7th Day, He 'took away', 'got rid of,' or 'placed back' from the 7th Day and all future days of the week, all of those billions of Earth-years those 'creation days' represented and shortened the 7th Day and all future days by setting the duration of 'a day' to the same 24-hour day we now experience.

So, the Genesis Code informs us — instead of simply 'resting' on the First Sabbath, the Creator caused a repose to encompass the entire universe He had made during the first six days of creation. Just how did Elohim's universal repose affect the Earth?

> *Maimonides concluded when God had finished His Creation and, on the 7th Day established the First Sabbath on Earth, 'the repose' He ordered changed the flow-of-time on our planet and established the parameters that from that moment onward, would define the limits of what we now experience as 'a day.' That is why we can say Adam's first day was the First Sabbath; and Adam's first day began that portion of the Biblical Calendar that satisfies our perception of reality. That First Sabbath marked the start of Adam's time, and the post-Adam period. How did that affect us? That First Sabbath was the point when the time-flow we experience was established!*

For us, based upon the historically prevalent superficial interpretations of the Genesis Creation Account, the flow-of-events that occurred during the first six days have appeared *illogical*, as if the laws of time and nature have been *violated* by the Biblical Account. This has produced a challenge and a problem of understanding in relation to common perceptions of time-flow that have confounded and puzzled believers through the ages. At the same time, the result of this apparent conundrum has caused great glee among

---

[932] Schroeder *Genesis and the Big Bang* Chapter 2 p 53*d* and 54*a*

nonbelievers who ridicule the Biblical Account of our origins.[933] *The time conundrum, which has resulted from a misinterpretation of the Genesis Creation Account, is one of the major reasons nonbelievers have labeled the Biblical Account of Creation a myth and a simple fairy tale for children.*

What is truly extraordinary is the fact that Einstein's discovery of the Law of General Relativity has extended the validity of the Biblical Calendar into those first six days. Because we now understand that time-flow throughout the universe is truly relative, there is no longer any need to try to explain away the presence of fossils in ancient rock strata as being placed in our world by the Creator to test our belief in an erroneous interpretation of Genesis that claims the Earth is very young. Radioactive decay in rocks, meteorites, and fossils, accurately records the passage of time. Furthermore, measurements of time based on the principle of radioactive decay are correct from the Earth's specific time-flow-perspective.

> *However, the passage of time that is measured — is the rate of time-flow as it was and is measured by the clocks of our Earth-bound time-reference-frame. That time-flow was, and still is, only relatively (i.e., only locally) correct. Other clocks in other reference-frames record Earth-bound events at very different, but equally correct times. This will always be the case so long as the universe follows the laws of nature, which God set during His repose on the 7th Day of Creation.*[934]

Summary Points:

- On the 7th Day the Creator did three things:
    - He blessed the 7th Day.
    - He sanctified the 7th Day.
    - And He rested from all of His work He had done on the Six Days of Old.
- When God blessed the 7th Day, He made it holy; meaning He set it apart.
- When God sanctified the 7th Day, He not only set it apart, but He declared it to be sacred, pure, and decreed it be kept free from sin.
- In the Genesis account, no specific command was given to Adam and Eve 'to keep' the 7th Day Holy. Perhaps that is because, at that moment — man had not sinned.
- However, later in the Exodus, the command 'to keep the Sabbath' was given to Moses as the 4th of the Ten Commandments that God decreed Israel should obey.
- God decreed the Israelites must:
    - Faithfully observe each and every 7th Day.
    - They must call that day of observance, 'the Sabbath.'
    - On each Sabbath they shall cease from work, and they must rest.
    - They must also understand the observance of the Sabbath was established by God as a Sign between God and His people which acknowledges that:
        - He alone is God!
        - Without any help, He single-handedly created all that exists!
- The Sabbath gets its name from the Hebrew word, 'shabat/and or shabath' that appears in Gen. 2:2-3.
- The first meaning of shabat is 'rest.'

---

[933] Schroeder *Genesis and the Big Bang* Chapter 2 p 53d-54a
[934] Schroeder *Genesis and The Big Bang* Chapter 2 p 54b

- However, when Maimonides realized the deeper meaning of shabat is 'to repose, to take away, or be rid of,' he concluded the deeper meaning of the original Hebrew of the Creation Account was informing us—From the moment God instituted the First Sabbath and for all time thereafter, the laws of nature, including the flow-of-time, would function in a 'normal' manner.

- What is meant by 'normal manner' is — the time-flow Adam would experience would be different from the time-flow that occurred during the six days of creation. It would be Adam's time-flow. And Adam's time-flow would be the same rate of time-flow all of the generations after Adam would experience.

- Therefore, when God had finished His Creation and, on the 7th Day established the First Sabbath on the Earth — during 'His repose' on the First Sabbath, He changed the flow-of-time on our planet and established the parameters, which (from that moment onward), would define the limits of what we now experience as 'a day.'

- That is why we can now say Adam's first day was the First Sabbath — and Adam's first day began that portion of the Biblical Calendar, which satisfies our perception of reality.

- That First Sabbath marks the start of Adam's time, and the Post-Adam Period — which is our Post-Adam Calendar in which the time-flow we experience was established.[935]

I have said God's command to keep the Sabbath Holy is the 4th Commandment. This 'opinion' is based on the way most Protestants *number* the *Ten Commandments*. Jews consider Ex.20:2 to be the First Commandment:

Ex.20:2 *"I am the LORD your God, who brought you out of the land of Egypt, Out of the house of slavery."*

Jews regard verses 3-6 as the 2nd Commandment:

Ex. 20:3 *"You shall have no other gods before Me."*

Ex. 20:4 *"You shall not make for yourself an idol. . . . . . ."*

Ex. 20:5 *"You shall not worship or serve idols...For I am a jealous God, visiting the iniquity of the fathers on the children to the 4th generation of those who hate Me."*

Ex. 20:6 *"But showing loving kindness to thousands, to those who love Me and keep My commandments."*

Roman Catholics also group verses 3-6 but regard them as the First Commandment. Then, they divide verse 17 into two commandments in order to have a total of ten.

Ex. 20:17 *"You shall not covet your neighbor's house; You shall not covet your neighbor's wife or his male servant."*

Most Protestants number the Ten Commandments in this way:

1) Ex. 20:2-3 *"I am the LORD your God. . .You shall have no other gods before Me."*
2) Ex. 20:4 (a paraphrase) *"You shall not make any idols of any kind."*
3) Ex. 20:7 *"You shall not take the name of the LORD your God in vain."*
4) Ex. 20:8 *"Remember the Sabbath day to keep it holy."*
5) Ex. 20:12 *"Honor your father and your mother."*
6) Ex. 20:13 *"You shall not murder."*

935 The Ryrie Study Bible: Reference Note on Ex. 20: 2

7) Ex. 20:14 *"You shall not commit adultery."*
8) Ex. 20:15 *"You shall not steal."*
9) Ex. 20:16 *"You shall not bear false witness."*
10) Ex. 20:17 *"You shall not covet."* From the NASB

WHY DO CHRISTIANS WORSHIP ON SUNDAY?

There is a relationship between the *Crucifixion of Jesus Christ* and the 1st and 2nd of the annual religious feasts of the Jews (¹ *The Feast of Unleavened Bread* and ² *The Passover*). *The Resurrection of Jesus Christ* and the third of the annual religious feasts of the Jews (³ *The Feast of First Fruits*) are also related. And *The birthday of the Christian Church* and the fourth of the annual religious feasts of the Jews (the feast that Jews call ⁴ *The Feast of the Harvest or The Feast of Seven Weeks* — and that Christians call "*Pentecost*") are likewise, related.

¹ THE FEAST OF UNLEAVENED BREAD

The first of the annual feasts of the Jews is *The Feast of Unleavened Bread*. The Thursday before the Sabbath celebration of the Passover is the first day of the Feast of Unleavened Bread. On that day, Moses instructed each family of the Israelites to prepare unleavened bread and sacrifice an unblemished lamb. For the Jews, leaven (or yeast) symbolizes sin. Each year, the Feast of Unleavened Bread spans the seven-day celebration of the ² *Feast of the Passover*. The Feast of Unleavened Bread is intended to celebrate and commemorate the meal the Jews were instructed by Moses to prepare on the night of the First Passover. For the first seven days of their exodus from slavery in Egypt, Moses commanded them to eat the unleavened bread they had prepared before the Passover (Ex. 12:17).

In the week in which the crucifixion of Jesus Christ took place (on Thursday) — on the first day of the Feast of Unleavened Bread — *Christ presided over the Lord's Supper in the Upper Room* (Luke 22:7-38). After Judas Iscariot left to betray Him (John 13:21-30), Jesus and His disciples walked to *the Garden of Gethsemane* (on the Mt. of Olives) where they planned to spend the night. Jesus was in anguish and prayed very fervently to the Father for the cup of sacrifice to be removed from Him. Yet, He pledged His obedience to God's will and the Father sent an angel from heaven to strengthen Him (Luke 22:40-46). Later that night, Jesus was arrested. On the very night the Feast of Unleavened Bread begins, *'the Lamb of God'* (Jesus Christ) was arrested and tried! After that, He was crucified! Through His crucifixion, He became *The Sacrificial Lamb for all of humanity — past, present, and future* (Hebrews, Chapters 7-10).

² THE PASSOVER

The second of the annual religious feasts of the Jews is *The Passover*. It commemorates the night the angel of death *'passed over'* the homes of the Jews who were enslaved in Egypt when they marked their homes with the blood of a sacrificial lamb as instructed by Moses. That night, all of the first-born males of the Egyptians (including the first born of their animals) died (Ex. 12). The blood of the lamb saved the Jews from death.

THE JEWISH RELIGIOUS AUTHORITIES OF CHRIST'S TIME—NOT THE JEWISH PEOPLE demanded the death of Jesus Christ, and the Roman Governor of Judea, Pilate, gave his consent and ordered his soldiers to carry out the death sentence. During the night of the first day of *The Feast of Unleavened Bread*, a Thursday night, while in *The Garden of*

Gethsemane, and after He had finished praying, Jesus was arrested by a *cohort* of Roman soldiers — somewhere between 300-600 soldiers (cf. John 18:3)! He was then taken to the house of the high priest. That night Jesus was tried before the Sanhedrin. This happened on the night before the day of preparation for *the Sabbath Feast of the Passover* (Matt. 26:17-27:75).

JEWISH LAW PROHIBITED TRIALS AT NIGHT![936]

Hence, the Sanhedrin broke its own law. In the trial, *'many were giving false testimony against Him, and yet their testimony was not consistent'*— that is, their testimonies did not agree (Mark 14:56). Jewish law required two agreeing witnesses to establish a charge — cf. Deut. 19:15. They asked Him: *"Are you the Son of God, then?" And He said: "Yes I am." So, they said: "What need do we have of further testimony? For we have heard it ourselves from His own mouth."* (Luke 22:70-71.

They then convicted Him of *Blasphemy*, took Him to the Roman Governor Pilate, and demanded He be crucified (Luke 23:21)! Christ was murdered *on the very day* of *the beginning* of the Jewish *Passover*, which started on the evening of the day that Christ died. The day they murdered our Lord was on *the* Friday which was *during the time of preparation for the Sabbath of the Passover celebration*. The Passover began on *that* Friday *at sunset* — the day after He was arrested, tried, ruthlessly scourged with a scorpion, and crucified! Although the Jewish religious authorities say Christ died before the Passover began, Christians see that claim as a façade!

THEY CRUCIFIED JESUS ON THE VERY DAY THE PASSOVER CELEBRATION BEGAN!

The Jewish religious leaders were so anxious Christ die *before* the beginning of the Sabbath Feast of the Passover (which would begin at sunset on the night of the day He was murdered), and His body be removed from the cross — that they asked for His legs to be broken to hasten His death. However, Christ's blood loss from the severe lacerations caused by the scorpion, and the blood loss that also resulted from the crown of thorns that pierced his scalp, and the nails in his wrists and feet — that He died of exsanguination while on the cross. The soldiers found it unnecessary to break His legs to hasten His death.[937*] Seeing that He was already dead, they did not break His legs, but pierced His side with a spear instead (see John 19:30-34 and 19:36-37 — cf. with Isaiah 52:13 – 53:12 and Psalm 22, Psalm 34:19-20, and Psalm 69). This fulfilled in every detail the prophecy of the Suffering Servant as recorded in the scriptures referenced.

³ THE FEAST OF FIRST FRUITS

The third of the annual feasts of the Jews is *The Feast of First Fruits*. This feast serves as an earnest or pledge of the full harvest yet to be gathered,[938] and is held on the day after the Passover. Therefore, the Jewish Feast of First Fruits is always celebrated on the Sunday after the Passover Sabbath. The feast of First Fruits that occurred after the crucifixion of Christ was on the third day after His Crucifixion. That day was a Sunday. Because Christ arose from the dead on the third day (the day after the Sabbath of the Passover and the same day of the Feast of First Fruits), Christians say that *Jesus Christ is the First Fruit of Salvation of those Risen from the Dead* (1 Cor. 15:20,23).

---

[936] Article: *12 Reasons Jesus' Trial was Illegal* by Grabriel N. Lischak http://reg.org/pillar/0902pp-trjtwi.html
[937*] Breaking the legs of the crucified, caused death by suffocation, because diaphragmatic breathing became impossible once the legs were broken.
[938] Ryrie Study Bible Note on Leviticus 23:10-14 concerning the Feast of First Fruits.

⁴ THE FEAST OF THE HARVEST (FOR JEWS) OR PENTECOST (FOR CHRISTIANS)

The fourth of the annual feasts of the Jews is *The Feast of the Harvest* (also called The *Festival of Seven Weeks*). This feast is celebrated the day after an interval of seven weeks has followed the Feast of First Fruits. That is why the Feast of the Harvest is also called the Festival of Seven Weeks. This allows a time interval of 49 days to pass after the planting of the harvest. Thus, the Feast of the Harvest is celebrated on the 50th day after the Feast of First Fruits. For Jews the Feast of the Harvest also commemorates *the giving of the Law at Mount Sinai*. That occurred fifty days after the Exodus from Egypt. *The giving of the Law to Moses at Mount Sinai is considered to be the birthday of the nation of Israel.*

Christians call the day of the Feast of the Harvest — *The Day of Pentecost* — because on the 50th day after the Resurrection of Christ, the Holy Spirit came to the apostles in the Upper Room in Jerusalem.[939] Pentecost means "50th day" in Greek. Thus, it is, the Jewish Feast of the Harvest and the Christian day of the first Pentecost occur on the same day — 50 days after the Resurrection of Jesus Christ. The command to keep the Sabbath holy is chronicled in Exodus 20:8-11. This is the only one of the Ten Commandments *not* repeated (by Christians) after that first day of Pentecost (in Acts 2). On that day, the Holy Spirit came to the disciples in the upper room as Christ had promised.[940] On that first day of the Pentecost — after the crucifixion, resurrection, and ascension of Christ — the Christian Church was born. *Thus, the birthday of Israel, and the birthday of the Christian Church are celebrated on the same day.*

CONCLUSION

What were the Jewish religious leaders doing on Friday, the day of preparation for the Sabbath celebration of the Passover in the week that Christ died? They, with the help of the Romans, were torturing and murdering the Son of God. When the Jewish religious leaders violated the 6th Commandment (thou shalt not murder) and murdered the Son of God on the day of preparation for the Sabbath of the Passover, they desecrated and forever hereafter defiled the Sabbath. From that moment onward, many Christians no longer venerated the Sabbath. In the 1st Century AD, the practice of Christian worship on Sunday (the 1st day of the week) was well established. Today, many Christians venerate the day Christ arose from the dead. That day was the 3rd day after His crucifixion. That day occurred on the day after the Sabbath of the Passover celebration that followed that infamous Friday when Christ was murdered. That day of Resurrection occurred on a Sunday, the first day of the new week that followed the crucifixion of Christ. Christians worship on Sunday for this reason. For many Christians, Sunday is venerated and celebrated as the Christian holy day.

THE APOSTLES STARTED AND CONTINUED THE TRADITION OF CHRISTIAN WORSHIP ON SUNDAY.[941]
The Christian Church has honored that tradition ever since. This practice is called "*1st Day Sabbatarianism.*" 7th Day Adventists may be the only exception among Christians. It was on a Sunday that Christ arose from the dead and became *the First Fruit of all*

---

[939] Ryrie Study Bible Note on Acts 2:1
[940] Ryrie Study Bible Note on Exodus 20:8-11
[941] Article: *Sabbath or Sunday?* http://www.catholic.com/trcts/sabbath-or-sunday NIHIL OBSTAT: *"I have concluded that the materials presented in this work are free of doctrinal or moral errors."* Signed by Bemadeane Carr, STL, censor Librorum, August 10, 2004.

believers (past, present, and future) who will be resurrected and glorified on the *Day of Christt* [942] when Christ comes again to inaugurate the *Day of the Lord* (a protracted period commencing with *the Second Advent of Christ* and ending with the cleansing of the heavens and the earth by fire preparatory to the new heavens and the new earth of the eternal state — cf. Isa 65:17-18, II Peter 3:10-13, and Rev. 21:1).

Many early Christians believed the resurrection and ascension of Christ signaled the renewal of creation, making the day on which Christ arose a day analogous to *Day One* of Creation when God made light. Many believe the Christian tradition of Sunday worship began in New Testament times because *the Sabbath* had been defiled by the murder of Christ. On the 3rd day after His crucifixion — on Sunday — Christ arose from the dead. In numerology, the number "3" is holy.

When we think of the Crucifixion of Christ, we must always be mindful God the Father willed it, and Christ was obedient to His Father's will. Otherwise, the Jewish religious leaders and the Romans who crucified Christ, could not have murdered the Son of God (cf. John 19:10-11). We must also remember, from the cross, Jesus asked the Father to forgive them for they did not know what they were doing (cf. Luke 23:34). Through Christ's sacrificial death, He became the redeemer of all mankind and the guarantor of God's New Covenant with man.

Because Christ died for our sins and arose from the dead, we now no longer live under the Dispensation of the Law. We now live under God's New Covenant of the Dispensation of the Grace of Jesus Christ — which the sacrifice of Jesus Christ ushered in — and under which repentant believers are granted full pardon. (Read the entire letter of I John.) I like to think of Sunday as: The Son's Day. Every Sunday, on the Son's Day, I worship and celebrate the Resurrection of my Lord and Savior, Jesus Christ. Because I believe in Him, and the fact of His Resurrection from the dead, I and all Christians, have the promise that we too will be raised from the dead and dwell in the eternity of Heaven with The Father, The Son, The Holy Ghost, His Heavenly Hosts, and all of Christ's Resurrected Saints.

---

[942] Ryrie Study Bible Note on Philippians 1:6

CHAPTER 26: WHEN EARTH CHANGED FROM A FIERY BALL INTO A TOXIC WATER WORLD—A RETROSPECTIVE OF A PART OF THE 2ND DAY (GENESIS 2:4-6)

In Book II, Part 7 of Chapter 9, The 2nd Day — I talked about ("A Perplexing Mystery — The Enigma of Genesis 2:4-6") and said that part of the Second Chapter of the Genesis Creation Account talks about a colossal event that happened near the end of the 2nd Day of Creation. Moses omitted that event from his initial account of the 2nd Day, which he gave in the First Chapter of Genesis. In the 2nd Chapter of his Book of Genesis, he revisited the 2nd Day. Using the literary devise of a retrospective review, he told us the 2nd Day was when the earth's first rain occurred. Now is the time to talk about the "nuts & bolts" of that perplexing retrospective mystery and how the Genesis Code enlightens us so that we can understand exactly what happened to the earth near the end of the 2nd Day. As you shall see, the Jewish sages believed this retrospective review (in Genesis Chapter Two) proves Moses not only wrote the Genesis Creation Account, but he also wrote Genesis Two — *after* he wrote Genesis One!   O. David

THIS IS WHAT THE MODERN LANGUAGE BIBLE (THE MLB) SAYS ABOUT GENESIS 2:4-6

(Gen. 2:4a) These are the generations of the heavens and the earth in their creation,

(Gen. 2:4b) when the LORD GOD made the earth and heaven.

(Gen. 2:5a) There was as yet not a shrub on the earth, nor any plant sprouting in the field.

(Gen. 2:5b) For the LORD GOD had not made it to rain on the earth,

(Gen. 2:5c) and there was no man to cultivate the soil.

*(Gen. 2:6) But a **vapor** used to rise from the earth to moisten all the surface of the ground.*

THE NEW AMERICAN STANDARD BIBLE (NASB) RELATES GENESIS 2:4-6 THIS WAY:

(Gen. 2:4a) This is the account of the heavens and the earth when they were created,

(Gen. 2:4b) in the day that the LORD GOD made earth and heaven.

(Gen. 2:5a) Now no shrub of the field was yet in the earth, and no plant of the field had yet sprouted,

(Gen. 2:5b) for the LORD GOD had not sent rain upon the earth,

(Gen. 2:5c) and there was no man to cultivate the ground.

*(Gen. 2:6) But a **mist** used to rise from the earth and water the whole surface of the ground.*

THE INTERLINEAR BIBLE (THE TIB) SAYS:

(Gen. 2:4a) These are the births of the heavens and of the earth when they were created,

(Gen. 2:4b) in the day that Jehovah was making earth and heavens—

(Gen. 2:5a) & every shrub of the field was not yet on the earth, & every plant of the field had not yet sprung up.

(Gen. 2:5b) For Jehovah-Elohim had not sent rain on the earth,

(Gen. 2:5c) and there was no man to till the ground.

*(Gen. 2:6) And a **mist** went up from the earth and watered the whole face of the ground.*

I have shown you these three English translations of Genesis 2:4-6 so that you can see how similar they are. They *all understate* the main event, and by understating it, they completely *'miss the boat'* (Pun intended)! They do not convey the deeper meaning of the original Hebrew. After we have reviewed the deeper meaning of Genesis 2:4-6, you will

515

see these verses talk about the first time it rained on the earth. That happened late on the 2nd Day of Creation. However, the first rain on earth was not mentioned in the account of the 2nd Day that is in the 1st Chapter of Genesis (cf. Gen 1:7-8). That account focuses on the expanse (firmament) which God placed *'in the midst of the waters'* so as to divide *'the waters above from the waters below.'*

(Gen. 1:7) "And God made the expanse, and He separated between the waters which were under the expanse and the waters which were above the expanse." (Gen 1:8) "And then, 'God called the expanse heaven" (*TIB*).

In Chapter 9, I previously concluded the *'expanse'* God called *'heaven'* (in the singular), *is the earth's atmosphere.* And I talked about *the first rain the earth experienced* when I briefly mentioned Gen. 2:4-6 in Chapter 9 in Book II. Like the three examples above, most English translations of Genesis 2:6 say *a mist or vapor rose from the earth and watered the whole surface of the ground.* Let's take another look at the words of *The Interlinear Bible* in verse 2:6 so we can discover *the transliterated Hebrew word the Interlinear Bible translates as 'mist' and the transliterated Hebrew word it translates as 'watered.'*

> *"And mist ('ed) went up from the earth and watered (shaqah) the whole face of the ground (Gen. 2:6 The Interlinear Bible)."*

One meaning of the Hebrew *word ('ed)* is: *"an enveloping fog, mist, or vapor."* So, you can see why English translations use these words. But you will soon see there is a deeper meaning of (*'ed)* that conveys an entirely different impression of what actually happened.

Shaqah means *"to water or make to drink."* However, it can also mean *"to drown."*

Dr. Schroeder tells us the deeper meaning of 'ed is — **"steam."**
Therefore, Dr. Schroeder says the deeper meaning of Genesis 2:6 is:

> "And **steam** would go up from the Earth,
> **And water *all* the face of the ground."** [943]

From the discussion that follows you will see *the Genesis Code* meaning of Genesis 2:6 is:
"And *'steam'* rose from the earth and *'drowned'* the whole surface of the ground."

The significance of *steam* rising from the earth and *drowning* the whole surface of the ground as opposed to a *mist* or *vapor* rising from the earth and (simply) *watering* the whole face of the ground is poles apart. From our previous discussions of the deeper meaning of the Hebraic script in Genesis One, and our previous comparisons of what modern science has learned and how theology and science are now in agreement — we can understand the Genesis Code in the First Chapter of Genesis explains how, during the 2nd Day:

- The earth was *'born in fire'* because its mass was formed by the impact-accretion of the debris in its orbital path deposited by the death of a preceding supernova. Compare*: 'Focus on Earth'— 'Scripture says The Lord God touched the Earth so*

[943] Schroeder *Genesis and the Big Bang* Chapter 8 p 126*a*

that it melted.' Also see: **'*Impact-accretion: the Earth was formed in Fire*'** —
(both in Chapter 9 of Book II).

And, in Genesis 2:4-6, we now see the Genesis Code also explains how:

- ***On the 2nd Day of Creation, the earth got its first atmosphere and its first ocean as it changed from a fiery ball in space into a primordial water world.***

We will now review what science says about the first rain that fell on the earth. It happened near the end of the 2nd Day of Creation (in the late Hadean Eon—cf. the last part of Chapter 12). Furthermore, the duration of that rainfall, and the volume of rain that fell was unlike any rainfall the earth has ever experienced since. **Scientists now believe the 1st rainfall the Earth experienced occurred late on the 2nd Day of Creation. That deluge was longer in duration than the duration of Noah's Flood (i.e., a 100 million years of a continuous downpour of rain according to modern-day Cosmology — vs. the 40 days and 40 nights of rainfall in Noah's Flood—Genesis Chapter 7).**

SCIENCE AGREES WITH THE BIBLE

In 1931, R.W. Garanson discovered — the molten basaltic and granite lava in earth's volcanic eruptions and the molten silicate in both types of lava, contain large amounts of absorbed water. He also observed, when the lava cools, the absorbed water in all types of lava is emitted as steam. *Furthermore, scientists have analyzed the chemical composition of volcanic steam and have discovered it is very similar to the chemical composition of the earth's ocean waters.* [944] Scientists have concluded the duration of the volcanic outgassing that began ~ 4.1 billion years ago in the last part of the Hadean Eon (i.e., during the 2nd Day of Creation), and the deluge of continuous rain that it caused — may have lasted for as long as 100 million years! By comparison, in Noah's Flood, "the fountains of the great deep burst open; the floodgates of the sky were opened, and rain fell for 40 days and 40 nights (Gen. 7:11 & 12)." So, the volume of water involved in the earth's 1st rain, which caused the Earth's 1st global flood (on the 2nd Day of Creation), may have been greater than in Noah's Flood! There is now a consensus of opinion among scientists this is the best explanation and the most likely scenario of how the earth's primordial atmosphere and primordial ocean were formed on the 2nd Day. [945,946,947,948,949]

So, we see the sequence of events on the 2nd Day was:

- Earth's atmosphere began forming late on the 2nd Day of Creation when the rocky debris in the earth's orbital pathway was finally cleared by impact-accretion.
- Next, the volcanically produced steam and other products of the earth's first and most prolonged epoch of volcanic-outgassing continuously rose above the earth's slowly cooling surface crust—
- And initiated the formation of the earth's primordial opaque and toxic atmosphere.
- At the same time, the steam rising from the slowly cooling lava-flows that accompanied the volcanic-outgassing triggered the greatest deluge of continuous rain in all the earth's history!

---

[944] Schroeder *Genesis and the Big Bang* Chapter 8 p 126*b*
[945] Schroeder *Genesis and the Big Bang* Chapter 8 p 126*b*
[946] Schroeder *Genesis and the Big Bang* Chapter 8 p 124*c*
[947] Schroeder *Genesis and the Big Bang* Chapter 8 p122*e*
[948] Article: Volcanic Gases and Their Effects ***volcanoes***.usgs.gov/hazards/gas/***index***.php
[949] The History Channel: *How the Earth Was Made: Part I*

- It rained for a hundred million years until, near the end of the 2nd Day (in the late part of the Hadean Eon), the earth's cooled volcanic surface crust was completely submerged by a great depth of ocean water.
- Thus, the earth's first ocean was formed, and the earth was changed from a fiery ball in space into a toxic water world.

Our English translations of the Bible give us the idea the earth's first rain was the result of a mist or a vapor that rose from the earth, and do not give us any indication the volume of rain produced was anything other than ordinary. But now, because of the Genesis Code, we can see the Biblical mention of the first time it rained on the earth (Genesis 2:4-6), informs us:

- *The earth's first rain* happened late on the 2nd Day of Creation.
- It was caused by *'volcanic steam'* rising from the earth—
- It lasted approximately 100 million earth-years,
- And the amount of *rain* that fell — *'drowned'* the whole surface of the ground.

Modern science has not only theorized it happened but has also proposed how and when it happened. Because the Genesis Code is not generally known, it is doubtful many scientists today are aware their theory of how and when the earth got its first atmosphere and ocean is in perfect agreement with the Bible. The deeper meaning of Moses' language in Genesis 2:4-6 tells us — the most recent scientific theory of how earth's first atmosphere and ocean formed is correct!

THE SCHOOL OF HIGHER CRITICISM VERSUS TRADITIONAL JEWISH LITERALISM [950]

The advocates of the School of Higher (Biblical) Criticism see *Genesis Two* as an example of a different literary style from the literary style used in *Genesis One*. They claim the use of two different names for God — i.e., *'Jehovah'* in Genesis 2:4b — and *'Jehovah-Elohim'* in 2:5b (as opposed to the *'Elohim'* of *Genesis One*), is the reason they think two different people authored the first two chapters of Genesis. They also allege writing had not become sophisticated enough for the *Torah* to have been written in Moses' time. The *'Higher Criticism'* argues writing did not achieve the level of sophistication the *Torah* exhibits until somewhere around 800 BC.

DR. PAOLO MATTHIAE & THE EBLA ARCHIVE

However, numerous archaeological discoveries have been made after the last prominent scholar of the *Higher Criticism* (Julius Wellhausen) died. These discoveries have completely discredited the *Higher Criticism's* notion that the art of writing in Moses' time was unsophisticated. Dr. Paolo Matthiae, the Director of the Italian Archeological Mission in Syria, reported one of the most significant archeological discoveries of all times. In 1975, he discovered the greatest third millennium (3000 BC) archive ever unearthed. It included more than 15,000 cuneiform tablets and fragments, which unveiled a Semitic empire that dominated the Middle East more than four thousand years ago. Its hub was Ebla (in the Levant, in northern Syria near Aleppo), where educated scribes filled ancient libraries with written records of history, people, places, and commerce. He concluded writing had been in use at Ebla for a long time even before 2500 BC! The names of cities thought to have been founded much later, such as *Beirut* and *Byblos*, 'leap' from the

[950] Article: *On Bible Criticism and Its Counterarguments—A Short History*: By Rabbi Nathan Lopes Cardozo, 1995: http://www.aishdas.org/toratemet/en_cardozo.html

tablets. *Damascus* and *Gaza* were also mentioned, as well as two of the Biblical cities of the plain — *Sodom* and *Gomorrah*. Most intriguing of all are the personal names found on the Ebla tablets. They include *Abraham* and *Esau*. [951,952,953]

From the Bible we know — centuries later, Moses was trained *'in all the wisdom of the Egyptians'* (Acts 7:22). There are also secular sources that confirm this. The Jewish historian *Josephus* tells us — not only had Moses been given the education of the Egyptian ruling class, but he was also a great general who led Pharaoh's army to victory over the kingdom of Ethiopia, which had (prior to their defeat by Moses) — conquered most of Egypt. According to Josephus, while Moses was attacking the Ethiopian capital city of Tharbis, the daughter of the king of Ethiopia became enamored of Moses. Seeing his valiant exploits, she bargained to deliver the city into his hands if he would but marry her. Moses agreed, and she fulfilled her promise. [954] Josephus said this occurred sometime before 1532 BC, when Moses was driven out of Egypt for slaying an Egyptian. Having been raised at Pharaoh's court, *Moses learned to write on fragile papyrus as well as clay tablets.* [955, 956, 957]

THE TEL EL-AMARNA LETTERS AND THE ROYAL EGYPTIAN ARCHIVES

The 1988 discovery (in Egypt) of the *Tel El-Amarna letters* show us written messages were an important part of Moses' culture. Furthermore, about four hundred cuneiform tablets have also been discovered in the royal archives of Amenhotep III, and Amenhotep IV (Akhenaten) — who reigned about 1400 BC. Among them were letters written in Babylonian cuneiform script to these Pharaohs of Egypt by various kings dwelling in the land of Canaan and Syria — all written during the time of Moses and Joshua. They provide the earliest discovered secular (i.e., non-biblical) evidence of the Hebrew tribes entering into the land of Canaan in ancient times. These letters also discuss the completion of the Biblical Exodus. Thus, these ancient letters in the royal Egyptian archives confirm the Biblical Account of the Exodus led by Moses and provide a contemporaneous 'non-biblical' historically documented source that describes the journey of the Israelites out of the bondage of Egypt and into the land God had promised them. [958]

OTHER ARCHAEOLOGICAL DISCOVERIES

Archaeological discoveries have documented the following dates for Abraham (~ 1900 BC), Joseph (~1700 BC), Moses (the Exodus ~ 1447 BC), and David (~ 1000 BC). The famous British born Archaeologist, William F. Albright said:

[951] Article: *Abraham didn't exist? Moses a myth? Archeological and Historical Evidence of Biblical Accuracy:* by Andy and Berit Kjos— http://www.crossroad. to/articles2/08/archeology.html
[952] Article: *EBLA: Its Impact on Bible Records* by Clifford Wilson, M.A., B.D., Ph.D.: **http://www.icr.org/article/92/**
[953] Article: *Ebla in the 3rd Millennium BC*. http://www.metmuseum.org/toah/hd/ebla/hd_ebla.htm
[954] Article: The **Antiquities** of the Jews, by Flavius **Josephus** - Project ...free eBook... www.gutenberg.org/files/2848/2848-h/2848-h.html Book II; Chp. 10: How Moses Made War with the Ethiopians.
[955] Ibid: How Moses Fled Out of Egypt into Midian
[956] Article: **The Ethiopian Connection** — *The **Dynasty of Moses and the Queen of Ethiopia*** http://www.hope-of-israel.org/dynmoses.htm
[957] Article: **Did Moses Marry a Cushite?** by J. Daniel Hays http://fontes.lstc.edu/~rklein/Documents/did_moses_marry_a_cushite.htm
[958] Article: **Abraham didn't exist? Moses a myth? Archeological and Historical Evidence of Biblical Accuracy:** by Andy and Berit Kjos— http://www.crossroad. to/articles2/08/archeology.html

"The excessive skepticism shown toward the Bible by important historical schools of the 18th and 19th centuries, certain phases which still appear periodically, has been progressively discredited. Discovery after discovery has established the accuracy of innumerable (Biblical) details and has brought increased recognition to the value of the Bible as a source of history." [959]

These are things that Wellhausen and the other proponents of *the School of Higher Biblical Criticism* never knew because these discoveries were made after their deaths.

THE VIEW OF JEWISH TRADITIONALISM

On the other hand, Jewish traditionalists attribute the authorship of the entire Torah to Moses. So, the question is: *How does one explain the different narrative approach that is taken in Chapter Two?* I think Moses exercised an author's poetic license and changed the perspective of the narrative in Chapter Two. I also think his novel approach to Chapter Two cleverly introduced new information about the 2nd Day.

THE DIFFERENT PERSPECTIVE OF THE SECOND CHAPTER OF GENESIS

From Genesis 2:4a to the end of the 2nd Chapter of Genesis, Moses re-tells portions of the Creation Account (what I have called *the 3rd Telling*), using a different perspective from the one he used in Chapter One. *Chapter One of the Book of Genesis represents God's perspective.* However, the perspective of the Creation Account *switches to the perspective of the Earth in Gen. 2:4-6 and then to Adam in the rest of Chapter Two.*

Genesis 2:4a-6 is that part of *the 3rd Telling, which represents the perspective of the Earth.* In the Mosaic narrative of Genesis Two, once God breathed *'His breath of Life'* into *'the Adam'* in Genesis 2:7 — *it is as if Adam himself is telling the story.* Thus, the *perspective* of the 3rd Telling is both that of *the Earth and of Adam.*

THE DIFFERENT NAMES FOR GOD

At the same time (beginning with Genesis 2:4b), Moses added to the Creator's name **"Elohim,"** His personal, explicit, and most holy name **("Jehovah"),** because God wished to establish with Adam a personal degree of intimacy. (We discussed this in Part IX of the Introduction.) The new information about the 2nd Day that is given in Genesis 2:4-6 **concerns the first rain on earth** and explains how, on the 2nd Day:

- *"Jehovah-Elohim"* established the waters *below* the expanse after He had separated them from the waters *above.*
- It also explains *how* the earth came to be *completely encased* by water at the end of the 2nd Day.
- Moreover, it would have been necessary for the Earth to have been completely submerged under *an ocean of water* by the end of the 2nd Day, for the emergence of the dry land to cause a separation of *the waters below* into the *seas* that *developed* on the 3rd Day.

In Chapter 23, I discussed the reasons the Jewish Sages believed Adam had been *made* and then *created* near the end of the 6th Day. In Chapter 25, I also said they thought the first day after the end of the 6th Day of Creation *was Adam's first full day.* The sages believed that day was the beginning of the time-flow Adam and all of humanity since Adam have experienced. According to them, Adam's first day began that portion of the

[959] Article: Query—***Debate.org.uk: The Bible's Archaeological Evidence***: http://www.debate.org.uk/debate-topics/historical/the-bible-and-the-quran/the-bibles-archaeological-evidence/

Biblical Calendar that satisfies our perception of reality. *His first full day on Earth was the First Sabbath.* Therefore, the First Sabbath marks the start of Adam's time, and the Post-Adam Period — which is our Post-Adam Calendar in which the time-flow we experience was established.

Now, we have introduced the concept that, beginning with *the breath of God* in Genesis 2:7, not only was the earth's time-flow readjusted to the same 24-hour day we experience, but the perspective of some specifics of the Genesis Creation Account switches to the perspective of Adam and the Earth. While this chapter is devoted to the discussion of how and when the Earth got its primordial atmosphere and oceans — in the chapters that follow, you shall see those specifics, which Moses relates to us in the Second Chapter of Genesis also include:

- How Adam was *created* after he had been *made.*
- The special place God made for Adam.
- When Adam *named* the animals and the other living creatures God *made.*
- And *how* God *made* Adam's special helpmate.

THE LITERARY STYLE OF RETROSPECTIVE ANALYSIS,

For the rest of this chapter, we will re-examine *the poetic license* Moses took when he wrote Genesis 2:4-6. By employing the literary style of *retrospective analysis*, Moses used his statements in each succeeding verse of Genesis 2:4-6, to focus our attention on an important event, that happened on the 2nd Day — **the earth's first rain.** Just as one might use the telescopic lens of a camera to zoom in on an important feature — with each statement Moses makes in Gen. 2:4-6 — he is causing our mind to go backward in time from the 6th Day of Creation to the 2nd Day when he will tell us about a key event God caused to happen to the Earth and its atmosphere on the 2nd Day. I think it is important to discuss the literary style Moses used to accomplish this. This review will bring with it a sense of *déjà vu.* That is because I briefly mentioned the perplexing mystery of Genesis 2:4-6 in Chapter 9. However, I will now take a detailed look at Genesis 2:4-6 and discuss the deeper meaning of this here-to-fore enigmatic retrospective regarding the 2nd Day that Moses placed at the beginning of the 2nd Chapter of his Genesis Creation Account. The deeper Genesis Code meaning of *'ed* and *shaqah* in Gen. 2:6 tells us what actually happened.

(Gen. 2:4a) "This is the Account of the heavens and the earth when they were created."

- Gen. 2:4a is like the statement that opens The 1st Telling of the Creation Account (i.e., Gen. 1:1): *"In the beginning God created the heavens and the earth."* The *1st Telling is told from God's perspective.* We know this because *the heavens* are mentioned *before* the earth in the 1st Telling. Here, in this first phrase of The 3rd Telling, *the heavens are likewise mentioned first,* and the word *'heavens'* similarly appears in *its plural form,* indicating this statement *is also from God's perspective.* The use of the plural form of *'the heavens'* in Gen. 1:1 and in Gen.2:4a means — *in both of these verses, Moses is talking about the universe at large.*
- The 1st Telling (i.e., Gen. 1:1-5) ends when Elohim causes light to emerge from the darkness of the beginning. This happens at the end of *Day One.* The cardinal form of ordering is used for *Day One* because there was no other day that preceded it.

- The 2nd Telling (Genesis 1:6-25), is also told from God's perspective and is a narrative of the order of creation continued in a time reference-frame of six days. However, the Bible uses the *ordinal form* of listing each day in The 2nd Telling because what happens on each succeeding day is dependent upon what happened on each *preceding day.*
- In The 3rd Telling, Genesis 2:4a is a repetition of a portion of the earlier theme of Gen. 1:1 and tells us the rest of the Second Chapter of Genesis will be a retrospective review of portions of the First Chapter of Genesis — i.e., portions of some of those original "*Six Days of Old.*" The Bible often gives emphasis by being repetitive and redundant. This statement in Genesis 2:4a is Moses, using his poetic license, to set up something new in his Creation Account that he had not mentioned before. By using the literary style of *retrospective analysis*, Moses thickens the plot, and tweaks our interest. Here, in Genesis 2:4a, not only does he prepare us for something new, but each following statement in Gen. 2:4b-5 will sharpen our focus, stimulate our curiosity, and draw our attention to an important event that occurred *on a particular day* in those *Six Days of Old*, when God started making and forming the earth. That important event will be revealed to us in Genesis 2:6.

(Gen. 2:4b) "In the Day that Jehovah made earth and heaven."

- The second phrase in *the 3rd Telling* (Gen. 2:4b), starts with these words: *'In the Day.'* This means the verses of *the 3rd Telling* will focus upon a specific day in those *Six Days of Creation*.
- Also note the earth is mentioned *before* heaven. This means the verses that follow Genesis 2:4b will specifically focus on the earth. In the New American Standard Bible, and the Modern Language Bible, Moses mentions *'heaven'* in its singular form. So, unlike *the heavens* in Gen. 1:1, and Gen. 2:4a, which refer to the universe at large — here in Gen. 2:4b, *'heaven'* does *not* refer to the universe at large. The *'heaven'* in Gen. 2:4b is *the earth's 'heaven'* — i.e., *the earth's atmosphere.* Since *all* English translations of the Bible *mention the earth before heaven* in Genesis 2:4b, we should understand — (beginning with Genesis 2:4b), the perspective of the Second Chapter of Genesis *switches from the universe at large to the earth and its atmosphere.*
- In Chapter Two of Genesis, the perspective of the earth and Adam's perspective *become one and the same after God breathes His 'Breath of Life' into Adam's nostrils in Gen. 2:7.*
- Note: in Gen. 2:4b, Moses introduces us to the personal, explicit, and most holy name for God. This is the first time the word *'Jehovah'* appears in the Bible. We have already talked about this in the Introduction — Part IX.
- Since we now know, from our prior discussions of the deeper meaning of the original Hebrew in Genesis One, that God started forming the earth on the 2nd Day (when He separated the waters below from those above) — we begin to think the waters above must have pre-existed the waters below. Since the earth is mentioned before heaven in Gen. 2:4b, we suspect we are going to learn something new about the earth that was not mentioned in Chapter One.

- Already, our interest is aroused. Imagine you are focusing the telescopic lens of your camera on a distant object. By doing so, you are seemingly bringing that object closer so that you can see it in more detail and learn more about it. In a similar way, Moses cleverly uses each verse that follows to serve the purpose of changing the focus of our attention. With each statement Moses makes, he is causing our mind to go backward in time from the 6th Day of Creation to the 2nd Day. He is causing us to 'focus' our attention on the 2nd Day when he will tell us about *the key event* that *Jehovah* caused to happen to the earth that initiated the formation of its atmosphere on the 2nd Day. If Moses had written this for us in Modern English, he would most probably have written Gen. 2:4b to say: *"On the 2nd Day of Creation when Jehovah began to form the earth and its atmosphere."*

Verses 5a, b, & c set the stage for the main event Genesis 2:6 will address.

(Gen. 2:5a) "Now no shrub of the field was yet in the earth, & no plant of the field had yet sprouted,"

The *2nd Telling* informed us Elohim made shrubs and plants on the 3rd Day. Since, at this point in *The 3rd Telling* vegetation did not exist, we intuit the main event, which will be described in verse 6, happened before the 3rd Day.

(Gen. 2:5b) "For Jehovah-Elohim had not sent rain upon the earth;"

Since we have just been told it had not yet *rained* on the earth, this phrase focuses our attention *on rain* and prepares us to expect an announcement of when and how the earth will experience its first *rain*. Also notice the most intimate and personal name for God (*Jehovah)* has been added to the Creator's name (*Elohim*) that appears in the 1st Chapter of Genesis.

(Gen. 2:5c) "And there was no man to cultivate the ground."

We know (from Chapter One) man was formed by *Elohim* near the end of the 6th Day. So, the main event of Genesis 2:4-6, which is not yet described, took place long before the 6th Day. We also know (from Chapter One) *the ground* which man would eventually cultivate (i.e., the continents *Elohim* brought forth), did not emerge to cause the 2nd separation of the waters (i.e., the separation of the *waters below heaven*), until the 3rd Day. So, the main event Moses is preparing us for — happened *before* the 3rd Day. With these words, Moses has focused the 'telescopic lenses' of our minds on the 2nd Day of Creation. We are now prepared for an announcement in the next verse that *the earth's first rain fell on the 2nd Day of Creation.*

(Gen. 2:6) "But steam rose from the earth & drowned the whole surface of the ground!"[960]

- On the 2nd Day of Creation, the earth formed as a fiery ball in space because its mass was formed by a relentless bombardment of countless numbers of meteorites that were the debris deposited in its orbital path from the rebounding shock wave of the dying supernova that preceded our sun.
- This bombardment continued for millions of years until the vast majority of the meteors that were in the earth's orbital path were accreted into the earth's mass.

[960] Schroeder *Genesis and the Big Bang* Chapter 8 p. 126 *b*

- As the debris-field slowly cleared, the incidence of impacts lessened, and the earth's surface crust slowly began to cool.
- The Genesis Code informs us — on the 2nd Day, *steam* rose from the earth and *drowned* the whole surface of the ground.
- Other English translations say *'a mist'* or *'a vapor'* used to rise from the earth. However, the words, *'vapor'* and *'mist'* covey the idea that the water, which rose from the earth on the 2nd Day was merely evaporating and rising into its atmosphere.
- But *the Genesis Code* tells us something *more* than simple evaporation was involved.
- The *'steam'* that rose from the earth on the 2nd Day *was the super-heated water vapor that was the product of the volcanism within earth's fiery interior;* something that continues to this day on a much smaller scale.
- *Steam rising from the earth is the main focus of this scripture and is the starting point for the formation of earth's early atmosphere and oceans.*
- When we read: *'And there was no man to cultivate the ground'* (in 2:5c) — and when we read: *'But steam rose from the earth and drowned the whole surface of the ground'* (in 2:6) — we must realize *'the ground'* in 2:5c is not the same 'ground' as *'the ground'* in 2:6.
  - Verse 2:5c refers to the 3rd Day of Creation. Therefore, the ground of 2:5c is the ground that was lifted up to separate the waters that God had placed below the waters that were already above. Thus, 'the ground' of 2:5c is the ground of the earth's *first continents* which were lifted up from the seafloor by God on the 3rd Day.
  - The 'ground' in verse 2:6 refers to the *thin surface crust* that developed on the slowly cooling fiery ball of the earth late on the 2nd Day when the epoch of impact-accretion slowed as the earth acquired and cleared the meteorite debris in its orbital path. Thus, 'the ground' of 2:6 became the *ocean floor* after the early earth had been completely submerged by the extended epoch of rain that fell at the end of the 2nd Day. It actually preceded *'the ground'* of 2:5c.

I must emphasize — Moses gave us a chronological sequence of creation in Genesis One which laid the foundation that made it possible for us to understand the literary style Moses used when he wrote Genesis Two. He employed the style of a retrospective review of a portion of the 2nd Day of Creation when he wrote Genesis 2:4-6. **Without an understanding of the "daily" sequences of creation that Moses explained in** Chapter **One, we would not have been able to understand Genesis 2:4-6.** This is one of the reasons why the ancient Jewish sages believed Genesis One was written before Genesis Two and why they believed both chapters were written by the same man—Moses!

WHEN DID THE EXODUS OCCUR?

The Bible says Moses was 40 years old when he fled Egypt and settled in the land of Midian (Acts 7:23-29). Forty years later (Acts 7:30), when Moses was 80, he had his 1st encounter with God in the burning bush incident on Mt. Sinai. That is when God told him to go back to Egypt and free the Israelites. The Bible says Moses died when he was 120 (Deut. 34:7).

- I Kings 6:1 tells us the Exodus occurred 480 years before the fourth year of Solomon's reign (~967 BC according to the Ryrie Bible study note on I Kings 6:1) — placing the Exodus at ~1447 BC (967 + 480 = 1447BC). Thus, this biblical calculation agrees with the archeological date for the Exodus given in the reference quoted earlier in this chapter when I listed some findings of *"Other Archaeological Studies."* If the 1447 BC date is correct, this would mean Moses was born 80 years earlier, in 1527 BC.

- Josephus says it was in 1532 BC when Moses fled as a refugee to Midian. If Josephus is correct, that would place the Exodus in 1492 BC if Moses was 40 when he went to Midian and 40 years later at the time of the Exodus he was 80 years old (1532 – 40 = 1492 BC). Therefore, Josephus places his birth in 1572 BC (1492 BC Exodus + 80 = 1572 BC his birth).

- Therefore, of the three sources quoted, two point to 1447 BC as the year of the Exodus, and one (Josephus), points to 1492 BC. That is a difference of only 45 years. I calculate that 45-year difference in two ways.
  1) The difference in the dates of the Exodus — (1492 – 1447 = 45).
  2) And using the differences in the dates of his birth — (1572 – 1527 = 45).

- For an event that occurred somewhere around about 3400-3500 years ago *Before the Present* — I think that is *pretty close*.

WHY DID MOSES FLEE EGYPT?

Although he was born a slave, Moses had been raised and educated as royalty in the house of Pharaoh's daughter. He had distinguished himself in the eyes of Pharaoh because he was the Egyptian general that defeated the Ethiopians in their war against Egypt. However, when he was 40 years old, he became so enraged at an Egyptian who was beating a Hebrew slave — he killed him. Fearing the punishment of death from Pharaoh, he fled from Egypt into the land of Midian and spent the next 40 years of his life tending sheep in the bleak Sinai Peninsula. When he was 80, God gave him the mission to lead His people out of Egyptian slavery. We all know the story. *Some have said Moses lived his first 40 years thinking he was a 'somebody' — his next 40 years thinking he was a 'nobody'— and his last 40 years — finding out 'what God can do with a nobody!'*

Summary Points on the 2nd Day of Creation:

1. **EARTH BEGINS TO FORM.**

   4 ½ billion years ago (about 750 million years before the end of the 2nd Day), when the universe was about 11.25 billion years old, the earth began forming from the collisions of countless numbers of meteors in our young solar system. Those meteors were the debris that had been spewed out from the center of a dying supernova.

2. **THE 2ND DAY WAS THE DAY THE EARTH WAS BORN.**

   On the 2nd day Elohim created *heaven* (in the singular, i.e., *the earth's atmosphere*) to separate the waters above from the waters below. He created *'the highest heavens'* earlier. So, the Bible states — before the earth was formed, there was water in space: *the waters of the highest heavens.* Since the Bible says the waters *above* were separated from *the waters below* on the 2nd Day, the earth's core and mass would have started forming *early* on the 2nd Day in order to provide the place for the separation of the waters below. This means *the waters above are those waters that are in the deep of space* — i.e., above the earth's atmosphere. *The waters below* are those waters that are located *on* the earth's surface, *inside* the earth's interior, and *in* the earth's atmosphere.

3. **EARTH WAS BORN IN FIRE.**

When the earth began to form on the 2ⁿᵈ Day, earth's temperatures were so high that our planet's surface was *'on fire.'* Back then, the surface of the earth was an *'ocean'* of molten rock miles deep. Temperatures exceeded 8,000 degrees Fahrenheit — similar to the surface temperature of our sun. Huge meteorites reigned down in a relentless bombardment.

4. **THE METEORS IMPACTING THE EARTH CAME FROM OUTER SPACE & CONTAINED PORTIONS OF THE WATERS FROM ABOVE.**

The meteorites that bombarded and accreted to form the earth's mass contained the ice-coated building blocks Elohim had made and formed in the nuclear furnaces of the supernovae of the universe and the first-order stars that were at least ten times the size of our Sun. *Water-ice* was one of those 'building blocks.' No rocks survived the impact-accretion period, but countless tiny crystals of *zircon* did. *Uranium carrying zircon crystals,* help date the earth. They are only found in erupted magma-lava-rocks. They formed deep within the earth's semi-liquid molten mantle-rocks when earth's subterranean waters, which had been brought to the earth by meteorites — mixed with the super-heated mantle-rock and caused them to melt and boil up to erupt through surface vents in the crust of the primordial earth. These crystals contain the evidence that water molecules had once been trapped within the zircon.[961] *Zircon crystals are the evidence that tells us our planet's water arrived from outer space.* It had been carried to the earth by the billions upon billions of meteorites that impacted our fiery ball as the mass of our earth formed.[962] Approximately 5% of the mass of meteorites is water.

5. **WHEN THE METEORS IN THE ORBITAL PATH OF OUR PLANET WERE ACCRETED INTO THE EARTH, OUR FIERY 'BALL' COOLED. THIS CAUSED A METAMORPHOSIS OF OUR PLANET.**

We now think — 4.4 billion years ago (about 650 million years before the end of the 2ⁿᵈ Day, when the earth was about 100 million years old), meteors still crashed into the planet, but the number of impacts per-unit-time declined as the debris in earth's orbit began to clear. As the debris-field cleared, the ever-decreasing frequency of collisions allowed cooling to begin, and the earth's surface solidified into a thin crust of dark volcanic basaltic-rock. The radioactivity that provided much of the heat was slowly declining, paving the way for earth's second radical change, *its transformation from a fiery ball in space into a water-world.* [963]

6. **THE EARTH'S 1ˢᵀ PROLONGED EPOCH OF VOLCANIC OUTGASSING:**

As the earth cooled, the volcanic activity in the earth's subsurface semi-liquid mantle of molten rock caused cracks in the earth's thin surface crust. For eons of time, volcanic eruptions caused a *continuous spewing out* of tons of carbon dioxide, sulfur dioxide, and copious volumes of super-heated vaporized water molecules in the form of steam.[964]

[961] Article: Precocious Earth http://science.nasa.gov/headlines/y2001/ast17jan_1.html
[962] The History Channel: *How the Earth Was Made: Part I*
[963] The History Channel: *How the Earth Was Made: Part I*
[964] Article: Volcanic Gases and Their Effects **volcanoes**.usgs.gov/hazards/gas/**index**.php

7. **THE EARLY EARTH WAS ENVELOPED BY A THICK, DARK, POISONOUS CLOUD.**

So, 4.1 billion years ago, about 350 million years before the end of the 2nd Day, when the earth was about 400 million years old, and the universe was about 11.65 billion years old; as the super-heated water evaporated off the surface of the earth, huge amounts of water vapor rose to join the carbon dioxide, sulfur dioxide, and other noxious vapors, ashes, silicates, and other materials of volcanism that continuously spewed forth into the young earth's poisonous primordial dark, and opaque atmosphere. The young earth was blanketed by a thick, dark poisonous cloud. This is the process Dr. Schroeder refers to as volcanic eruptions and science calls volcanic out-gassing. [965,966]

8. VOLCANISM CAUSED AN EPOCH OF RELENTLESS RAIN THAT FORMED THE EARTH'S OCEANS.

As vast quantities of volcanically produced steam were vented onto and above the earth's cooling surface, the colossal amounts of super-heated water vapor rose to join the carbon dioxide, other volcanic gases, and the other products of volcanism in the early atmosphere of the earth 4.1 billion years ago. [967] *So, when the earth was only about 400 million years old, this condensing water would trigger the first and greatest continuous down-pour of rain the earth would ever see. Scientists believe it rained continuously from thunderstorms for about one hundred million years.[968] The result was a toxic water-world.* At the end of this deluge, our fiery planet was converted from a fiery ball into a planet covered by a great depth of toxic ocean water.

9. **THE STAGE WAS SET FOR THE 3RD DAY.**

4 billion years ago, when the earth was about 500 million years old, its surface was a vast ocean. Its monstrous seas were iron-rich, making them an olive-green color. Carbon dioxide, sulfur dioxide, and other noxious gases and silicate products of volcanism still filled earth's atmosphere so thickly that the skies appeared purple red. The dense atmosphere produced enough pressure to crush a human body flat. It was also incredibly hot — with temperatures exceeding 200 degrees Fahrenheit. This toxic water-world would remain for another ½ billion years. But further dramatic changes were on their way. A 2nd epoch of renewed volcanic activity would trigger the construction of the continents by creating an entirely new kind of rock. On the 3rd Day of Creation, earth's continental land masses would appear, and earth would become a *Granite Planet.* [969] By the end of the 4th Day of Creation, the Creator would give the earth its life-friendly atmosphere and oceans.

Does any other scripture in the Bible give us any hint the earth formed in fire, and then changed into a water-world? We have already mentioned *the Vision of Amos.* Please review the discussion of the Vision of Amos in the last part of Chapter 9 in Book II.

[965] Schroeder *Genesis and the Big Bang* Chapter 8 p. 122 *e*—123 *a*
[966] The History Channel: *How the Earth Was Made: Part I*
[967] Schroeder *Genesis and the Big Bang* Chapter 8 p. 122 *e* & 126 *b,c*
[968] Article: Earth in the Beginning by Tim Appenzeller, National Geographic Magazine Dec. 2006
Search: Early Earth Article, Hadean Information, Earth History Facts
http://science.nationalgeographic.com/science/space/solar-system/early-earth.html
[969] Article: *Igneous Rocks* http://www.tulane.edu/~sanelson/geol111/igneous.htm

❧
CHAPTER 27: YUDS—LAMEDS—THE NEFESH HAIYAH—THE NESHAMA—&—THE NEPHILIM.

We will now turn our attention to Genesis 2:7 and we will make a comparison with Genesis 2:19.
In this chapter, we will examine:

I.   The extra *Yud* in the spelling of the Hebrew word for *'formed'* in 2:7.
II. The *superfluous lamed that is prefixed to the Hebrew word for the animal 'soul' in 2:7.*
III. The meaning of *nefesh, & nefesh haiyah,* and the different interpretations Onkelos made in regard to the nefesh haiyah in Gen. 1:20-21, 1:24, and 2:7.
IV. We will also introduce something *new* about the *neshama.*
V.   Then, we will talk a bit about what Dr. Schroeder said about the *Nephilim.*   O. David

In the five English Translations of Genesis 2:7 listed below, notice two do not mention the word — *'soul.'* Three do. (Note: The Revised Standard Version & the New American Standard Bible are identical.)

(Gen. 2:7) "Then the LORD GOD formed man of dust from the ground and breathed into his nostrils the breath of life; and man became a living 'being.'"   RSV

(Gen. 2:7) "Then the LORD GOD formed man of dust from the ground and breathed into his nostrils the breath of life; and man became a living 'being.'"   NASB

(Gen. 2:7) "And the LORD GOD formed the man from the dust of the ground and breathed into his nostrils the breath of life, and the man became a living 'soul.'"   MLB

(Gen. 2:7) "And the LORD GOD formed man of the dust of the ground and breathed into his nostrils the breath of life; and man became a living 'soul.'"   KJV

(Gen. 2:7) "And Jehovah-Elohim formed (ya-tsar) *the man out of dust* (`aphar) *from the ground* ('adamah) *and blew* (naphach) *into his nostrils* ('aph) *the breath of life* (the neshama); *and man became a living* 'soul' ('to' a nephesh haiyah)."   TIB

The Hebrew words (in parenthesis above), have the following meanings:
- *Ya-tsar* means 'to mold into a form, using some already created substance.'
- The meaning of `aphar is 'dust, clay, earth, mud, ground, or ashes.'
- *Adamah* means 'the earth, ground, land, or country.'
- *Naphach* means 'to blow, blew, or breathe into, inflate, or to puff.'
- *'Aph* means 'nostril.'
- And, in both Gen. 1:20-21 and Gen. 1:24, *nefesh haiyah* means 'a living animal soul.'
- But, in Genesis 2:7, the phrase "*'to' a nefesh haiyah*" has been translated by Onkelos as *'a communicating spirit.'* We'll talk about that in this chapter.

I.   THE EXTRA YUD (IN GEN. 2:7) IN THE HEBREW WORD FOR 'FORMED.'

The Bible says the body of mankind was *formed* from the *dust of the ground*. The Hebrew word for man, *adam*, derives directly from the Hebrew word *adamah*, meaning *ground or soil*. In his book, *The Science of God*, Dr. Schroeder said the Hebrew Bible tells us: *(Genesis 2:7) "And the LORD GOD formed the adam dust from the adamah..."* [970]

---

[970] Schroeder *The Science of God* Chapter 9 p. 139*b*

The Bible also says the bodies of all of the animals were formed from the same material as Adam, the ground: *(Gen. 2:19) "And the LORD GOD formed from the adamah all the animals."* [971]

However, the Hebrew script Moses wrote shows a crucial difference between these two verses. In the verse that relates to the forming of man (Genesis 2:7), the Jewish Bereshit Hebrew word for 'formed' is spelled with *two* Yuds (two Hebrew marks called '*Yud'*). Although the structure and grammar are the same in 2:7 and 2:19 — in Genesis 2:19, the Jewish Bereshit Hebrew word for '*formed,*' that is used for the formation of the animals, is spelled with *one* Yud. Go into any synagogue in the world — it doesn't matter if the synagogue is in Africa, the Americas, Europe, Australia, or Asia — every Torah scroll is written this way.

Yud is the *abbreviation of God's explicit name.* According to Dr. Schroeder, the '*Yud'* is best translated as '*the Eternal.*' Three influential ancient Jewish commentators — Rashi, Maimonides, and Nahmanides — explain the extra *Yud* in Genesis 2:7 this way. In Genesis 2:7, the extra *Yud* in the verb that involves the forming of mankind, means the Bible is telling us that even though mankind and animals may share a common physical origin, *there is an extra spiritual input into humans. That extra input,* according to these commentators, *is the Neshama — the spiritual human soul of life-eternal Jehovah-Elohim breathed into the nostrils of the first man. In Hebrew Cosmogony, this Neshama is the one thing that distinguishes man from beast!* [972]

II.   THE SUPERFLUOUS LAMED PREFIXED TO THE HEBREW WORD FOR THE ANIMAL 'SOUL:'
The Bible distinguishes man from beast. Nahmanides noticed something about the phrasing of *nefesh haiyah* in Genesis 2:7 that was different from the way it was phrased in 1:20-21, and 1:24. The Hebrew text of Genesis 2:7 says: *"And the adam became <u>to</u> a nefesh haiyah (i.e., **to** a living soul)."*

This '*to'* addition is the result of an extra Hebrew letter that is called the *lamed,* which was 'prefixed' to the word for 'soul' in this verse. From a grammatical standpoint, Nahmanides felt the lamed was *superfluous.* So, he reasoned it was there in 2:7 to teach us something. He wondered if it meant — *"perhaps the making of man involved a change in form."* Could the *lamed* in 2:7 mean that mankind might have progressed through different stages of development when he was made and formed by the Creator? If so, Nahmanides reasoned: *When the creature (that Elohim had already formed), received the Neshama in Gen. 2:7 — it became a human!* Nahmanides wrote a rather lengthy commentary on this conjecture about the implications of the *lamed* in 2:7 and concluded his comments with these words: *"Or it may be that the verse is stating that prior to receiving the Neshama, it was a completely living being and by the Neshama it was transformed into another man."*

So, according to Nahmanides, the biblical text has told us — before the Neshama, there was perhaps — *something like-a-man that was not quite human.*[973] Suddenly, *cavemen* (i.e., the Neanderthals and the Cro-Magnons), that science has proved existed prior to Adam, by many thousands of years — make sense.

---

[971] Schroeder *The Science of God* Chapter 9 p. 139*b*
[972] Schroeder *The Science of God* Chapter 9 p. 139*b,c,d,e*
[973] Schroeder, *The Science of God,* Chapter 9 p. 140

In the last part of Chapter 22, we mentioned Maimonides had similar thoughts. Please refer to the discussion in Chapter 22, which concerns the deeper meaning of *'The Beasts of the Earth and/or The Rulers of the Field.'* We concluded that discussion with these words: *"Thus, it is that there are ancient, accepted sources that describe animals (i.e., the Cro-Magnons), with human shape, form, intelligence, and judgment that looked exactly like human beings, but were nevertheless not truly human. Suddenly cave paintings that predate Adam by 20,000 years and the archeological evidence that proves the pre-Adam 10,000-year-old inception of agriculture (4000 years before Adam), and the pre-Adam 8,000-year-old inception of pottery (2000 years before Adam), become understandable. These less-than-human creatures had human-like skills. According to the Talmud and ancient Jewish tradition, what they lacked was human spirituality.[974]"*

Thus, we can surmise the Cro-Magnons lacked the God-breathed spiritual soul of eternal life — *the Neshama* — which is the defining otherworldly essence of human beings. Therefore, it is *possible* that *the Rulers of the Field were Cro-Magnons.*[975] And it is possible that when God first made *Adam* (in Genesis 1:26), he was a Cro-Magnon. Then, when God breathed the *Neshama* into his nostrils in Genesis 2:7, *the Neshama changed him into the world's first human being.* The ancient sages certainly knew nothing about the fossil evidence of the existence of Cro-Magnon creatures when these ancient commentaries were written, but the paleontological discoveries of modern science *certainly prove Cro-Magnon creatures existed on Earth in Adam's day.* However, Neanderthals died out ~25,000 years before Adam was created. They were not contemporaries of Adam. They were long gone when Adam arrived.

III. THE ANIMAL 'NEFESH HAIYAH' IS DIFFERENT FROM OUR HUMAN 'NEFESH HAIYAH.'

Moses tells us animals have a soul. He uses the same words for the soul of animal life (i.e., *nefesh haiyah*) in Gen. 1:20-21, and 1:24. However, in Genesis 2:7 Moses changed the spelling of *nefesh haiyah*. He added *the lamed* — *'to'* (i.e., *'to'* a nefesh haiyah). This is the same superfluous *lamed* we have just discussed. Nevertheless, English translations of the Bible do *not* mention there is such a thing as *an animal soul* in 1:20-21, and 1:24.

The King James Bible and the Modern Language Bible *do* mention the word *'soul,'* but only in relation to the soul of man in Genesis 2:7. In that verse, both say: *'and man became a living soul.'* However, in Genesis 2:7, the Revised Standard Version and the New American Standard Bible make no mention of a soul and simply say: *"And man became a living being."*

Hebrew has two terms for soul: *nefesh haiyah* and *Neshama*. The first 'soul of life' mentioned in the Moses Creation Account is *the animal nefesh haiyah* in Genesis 1:20-21. The 2nd mention of *the nefesh haiyah* is in Genesis 1:24. Why would our English translations of the Bible leave out the vital fact that **Animals have a soul?** Was the omission of this very important detail in Genesis 1:20-21, and 1:24 the result of an oversight committed by the Jewish translators employed by Ptolemy when they translated the Torah into Greek? Or did the error occur in other translations centuries later? The *Torah*, the *Talmud*, and *Jewish tradition* teach *all animals* have the soul of animal life — the *nefesh haiyah*. Biblically, an animal is defined as a *living nefesh* (i.e., *a nefesh*

---

[974] Schroeder, *The Science of God*, Chapter 9, p. 141*e*
[975] Schroeder, *The Science of God*, Chapter 9, p. 141*f*

haiyah). The ancient Hebrews believed the 'soul of animal life' gives all animals (including man), the decision-making program that science calls *'first-order instincts.'* Our first-order instincts direct us and all animals to:

- Seek pleasure and avoid pain.
- Seek shelter and avoid discomfort.
- Seek nourishment, nurture our kind, and avoid hunger.
- Seek to survive, thrive, reproduce, and avoid injury and death.[976]

So it is Elohim placed this soul of animal life, this *nefesh haiyah*, in all animals, including man. It is a bit of divinity that Elohim placed in *all* living animals.

ONKELOS' DIFFERENT INTERPRETATION OF NEFESH HAIYAH IN GENESIS 2:7

The descriptive essence of animal life (*the nefesh haiyah* — in Hebrew), appears three times in the Torah in the first two chapters of Genesis.

- In Genesis 1:20-21 *the nefesh haiyah* relates to the establishment of the *first animal life* on Earth. This is the *aquatic* life the Bible mentions on the 5th Day.
- Next, it is found in the mention of the *first land animals* at the start of the 6th Day in Genesis 1:24.
- Finally, the phrase: *'to a nefesh haiyah'* is found in *the 3rd Telling* of the Creation Account in Genesis 2:7 near the close of the 6th Day when *'the adam'* is mentioned.[977]

In each of the first two instances, Onkelos translates *nefesh haiyah* as *'a living animal'* — the literal meaning of the Hebrew. But when Moses mentioned *mankind in Genesis 2:7*, the Hebrew text has a *slight variation*. The text says: *"The adam became 'to' a nefesh haiyah."* Based on the *lamed* (*'to'*), which was added, Onkelos translated *'to a nefesh haiyah'* as — *'a communicating spirit.'*

> *"And the eternal God formed the adam dust from the ground and breathed into his nostrils the Neshama of life and the adam became a communicating spirit (i.e., 'to' a nefesh haiyah)"* — (from The Onkelos Aramaic Translation of Genesis 2:7).

So, it is we see the animal that became Adam was *different* in *three very special ways* from the other man-like hominids God formed and made on the 6th Day.

- His *nefesh haiyah* was different. Adam's *nefesh haiyah* possessed the *lamed*. It was: *'to a nefesh haiyah,'* as opposed to the *'nefesh haiyah'* the other animals received. The Onkelos translation informs us this meant Adam would become *'a communicating spirit.'* Adam would not only speak. **He would also learn to write!**
- His *forming* was special and different. Adam's *forming* involved two *Yuds* as opposed to the one *Yud* involved in the forming of all of the other animals. The *Yud* is an abbreviation of God's explicit holy name which means *'the Eternal.'* Therefore, when Adam was formed, this signaled he would receive *an extra spiritual input*.
- Finally, he alone, among all of the animals, was next *created*. This means — Adam received the extra spiritual input that had been foretold by the extra *Yud* in his forming when God breathed the breath of life into his nostrils in Genesis 2:7. That breath of life was the divine human spirit of eternal life —*The Neshama*.

---

[976] Schroeder, *The Science of God* Chapter 11 p. 171-172
[977] Schroeder *The Science of God* Chapter 9 p 145a

The vital *qualitative* characteristic that sets humans apart from all other animals *is our immanent spirituality <u>and our ability to share that spirituality with others</u>*. The *Neshama* is the distinguishing *qualitative* factor that differentiates humans from other animals. It cannot be measured or quantitated. When a human dies, the *Neshama* leaves the body. *It leaves no imprint.* <u>It is the only part of humans that is *Eternal.*</u> Archaeologists can never discover the fossil remains of the *Neshama* because the *Neshama* is *totally spiritual.*[978]

ADAM'S COMMUNICATING SPIRIT, HIS NESHAMA, AND WRITING

Dr. Schroeder makes a startling statement and proposal in Chapter 9 of his book, *The Science of God.* On page 143, under the heading of: *'Writing Humanity in the Record,'* he talks about a *qualitative leap* that occurred about six thousand years ago at the *"creation"* of Adam. That qualitative *leap* was the *Neshama.* Archaeology has provided us with an impressive record of that change. Though the soul leaves no material remains, the effects of the spirituality brought by the *Neshama* are written loud and clear in the remnants of ancient Mesopotamia.

In all the major museums in the world, the division between history and *prehistory* has been set at *the invention of rudimentary writing.* Therefore, when we refer to something as *'prehistoric,'* we are really saying — it happened *before* the invention of the first form of rudimentary writing. We are not referring to the *pictographs* the Neanderthals and the Cro-Magnons drew on the walls of their caves. Those pictographs illustrated the main theme of the event they were meant to convey. But the pictographs still required an oral interpretation to convey the complete *history.* Furthermore, we are not talking about the sophisticated form *of writing* Moses used, because Moses wrote with a fully developed and sophisticated Hebrew *aleph-bet*, which arguably may have predated the Greek alphabet.

No. Even though the beginning of written communications started with the *pictographs* of the Neanderthal and Cro-Magnon *man-like hominids*; several thousands of years passed before the pictographs were developed into *cuneiform's six hundred stylized symbols.* It is generally accepted — *cuneiform* is the earliest form of communication that can be called *the first form of rudimentary 'writing,'* because cuneiform *could be fully interpreted by any reader and did not require an oral interpretation* to convey *the complete 'history.'* The invention of cuneiform occurred in Mesopotamia, in Adam's time, approximately 2000 years before the birth of Abraham. Archaeologists date that first writing at five to six thousand years Before the Present — the exact period the Bible tells us the Neshama was breathed into 'the man' and Adam was created!

As the populations of man-like hominids grew, improvements in agriculture and animal husbandry led to greater food supplies which freed large segments of the population from the necessity of providing food. Man-like hominids were no longer tied to the land. As *'people'* moved into progressively larger communities, the need for an increasing number and variety of goods and services grew. This caused a division of labor which inherently accompanies any move from farm to city. All of this happened *after* the advent of large cities. Commercial transactions followed as goods and services were

---

[978] Schroeder *The Science of God* Chapter 9 p 145*b*

traded for food and other essentials. As the population of cities grew, the demand for civil administration grew. *All of this made the invention of writing inevitable.*

THE PARALLEL BETWEEN ADAM AND WRITING IS NO MERE COINCIDENCE.

As just stated, commercial transactions became necessary when people began to congregate into larger groups — eventually giving rise to big cities. One of the first of those cities was *Uruk* which was located on the banks of the Euphrates River in Mesopotamia, some 60 miles northwest of *Ur* — the city the Bible says was the birthplace of Abraham (Genesis 11:27-28). Dr. Schroeder says there is a graphic description of the parallel between Adam and writing on display in the Mesopotamian rooms of the British Museum, where a plaque states: *"The earliest cities evolved before 5500 years ago as local centers. But, about this time there was also a change in scale. The most important innovation of the period, however, was the invention of writing. The stimulus for the emergence and development of writing was the need to record economic transactions. So, the start of writing was directly tied to the need for bartering, which related to the formation of large cities."*

WHY DID LARGE CITIES APPEAR AT THAT TIME? WHY NOT EARLIER?

With the invention of agriculture, the land could support larger populations. It is, however, unlikely that a population explosion was the sole cause of the start of large cities. Man-like hominids had invented agriculture almost 4000 years before the creation of Adam and for those thousands of years they did not live in large cities. A key element that would facilitate the transition from village to city was missing. Dr. Schroeder thinks the missing factor was the *Neshama*.[979] Ergo, large cities came into being shortly after the creation of Adam. And Adam was the first '*animal*' to receive the *Neshama*. The same verse in the Bible that tells us when and how *'the adam'* received the *Neshama* and became *'Adam,'* also tells us the hominid that was *the adam* before it received the *Neshama* was the one that became " *'to' a nefesh haiyah"* when it received the *Neshama*. So, *the adam* that became *Adam*, became the first hominid to possess — *"a communicating spirit."* We get that from the *lamed* — *'to'* (i.e., *'to' a nefesh haiyah*) in Genesis 2:7. Thus, the Earth's 1st human was *"created."*

THE BEGINNING OF WRITING IS ASSOCIATED WITH THE ADVENT OF ADAM.

This puts a whole new level of meaning on the Onkelos Aramaic translation of the ending phrase of Genesis 2:7, doesn't it?

IV.   SOMETHING NEW ABOUT THE NESHAMA.

We and all animals are pleasure seekers, but the 2nd Divine Creation the Torah mentions in Genesis 2:7 is the *Neshama*, which is *the soul that is unique to humankind*. Humans have an additional source of pleasure that is not evident in other animals. That additional source of pleasure is our Neshama. Our Neshama is *our God-breathed divine human soul of life-eternal*. Our Neshama is our link to God. God is the all-encompassing Unity that underlies all He created — the universe, and all that exists — including us and our Earth. The Neshama was given to all humans. Adam was its first recipient. And, according to Hebrew Cosmogony, *the Neshama* is what distinguishes humans (i.e., the hominids

---

[979] Schroeder *The Science of God* Chapter 9 p 143-144

that descended from Adam and Eve through Seth)[980] from all other animals — both those that preceded Adam and those that would follow. Among the most recent of those who preceded Adam were the Cro-Magnons. They were also Adam's contemporaries. Again, I wish to emphasize — according to the Talmud and ancient Jewish Tradition, Adam *may* have been one of their number when he was first made and formed by God. After God breathed His Neshama into the nostrils of *the adam* (whom He had previously formed), *the adam* became *the Adam* (*the first man*). At that moment, Adam became aware of a pleasure that transcended his animal nefesh — i.e., his heretofore sense of a limited physical existence. In addition to the first divine gift of his nefesh, which gave him his animal instincts for physical pleasure (*eros*) and survival, Adam *now had* God's 2nd Divine Creation, *the Neshama*. Thus, God gave man both the *nefesh* and the *Neshama*. Once Adam received the *Neshama, he was capable of an awareness of God's grand divine spiritual goals for man.*

How we choose to achieve our pleasure determines the quality of our person. The Neshama informs us there is something out there that is bigger than ourselves. We become more aware of that something we call "the community of mankind," and can feel the sense of an obligation to contribute in positive ways. We recognize "the me that I am" and can realistically compare 'it' with "the me that I should be and can become." And we can at least identify with "the me I want to be" even before we have achieved 'it!' Our "God-breathed Neshama" gives us the capacity to love in ways that surpass the motivation our nefesh-driven eros provides. Our Neshama is the engine which gives us the capacity for brotherly love (philia), and sacrificial love (agape). It is our Neshama that can guide us on our journey through this thing we call life, and can motivate us to make the sometimes hard, but correct choices that contribute to the welfare of others.[981, 982] With the Neshama, man is equipped to recognize the existence of a higher power. Man becomes sensitive to the existence, presence, and Will of God.

According to Dr. Schroeder, the Bible teaches the age of responsibility is 20. Only after one has become twenty years of age, does one become responsible for his actions (Num 1:3, 14:29).[983] Hebrew cosmogony holds it is our Neshama and not any physical attribute we possess, which separates us from all other life. It is our Neshama that makes us *moral beings* who possess *the spirit of the Eternal.* Our Neshama *sets us apart from amoral animals.* Perhaps this is the underlying reason for the Jewish legend that *Adam was created when he was twenty years old* — and caused the ancient Jewish sages to think perhaps "*the adam*" was formed as a *man-like animal 19 years before* he received the *Neshama. He may have lived his first 19 years without the Neshama* — possessing only *the nefesh* for that period of time.[984]

[980] Since Cain killed Able before he had any descendants, and Cain and his descendants died in Noah's flood — (according to the Bible), all humans are descendants of Seth (Adam and Eve's 3rd son). Noah is in the lineage of Adam through Seth.

[981] Schroeder *The Science of God* Chapter 9 p 144

[982] Schroeder *The Science of God* Chapter 11 p 172

[983] In Moses' time, the age of eligibility for military service (i.e., 20 years old) was considered to be the '*age of responsibility.*'

[984] Schroeder *The Science of God* Chapter 9 p 137*d,e*

Humans have *both* the nefesh and the Neshama. But, according to the ancient Hebrew belief, the mention of the Neshama only in relation to Adam and Eve means — *all other animals have only the nefesh.*[985]

V.   THE NEPHILIM

In Chapter 22 and Chapter 23 I mentioned the Jewish Sages thought the possession of both the nefesh and the Neshama is what distinguished Adam from the anatomically modern humans they called the Nephilim (what others call the Cro-Magnons). In referring to the generations following Adam and Eve, in Genesis 6:1-4, The New American Standard Bible talks about the *Nephilim* —*"Now it came about, when men began to multiply on the face of the land, and daughters were born to them, that the sons of God saw that the daughters of men were beautiful. And they took wives for themselves, whomever they chose. Then the LORD said, 'My Spirit shall not strive with man forever, because he also is flesh; nevertheless, his days shall be one hundred and twenty years.' The Nephilim were on the earth in those days, and also afterward, when the sons of God came into the daughters of men, and they bore children to them. Those were the mighty men who were of old, men of renown."*

The Interlinear Bible gives us a different take on Genesis 6:4—

"The giants (nᵉphil) were on the Earth in those days, and even afterwards when the sons of God came into the daughters of men, and they bore to them. They were heroes (gibbor) who existed from ancient time ('olam) the men of name."

`OLAM = ANCIENT TIMES—ANCIENT DAYS

In the Bible, whenever you see the terms: *'ancient times,'* or *'ancient days,'* the reference is to a time in the very remote past. In Genesis 6:4, the Hebrew root word *('olam)*[986] that is interpreted as *'ancient time'* means *'time out of mind, of old time, or the beginning of the world.'* Since Genesis 6:4 is talking about the time when *"men began to multiply on the earth:"* that time was *the time* that occurred *after* the end of the 6th Day. The *end of the 6th Day* was the time of the *advent* of *Adam.* It was also the time God completed His Creation. That *'ancient time'* would have occurred after the events of creation were complete. In all likelihood, it occurred in *the early Holocene Epoch, in the immediate Post-Adam Period.* Therefore, the *'ancient time'* in Genesis 6:4 was most likely a part of the early Holocene Epoch, *after* but *near, the advent of Adam and Eve.* Why think it was *after* the advent of Adam and Eve? Because the Bible says it was the time when men had begun to multiply on the face of the land, meaning enough time had occurred after Adam that the population of humans was notably increasing. The Hebrew root word *(nᵉphil)*[987] in Genesis 6:4 that the Interlinear Bible interprets as *'giants'* can also mean: *'a bully or tyrant.'* But, in the same verse, The Interlinear Bible says these *'giants'* were *'heroes'* (from the Hebrew root word, *gibbors*).[988] *Gibbor* can also mean: *'powerful warriors, champions, chiefs, giants, mighty men, strong men, or valiant men.'* These are *the laudatory meanings.* Hence, the Interlinear Bible decided to interpret these *'men'* as

[985] Schroeder *The Science of God* Chapter 9 p 139 *e*
[986] The Interlinear Bible and the Hebrew and Chaldee Dictionary
[987] The Interlinear Bible and the Hebrew and Chaldee Dictionary
[988] The Interlinear Bible and the Hebrew and Chaldee Dictionary

'heroes.' However, the root word can also mean: 'bullies, tyrants, fugitives, inferiors, or fallen.'[989] The King James Bible and the Modern Language Bible also translate n^{e}phil as 'giants;' but, the Revised Standard Version and the New American Standard Bible translate the Hebrew root word n^{e}phil as 'the Nephilim.' The only other time in the Bible that the word Nephilim is found is in Numbers 13:33.[990] That verse refers to the report of some of the scouts Moses sent into the Holy Land 'to spy out' the land God told them to enter and possess. The scouts reported they saw men of great size (the Nephilim who were sons of Anak) — who looked upon them as if they were grasshoppers because the Israelite spies were so small. The 'sons of Anak' were supposedly Giants. The Nephilim could have been Cro-Magnons!

The Ryrie Study Bible note on Genesis 6:4 says the Hebrew root word for the 'Nephilim' means 'to fall'—as in 'to fall upon others because they were men of strength.' However, in his book The Science of God, Dr. Schroeder gives us a different take on 'fallen.' He says — Nephilim means 'fallen or inferior,' and explains that Adam, having the Neshama — would have found the Cro-Magnon inferior in spirit although not in body.[991] Nevertheless, we know the Cro-Magnons were very tall. They towered over the Neanderthals and other hominids that were (for a short time) their contemporaries.

The phrases: 'the men of name,' and 'men of renown,' come from a Hebrew root word that can mean: 'honor, authority, character, famous, renown, or report.' — but can also mean — 'shame,' or 'connoting the idea of definite and conspicuous position.' So, you can easily understand why there is so much mystery and mysticism concerning just who these 'people,' or 'things,' or 'animals' were (i.e., the Nephilim), that found the daughters of men so beautiful that they cohabited with them.

AN OLD TALMUDIC LEGEND ABOUT EVE

There is an old Talmudic legend which posits — after Eve ate the forbidden fruit from the Tree of the Knowledge of Good and Evil, she realized she was destined to die. She also realized if Adam did not eat the forbidden fruit, he would live forever. So, the legend states Eve became so distressed Adam might take another wife (after her death), that she persuaded him to eat the fruit so he would also be mortal.[992] Interesting myth? Psychological speculation? Perhaps, except for one thing — the possibility of Adam taking another wife. According to the Bible, Adam and Eve were the only human beings at the time. So how is it possible another woman could enter into the picture? Is the Talmud proposing there were other non-human females present who were so much like Eve that they might attract Adam's interest? I think Eve might have considered that after God evicted them from the Garden of Eden — but not before.[993] The Bible leads us to believe Adam and Eve were the only ones of their 'kind' in the Garden.

Today, there is a considerable amount of religious controversy concerning the claims for the existence of pre-Adam creatures similar to humans in shape and intellect

989 The Ryrie Study Bible: Note on Genesis 6:4—the Nephilim
990 The Ryrie Study Bible: Note on Genesis 6:4
991 Schroeder The Science of God Chapter 9 p 142b
992 Schroeder The Science of God Chapter 9 p 142 d & e
993 I can see Eve might have discovered the existence of Cro-Magnon women after their expulsion from the Garden of Eden. But the Bible says the Garden of Eden was the place where God put Adam and Eve. I don't believe any Cro-Magnons were in the Garden.

but less than human in spirit. However, when the ancient commentaries were being written, paleontology did not exist. No one was digging up old bones and claiming to discover relics of intelligent pre-human creatures. *There was no incentive* to prompt the commentators of one and two thousand years ago *to speculate about pre-human hominids.* Their idea of the existence of pre-Adam human-like creatures was learned directly from the special wording of the Bible. Science has confirmed the Bible's description of life starting immediately on the Earth after it had cooled. The Bible has also documented the literal explosion of life on the 5th Day, and the progression from the simple biosphere of the 5th Day to the complexity of the modern biosphere on the 6th Day. Science has also confirmed the ancient Hebrew assertion that *less-than-human creatures with human-like bodies and brains existed before Adam but were also on the Earth after Adam.*[994]

No one knows for certain *who* the Nephilim were or *where* they came from. All sorts of ideas have been proposed that range from the speculation they were *fallen angels* who were formerly *'sons of God'* that rebelled and came to Earth to have sexual intercourse with human women — to *extra-terrestrial aliens* from outer space who visited Earth from time to time in their spaceships and cohabited with some Earth-women. Whoever they were, they were giants — supposedly.

OCCAM'S RAZOR

There is an axiom known as *Occam's razor*. It is a principle that states — *Among competing hypotheses, the one which makes the fewest assumptions is most probably correct.*

Here, we have ancient Jewish Talmudic Sages who have proposed what *may be the most likely hypothesis for the origin of the Nephilim.* The Bible says they were *the mighty men of old, men of renown who came into the daughters of men who bore children to them.* Science has discovered there *is* evidence some Cro-Magnons (i.e., *'AMHs'* — for *anatomically modern humans*), and Neanderthals interbred. We now know some modern humans carry immune genes that originated in Neanderthals and Cro-Magnons. [995,996] The idea that Cro-Magnons interbred with humans in ancient Biblical times is *at least as plausible as* the idea that the Nephilim were extra-terrestrial space aliens. *In my view, the idea that Cro-Magnon Giants were the "fallen Nephilim" that procreated with the beautiful daughters of men in 'ancient times' — is more plausible.*

There is enough scientific evidence that fills major museums the world over, which *proves* Cro-Magnons not only pre-existed Adam, but were also his contemporaries. Furthermore, there has been enough DNA research that confirms the idea that crossbreeding between humans and Cro-Magnons *actually happened.* Cro-Magnons were a breed which were *so much like humans* that the term, *Cro-Magnon*, has now been dropped. Modern science now calls them *Homo sapiens sapiens, and states they were 'anatomically modern humans.'*

---

[994] Schroeder *The Science of God* Chapter 9 p 142*c,d,e,f* & 143*a*
[995] Article: The Downside of Sex with Neanderthals:
http://www.guardian.co.uk/science/blog/2011/aug/25/neanderthal-denisovan-genes-human-immunity
[996] Article: *N.Y. Times* April 25, 1999, Discovery Suggests Humans Are a Bit Neanderthal By JOHN NOBLE WILFORD
http://cogweb.ucla.edu/ep/Neanderthal.html

So, if we were to apply Occam's razor to the proposition, we would find the ancient Jewish Sage's idea concerning the Nephilim is *the most likely hypothesis*. Nevertheless, I doubt Eve had any idea that Cro-Magnons existed when she and Adam were in the Garden of Eden.

Summary Points on Genesis 2:7—

- At the end of the 6th Day of Creation, God formed man from the dust of the ground.
- Then, God breathed into his nostrils the Neshama (the divine human spirit of life eternal), and man became *'to'* a nefesh haiyah (a living communicating spirit).
- The extra 'Yud' in the Hebrew word for 'formed' indicates Adam would receive an extra spiritual input which other animals did not possess — the Neshama.
- The superfluous 'lamed' prefixed to the Hebrew word for 'the soul of animal life' indicates two things:
    o The first man was formed before he was created.
    o When he was formed, his forming prepared him to receive the extra spiritual input that God would give him when God later created him by breathing His breath of life into his nostrils (i.e., the Neshama).
- The Neshama is the defining quality that differentiates mankind from the other animals.
- The Neshama gives us the capacity for brotherly love (philia) & sacrificial love (agape).
- The Neshama is eternal.
- The advent of Adam was commensurate with the invention of writing.
- The advent of Adam marks the beginning of history and society.

THE SYMBOLISM & SUBSTANCE OF CLAY

Adam was formed out of the *'dust (i.e., the `aphar, meaning ashes, dust, or clay) of the ground'* (Gen. 2:7 The Interlinear Bible). Job said: *"You have formed me as chomer (i.e., dry measure, clay, or dust) and will You bring me to `aphar (i.e., to dust or clay) again"* (Job 10:9 The Interlinear Bible)? A descendant of a nephew of Abraham, Elihu, also said: *"I am formed out of chomer (that is, formed out of a dry measure, clay, or dust)"* (Job 33:6 The Interlinear Bible). Jesus Christ *spat* on the ground and made *pelos* (Greek for *clay*) with His *spittle*. He applied the *clay* to the eyes of a man who had been blind since birth and instructed the blind man to go to the pool of Siloam and wash. When he did, he received his sight (John 9:1-11 The Interlinear Bible). So here, in John 9:1-11, we find just one of many *threads of continuity* in the *Bible that links the beginning to Jesus Christ.* Let us now re-exam the thread of continuity & *connect those 'dots.'*

- In Genesis we learn the first man was formed *'of the dust of the ground'* (the `aphar of the *adamah*). As was just demonstrated, both `aphar and *chomer* mean 'clay.'
- Job said he was made of *a dry measure of clay.* Elihu, the youngest of Job's friends, also told Job that God had formed him from *a dry measure of clay.* Elihu was the last one of Job's four friends to tell Job his suffering was due to some unconfessed sin. The fact that Elihu was descended from a nephew of Abraham — was common knowledge. From this we can deduce Job would have known about Abraham. Job also would have known he and Abraham worshipped the

same God — *Jehovah*. Job certainly would have known of *the Genesis Creation Account* and would have also known Adam had been created by Elohim from *clay*.

- The story of the healing of the blind man by Christ in the Gospel of John comes from a time that was about 2,000 years after Job. John tells us Jesus Christ made *clay* from the *ground* with His *spittle* and applied it to the eyes of a man who had been blind from birth. When the blind man did as Jesus instructed, he received his sight. Jesus Christ could have healed this man by touching him or telling him he was cured, or by saying to him: *'Open your eyes and see.'* Instead, *He made clay from the dry ground with His spittle* and healed the blind man. The *symbolism* of *making and using 'clay in healing'* would not have been missed by those Jews who believed in Jesus, or even by those who opposed Him. It demonstrated to all who witnessed this particular healing — *Who Jesus was.* So, in John 9:1-11, we have Jesus Christ, Who is *the First Wisdom* through Whom *Elohim* created *all things*, performing an act of healing by using *the same thing* He used to form *all living things in the beginning.* He used His spittle to make clay from the dust of the ground. He then applied it to the blind man's eyes. This thread of continuity, this use of the clay to heal, demonstrated to the people who witnessed it and reminds us today *that Jesus Christ is the Son of God. He is the 'King of kings, and the LORD of Lords.' Everything Jesus Christ did in the New Testament not only had substance but was also symbolic.*

Elihu attributed Job's suffering to some unconfessed sin. Job answered that he was blameless. In the case of the man who had been blind from birth, the disciples asked Jesus who sinned — the blind man or his parents? Jesus answered: *"Neither this one sinned nor his parents, but that the works of God might be revealed in him."*

Too often we attribute unfortunate circumstances as punishment for unconfessed sin. The healing of the man who had been blind since birth demonstrated to the disciples and to us how wrong such judgments can be.

THE GRACE OF JESUS CHRIST

Jesus Christ *still lives.* He is eternal. He was crucified, dead, and buried.[997] But, on the 3rd day, He arose from the dead;[998] ascended into Heaven, [999] and now sits at the right hand of God the Father Almighty.[1000] From thence, He shall come again to judge the quick and the dead.[1001] At His 2nd Advent,[1002] He will be *the advocate for all who believe in Him at the time of the final judgment.*[1003] It is through *His blood sacrifice* that the sins of all who believe in Him (past, present, and future) are washed away so that we are made whole, rendered acceptable to the Father, and granted entry into eternal life.[1004,1005]

[997] Matthew Chapter 27; Mark 15:21-47; Luke 23:26-55; John 19:1-42.
[998] Matthew Chapter 28; Mark 16:1-8; Luke 24 1-12; John 20:1-21:25.
[999] Acts 1:9; Mark 16:19-20; Luke 24:50-53.
[1000] Mark 16:19; Hebrews 10:12.
[1001] Acts 10:38-43
[1002] Acts 1:10-11
[1003] I John 2:1; John 14
[1004] I John 2:2.
[1005] Romans 8:1-11; Hebrews 10; I Peter 3:18-20.

The apostle Peter told us the blood sacrifice of Jesus Christ also covers those who perished in Noah's flood — because Jesus Christ went to them and preached the gospel to them after his crucifixion. Peter said: *"For Christ also died for sins once for all, the Just for the unjust, in order that He might bring us to God, having been put to death in the flesh, but made alive in the spirit; in which also He went and made proclamation to the spirits now in prison, who once were disobedient, when the patience of God kept waiting in the days of Noah, during the construction of the ark, in which a few, that is, eight persons, were brought safely through the water...For the gospel has for this purpose been preached* (by Jesus) *even to the those who are dead, that though they are judged in the flesh as men, they may live in the spirit according to the will of God."* II Peter 3:18-20 & 4:6.

Therefore, God made provision for a second chance for those who died in Noah's flood who denied Jesus Christ in life. But, to those who die after Noah's flood, can we still assume Jesus will preach to those who die in a state of unbelief? Will they get a second chance? The majority of evangelists say — NO! They say that exception in the Book of 2nd Peter was a one-time thing. They teach the rejection of the opportunity to believe in Jesus is *"the one unforgivable sin."* They preach the choice to accept Jesus as your savior must be made before your mortal death.

Dr. David Jeremiah preached the most informative sermon on "The One Unforgivable Sin" I have heard. You can listen to his sermon. It is S2016 E27: "Is There a Sin God Can't Forgive?" Dr. Jeremiah convinced me: If anyone hardens their heart to the point that they repeatedly refuse to believe Jesus is the Son of God, they can form a "callus" around their heart. Dr. Jeremiah has convinced me the repeated refusal to believe in Jesus Christ is — "The One Sin God Absolutely Will Not Forgive!" I believe those people who do this have personally crucified Jesus on that cruel cross again and again and again! Christians also believe Our Abba, our Father, is perfect. His Judgments and His Justice are true, fair, just, and perfect!

If you have rejected Jesus Christ. If you have refused to believe He is the Son of God, and our only pathway to God, don't wait any longer. Don't wait until after death to discover whether or not Jesus will come preach to you. The majority of Christians and Christian Evangelists believe and teach — people need to confess their sins to Jesus, ask for forgiveness, and accept Jesus as their Lord and Savior — before they die. The majority of Christians believe we must make our choice between Eternal Life and Eternal Death — before we die.

For a Life full of Meaning, and Filled with Purpose: Agape's the Way, Belief's the Seed, and Faith's the Kernel, That Lead Believers to Life Eternal."

GO TELL IT ON THE MOUNTAIN: JESUS CHRIST IS LORD!
O. David

❦
CHAPTER 28: THE GARDEN OF EDEN

The 2nd Chapter of Genesis isn't the only place the Garden of Eden is mentioned in the Bible.

(Isaiah 51:3 NASB) *"Indeed, the LORD will comfort Zion. He will comfort all her waste places. And her wilderness He will make like Eden. And her desert like the garden of the LORD. Joy and gladness will be found in her. Thanksgiving and the sound of a melody."*
(Joel 2:1-3 NASB) *"Blow a trumpet in Zion and sound an alarm in My holy mountain! Let all the inhabitants of the land tremble! For 'the Day of the LORD is coming.' Surely it is near. A day of darkness and gloom. A day of clouds and thick darkness. As the dawn is spread over the mountains, so there is a great and mighty people. There has never been anything like it. Nor will there be again after it, to the years of many generations. A fire consumes before them, and behind them a flame burns. The land is like The Garden of Eden before them. But a desolate wilderness behind them. And nothing at all escapes them. Their appearance is like the appearance of horses; and like war horses, so they run."* (This is part of Joel's Prophecy of God's special intervention in the affairs of human history in the End Times.)

(In Ezekiel 28:12-13a; & 15, 19 NASB God speaks to Satan) *"Thus says the LORD GOD (to Satan). You had the seal of perfection, full of wisdom and perfect in beauty. You were in the Garden of Eden. Every precious stone was your covering"...You were blameless...until unrighteousness was found in you...and you sinned; Therefore, I have cast you as profane from the mountain of God...You profaned your sanctuaries. Therefore, I have brought fire from the midst of you. It has consumed you...All who know you among the peoples are appalled at you. You have become a terror, and you will be no more."*

(Rev. 22:1-5 NASB) *"And he showed me a river of the water of life, clear as crystal, coming from the throne of God and of the Lamb, in the middle of its street, and on either side of the river was The Tree of Life, bearing 12 kinds of fruit, yielding its fruit every month, and the leaves of the tree were for the healing of the nations. And there shall no longer be any curse: and the throne of God and of the Lamb shall be in it and His bondservants shall serve Him; and they shall see His face, and His name shall be on their foreheads. And there shall no longer be any night; and they shall not have need of the light of a lamp nor the light of the sun, because the LORD GOD shall illumine them, and they shall reign forever and ever."* (John's vision of The New Jerusalem in Heaven.)

Thus in Rev. 22:1-5, in Heaven, after almost 4,000 years of human history, through *the Revelation of the Apostle John* (in the 1st Century AD—i.e., from Adam to John), the Bible *'comes full circle'*— back to the other tree in the middle of *the Garden of Eden— The Tree of Eternal Life.* (Genesis 2:9)

THE SUBJECT OF THIS CHAPTER IS MAN'S FIRST HOME: THE GARDEN OF EDEN.
There is much mystery about the Garden of Eden. Since the time of Adam, humankind has been perplexed by the story of the Garden of Eden.
* Was Eden a metaphorical garden, a mythical garden, or was it a real garden?
* If the Garden of Eden was real, why was it created?

- ○ What purpose did the Garden serve?
- ○ Where was it located?
- ○ What are the lessons of the Garden?

THIS IS WHAT THE INTERLINEAR BIBLE SAYS ABOUT THE GARDEN OF EDEN.

(Gen. 2:8) *"And Jehovah-Elohim planted a garden in Eden, to the east; and He put the man whom He had formed there.*

- Eden: (Eden is from 'adan' meaning to live voluptuously and delightfully).
- East: (qedmah, or qadam, meaning toward the east).

(Gen. 2:9) *And out of the ground Jehovah-Elohim made to spring up every tree that is pleasant to the sight and good for food. The Tree of Life was also in the middle of the garden; also, the Tree of the Knowledge of Good and Evil.*

- Knowledge: (da'ath— from yada meaning awareness, knowledge, cunning, or wit).
- Good: (tᵉhowr— meaning purity, or pureness).
- Evil: (ra'— meaning incompleteness, lack of wholeness, soreness, sorrow, trouble, wickedness, wretchedness, wrong, adversity, affliction, calamity, distress, harm, hurt, heavy, misery, bad — the opposite of peacefulness — and all resulting from the absence of God).

(Gen. 2:10) *And a river went out of Eden to water the garden, and from there it was divided and became four heads.*

(Gen. 2:11) *The name of the first was Pishon. It is the one surrounding all the land of Havilah, where gold is.*

- Pishon (from another Hebrew word that means 'dispersive, to spread, or to grow up').
- Havilah: (literally meaning 'circular,' or as some claim, 'the sand region').

(Gen. 2:12) *And the gold of that land is good. There is bdellium gum resin, and the onyx stone.*

(Gen. 2:13) *And the name of the second river is Gihon. It is the one surrounding all the land of Cush.*

- Gihon (meaning 'stream,' from another Hebrew word that means 'short,' or 'to gush forth or break forth').
- Cush (see the discussion that follows).

(Gen. 2:14) *And the name of the third river is Hiddakel. It is the one going east of Assyria. And the fourth river is Euphrates.*

- Hiddakel: (Chiddequel or Chiddekel or Hiddekel — according to The Hebrew and Chaldee Dictionary in Strong's Concordance of the Bible — 'probably the Tigris River').
- Euphrates: (from Pᵉrath meaning 'rushing' — i.e., the Euphrates River of the East).

(Gen. 2:15) *And Jehovah-Elohim took the man and put him into the Garden of Eden, to work it and to keep it.*

(Gen. 2:16) *And Jehovah-Elohim commanded the man, saying, 'You may freely eat of every tree in the garden.'*

(Gen. 2:17) *'But of the Tree of the Knowledge of Good and Evil you may <u>not</u> eat, for in the day that you eat of it, you shall surely die.'"*   *The Interlinear Bible*

I.   THE GARDEN OF EDEN — MYTH, METAPHOR, OR REAL?

Much has been written about the Garden of Eden. Skeptics consider it a myth. Many, including a number of people who believe in God and the Bible, consider the Garden a metaphorical concept that was intended to teach us something about obedience to God and the consequences of disobedience to His will.

However, the ancient Jewish sages and Jewish tradition consider the Genesis Creation Account to be accurate, factual, and true — *all of it.* They never considered it could be mythical or metaphorical. Why? Because they believed every word of the Torah to literally be *words Jehovah-Elohim spoke to Moses — words that Moses faithfully wrote down in his Genesis Account of Creation, and his 5 books of the Torah — Genesis, Exodus, Leviticus, Numbers, and Deuteronomy.*

When I started writing this book, I had a concept of how I wanted to approach the Genesis Creation Account. But I had no idea what the end result would be or how this task would influence me. My decision to attempt to write this book was an act of faith — faith that my belief in the Bible (as the true word of God) would stand the test of what modern science has discovered. However, I also considered this work would serve as a test of my faith and a test of the claim of the ancient Jewish sages. They said all conflicts between science and the Bible result either from faulty science, or faulty interpretations of the Bible. I told myself — *if I should find otherwise* — I would stop this quest, and this book would never see the light of day. Truthfully, I still doubt this book will "see the light of day." I knew that writing this book would be a daunting task, but it would only be the first hurdle. Bringing it to the attention of other people would be another intimidating obstacle. However, as I write these words, I have found the Biblical statements about our origins have all been *'spot on,'* and I have not yet found any reason to stop writing. I have found numerous instances where scientific opinions in the past that contradicted the Bible were faulty science. I also discovered every scientific conflict has been resolved by further scientific inquiry. In all of those conflicts, the correction was the result of the work of another generation of scientists. I have also mentioned other times where faulty interpretations of the Bible have led past generations of believers astray. Yet, modern-day theological inquiry has corrected many of those inconsistencies.

So, it should not be any surprise this discussion considers the Garden of Eden was a *real* place — a place that actually existed and served a specific purpose God intended. That specific purpose fits into God's grand plan for the salvation of man.

John's vision of The Tree of Life in Heaven (in Revelation Chapter 22) *is one of the reasons I believe Eden was a real place. It neatly completes the whole Biblical story of man. The Tree of Eternal Life is something Adam saw in the Garden of Eden. We will also see it when we get to our eternal home—our heavenly Garden of Eden. But in Heaven, we will have full unrestricted access to the Tree of Life.*

II.   WHY DID GOD CREATE THE GARDEN OF EDEN?

The Bible says — after the Creator breathed the soul of life into *'the adam,'* He placed *'Adam'* in a special garden He planted for him. That garden was in a place the Bible calls

'*Eden.*' Eden was indeed a special place. Its name tells us this. *Eden means 'delight.'* [1006] It was the ideal home for Adam and his helpmate, Eve. It contained '*every tree that was pleasant to the sight and good for food.*' Man's first home on earth was a veritable paradise. God intended Eden to be a glorious place — a place where man could experience blissful joy, delight, and the ecstasy of daily communion with his Creator. It was a place where God could experience the delight of a perfect communion with His penultimate creation — Adam — and His ultimate creation — Eve.

Bliss, joy, delight, glory, and ecstasy are all synonyms of '*paradise.*' Another synonym for paradise is '*heaven.*' The Garden of Eden was literally intended to be — '*Heaven on Earth.*'

III.   WHAT PURPOSE DID EDEN SERVE? ANSWER — SEPARATION FOR HOLINESS.

Perhaps the answer can be found in the story of another important man in the history of Israel, Christianity, and Islam. Consider '*the Call of Abraham,*' which is told in the 12th Chapter of Genesis. Why was Abraham important?

(1.) He was the father of the Israelites.

(2.) He was also the father of the Arabs, and

(3.) He was in the lineage of Jesus Christ.

Abraham's story actually starts in the 11th Chapter of Genesis with his father, *Terah*. Terah was the 19th descendant of Noah's son Shem. Terah had three sons — Abram, Nahor, and Haran. *Abram* means *exalted father*.[1007] God later changed his name to *Abraham* (Gen. 17:5), which means *father of a great multitude.* [1008] Genesis 11:28 tells us Abram's brother (Haran) died in the presence of his father (Terah), in the city of his birth, *Ur of the Chaldeans*. A Ryrie Study Bible footnote on this verse informs us *Ur* was a wealthy, populous, and sophisticated pagan center in southern Mesopotamia that was located 220 miles SE of current-day Baghdad, Iraq. Some have said its most prosperous and literate era was during the time of Abram. Modern-day Iraqis would be justifiably offended by that statement. But there is no denying several ancient Mesopotamian civilizations were established in the *Neolithic Period* by intelligent, sophisticated, and culturally advanced ancient "*people.*" A great ziggurat was built there by Nimrod, and Abram must have seen it. It is known in Biblical history as *The Tower of Babel* (Genesis 11:1-9).

In the last part of the 11th Chapter of Genesis, the Bible tells us Terah took Abram and Abram's wife Sarai, and Lot (the son of Abram's brother Haran who had died), and left Ur of the Chaldeans after his son Haran died. But they got only as far as a place in modern-day southeastern Turkey (north of Ur, and near the modern-day Syrian border) — called '*Haran.*' Terah died there. After Terah died (Chapter 12 of Genesis), God said to Abram: "*Lech-Lecta,*" which means: "*Go-for-you/ Get going/ Get out/ Go for your own good/ Go Forth...*"[1009]

GOD'S COVENANT WITH ABRAHAM

(vs.1)"*Now the Lord said to Abram: 'Go forth from your country, and from your relatives, and from your father's house, to the land which I will show you;* (vs.2)*And I will make you a*

[1006] The Ryrie Study Bible: footnote of Genesis 2:8

[1007] Ryrie Study Bible note on Genesis 11:27

[1008] The Ryrie Study Bible: footnote of Genesis 11:27

[1009] Lech-Lecha: "Get Yourself Going" – Reb Jeff www.rebjeff.com

great nation, and I will bless you, and make your name great; and so you shall be a blessing; (vs.3)*And I will bless those who bless you, and the one who curses you I will curse. And in you all the families of the earth shall be blessed.* (Genesis 12:1-3 NASB).'"

The Bible next says: (vs.4) *"So Abram went forth as the Lord had spoken to him; and Lot went with him...* (vs.5) *And Abram took Sarai his wife and Lot his nephew, and all their possessions...and the persons which they had acquired in Haran, and they set out <u>for the land of Canaan</u>* (my underlining)*; thus, they came to the land of <u>Canaan</u>."* (Genesis 12:4-5 NASB)

Why did God command Abram (Abraham) to leave his pagan roots and go to the land of Canaan? So that Abraham would *separate* himself from the wickedness and influences of the pagan practices of the people in Ur and Haran. In *Canaan*, Abraham would begin to experience a close communion with God, and he would become the patriarch of a great nation — the nation of Israel — the nation God would separate unto Himself to be an example of holiness to the world. Israel was the nation to which He would send His Son (*Jesus Christ*) to inaugurate His plan for the salvation of *all* mankind.

"Just as Abraham was sent to Canaan to nurture his knowledge of God, Adam and Eve had also been set apart (in the Garden of Eden) to nurture their belief."[1010]

(This statement is a direct quote from Dr. Schroeder — taken from his book: *The Science of God*.) So, we see, God removed Abraham from the idolatrous society of his birthplace — *Ur of the Chaldeans*. We have already discussed *the principle of the separation of God's people for religious purposes* in Chapter 8 in Book I, when we talked about the Genesis Code meaning of the Hebrew word for holy — *kodesh* — which means *"separate and set apart for God."*

But from whom was God separating Adam and Eve when He placed them in the Garden of Eden? Why set them apart? Could it be God intended Adam and Eve to be separated from the other man-like hominids (i.e., *the beasts of the field*) who preceded Adam and Eve but were also their contemporaries? The "beasts of the field" didn't know Jehovah-Elohim. They worshipped their false gods of nature and made ritual sacrifices of their children to them!

I have already talked about the fictional character that the authors of *Inherit the Wind* invented, i.e., *Scopes' fiancé*. And I pointed out Bryan's abuse of her on the witness stand was fabricated. But when Darrow questioned Bryan about the Bible's claim that God caused the sun to stop for a day during the Battle at Aijalon, he assumed Joshua 10:12-14 could not have happened, because for the sun to suddenly stop its setting would mean the earth would have to suddenly stop spinning. Scientists think that would be disastrous because the momentum of the spin would cause things on earth's surface to start flying eastward. Moving rocks and oceans would trigger earthquakes and tsunamis, and the still-moving atmosphere would scour landscapes. However, all of this assumes the Creator would be unable to control the things He created. Let me remind you, God created light and gave it a speed man cannot achieve. And yet, light is the fastest thing in the universe! *Nothing is impossible for God!* Nevertheless, this discussion of *Separation*

[1010] Schroeder *The Science of God* Chapter 9 p 137*b*

in the Garden of Eden reminds me of a question Darrow *factually asked* William Jennings Bryan during the Scopes Monkey Trial. In his cross-examination of Bryan, Darrow read from the Bible: *"And Cain knew his wife and she conceived..."* (Gen. 4:16-17). He then asked Bryan: *"Where do you suppose she came from?"* Bryan said something like —(I'm paraphrasing now)— *What do you mean?* Darrow responded with something like — *Well now, Adam and Eve were the only people living at the time. The Bible says Cain and Able were born to them. There is no mention of a daughter. So where did Cain's wife come from?* Bryan was stumped. I wish he had responded that Genesis 5:4 makes it clear Adam had *"other sons and daughters."* Notice the Bible doesn't say he had *all of them with Eve!* Furthermore, we have already talked about God's command for Adam and Eve to be fruitful and multiply and fill the earth with their children. Darrow made the mistake of taking it for granted that the narrative in the Bible is strictly linear.

However, I think it is a good thing William Jennings Bryan didn't know about the ancient Talmud scholar's interpretation of *"the beasts of the field;"* and that they considered the possibility Adam was *"created from one of the beasts of the field that God had already formed before God breathed the Neshama into his nostrils."* If he had known that — and if he had known some ancient Jewish sages also thought Adam may have separated from Eve and cohabited with some female *"beasts of the field for 130 years after Cain killed Able"* — he could have shocked Clarence Darrow right out of his fancy suspenders *and* his socks! But if he had used that argument, I think Bryan would have discredited himself in the eyes of the good people of Dayton, Tennessee! In 1925, that argument would have been called — *blasphemy!* Furthermore, I bet a lot of current-day Christians would agree.

Nevertheless, God's original purpose for creating the Garden of Eden was to separate Adam and Eve *apart for God* so that they could be holy to Him alone. They were very definitely different from the other man-like hominids that we now know existed at the time, because God had breathed into Adam's nostrils His *'breath of life'* — *His Spirit of Life Eternal,* or as the Hebrews say — *God's Neshama.* All that was required from Adam and Eve, was *obedience* to God's one prohibition concerning the forbidden fruit of the *'Tree of the Knowledge of Good and Evil.'*

The Garden of Eden was the first physical expression of *God's Love and Grace toward humankind.* It was the first place God created where Adam and Eve could experience a perfect communion with God. Genesis 3:8-13 tells us it was God's practice to walk in the garden with Adam and Eve in the cool of the evening. After they sinned, they were so ashamed and frightened that they hid from God.

Since God is all knowing, God knew they had betrayed His trust and had fallen from His Grace. Adam and Eve failed the test of obedience to God. In failing God, they also failed and disgraced the entire human race. Their failure ushered in mortal death for all humankind!

IV. WHERE WAS THE GARDEN OF EDEN LOCATED?

The Bible says the garden was located to the east, meaning *'toward'* the east. We ask: *'To the east of what?'* The assumption most make is Eden was located to the east of the Holy Land, which was the region called *Canaan* in ancient times. *Canaan* was the land to which God commanded Abraham to go after he left *Haran*. A Ryrie Study Bible note on

Genesis 2:8 says Eden was apparently somewhere in Mesopotamia since two of its four rivers are the well-known *Tigris and Euphrates*. Ancient Mesopotamia was located to the east of ancient Canaan, and today is known to us as the modern-day country of Iraq, which among other things, is famous for its two well-known rivers — *the Tigris and the Euphrates*.

Jewish traditionalists believe the original story of the Garden of Eden was told by *Adam* himself and was handed down by an *oral tradition* to succeeding generations of *Adam's* descendants. Jewish tradition also holds that the *first Jewish written record* of the Garden of Eden was recorded by *Moses* in the first book of the *Torah* (i.e., Genesis), when God dictated it to him.

God had planted a garden in Eden and caused trees to spring up that were pleasant to the sight and produced good food for *the man*. We are also told — *in the middle of the garden* was *the Tree of Life,* and also in the middle of the garden was another tree — *the Tree of the Knowledge of Good and Evil.*

The Bible says a river that watered the garden flowed out of the garden. Outside of the garden, that river divided into four other rivers — the *Pishon* River, the *Gihon* River, the *Euphrates* River, and the *Hiddakel* River (called the *Tigris* River in the Modern Language Bible, and the Revised Standard Version of the Bible).

- The river *Pishon* (or *Pison*) is unknown in modern times, but, according to the Bible, it nourished a land called *Havilah* which contained *gold, bdellium gum resin* and *onyx stone.* The Bible says the gold of that land was good.

- *Havilah* is also the name of an individual. He is listed in the genealogy of Ham, who was one of Noah's three sons. *Havilah* was one of *Ham's* grandsons. He was the second of the five sons of *Cush* that are listed in Genesis 10:7-8. *Cush* was one of the four sons of *Ham* (see Genesis 10:6). He was the father of Nimrod (Gen. 10:8).

- *In ancient times an area of land was called by the name of the principal person who first settled that land.* For example, when God told *Abraham* to go to a land that He would show him, God directed him to *the land of Canaan. Canaan* was the 4th son of *Ham. The land of Canaan* was the small area along the eastern shore of the Mediterranean Sea where *Canaan* settled after Noah's Flood. *The land of Canaan* was also the place where, centuries later, *Moses* and *Joshua* led the Israelites in their exodus from slavery in Egypt. *Today, the land of Canaan is the country of Israel.*

- So, *the land of Havilah* was the Hebrew name for the place that *Havilah,* a great-grandson of *Noah,* a grandson of *Ham,* and the second son of *Cush* settled. He settled somewhere within the Arabian Peninsula (the area today that is Saudi Arabia and Yemen). THE LAND CALLED HAVILAH is next mentioned in the 25th Chapter of Genesis as the land where the 12 tribes that descended from *Ishmael* settled after *Ishmael's* death (see Genesis 25:12-18). *Ishmael* was Abraham's 1st son — born of the union of *Abraham* and his concubine — *Hagar.*[1011] Genesis 25:18 says the descendants of Ishmael settled from *Havilah to Shur* which is east of Egypt as one goes toward Assyria. A Ryrie Study Bible footnote on this verse says *Havilah* was located in central Arabia — north of modern-day Yemen. *Shur* (referring to another note on Genesis 16:7) was somewhere on the road from *Beersheba to Egypt.* Beersheba is an ancient

---

[1011] Sarah was Abraham's 1st wife. Hagar was her Egyptian handmaiden.

city which is south of Jerusalem. Today, it is the largest city in the Negev desert of southern Israel. *Hagar* (the mother of *Ishmael* by *Abraham*) had collapsed near a spring on the road to *Shur* when she fled from *Sarah* because of *Sarah's* harsh treatment of her after *Ishmael's* birth (see Genesis 16:3-16). Today, gold mines, bdellium gum resin, and onyx stone have been found in abundance in modern-day Saudi Arabia and Yemen.*[1012,1013,1014,1015,1016,1017]*

- The river *Gihon* nourished a land called *the land of Cush* (son of Ham and grandson of Noah — Gen. 10: 6-12) — referred to as *Ethiopia* in the King James Bible but, *arguably,* some think may have referred to the land of the Kassites in the mountains east of Mesopotamia.[1018] The river *Gihon* is also *unknown* in modern times.

- *The land of Cush* should probably be called the *lands* of Cush because the *descendants of Cush* settled over a very wide area. *Cushites* appear to have spread from the upper Nile to the Tigris and Euphrates River valleys from Ethiopia through Arabia, and Babylonia, and then onward into Persia and Western India. So it is that more than one land of Cush existed.[1019] For example, *Nimrod* (Genesis 10:8 and I Chronicles 1:10) may have been the most prominent descendant of *Cush.* Genesis 10:9-12 tells us *Nimrod was a mighty hunter before the Lord.* The beginning of his kingdom was *Babel, Erech, Accad,* and *Calneh* in *the land of Shinar.* These are cities in ancient Babylonia (also known as *the land of Shinar*) that *Nimrod* founded. After *Nimrod* started building the *Tower of Babel* (described in Gen. 11:1-9), that according to the Bible God stopped — he went to Assyria (Micah 5:6). There, he founded the city of *Nineveh* (Genesis 10:11), which became the capital of the Assyrian empire. Both the Babylonians and the Assyrians became enemies of Israel centuries later.

- The river *Hiddakel* (or *Tigris* River) went east of Assyria. The *Tigris River* is known today. It is the eastern most of the two major rivers of the current-day country of Iraq. The Tigris River flows through its capital — Baghdad.

- The fourth river was called *Euphrates* — the companion river of the *Tigris* — thought to be the river by the same name in the modern-day country of Iraq. In ancient times, the land between the *Tigris* and the *Euphrates* was called *Mesopotamia,* which means '*the land between the two rivers.*' It was the ancient land of the *Sumerians* (who preceded the Babylonians), and the *Babylonians* (both, in the southern *Mesopotamia*). It was also the land of the *Assyrians* (who settled in the northern part of the *Tigris-Euphrates River valley*).

[1012] Article: *Eden* (Originally titled "*The Land of Eden Located*:" by David J. Gibson, http://nabetaena.net/eden4.html

[1013] Article: *The Garden of Eden:* by **Eric H. Cline** Department of Classical & Semitic Languages & Literatures, The George Washington University, October 2009 http://www.bibleinterp.com/articles/eden357918.shtml

[1014] Article: *Investigating Genesis Series:* © 2002 by Stephen Caesar *"Lost River of Eden Discovered by Satellite"* http://www.creationism.org/caesar/eden.htm

[1015] Article: The Rivers of the Garden of Eden: Ancient Geography: The Lost River of Eden and Recent Geological Discoveries Jan. 27, 2007, http://www.mauenvios.com/trujillo2001/The_Lost-River-of-Eden.htm

[1016] Article: Recent Discoveries Confirm Old Testament Accuracy—Part I: by Stephen Caesar: http://www.pulpithelps.com/www/docs/976-4899

[1017] Article: *Whatever Happened to the Garden of Eden?* 2008 http://scienceandthebible.xanga.com/679729999/item/

[1018] *The Interpreter's One Volume Commentary on the Bible*: Edited by Charles M. Laymon: Abingdon Press, Nashville, TN.; © 1971 by Abingdon Press.

[1019] Article: *Eden* (Originally titled "*The Land of Eden Located*:" by David J. Gibson, http://nabetaena.net/eden4.html

- Let us now turn our attention to the two rivers that are *unknown* today — the *Pishon* and the *Gihon* Rivers.

V.   THE JURIS ZARINS THEORY

An interesting but controversial theory has been proposed by *Dr. Juris Jarins*, a retired Anthropologist and Archeologist who was a Professor at Missouri State University when he proposed his theory. Dr. Zarins believes *the Biblical Garden of Eden* was located at the northern most extent of the Persian Gulf. *He thinks Eden was flooded by the rising waters of the Persian Gulf ~ 6,000 years ago!* Using LANDSAT satellite images from space, Dr. Zarins has found a *'fossilized'* riverbed, which today is called the *Wadi Rimah and the Wadi Batin River system.* He thinks these dry wadis represent the ancient *Pishon* (or *Pison*) *River*. The *Wadi Rimah and the Wadi Batin* once drained the now dry, but once fertile central part of the Arabian Peninsula. Today they connect to form a single dry *'fossilized'* channel that begins in the Hijaz Mountains near Medina and runs northeast through Kuwait. That fossilized channel connects with *the confluence* of the Tigris and Euphrates Rivers just before they flow into the Northern most *head* of the Persian Gulf. Dr. Zarins thinks *the Karun River* in current-day Iran represents the Biblical *Gihon River*. The Karun River drains a basin in Persia to the east. It flows into the confluence of the Tigris and Euphrates Rivers only a short distance before their common channel flows into the Northern head of the Persian Gulf.

Zarins' theory proposes the most recent time that the *Pishon River* would have flowed with water would have been during *the Neolithic Period, about 6,000 years ago.* That was the time of the advent of Adam (cf. *Neolithic Period Cultures* in Chapter 22 in Book II). According to Dr. Zarins' theory, sea levels were anywhere from 200 to 300 meters lower in *Adam's* time than they are today, and the place where the four rivers met was *the Biblical Garden of Eden* which would have been a verdant river valley in *Adam's* time. Today, that region is completely submerged under the Northern most part of the Persian Gulf. According to Zarins' theory, when the last of the major Ice Ages ended at the end of the Pleistocene Epoch, the melting of the ice caps in the Polar Regions would have caused an uplift of those land masses that had been depressed by the weight of the ice. However, in the case of the land masses in more temperate regions, sea levels would have slowly risen and eventually caused flooding of those inland regions that were close to the seas. Jarins thinks the Persian Gulf flooded the Garden of Eden ~ 6,000 years ago BP (*Before the Present*) when the melting of the ice caps caused the Persian Gulf to flood the fertile lowland that today represents *the seabed* of the Northern part of the Persian Gulf. Once again, I want to emphasize the date of ~ 6,000 years Before the Present *corresponds to the advent of Adam.*

Dr. Zarins' theory about the *Pishon* and *Gihon Rivers* was supported by *James A. Sauer* (1945-1999) of the American Center of Oriental Research and a former curator of the Harvard Semitic Museum.[1020] This map illustrates the basics of Dr. Zarins' theory.

[1020]   James A. Sauer, *"The River Runs Dry,"* Biblical Archaeology Review, Vol. 22, No. 4, July/August 1996, pp. 52-54, 57, 64

549

Dr. Zarin's Theory about the Location of the Garden of Eden

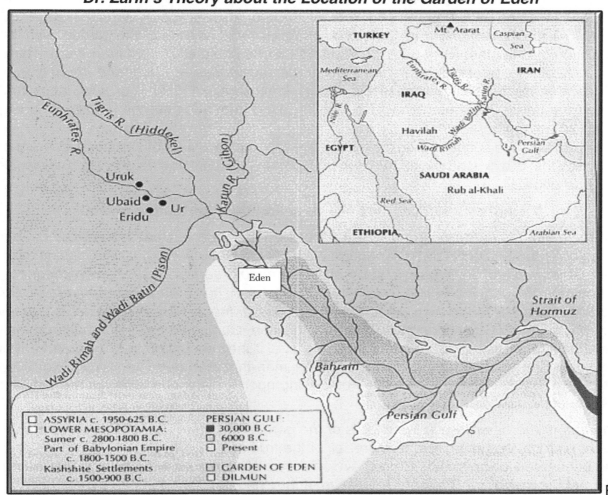

The submerged oval area in the 'head' of the Persian Gulf (labeled "Eden") is the location of the Garden of Eden. Image courtesy of http://www.ldolphin.org/eden/ [1021]

Truthfully, all of what has been said about the location of *'Eden'* is controversial. Literally, volumes have been written speculating on the location of the Garden. Sadly, in some circles the controversy is *very heated.* However, at least when folks debate the location of the garden, they are not questioning it existed. However — for believers — the *location* of the garden should *not* be the most important thing about the garden. Christians should instead focus on *the lessons* of the Garden of Eden.

VI.   THE LESSONS OF THE GARDEN OF EDEN

The Lord God put *the man* in the garden to work it and keep it. *The Garden of Eden* was full of all sorts of wonderful trees. Apparently, all of the trees in the garden produced edible food for man. One particular tree gave *Eternal Life,* and another gave *the awareness of*

Article: ***Has the Garden of Eden been located at last?*** by Dora Jane Hamblin http://www.ldolphin.org/eden/

good (purity) *and evil* (incompleteness, lack of wholeness, etc. — the opposite of peacefulness and happiness — and all resulting from an absence of God).

God gave *man* only one command. *Adam* was told all trees in the garden, with the exception of only one, were given to him and that he could eat freely from them. There was only one forbidden thing — *the Tree of the Awareness of Purity and Impurity* (i.e., the Awareness of the wholeness that Purity imparts and the lack of wholeness that Impurity imparts). If the man should disobey and eat from this tree, the penalty for doing so would be death.

Some have accused God of wanting to keep man in a state of perpetual ignorance. They say that is why God prohibited man from eating the fruit of the *Tree of the Knowledge of Good and Evil.*

When they say that, they are revealing their ignorance of God!

We have already indicated that tree was special. The Genesis Code tells us the deeper meaning of the ancient Hebrew language explains the Hebrew word for evil means more than being wicked. *It reveals a state of indescribable sorrow, trouble, wretchedness, wrongness, adversity, affliction, calamity, distress, harm, hurt, heaviness, and misery. But God had meant Eden to be a place of delight, pleasantness, blissful happiness, and joy for both man and God. Eden means delight.* In Eden, God could delight in man and man could delight in God. God warned Adam and Eve, if they should disobey Him and eat of the fruit of the forbidden tree, the paradise for man that God had intended — would be destroyed. By disobeying God, man would bring upon himself and all of his progeny the penalty of mortal death.

The fruit of the other tree in the middle of the garden (i.e., the Tree of Eternal Life), had not been forbidden man. Furthermore, *all* of the fruit and food from *all* of the *other* trees had been freely given to him. Some have said it was fortunate that Adam and Eve did not also eat the fruit of *the Tree of Eternal Life.* If they had, they would have experienced an eternal death and an eternity of separation from God after they ate the fruit of the forbidden *Tree of the Knowledge of Good and Evil.* So, the argument can be made that, the ultimate choice given to the Earth's first man and woman was not between choosing evil over good — *it was basically the choice between life and death!* By disobeying God, Adam and Eve were not choosing to be *like* God, as the serpent had deceptively convinced *Eve. They were actually choosing mortal death.* (See Chapter 3 of Genesis.)

The fact man was given a choice indicates when our Creator created Adam and Eve, *He gave them free will—the choice to obey or disobey.* If man chose to obey God, he would also be choosing life. If man chose to disobey God, he would be choosing death. *God made the consequences of those choices abundantly clear!*[1022]

Just before Moses completed writing the Torah, he stated the choice our free will faces.

> *"I call heaven and earth to witness against you this day that I have set*
> *Before you life and death, the blessing, and the curse; therefore choose*
> *Life that you may live, you and your progeny."*   Deut. 30:19

[1022] Schroeder The Science of God Chapter 11 p 174

The apostle *Paul* eloquently stated the choice that we all have in I Corinthians 15:20-26.

"But now Christ has been raised from the dead, the first fruits of those who are asleep. For since by a man (Adam) came death, by a man (Jesus Christ) also came the resurrection of the dead. For as in Adam all die, so also in Christ all shall be made alive. But each in his own order: Christ the first fruits, after that, those who are Christ's at His (second) coming. Then comes the end, when He delivers up the kingdom to the God and Father, when He has abolished all rule and all authority and power. For He must reign until He has put all His enemies under His feet. The last enemy that will be abolished is death."

Summary Points: the choice our free will faces—The lessons of the Garden.

- We now know the consequences of the choice Adam and Eve made.
- Because they chose to disobey God, we will all suffer the penalty of mortal death.
- As individuals, we are still faced with the same choice they had. We must also choose between eternal life and eternal death.
- The choice is ours to make. It is our free-will God-given choice.
- If we choose to obey God, and profess our belief in Jesus Christ, we are choosing life eternal.
- If we choose to obey God, we are choosing to live our lives according to the teachings of God and Jesus Christ. We are pledging to follow the example of Christ.
- Belief in Jesus Christ and choosing to follow His teachings will grant us the reward of eternal bliss in Heaven with the Father, the Son, and the Holy Ghost.
- Our choice to obey God is the choice to subjugate our free-will to God's will.
- When we do that, we stop living our lives for ourselves, and begin to live our lives for God by serving others.
- The punishment for disobedience is eternal death and an eternal separation from God.
- Nothing could be more simple or more clear. There is nothing ambiguous about it.
- By choosing to obey God, we are showing others we love Him and honor Him.

CHAPTER 29: ADAM NAMES THE ANIMALS—GOD MAKES ADAM'S HELPER

We have now come to the last two topics for discussion in the Genesis Creation Account:
* *The naming of the animals.*
* *The making of a suitable helpmate for Adam.*   *O. David*

I.   **THE NAMING OF THE ANIMALS.**

(Gen. 2:18) *"And Jehovah-Elohim said: 'It is not good, the man being alone. I will make a helper suited to him.'*

(Gen. 2:19) *And Jehovah-Elohim formed every animal of the field, and every bird of the heavens out of the ground. And He brought them to the man, to see what he would call it. And all which the man might call it, each living soul, that was its name.*

(Gen. 2:20) *And the man called names to all the cattle, and to the birds of the heavens, and to every animal of the field. But no helper suited to man was found for a man."* (The Interlinear Bible)

In Chapter 24 when I examined Genesis 1:28-31, I talked about the deeper meaning of God's blessing and charge to the Earth's first man and woman. That is when God commanded them:
* *To be fruitful and multiply.*
* *Fill the Earth and subdue it.*
* *And Rule over:*
  * *the fish of the sea—*
  * *the birds of the heavens—*
  * *and all living things that creep on the Earth.*

That is when God announced his intent for man to have *dominion and control over the Earth and all living things on Earth.* God's intent for man to have dominion and control is the reason David later wrote in Psalm 8 that God had crowned man with glory and honor — had given man dominion over the works of God's hands (God's Creation) — had put all things under man's feet — *and thus, had made man "A little lower than the angels."*

Now, in Genesis 2:18-20, God accomplished what He intended in Genesis 1:28-31 (cf. Chapter 24). For it is here, when God paraded all the animals and birds before *'the man'* so that *'the man' could name them* — that God demonstrated to Adam and to all future generations — *Man had been given dominion and control over all living things God created.* The act of Adam's naming the animals is the sign of Adam's lordship over all living things. Adam's lordship was given to him by *Jehovah-Elohim. And Adam's Lordship over all things was also the sign Adam was the quintessential and penultimate creature in all God's Creation.*

IN CHAPTER 24, UNDER THE DISCUSSION OF GENESIS 1:31, WE TALKED ABOUT—

> *"And God saw everything that He had made. And behold, it was very good.*
> *And there was evening and there was morning, the Sixth Day."*

At that time, we mentioned — the addition of the word *'very'* to the phrase *'it was good,'* which had appeared at the end of God's work on each of the preceding five days of creation — caused Onkelos to translate — *"And it was very good"* — differently. In his

Hebrew-Aramaic translation of Genesis 1:31 Onkelos interpreted — *"And it was very good"* as:

"It was a unified order."

Thus, according to Onkelos, all of God's labor during *"The Six Days of Old"* forged a state of *'Unity and Order'* out of the extreme chaos of the beginning. *Unity and Order* are the hallmarks, the trademarks, the stamp of completion, and the end result of God's creative activity in the First Chapter of Genesis! [1023] The end result of unity and order out of the chaos of the beginning would not have happened if the universe had developed through the devices of *random chance* as the disciples of Darwin have claimed. If that had been the way the universe came into being, nothing would have changed from the chaos of the beginning and no development of the universe would have occurred. The chaos would have continued and would have prevailed. *All would have ended in the overwhelmingly fatal gravitational vortex of a super black hole!* We have already discussed this in Chapter 7 (in Book I) when we said — *"the Singularity was the first black hole."* However, God intervened with His *Ruach Elohim* (i.e., *the Wind of God &/or the Holy Spirit*), and *unity and order were the end-result.* Six times over, the Bible tells us of the unifying passage to ever more complex and orderly arrangements of the chaotic matter of the beginning that resulted from God's labor on each and every one of *the Six Days of Creation* by this simple statement that appears at the end of each of the six days:

"And there was evening (erev) and there was morning (boker)."

As we discussed in Chapter 8 (in Book I) the Genesis Code meaning of *'erev'* is *chaos*; and the deeper meaning of *'boker'* is *order.* Nahmanides concluded the deeper meaning of the text tells us something crucial about the God-directed flow-of-matter in the universe. God caused a systematic flow of order to emerge out of the chaos of the beginning on each and every day of creation. That is, there was a systematic flow from disorder (*the chaos of evening*) to order (*the unifying cosmos of morning*) that resulted from each Day of His labor. It must be emphasized this is the *opposite* of what would have happened if the chaos of the universe had been left to the governing forces of *random chance.*

The entire saga of God's creation ends with the appearance of human life. Approximately eight hundred years ago, Nahmanides (circa 1194-1270 AD) agreed with Onkelos. In his commentary he interpreted the deeper meaning of the original Hebrew text of Genesis 1:31 to mean:

"And God saw everything that was made and behold it was a unified order."

Dr. Schroeder (commenting on the general consensus of other ancient Jewish sages — many of whom preceded Nahmanides by several hundreds of years), puts it this way:

"Two thousand years ago, the commentators on the Hebrew text of Genesis 1:31 saw within the words a wondrous transition from chaos to cosmos; from a jumble of energy and atoms to the dazzlingly complex and unified order of life."— a direct quote.[1024]

[1023] Schroeder: *The Hidden Face of God*, Chapter 3, p 33c
[1024] Schroeder *The Hidden Face of God* Chapter 4, p 59

When God paraded all the animals before Adam for him to name them, He demonstrated that a perfect harmony and order existed in the garden He planted in Eden. This was before Adam and Eve were tempted by Satan and committed the original sin that destroyed the paradise of Eden. Their disobedience brought death and enmity to all living things. It brought death and enmity:

- between man and the Earth,
- between man and nature,
- between man and the animals,
- and between *'man'* and man, and
- It also brought *separation between man and God.*

> **This book is only about God's Creation.**
> **The death, the enmity, and the separation that resulted from the events the Bible details in the 3ʳᵈ Chapter of Genesis are not topics for discussion in this book. That's because the 3ʳᵈ Chapter of Genesis is about "The Fall of Man," and the rest of the Bible is about the historical saga of God's provision for the redemption of man that the rest of the Old Testament and the New Testament address.**

Nonetheless, the parade of the animals that occurred when they were named demonstrated there was no enmity between the animals at that time. There were no predatory instincts at that time.

I have mentioned Adam's naming of the animals in Genesis 2:19 was the sign that Adam was the quintessential (*i.e., the purest and most perfect being*) and the penultimate creation in all God's creation. Why was Adam the penultimate creation? Because he was the next to the last quintessential creation of God. Go back and look at the first statement of Genesis 2:18 and then look at the last sentence in Genesis 2:20. When you do, you will find:

"And Jehovah God said: 'It is not good, the man being alone. I will make a helper suited to him (Gen. 2:18)."

And there was: *"…no helper suited to man was found for a man* (Gen. 2:20b)."

Since all of God's living creatures had passed before Adam when he named them, and since at that time, not one was found to be a suitable helper for him, God immediately goes about the business of making and creating Adam's helpmate.

II.   THE MAKING OF A HELPER FOR ADAM.
(Gen. 2:21) *"And Jehovah-Elohim caused a deep sleep to fall on the man, and he slept. And He took one of his ribs and closed up the flesh underneath.*

(Gen. 2:22) *And Jehovah-Elohim formed the rib which He had taken from the man into a woman; and brought her to the man.*

(Gen. 2:23) *And the man said, 'This now is at last bone of my bones, and flesh from my flesh; For this shall be called Woman, because this has been taken out of man.'*

(Gen. 2:24) *Therefore, a man shall leave his father and his mother, and shall cleave to his wife; and they shall become one flesh.*

(Gen. 2:25) *And they were both naked, the man and his wife, and they were not ashamed."*
The Interlinear Bible

In his commentary on Genesis 2:21 and 2:22 Dr. Schroeder says the Hebrew word that has been interpreted in all English translations of the Bible (including the Interlinear Bible) as one of Adam's 'ribs' — is the same word that is used in Exodus 26:20, which talks about the building of the 'sides' of the tent tabernacle.[1025] However I find the transliterated Hebrew-to-English word in Dr. Schroeder's scriptural reference — is *"tsal'ah."* The Hebrew-Chaldee Dictionary says *tsal'ah* comes from the Hebrew word — *tsala'.* However, the *word* in Exodus 26:20 that is translated as *'side'* in most English Bibles is stated by the Interlinear Bible to be — *pe'ah*, which means: *corner, end, quarter, or side.*

Dr. Schroeder may be making a moot point here because the Hebrew-Chaldee Dictionary says the following about the Hebrew word *tsal'ah* (in Genesis 2:21-22):

"Reference word number 6763 (i.e., tsal'ah) for rib is taken from reference word number 6760 (i.e., tsala'); a rib as curved of the body, or figuratively of a door, or a leaf; hence a side of a person—also can be taken to mean a beam, board, chamber, corner, leaf, plank, **side, or rib**.*"*

So, it seems to me that tsal'ah and pe'ah are synonyms. Therefore, whether a *rib* or a *side* or *neither*, the event of the making and creating of *the woman* that God formed in Genesis 2:22 is not likely to be proved by any physical evidence in any archaeological finds. Perhaps the most important point for men to remember is that Eve was not only the last quintessential creation of God; she was also the *ultimate* creation of God. *Women represent the best of humankind.* They are the *acme* of God's Creation. For that reason, men should consider women to be the *crown of all of God's creations and should treat them with the utmost respect.*

For Biblical literalists however, the fact remains that the Hebrew word for woman (*ishah*) comes from another Hebrew word for man, (*ish*). [1026] When used in the context of the forming of the suitable helper for *'the man'* that God later named *'Adam:'* Adam's *helper* was formed by God out of *the man* He had just made and created — and then, *the two of them became one flesh*. The man then looked upon his wife and acknowledged she had been formed out of his flesh when he uttered these words:

"And the man said, this now is at last bone of my bones, and flesh from my flesh. For this shall be called Woman because this has been taken out of man (Gen. 2:23)."

The next verse, Genesis 2:24, introduces the ordination of marriage between men and women.

"Therefore, a man shall leave his father and his mother, and shall cleave to his wife; and they shall become one flesh."

[1025] Schroeder: *Genesis and the Big Bang* Chapter 2 p 28*c*
[1026] Article: from the Makor Hebrew Foundation: **The Importance of Hebrew in the Tanakh** (the Old Testament) http://www.makorhebrew.org/tanakh.shtml

THE BIBLICAL CREATION ACCOUNT ENDS WITH THE FOLLOWING WORDS:

*"And they were both naked, the man & his wife, & they were not ashamed (*Gen. 2:25).*"*

Thus, begins what Biblical Scholars commonly refer to as *the Age of Innocence, or the Dispensation of Innocence.* However, it was short-lived because the next saga in the history of man (i.e., in the 3rd Chapter of Genesis), continues with the sad tale of *The Fall of Man.* Those of you who are familiar with the Bible know the story and know the history of how God has provided for *the reconciliation and redemption of man.* For those of you who do not know *'the rest of the story'* (as Paul Harvey would have said), it is there in the Bible for any and all to read.

Remember, the Bible is not only a book about the *history* of man. It is also a book about *belief and faith in God.* It is also a book about *science,* and *religion.* However, so far as creation is concerned, science can only take us so far. *Only belief and faith in God can take us to those places science can never go. Praise be to God.*   O. David

THIS IS WHAT MY STUDY OF THE GENESIS CREATION ACCOUNT HAS TAUGHT ME.

1. The Bible is the inspired Word of God.
2. The Biblical Account of Creation is truth. It is *Science, Religion, and the History* of all God's Creation.
3. The Pre-incarnate Jesus Christ was in the beginning with Elohim.
4. He is the First Wisdom of God through Whom God created and made all that exists.
5. Jesus Christ our Lord and Savior.
6. He is our pathway to God.
7. If we invite the Holy Spirit (i.e., the *Ruach Elohim* — the Hebrew name for *the Wind of God),* into our lives, He will dwell in us and bring *Unity and Order to our Chaos. God's Holy Spirit will do that for us — in our Present. God's Holy Spirit will dwell in us, and we will experience God's inner peace in the here and now — and also in Eternity Future.*

❧
APPENDIX II: "WHEN THE FULLNESS OF TIME HAD COME."

"When the fullness of time had come, God sent forth His Son, born of a woman, born under the Law, in order that He might redeem those who were under the Law, that we might receive the adoption as sons (Gal. 4:4-5 NASB)."

This Appendix summaries the historical events that prepared the world for the 1st coming of the Messiah—Jesus Christ of Nazareth.

BETWEEN THE TESTAMENTS (400 YEARS)

During the 400 years between the close of the Old Testament and the birth of Jesus Christ, several important events happened. [1027]

1. The Greeks under Alexander the Great ruled the world for a time and introduced Greek culture and the Greek language throughout all of Alexander's empire. Greek became the commercial language of the known world.

2. After Alexander's death, his empire was divided between the four generals in his army.
   - Ptolemy I (323—282 BC) ruled Egypt, Palestine, Cilicia, Petra, and Cyprus.
   - Seleucus I Nicator ruled Mesopotamia, The Levant, Persia, and part of India.
   - Lysimachus took Thrace and Asia Minor.
   - Cassander ruled Macedonia and Greece.

3. Later, the Ptolemies were overthrown by the Seleucids, who took control of Palestine and the lands previously ruled by the Ptolemies.

4. When the Seleucids took control of Palestine, the Jewish Maccabees revolted and broke away from the rule of the Greeks.

5. A brief period of Jewish independence followed the revolt of the Maccabees, and Hebrew traditions were once again taught and openly practiced in Palestine.

6. The Roman Empire succeeded the Greeks, crushed the Maccabees, and ruled the known world when Jesus Christ was born.

7. Roman military roads made travel easier between the far reaches of the Roman Empire, and the Pax Romana (i.e., the peace enforced by Roman rule) made possible the rapid spread of Christian doctrine and the Christian Church after Christ's death and resurrection.

8. The Jewish synagogue, the Sanhedrin, and sects such as the Pharisees and Sadducees developed.

9. Into the mix of Greek and Roman culture, with their worship of idols and false gods, great spiritual confusion and moral deterioration developed, and out of this morass a great spiritual hunger and awakening was born.

All of these events set the stage for the birth and ministry of Jesus Christ, and the birth and early growth of the Christian Church. It was indeed — *"When The Fullness of Time Had Come."*

[1027] Query: **The Hellenistic World: The World of Alexander the Great**

THE DISPERSIONS OF THE JEWS IN 722 BC AND 586 BC WERE PART OF GOD'S PLAN.

Before all the above, Isaiah and Jeremiah prophesied to the Jews. Beginning with Solomon, the Jewish people abandoned their God Jehovah, and worshiped pagan gods. They made sacrifices of innocent children to pagan gods in all the high places of Israel. They also adopted licentious sexual pagan rituals. Isaiah and Jeremiah warned the Jews Jehovah would bring about the destruction of Jewish hegemony. But the people and their kings didn't listen. The nation forged by King David and glorified during the reign of his son Solomon — would be completely destroyed. We have already mentioned the Civil War that broke out between the 12 tribes of Israel that split Solomon's Kingdom in two after Solomon's death. Both Jewish Kingdoms were conquered, and their people were deported to the lands of their conquerors.

In 722 BC, Assyria conquered the Kingdom of Northern Israel and took all the Jews of Northern Israel in chains (with hooks in their noses), to their capital city — Nineveh.

"So (northern) *Israel was carried away into exile from their own land to Assyria... (II Kings 17:23c)."*

II Kings 17:24-41 tells the story of what happened when the Assyrians resettled the land of the former northern kingdom of Israel. They resettled northern Israel with slaves from the conquered kingdoms of Babylon, Cuthah, Avva, Hamath, and Sepharvaim. Many of those former Assyrian slaves settled near King Omni's 9th century BC capital city *Samaria and intermarried with some Jews who escaped deportation to Nineveh.* Their offspring were considered *a mongrel race* by the Jews of the Southern Kingdom of Judah and Benjamin. That is why the foreign settlers and those Jews in the north who married them were called *"Samaritans."* The resettled Assyrian slaves brought with them a syncretism of foreign pagan religions. II Kings 17:25 says they did not fear Jehovah, so Jehovah sent lions among them. Consequently, they believed their bad luck was because they had offended the god of Northern Israel. After they complained, the Assyrians sent a captured Jewish priest of Jehovah back to Samaria so that he could indoctrinate the Samaritans in the beliefs and practices of Judaism. The reason the Jews in Jesus' time had such disdain for the Samaritans was because they were not only considered a mongrel race, but their ancestors simply added Jehovah to the list of the pagan gods they worshipped. So, the religion of the Samaritans of Northern Israel was not pure Judaism — far from it.

The captured and deported Jews of the Northern Kingdom never returned to Northern Israel. They disappeared as a people after 722 BC and became known in Jewish history as *"The Ten Lost Tribes of Israel."*

THE BATTLE OF NINEVEH 612 BC

Determined to end Assyrian ascendancy in Mesopotamia, Babylon led an alliance with Medo-Persia in an attack on the Assyrian capital, Nineveh. In the Battle of Nineveh (612 BC), Nineveh was destroyed, sacked, and the Assyrian king was killed. After their Assyrian masters and their capital were defeated and destroyed, the Jewish slaves from the former Northern Kingdom of Israel left Nineveh and dispersed throughout Asia Minor, Greece, and Macedonia. This became known as *the Great Diaspora of the Jews.* However, when Paul made his missionary journeys to Asia Minor and Greece after the death and resurrection of Jesus Christ, he visited the synagogues of the descendants of the Jews of the former Northern Kingdom. There, in his three missionary journeys in New Testament times, he found his converts to Christianity.

THE BATTLE OF CARCHEMISH IN 605 BC

After Nineveh was destroyed, remnants of the defeated Assyrian army joined with an Egyptian army at the Egyptian-controlled city of Carchemish (on the banks of the Euphrates River). The Babylonians & their allies (under the command of Nebuchadnezzar II) warred against them at the Battle of Carchemish and won. After Carchemish, Judah became a vassal state of Babylon. The Egyptians and Assyrians never regained their supremacy in the middle East.

NEBUCHADNEZZAR II WARRED AGAINST THE SOUTHERN KINGDOM OF JUDAH (601-586 BC)

His 1st siege of Jerusalem occurred in 598 BC. The king of Judah (Jehoiakim) died during that 3-month siege. At the end of the siege, Jehoiakim's successor son, Jehoiachin was captured and deported to Babylon along with the aristocracy, elite "men of valor," artisans, smiths, and craftsmen of Judah. (Daniel had been taken captive in 605 BC when Judah became a vassal state after Carchemish.) Only the poorest of the poor were left behind. Nebuchadnezzar sacked Solomon's Temple and stole the Golden Temple goblets and other valuable artefacts. The original and all of the copies of the sacred Torah and Tanakh, and the Ark of the Covenant (*all kept in Solomon's Temple*), disappeared and have not been found. What happened to them is a mystery.

Before Nebuchadnezzar returned to Babylon, he made Zedekiah a vassal- puppet-king of Judah. But nine years later, Zedekiah rebelled and formed an alliance with Egypt. This brought about a 2nd campaign against Jerusalem.

Some claim Solomon had a son with the Queen of Sheba. His son, Menelik, was born in Ethiopia after his mother returned to Ethiopia. According to legend, Menelik visited his father Solomon when he was twenty. Upon his return to Ethiopia, he was informed someone in his company had stolen the Ark of the Covenant. A Jewish sect of Ethiopians claim the Ark is in Axum (Aksum), Ethiopia.[1028] Some claim a copy of the Ark was made in Solomon's time and placed in the Temple. The original and its contents were secreted in a cavern in the Temple Mount beneath the Temple. After Menelik's visit, this legend claims Solomon returned Menelik to be with his mother in Ethiopia (accompanied by bodyguards). According to this legend, the real Ark and its contents were secretly sent with Menelik to Ethiopia at that time. There is much mystery surrounding the disappearance of the Ark and the original Tanakh.

NEBUCHADNEZZAR RAZED JERUSALEM & DESTROYED SOLOMON'S TEMPLE (586 BC).

When Nebuchadnezzar heard about Zedekiah's treachery, he returned to Jerusalem. This time, he razed the city and destroyed Solomon's Temple. He blinded Zedekiah and took him captive to Babylon in chains. Nebuchadnezzar's campaigns against the Southern Kingdom caused the *2nd Diaspora of the Jews.*

[1028] Search for: Keepers of the Lost Ark?

BABYLON FALLS IN 539 BC.

After the death of Nebuchadnezzar II, the Babylonians were defeated by a Medo-Persian coalition that had been formed under the leadership of Cyrus II of Persia. 200 years before Cyrus was born, Isaiah prophesied Cyrus would free the Jews from Babylonian captivity. It all happened as Isaiah and Jeremiah had prophesied. The capital of the Babylonian empire (Babylon) was captured, and their king (Belshazzar) was killed in 539 BC. We talked about that in the Introduction—Part I Synopsis in Book I. Seventy years after the Babylonians enslaved the Judean Jews, King Cyrus II of Persia, freed them and allowed a small remnant of the Judean Jews to return to Jerusalem to rebuild their capital city and erect their 2nd Temple to Jehovah. Under the leadership of Ezra and Nehemiah, that tiny remnant rebuilt Jerusalem and The 2nd Temple. At the same time, the dispersions of 722 BC and 586 BC had scattered Judaists to every corner of the globe. As the centuries passed, parts of the Hebrew traditions were handed down from one generation to another and the hopes of the prophets concerning the coming of the Messiah were kept alive. They were kept alive not only in the small remnant that returned to Judea, but also in countless conclaves of Jews scattered throughout the entire world.

CORRUPTION OF THE JEWISH PRIESTHOOD

The Persians continued to rule Judea for another 100 years after Nehemiah. During this time, Judah enjoyed religious freedom under the religious rule of Jewish priests responsible to Persia. However, as the result of this melding of church and state, the priesthood degraded into a pollical office. Hebrew traditions continued, but corruption of the priesthood created a leadership vacuum leading to moral deterioration and spiritual confusion. This was undoubtedly greatly exacerbated by the imposition of Greek and Roman culture. Yet, this eventually resulted in a genuine spiritual hunger.

ALEXANDER THE GREAT CONQUERED PERSIA IN 333 BC.

Alexander conquered the known world in 13 years! He dealt kindly with the Jews and allowed religious freedom. Alexander introduced Greek culture, and Greek mythology. The Greek language became the universal commercial language of his entire realm. For the first time since the dispersion caused by the confusion of tongues in the time of Nimrod and his tower of Babel — the world had a common language. The Greek language became commonly known and was widely written and spoken. This allowed communication and commerce on a world-wide scale. Alexander sought more than a power over nations. He also wanted to 'enlighten' the world through the introduction of Hellenistic culture. An avid advocate of Greek culture, He sought to distribute its 'benefits' to all his subjects.

After Alexander's death in 323 BC, his empire was divided among his generals. Ptolemy the 1st controlled the western provinces of Egypt and Judea, while Seleucus controlled Syria and the eastern Provinces. Alexander's Generals also continued to introduce Greek culture to the provinces they ruled.

GOD USED ALEXANDER TO ESTABLISH A UNIVERSAL LANGUAGE.

With the Greek ideal went its language. Consequently, when Jesus came into the world, He met a world that shared a common commercial tongue. Wherever His message was taken (India, Spain, Egypt, Galatia, or Rome) — everywhere there would be people who could understand it.

GOD USED PTOLEMY II TO CREATE THE SEPTUAGINT.

There were 7 Greek Kings of Egypt after Alexander died. All had "Ptolemy" in their name. From a religious viewpoint, Ptolemy II (also known as Ptolemy Philadelphus 285-247 BC) was the most important. Up until 198 BC, when Ptolemy V lost control of Judea to a descendant of Seleucus, Judea was ruled by the Ptolemies whose capital was Alexandria, Egypt. The Ptolemies followed Alexander's example and also dealt kindly with the Jews. They permitted religious freedom. Alexandria (the pre-eminent city in Egypt named for Alexander the Great), became an important center of Jewish culture.

Ptolemy II commissioned the translation of the Hebrew Torah into Greek. *The Torah* (which contained the canon of Jewish Law) was translated into Greek in Alexandria. The Greek translation of the *Five Books of Moses* was called *"the Pentateuch"* — for *"5-fold vessel."* Seventy Jews, who were skillful linguists, were sent from Jerusalem to Alexandria. The Pentateuch was translated first. Later the rest of the Hebrew Old Testament books were added to the translation. That complete volume was called the *"Septuagint,"* for the 70 translators who did the work. It is believed the translators were inspired by God to produce an infallible translation. The translation was made because Greek was the commercial language of the world at that time. The Septuagint was in common use in the Days of Christ. The New Testament was also written in Greek. Many of the quotations in our English Old Testament are translated from the Septuagint.

JUDEA UNDER THE SELEUCIDS:

There were 13 Greek Seleucid Kings of Syria. From a religious viewpoint, the infamous Antiochus Epiphanes IV (175-164 BC) was the most important.

GOD USED THE TYRANNY OF ANTIOCHUS EPIPHANES IV AGAINST HIM.

In 198 BC, Judea was taken from the Ptolemies by Antiochus III, a Seleucid. In 168 BC, *Antiochus Epiphanes IV* sided with the Hellenists against Orthodox Jews and imposed Hellenistic rule with its worship of Greek gods. He was violently bitter against the Jews and made a furious and determined effort to exterminate them and their religion. He devastated Jerusalem in 168 BC, defiled the Temple by offering a sow on its altar, and erected an altar to Jupiter in the place of the Jewish altar. He prohibited Temple worship, forbade circumcision on pain of death, sold thousands of Jewish families into slavery, destroyed all copies of Scripture that could be found, and slaughtered everyone discovered in possession of scripture copies. He resorted to every conceivable torture to force Jews to renounce their religion. Many have interpreted this as the *"abomination of desolation"* mentioned in Daniel 12:11 as something that has already occurred.

There is another interpretation of the *"abomination of desolation"* as something that will occur in the future. A Ryrie Bible note on Daniel 12:11 says: *"At the mid-point on the Tribulation week* (in the end-times), *the Antichrist will abolish the Jewish sacrifices* (cf. Daniel 9:27, Matt. 24:15, and II Thessalonians 2:4)." It is possible both interpretations are valid, as prophecies may have more than one time-space-continuum application.

The tyranny of *Antiochus Epiphanes IV* led to the Maccabean revolt — one of the most heroic feats in Jewish history.

GOD USED THE MACCABEES TO REINSTITUTE HEBREW TRADITION, CAUSE A SPIRITUAL REVIVAL, AND INFLUENCE FUTURE ROMAN POLICY.

The period of independence under the Maccabees is also referred to as the Maccabean (*or Asmonean, or Hasmonean*) Period. *Mattathias,* an intensely patriotic priest with unbounded courage, became infuriated at the attempt of Antiochus Epiphanes to destroy the Jews and their religion. When the emissaries of Antiochus arrived at the small town of *Modin* (about 15 miles west of Jerusalem), they expected the aged Mattathias, to set a good example for his people. They expected him to offer a pagan sacrifice on Jehovah's altar in Modin. He not only refused, but he killed an apostate Jew — and he also killed the Greek officer who was presiding at the ceremony. Mattathias fled to the Judean highlands. He and his sons waged a guerrilla war against the Seleucid rulers of Syria and Judea. Although the aged priest did not live to see his people freed from their Greco-Syrian yoke, he commissioned his sons to complete the task.

Mattathias had five heroic, warlike sons — *Judas, Jonathan, Simon, John, and Eleazar.* When Mattathias died in 166 BC, his mantle fell on his son *Judas* — a warrior of amazing military genius. He won battle after battle against unbelievable and impossible odds. He re-conquered Jerusalem in 165 BC, and he purified and re-dedicated the Temple. (*This was the origin of the Feast of Dedication*). Judas united the priestly and civil authority in himself and established the line of *Hasmonaean priest-rulers who* (for the following 100 years) governed an independent Judea. Under the Maccabees, Hebrew traditions were renewed, and a spiritual revival occurred. The revolt of the Maccabees against religious tyranny was a lesson that was not lost on future Roman conquerors.

JUDEA UNDER THE ROMANS

Rome threatened all factions of Alexander's divided house. Founded as a city-state in 753 BC — by 266 BC Rome controlled the entire Italian Peninsula. The Romans then embarked on a conquest of the entire Mediterranean Basin. First, they defeated their great rival *Carthage,* whose possessions included Sicily, Spain, and North Africa. All eventually became Roman provinces. During the 2nd and 1st centuries BC, Rome's military legions fought against kings and city-states in the eastern Mediterranean to bring Greece, Asia Minor, Syria, Mesopotamia, Persia, Judea, and Egypt under Roman control. In the west, Julius Caesar conquered Gaul, which included all of modern France, Belgium, and parts of the Netherlands, Germany, and Switzerland. Austria, Hungary, and the Balkans also fell under Roman rule so that the Roman frontiers extended (west to east) from the Atlantic to the Caspian Sea, and from North Africa to the Euphrates. From (north to south) Roman hegemony extended from Britain to the Nile. The Mediterranean Sea became a *"Roman Lake."* Everywhere, the Roman standards were seen. Everywhere, the barriers of nationalism had been cast down and all elements of many divided kingdoms were welded into one great Roman Empire. Rome ruled the world!

HOW ROME GOT INVOLVED IN PALESTINE

Although *Judas Maccabeus* championed a revolt against the Seleucids and won Judea's independence, another power struggle soon developed that led one of the Jewish kings to seek the aid of *Pompey* (106-48 BC). Pompey was a Roman General, statesman and a member of *The First Triumvirate.* Pompey obliged, and in 63 BC, Judea was conquered by the Romans. *Antipater (an Idumean and therefore an Edomite descended from Esau),* was appointed ruler of Judea. Antipater was succeeded by his son *Herod the Great,* who became king of Judea with Roman support. Herod was king of Judea from 37 — 3 BC. To gain the favor of the Jewish people, Herod rebuilt the small 2ⁿᵈ Temple (i.e., *Ezra's and Nehemiah's Temple*) in Jerusalem with great splendor. However, Herod was one of the most brutal and cruel rulers of all time. According to *Josephus*, Herod murdered his political opposition. Because of jealousy over their popularity, he executed his two sons! When *Augustus Caesar* heard about that, he said: *"It is better to be Herod's dog than one of his children."*

Herod's sister, *Salome*, slandered Herod's wife, *Miriam* (a Hasmonean princess descended from the Maccabees), and *poisoned* Herod's mind with false tales of a love affair between Miriam and a man maned *Joseph*. In a fit of ungovernable jealousy and rage, Herod had Joseph immediately killed. Miriam was falsely accused of adultery, and was subsequently tried, convicted, and executed.

Herod the Great was the king who ruled Judea when Jesus was born. He was the king who ordered the slaughter of all the male children of Bethlehem and in all of its environs from two years-old and under — because he heard *The King of the Jews* (Jesus Christ) *would soon be born* (Matt. 2:16). This fulfilled the prophecy of Jeremiah when he foretold weeping and great mourning for Rachel's children... *"because they were no more"* (Jer. 31:15).

An Angel of the Lord appeared to another *Joseph (the* husband of Mary, the mother of Jesus*)* in a dream and warned him to: *"Arise and take the Child and His mother, and flee to Egypt, and remain there until I tell you; for Herod is going to search for the Child to destroy Him* (Matt. 2:13)."

This was a fulfillment of the prophecy of Hosea when he said:

"Out of Egypt did I call My Son (Hosea 11:1)."

Some 33 years later, Herod's son, *Herod Antipas* killed *John the Baptist* (Mark 6:14-29), and mocked Christ (Luke 23:7-12). Fourteen years after the beheading of John the Baptist, his grandson, *Herod Agrippa I* murdered *James the Apostle* the brother of *the Apostle John* — Acts 12:1-2. Sixteen years after the death of James, Herod's great-grandson (*Herod Agrippa II*) was the king *who tried the Apostle Paul* (Acts 23:12—26:32).

THE JUSTINIAN CALENDAR MADE A MISTAKE REGARDING CHRIST'S BIRTH.

If *Herod the Great* was King of Judea when Christ was born, how is it possible that history records the length of his rule as being from 37 — 3 BC (supposedly ending three years before Christ was born)? When Christ was born, time was reckoned in the Roman Empire from the founding of the city of Rome (supposedly in the year 753 BC). When Christianity became the universal religion over what had been the Roman World, a monk named *Dionysius Exiguus* (at the request of the Roman Emperor *Justinian*), made a calendar (in 526 AD) that superseded the Roman Calendar and reckoned time from the birth of Christ. Long after the Christian calendar had replaced the Roman calendar, it was found that Dionysius had made a four-year mistake.

GOD USED ROMAN MILITARY ROADS TO SPREAD THE GOSPEL.

Meanwhile, *Caesar Augustus* was a worried man. As he surveyed the vast expanses of the world he ruled, he feared rebellion from within. His solution was military roads. He commanded 10,000 laborers to build a network of military roads from one end of his empire to the other. With these roads in place, he could quickly march his legions to any trouble spot to strike down any rebellion.

THE PAX ROMANA CREATED A PERIOD OF PEACE SO THAT THE GOSPEL COULD BE HEARD.

Not before or since in the annals of recorded human history has the world enjoyed such an extended period of relative peace. During the Pax Romana the people under Roman rule felt safe. Wherever Caesar's subjects were found, they could scan their horizons and see no signs of an enemy. Rome ruled with a strong hand and no nation anywhere was big enough or powerful enough to attack her. Peace and quiet reigned. With the multitudes no longer pre-occupied with the struggle to keep alive, the peaceful words of Jesus Christ could be heard by all.

GOD CAUSED THE ROMANS TO GRANT RELIGIOUS FREEDOM TO JUDEA.

Just like the Greeks, the Romans were idol worshippers. Their mythology closely mirrored the Greeks. They worshipped many of the same gods but gave them Latin names. When Julius Caesar acquired absolute power, the 500 year-long period of Roman Republican Government came to an end. After the conclusion of the Civil War that erupted after his murder, Rome entered into a period of Imperial Government. Romans began to *deify* their emperors and required all Romans and all subjects of the Roman Empire to worship their Roman Emperors as gods. This combination of military and spiritual power insured absolute rule.

THE FISCUS JUDAICUS.

However, the Romans were no fools. They saw what happened to the Seleucids when they tried to impose their Greek gods and their Hellenistic culture on the Hebrews. The Maccabees had won against overwhelming odds. The Hebrews had refused to bow to foreign gods and had revolted rather than submit to the reinstitution of idol worship. The Romans wisely made an exception for the province of Judea. The Jews were granted an exemption from the official Roman state-religion. In Judea, they allowed the Jews religious freedom and did not impose the worship of their Caesar. For this "privilege" the Jews were required to pay a punitive tax called the *Fiscus Judaicus*. In effect they said to the Jews: *"So you want to be exempt from the state-religion? Okay, as long as you pay for the privilege."*

GOD USED JEWISH RELIGIOUS GROUPS & THE SANHEDRIN TO OPPOSE HIS SON SO THAT HIS PLAN OF SALVATION COULD COME TO FRUITION.

The three religious groups who opposed Christ were the Pharisees, the Sadducees, and the Scribes. The Essenes were a 4th group that pretty much kept to themselves. However, we owe them a great debt of gratitude. They are the ones who transcribed and preserved the Dead Sea Scrolls at Qumran.

WHO WERE THE PHARISEES?

The word "*Pharisee*" means "*separatist*." They were the spiritual descendants of the pious Jews who had fought the Hellenizers in the days of the Maccabees. They were probably given the name of "*pharisee*" by their enemies to indicate they were nonconformists. Their stronghold was the synagogue. Their strictness separated them from their fellow Jews. Loyalty to "*truth*" sometimes produces *pride* and *hypocrisy*, and it is this perversion of the earlier Pharisaic ideal that was denounced by Jesus (Mark 7:8-9). See also *the Parable of the Pharisee and the Publican* (Luke 18:10-14). Before his conversion, Paul reckoned himself a Pharisee (Phil. 3:5).

WHO WERE THE SCRIBES?

The Scribes were not a sect but were members of a profession. They were *copyists* of the Law. They came to be regarded as the authorities on the Scriptures, and thus exercised a teaching function. Their thoughts were usually akin to those of the Pharisees, with whom they frequently associated. Jesus warned against the scribes when He said:

"Beware of the scribes, who like to go about in long robes, and love salutation in the marketplaces and the best seats in the synagogues and the place of honor at feasts, who devour widows' houses and for a pretense make long prayers. They will receive the greater condemnation (Luke 20:46-47)."

WHO WERE THE SADDUCEES?

The Sadducean party denied the authority of tradition and looked with suspicion on all revelation later than the Mosaic Law. They denied the *Doctrine of Resurrection,*[1029] and they did not believe in the existence of angels or spirits. They were largely people of wealth and position, and they gladly cooperated with the Hellenism of the day. In New Testament times they controlled the priesthood and the Temple ritual.

WHO WERE THE ESSENES?

Essenism was an ascetic reaction to the externalism of the Pharisees and the worldliness of the Sadducees. The Essenes withdrew from society and lived lives of asceticism and celibacy. They gave attention to the reading and study of scripture, prayer, and ceremonial cleansings. They held their possessions in common and were known for their industry and piety. Both war and slavery were contrary to their principles. *John the Baptist* is said to have been an *Essene.* The monastery at *Qumran,* near the caves in which the Dead Sea Scrolls were found, is thought by most scholars to have been an Essene center in the Judean wilderness. The scrolls indicate members of the community had left the corrupt influences of the Judean towns to prepare in the wilderness *"The way of the LORD."* They had faith in the coming *Messiah* and thought of themselves as *the true Israel to whom He would come.*

THE DEAD SEA SCROLLS

The Dead Sea Scrolls validate the accuracy of the Septuagint Translation. Although many think much of the pottery found at Qumran was only used to store food — from a very recent analysis of the composition of the clay pottery jars that contained the Dead Sea Scrolls, we now know the chemical composition of the clay used to make those jars is identical to the chemical composition of *Qumran clay.* Scientists say: *all clay from one site has a distinctive chemical composition. No clays from other sites are identical. Each site is different.* According to a recently aired *History Channel Dead Sea Scrolls Documentary* (on the televised History Channel — on Sunday, March 21, 2021), we now have the proof that the pottery jars, which contained the Dead Sea Scrolls in the caves near Qumran, *were made from Qumran clay!* Furthermore, chemical analysis of the ink on the Dead Sea Scrolls has proved: *the ink was also made at Qumran!* Other scientific studies have dated the clay jars and the ink on the Dead Sea Scrolls *to the exact time of*

[1029] Some have joked the Sadducees denial of the resurrection *"made them — 'SAD-YOU-SEE.'"*

the Essene community at Qumran! **So, we now have proof the Essenes at Qumran transcribed and preserved the Dead Sea Scrolls! We are greatly indebted to them for their preservation of the ancient Hebrew Bible.**

WHAT WAS THE SANHEDRIN?

The Sanhedrin was the highest court and council of the ancient Jewish nation. The Sanhedrin functioned as the Jewish religious "Supreme Court" during the *Pax Romana.* Therefore, the Sanhedrin was the recognized headship of the Jewish people in the days of Christ. It was composed of 71 members, mostly priests and Sadducean nobles — but also included some Pharisees, Scribes and Elders. The High Priest of Israel presided over the Sanhedrin. The Sanhedrin was the Jewish high court that tried Jesus after His arrest before He was sent to Pontius Pilate for sentencing (John 18:12-24). The Sanhedrin denied Jesus *the due process of law* during His trial. His trial was held at night. Jewish Law specifically prohibited trials at night.

REBELLION OF THE JEWS AGAINST ROME:[1030]

The Romans had ruled Judaea since 63 BC. Political and religious tensions between the Jews and Rome had always existed. But it began to come to a "*head*" when Several Roman Emperors began imposing punitive taxes and religious persecution. In 39 AD, Caligula ordered his statue be placed in every temple and religious site in his empire. Open rebellion and warfare against Rome broke out in 66 AD after the Roman Emperor Nero plundered the treasures in Herod's Temple to God in Jerusalem. The last stand of a particularly dangerous group of rebels (known as the Sicarii) was crushed when Rome captured Masada later in the same year. After a long siege, when the Romans finally stormed into that mountain-top fortress, they found all of the rebels (including all of their women and children), had committed suicide! Under the Emperor Vespasian, the Roman army crushed the Jewish rebellion. The Sanhedrin was abolished when Titus, the son of Vespasian, destroyed Jerusalem and Herod's Temple to Jehovah on the Temple Mount in 70 AD.

SUMMARY POINTS:

JEWS & CHRISTIANS SEE HISTORY AS THE JUDGMENT OF GOD. CHRISTIANS BELIEVE—

- God used Assyria and Babylon to chasten His people and scatter them throughout the world.
- God used Cyrus to free His people and rebuild Jerusalem and the 2nd Temple.
- God used Alexander the Great to give the world a common language so that the message of Christ could be carried to the four corners of the world and be understood.
- God used Ptolemy II to bring about the translation of His written word from the Hebrew into a universal world language in the time of Jesus Christ—i.e., The Greek Septuagint.
- God used the abomination and tyranny of Antiochus Epiphanes IV to incite the Maccabean revolt.

[1030] **66 AD: Was the Great Jewish Revolt Against Rome a ...**

567

- God used the Maccabean revolt to reinstitute Hebrew Traditions of Worship and cause a Spiritual Revival.
- God used the Romans to enforce an extended period of World Peace, and build an extensive network of roads, so that Christ's message and example could be rapidly carried to the four corners of the world. This allowed the rapid spread of the Christian Gospel and Christian Church after Christ's death and resurrection.
- The lesson learned from the Maccabean revolt caused the Romans to exempt Judea from Roman state-religion and allow the Jews religious freedom.
- God used the spiritual confusion and moral deterioration of the period to cause the resurgence of a true spiritual hunger.
- God used three of the four Jewish religious groups and the Sanhedrin to oppose his Son so that his plan of *Salvation* could come to fruition.
- God used the Essenes to write the Dead Sea Scrolls, which centuries later would validate the Septuagint by demonstrating the accuracy of its translation.
- God had been everywhere, shaping the course of history for the coming of Jesus Christ.
- God used all of these historical factors to create a nourishing environment so that when He sent His Son to redeem the world, His message would capture the hearts and souls of men and women everywhere.
- The moment the Father chose to bring His Son into the world was the optimum moment for the announcement of God's New Covenant with Man with the introduction of His Dispensation of Grace through the sacrifice and death of His Son Jesus Christ!
- The Resurrection of Jesus Christ gives all Christians the hope of Life Eternal in Heaven with the Holy Trinity.
- Indeed: *"The time had fully come for God to send forth His Son!"*

JERUSALEM IS ONE OF THE OLDEST CITIES IN THE WORLD.

Christians & Jews believe *all the roads of world history meet at Jerusalem*. The oldest part of Jerusalem was settled ~ 4,000 BC making Jerusalem one of the oldest cities in the world. A priest of God (Melchizedek) lived there in the time of Abraham in ~ 2,000 BC. His city was called *Salem*. Some have said King David was the first conqueror of Jerusalem when he captured it and made it (i.e., *the City of David*) his capital in ~ 1,000 BC. Jesus Christ was crucified and rose from the Dead there. Jerusalem has been attacked 52 times, captured 44 times, besieged 23 times,[1031] and completely destroyed twice. The city also figures prominently in Bible prophecy concerning the end-times and the future millennial peaceful rule of Jesus Christ when Jesus comes again as *the Conquering Messiah*. Jerusalem truly sits at the center of world history. Three great monotheistic religions lay claim to it.

[1031] What is the difference between "attacked" and "besieged?" An "attack" is a military assault. Successful attacks capture the city. However, attacks can be repulsed and fail. A city that is "besieged," is surrounded by the enemy army for a long period of time and "starved" into surrender.

APPENDIX III: HEAVEN IS "FOR REAL!" HEAVEN REALLY DOES EXIST!

In Chapter Three of Book I, when I talked about *The First Wisdom of God, His Intelligent Design and Eternity,* I also presented the scientific evidence that defined the connection between the Laws of Relativity, the Speed of Light, and Eternity. Furthermore, I also talked about Time—Space—Matter—Time-reference-frames—and the fact they are all *'Relative'* and *'Relevant.'* The connections between Electromagnetic radiation—Radiant energy—and Time-Flow were also presented. Then, we talked about *'When Time Stands Still,'* and the scientific reality of Heaven. All of this led to the conclusion — Heaven is not a myth. Ladies and gentlemen: *Heaven is a real place! Heaven really does exist! Nothing is impossible for God!*

In Chapter 8 of Book I (when we discussed the physical and the metaphysical aspects of light), we talked about ***"The Light of Jesus Christ"*** — and how the Light of Jesus changed Saul into Paul. That story (in the Book of Acts) told us Jesus appeared and spoke to Saul in the form of a flashing light from heaven that blinded him. The Bible says the men with Saul heard the voice of Jesus but saw no one. The Bible is silent on whether or not the men with Saul saw the flashing light. However, they certainly understood Saul was blind after Jesus spoke; because afterward, they had to lead Saul *'by the hand'* into Damascus. There can be no doubt the light of Christ that blinded Saul was — *the light of Christ in a physical sense.*

In *Revelations 21:23*, John had a vision of the Holy City in Heaven. He saw that—*"The city has no need of the sun or of the moon to shine upon it <u>for the glory of God has illumined it and its lamp is the Lamb</u>"* (Who is Jesus the Christ.) Also consider this statement concerning the Holy City in Heaven: *"And there shall no longer be any night; and they shall not have need of the light of a lamp nor the light of the Sun <u>because the LORD GOD shall illumine them</u> (Rev. 22:5)."*

The discussion of Time-Flow led us to the subject of light. The subject of light led us to God, and to the concept of God's timeless existence. The belief in the timeless existence of God (i.e., *the Eternal Nature of God),* led us to the concept of Life Eternal in Heaven after death, and the eternal life that has been promised to those who trust and believe in Jesus Christ.

O. David

LADIES AND GENTLEMEN HEAVEN IS FOR REAL!

Before we leave the subject of timeless existence and the assertion that the Laws of Relativity have changed the Biblical concept of timeless existence (i.e., Eternity) from a theological claim to a possible physical reality—meaning Heaven really does exist—I need to mention two books you should read. The books are:

* *Akiane, Her Life, Her Art, Her Poetry.*
* And: *Heaven is For Real.*

These books are truly inspiring. They have nothing to do with science. They are books about faith in God. They deal with the religious experiences of two innocent and guileless children who encountered God when they were four years old. I consider these books two of the most important books I have ever read. For children who experience the love of grateful parents and are raised in an environment where peace prevails, their early years are the time in their lives when their innocence prevails. They have not reached an age where innocence begins to erode. The stories of these two children and their experience of God should convince you Heaven really does exist.

AKIANE, HER LIFE, HER ART, HER POETRY

Akiane Kramarik lives in rural Idaho. She was <u>not</u> born into a religious family. Her mother was raised an atheist in Lithuania. One morning, when Akiane was *four*, she whispered to her mother, *"Today I met God."* Her mother had never mentioned God to her, and so far as she knew, Akiane had never heard the word *God*. *"What is God?"* — her mother asked. *"God is light — warm and good. It knows everything and talks with me. It is my parent:"* Akiane replied. Her mother wanted to know who taught her such a word as — *God?* Akiane told her: *"You won't understand."* **Notice: 4-year-old** Akiane said: ***"God is light"*** — (cf. I John 1:5, John 1:4-5, 8:12, 9:5; Ps. 18:28, 27:1: Isa. 60:1; and Rev. 21:23*)*.

If you read Akiane's book you will discover she has been to Heaven (in spirit) through her visions many times. This girl regularly communes with God. She has seen Jesus many times because He is in all of her visions of Heaven. Although she writes religious poetry, she is distinguished by her art. Akiane says God taught her how to draw and paint. The process took several years, but Akiane has become a famous artist. Her two portraits of Jesus are her most famous works. The story of how she prayed for a model with the right face is truly intriguing.

HER EN FACE PORTRAIT OF JESUS CHRIST: "THE PRINCE OF PEACE"

Desperately wanting to paint portraits of Jesus (whom she had seen in her dreams), she spent a lot of time searching for the right face. For over a year she stood by supermarkets, shopping malls, parks, and on city streets — all the while searching the crowds looking for the perfect representation of Jesus — only to shake her head in disappointment. One morning, when she was 8 ½ years old, she prayed: *"I can't do this anymore, God. This is it. I can't find anyone by myself."* Then, she tearfully prayed to God: *"I need You to send me the right model and give me the right idea. Maybe it is too much to ask, but could You send him right through our front door? Yes, right through our front door."*

The next day, in the middle of the afternoon, the doorbell rang. An acquaintance brought her friend — *a carpenter* — right through the front door of Akiane's home. As the almost seven-foot-tall carpenter (with his strong hands, long hair, and beard, and with his warm smile) stood there — Akiane said (in Lithuanian): *"This is he! This is the man who will model for the Jesus painting. He resembles the image that keeps coming back to me in my visions. Maybe he's the reason God moved us to this town"* (pages 26-27 of her book).

Akiane worked at a feverish pace. She choreographed the poses, studied the carpenter's face and took several pictures. She was most anxious to begin her sketching, and right away she decided to start with a resurrection-scene (i.e., the painting she entitled: *"The Prince of Peace)."* She cut a strand of her own hair to make a fine brush to paint the eyelashes. Forty hours after she started, her first portrait of Jesus was finished. Every viewer quickly noticed — no matter where you stand — the eyes of Jesus follow you. Although the portrait resembled the model, Akiane had altered his expression and features to mimic the resurrected Jesus she remembered from her dreams.

"FATHER FORGIVE THEM"

After she finished her first portrait of Jesus, she immediately began sketching the profile for her next portrait which she named: *"Father Forgive Them."* Her second portrait depicts a kneeling Jesus in profile with His hands and face lifted toward Heaven, pleading with the Father to forgive those who crucified Him. This powerful image took seventy hours to paint. Like the first portrait, Akiane worked at a frantic pace. For a while, she struggled to represent Christ's hands. *"They have to lift up the world to the Father. They have to be strong, strong hands"* — she said.

Months later, thousands of people were discussing her two portraits of Jesus. Some scientists from Russia said her *Prince of Peace* portrait bore a remarkable resemblance to the mysterious image taken from the *Shroud of Turin*. Scholars from India were fascinated by Akiane's depiction of the towel-robe Christ wore. At the time she painted the portraits, Akiane knew nothing about the clothing of the ancient Israelites. However, the scholars from India claimed adult Jews wore similar robes during worship two thousand years ago! Hundreds of people (the world over) wrote to her that her portraits of Jesus were the exact images of Christ they had seen in their dreams!

Many of her paintings have been exhibited in *the Museum of Religious Art in Iowa*. Once, when she was there during an exhibition of her art, a man approached her and said: *"I am a Buddhist. You called Jesus the 'Prince of Peace,' yet in His name so many people were massacred. How do you explain that?"* Akiane replied: *"Jesus is peace, just like calm water. But anyone can drop a stone into water and make it muddy."* Another person asked her: *"Why did you choose Christianity instead of another religion?"* Akiane said: *"I didn't choose Christianity; I chose Jesus Christ. I am painting and writing what God shows me. I don't know much about the religions, but I know this: God looks at our love."*

COLTON BURPO— "HEAVEN IS FOR REAL"

This book is about a little boy from Imperial, Nebraska. His father, Todd Burpo, is a minister. Pastor Burpo's son, *Colton*, had a *near death experience* during surgery for a ruptured appendix when he was *four* years old. Pastor Burpo says: *"Young children have a call-it-like-you-see-it innocence. At four years old, they haven't learned either tact or guile. They might loudly ask an embarrassing question—like when they point to a pregnant lady and ask: 'Why is that lady so fat'…or laugh and point and say, 'You've got a booger in your nose!'"*

Colton told his parents — when he was so sick, he had gone to Heaven for three minutes. The first person he saw in Heaven was Jesus. The things this *4-year-old* told his parents about Heaven are truly amazing. They are things no one would expect a 4-year-old to know. After surgery, the doctors thought little Colton would die and they told the nurses to refrain from giving the family any hope of his recovery. However, when all truly seemed hopeless, Colton suddenly began to improve and eventually recovered.

COLTON'S STILLBORN SISTER

Over a period of several months following his complete recovery from that illness, Colton slowly revealed to his parents the facts of his visit to Heaven. They were astounded by his descriptions of Heaven and the people he saw there. A little girl with dark hair came up to Colton and told him she was his sister. She wouldn't stop hugging him. She told him she had died in her mommy's tummy before she was born. She had not been named and she could hardly wait for mommy and daddy to get to Heaven so that she could see them, and they could give her a name. In the meantime, God had adopted her. When Colton's mother, Sonja, said: *"You mean Jesus adopted her."* Colton replied: *"No, His Dad did."*

Sonja was struck and astounded by Colton's *matter-of-fact statements*. Here was her almost 5-year-old son talking about his experience of God and Jesus in Heaven — during a surgical operation when he was a 4-year-old and deathly ill — as if it should be something people should just understand — as if his experience was nothing out of the ordinary!

After Colton was born, Sonja had a miscarriage, and a little premature baby was stillborn. The stillborn child had not been shown to her or her husband, and they did not know the baby was a girl. Neither did they know she had dark hair. She had not been named. I guess that was the way they handled stillborn births in those days — because the same thing happened to us at the Jefferson-Hillman Hospital (the main teaching hospital at the University of Alabama Medical School in Birmingham, Alabama) in 1966!

Sonja and Todd had never mentioned their stillborn baby to Colton! They had explained it all to Colton's older sister, Cassie, because she was old enough to understand — or so they thought. (If the stillborn infant is anatomically normal, I don't think it is possible for us to understand the *"why"* of stillborn birth.)

Sonja once said to her husband Todd: *"I carry these children for nine months and they all come out looking like you."* You see, Cassie, Colton, and their younger brother Colby, all have blond hair — like their dad. Now, Sonja and Todd have the peace of knowing that their little dark-haired daughter has been adopted by God and is in Heaven with God and Jesus. She has been spared the sorrows of this world. And yet, even though she is in Paradise with God, she feels incomplete because she had not met her parents, and she had not been named. She is anxious to meet them when they get to heaven. The thought I have unnamed twin boys in heaven, gives me an extra incentive to — *"make it to heaven."* Oh, how I long to meet them, hug them, and name them!

While Colton was in Heaven, he also told his parents about the things he saw them doing on Earth while he was in surgery. This astounded them too because they *were doing those things* while Colton was in surgery. Colton also told them the whole time he had been in surgery, he was *"so scared."* However, Jesus held him in His lap and the angels sang to him to make him feel better. They sang *"Jesus loves Me"* and *"Joshua Fit the Battle of Jericho."* Colton asked them to sing: *"We Will, We Will Rock You,"* but they wouldn't sing that — he said.

As I read the book I was stunned by Colton's descriptions of Heaven. They coincided with the descriptions of Heaven that are in the Bible! Everything this 4-year-old said about Heaven is scriptural — and his parents know they are things no one (not them and not his Sunday school teachers) ever told him when he was 4 and 5 years old!

Next to the Bible, I consider this little book the second most important book I have ever read. If you read *"Heaven is For Real,"* you will be rewarded with a picture of Akiane's *Prince of Peace*, because Akiane gave Pastor Burpo permission to print that portrait of Jesus in *"Heaven is For Real."* The story of how Akiane found the model for her first portrait of Jesus is included in Pastor Burpo's book, *"Heaven is For Real."*

For several years Colton's parents had been showing him various portraits of Christ. Colton always said Jesus did not look like the portraits they showed him. It got to the point they would say: *"OK Colton, what's wrong with this one?"* After a friend of theirs told them about Akiane and showed them pictures of Akiane's two portraits of Christ, the

Burpos showed Colton the picture of Akiane's *Prince of Peace.* Colton looked at the portrait for a long time but said nothing. *"What's wrong with this one?"* — Pastor Burpo asked. Finally, Colton said — *"Dad, that one's right."*

THERE ARE NO OLD PEOPLE IN HEAVEN.

The New Testament tells us: *"We Christians...also groan to be released from pain and suffering. We, too, wait anxiously for that day when God will give us our full rights as His children, including the new bodies He has promised us — bodies that will never be sick again and will never die (The Living Bible paraphrase of Romans 8:23)."*

Other English translations of the Bible say something about how we ourselves groan within ourselves, waiting for the adoption, *"to wit, the redemption of our body."* I like the way the Living Bible paraphrases Romans 8:23 because it brings meaning to the awkward 17th century phrase: *"the redemption of our body."*

Regarding the promise of new bodies when we get to Heaven, Colton told his Dad something that seems to confirm this. He told his Dad he had met his great-grandfather, Pop (Lawrence Barber), in Heaven. Colton said: *"Pop was really nice and had really big wings."* This caught Pastor Burpo's attention because Pop had died a few decades before Colton was born. Pastor Burpo showed Colton the only photo of Pop he had. It was taken when Pop was 61. Colton didn't recognize the man in that picture. Instead, Colton said:

"Dad, nobody is old in heaven, and nobody wears glasses."

So, Pastor Burpo called his mother in Ulysses, Kansas and asked if she had any pictures of Pop when he was younger. A few weeks later, an old photo of Pop arrived that was taken when he was 29 years old. When the photo was shown to Colton he said,

"Hey! How did you get a picture of Pop?"

Colton had recognized his great-grandfather in a photo that had been taken a half century before Colton was born! Please stop a moment and think about that!

Once, Colton's dad tried to *'trip him up.'* He told him he remembered Colton had said he stayed with Pop when he was in Heaven. So, he asked him what they did when it got dark. Did they go home together? Colton suddenly got serious and scowled and said: *"Who told you that? It doesn't get dark in Heaven, Dad!"* Testing him further, his dad replied: *"What do you mean it doesn't get dark?"* Colton then told him:

"God and Jesus light up Heaven. It never gets dark. It's always bright!"

Pastor Burpo realized: not only had Colton not fallen for the *'when it gets dark in Heaven trick,'* but Colton told him *why* it didn't get dark—

"The city does not need the sun or the moon to shine on it for the glory of God gives it light, and the Lamb is its lamp (Rev. 21:23)."

Colton and Akiane say *they belong to God.* Like Colton, Akiane has seen Jesus, but Akiane has seen him several times since He is in all of her visions of Heaven. Both children say Jesus is really tall and has the most beautiful eyes. They also say He is very masculine. Colton says He wears a white robe with a beautiful purple sash (the color of royalty) that forms a diagonal from His left shoulder to the right side of his waist. According to Colton, Jesus is the only one in Heaven who wears purple. He also has red marks on both hands and feet (the marks of the nails used in His crucifixion). I think Colton didn't mention the spear mark in Christ's side because the robe Jesus wore covered it. Both children say Jesus really loves children.

Although Jesus is really tall, God is even bigger and sits on a majestic throne. God is the biggest person in Heaven — Colton says. Jesus sits on God's right side, and the angel Gabriel sits on God's left.

Akiane's descriptions of Heaven, God, Jesus, and the Holy Spirit are identical to Colton's. Like Colton, she says the *colors in Heaven* are much more vibrant and beautiful than anything on Earth. Furthermore, Heaven has more of them. Both children give identical descriptions of God, Jesus, the Holy Spirit, the angels, and the people and animals in Heaven. Both children agree — *There are no old people there.*

"Dad, God really loves us! You can't believe how much He loves us!" Colton said.

If you have any doubts about Heaven, and the Trinity, you must read these two books. As I read these two books the following scriptures repeatedly came to mind.

"The wolf also shall dwell with the lamb, and the leopard shall lie down with the kid; and the calf and the young lion and the fatling together; and a little child shall lead them. Isaiah 11:6 (a prophecy of the harmony that will prevail during Christ's reign in the future Millennial Kingdom—KJV)."

"And He (Jesus) called a child to Himself and set him before them, and said, 'Truly I say to you, unless you are converted and become like children, you shall not enter the kingdom of heaven. (Matthew 18:2-3—NASB).'"

"And they were bringing children to Him so that He might touch them; and the disciples rebuked them. But when Jesus saw this, He was indignant and said to them, 'Permit the children to come to Me; do not hinder them; for the kingdom of God belongs to such as these. Truly I say to you, whoever does not receive the kingdom of God like a child shall not enter it at all' (Mark 10:13-15 and Luke 18:15-17—NASB)."

"But when the Pharisees heard that He had put the Sadducees to silence, they gathered themselves together. And one of them, a lawyer, asked Him a question, testing Him. 'Teacher, which is the greatest commandment in the Law?' And He (Jesus) said to him, 'You shall love the Lord your God with all your heart, and with all your soul, and with all your mind. This is the great and foremost commandment. And a second is like it. You shall love your neighbor as yourself. On these two commandments depend the whole law and the prophets' (Matthew 22:34-40—NASB)."

Remember, Akiane said: "But I know this: God looks at our love."

Summary Points:

Like the apostle Thomas, I think many of us have *doubts* about God, Jesus, Heaven, Life after death, and the Bible. But for believers, the life experiences, and words of these two innocent children should be convincing evidence that:

- o God is real. Jesus is real.
- o God and Jesus *"are light and life (John 1:4)!"*
- o The Holy Spirit is real.

- o Heaven is *For* real.
- o Eternal Life is promised after death for those who believe in Jesus.
- o And the Bible is a serious book. It is the true written *WORD of GOD.*

Unbelievers who say there is no proof God exists must concede there is no way to prove He doesn't. If you don't believe in God and Jesus, you should seriously look at the risk you are taking with your life. Everyone should consider this; *if* we would live our lives according to the teachings of Jesus — *if* we truly lived by loving each other as we love ourselves — this world would be a different place. It would literally be *a paradise on Earth.* How do we love others as we love ourselves? We should *always* treat others like we would want to be treated. (See Matthew 7:12 and Luke 6:31 — *The Golden Rule.*) Like Jesus, we should live our lives serving others.

OUR TWIN BOYS

My wife and I lost twin boys in the 5th month of our first pregnancy. The twins were stillborn. Their lives were taken because of — *polyhydramnios* — an excess of amniotic fluid, which the uterus cannot accommodate. Polyhydramnios causes premature birth. Though not common, it usually happens with twins — I was told. Sometimes the twins have fetal abnormalities. But I was told our twin boys were normal. Although the doctors showed them to me, they did not feel it wise to show them to my wife. They feared her postpartum depression would be gravely prolonged if she saw them and carried *that* memory. I agreed — because it hurt me so bad when I saw them. So, Sarah never saw them. Since they were stillborn, they were not named. We were told: *the hospital would take care of them — we need not worry about that.* We acquiesced. In the moment of decision that was thrust upon us, we were *shocked* to the point of being absolutely *stunned!* We let the hospital — *"take care of them."* We didn't name them! We didn't give them a proper burial!

The next day, as her mother (who had rushed from Georgia to be with us) and I sat by Sarah's side in her hospital room, we were still too stunned to say much of anything. The day after that, like a robot, I returned to work at Lloyd Noland Hospital where I was an intern. Getting busy again with patients diverted my attention from the tragedy of it all. About two weeks later, we received mail from the county health department. They sent us our twin boy's birth certificates and death certificates! Our doctor had told us: *"They never lived!"* Their birth certificates said they were — *"unnamed!"* Their death certificates said — *"disposed of by hospital."* That's when we both — *"lost it!"* We were once again — *overcome with grief. But this time we were also burdened with an unbearable sense of guilt and profound regret!* The people who served us at the hospital had — "heart." They were kind and sympathetic. But government bureaucracy is cold and heartless!

For years the memory of our tiny innocent lifeless boys haunted me until I read *"Heaven is For Real."* The story of Colton's little stillborn sister rushing up to meet him when he was in heaven did wonders for me. Learning that God had adopted her, that she had grown into a little girl, she was happy and glad to see Colton, and she looked forward to meeting her parents when they came to heaven to give her a name — had a miraculous healing effect on me. A cascade of tears poured forth. The floodgates of tears burst open!

I hadn't realized how much of an emotional burden I had been carrying and had suppressed all of those years! **After reading** *Heaven is For Real,* **my wife and I prayed and thanked God for letting us know our twin sons are in Heaven under His care. We now know** *"Our Abba Father"* **(cf. Introduction—Part VI: "Myth vs. Fact," Book I) adopted them**. Praise the LORD, they have been with Him ever since! When we prayed, we asked our *"Abba"* to tell them we love them and look forward to seeing them. We also told God the names we wanted to give them — *Joshua and Stephen. Joshua* — because Hebrew for *"Jesus"* is *"Jeshua"* (short for *"Yehoshua")*, which translates to *"Joshua"* in English. It means *"Yahweh is salvation."* Joshua was the faithful lieutenant of Moses in Egypt and during the Exodus. He was one of the two spies (out of 12) who saw the giants in the holy land but unlike the other 10 spies, his and Caleb's faith in God made them willing to carryout God's command to go into the promised land. *Stephen* — because he was the one who was faithful unto death. When accused of blasphemy, he stood before the Sanhedrin, recited the history of Israel to them and bravely told the Sanhedrin they were responsible for murdering God's Son. During his trial, Stephen's face looked like the face of an angel (Acts 6:15). Stephen was stoned to death. (cf. Numbers 13 and 14 and Acts 6 and 7.)

Little Colton Burpo has helped me understand our twin sons (Joshua and Stephen) were taken straight to Heaven. They have been spared the trials and the sorrows of this cruel world. They were "born" to Eternal Life in God's Paradise — Heaven! When I learned that, I prayed, and still pray this prayer.

***"The Lord giveth and the Lord taketh away. Blessed be the Name of the Lord.
And blessed are they who the Lord taketh unto Himself."***

Now, I Corinthians 13:12-13 has new meaning for me. *"For now, I see in a mirror dimly, but then face to face. Now I know in part, but then I shall know fully—Just as I also have been fully known. But now abide faith, hope, love, these three. But the greatest of these is love."*

Thank you Dear Abba Father for Loving and Saving Joshua and Stephen. I know that my Redeemer liveth. And I know that someday I shall see God face to face. I also know I shall see all of my loved ones who have preceded me in death.

⚜

BAD THINGS HAPPEN! LOOK AT JOB! WE CANNOT KNOW WHY!

Maimonides believed the Book of Job is a parable, [1032] and the Land of Uz is a place-name — meaning *"to take counsel."* Thus, according to Maimonides,

"Job said all he said because he had no true knowledge. He relied only on authority and tradition. He assumed with tradition that happiness consisted of wealth, children, and health. When they were taken away, he was perplexed. Only when he gained true knowledge of God at the end did he make peace with his misfortune and experience true happiness (a direct quote of Seow's book, p. 133)."

[1032] *Job 1-21, Interpretation & Commentary:* William B. Eerdmans Publishing Company, Grand Rapids, MI/Cambridge, UK: Copyright © 2013 C. L. Seow. Cf. p. 133

Others have argued Job was a real person, who God said was blameless and upright. God said Job feared (respected) God and turned away from evil (Job 1:1 and 1:8). In Job 1:8, God told Satan, Job was so faithful and exemplary in his faith that there was no one else on earth like him. I am inclined to believe Job was a real person. I also think (like Maimonides), a lot of us have no true knowledge of God. We also rely on "authority and tradition." We are all perplexed when we see good people suffer. We all cry — Why?

In all of his suffering, Job complained about his misery, but he never once blamed God! His friends were convinced Job's suffering was because he had sinned. They said he arrogantly refused to confess his sin. But Job said — No! This argument goes on and on from Chapter 3 through chapter 37! God's response begins in Chapter 38 and continues through Chapter 41. Finally, in Chapter 42 Job repents. He confesses he complained about — *"that which he did not understand."* Heretofore, Job told God he had heard about God, but after his suffering, he now could see God with his eyes! Job acknowledged his ignorance of God's thoughts and ways and repented his complaints saying he must now be silent before God. In Job 42:10, God restored the fortunes of Job after Job prayed for his friends. Job is the example for all believers.

Bad things can and do happen to good people through no fault of their own. Through good times and bad we must trust God.

I now know I must hold to my faith and trust in God. It is my greatest desire that through my life-experiences (even if it happens that I must suffer), I may also gain a true knowledge of God, and like Job (when I come to know God), I may also be granted the experience of true happiness in heaven with the Holy Trinity, in the presence of my loved ones who have preceded me in death. If I must suffer, I also know no amount of suffering I might experience can compare to the suffering of Jesus Christ when he died on that cruel cross for us all!

❧
APPENDIX IV: "MADE FROM MONKEYS?" [1033]

In their scheme of the *'Man Made from Ape Theory,'* today's Neo-Darwinists tell us we are the result of a series of random point mutations of DNA in gametes (i.e., mature sex cells) that united to form mutated zygotes which grew into mutated offspring. They claim nature then selected for or against the change expressed by the mutations. In those instances where random chance selected for, they posit — through many generations of interbreeding, the beneficial mutations gradually became the dominant traits in an improved population. They now claim this random plus selective process was repeated a myriad of times until the needed number of mutations for the success of their proposed natural selection process reached the present. This is the way Neo-Darwinists now claim you can get the complexity of a Homo sapiens out of a less-complex ape — an ape out of a still less-complex reptile — and a reptile out of an even less-complex fish. Their proposal creates a common putative ancestor for apes and humans that evolved from reptiles.

O.David

RICHARD DAWKINS, AN AVID DARWINIAN EVOLUTIONIST, ONCE SAID:

"Measuring the statistical improbability of a suggestion is the right way to go about assessing its believability." [1034] So, let's do that. What is the statistical improbability that man was — "Made from Monkeys?"

- *First*: There is no evidence of a recognized common ancestor of apes or humans in the fossil record.
- *Second:* There is no evidence of a common ancestor of either of the two man-like hominids (Neanderthals and Cro-Magnons).
- *Furthermore:* The fossil record shows Cro-Magnon fossils overlap with the more primitive Neanderthal fossils.
- The discovery of this overlap countered the theory that Neanderthals evolved into the more modern Cro-Magnons.
- So, there is no fossil evidence that connects humans to apes to reptiles.
- However, if we are going to construct a favorable statistical model for the Neo-Darwinian "Man from Ape Theory,"
- We need to ignore the fossil record — like Darwin did!

We now know the Cro-Magnons were anatomically identical to us. That is why scientists now say they were AMHs (i.e., Anatomically Modern Humans). We also know Chimpanzees are the hominids that are genetically closest to us. Humans and chimps belong to the same phylum, the same subphylum, same class, and same order of animals. Their Linnaean Classification does not diverge until the level of the genus is reached.

- Chimps are of the genus *Pan*.
- Humans are of the genus *Homo*.

Nevertheless, some geneticists say Chimps are "genetically almost human" and argue they rightfully belong to the same genus we do. Be that as it may, we absolutely need to forget about Monkeys because their genetic differences are even greater, and they are also further removed from apes and humans in the Linnaean Taxonomy.

An intense effort is underway to map the Human genome. Only a tiny fraction of the Chimp genome has been studied. But, if we take the known data and assume (there is that word

[1033] Schroeder *The Science of God* Chapter 8 p 116-124
[1034] R. Dawkins *The Blind Watch Maker*, W. W. Norton, New York, 1986

again), "*assume*" the data is indicative of the entire genome, then the genetic difference between Chimps and Humans is only 1-5%, depending on which sequence of amino acids is being compared. At first glance, 1-5% doesn't seem like much. Actually, it is huge!

So, statisticians ignored the fossil evidence and seriously considered the Neo-Darwinian conjectures. They constructed a scenario that favors the Neo-Darwinian Man from Ape Theory and created a favorable statistical model that eliminated all bias against the Neo-Darwinian assumptions. If an error were to creep into the statistical model, they wanted the model to err on the side that is favorable to the Neo-Darwinian scheme.

THE GENOME

The genome is the genetic package of information carried on the chromosomes. It is about the same size in all mammals. It consists of about 3 billion nucleotide base pairs per cell. These are the molecular points of information within the double-helical strands of chromosomal DNA. At each one of those 3 billion points, one of four specific bases resides — *guanine, cytosine, adenine, and thymine (or G-C-A-T)*. Sets of three of these bases (called codons) determine which one of twenty naturally occurring amino acids will be produced in the offspring. A combination of several hundred linked amino acids are folded into a specific three-dimensional structure of DNA to produce one of the thousands of the proteins that are found in life.

CONSTRUCTION OF THE FAVORABLE STATISTICAL MODEL

The statistically favorable model starts with the *assumption: To form a Chimp and a Cro-Magnon from their assumed common ancestor that lived 7 million years ago, only the active part of the genome need be changed.*

The active part of the genome is 3% of the bases. That is 90 million bases — (3% of 3 billion base sites is 90 million base sites) — each one of which will host one of four possible bases (G-C-A-or-T).

The most favorable statistical model takes the lower range of the estimated 1-5% difference between Chimp DNA and human DNA and assumes the actual difference is only 1%. Therefore, within the 90 million bases which comprise the active part of the genome that needs to be changed, the supposition was made: there is a 1% difference between the imagined common ancestor of Cro-Magnon and Cro-Magnon. (Remember, in this model, Cro-Magnons are assumed to have been anatomically and genetically identical to humans.) This would mean the genetic difference between humans and the putative ancestor of Chimps and Humans would be 1% of 90 million bases = 900 thousand (900,000) differing bases.

ADDITIONAL ASSUMPTIONS

So, to evaluate the *improbability* of the *Man from Ape Theory*, the model *assumes* that:
- A common ancestor evolved from reptiles and produced two new animals — the Chimpanzees and the Cro-Magnons.
- The Cro-Magnon was the first human.
- There needed to be a change in 900,000 differing bases in the active expressed region of the genome of the Common Ancestor (that was similar to a Chimpanzee), to produce the first Cro-Magnon (and/or the first Human).
- All of this supposedly happened over a period of 7 million years — because Neo-Darwinian Theory posits the tectonic plate-shift which caused the Afro-Syrian rift

isolated the population of primates in Africa 7 million years ago and changed the environment so much that the development of the rift *was* the seminal environmental event that caused the expression of the genetic changes the Neo-Darwinists imagined.

THE QUESTIONS

The first question the favorable statistical model needs to answer is:

- *"Can we expect to have 900,000 beneficial point mutations in DNA and have them passed on to become the dominant traits in the entire population of the herd in the 7 million years that the fossil record and the Neo-Darwinist conjecture tells us are available?"*
- The next question the statistical model needs to answer is: *"Which mutations are necessary to change a common ancestor similar to a Chimp into a Cro-Magnon (i.e., a Human)?"*

Neo-Darwinists will naturally object to this last question because it suggests a purposeful intention is involved. They claim their conjecture of natural selection lacks all intention. However, we must ignore their objection — because if evolution lacks intent, then we must deduce — if we humans did not evolve, then one of a multitude of other life-forms would now be the top-of-the-line creature. If we take the stance that humans are *the only* top-of-the-line form capable of meeting the challenges of nature — the problem of producing us by the random plus selective natural process becomes insurmountable in the time the Neo-Darwinists postulate was available.

THE PARAMETERS OF THE STATISTICAL MODEL

Nevertheless, the question still needs to be answered. To do this, the statisticians proposed a set of five highly improbable parameters. They proposed a *most favorable* statistical model that—

- [1]Allows the mutations to be *random* at the level of DNA.
- [2]Postulates *in every case,* that nature selected *for* the mutations.
- [3]Assumes *all* mutations will be *beneficial,* and *none* will be *fatal*.
- [4]Assumes *none* of the beneficial mutations will be lost by *any subsequent detrimental nonfatal* mutations.
- And [5]*assumes* the mutations that occur will become *the dominant traits* which will be *expressed* throughout the entire population of progeny in the herd in the 7 million years the Neo-Darwinist supposition allows.

ROADBLOCKS TO THE MODEL

The maximum reported mutation rates in human body cells are one per ten cell divisions. In gametes (i.e., the mature sex cells in which the 900,000 different base changes need to occur), the mutation rate is much lower — one mutation per every 10,000 to one per 100,000 generations! This lower mutation rate of gametes is nature's way of maintaining the status quo. It guards against mutations. Nevertheless, since successful mutations are the engine of change in the Neo-Darwinian belief, the favorable statistical model needed to get around this roadblock. The statisticians did so by ignoring the lower mutation rates that occur in gametes. They factored in the higher mutation rates that characterize common body cells. They realized they were constructing a statistical model that had nothing to do with reality. However, if this statistically biased model, which favored the

Neo-Darwinian assumption were to fail, the Neo-Darwinists would at least have to recognize — the failed model was the most favorable model that could have been constructed.

FINDINGS

The usual breeding population for herds of large animals is 10,000 members. Assuming all sexually mature animals in the herd participate during the mating season (an unrealistic assumption); at a gamete mutation rate as high as that of a common body cell — one per ten matings — one can expect 500 mutations in the herd each year. Three percent of these, or 15, will occur in the expressed region of the genome. At each point on the chromosome, any one of four bases may reside. On average, only one in four of the expected 15 mutations will cause a positive improvement of the host animal. These mutations must then spread through the entire herd by the interbreeding of the mutant with its nonmutated relatives.

- If a mutated trait is neutral — (i.e., causes no advantage), and if it is not lost by subsequent mutations — it will spread through the herd in 5000 generations.
- If each mutated trait conveys as much as a 1% advantage to the mutant over the others in the herd, 500 generations will be required for each new mutated trait to spread through the herd and express itself as a dominant trait.
- If this happened with the alleged common ancestor of Chimps and Cro-Magnons, the 500 generations of interbreeding would have required over 3000 years.

Here, we are talking about 3000 years for only **ONE** *successful mutated trait to become dominant within the herd!*

However, the bar is much higher than **ONE**. More than one trait is needed to achieve the evolutionary changes. Traits such as [1]hip structure, [2]hair cover, [3]cranial shape, [4]changes in facial characteristics, [5]shortening of the upper extremities, [6]lengthening of the lower extremities, and [7]lengthening of the back, [8]trunk, and [9]neck, for example, *and many more than just these 9 are needed.* 70,000 successful mutated altered sites are needed for *each* new trait. Furthermore, the 70,000 altered mutated sites must always fall within the narrow 900,000 site band (out of the total of 90 million active sites) that harbors the basis of change. *Assuming* only 15 concurrently changing traits are needed, the problem becomes colossal — because — at each nucleotide location, one of four bases may be selected, but only one of the possible four will be correct. The probability (P), of filling *the first site correctly* is 1 minus the probability of failure (q).

$$P = 1 - q = 1 - (279{,}999/280{,}000)^r$$

Where *r* is the number of generations, and 280,000 represents the 70,000 sites of each trait, each site having one of four possible bases (4 x 70,000 = 280,000).

500,000 generations are required for an 83% probability the first of the required 70,000 mutations will have occurred. Hundreds of millions of generations will be required to complete the task. The time is just not there. The fossil record and the Neo-Darwinist conjecture tell us it all happened in seven million years. So, the most favorable model for their random plus selective mutation process falls woefully short. It fails miserably. Even if the size of the herd is increased from 10,000 to 100,000, we still need over a thousand generations for each mutation to spread through the herd. Increasing the size of the herd does not solve the problem of how to get the needed mutations in the available time. If the herd is larger, more time will be required for a mutated trait to express itself throughout the entire herd.

What if the model allowed the needed 900,000 mutations to occur *in any order*, but still required the needed 15 annual mutations *to be distributed randomly* over the 90 million basses? This model found there was only a 17% chance a mutation would occur at a potentially beneficial site. It was also found there was only a one in four chance the mutation would select a beneficial site. The *probability for success* in the first generation of mutants in this model is only 4%.

$$P = .017 \times .025 = 0.0425 \text{ or } 4\%$$

The probability of failure is $q = 1 - P = 0.9575$ or 96%

The probability of success in subsequent generations is $P = 1 - q^r = 1 - (.09575)^r$

Forty generations must pass before there is an 82% probability any one of the potentially useful mutations will have occurred. Nature requires 900,000 changes and forty million generations, even if one neglects the 500 to 5000 generations required for each mutation to spread through the herd. However (once again), the fossil record gives us only seven million years for all of this to be accomplished.

Today, even avid evolutionists agree the scheme of the Neo-Darwinian Theory of *'Man Made from Apes'* cannot win if the classic concept of randomness at the point molecular level of DNA is the driving force behind the mutations. Not only does the math not work — but the time is just not there.[1035]

CONCLUSIONS

1) Statistical analyses, based on models that *'bend over backwards'* to favor the Neo-Darwinian conjecture that man was made from apes, *have proved the statistical improbability of their scheme beyond every shadow of a doubt! Every attempt of Atheists and antitheists to exclude God from the Creation Equation has failed!*

2) The Biblical Account of Creation proclaims a *God-directed orthogenesis of man.* I suggest you review Chapter 18 (Book II) and pay close attention to the discussion about the statistical improbability of the idea that *gradual random mutations were the mechanism of change.* Also review Chapter 20 and carefully consider the discussion of the possibility of common ancestry. In Chapter 22 — in Chapter 23 — and again in Chapter 27 — the belief of the Jewish sages that God *'made'* Adam before He *'created'* him was presented. You might review those pages as well.

3) The problem with the Neo-Darwinian conjecture of *'Man Made from Apes'* is — *their scheme excludes God!*

4) The fossil record tells us Cro-Magnons suddenly appeared 50,000 years ago as a distinctly separate and different species of hominids. They were anatomically identical to us. We are smaller, but today's young people are the evidence humans are getting bigger. The ancient Hebrew sages believed when God formed man, the forming took time. They also believed it was possible God changed (evolved) the form of the creature that eventually became the first "man." According to their

[1035] Schroeder *The Science of God* Chapter 8 p 123-124

belief, it was possible God started the formation of man by first making a putative common ancestor and by gradually changing that ancestor, finally formed the "*animals*" the Hebrews called the *Nephilim*. Today, we call them — *Cro-Magnons*.

5) So, it is possible that chimps and man may have had a common ancestor. Science tells us there is "*only*" a 1-5% genetic difference.

6) According to the Hebrew Cosmogony, the only difference between the Nephilim and humans was the *Neshama*. The ancient Hebrew sages believed the difference was qualitative, not quantitative. The ancient Hebrew sages also believed the deeper meaning of the Hebrew narrative of the Bible (the Genesis Code) was telling them that ~ 5700 years ago, Elohim took one of the Nephilim and blew into his nostrils 'God's breath of life' (the Neshama), and Adam was created.

7) The Ancient Hebrew Sages believed the Hebrew Bible also described the event that caused the demise of the Nephilim — *Noah's flood*. Since Noah was descended from Adam, and we are descended from Noah, we are the evidence that the species that initially was a Cro-Magnon and then became human (when Elohim blew the neshama into Adam's nostrils), did not become extinct altogether — because Noah and his family survived the flood.[1036]

8) Although the Neo-Darwinist conjecture has been statistically proved impossible, the irony is, if you put God back into the creation equation, *the 'Man Made from Apes' slogan becomes plausible—BECAUSE NOTHING IS IMPOSSIBLE FOR GOD!*

[1036] The Nephilim are not mentioned in the KJV, the NKJV, or the Living Bible. These versions talk about giants being in the land and refer to the giant sons of Anak. The Nephilim are mentioned in the MLB, RSV, and the NASB. And, the RSV says the sons of Anak come from the Nephilim. The Bible mentions other giants in the post-flood Holy Land (i.e., Goliath and King Og—also the Emim & Raphaim for example). It is not clear to me if these races of giants were the same as the antediluvian Nephilim. (cf. Gen. 6:4 & Numbers 13:33.)

✤
APPENDIX V: COMMENTARY ON AGNOSTICISM, GNOSTICS, & GNOSTICISM

'Gnosticism' comes from the Greek word 'gnosis' meaning "to know." Gnosticism flowered in the 1st and 2nd centuries after the crucifixion and resurrection of Jesus Christ.   O. David

AGNOSTICISM

Agnostics say they don't know God exists. Their uncertainty is an admission of their doubt. They say they cannot commit to something that is unknowable. As Darwin put it:

"I feel most deeply that the whole subject is too profound for human intellect.
A dog might as well speculate on the mind of Newton."

GNOSTICS CLAIM:

*They possess a special **secret self-knowledge** of the Divine and of Jesus Christ — not known to Christ's Apostles!* Gnosticism is that belief! Several schools of Gnosticism developed in the 1st and 2nd centuries AD. While Atheists deny the *Divinity* of Christ, Gnostics deny His *humanity.* Furthermore, they slander God! According to the Ryrie Study Bible's Introduction to the First Letter of John — *"The heresy of Gnosticism had begun to make inroads among churches in the days of John the Apostle."*

FIRST AND SECOND CENTURY GNOSTICS BELIEVED:

(1) Knowledge is superior to virtue.
(2) The non-literal sense of Scripture is correct. Only a select few can understand it.
(3) Evil in the world precludes God's being the only Creator.
(4) Deity can't exist in human form. Therefore, *The Incarnation of Jesus* was a myth.
(5) There is no resurrection of the flesh.

GNOSTICS ALSO CLAIM:

- Only Gnostics possessed the **secret** knowledge of the Divine.
- The world was created by evil angelic powers who kept the human soul trapped in a physical body.
- Matter and the physical body are evil. Only the spirit is good.
- Since the body is evil, one is allowed all indulgences of the flesh without fear of any spiritual consequences, for one's spirit is pure and cannot be defiled.
- Since the flesh is evil, the story of the incarnation is false, for Christ would not have come in human form, because deity cannot unite itself with anything material such as an evil body. Jesus Christ's body only seemed real. It was a phantom body.
- Christ was not crucified because one cannot kill a god. Christ only seemed to experience crucifixion. At the time of the crucifixion, He was above in spirit and was laughing at the deception. Therefore, the testimony of the apostles concerning the crucifixion was a hoax.
- **Since all flesh is evil, there is no such thing as the resurrection of the flesh.**
- Belief in Christ alone is not sufficient for salvation. Salvation is accomplished through the descent from heaven of a feminine savior who brings knowledge of the heavenly, spiritual world and thereby enables men to escape the prison house of the flesh.
- The God of the Old Testament is evil, jealous, vindictive, and an arrogant, ignorant *"Demiurge"*— a term adopted by Gnostics, who, in their dualistic worldview, saw the Demiurge as one of the forces of evil, who was responsible for the creation of

the despised material world and was wholly alien to the supreme God of goodness.

Gnosticism was and is a system of religious and philosophical doctrines combining Christianity with Greek Mythology and Oriental Mysticism. Not all Gnostics believed the same things. Several schools of Gnosticism developed. Their beliefs were varied, but most all Gnostics believed all the above, and lived their lives accordingly. Gnostic beliefs are complicated and are just as dangerous as ever. This just gives us some idea of the heresies Paul and the Apostles faced when they went into the world teaching the Gospel to all nations. Elaine Pagels' 182-page book: *"The Gnostic Gospels,"* has received much acclaim. While reading it, I wondered if Pagels was a Gnostic. However, on page 151 she wrote: *"That I have devoted so much of this discussion to Gnosticism does not mean, as the casual reader might assume, that I advocate going back to Gnosticism — much less that I 'side with it' against orthodox Christianity...But the task of the historian, as I understand it, is not to advocate any side, but to explore the evidence — in this instance, to attempt to discover how Christianity originated...For the Christian, the question takes a more specific form: What is the relation between the authority of one's own experience and that claimed for the Scriptures, the ritual, and the clergy?"*

I suppose Pagels would consider me — *a casual reader.*

Some have claimed Kabbalah is a form of Gnosticism. Not so! Maimonides and Nahmanides (both Kabbalists), worshipped Jehovah-Elohim! They were faithful followers of our Abba, Father. They believed Gnostics are heretics!

I reject Gnosticism. I also believe they are heretics. I side with Paul who said: *"For by grace you have been saved through faith, and that not of yourselves; it is the gift of God, not of works, lest anyone should boast (Ephesians 2:8-9 NKJV)."*

Thus, it is through belief and faith in Jesus Christ alone that we are saved!

Jesus Christ alone is sufficient for salvation!

JESUS CHRIST WAS CRUCIFIED, DIED, & WAS RESURRECTED IN THE FLESH!!!

I believe Jesus Christ was **Crucified and Died "In The Flesh,"** as the multitude at Golgotha watched! I also believe **Jesus Christ was Resurrected In The Flesh**—as the apostles and the crowd of more than 500 in Galilee witnessed (I Cor. 15:6)! In Luke 24, they saw his wounds, He broke bread with them, and ate broiled fish! And in John 20, Thomas put his hands into Christ's wounds. A Spirit has no need of food, and one cannot touch a Spirit!

Furthermore, I believe Jesus when He said: *"I have always spoken openly to the world. I have always taught in synagogues, and in the temple where all the Jews come together;* ***And I spoke nothing in secret (John:18:20)!"***

Satan has lost!
Christ has won!

God made me captain of my God-given soul. I gave it back to Jesus and my Father long ago. For my Abba-Father, and His Only Begotten Son— Are Creator, Lord, and Savior—Are truly, truly — ONE!   O. David

Are you uncertain God exists? If you are uncertain, or if you wonder about what God thinks about you, consider how King David felt after his adultery with Bathsheba and his murder of her husband became known.

DAVID PRAYS FOR FORGIVENESS

After God rejected Saul from being king over Israel, God sent Samuel to Bethlehem to anoint a new king. God had selected a new king for Himself among the sons of Jesse (1st Samuel Chapter 16). When Samuel looked at Jesse's son Eliab, he thought God's choice was standing before him. But God told Samuel: *"Do not look at his appearance or at the height of his stature, because I have rejected him; for God sees not as man sees, for man looks at the outward appearance, but the Lord looks at the heart (vs. 7)."* Then Samuel asked Jesse if those present were all his sons. Jesse said the youngest, David, was in the fields tending the sheep. Samuel told Jesse to send for him. David was the youngest and least physically impressive of Jesse's sons. But as soon as Samuel saw the young boy, he knew he was — *"The One."*

All Christians know David's story. Raised by his father to be a shepherd boy, God made him the 2nd king of Israel. When still a boy, David killed Goliath, and the people learned of David. There were many trials ahead for him, but he eventually became the king that united the 12 tribes of Israel. David was a nation builder. But as so often happens, once his power seemed secure, David relaxed. He did not accompany or lead his army one spring, when kings went forth to war. He remained behind in his newly established capital (Jerusalem) when his army sallied forth to besiege Rabbah and destroy the sons of Ammon in one of his last military campaigns. There, while walking on the roof of his palace one spring night, David saw Bathsheba bathing, and he fell from grace. He committed adultery and murder. The story is in the Book of 2nd Samuel. After David's hegemony was well established, great turmoil within David's family developed. His favorite son, Absalom, rebelled against him. David fled from his capital. Absalom marched on Jerusalem, took control of David's kingdom, slept with David's wives, and forced a final battle, in which he was killed. The story is in the last part of the Book of 2nd Samuel.

After his sin with Bathsheba, the death of their first son, and again with the death of his favorite son, Absalom, David was shaken to his roots. At first, David refused to acknowledge his sin. In Psalm 32:3-4 David tells us when he did not immediately confess his sin (*"When I kept silent about my sin"*), God chastened him physically and emotionally and David wasted away and groaned all day long. Eventually, David repented his sins, and prayed this prayer: *"Restore unto me a clean heart, O God. And renew a right spirit within me. Cast me not away from Thy presence and take not Thy Holy Spirit from me. Restore unto me the joy of Thy salvation and uphold me. Uphold me with Thy Spirit. Thy Holy Spirit. Then I shall teach transgressors Thy ways. And sinners shall be converted unto Thee. Restore unto me a clean heart — O God* (Psalm 51)."

When God forgives, He forgets our sin! It is with God as if our sin never happened! (***Hebrews 8:12***, also see Psalm 32:1-2, Isaiah 44:22, & Romans 8:1-2)

Paul said: "All have sinned and have fallen short of the glory of God (Romans 3:23)."

If we are truly sorry, every time we sin, we can find our way back to Jesus—if we earnestly repent, ask for forgiveness, sincerely pray David's prayer—and focus on Jesus!

WE MUST BECOME LIKE A LITTLE CHILD.

Jesus called a little child to Him, set him in the midst of them, and said: *"Assuredly, I say to you, unless you are converted and become as little children you will by no means enter the kingdom of heaven. Therefore, whoever humbles himself as this little child, is the greatest in the kingdom of heaven. Whoever receives one little child like this in My name receives Me (Matthew 18:2-5 NKJV)."*

Remember this little song we sang as children? "Jesus loves me this I know. For the Bible tells me so. Little ones to Him belong. We are weak, but He is strong. Yes, Jesus loves me. Yes, Jesus loves me. Yes, Jesus loves me. The Bible tells me so." I have so often been reminded through my trials and life-experiences — the little songs we were taught as children — taught us some of the most profound things.

Are you discouraged? Does the future seem hopeless and dark? Are you struggling with your health — your work — your family relationships? Are you threatened by circumstances you can't control? We all face these problems and many, many more that are common to all mankind.

If you are harboring some unconfessed sin. If you have refused to acknowledge it, you must repent you sin, and earnestly ask God for forgiveness. You need to do it NOW. Don't delay. DO IT, and then pray this prayer:

"Dear God, Thank you for the gift of your Son, Jesus Christ. I acknowledge He died for me and all people so that through His shed blood, he crucified all sins for all people for all time on that cruel cross. All praise, glory, and honor be to you Oh Father for Christ's gift of salvation. Now, I pray for forgiveness, and I pray You grant me the serenity to accept the things I cannot change, the courage to change the things I can, and the wisdom to know the difference."

Then, Meditate on Matthew 11:28-30 *"28 Come unto me, all ye that labor and are heavy laden, and I will give you rest. 29 Take my yoke upon you and learn of me; for I am meek and lowly in heart: and ye shall find rest unto your souls. 30 For my yoke is easy, and my burden is light."*

As you pray:

FOCUS ON JESUS!

FOCUS ON JESUS!

"When the great scorer comes to score against your name, He marks not that you won or lost, but how you played the game (Grantland Rice)."

Come Little Davids, Come Blow Your Horns. Sheep in Our Meadows. Cows in Our Corn. We Must Contend with Satan's Scorn. ALL WE NEED — IS JESUS!!!

Soli Deo Gloria,
Love to All,
O. David

⚜ EPILOGUE

If you have read this far, perhaps you will agree this book is about our origins. I have not only focused on what the deeper meaning of the Hebrew Bible says about the Creation Account but have also attempted to explain that Modern Science now agrees with the deeper meaning of Moses' words. I also hope you will agree this is also a book about Belief and Faith in God and one that emphasizes Jesus Christ told us and showed us how we can live our lives "*In God's Way*" — by loving and serving others. O. David

FAULTY RELIGIOUS INTERPRETATIONS CAUSED CONFLICTS BETWEEN RELIGION & SCIENCE.

We have reviewed some of the doctrines of the Western Christian Church that were based on faulty interpretations of the Bible. And, we have seen there were some instances when the conflict between faulty Church doctrines and the scientific hypotheses of the time resulted in much pain, suffering, and even the deaths of some scientists that a judgmental and self-righteous Church persecuted because the Church labeled them heretics. Maimonides lived three centuries before the Spanish Inquisition, but because he was Jewish, he suffered religious persecution by Muslims in Spain and Morocco. When he fled to the Holy Land, Christian Crusaders also persecuted him. They expelled him from Jerusalem. He finally found acceptance in Egypt. There, he was a physician who treated the common people (without charge). Such was his skill that the excellence of his service came to the attention of Saladin (a Muslim who was the Sultan of Egypt). Saladin made Maimonides his personal physician. Maimonides also became the revered spiritual head of the Jewish community in Egypt. He believed:

"Conflicts between science and religion result from misinterpretations of the Bible." [1037]

Sadly, misinterpretations of the Bible continue, and people who follow the doctrines of men as if they are a test of religious fellowship, continue to judge and exclude others unjustly.

Today, the most egregious examples of misinterpretations of the Bible are the failed documentary hypotheses of *the School of Higher Biblical Criticism*. The opinions of this school reached their peak through the writings of Julius Wellhausen. His writings are still taught in some Western Protestant Christian Seminaries, even though archaeological discoveries (made after his death) have contradicted many of his opinions. The seminaries that teach Wellhausen's documentary hypotheses ignore the fact that the highly competent and intellectually respected *Rabbi Chaim Heller* (1878-1960) showed the divergences from the Torah in the various lectionaries in the possession of the School of Higher Criticism were due to the school's *misinterpretations* of the texts *rather than to the way the texts were written.*

Rabbi Heller also showed *all* the differences stemmed from the misapplication of one or more of the 32 rules of Biblical interpretation enumerated by *Rabbi Elazar ben Shimon*. Rabbi Heller's arguments have proved *unimpeachable* because he showed how the translators misapplied each rule in their versions.[1038] (See Introduction—Part VIII, Book I, Rabbi Chaim Heller.)

[1037] Schroeder *Genesis and the Big Bang* Chapter 2 p. 27
[1038] Article: *On Bible Criticism and its Counterarguments* by Rabbi Nathan Lopez Cardozo 1995
http://www.aishdas.org/toratemet/en_cardozo.html

Current-day Protestant Seminarians who teach Wellhausen's Documentary Hypotheses have apparently lost sight of the fact that Wellhausen resigned his Seminary Professorship at the University of Greifswald in 1882 because he realized there was a conflict between what he was teaching his students and what he was obligated to do — *train them to be Protestant clergy!* In his letter of resignation Wellhausen wrote: *"I became a theologian because the scientific treatment of the Bible interested me; only gradually did I come to understand that a professor of theology also has the practical task of preparing the students for service in the Protestant Church, and that I am not adequate to this practical task; but that instead despite all caution on my own part I make my hearers unfit for their office. Since then, my theological professorship has been weighing heavily on my conscience."* [1039]

His crisis of conscience caused him to resign his Seminary Professorship and leave the Ministry. He then joined the faculty of a liberal philosophy *'think-tank'* at the University of Halle where he became a professor of oriental languages. He later joined the faculty at Marburg as a full professor where he studied and wrote about Islam. His last appointment was at Göttingen where he taught Hebrew and Aramaic.

It must not be widely known Wellhausen suffered a crisis of his conscience when he realized the teaching of his theory conflicted with his duty to prepare his seminary students for service in the Lutheran Church. Sadly, Wellhausen favored *'his facts'* over his faith!

FAULTY SCIENCE CAUSED CONFLICTS BETWEEN SCIENCE & RELIGION.

Maimonides must have realized he was only partially correct about the reasons for the history of conflict between science and religion. The historical record of scientific hypotheses shows a number of times that science — *'got it wrong.'* Many faulty platforms of scientific opinion were constructed over the years that have been *disproved* by the research and discoveries of later generations of scientists. Perhaps that is why Maimonides also wrote: *"We must form a conception of the existence of the Creator according to our capacities; this is, we must have a knowledge of metaphysics* (i.e., the Science of God), *which can only be acquired after the study of physics* (i.e., the Science of Nature); *for the science of physics is closely connected with metaphysics and must even precede it in the course of studies. Therefore, the Almighty commenced the Bible with the description of creation — that is with physical science."*

As we have seen, there was so much opposition by the church to his premise — *an understanding of science could add to mankind's understanding of spirituality* — that his book was burned by Jews and Christians alike. [1040] And yet, we now know science can only take us so far. I firmly believe Maimonides was wrong in his premise that the study of physics (i.e., the science of nature) can lead us to an understanding of metaphysics (i.e., the science of God) — because the science of nature cannot help us understand the mind of God, let alone prove God's existence. I think Belief in God, and Faith in God are our only pathways to God!

THE IMPACT OF THE FAILED HYPOTHESES OF CHARLES DARWIN

The prime example of *faulty science* concerns the failed hypotheses of Charles Darwin.

[1039] *The Bible Without Theology:* Robert A. Oden: books.google.com/books?isbn=025206870X
[1040] Schroeder *The Hidden Face of God* Chapter 2 p. 23-24

- His mistaken idea that life originated through gradual random chance abiogenic chemical reactions—
- His erroneous hypothesis of macroevolution—
- His imaginary tree of evolution—
- And his one-dimensional hypothesis of natural selection by the survival of the fittest—

have *all* been disproved by scientific discoveries made over the last 85 years. Nevertheless, it was Darwin's ascendancy in his field of biology that motivated Wellhausen to make a similar impact in his field of theology. The ideas of both men gave the anti-God people of their day and succeeding generations of a host of atheists and anti-theists — the motivation to promote their worldly, prejudiced, political and social agendas. Furthermore (like Wellhausen), some Protestant Christian ministers and academics turned their backs on the Christian Church. In the 19th century several prominent people in Britain and the USA were so taken with Darwin and Wellhausen and were so outspoken in their denial of the truth of the Old Testament, that they were accused of heresy, tried by their Christian churches, and were excommunicated! All pointed to Darwin's and Wellhausen's ideas as the *well-spring* for their rejection of the Old Testament.

In the 20th century, politicians joined in and made changes to governing laws and social institutions, which have excluded God and prayer from our schools. Their actions have led millions astray and away from God! The majority of people are still unaware Modern Science has disproved Darwin's ideas of life's origins and evolution. Furthermore, candid theological, archeological, and academic rebuttals of Wellhausen's Documentary Hypotheses are beginning to gain traction. So far as Darwinism is concerned, the argument is not about *if* evolution occurred. It is about the *specifics* of *how* evolution occurred. The faculties of prestigious universities around our globe are not only content in doing nothing to correct Darwin's incorrect assumptions, but they still teach Darwin's ideas as if they have been proven to be law. (Take another look at Chapter 18: Evolution—Darwin vs. Modern Science and the Bible—in Book II).

THE CONVERGENCE OF AGREEMENT BETWEEN MODERN SCIENCE & THE CREATION ACCOUNT:
On the other hand, science has now proved the Bible right about the inauguration of life on Earth at the appearance of liquid water. And science has made it possible for us to understand the first life-forms on our planet were *microscopic* forms of life. Furthermore, Modern Science has also made the most important step it can ever make in closing ranks with the Bible through its discovery that:

1. There actually was a beginning to our universe, and—
2. Life started rapidly on Earth and not via eons of random chemical reactions.[1041]

Even though science has discovered Nahmanides was correct that the universe and all existence began with a Big Bang, science still doesn't know how, and has not been able to discover what caused the Big Bang, or what caused the start of life itself.

We have discussed the reasons Science can only take us *"so far."* In an acknowledgment of the limitations of science, a majority of scientists now agree — *science cannot adjudicate the issue of God's superintendence of nature.* However, an

[1041] Schroeder *The Science of God* Chapter 2 p. 29

increasing number of scientists who believe in God — *are now confident God actually did create and make all that exists!*

CONCLUSIONS

In Chapter 4 (Book I), we discussed how Nahmanides concluded man would never be able to discover what happened *before* the beginning. But what happened after the moment of the beginning — would be open to man's discovery. He also reasoned — the deeper meaning of the first verb in the Bible (*barah*) meant Elohim created all that exists from nothing. Therefore, nothing existed *before* the beginning — *but Elohim.* We now know Modern Science agrees with Nahmanides' concept of *the Beginning.*

In preceding chapters, we discussed the deeper meaning and nuances of the ancient Hebrew language Moses used when he wrote the Genesis Creation Account. And I explained why I have called the ancient Jewish sages' explanation of the deeper meaning of the Hebrew language— *"The Genesis Code."*

Can we assume Moses fully understood the meaning of the words God dictated to him when he wrote the Genesis Creation Account? Would it have been necessary for Moses to understand *how* the ancient Jewish sages would interpret his words? Would it have been important for him to know modern science would make the discoveries it has? And would it have been an imperative for him to understand the recent discoveries of modern science now show a convergence of opinion which agrees with the deeper meaning of God's Creation Account? There is really no way for us to know.

But I do think Nahmanides was *'spot on'* in his interpretation of the meaning of *the bet* (and/or the *beth),* and *barah* in the first verse of the first chapter of the Bible. And, for me, this is just one of the many examples that prove the Bible is *the* book for all men in all times. The meaning of the Holy Scriptures has been and will continue to be *relevant to all men in all times.* God's Word is written is such a way that it reaches each one of us *at our own individual level of understanding.*

Please understand, I do not believe it is necessary for a person to know *anything* of what I have written — to understand the Biblical Account of Creation is serious and important. People of faith, who believe in God, and through their belief, know in their hearts that God created the earth and the heavens and all that exists — really don't need to speculate about *how* or *by what mechanisms* Elohim created. They know *God is God,* and their *trust* in *the Bible* and *all* the various translations of the Bible is what is important to them. They know there is no need to try to *'prove'* the existence of God because they understand *that* is not possible. More importantly, they know *no one can disprove the existence of God!* Furthermore, they don't need any of what I have discussed to convince them their faith and trust in God is right and true. **Nothing mentioned in this book is necessary for the salvation of any individual! The message of all translations of the Bible concerning salvation, is crystal clear and is easily understood by all.**

THE RELEVANCE OF THE GENESIS CODE

Perhaps the Genesis Code is only relevant to those who wish to argue against the skeptics who ridicule God's Word. *Perhaps* knowing there is an ever-converging agreement between what Modern Science has been discovering about our origins over the last 85 years, and what the Bible has stated for the last 3300 years, is important when Christians are confronted with the erroneous claims of non-believers as they attack God's

Word. *At least we now know how to answer the skeptics. And we also know modern science agrees with the Bible's Creation Account. Furthermore, we are now better equipped to recognize pseudoscience when we hear and see it.*

Can we change the opinions of those who ridicule the Creator? Not if a change of opinion would threaten whatever agenda a person has for not believing. What a person believes depends on what is in his heart. Is he possessed with the desire for riches or power? Once a person achieves power and wealth, does he measure his value and the worthiness of others by how much wealth can be accumulated, or by how much power and influence can be acquired? Does he consider the laws of God an intrusion upon his individual freedom of expression — his indulgence of sexual experience — or his freedom to use his power for acquisition, possession, and control? Does *God's Word* interfere with the exercise of his influence? Does it encroach or interfere with any grand plans for his personal hegemony? The important questions for you are:

- How do you see things?
- What is the treasure of your heart?
- Are you the center of your agenda, or is God?
- Do you wish to be close to your Creator?
- Or do you have a heart of stone?

The Bible has a lot to say about how we perceive things, what is in a person's heart, and how the Creator views our hearts. Here are but a few examples.

✓ *"The fool has said in his heart, 'There is no God" Ps. 53:1.*

✓ *"Do not harden your hearts, as at Meribah…" Ps. 95:8.*

✓ *"For forty years I loathed that generation, and said they are a people, Who err in their heart, and they do not know My ways. Therefore, I swore in My anger, truly they shall not enter into My rest" Ps. 95:10-11.*

✓ *"If your eye is bad, your whole body will be full of darkness. If therefore the light that is in you is darkness, how great is the darkness?" Matt. 6:23.*

✓ *"The good man out of the good treasure of his heart brings forth what is good; and the evil man out of the evil treasure brings forth what is evil; for his mouth speaks from that which fills his heart" Luke 6:45.*

✓ *"Thus says GOD, 'I will give you a new heart and put a new spirit within you & I will remove the heart of stone from your flesh and give you a heart of flesh'" Eze. 36:5.*

✓ *"With all my heart I have sought Thee; Do not let me wander from Thy Commandments. Thy word I have treasured in my heart, That I may not sin against Thee" Ps. 119:10-11.*

✓ *"There are six things which the Lord hates, Yes, seven which are an abomination to Him:*
[1]Haughty eyes, (i.e., arrogant, prideful, self-importance)
[2]A lying tongue,
[3]And hands that shed innocent blood,
[4]A heart that devises wicked plans,
[5]Feet hat run rapidly to evil,
[6]A false witness who utters lies,
[7]And one who spreads strife among brothers." Proverbs 6:16-19

These words were written thousands of years ago. Do these words remind you of the activities of any people in our country today?

PAY HEED TO THE PARABLE OF THE SOWER:

"Hear then the parable of the Sower. When anyone hears The Word of the Kingdom, and does not understand it, the evil one comes and snatches away what has been sown in his heart. This is the one on whom seed was sown beside the road.

And the one on whom seed was sown on the rocky places. This is the man who hears The Word, and immediately receives it with joy. Yet he has no firm root in himself but is only temporary. When affliction or persecution arises because of The Word, he immediately falls away.

And the one on whom seed was sown among the thorns, this is the man who hears The Word, And the worry of the world, and the deceitfulness of riches choke The Word, and it becomes unfruitful.

And the one on whom seed was sown on the good soil, this is the man who hears The Word and understands it. He indeed bears fruit, and brings forth some a hundredfold, some sixty and some thirty" Matthew 13:18-23.

Which verses apply to you? We have all been made from the dust of the earth. But what kind of soil do you represent:

- The hard pan of the roadbed—
- The scant soil among the rocks—
- The soil that is overgrown with thorns—or
- The good soil you have prepared for the LORD's work.

Where do you stand with the LORD? We know where Joshua stood.

"So, revere Jehovah and serve him in sincerity and truth. Put away forever the idols, which your ancestors worshiped when they lived beyond the Euphrates River and in Egypt. Worship the LORD alone. But if you are unwilling to obey the LORD: Then decide today whom you will obey. Will it be the gods of your ancestors beyond the Euphrates or the gods of the Amorites here in this land (Canaan)? But as for me and my family, we will serve the LORD" Joshua 24:14-15 (The Living Bible).

And we also know where David stood. In the King James Version of Psalm 8, this is what David said. *"O LORD our GOD, how excellent is thy name in all the earth! Who hast set thy glory above the heavens? When I consider thy heavens, the work of thy fingers, the moon, and the stars which thou hast ordained. What is man, that thou art mindful of him? And the son of man, that thou visitest him? For thou hast made him a little lower than the angels. And hast crowned him with glory and honour. Thou madest him to have dominion over the works of thy hands. Thou hast put all things under his feet. All sheep and oxen, yea, and the beasts of the field; the fowl of the air, and the fish of the sea, and Whatsoever passeth through the paths of the seas. O LORD our LORD, how excellent is thy name in all the earth!"*

THE CHOICE WE FACE

We all face the same choice Adam and Eve faced. But our choice is not in choosing to be like God, as Satan put it to Eve. Like Adam and Eve, our choice is between *Life Eternal* and *Eternal Death*. We can choose the way of the world, or we can choose God's Way.

Macbeth decided life was *'but a walking shadow, a poor player, that strutted and fretted his hour upon the stage,'* only to be *'heard no more.'* Instead of walking in God's shadow, he went his own way and chose to walk in the ways of the world. Near the end of his life, he decided the path he chose had led him to a life that was full of sound and fury signifying nothing.

The Bible points to another way. That way is God's Way. If we choose to live in God's shadow, we *will be living in* God's Way. Our lives will be full of meaning and filled with purpose.

In Chapter 23 (of this Book — Book III) we discussed the Genesis Code meaning of man being *"made in God's image."* We discovered God intended us to act like *His shadow.* That is, we should emulate Him as we perceive His interactions projected within our world. We must be as close to our Creator as we can be. How can one be close to God? One must do as Christ advised.

- *We must love the Lord our God with all of our heart, soul, mind, and strength.*
- *And we must love our neighbor as we love ourselves. How can we do that?*
- *We must always treat others as we would want them to treat us.*

In the final analysis, *we must Love Others in the same way God Loves Us.* Just how does one love others as God does? We must first realize God's Love is *Agape.* Perhaps the best example of *how to show others our version of God's Agape* is given us in the following scriptures.

AGAPE—SACRIFICIAL LOVE—UNSELFISH LOVE

"But when the Son of Man comes in His glory, and all the angels with Him, then He will sit on His glorious throne. And all the nations will be gathered before Him. And He will separate them from one another, as the shepherd separates the sheep from the goats. And He will put the sheep on His right, and the goats on the left.

Then the King will say to those on His right: 'Come, you who are blessed of My Father. Inherit the kingdom prepared for you from the foundation of the world. For I was hungry, and you gave Me something to eat. I was thirsty, and you gave Me drink. I was a stranger, and you invited me in. Naked, and you clothed Me. I was sick, and you visited Me. I was in prison, and you came to Me.'

Then the righteous will answer Him, saying: 'Lord, when did we see You hungry, and feed You. Or thirsty, and give You drink? And when did we see You a stranger, and invite You in, or naked, and clothe You? And when did we see You sick, or in prison, and come to You?' And the King will answer and say to them. **'Truly I say to you. To the extent that you did it to one of these brothers on Mine, even the least of them, you did it to Me.'**

Then He will also say to those on His left. 'Depart from Me accursed ones, into the eternal fire which has been prepared for the devil and his angels. For I was hungry, and you gave Me nothing to eat. I was thirsty, and you gave Me nothing to drink. I was a stranger, and you did not invite Me in. Naked, and you did not clothe Me. Sick, and in prison, and you did not visit Me.'

Then they themselves also will answer saying: 'Lord, when did we see You hungry. Or thirsty, or a stranger, or naked or sick, or in prison, and did not take care of You?' Then He will answer them, saying: **'Truly I say to you, to the extent that you did not do it to one of the least of these, you did not do it to Me.'**

And these will go away to eternal punishment. But the righteous to eternal life." *Matt. 25:31-46*

"Love is patient and kind. Love is not jealous or boastful. It is not arrogant or rude. Love does not insist on its own way. It is not irritable or resentful. It does not rejoice at wrong but rejoices in the right. Love bears all things, believes all things, hopes all things, endures all things. Love never ends." I Cor. 13: 4-8

"But now abide faith, hope, love, these three. But the greatest of these is love" I Cor. 13:13.

Remember, Akiane said: *"But I know this: God looks at our love."*
We must choose, but we must also understand science cannot help us in our choice. Only Belief and Faith in God can take us to those places Science can never go. So, in the twilight of my life, as I look around me, like David and Job, all those many thousands of years ago — when I look into the night skies, I see the works of my Maker and my Creator. I see the handiwork of my LORD and my GOD. Like David, Job, Moses, and Joshua, I choose to serve the Triune God — *Jehovah Elohim.*

We must always remember we have been blessed to be a blessing. (Gen. 12:2)

In The Introduction—Part IV: Belief and Faith (Book I) I talked about 'The Three Great Questions' — What was the origin of:

- The Universe?
- Of Life?
- Of Humans?

And, from that moment until now we have been talking about those questions. However, there is one other question we must ask. At the conclusion of one of the most thought-provoking sermons I have ever heard; my pastor asked and answered what he considered the most important question man can ever ask.

"If you were the only person ever created by God, would Jesus have died for you? Yes! That is how much God loves you!"

Rev. Jim Giddens, Skidaway Island United Methodist Church, Savannah, GA. 2004

AN EXAMPLE OF THE AGENDA OF MODERN-DAY ATHEISTS[1042]

Have you ever told God you love Him? If you haven't, a key ingredient in your prayer-life is missing. The following is an anecdote from Father Stephen Parker's book: *Bridges— Reconnecting Science and Faith*. Practically from his earliest memory, Stephen Parker had decided he wanted to be an Episcopal Priest. However, his first crisis of faith happened during his college days at *the College of William and Mary* in Williamsburg,

---

[1042] S. Parker *Bridges: Reconnecting Science and Faith* p. 27-30

Virginia — and was most acute in his sophomore year. *"After initially immersing myself in philosophy, and dipping my toes into the waters of psychology,"* he writes, *"I settled on a major in the Department of Anthropology and Sociology."* He further relates—*"All of his professors were agnostics or atheists. Most were in the science of — 'The Uncommitted.'"*

It seemed to Parker — *"Their disciplines derived power from their refusal to commit or believe in any one specific idea."* Consequently, Parker began to question his own faith and found his faith was at a crossroads — faith seemed to be entirely subjective, and other religions seemed to have their own validity. What he was being taught by his professors about science and world cultures caused him to doubt his rather orthodox, though not very well-formed view of the Bible. He found himself floundering in his own lack of direction, and his sense of purpose was diminished. We have already mentioned *"The Militancy, Aggression, and Mission of Modern-Day Atheists"* in Chapter 21 (Book II). In this anecdote, Farther Parker relates his own experience with *that* mission.

Fortunately, after having met the Episcopal Bishop of Puerto Rico (Irvine Swift) when he was eleven years old, student Parker had corresponded with him during his high school years, and Bishop Swift became *his mentor in absentia*. So, in his first crisis of faith, Parker turned to his mentor for advice.

Have you ever told God you love Him?

Bishop Swift replied: *"Have you ever told the Lord you love Him?"* Parker had not. Bishop Swift then urged his young college protégé to pray this simple prayer:

> *"Dear Lord, I love you.*
> *Thank you for loving me."*

Furthermore, Bishop Swift urged him to pray this prayer fervently and often. Parker replied this would be impossible for him in his current state of mind because, as things stood, he didn't feel he loved God, and wasn't even sure he believed in God anymore. The hypocrisy of saying *that* prayer seemed intolerable to him at *that* moment.

Bishop Swift then advised Parker to trust him and say the words anyway. He told him: *"Let God handle the hypocrisy of it."* So, he followed Bishop Swift's advice and committed to praying this prayer on a daily basis for three months. At times he *"choked on the prayer again and again, and almost gave up."* Eventually, he was able to pray these words to God with *"great sincerity."* When the three months were up, he was free of his promise but was surprised he could not give it up. He began to pray it on his own and realized his new relationship with God *owned* him. *Father Parker now considers this simple prayer the most important prayer he has ever uttered because it restored his faith and brought him into a new relationship with his Creator. He cherishes it to this day.* In closing, my prayer for you is this prayer of blessing The Lord God spoke to Moses:

> *"Then the Lord spoke to Moses, saying: 'Speak to Aaron and to his sons,*
> *saying: Thus, you shall bless the sons of Israel. You shall say to them:*
> *The Lord bless you and keep you. The Lord make His face to shine on*
> *you, and be gracious to you: The Lord lift up His countenance on you,*
> *And give you peace'" Numbers 6:22-26 NASB.*

This blessing is now universally known as "The Aaronic Benediction." It may be the most recognizable benediction in the world today. I wonder how many people know — These are God's words — Words God spoke to Moses so they would be spoken as God's Blessing to the Children of Israel. They are words that convey God's compassionate and all-encompassing love for us.

The Lord wants us to choose to belong to Him. He wants us to be His people.
If you ever think God doesn't love you, know this—that thought came from Satan! I believe self-loathing is a sin. It's what Satan wants you to do. Remember: God made you! Also know this: **God doesn't make mistakes!**

Remember, little four-year-old Colton Burpo told his dad:
"Dad, God really loves us! You can't belieeeeve how much He loves us!"
Akiane said: *"God is Light ... and Love!"*
In John 1:4, John said: *"...Jesus was light, and the light was the life of men!"*

Isaiah 50: 10. *"Who is among you that fears the LORD, that obeys the voice of His servant* (i.e., Jesus Christ), *that walks in darkness and has no light? Let him trust in the name of the LORD* (Jesus Christ) and *rely on his God* (our Father).

I believe this verse is especially true for the millions of Christians today, and throughout history who have been and are being persecuted (often to death) for following Jesus Christ. They are imprisoned by the darkness of their persecutors. The persecution of followers of Jesus is ever growing today in many countries and is more rampant in our present than in any other time in history! It is even happening right now in the USA, and I believe will only get worse. That is because the world hates Jesus Christ. And yet, Jesus Christ is the only answer to all our problems. We must persist in our faithfulness to Him, even to mortal death. The reward for all faithful believers is Eternal Life. Christians see death as their doorway to Heaven.

Isaiah 50:11. *"...all you who kindle a fire and walk in the light of your own fire...will lie down in torment."* This means — the unbelievers who try to illume their darkness by their own efforts, will only know sorrow.

Each one of us should fervently pray this prayer every day.

Dear Lord, I love you. Thank you for loving me. The Lord giveth, and The Lord taketh away. Blessed be the name of the Lord. And Blessed are they — that the Lord taketh unto Himself.

I leave you now with these last thoughts. The ancient Greeks believed there were only four elements: Earth—Air—Fire—and—Water. This image of a solar eclipse was made in a unique place and on an unusual day.

A total eclipse of the Sun reveals the Milky Way (Public Domain Image courtesy of History. Com).

In many images of a solar eclipse, it may not be possible to see the Milky Way, because the ambient light on the horizon of earth's populated continents prevents it. But in this day-time picture, taken on an island in the middle of the ocean, which was in the middle of the path of totality during an eclipse of the Sun — the Milky Way shines out. This image depicts:

- Earth—the tall rock on the left, and the rocky islands in this image—
- Air—the atmosphere of the Earth—
- Fire—the stars in the Milky Way—
- And Water—Earth's *"Waters Below"* (on Earth) and *"The Waters Above,"* that are in *"The Highest Heavens."* The water in the highest heavens is made in the stars of the Milky Way and all of the other stars in the universe, which are larger than our Sun.

I want to emphasize — the Eclipse image on the preceding page is a daytime image. The black ball near the center is the Moon. The Moon is completely covering the Sun. This creates the impression the image was made at night. The Sun's light is blocked by the Moon at the moment of a total eclipse of the Sun — thus revealing *the fires in the Milky Way, and the fires in the Highest Heavens—*

ALL OF IT CREATED AND MADE BY GOD!

Deus est regit omnia — There is a God Who rules all things.

In Excelsis Deo — Glory to God in the Highest.

Soli Deo Gloria — Glory to God Alone.

Dirige nos Domine — Direct us, O God.

*For a Life full of Meaning, and
Filled with Purpose:
Agape's the Way,
Belief's the Seed, and
Faith's the Kernel,
That Lead Believers
to Life Eternal.*

Now, Go Tell It on The Mountain — ***JESUS CHRIST IS LORD!!!***

*Love to All,
David*

Made in the USA
Las Vegas, NV
09 November 2024

10924276R00328